Women's Rights
and the Law

Barbara A. Brown
Ann E. Freedman
Harriet N. Katz
Alice M. Price

edited and with
an introduction
by **Hazel Greenberg**

Women's Rights
and the Law

The Impact of the ERA
on State Laws

PRAEGER PUBLISHERS
Praeger Special Studies

New York • London • Sydney • Toronto

Library of Congress Cataloging in Publication Data
Main entry under title:

Women's rights and the law.

   (Praeger special studies in U.S. economic, social,
and political issues)
   1. Sex discrimination against women—Law and
legislation—United States—States.   2. Women—Legal
status, laws, etc.—United States—States.   I. Brown,
Barbara A., 1946-
KF4758.Z95W65   342'.73'087   77-9961
ISBN 0-03-022316-4 hb.
ISBN 0-03-022311-3 pb.

PRAEGER PUBLISHERS
PRAEGER SPECIAL STUDIES
383 Madison Avenue, New York, N.Y. 10017, U.S.A.

Published in the United States of America in 1977
by Praeger Publishers,
A Division of Holt, Rinehart and Winston, CBS, Inc.

89   038   98765432

All of the authors of this book have a deep commitment to the
struggle for equal rights for women. The equal rights amendment
(ERA) seems an important and proper vehicle to rid our laws of sex
discrimination and stereotyping. This book grew out of our awareness
that congressional understanding of the meaning of sex equality, and
even the ratification of the amendment by the states, would only be
the beginning of a long effort to eliminate sex discrimination from the
law and governmental institutions. Indeed, an awakening to the magni-
tude of this task often has been a major impetus for ERA ratification
in the states.

When we began work on the book, nearly three years ago, the
exciting swell of activity at the state level reported here was still in
its early stages. The ratification of the federal ERA was expected
within months. While that expectation has not yet been fulfilled, the
ratification process appears to be coming to a successful conclusion.
As of this writing, 35 of the necessary 38 states have ratified, and
several other state legislatures are in the final stages of consideration.

Legislative reform aimed at eliminating sex discrimination
from state statutes began in earnest in 1971 and 1972, just at the time
of serious congressional consideration of the ERA. Often the search
for statutes that would be affected by the ERA, done as part of the
ratification process, prompted legislative action. In other instances,
a particular issue received national attention and was the subject of
legislation in a large number of states. The pace of activity has ac-
celerated over the past several years, producing an uneven but encouraging picture of reform accomplishments. This legislative reform paralleled and was affected by a dramatic shift in judicial treatment of sex discrimination. The standards for judging and the toler-
ance for sex distinctions have changed markedly, in both the federal
and state systems, since 1970.

Much remains to be done, however, both in terms of a firm
theoretical basis for equality and the translation of that theory into
state law and administration. Some may ask why the ERA is important
now that this process is on its way. There are a number of reasons.
First, the ERA ratification has been and continues to be a spur to action in many states. The ERA has been a force in public opinion concerning discrimination against women and has been instrumental in
bringing about consensus on the need for reform of existing laws or

enactment of new affirmative legislation. Second, the ERA will set a uniform standard of equality across the nation, so that men and women will not be subject to treatment held lawful in one state and unlawful in its neighbor. And, of course, there is still a great deal to be done before we can feel confident that sex equality is really the law of the land. The ERA is a mandate for the states to undertake or complete this process of reform and will create deadlines for action, set standards for new laws, and encourage interstate cooperation on law reform. It will preclude the need for a case-by-case definition of equality, with its unpredictability and, thus far, its clear shortcomings in terms of results. It will assure the women of this country a permanent commitment to equal treatment of the sexes. We clearly need it.

This book hopefully will serve as a guide to the process of conformance of state law to principles of sex equality. It is intended for use by both lawyers and lay persons interested or involved in that process. It assumes that the ERA will continue to be the moving force behind that reform and treats it as a comprehensive theory of sex equality. Of course, whether the ERA is ratified or not, the need to press for legislative reform in the states is evident. We think the presentation and critique of state law will be relevant whether or not the amendment is ratified by 38 states.

Chapter 1, written by Dr. Hazel Greenberg, explores the sociological aspects of the equal rights amendment, both in terms of its legal implementation and its role in changing social ideology. The remainder of the book is divided along substantive lines, with background material on ERA theory, the methodology of state law reform, and an analysis of cases decided under equal rights amendments to state constitutions. There are chapters on criminal law, public obligations, domestic relations, employment, social insurance, and affirmative laws. Within each substantive area, the material is introduced with a background section reviewing the common forms of discrimination historically found in that area of law. The current state of the law is also presented to indicate whether the traditional discriminations are largely a thing of the past or are still very much with us. The second section for each topic examines the impact of the ERA on that area of law—what it prohibits and what it requires—and is a statement of the minimal level of reform required. This section treats explicit discrimination separately from those laws and practices that, though neutral on their face, have a discriminatory impact. The next section discusses the policy considerations that should enter into the decision on how to revise laws that violate the amendment. It goes beyond what the ERA strictly requires and points out the fundamental forces and policies that might argue for one sex-neutral solution to current discrimination rather than another, or for a broader sweep of reform.

This section often includes or refers the reader to a model law that we think is a good starting point for state reform; this model may be adapted to a state's particular needs, but often it can be taken as is. In some areas we make no such recommendation, either because the reform is straightforward or because state law is so varied that no one formula will satisfy any sizable number of jurisdictions. The last section reviews the reform efforts of the states to date. In areas in which there has been extensive reform we indicate the merits and shortcomings of various alternatives. Reading these sections, it is clear that we have come far, but we have far to go. We hope that this book will help us on our way.

We have many people and organizations to thank for their role in the work. Grants from the Ford Foundation, the Rockefeller Family Fund, the Philadelphia Foundation, Shalan Foundation, Laras Fund, and the Women's Fund—Joint Foundation Support made the project possible. A great deal of the work and more than their share of trauma was borne by the legal workers of the Women's Law Project, Rachel Rubin and Gina McQuinn, by our expert editor, Hazel Greenberg, and by the countless law students who joined us throughout the years. We also thank the Trustees of the Women's Law Project, who have supported us so faithfully in this and other endeavors.

CONTENTS

LIST OF TABLES

THE EQUAL RIGHTS AMENDMENT

Proposed Amendment XXVII
(Proposed by Congress on March 22, 1972)

Section 1. Equality of rights under the law shall not be denied or abridged by the United States or by any State on account of sex.

Section 2. The Congress shall have the power to enforce, by appropriate legislation, the provisions of this article.

Section 3. This amendment shall take effect two years after the date of ratification.

1

THE ERA IN CONTEXT:
ITS IMPACT
ON SOCIETY

Hazel Greenberg

INTRODUCTION

"Equal protection of the laws" is guaranteed to the people of the United States by the Fifth and Fourteenth Amendments to the Constitution. That mandate, however, has never been interpreted to prohibit all discrimination against women as a class. As a result, public laws and policies often limit opportunities or disadvantage people in other ways solely on the basis of sex. This is the simple necessity for the equal rights amendment (ERA), an unresolved issue troubling the conscience of America since 1923.

The language of the amendment is straightforward: "Equality of rights under the law shall not be denied or abridged by the United States or any state on account of sex." It is a declaration that laws distinguishing between people on the basis of gender are illegal. As a constitutional amendment, the ERA mandates the revision or repeal of federal and state laws that treat men and women differently and the incorporation of the concept of sex equality into judicial interpretation.

The significance of the ERA from a social policy standpoint is that it can provide a universal legal definition of equality, at once activating widespread and consistent change throughout the nation. From a moral standpoint, a constitutional amendment is the highest sanction in our legal system.

Hazel Greenberg is Director of Research at the Institute for Studies in Equality, a nonprofit, tax-exempt research corporation, funded by the Rockefeller Foundation, that evolved from the Equal Rights Amendment Project of the California Commission on the Status of Women.

In many ways, the ERA has less to do with equal rights than with treating each person as unique. For example, government no longer can assume that all women are incapable of combat duty, for many individual women are as strong, as physically rugged, as capable of long-term struggle as men. It is a matter of individual life-style and constitution. The ERA guarantees that each person must be treated as an individual. In view of the multitudinous differences among people, sex is too broad a classification. Sex-based laws are unjust and irrational because they use gender rather than ability or need to determine an individual's rights, responsibilities, and benefits. The effect of sex-based laws is to steer people into sex tracks and to deny them freedom to choose the path of their own capacities and aspirations.[1] The point is not laws that require sameness but laws that tolerate individual differences.

Once ratified, the ERA will be more and less than law; it will be both end and means in the drama of social change. This chapter takes the position that the ERA will have specific beneficial effects on our legal system and on society generally, in terms of both ideology and implementation. These results could not be achieved as easily or as completely in any other way. On the other hand, if complacency sets in, with the attitude that legal and social change will automatically follow ratification, then the effect of the amendment will be substantially reduced. The first section of this chapter considers the legal impact of the ERA on society. The second treats its ideological impact and assesses the potential for substantial social change.

LEGAL IMPLEMENTATION

Skeptics about the legal process have observed that meaningful implementation of any law is not guaranteed by mere passage, an observation illustrated by the fact that 14 years after passage of the Equal Pay Act, the earnings gap between men and women has actually increased. It is possible for the ERA's egalitarian ideology to be given a similarly limited social reality. Sex discriminatory language would be removed from the statutes, but discrimination might still persist. On the other hand, the ERA could generate widespread reform, not only of public but of private discrimination against women.

Which result occurs depends upon the outcome of the process of interpretation and application by the executive, legislative, and judicial branches, a process affected not only by legal considerations but by political, economic, and psychological ones as well. Let us examine the specific dynamics of implementation at each of these levels.

Legislative Implementation

The ERA's direct impact is the rewriting of laws to eliminate sex discrimination. In this arena, the ERA's meaning will be determined by conflict, for legislative changes are authorized but not activated by the amendment and some changes are better, from a social policy standpoint, than others. Conforming legislation will call forth responses from a multiplicity of interest groups that have a stake in the proposed changes. Those in the legislative minority who oppose the amendment will not automatically become its supporters after passage, and they may respond minimally to law enforcement efforts. "The whole political process of law making, law breaking, and law enforcement becomes a direct reflection of deep-seated and fundamental conflicts between interest groups and their more general struggles for the control of the police power of the state."[2] The struggle between the supporters and opponents of the law that existed in the community before it actually became law—the basis for the legislative battle—carries over to the process of enforcement: "The principle of compromise from positions of strength operates at every stage of the conflict process."[3]

This is not to say that implementation is a fantasy or that it cannot proceed within realistic expectations; it is merely to say that it must be made to happen. To minimize these impediments, political activists must keep the conflict process alive. Delaying tactics must be brought out into the open; devices such as grievance procedures, periodic evaluation of programs and agencies, ombudspersons, legislative oversight, judicial review, and citizen participation in bureaucratic decision making, can be incorporated into implementing legislation; coalition building can be used to mobilize power and resources; group members and the community can be educated about the law and the issues; direct pressure can be exerted on legislators; and individuals from previously unrepresented parts of the community can be mobilized to seek power positions.[4]

Administrative Implementation

Administrative regulations often provide more detailed interpretations of legislative intent and can either strengthen or weaken the law's impact. Since the nature of the political process makes it much easier to resist change than to institute it, legislators must begin to specify the direction and method of change as thoroughly as possible and leave little to bureaucratic discretion. In many cases, however, guidelines and administrative decisions still will be needed to adapt legislation to the changing conditions and varied situations that arise.

There are many reasons for the agonizing slowness with which antidiscrimination laws often have been enforced.[5] The pervasiveness of the necessary changes, the number and complexity of institutions covered, and the lack of individual accountability within such large and complex organizations make the task very difficult, especially when sentiment is openly or tacitly against it. Bureaucratic realities, including the work load of those who implement the laws, assure delay. Bureaucratic discretion allows rules and regulations to be changed readily so that they easily can be weakened. Bureaucratic priority shifting, subject to political pressure and psychological preference, can result in a policy of inaction even after regulations are drawn. Finally, internal inconsistencies within an enforcement agency, among its regional offices, or among agencies that administer similar laws obstruct the development of uniform definitions and impact.[6]

On the other hand, effective, well-drafted regulations can provide needed guidance to those affected by a legislative change and can forestall the development of loopholes in the law. Therefore, it is of critical importance that those concerned with the implementation of equal rights for men and women focus on the administrative process as well as on the more public legislative arena. That such a focus can have beneficial effects is well-illustrated by some of the rule making of the Equal Employment Opportunity Commission, the agency that administers Title VII of the Civil Rights Act of 1964.

Judicial Implementation

The ERA's meaning will depend to a large extent upon judicial interpretation. In addition to giving people the right to challenge what they perceive to be discriminatory laws and practices, the ERA establishes a particular standard—the prohibition of sex classifications in the law—thus incorporating the theoretical principle of equality into judicial interpretation. But the application of this standard is not cut-and-dried. Certain factors that will influence the process arise from the nature of the judicial system rather than the amendment itself. First, not only procedural but also psychological restrictions affect the very selection of cases the Court and lower courts will hear. Lingering doubts about sex equality may delay the widespread consideration of ERA-related cases. Second, conflicting political interests are often a factor in both the selection of cases and the outcome of constitutional decision making. Those interests represented by the groups that have power and access to the formulation of public policy will carry great weight before the Court. Third, the fact that the concept of "equal protection" under the Fifth and Fourteenth Amendments has not been given uniform articulation, even for groups other than women, inevitably will affect ERA interpretation.

This is because the equal protection experiences of America represent an ultimate and central struggle in our system between sub-group and government, and between individual and legal category. Also, political and judicial clashes concerning equal protection have formed precedents, shaped approaches, and revealed biases and beliefs about equality that ratification of the Equal Rights Amendment, by itself, can neither dissolve nor reconcile. [7]

The application of constitutional standards of review grows in the process of judicial decision making; it is not written in a set of rules. Similarly, individual mind-sets and prejudices inevitably affect court decisions, for judges are human beings, not robots. The way in which courts will apply principles of sex equality in difficult cases in part depends upon the judges' own socialization and expectations about men and women, especially where biology is concerned. For example, the Court may be psychologically predisposed, as it has been in the past, to approve sex classifications related to pregnancy. The equal rights amendment's legislative history makes congressional intent to prohibit such discrimination apparent. Nonetheless, obtaining judicial acceptance of this proposition is likely to require persuasive and expert litigation.

While the Supreme Court and other courts have exhibited a great deal of ambiguity about the meaning of sex equality, the ERA is designed to eliminate that ambiguity. Moreover, the courts also have shown progress in reevaluating the legal relevance of the biological distinctions between the sexes. Ambiguity is itself a giant step beyond the unwavering belief in the universal appropriateness of legal distinctions based on sex that characterized constitutional interpretation until 1971.

Perhaps the key to the usefulness of law as a catalyst of change is that it invites conflict; it gives people the opportunity to claim their rights as they perceive them. Equal rights laws legitimate the attack on the patriarchy. This is a very important function of law, one that is often denigrated because people expect law to answer rather than to raise questions. Definitions of equal rights will evolve from the conflicts that take place in the rewriting of legislation, the construction of administrative guidelines, and the development of judicial opinion after the amendment is ratified. Its social reality will be the result of this multifaceted conflict. As the means by which new values are incorporated into the social fabric, conflict is a necessary condition for progress and growth.

Probably the most basic attack leveled against legislation as a tool for social change is its inability to affect social values, on the macrocosmic level, and psychological attitudes, on the individual level. The law is quite often only a reflector of social values. Insofar as the ERA challenges traditional sex role differences, it challenges deeply internalized social values of the society; yet, insofar as social values have changed enough to pass the ERA, they have the potential to encourage cooperation with implementation following passage.

In many areas of legal change, social values will activate resistance or determine the nature of conformance. Whether prostitution is decriminalized or prostitution laws and enforcement simply sex neutralized will depend upon social values. The sex neutralization of rape laws will not in and of itself prevent a rape victim from being treated as if she herself were the criminal. Social values will determine whether specific protective labor laws are extended to men or repealed; whether differential definitions of male and female delinquency are equalized by criminalizing certain behaviors for boys or legalizing them for girls; whether women will retain or change their own names upon marriage; and whether Congress is likely to reenact the draft or rely on voluntary enlistments of both men and women.[8] Wherever discretion is used by judges and other government officials, as in custody and alimony cases, and wherever a benefit may be sex neutralized by repealing or extending it, social values will continue to influence and delimit the establishment of equal rights.

Indeed, the law often lags behind social reality. The law is a notoriously conservative institution, and the legislative majority needed to pass a law, especially at the constitutional level, requires pervasive change in the cultural climate. Legal reform is often necessary, not to initiate and institutionalize change in custom but to recognize already changing custom. In fact, the law must sometimes acknowledge social change in order to preserve its influence as an institution.

However, the law can affect attitudes over time. Insofar as the sanctions of the law change behavior through the threat of enforcement, this process will eventually result in attitudinal change—by two means. First, it is the psychological nature of human beings to resolve cognitive dissonance; that is, people cannot long behave in a way that is antithetical to their beliefs and emotions without mentally adjusting them one to another. Changes in behavior to conform to law will eventually involve concomitant intellectual and emotional changes. While there is an inevitable cultural lag between these responses, immediate resistance eventually will give way to psychological conformance. We have seen this happen with racial discrimination.

Attitudinal accommodation to law is not merely rationalization, however. The second means to psychological conformance is created by opportunity. Changes in the economic and political rights of women will give them the opportunity to change traditional opinion about their abilities and their proper "place." Sexism is a self-fulfilling prophecy: women do not achieve because they think they cannot, because they are told that they cannot, and because they are not allowed to; yet the fact that they do not is taken as proof that they cannot. New role models can change this circular lie; once women have the right and opportunity to prove their worth, they will be accepted as worthy. They will be able to disprove the myths. In this way, egalitarian ideology in the private sector is likely to be reinforced by changes in the public sector.

To summarize the interaction of law and the social system in terms of the psychological realities discussed above, the law can be seen as a midpoint in the process of social change. Legal change takes place as a response to cultural change and then carries its own literal and symbolic weight as an effector of behavioral and attitudinal change. It is an important step in the process, and with or without pervasive implementation, its influence cannot be gainsaid.

IDEOLOGY

As law, then, the ERA is a potentially influential effector of social change. A second issue related to its effectiveness as a tool for social change arises from the ERA's extralegal nature—the ideology it embodies and the extent to which that ideology can be institutionalized.

In constructing social law on the basis of natural law, man has made much of the difference between male and female. [9] He has given this factual differentiation a value and, by doing so, has imposed a patriarchal definition of reality on society. This definition assigns moral, practical, and psychological meanings to neutral biological differences. This has resulted in sexuality being the first and foremost classification of persons and in females being defined as unequal to males within that classification system. The "social reality" of the ERA—the meaning given to it by society and the amount and character of social change likely to result from it—will partially depend upon its ability to create a new definition of reality, specifically of sexual differentiation.

Redefinition of Reality

Kate Millet grounds her criticism of the suffrage movement in "its failure to challenge patriarchal ideology at a sufficiently deep and radical level to break the conditioning processes of status, temperament and role." She generalizes this comment to "the superficial change which legislative reform represents," asserting that legal reform movements were not even capable of utilizing their new rights, let alone proposing

> the sweeping radical changes in society necessary to bring about the completion of a sexual revolution—changes in social attitudes and social structure, in personality and institutions. . . . Despite the reform of its legal system and the (finally minor) humiliation to its political pride, the patriarchal mentality reasserted itself with great strength. . . . Patriarchy, reformed or unreformed, is patriarchy still: its worst abuses purged or foresworn, it might be actually more stable and secure than before.[10]

Harriet Holter, a Swedish sociologist, denigrates the official egalitarian ideology of her country in that it has not affected a change in values despite equal rights and the equal participation of women.

> The . . . entrance of women into secondary institutions in present-day society has taken place on male premises. Women have accepted the dominant norms and values of secondary affairs, be it "efficiency" or "competition" or "universalism," and these very values have often in the debates provided the justifications for women's participation in work, education, and politics. No wonder, then, that male values persist in the face of female participation.[11]

She labels the form of equality obtained within the framework of present Western societies "masculine equality," as opposed to a form of equality that might be obtained in a qualitatively different society, one not dominated by masculine values as we know them. Masculine equality is the 50-50 distribution of both sexes in all positions throughout society, while maintaining the same economic and political order. Institutions remain intact, and, in order to participate in them, women have to become more like men, conforming to male ideas of efficiency, profit, competition, and power, since male-dominated institutions operate on the basis of these values. Moreover, the maintenance of female values in primary institutions, such as the family, despite increased male participation in them, heightens the polarization of male and female values in society rather than effecting a synthesis, according to Holter.[12]

Attempts to institutionalize only masculine equality are based on a static or "order" view of society rather than a conflict view.

Such a perspective assumes several things about the social order. It assumes, for example, that society is stable, persistent, and well integrated; that it is held together by a consensus of values; and that all parts function to maintain the system as it is. Consequently, conflict disrupts society. Social disorganization is considered an imbalance of means and ends, the solution to which is administrative action to correct that imbalance without changing the basic framework or value structure of the organization. In other words, the status quo is sanctified. Minority group dissatisfaction constitutes a moral dilemma for the system because it represents an incongruity between legitimate social goals and the socially available opportunities to achieve these goals.[13] It is not viewed as an essentially healthy expression of dissension. Legislation is one primary tool used in this context to restore social order by expanding opportunities for mobility. In this "order" view, by legitimating changes in the opportunity structure, legislation functions to reinforce the dominant values and definition of reality.

The motive of social analysts who sanction the "women's rights" movement, while they treat "the libbers" pejoratively, is to control the type of equality achieved, that is, to institutionalize only masculine equality. Incorporating the women's rights movement into the dominant system is a way of preserving the system because it does not seem to question traditional values, only women's access to them. Social change of this kind results in minority group assimilation into the dominant society, accompanied by the obliteration of the group's distinct and conflicting values. The "women's liberation" movement, on the other hand, is seen as a danger to the status quo because it does not take the form of female capitulation to the patriarchal value system in a trade-off for a bigger piece of the pie; rather, it is a process that will change the values of both sexes.

These analysts see the ERA as the culmination of the women's rights movement: it is a legal instrument that explicitly states only that both sexes will be given equal rights under the law, to share in that sanctified, traditional, male value system. This view is too limited because the ERA is premised on the idea that there is no absolute social order. It is a legal instrument, but one that attempts to generate new laws as well as apply existing law more equitably.

More centrally, it is naive to believe that one aspect of the movement can exist without the other. The avid opposition to the amendment derives precisely from a perception of its second dimension. Why else would the 1976 Republican platform committee even consider not endorsing the ERA at the same time that it unhesitantly commended strong enforcement of present antidiscrimination law? Why else would Phyllis Schlafly, a self-proclaimed women's rightist, be its arch-opponent? Why else would conservatives prefer the status quo methods

of piecemeal state legislative reform, legal challenge in the lower
courts, or appeal to the Supreme Court under the Fifth and Fourteenth
Amendments? The ERA as a legal statement plugs into the traditional
and sacred American value system honoring justice, equality, and
equal protection for all social groups—the democratic values upon
which the society and its government were founded. The matter of
simple justice, the matter of equal rights, the matter of individual
freedom take precedence over all other social values because they
are so basic. Assuring women equal rights, therefore, is surely
compatible with this system and this philosophy. Why then, did it
take 49 years for the ERA to pass Congress, and why, after five more
years, is it still not ratified? Were the question of values not involved
at some level, the ERA would have become reality long ago.

The ERA partakes of two worlds and is a prelude to far-reaching changes because of its implications, as well as its direct impact.
It reaches not only the "equal opportunity" areas but also our deepest
stereotypes. Underlying all questions of tactics, all objections to the
ERA's comprehensive nature, is the biological rationale for traditional
sex roles that has been a persistent barrier to enforcement of antidiscrimination law. Women may be given selected rights and opportunities, so long as other more fundamental, more sensitive areas
are left untouched.

The ERA is an attack on that patriarchal definition of reality
that sees society as organized primarily by sex. Its limitations and
possibilities are determined by the very same fact: sex distinction
is ultimately more basic to our social structure than equality. It is
this fact that causes the ERA to frighten the patriarchy, making implementation difficult. But it is also this fact that challenges "patriarchal ideology at a sufficiently deep and radical level to break the
conditioning processes of status, temperament and role." It heralds
far more than "masculine equality."

The ERA's negative phraseology will allow free reign to the conflict of values that results from a change in the way men and women
perceive reality. It does not instruct people to do something; rather,
it prevents them from doing anything to inhibit possibility. Negatives
are the most influential normative rules (for example, taboos), partially because they tend to be so far-reaching. The ERA is an invita-
tion for new values to enter the social arena.

If we view society as a natural and constant struggle of values,
we see the ERA as a strong statement of pluralism—of freedom from
the straitjacket of stereotypes and traditions and freedom for diversity.
It challenges false homogeneity by discouraging unnecessarily broad
classifications of people that deny their uniqueness. Viewing society
and the ERA from this perspective reveals the possibility for change
in both social values and the social structure.

Symbolic Impact

The ERA also has an important symbolic function, for the Constitution is itself a symbolic creation that serves as a "myth of origin," articulating and explaining the structure of our society. Appeal to its symbols—for example, equality and justice—resolves intergroup conflicts and shapes human relations. The ERA "will codify and make explicit the belief that 'equity' and 'justice' transcend the various conflicts engendered by the meanings we attach to the man-woman polarity in our culture,"[14] or that they <u>should</u>.

It will not only revise the social order created by the symbolism of the Constitution but also it will legitimate the claim for equality and dramatize the need for a new commitment to equality. Legal recognition of freedom makes one sensitive to violations of one's freedom previously ignored or fearfully suppressed. The ERA has the potential to unite women, raise their consciousness, and increase their perception of themselves as an oppressed group at the very moment of their liberation. Ironically, its symbolic power will be increased by the difficulty of its 53-year career, having been an elaborate rite de passage for women. It may seem foolish to assume, in view of its long history, that women have not already been instilled with that "consciousness of servitude" so necessary to liberation. Of course, the movement could not have existed without such an awareness on the part of many women, but there is a multitude only vaguely aware of discrimination who would, if queried, question the legitimacy of the demand for equality. A constitutional amendment based on the fact of discrimination gives credibility to the need for equality and legitimacy to the demand.

Further, the ERA will sanction the instinct to move out of traditional roles because of its emphasis on uniqueness and individuality rather than classes of people. More than merely allowing women to demand equal rights and to make nontraditional role choices without guilt, the ERA will encourage them to do so. The importance of this psychological growth cannot be overemphasized, for the internalization of social expectations and the consequent development of self-esteem differentially by sex create the most damaging difference between women and men. Social expectation determines both behavior and self-esteem, which themselves are integrally related. Self-esteem is necessary to aspiration; people seldom aspire to what they are told they cannot achieve or do not deserve. In a world where the expectations of women are the same as those of men, women are likely to think better of themselves, expect more from themselves, and therefore achieve more. Successful achievement in turn increases self-esteem. In a complementary manner, by symbolically sanctioning achievement goals for women, the ERA may increase society's respect for women's potential, and this too enhances their self-esteem, the very prod necessary for aspiration and achievement. In other words, discrimination not only prevents professional advancement for competent women but, by encouraging low self-esteem through the expectation of incompetence, also prevents the development of competence in the first place. The cycle is thus perpetuated. In this realm, the legal and extralegal impact of the ERA work in tandem, providing women legal opportunities as well as psychological motivation to expand their horizons.

Thus, the extralegal ability of the ERA to effectively challenge patriarchal values is greatly enhanced by its symbolic power as a constitutional commitment to equality. Its extralegal impact is further expanded by the fact that changes in society are systemic, acting like concentric circles, causing at first minor changes here and there, effecting in their turn other changes, and so on. These formal and symbolic advantages in conjunction with its "radical" ideology provide the potential for constructing a new social reality. The very passage of the ERA by Congress and by over two-thirds of the states means that large numbers of people are ready to give it a significant social meaning in the conflict of values that it will mandate and invite. In that conflict, its meaning for and impact upon society will be developed, and the patriarchal sense of reality as necessarily sex differentiated can be redefined. The changes, as they nourish one another, will not simply incorporate women into the present social structure but can qualitatively change that social structure—for the greater good of humankind.

2

EQUAL RIGHTS
AMENDMENT THEORY

LEGISLATIVE HISTORY OF THE FEDERAL
AMENDMENT

While significant advances have been made in securing equal opportunity for women in recent years, the United States Supreme Court
has been slow in accepting sex equality as a constitutional doctrine.
The Fourteenth Amendment, ratified in 1868, provides in its equal
protection clause: "Nor [shall any state] deny to any person within
its jurisdictions the equal protection of the laws." Early feminists
were strongly involved in the antislavery struggles that prompted passage of this amendment, but they lost their campaign to have "sex"
explicitly included in the Constitution as a protected class.[1]

Not until 1971 did the Supreme Court hold a statutory classification based on sex to be a denial of equal protection under the Fourteenth Amendment. Indeed, in two earlier cases, one decided in 1948
and one in 1961, the Supreme Court expressly upheld sex-based classifications as constitutional. In Goesaert v. Cleary,[2] a Michigan statute
prohibiting a woman from serving as a barmaid unless she was the
daughter or wife of a bar owner was held to be a reasonable classification, even though the ostensible legislative intent of protecting women
was not factually substantiated as either a reason for or consequence
of the statute. In Hoyt v. Florida,[3] Florida's jury selection statutes,
which automatically exempted women by requiring a special registration process for them but not for men, also were upheld as a "reasonable," and therefore constitutional, classification. As the Court said,
"It is still true that a woman's place is in the home."

Finally, in 1971, the Supreme Court relied on the equal protection clause to invalidate an Idaho statute preferring male over female
relatives in appointing the administrator of a decedent's estate.[4]

While this decision signaled the possibility that the Fourteenth Amendment would be interpreted as a broad prohibition against sex discrimination, the Court has since wavered in its application of the equal protection clause to sex distinctions in the law.[5] In 1972, for example, eight of the nine justices voted to strike down an Air Force regulation requiring husbands of officers to prove dependency in order to receive special benefits while wives of officers receive dependency benefits automatically.[6] Four of the justices even spoke of sex as a "suspect" classification, the strictest form of protection now available under the Fourteenth Amendment. Two years later, however, the same Court failed to find sex discrimination in a California disability insurance plan that excluded from coverage all disabilities related to pregnancy.[7] Other sex-based classifications also have been upheld by the Court since that time.

In light of this erratic history, the need for the equal rights amendment (ERA) as a clear and uncompromising constitutional standard of sex equality is apparent. Moreover, the ERA includes a mandate for the legislative implementation of sex equality by the states, a methodology for achieving equal legal rights for men and women that is more sensible and more in keeping with our lawmaking ideals than case-by-case judicial scrutiny.

Congressional passage of the equal rights amendment in 1972 marked the end of a struggle to secure approval of the ERA that first began in 1923.[8] Early debates on the amendment, particularly in the late 1940s and early 1950s, were never clear about what constitutional standard should, in fact, determine equality of rights for women. The Congress that passed the ERA in 1972, however, engaged in extensive debate on the theory of the amendment, and, by the time the amendment was finally approved, the standard Congress wanted incorporated into the Constitution was clear: a principle of absolute sex equality under the law. That is, under the ERA, sex is an impermissible classification for drawing lines in any law or policy in which the government is directly or substantially involved. The only qualifications to this absolute principle recognized by Congress are those instances in which the constitutional right of privacy or a physical characteristic unique to one sex necessitates taking sex into account in legislation or other governmental action.

The theory of the ERA is clearly set out in the Senate committee report recommending its approval in 1972. As the report states:

> The general principles on which the Equal Rights Amendment rests are simple and well-understood. Essentially, the Amendment requires that the federal government and all state and local governments treat each person, male and female, as an individual.

It does not require that any level of government establish quotas for men or for women in any of its activities;
rather, it simply prohibits discrimination on the basis of
a person's sex. The Amendment applies only to governmental action; it does not affect private action or the
purely social relationships between men and women. [9]

The basic premise of the ERA set out in this report is "the fundamental proposition that sex should not be a factor in determining the legal
rights of women or of men."[10] The legal principle underlying this
premise is that the law "must deal with the individual attributes of the
particular person and not with stereotypes of over-classification based
on sex."[11]

In determining that sex should be an impermissible factor under the ERA, Congress clearly went beyond current interpretations
of the Fourteenth Amendment's protections against discrimination.
As described in a law review article read into the Congressional Record as part of the legislative history of the ERA, "The issue under
the equal rights amendment cannot be different but equal, reasonable
or unreasonable classification, suspect classification, fundamental
interests, or the demands of administrative expediency. Equality of
rights means that sex is not a factor."[12]

This absolute standard is subject to only two narrow qualifications. One is the constitutional right to privacy. This right, which
has been articulated by the Supreme Court in a number of constitutional
decisions, stands on an equal footing with other constitutional rights
and thus must be harmonized with them. The Senate report recognized
this in noting:

Another collateral legal principle flows from the constitutional right of privacy established by the Supreme Court
in Griswold v. Connecticut, 381 U.S. 479 (1965). This
right would likewise permit a separation of the sexes with
respect to such places as public toilets, as well as sleeping quarters of public institutions. [13]

The Supreme Court has upheld in its privacy cases an individual's
right to control his or her private activities and bodily functions without interference by the state. Even in the context of strict sex equality,
then, a state can protect an individual's right to perform personal
functions, such as disrobing, sleeping, or showering, without intrusion by members of the opposite sex.

The second area of qualification concerns "unique physical characteristics." When classifications based on characteristics unique to
one sex are incorporated into legislation or public policy, Congress

intended a constitutional standard known as strict scrutiny to be applied to insure that the basic premise of sex equality under the ERA is preserved. This test can be expressed most simply by three questions: (1) is the unique physical characteristic closely related to the purpose of the classification? (2) is the state interest in legislating on this particular subject compelling? and (3) if so, is there some other way in which this interest can be satisfied? Almost no sex-based classifications can pass this rigorous test. Among the few examples that have been cited are laws regulating wet nurses or sperm banks. It is clear, however, that the "unique physical characteristics" exception does not allow broadly differential treatment of sex-based characteristics, such as pregnancy, which traditionally have been used arbitrarily to restrict women's opportunities. Indeed, the legislative history of the amendment indicates that it is just that kind of invidious discrimination, such as the noncoverage of pregnancy under a state disability program, against which the amendment is aimed. Similarly, the exception does not sanction legislative classifications based on traits commonly but not necessarily or uniquely found in one sex or the other. Thus, a regulation or statute excluding girls or women from certain strenuous athletic or occupational activities on the theory that most women are physically unable to successfully participate in them would not withstand scrutiny under the ERA.[14]

In addition to the two areas of qualification discussed above, one other issue must be explored in order to understand fully the theory of the equal rights amendment. This concerns the application of the ERA to legislative classifications or legal doctrines that, though neutral on their face, have a disparate impact on members of one sex. In many ways, these so-called neutral rules embody the most invidious form of sex discrimination in the law. A principle of strict sex equality, then, must look behind apparent neutrality to the practical effect of various laws and policies.

The disparate impact on one sex of a facially neutral rule may derive from a number of sources. It may be that a history of explicit discrimination causes an ostensibly neutral policy to weigh more heavily on women than men. For example, a civil service program granting preference to veterans may be phrased in sex-neutral language, but women civil servants clearly suffer disproportionately because of a history of explicit discrimination against women seeking to enlist in the military and to gain the benefits therefrom. Other laws have a disparate impact not only because of a tradition of explicit legal distinctions but also because of social and cultural forces that have led to sex role stereotyping. For example, since women make up the overwhelming percentage of homemakers, it is they who feel the primary burden of the law's disparaging attitude toward that role and of society's refusal to value the homemaker's contributions in tangible ways. A state law providing that property at divorce be given to the spouse who put up the purchase money, for example, clearly disadvantages homemakers, which is to say it affects women more than men.

Laws phrased in neutral language but having a disparate impact on one sex are not absolutely prohibited by the equal rights amendment. Like laws relying on a "unique physical characteristic," however, they are subject to a strict scrutiny test. In order to withstand constitutional challenge, the law must be closely related to a compelling state interest and there must be no way to accomplish that purpose in a less severely discriminatory manner. This latter requirement often will be the focus of the inquiry under the amendment since many neutral rules further important state interests but do so in ways that unnecessarily burden members of one sex. For example, while it is valid for the state to take steps to reintegrate veterans into civilian society, a rule giving them an absolute preference over all qualified women applicants for state employment is unacceptable under the ERA because alternate solutions are available that impact women less severely.

The intent of Congress to subject even facially neutral laws to strict scrutiny under the ERA is clear from the legislative history:

> Protection against indirect, covert or unconscious sex discrimination is essential to supplement the absolute ban on explicit sex classifications of the Equal Rights Amendment. Past discrimination in education, training, economic status and other areas has created differences which could readily be seized upon to perpetuate discrimination under the guise of functional classifications. The courts will have to maintain a strict scrutiny of such classifications if the guarantees of the Amendment are to be effectively secured.[15]

Although no state court in a jurisdiction with an equal rights amendment has yet faced a challenge to a neutral rule discriminatory in its impact, the theory set forth above and adopted by Congress as the official purpose of the amendment should govern.

The United States Supreme Court recently has cut back on its scrutiny of neutral rules with a discriminatory impact under the Fourteenth Amendment. In the case of Washington v. Davis,[16] the Court held that a test used by the District of Columbia Police Department was not unconstitutional under the Fourteenth Amendment merely because more black than white applicants failed, especially since other efforts by the department to encourage minority applicants indicated a lack of any intent to discriminate. There are a number of reasons why the holding in Washington will not be an appropriate standard under the ERA however.

Foremost, the legislative history of the ERA clearly indicates an intent on the part of Congress to subject neutral rules to strict scrutiny. This history is critical since courts called upon to interpret a statute or an amendment generally defer to the congressional understanding of that law. Moreover, the Court in Washington did not say that differential impact should not be a consideration in determining the constitutionality of a classification but merely that differential impact alone will not trigger a strict scrutiny test:

> This is not to say that the necessary discriminatory racial purpose must be express or appear on the face of the statute, or that a law's disproportionate impact is irrelevant in cases involving Constitution-based claims of racial discrimination. A statute, otherwise neutral on its face, must be applied so as invidiously to discriminate on the basis of race [citations omitted]. It is also clear from the cases dealing with racial discrimination in the selection of juries that the systematic exclusion of Negroes is itself such an "unequal application of the law . . . as to show intentional discrimination."[17]

On this very basis, the Washington case can be distinguished from the neutral rule situations likely to arise under the ERA. Most of the identifiable rules that are neutral on their face but sex discriminatory in impact fit well within the Court's enumeration of conditions that would trigger the strict scrutiny test. Most, if not all, arise from a tradition of explicitly discriminatory laws or application of the laws. Many grow out of a systematic exclusion of women from certain roles, jobs, and positions in the public sector. Others grow out of the traditional role allocation in the family. Yet, women's family role has been determined in part by a history of sex discrimination and sex stereotyping in domestic relations law. Discrimination in other areas, most notably education and employment, has made that role division all the more inevitable. Thus, the disproportionate impact of a facially neutral rule is often only one of a number of factors showing the presence of invidious sex-based discrimination, and the discriminatory purpose demanded by the Washington Court in order to apply a strict scrutiny test is clear in the large percentage of these cases. Nor, in most instances, will there be any evidence, such as that in Washington, of affirmative efforts by the state or federal government to cure the discriminatory situation in which the neutral rule arises.

Thus, many neutral rules can be distinguished from the one in Washington. Further, and more fundamentally, the ERA is not merely the equal protection clause of the Fourteenth Amendment applied to

sex. It is a new and more pervasive prohibition of all forms of state
action that hamper the ability of members of either sex to fulfill their
potential by treating them first and primarily as men or women rather
than as individuals. To do this, the ERA must encompass not only
explicitly discriminatory laws and policies but also practices that impact members of one sex disproportionately and result indirectly in
sex role determinism in the law.

STATE ERA CASES

Because there is no federal ERA, the application of the theoretical
principles delineated in its legislative history is to be found only at
the state level—in the interpretation of state equal rights amendments
by state judiciaries. To date, 16 states* have enacted constitutional
provisions directly prohibiting discrimination based on sex. For the
text of these provisions, see Table 2.1. Nine[†] of the 16 state equal
rights amendments closely resemble the federal amendment, which
states that equality under the law shall not be denied or abridged because of sex. The language of recent amendments in five other states
varies but generally is more like that of the equal protection clause
than the federal ERA.[‡] Utah and Wyoming added broad equal rights
provisions to their constitutions near the end of the nineteenth century,
rather than as part of the current movement for sex equality, and have
experienced less recent implementation activity than the other ERA
states.

Of these 16 state provisions, the Pennsylvania amendment has
been the most widely used by litigants. Since its adoption in 1971,
the Pennsylvania ERA has been the basis for decisions in approximately 24 reported cases, eight of which have culminated in opinions
by the Pennsylvania Supreme Court (a list of ERA cases, by state, is

---

*Alaska, Colorado, Connecticut, Hawaii, Illinois, Maryland,
Massachusetts, Montana, New Hampshire, New Mexico, Pennsylvania,
Texas, Utah, Virginia, Washington, and Wyoming.
   [†]Colorado, Hawaii, Maryland, Massachusetts, New Hampshire,
New Mexico, Pennsylvania, Texas, and Washington.
   [‡]Connecticut, Illinois, and Maryland have equal rights provisions
phrased in terms of "equal protection." Virginia's provision includes
the language of the federal ERA as part of a broad equal rights provision that makes an exception for "mere separation of the sexes." Alaska's provision, which has had little interpretation since its enactment,
parallels neither the federal ERA nor the equal protection clause in
language and thus is harder to assign to a particular interpretive category.

TABLE 2.1

State ERA Cases

State	Constitutional Provision	Significant ERA Decisions
Alaska	No person is to be denied the enjoyment of any civil or political right because of race, color, creed, sex or national origin. (Art. 1, § 3, October 1972)	Schreiner v. Fruit, 519 P.2d 462 (Sup. Ct. 1974). Extended right to sue for loss of consortium to women.
Colorado	Equality of rights under the law shall not be denied or abridged by the state of . . . Colorado or any of its political subdivisions on account of sex. (Art. 2, § 29, November 1972)	People v. Elliot, 525 P.2d 457 (Sup. Ct. 1974). Upheld felony nonsupport provision applying to men only. (Statute has since been sex neutralized by legislature.) People v. Green, 183 Col. 25, 514 P.2d 769 (Sup. Ct. 1973). Upheld statutory rape provision assigning higher offense and punishment to male offenders. Mora v. St. Vrain Valley Sch. Dist., Civil No. 75-3182-1 (Boulder Co., Colo., filed Dec. 3, 1975). Invalidated rule that girl student could not practice or play with any boys' team at public school.
Hawaii	Equality of rights under the law shall not be denied or abridged by the State on account of sex. (Art. 1, § 21, November 1972)	Cragun v. Hawaii and Kashimoto, Civil No. 43175 (1st Cir. Ct. 1975) [cited in 1 Women L. Rep. 1.162 (Mar. 1, 1975)]. Gave married women right to use birth-given name to vote. (Statutory restriction requiring use of husband's name for all purposes repealed.)
Illinois	The equal protection of the laws shall not be denied or abridged on account of sex by the State or its units of local government and school districts. (Art. 1, § 18, July 1971)	Anagnostopoulos v. Anagnostopoulos, 22 Ill. App. 3d 479, 317 N.E.2d 681 (1974). Custody granted to father based on "best interests of child." Court recognized no rule requiring maternal custody. Borowitz v. Borowitz, 19 Ill. App. 3d 176, 311 N.E.2d 292 (1974). Proper to look at wife's as well as husband's own financial means in determining alimony, in addition to age of parties and length of marriage.

People v. Boyer, 24 Ill. App. 3d 671, 321 N.E.2d 312 (1974).
Struck down higher penalty provision for incest between father and daughter—remanded for resentencing under penalty provision formerly applicable to incest between mother and sons or brothers and sisters (but see People v. York, below).

People v. Ellis, 57 Ill. 2d 127, 311 N.E.2d 98 (Sup. Ct. 1974).
Invalidated statutory provision extending juvenile status to female delinquents up to 18 and males up to 17—interpreted statute to apply to both males and females up to age 17.

Garland v. Garland, 19 Ill. App. 3d 951, 312 N.E.2d 811 (1974).
Upheld presumption favoring maintenance of original custody award to mother even though she was leaving state, not because of mother's sex but because of children's welfare.

In re Estate of Karas, 61 Ill. 2d 40, 329 N.E.2d 234 (Sup. Ct. 1975).
Upheld statutory scheme allowing illegitimate children to inherit from mother's but not father's intestate estate.

Marcus v. Marcus, 24 Ill. App. 3d 401, 320 N.E.2d 581 (1974).
No inflexible rule found requiring maternal custody for child of "tender years"—even if mother is fit custodian, best interest of this child is placement with father.

People v. Medrano, 24 Ill. App. 3d 429, 321 N.E.2d 97 (1974).
Upheld rape statute covering only male aggressors, based on what court saw to be physiological and sociological differences between the sexes.

Pancio v. Robinson, 23 Ill. App. 3d 848, 320 N.E.2d 101 (1974).
Cosmetologists, who formerly were restricted to cutting hair incidental to styling females' hair, can now cut hair of both sexes if only incidental to styling.

Phelps v. Bing, 58 Ill. 2d 32, 316 N.E.2d 775 (Sup. Ct. 1974).
Struck down statutory difference in age of marriage for men and women; now men are subject to lower age restrictions of women.

(continued)

TABLE 2.1 (continued)

State	Constitutional Provision	Significant ERA Decisions
Illinois (continued)		Randolph v. Dean, 27 Ill. App. 3d 913, 327 N.E.2d 473 (1975). Presumption favoring maternal custody not unconstitutional if it is only one factor among others rather than an inflexible rule.
		Slavis v. Slavis, 12 Ill. App. 2d 467, 299 N.E.2d 413 (1973). Neither ERA nor amended statute requiring support obligations for both men and women relieves father from payment of child support arrearages—past support obligations are a vested right of children.
		Tan v. Tan, 3 Ill. App. 3d 671, 279 N.E.2d 486 (1972). Proper to terminate alimony after seven years, as the couple had lived together only seven months and had no children—court noted that wife is employable and has responsibility for own support.
		People v. Yocum, 31 Ill. App. 3d 586, 335 N.E.2d 183 (1975). Conviction for aggravated incest between father and stepdaughter overturned because statute did not prohibit sexual conduct between mother and adopted or stepson.
		People v. York, 29 Ill. App. 3d 113, 329 N.E.2d 845 (1975). Upheld higher penalty for father's incest with daughter than for mother's incest with son because of high proportion of incest committed by men (but see People v. Boyer, above).
Maryland	Equality of rights under the law shall not be abridged or denied because of sex. (Declaration of Rights, Art. 46, December 1972)	Brooks v. Maryland, 24 Md. App. 334, 330 A.2d 670 (Ct. Spec. App. 1975). Upheld rape statute penalizing only male aggressors because of physiological differences between sexes because only women can become pregnant.
		Colburn v. Colburn, 20 Md. App. 346, 316 A.2d 283 (Ct. Spec. App. 1974). Husband challenging statute allowing alimony and attorney's fees to women only was found not to have standing since he was not seeking alimony or fees for himself.
		Cooke v. Cooke, 21 Md. App. 376, 319 A.2d 841 (Ct. Spec. App. 1974). Maternal preference in custody is constitutional if all other factors are equal and application is limited to situations where factual determination is otherwise impossible to make.

Maryland State Board of Barber Examiners v. Kuhn, 270 Md. 496, 312 A.2d 216 (Ct. App. 1973).

Statutory scheme prohibiting cosmetologists from washing and cutting men's but not women's hair found to be an unreasonable classification—court relied on "due process" rationale rather than ERA, however.

Minner v. Minner, 19 Md. App. 154, 310 A.2d 208 (Ct. Spec. App. 1973). Same as Colburn, above.

Tignor v. Tignor, Divorce No. 12601 (Anne Arundel Co. Cir. Ct. 1974). Allowed alimony to blind man whose wife had substantial assets and income over $10,000 per year (alimony provision now sex neutral).

In re Kujath, 1 Family L. Rep. 2533 (Sup. Ct. 1975). Struck down statute prohibiting wife to alienate over two-thirds of her estate by will without her husband's consent.

Montana	The dignity of the human being is inviolable. No person shall be denied the Equal Protection of the laws. Neither the State nor any person, firm, corporation, or institution shall discriminate against any person in the exercise of his civil or political rights on account of race, color, sex, culture, social origin or condition, or political or religious ideas. (1972 Constitution, Art. 2; Declaration of Rights, July 1973).	
New Mexico	No person shall be deprived of life, liberty or property without due process of law; nor shall any person be denied equal protection of the laws. Equality of rights under law shall not be denied on account of the sex of any person. (Art. 2, § 18, July 1973).	Schaab v. Schaab, 87 N.M. 220, 531 P.2d 954 (Aup. Ct. 1974). Alimony statute, already sex neutral on its face, upheld under ERA as to its application to appellant husband, whose wife had custody of all but one child and needed financial help of former spouse.

(continued)

TABLE 2.1 (continued)

State	Constitutional Provision	Significant ERA Decisions
Pennsylvania	Equality of rights under the law shall not be denied or abridged in . . . Pennsylvania because of the sex of the individual. (Art. 1, § 28, May 1971; Ann. Code § 27)	Com. ex rel. Buonocore v. Buonocore, 340 A.2d 579 (Super. Ct. 1975). Child support order against wife upheld since husband's income was inadequate and children were living with him and since wife had an ability to contribute—otherwise, children would have become "indigent" under "poor law."
		Butler v. Butler, 2 Family L. Rep. 2092 (Sup. Ct. 1975). Presumption that wife does not intend husband to benefit from her contributions to "entireties" property no longer valid. Court held that "entireties" property should be divided equally at divorce.
		Commonwealth v. Butler, 458 Pa. 289, 328 A.2d 851 (Sup. Ct. 1974). Upheld minimum sentence of male defendant under Muncy Act but declared portion of act providing for no minimum sentence for women to be unconstitutional.
		Conway v. Dana, 456 Pa. 536, 218 A.2d 324 (Sup. Ct. 1974). Parents have equal responsibility for child support according to their capacities. Presumption that fathers alone are responsible is no longer valid. Court should assess financial abilities of both.
		Corso v. Corso, 59 D. and C. 2d (Allegheny Co. Ct. C.P. 1972). Allowing "bed and board" divorce for women only no longer constitutional. Thus, this cause of action is no longer recognized in this county.
		DeRosa v. DeRosa, 60 D. and C. 2d 71 (Delaware Co. Ct. C.P. 1972). Statutes allowing alimony and counsel fees to women without adequate resources do not violate the ERA. (Statutes now sex neutralized.)
		DiFlorido v. DiFlorido, 331 A.2d 174 (Sup. Ct. 1975). Presumption favoring ownership of all household goods by husband is invalid. Nonmonetary as well as monetary contributions to household must be considered. Proper presumption in dividing goods on divorce is one of joint ownership.
		Einstein Medical Center v. Gold, 66 D. and C. 2d 347 (Phila. Co. Ct. C.P. 1975). Improper for wife to defend against payment of husband's medical expenses by relying on outmoded doctrine that only husbands are responsible for the "necessaries" of their spouses.

24

Frank v. Frank, 62 D. and C. 2d 102 (Lebanon Co. Ct. C.P. 1973).
Upheld statute allowing alimony pendente lite for women. (Now statute is sex neutral.)

Green v. Freiheit, Civil No. 1015, Docket No. 260259 (Family Div., 1st Judicial Dist., Oct. Term 1973).
Child support responsibility rests equally with both parents according to ability. Presumption charging father with primary obligation no longer valid under ERA.

Hakes v. Hakes, 67 D. and C. 2d 25 (Sullivan Co. Ct. C.P. 1974).
Real estate conveyed to wife in her own name did not create tenancy by entirety or constructive trust in favor of husband. Wife used no undue influence against husband and should not be bound by old presumptions about the marital unit.

Henderson v. Henderson, 458 Pa. 97, 327 A.2d 60 (Sup. Ct. 1974).
Found statutory provisions allowing alimony pendente lite and counsel fees for women only to use impermissible sex classification. Noted that statute had now been sex neutralized by legislature. Held that support rights and obligations depend not on sex but on relative financial circumstances of spouses.

Hopkins v. Blanco, 457 Pa. 90, 320 A.2d 139 (Sup. Ct. 1974).
Extended right to sue for loss of consortium to women.

Kaper v. Kaper, 227 Pa. Super. 377, 323 A.2d 223 (Sup. Ct. 1974).
Must consider mother's income and actual needs of child in assessing father's support obligation.

Keenan v. Penn Hills School District, 65 D. and C. 2d 764 (Allegheny Co. Ct. C.P. 1974).
ERA creates no new rights of one spouse in income of other during marriage.
Thus, it is proper for wives without outside income to be covered by school tax exemption, regardless of income of husbands.

Kehl v. Kehl, 57 D. and C. 2d 164 (Allegheny Co. Ct. C.P. 1972).
Statutory provisions allowing alimony and counsel fees to women only violate the ERA. (Provisions are now sex neutral.)

(continued)

TABLE 2.1 (continued)

State	Constitutional Provision	Significant ERA Decisions
Pennsylvania (continued)		Lukens v. Lukens, 224 Pa. Super. 227, 303 A.2d 522 (Super. Ct. 1973). Discrepancy in support provisions for wives and husbands does not violate the ERA because both spouses have a reciprocal and substantial right to support, despite the lack of mathematical equality.
		Murphy v. Murphy, 224 Pa. Super. 460, 303 A.2d 838 (Super. Ct. 1973). Upheld alimony and counsel fees for women only. (Statute is now sex neutral.)
		Norris v. Norris, 63 D. and C. 2d 239 (Phila. Co. Ct. C.P. 1974). ERA does not require precise equality in relationship to a substantial right to support for both sexes. Not unconstitutional to allow statutory "in rem" action for support by deserted wife but not by deserted husband.
		Commonwealth v. Pennsylvania Interscholastic Athletic Ass'n, 334 A.2d 839 (Cmwlth. Ct. 1975). By-law prohibiting competition by girls against boys in any athletic contest violates ERA. Sex averaging is prohibited.
		Percival v. City of Philadelphia, 317 A.2d 667 (Cmwlth. Ct. 1974). Exempting married women from arrest under writ of capias action to recover city wage taxes from nonresident employees violates ERA.
		Rogan v. Rogan, Civil No. 1934 (Luzerne Co. Ct. C.P. Oct. Term 1972). Neither husband nor wife should be allowed counsel fees under statutory scheme allowing such awards to women upon divorce. (Provision now sex neutral.)
		Commonwealth v. Santiago, 340 A.2d 440 (Sup. Ct. 1975). Common law doctrine of coercion of wife in crime by husband and wife no longer legitimate defense since wife's identity will no longer seem to merge with husband's on marriage.
		Wiegand v. Wiegand, 226 Pa. Super. 378, 310 A.2d 426 (Super. Ct. 1973), rev'd on other grounds, 337 A.2d 256 (Sup. Ct. 1975).

Texas

Equality under the law shall not be denied or abridged because of sex, race, color, creed, or national origin. (Art. 1, § 3a, November 1972)

Appellate court invalidated statutory provisions allowing "bed and board" divorce for women only. However, supreme court said ERA challenge not properly raised, so status of "bed and board" divorce remains in question in Pennsylvania.

Cooper v. Cooper, 513 S.W.2d 229 (Ct. Civ. App. 1974).
Unequal division of community property and child support obligations favoring wife on divorce does not violate ERA because court must consider sex-neutral factors such as wife's lower earning capacity.

Felsenthal v. McMillan, 493 S.W.2d 729 (Sup. Ct. 1973).
Tort of criminal conversation, available at common law to husbands only, must be made available to women, too.

Finley v. State of Texas, 527 S.W.2d 553 (Tex. Ct. Crim. App. 1975).
Upheld rape statute on "unique physical characteristics" rationale and fact that most rapes are by men against women.

Friedman v. Friedman, 521 S.W.2d 111 (Ct. Civ. App. 1975).
Family Code requires both parents to support children but does not require mathematically equal contributions. Services as well as money should be assessed.

Lipsky v. Lipsky, 525 S.W.2d 222 (Ct. Civ. App. 1975).
Upheld award of attorney's fees to wife as part of property settlement because her financial need, apart from her sex, justified such an award.

Mercer v. Board of Trustees, North Forest Ind. Sch. Dist., Civil No. 1302 (Houston Ct. Civ. App., filed June 2, 1976).
Improper for court to intervene in dispute over school regulation regarding hair length for boys, despite strict review standard of state ERA.

Perkins v. Freeman, 501 S.W.2d 424 (Ct. Civ. App. 1973), rev'd and remanded on other grounds, 518 S.W.2d 532 (Sup. Ct. 1974).
Upheld award of custody and attorney's fees to father because it was in best interests of child and because attorney's fees were "necessaries" for child. Like women, men should be awarded fees in proper situations under ERA.

(continued)

TABLE 2.1 (continued)

State	Constitutional Provision	Significant ERA Decisions
Texas (continued)		Scanlon v. Crim, 500 S.W.2d 554 (Ct. Civ. App. 1973). ERA extends right to action for common law breach of marriage promise to men as well as women. Texas Woman's Univ. v. Chayklintaste, 521 S.W.2d 949 (Ct. Civ. App. 1975). School must provide on-campus housing for men as well as women and must allow women as well as men to live off-campus. "Business judgment" was not an adequate defense to ERA challenge of policy not to build campus housing for men at formerly all-female campus.
Washington	Equality of rights and responsibility under the law shall not be denied or abridged on account of sex. (Art. 31, § 1, December 1972)	Ayers v. Employment Security Dep't, 85 Wash. 2d 500, 536 P.2d 610 (Sup. Ct. 1975). Husbands as well as wives should not be denied unemployment benefits for leaving work to follow their spouses to a new location under appropriate circumstances. Darrin v. Gould, 85 Wash. 2d 859, 540 P.2d 885 (Sup. Ct. 1975). Regulations prohibiting girls from playing on high school football team violate the ERA. Hanson v. Hutt, 83 Wash. 2d 195, 517 P.2d 599 (Sup. Ct. 1973). Unconstitutional to deny unemployment benefits to a woman automatically between the seventeenth week before childbirth and the sixth week subsequent. Singer v. Hara, 11 Wash. App. 247, 522 P.2d 1187 (1974). Statute prohibiting same-sex marriage upheld under ERA as not being sex discriminatory as between men and women. Smith v. Smith, 13 Wash. App. 381, 534 P.2d 1033 (1975). ERA requires equal responsibilities of parents for child support. Trial court erred in not considering income of both new marital units in assessing child support obligations from previous marriage. ERA does not require 50/50 breakdown, however.

Source: Compiled by the authors.

28

located in Table 2.1). Illinois has had approximately a dozen reported ERA cases; Maryland, Texas, and Washington have had approximately half a dozen cases each. The remaining states have produced little or no significant judicial interpretation of their equal rights provisions to date. This is attributable to the short time span since the enactment of their amendments, the successful implementation of the ERA through legislation, or, in the cases of Wyoming and Utah, the lack of recent political commitment to sex equality as an impetus for conformance efforts.

While the number of state ERA cases is not yet large, certain patterns are beginning to emerge. The results on the whole have been very positive. Courts are looking to the legislative history of the amendment and taking it as a strong mandate for sex equality in the law. In cases involving a benefit to members of one sex, judges have usually extended the statute or common law doctrine to cover both men and women. If a burden is imposed on members of one sex by the challenged law, the courts generally have struck it down and forced legislatures to enact sex-neutral legislation or have themselves redistributed the responsibility along sex-neutral lines.

However, the generally commendable judicial handling of this new constitutional principle should not obscure the fact that the results in the relatively small number of cases decided so far cannot offer unqualified assurance that the courts will continue to invalidate sex-based distinctions in the law. Further education of the judiciary is needed to bring deeper understanding of the principles involved in ERA cases. In addition, education of lawyers and the public generally to alert them to sex discrimination issues is necessary in order for the passage of an amendment to mean a real commitment to the elimination of sex discrimination.

Moreover, it is important to analyze the cases decided to date, for these cases will be the basis for the decisions of many persons, including judges, lawyers, and members of the public, about whether to press for ratification or implementation of the amendment in their respective states. What follows, then, is a discussion of both the results of cases in various substantive areas of law and the holdings concerning the appropriate standard of review for a court to apply under the ERA.

Scope and Standard of Review

Courts in jurisdictions with equal rights provisions have applied the principle of sex equality to a wide array of state law topics. As is consistent with the legislative history of the federal amendment, no substantive area of law has been excluded from review under the

amendment if the challenged practice is state action and not private
activity.* For example, an attempt by a lower court in Pennsylvania
to exclude marital support obligations from ERA scrutiny on the theory
that parties waive certain legal rights by signing the marriage "contract" was clearly laid to rest by that state's supreme court.[19]

The number of ERA cases remains small, despite the wide scope
of the state amendments, for two primary reasons. A number of
cases have not proceeded to a decision on the merits because of a
failure to meet procedural requirements. Counsels' failure to raise
the equal rights amendment issue in a timely manner has precluded
ERA review in several cases.[20] This problem should diminish as
the legal community and society at large become more sensitive to
questions of sex equality. Other cases have been dismissed because
the parties did not have standing to sue under the equal rights amendment.[21]

As discussed above, the standard of review mandated by the
legislative history of the federal amendment is an absolute ban on
sex discrimination. No state interest can justify sex distinctions in
the law. A court reviewing legislation under the amendment must,
consistent with this history, declare all sex-based laws and practices
unconstitutional. The only exceptions to this principle are constitutionally protected rights of individual privacy, which may justify sex
separation under certain circumstances, and laws based on "unique
physical characteristics," if the sex distinctions in the law are necessary for the accomplishment of a compelling state interest.[22]

This standard is more stringent than the one developed in sex
discrimination cases brought under the equal protection clause of the
Fourteenth Amendment. In that context, courts generally have required the state to show that the sex discrimination bears a direct
and substantial relationship to a valid state interest in order to withstand scrutiny.[23] Some courts have gone further and declared that
sex is to be treated in the same way as is race under the Fourteenth
Amendment; that is, a sex-based law will survive judicial scrutiny
only if it is necessary to a compelling state interest, the test under
the ERA for laws raising "unique physical characteristics" issues.[24]
Other courts, most notably the United States Supreme Court, have ap-

---

*The one issue exempted from ERA scrutiny by the courts has
been homosexual marriage. This is because of the clear legislative
history that the equal rights amendment does not preclude the states
from refusing to recognize that form of relationship as marriage.
This single exclusion from the amendment's coverage has no implications for the scope of review generally, and congressional intent has
been followed by the courts faced with an ERA challenge on this issue.[18]

plied varying standards in different cases raising sex discrimination issues, depending upon the substantive area under consideration and, more important, upon whether the Court perceives the law to be an attempt by the legislature to compensate women for past discrimination.[25]

The significance of the choice of applicable standard is that it determines which party bears the burden of proof and, in most instances, the result. In only one case has the Court found a compelling state interest that justified a racial classification; on the other hand, under a minimum scrutiny test the Court has almost always found some legitimate justification that is rationally related to the classification.[26]

The higher courts in those nine states (see p. 19) with equal rights provisions paralleling the language of the federal ERA generally have declared sex to be a "suspect" or "impermissible" classification or have applied some variety of "strict scrutiny" standard. Thus, sex-based classifications in those jurisdictions are, on the whole, being subjected to a higher standard of review than is common under the Fourteenth Amendment of the U.S. Constitution.[27] In the seven states with amendments more closely paralleling the equal protection clause,* the little existing judicial interpretation has tended to rely on a traditional or heightened "rationality" analysis.[28] An exception among the latter group is Illinois, where fairly extensive litigation in the area of sex equality has led to growing judicial articulation of a strict standard of review.[29]

Thus far, Pennsylvania has produced the body of judicial interpretation most in keeping with the legislative history of the federal ERA. While there has been some variation among the lower courts of that state as to the proper standard of review to be applied to sex-based classifications, the Pennsylvania Supreme Court has uniformly applied an absolute standard of review. In Henderson v. Henderson,[30] a case holding that the right of spousal support does not depend upon sex but upon the relative financial needs of the parties, the court declared:

> The thrust of the Equal Rights Amendment is to insure
> equality of rights under the law and to eliminate sex as a
> basis for distinction. The sex of citizens of this Common-
> wealth is no longer a permissible factor in the determina-
> tion of their legal rights and legal responsibilities. The
> law will not impose different benefits or different burdens
> upon the members of a society based on the fact that they
> may be man or woman (emphasis added).

---

*See p. 19, plus Utah and Wyoming.

Similarly, in Hopkins v. Blanco,[31] extending the right to sue for loss
of consortium to wives, and Commonwealth v. Butler,[32] requiring
minimum sentences for female as well as male offenders, the Pennsylvania Supreme Court enunciated a clear and unequivocal standard
of sex equality, in accord with the obvious purpose of the ERA.

In most of the other states with equal rights provisions, the decision about which standard will be adopted in interpreting the amendment is still pending. As discussed above, in substantive terms courts
are, for the most part, reaching the results being sought by advocates
of sex equality. Indeed, a heightened rationality test or some form
of strict scrutiny may well suffice in most instances to invalidate sex-
based classifications. However, if the courts follow the legislative
history of the federal amendment, the quality of analysis of cases
raising difficult questions (for example, unique physical characteristics issues) will be improved, and the results in these cases will not
have an adverse impact on the general ERA standard. For example,
in sustaining rape laws as permissible under the ERA because they
are directly related to unique physical characteristics of women and
men,[33] the courts have spoken of state interests in protecting women
or of the fact that a majority of rapes are committed by men against
women, thus lowering the standard of review in order to uphold the
laws. The use of this kind of reasoning may lead to a general weaken-
ing of the standard of review and to the serious consideration of state
interests that, under the absolute standard and its unique physical
characteristics corollary, would not justify a sex distinction.

Moreover, the application of minimum tests does not offer a
comprehensive theory of equality or uniform principles to govern case
decision. The absolute standard of the federal ERA is far more satisfactory from this point of view because its clarity and simplicity offer
a model for both judicial and legislative implementation of the principle of sex equality.

Remedies

The general trend, both in terms of common law doctrines and
statutory law, has been for courts in ERA jurisdictions to strike down
outdated or unreasonable restrictions on one sex and to extend important rights, benefits, and obligations to members of both sexes.
In reaching these results, state courts have relied on both the general
and specific legislative history surrounding the enactment of their
equal rights amendments, as well as their broad authority to engage
in statutory construction.

Overall, state courts' application of the ERA to nonconforming
statutes has utilized long-standing judicial rules of interpretation and

construction.[34] Of primary consideration in this process has been a determination of legislative intent. When such legislative intent is not explicit, courts have considered other factors such as the overall scheme of the law, the statutory language and intent of related laws, and the importance and feasibility of saving the law through construction, including the impact of eliminating or extending particular rights or liabilities on both the public and the covered class. In construing criminal statutes, court decisions in ERA jurisdictions have reflected a traditional bias against judicial enlargement of the scope of criminal liabilities. In the civil area, on the other hand, the courts have been more liberal in construction, often extending statutory coverage by reading in sex-neutral language and standards when necessary to save important rights and obligations.

Criminal

Criminal statutes concerning rape, incest, felony nonsupport, juvenile delinquency status, adult sentencing, and a wife's common law defense of criminal coercion by her husband have been challenged on ERA grounds. Based on approximately a dozen reported cases in five jurisdictions, two patterns are emerging: courts are not using the equality principle to extend criminal liability to previously uncovered groups and they are striking down sex-based provisions without disturbing the criminal liability of the particular defendant class making the ERA challenge.[35]

Cases challenging unequal sentencing standards based on sex are illustrative of these patterns. Pennsylvania had a statutory dual system of sentencing adult offenders. Men were sentenced to minimum terms under a traditional sentencing act, but a newer act covering only women did not provide for minimum sentences. After holding in Commonwealth v. Butler[36] that such a dual system was unconstitutional, the Pennsylvania Supreme Court had to decide how best to remedy the situation. The court reasoned that since the original sentencing act was neutral on its face, it was the later act exempting women from general coverage that created an unconstitutional result. Therefore, striking down the exemption would be more in harmony with overall legislative intent concerning sentencing and would avoid the undesirable result of removing the only existing authority for sentencing males.[37] Both men and women are now subject to generally applicable standards of minimum sentencing under the original act. The specific relief sought by the male defendant—potentially earlier parole in the absence of a mandatory minimum sentence—was denied as a consequence of the court's basic concern with preserving an overall statutory scheme consistent with legislative intent and public need.

In People v. Boyer,[38] the Appellate Court of Illinois struck down a penalty provision for incest between a father and daughter that

provided a higher sentence than could be given for incest between a
mother and son or between siblings. The court did not reverse the
male defendant's conviction, however, but simply remanded for resentencing under the lesser penalty provision for other forms of incest.
Thus, the court neither extended nor eliminated criminal liability
against the legislative or public will. Similarly, in People v. Ellis,[39]
the Illinois Supreme Court invalidated a statutory provision extending
juvenile status to female delinquents up to age 18 and males up to
age 17 by striking down the special extension for females and interpreting the statute to apply to juveniles of both sexes up to age 17.
Again the specific relief sought by the male defendant, a 17-year-old
seeking to avoid criminal prosecution, was denied.

There have been several cases challenging sex-based rape laws;
however, in many states, the legislatures have enacted sex-neutral
rape or sexual assault statutes offering protection to all victims of
sexual aggression. This is clearly the preferable response to the current crisis in rape law enforcement. The courts, when faced with
such challenges to sex-based rape laws, have sustained the laws in
question, generally because of the unique physical vulnerability of
women to forcible attack, although some courts have applied the standard too loosely by relying on noncompelling state interests. It would
be far preferable for the legislatures to preclude the need for court
action on these laws by acting to reform them; however, the results
that have been reached are undoubtedly in line with legislative intent
behind the ERA.

Civil

The large majority of ERA civil cases has involved challenges
to statutes or judicial doctrines in the area of domestic relations,
such as child and spousal support, child custody, and marital property. In deciding these cases, the courts have been liberal in fashion-
ing remedies to accomplish sex equality. For example, a number of
common law actions and remedies formerly available to only one sex
—breach of marriage promise, loss of consortium, criminal conversation, and the "necessaries" doctrine—have been extended by courts
in ERA jurisdictions to cover both sexes.[40] In Hawaii, where a
statute restricted a married woman's common law right to use the
name of her choice, a court simply struck down the restriction.[41]

Child and spousal support and child custody have been the most
frequent subjects of ERA litigation because of their long history of sex-
based standards and their critical relationship to overall sex equality
in the society. Courts have exerted their equitable powers fairly
broadly in such cases, extending sex-based statutory provisions concerning the rights and obligations of spouses and parents to both sexes

equally and replacing traditional sex-stereotyped judicial doctrines with sex-neutral standards. The general rule that has emerged in ERA jurisdictions is that intrafamily financial obligations must not be assessed on the basis of sex or sex-based notions but rather on the basis of the actual financial assets and needs of the parties involved. The critical underpinnings of this judicial doctrine of "equitable distribution" are the elimination of any rules stating that one or the other spouse is liable for a set amount of spousal or child support—that is, 100 percent or 50 percent—and judicial recognition of the value of unremunerated contributions to the household in assessing support obligations or dividing marital property upon divorce.

For example, Cooper v. Cooper[42] and Friedman v. Friedman,[43] two cases decided recently by the Texas Court of Civil Appeals, clarify the ERA's mandate concerning equal support obligations. That mandate has not been taken to mean that the court must make mathematically equal child support orders but that it should give due consideration to the ability of each parent to contribute money or services necessary for the maintenance of his or her children. The Cooper court also upheld against an ERA challenge an unequal distribution of community property in favor of the wife, relying on such sex-neutral considerations as her lower earning capacity. The Pennsylvania Supreme Court struck down a presumption that the husband owns the household goods, replacing it with a presumption of joint ownership and holding that nonmonetary contributions to the household must be considered in dividing goods at divorce.[44]

Similarly, in child custody disputes, judicial presumptions such as the "tender years" doctrine, which favors maternal custody of young children, have been largely repudiated when challenged under a sex equality standard. Courts in ERA jurisdictions where the legislatures have not already done so are now beginning to enunciate more clearly a number of sex-neutral factors to be considered in determining custodial placement "in the best interests of the child."

A few cases that have been widely publicized because they seem to impose unfair burdens on women in the name of sex equality in fact arise out of unusual situations, in light of which the result of the court makes good sense. For example, a court in Illinois terminated alimony to a woman under a sex-neutral standard. This result made sense because the marriage had lasted only seven months, there were no children born of it, and alimony had already been paid for seven years.[45] Similarly, a Pennsylvania case in which a woman was charged with child support is also fair when viewed in the context of its facts.[46] In that case, the woman had left her husband, who was caring for the children, and she had a salary commensurate with his. Undoubtedly, the existence of facts not sympathetic to the claims of the women in these cases motivated the husbands to persist in litigation. They represent a small number of cases and an even smaller number of marital situations.

When confronted with ERA challenges in civil cases outside the field of domestic relations, state courts have also exercised broad remedial powers. In one jurisdiction, the ERA was relied on to invalidate a law prohibiting cosmetologists from cutting men's hair, thus allowing them to serve customers of either sex, subject to state licensing requirements. [47] The Washington Supreme Court has recognized the right of husbands as well as wives to leave work to follow their spouses to a new location without jeopardizing their eligibility for unemployment benefits. [48] That court also has struck down an automatic denial of benefits to women between the seventeenth week before and sixth week subsequent to childbirth. [49] In education, courts in three ERA jurisidctions have struck down athletic regulations prohibiting girls from competing against boys in interscholastic sports. [50] Another struck down a state university rule prohibiting female students from living off campus and extended to male students the right to have on-campus housing made available to them. [51]

3

METHODOLOGY OF
STATE LEGISLATIVE
REFORM

INTRODUCTION

When the equal rights amendment (ERA) is ratified, the question will then naturally arise: What must be done to conform state law to the amendment's strict principles of sex equality? As illustrated by the preceding section on case law under state ERAs, the courts can play an important role in interpreting the equal rights amendment and applying it to cases before them. The courts are of necessity confined to piecemeal decision making, however, since they interpret legal principles only in light of the facts of each case that comes before them. Similarly, the executive of a state can influence the administration of the law but is not normally authorized to make sweeping changes in the law. The natural place to concentrate, then, is on the legislative body of each state, since the legislature is mandated to adopt general rules and formulate basic governmental policies. This political mandate and the fact-finding tools at its disposal make the state legislature the appropriate branch of government to oversee the process of review and revision that implementation of the ERA requires.

As of 1976, a majority of the states already have made some effort to identify sex-based laws, a process that has been simplified by the widespread use of computerization of state codes. Many also have taken steps to bring their laws into line with the requirements of the ERA. The strength of the legislative commitment to this activity and the degree of success attained vary widely from state to state. The mandate for conformance is paramount in those states that have adopted equal rights amendments to their own constitutions. Comprehensive efforts have not been limited to these states, however. Some of the most outstanding illustrations of reform can be drawn from

states in which the commitment to sex equality derives from ratification of the federal ERA or from the lobbying efforts of feminists
around selected issues of popular concern, such as rape.

States just beginning a systematic review of their laws can learn
much from the experience of those already well on their way. Certain fairly well delineated steps and resources can now be identified
to facilitate the processes of locating laws and policies in need of
change, consulting with those knowledgeable about their operation and
impact, bringing a feminist perspective to bear on the formulation of
new legislation, and organizing a coalition to effectively educate the
public and the legislature about necessary reform. Some states that
have undertaken comprehensive reform efforts have published reports
detailing both the methodology and the conclusions of their work.
These reports, most of which appear in the state-by-state bibliography
at the end of this book, are a major source for less experienced states.

This chapter, drawing on the experience of the states that have
enacted the various reforms discussed in the following chapters, discusses the basic steps in the ERA implementation process, offering
recommendations and identifying models from those jurisdictions in
which ERA conformance efforts are well under way. It should be noted
that these examples are chosen to illustrate patterns of reform and
do not comprise an exhaustive report on all conformance activity across the country.

ORGANIZATIONAL FORMAT

The first step in initiating comprehensive ERA implementation
is the selection of a group or person to oversee the conformance work
that ultimately will be presented to the legislature. This is a critical
matter since the person or persons primarily responsible for the initial recommendations may determine not only their substantive content
but also the political clout such recommendations eventually carry.
In New Mexico and Pennsylvania, for example, the early and strong
support of the traditional bar associations has been vital in lending
political clout, as well as expertise, to ERA conformance efforts.
The state reviews initiated to date have been carried out by a variety
of bodies with differing jurisdictions. Usually authorized by the legislature or the governor's office, these bodies have included standing
committees or subcommittees of the state legislature, ad hoc committees of the legislature, the staff of the legislative drafting council or
legislative review commission, and state commissions on the status
of women or special ERA commissions appointed from the public with
representation from the feminist and legal communities. Some early
studies were done by law professors and students or private coalitions,

often connected to the state law school, but these were generally confined to the identification of sex-based laws.*

The most effective model is probably one that begins with a central commission or committee officially authorized to undertake ERA
conformance. If headed by a well-respected person and funded adequately to carry out the task thoroughly, this group need not be large.
Its core should be drawn from the feminist and legal communities,
particularly feminist attorneys. It should also include some persons
knowledgeable about the legislative process, both in terms of statutory
drafting techniques and the political feasibility of various alternatives,
as well as those familiar with the organized groups available as resources. This central commission should be supplemented by task
forces or committees in particular substantive areas. This permits
the expertise of a large number of people to be tapped without involving people in areas unfamiliar to them. These task forces should include legislative staff, state agency personnel, representatives from
the governor's office, law professors, the organized bar, private
practitioners, and citizen and feminist groups interested in specific
reforms.

Ohio, for example, using a variation of this model, incorporated
into its conformance process a wide range of experience as well as the
requisite amount of political sensitivity and power.[1] In 1974, a few
weeks after ratifiaction of the federal ERA, the governor and the attorney general of the state joined in creating a citizens' task force to
study implementation of the amendment in state law. Soon thereafter,
an executive order was issued creating an official Ohio Task Force
for the Implementation of the Equal Rights Amendment. This task
force was charged with reviewing all statutes and regulations, drafting new statutes or amendments when necessary, and submitting a
final report of recommendations for ERA conformance. A bipartisan
membership was appointed, including 13 women and 12 men with back-
grounds in such varied fields as law, business or labor, social work,

---

*Special public commissions or projects of state commissions on
the status of women with a strong mandate for comprehensive ERA
conformance have been set up in a number of states, including Ohio,
Maryland, California, Pennsylvania, Washington, and Massachusetts.
Other states, including Connecticut, Kansas, Illinois, Indiana, Florida,
Montana, New York, Wisconsin, and Vermont, have relied on bodies
within the existing legislative structure to carry out preliminary reviews of sex-based laws. In a few states, such as Arizona, Indiana,
New Mexico, and Tennessee, state university professors and students,
bar associations, or private citizen groups have conducted the conformance studies.

education, homemaking, the military, and the legislature. This membership was then divided into six working committees, supplemented with outside experts, to study critical areas of law: marriage and family; children; employment; insurance, pensions, and tax; criminal law; and public obligations. A special ad hoc committee also was organized to study education questions. Beginning with a computer print-out identifying sex-based laws, these committees studied, consulted with experts, and formulated recommendations over several months. These committee recommendations were then debated by the full task force before being incorporated into a final report to the governor and attorney general. Unfortunately, because of a change in the balance of political power at the state level in Ohio during the time the report was being completed, only a few of its carefully thought out recommendations for ERA implementation have successfully passed the legislature to date.

Another model is that of Pennsylvania, where the state Commission for Women has overseen the conformance process with the assistance of the attorney general's office. Responsibility for the initial screening of the computer print-out of statutes and recommendations for change was distributed by commission staff to law professors, students, and feminist practitioners around the state. In addition, state agency liaisons were selected to review state laws and administrative policies under their agency jurisdiction that required revision. Then, the commission staff, with the assistance of the legislative drafting council, prepared a package of recommended bills. These bills are currently being given final review and approval by a special committee of the state bar association before they are submitted to the legislature.

IDENTIFICATION OF LAWS AND POLICY MAKING

The first task facing an ERA conformance task force or commission, of course, is the identification of all laws that are facially discriminatory on the basis of sex. In states that have computerized their laws, the most efficient way to locate sex-based laws is by means of a print-out of all statutory provisions containing at least one of a number of specially selected words likely to indicate sex distinctions. In Pennsylvania, for example, 75 words ranging from "pregnancy" to "grandmother" were fed into the computer to obtain a preliminary print-out of several hundred potentially discriminatory statutes. Student researchers then scanned these laws to eliminate those requiring no action, such as those referring to the treatment of female animals. The remainder were classified into substantive area groupings for distribution to the various experts around the state and in state agencies who were responsible for making recommendations for change.

At this stage, each substantive area of law should be scanned again to pull out those statutory provisions requiring only simple terminological changes. Some states have opted to avoid the widespread but minor changes necessary to eradicate all sex-based references in their statutes, particularly gender pronouns, by enacting a general provision stating that msculine references include women. Pennsylvania, as well as a number of other states, has chosen to approach the sex neutralization of language on a provision-by-provision basis, since the process is actually quite simple and prevents ambiguities that might arise from a general prescription about statutory language. The prophylactic and educational benefits of a state code that is, in fact, facially neutral throughout should not be minimized by states facing this choice.

In determining whether simple terminological changes are appropriate or whether repeal is preferable in the case of a sex-based law that appears to be obsolete, special attention should be given to laws granting specific legal rights to married women. Most of these laws, passed around the turn of the century, represent statutory repeals of the common law disabilities traditionally attached to married women. The statutes often extend to married women the same legal rights assumed by others in the population without question. Simple repeal of these laws, under the modern-day understanding that married women share a legal status equal to that of their husbands, may be a viable option for states seeking ERA conformance. However, the repeal of these special "affirmative" laws may be misinterpreted to revive the common law disabilities they were meant to displace. It is therefore important that legislative drafters clearly state at some appropriate point in the code that the repeal of these sex-based laws does not resurrect the common law doctrines that predated them. In addition, to the extent that such laws accurately reflect and serve to clarify the current legal status of married persons, they can be preserved with minor changes, such as changing "married women" to "married persons" or "spouses."

While the move toward sex-neutral terminology is an important first step, unfortunately some states have not yet moved beyond this mechanical approach to ERA reform. Once decisions have been made about straightforward terminological changes, the harder task of substantive law revision must be undertaken for those provisions where sex neutrality entails more than a change from "he" to "person," for example. As in the simpler process described above, each substantive provision must be scrutinized to determine whether it should be repealed, because it is archaic or places an unfair burden on one sex that should not or cannot be extended to the other, or whether it should be extended to cover both sexes in an otherwise undisturbed form. When neither of these solutions seems appropriate, the law must be

recast in order to reflect a new perspective of sex equality and to promote desirable social policy goals.

In order to fully conform state law to an absolute principle of
sex equality, study must not end with those statutory provisions or
policies that are discriminatory on their face. A second major group
of laws requiring scrutiny is those that, though neutral on their face,
have a disparate impact on members of one sex. While these provisions do not contain explicit discriminatory language, they may result
in some of the most invidious forms of discrimination. An exhaustive
computer search guided by an imaginative list of key words will locate
some of these laws. The bulk of this task, however, must be done by
experts in sex discrimination who are also familiar with the day-to-
day application of state laws. Of course, those areas in which there
is a well-known tradition of explicit discrimination, such as domestic
relations, employment, social insurance, and criminal law, are
prime targets in the search for laws that impact members of one sex
disparately. Another dimension of this task is the review of affirmative civil rights statutes to ensure that they protect all identifiable
victims of discrimination based on sex stereotyping. For example,
a fair housing law prohibiting discrimination based on sex might not
be interpreted to cover discrimination against single-parent families,
the vast majority of which are female-headed, unless additional
language prohibiting discrimination based on marital status is included.

When neutral laws with a disparate impact on one sex have been
identified, each must be subjected to the following test: are the social
policies furthered by the law consistent with an overall goal of sex
equality, and would a law with a less severe impact on one sex accomplish the same purpose? As specifically illustrated throughout the
substantive law chapters of this book, even when such laws further
important social goals, they often fail to pass the second aspect of the
test and thus require some form of amendment to comply fully with
the ERA.

In seeking efficient and intelligent ways to revise these impermissible "neutral rules," all of the resources already mentioned in
connection with facially discriminatory laws are available. Of particular importance at this stage is the assistance of feminist practitioners because of their heightened sensitivity to the law's subtle, as well
as direct, impact on women. Another resource that has proved successful in identifying targets for change and arriving at sound policy
decisions is the use of law school students, working for credit under
the supervision of law faculty or practitioners, to initially screen the
statutory provisions and collect materials helpful in recommending
policies in various substantive law areas. Student papers are then
submitted to task force members as part of the package of resources
available for debate and decision making. The model laws drafted by

the Commissioners on Uniform State Laws are critical contributions to this package, since they often span a whole legal area, such as marriage and divorce, changing both facially discriminatory and facially neutral provisions when necessary to create a rational scheme of modern state law. These model laws are excerpted throughout this book, with commentary on their strong points and their occasional drawbacks. Hopefully, this book, as well as the reports of state ERA conformance projects noted in the bibliography and the firsthand knowledge of individuals who have worked closely with ERA conformance in the past, can provide states undertaking this process with insight into the advisability of particular policy choices, examples of skillful drafting, and advice on model laws or articles to consult.

Once all statutes, library materials, and other resources have been collected and distilled by the staff of the ERA commission, they should be distributed to the relevant task forces. Since the general policies that inform the conformance review should be uniform throughout the process, the work of the individual task forces should be supervised and scheduled by the central commission. In this way, all recommendations will be doctrinally consistent, as well as free of any technical contradictions, overlaps, omissions, and so on. The actual drafting of legislation probably should be done by the legislative drafting council of the state in order to draw on its expertise and comply with the rigors of good statutory language and other technicalities of legislative drafting. The commission should submit its recommendations to the council with explicit instructions about the underlying goals of the reform and check each bill carefully before it is finally submitted to the legislature.

LEGISLATIVE IMPLEMENTATION

When policy decisions have been made concerning each law drawn into question by the ERA and proposed amendments have been drafted, the next critical step is the determination of the form in which recommendations for change should be presented to the legislature. Many states, including Arizona, Iowa, Kentucky, Montana, and Vermont, have chosen to gather all statutes identified for reform into a single omnibus bill, which is presented to the legislature as a comprehensive package to eliminate sex discrimination from the state code. Often these omnibus bills have been limited to terminological changes, however, which enhances their chance for complete or substantial acceptance by the legislature but undercuts their long-range impact. Other states, particularly those that have tackled some of the more subtle or controversial elements of sex discrimination, have opted against an omnibus bill approach, fearing that opposition to one or more provisions of the bill would delay or prevent passage of the remainder of the bill. In those cases, the more straightforward recommendations for change should be submitted at the outset, followed by piecemeal introduction of other bills carefully calculated to muster the broadest support. Ultimately, the decision of how best to present an ERA conformance package to the state legislature is a political one. The wisest course is to consult with sympathetic legislators and citizen groups familiar with the legislative process and the history of reform efforts in each particular state.

Legislative ERA implementation in many states has reached a level of expertise worth sharing with individuals working in locations where conformance efforts are now being initiated for the first time. Indeed, the availability of model organizational formats, written materials and commentary, and proposed legislative packages covering a wide variety of state law issues makes it relatively easy for states to move beyond simple facial neutrality to a state code that reflects a full commitment to sex equality throughout its provisions. This book is primarily concerned with this critical legislative process, the logical first step in state ERA conformance efforts. Hopefully, in the years to come, attention also will be turned to a methodology for ensuring sex equality in the policies and structures of the various administrative agencies and other institutions comprising the public sector.

4

CRIMINAL LAW

INTRODUCTION

Sexism permeates the criminal justice system. It appears most strikingly in the definition of substantive crimes involving sexual behavior; in law enforcement practices concerning sex crimes against women; in the double standard of delinquency for male and female juveniles; and in the very different treatment of male and female offenders in penal institutions. Most of the differences have been harmful to women. Both adult and juvenile women are imprisoned for activity tolerated in men or boys; rape law enforcement is so inadequate that it has been blamed for widespread underreporting of the crime; and opportunities available to male prisoners are routinely denied to women. At the same time, men's prisons stand out as very oppressive institutions compared to those in which women are incarcerated.

The ERA will be a powerful tool for the elimination of sexist laws and policies in criminal law enforcement and administration. This chapter discusses the major problem areas and possible directions of change and evaluates reforms that have already taken place.

RAPE

Background

Rather than protecting all adults and youths from sexual assault or coercion, rape laws traditionally have singled out women and girls as a vulnerable class needy of special protection against men. The traditional legal definitions of rape are explicitly sex-based.[1] Com-

45

mon law (or forcible) rape is defined as unlawful carnal knowledge by a man of a woman, forcibly and against her will.* Statutory rape is carnal knowledge by a man of a girl under a certain age. As of 1975, 25 jurisdictions still failed to protect male victims of sexual aggression in their forcible rape laws, while 22 failed to protect male youths from statutory rape (see Table 4.1).[†]

More critical in its social and legal impact, however, has been the practice of enforcing rape laws in ways that create wide disparity between the treatment of female victims of rape and victims of other crimes in the law enforcement process. In stark contrast to the seemingly protective stance toward women of the traditional definitions of rape, the enforcement of rape laws has evidenced distrust and fear of women. Rape victims who file criminal charges frequently find themselves humiliated by law enforcement personnel and the courts because of the prevailing belief that women provoke, acquiesce in, or even fabricate the rapes that they report. At the investigatory stage, male police officers' attitudes may lead them to focus questioning on the victim's rather than the assailant's behavior.[2]

In many states, if and when the victim testifies in court, she will face strict evidentiary standards peculiar to rape trials, which further reflect doubt on her honesty and general character. For example, some states still require special corroboration of the elements of a rape by evidence other than the victim's own testimony.[3] In addition, cross-examination about the victim's reputation or her sexual history may be permitted to impeach her testimony or rebut her claim of nonconsent.[4]

---

*The primary exception to the protection of women from assault has been the refusal of most states to permit a charge of forcible rape by a married woman against her husband, regardless of the circumstances and degree of coercion actually involved.

[†]Those jurisdictions that cover rape of males in their forcible rape statutes are: Colorado, Connecticut, Delaware, Florida, Illinois, Indiana, Michigan, Montana, New York, Ohio, Texas, and Washington. These statutes are aimed primarily at homosexual rape. Those jurisdictions that explicitly protect young males in their statutory rape provisions are: Arkansas, Colorado, Delaware, Florida, Illinois, Indiana, Kansas, Kentucky, Louisiana, Maine, Massachusetts, Michigan, Minnesota, Montana, Nebraska, New Hampshire, New Mexico, North Dakota, Ohio, Pennsylvania, South Dakota, Utah, and Washington. It should be noted, however, that other states that do not explicitly protect males from forcible or statutory rape may protect young or helpless males from various forms of sexual imposition or corruption in other criminal statutes (see Table 4.1 for citations).

TABLE 4.1

State Rape Law Reforms

State	Statutes	Statutory Rape	Date of Recent Amendment	Sex Neu-tral	Forcible Rape	Date of Recent Amendment	Sex Neu-tral	Evidentiary Rules: Recent Amendments
Alabama	Ala. Code (1959)	Tit. 14, §§ 398, 399 § 11.15.120		No	§ 395		No	No
Alaska	Alaska Stat. 1962 (1975 ed.)	§ 11.15.120		No	§ 11.15.120		No	No
Arizona	Ariz. Rev. Stat. Ann. (1956)	§ 13-611	L. 1962, ch. 52, § 1	No	§ 13-611		No	No
Arkansas	Ark. Stat. Ann. (1964)	§ 41-1803 et seq.	Acts 1975, No. 280, § 1803 et seq.	Yes	§ 41-1803 et seq.	Acts 1975, No. 280, § 1803 et seq.	Yes	No
California	Cal. Penal Code (1970)	§ 261.5	Added by Stats. 1970, ch. 1301, § 2	No	§ 261		No	Yes
Colorado	Colo. Rev. Stat. Ann. (1973)	§ 18-3-405	Repealed and reenacted by L. 1975, at 630, § 1	Yes	§ 18-3-402	Repealed and reenacted by L. 1975, at 628, § 1	Yes	Yes
Connecticut	Conn. Gen. Stat. Ann. (1975)	§ 53a-72		No	§ 53a-72		No	No

(continued)

TABLE 4.1 (continued)

State	Statutes	Statutory Rape	Date of Recent Amendment	Sex Neutral	Forcible Rape	Date of Recent Amendment	Sex Neutral	Evidentiary Rules: Recent Amendments
Delaware	Del. Code Ann. (1975)	Tit. 11, § 761 [§ 762-2d degree]	59 Del. Laws, ch. 547 (1974)	Yes	Tit. 11, § 764 [§ 763-2d degree]	59 Del. Laws, ch. 547 (1974)	Yes	No
District of Columbia	D.C. Code Encycl. Ann. (1967)	§ 22-2801		No	§ 22-2801		[No]	No
Florida	Fla. Stat. Ann. (1965)	§ 794:011	L. 1974, ch. 74-121, § 2 L. 1975, ch. 75-298, § 17	Yes	§ 794:011	L. 1974, ch. 74-121, § 2 L. 1975, ch. 75-298, § 17	Yes	Yes
Georgia	Ga. Code Ann. (1972)	§ 26-2018		No	§ 26-2001		No	No
Hawaii	Hawaii Rev. Stat. (1968)	§§ 730-32	L. 1972, No. 9, §§ 733-35	No	§§ 730-32	L. 1972, No. 9, §§ 733-35	No	Yes
Idaho	Idaho Code (1948)	§ 18-6101		No	§ 18-6101		No	No
Illinois	Ill. Ann. Stat. (Smith-Hurd 1972)	Ch. 38, §§ 11-4, -5		Yes	Ch. 38, § 11-1		Yes	No
Indiana	Ind. Ann. Stat. (Burns 1975)	§ 35-42-4-3	Acts 1976, ch. 148, § 2	Yes	§ 35-42-4-1	Acts 1976, ch. 148, § 2	Yes	Yes
Iowa	Iowa Code Ann. (1950)	§ 698.1		No	§ 698.1		No	Yes

State	Statute							
Kansas	Kan. Stat. Ann. (1974)	§§ 21-3503-04	L. 1975, ch. 193, §§ 1-2	Yes	§ 21-3502	No	1974, H.B. 232, § 81	No
Kentucky	Ky. Rev. Stat. Ann. (1975)	§ 510.040 et seq.		Yes	§ 510.040 et seq.	Yes		No
Louisiana	La. Rev. Stat. Ann. (1974)	§ 42	Acts 1975, No. 612, § 1	Yes	§§ 41, 41.1	No	Acts 1975, No. 612, § 1	No
Maine	Me. Rev. Stat. Ann. (1975)	Tit. 11, § 252 et seq.	L. 1975, ch. 499, § 1	Yes	Tit. 11, § 252 et seq.	Yes	L. 1975, ch. 499, § 1	No
Maryland	Md. Ann. Code (1976)	Art. 27, §§ 12, 462, 462A		No	Art. 27, § 461	Yes		No
Massachusetts	Mass. Gen. Laws Ann. (1970)	Ch. 265, § 23	Stat. 1974, ch. 74, § 3	Yes	Ch. 265, § 22	Yes	Stat. 1974, ch. 474, § 1	No
Michigan	Mich. Comp. Laws Ann. (1968)	§ 750.520a et seq.	Acts 1974, No. 266, § 1	Yes	§ 750.520a et seq.	Yes	Acts 1974, No. 266, § 1	Yes
Minnesota	Minn. Stat. Ann. (1964)	§ 609.342 et seq.	L. 1975, ch. 374; L. 1974, ch. 576, § 1	Yes	§ 609.342 et seq.	Yes	L. 1975, ch. 374	No
Mississippi	Miss. Code Ann. (1973)	§§ 97-3-65, -67		No	§ 97-3-71	No		No
Missouri	Mo. Ann. Stat. (Vernon 1953)	§ 559.260	L. 1975, H.B. No. 150, § A	No	§ 546.330, § 559.260	No	L. 1975, H.B. No. 150, § A	No
Montana	Mont. Rev. Codes Ann. (1969)	§§ 94-5-502 to -504	L. 1973, ch. 513, § 1; L. 1975, ch. 2, § 1; ch. 129, § 1	Yes	§§ 94-5-502 to -504	Yes	L. 1973, ch. 513, § 1; L. 1975, ch. 2, § 1; ch. 129, § 1	Yes
Nebraska	Neb. Rev. Stat. (1975)	§§ 28-408.01 to -408.05, as amended	L. 1975, L.B. 23, § 9	Yes	§§ 28-408.01 to -408.05, as amended	Yes	L. 1975, L.B. 23, § 9	Yes

(continued)

TABLE 4.1 (continued)

State	Statutes	Statutory Rape	Date of Recent Amendment	Sex Neutral	Forcible Rape	Date of Recent Amendment	Sex Neutral	Evidentiary Rules: Recent Amendments
Nevada	Nev. Rev. Stat. (1973)	§ 200.365		No	§ 200.363		No	Yes
New Hampshire	N.H. Rev. Stat. Ann. (1955)	§ 632-A:1 et seq.	L. 1975, § 302:1	Yes	§ 632-A:1 et seq.	L. 1975, § 302:1	Yes	No
New Jersey	N.J. Stat. Ann. (1969)	§ 2A:138.1		No	§ 2A:138.1		No	No
New Mexico	N.M. Stat. Ann. (1953)	§ 40A-9-20 et seq.	L. 1975, ch. 109	Yes	§ 40A-9-20 et seq.	L. 1975, ch. 109	Yes	Yes
New York	N.Y. Penal Law (McKinney 1975)	§ 130.05 et seq.		No	§ 130.05 et seq.		No	Yes
North Carolina	N.C. Gen. Stat. (1969)	§ 14-21		No	§ 14-21		No	No
North Dakota	N.D. Cent. Code (1976)	§ 12.1-20-03 et seq.		Yes	§ 12.1-20-03 et seq.		Yes	Yes
Ohio	Ohio Rev. Code Ann. (Baldwin 1972)	§ 2907.02 et seq.	L. 1972, H.B. 511	Yes	§ 2907.02 et seq.	L. 1972, H.B. 511	Yes	Yes
Oklahoma	Okla. Stat. Ann. (1958)	Tit. 21, § 1114 et seq.		No	Tit. 21, §§ 1111, 1114 et seq.		No	Yes
Oregon	Ore. Rev. Stat. (1953)	§ 163.355 et seq.		No	§ 163.355 et seq.		No	Yes
Pennsylvania	Pa. Stat. Ann. (1973)	Tit. 18, § 3122	L. 1976, Act No. 53	Yes	Tit. 18, § 3121	L. 1976, Act No. 53	Yes	Yes

State	Statute							
Rhode Island	R.I. Gen. Laws Ann. (1970)	§ 11-37-2		No	§ 11-37-1 et seq.		No	No
South Carolina	S.C. Code Ann. (1962)	§ 16-80		No	§ 16-71		No	No
South Dakota	S.D. Comp. Laws Ann. (1969)	§§ 22-22-1, -7	L. 1975, ch. 169, §§ 1, 5; L. 1976, ch. 158, §§ 22-1, -3	Yes	§ 22-22-1	L. 1975, ch. 169, §§ 1, 5; L. 1976, ch. 158, § 22-1	Yes	Yes
Tennessee	Tenn. Code Ann. (1975)	§§ 39-3705, -3706		No	§ 39-605 §§ 39-3701 to -3703		No	Yes
Texas	Tex. Penal Code Ann. (1974)	§§ 21.09, 21.11	Acts 1973, ch. 399, as amended	No	§ 21.02 et seq.	Acts 1973, ch. 399, as amended	No	Yes
Utah	Utah Code Ann. (1953)	§ 76-4-405	L. 1973, ch. 196	Yes	§ 76-5-402	L. 1973, ch. 196, § 101	No	No
Vermont	Vt. Stat. Ann. (1974)	Tit. 13, § 3202		No	Tit. 13, § 3201		No	No
Virginia	Va. Code Ann. (1950)	§ 18.2-63	L. 1975, chs. 15, 16, 606	No	§ 18.2-61	L. 1975, chs. 14, 15	No	No
Washington	Wash. Rev. Code Ann. (1975)	§ 9.79.200	L. 1975, ch. 14, § 10	Yes	§ 4.79.140	L. 1975, ch. 14, § 10	Yes	Yes
West Virginia	W. Va. Code Ann. (1966)	§ 61-2-15		No	§ 61-2-15		No	No
Wisconsin	Wis. Stat. (1958)	§ 944.10		No	§ 944.01		No	No
Wyoming	Wyo. Stat. Ann. (1957)	§ 6-63		No	§ 6-63		No	No

Source: Compiled by the authors.

This distrust of forcible rape victims is often heightened in the context of statutory rape, even though actual consent is not at issue. While some states have lowered their statutory age of consent in recent years to conform to changing sexual mores, over half still extend protection to girls until the age of 16 and even 18 in some cases. * Because the likelihood of prior sexual activity and apparent consent may be high in these older age brackets, a general disregard for statutory rape charges results, a disregard that then extends to victims in lower age ranges as well.

Disproportionate penalties, particularly for forcible rape, have posed a problem by encouraging juries to acquit the defendant or convict him of a lesser offense in order to prevent life imprisonment or death. [5] Several states still permit sentences of up to life imprisonment for forcible rape. [6]

Impact of the ERA

Explicit Discrimination

Statutes that penalize perpetrators and/or protect victims of crime in terms of their sex are subject to revision under the ERA. In the area of rape, however, statutory or judicial definitions that impose criminal liability on the forcible or attempted insertion of the penis into the vagina may be drawn narrowly enough to meet the "unique physical characteristics" exception to the equality principle. Because

---

*Alabama (girl up to 16/boy at least 16); Alaska (girl up to 16/ lesser penalty if boy under 19); Arizona (girl up to 18/boy at least 14); Arkansas (up to 16 for carnal abuse/ignorance of age a defense above 11); California (girl up to 18); Delaware (up to 16); D.C. (girl up to 16); Idaho (girl up to 18/boy at least 14); Illinois (girl up to 16/boy 4 years older); Iowa (girl up to 17/actor over 25; any girl up to 16); Kansas (up to 16); Maryland (up to 16 for carnal knowledge/actor over 18); Massachusetts (up to 16); Missouri (up to 16); Montana (up to 16/ actor 3 years older); Nebraska (up to 16/actor over 18 for 1st degree); Nevada (girl up to 16/penalty varies by age of actor); New York (girl up to 17/actor over 21 for 1st degree); Oregon (girl up to 16); Rhode Island (girl up to 16); South Carolina (girl up to 16); South Dakota (up to 16/actor 4 years older for felony); Tennessee (girl up to 18 for carnal knowledge); Vermont (girl up to 16/actor over 16); Washington (up to 16/actor over 18 for 3d degree); West Virginia (girl up to 16/actor over 16); Wisconsin (girl up to 18/penalty varies by ages of victim and actor); and Wyoming (girl up to 18 for 3d degree).

women's genitals can be penetrated by male genitals during an act of
sexual assault, this form of criminal aggression is unique in the sex-
based nature of its elements, and the legislative history of the federal
amendment indicates that forcible rape laws of this variety would
withstand strict scrutiny. [7] Courts in three states that have equal rights
amendments to their constitutions have upheld forcible rape statutes
under this type of analysis. [8] As the Court of Criminal Appeals of
Texas reasoned in Finley v. State:

> [A] unique characteristics test can be applied to justify
> the statutory classification. Hymen and uterine injury to
> female rape victims, the possibility of pregnancy, and
> the physiological difficulty of a woman forcing a man to
> have sexual intercourse with her all suggest a justification
> for the sexual distinction embodied in Art. 21.02. [9]

Such reasoning is not generally applicable to sex-based statutory
rape laws, however, since the critical element of forcible penetration
is not a factor. Statutory rape, by definition, involves consensual
sexual activity but with someone who is below the legal age of consent.
Thus, the special vulnerability of the vagina to unwanted penetration
cannot be relied upon as a justification for protecting young girls but
not young boys from sexual advances that this society finds undesirable or at least premature. Other traditional justifications, such as
the protection of young girls' virginity before marriage, cannot withstand ERA scrutiny since they are based on double social or sexual
standards rather than on actual physical differences between the
sexes. A possible exception might be a law designed to protect girls
who have not yet reached puberty from nonforcible, as well as forcible, intercourse because of the physical damage that could result
from penetration by the penis of an adult male.

Neutral Rules

In addition to explicit sex-based distinctions in the rape laws,
a number of ostensibly neutral rules have a severely disparate impact
on women because women comprise the overwhelming percentage of
rape victims. A number of evidentiary rules, derived from stereotypical views of women who "cry rape," unfairly call into question
the credibility and character of the victim by permitting instructions
to the jury on the unreliability of her testimony or wide-ranging cross-
examination on her prior sexual history.

As no credible, nonsexist rationales have been advanced for the
use of different evidentiary rules in rape cases than those applicable
in criminal proceedings generally, these special corroboration re-

quirements and instructions may fall afoul of the ERA because of
their disparate impact. Some of them may have to be repealed altogether; others, particularly those concerning the prior sexual conduct
of the complainant, should be replaced with provisions protecting the
legitimate interests of both the complainant and the defendant.

A second type of neutral rule that has a disparate impact on women is the prohibition against married persons charging their spouses
with rape. This virtually universal rule was an outgrowth of the common law view that a man has an absolute right to sexual relations
with his wife regardless of her desire. It has more recently been
justified on the basis of the constitutional right of privacy in the marriage relation, particularly in sexual matters. This reasoning is
unpersuasive. Marriage relationships are not now free from the
scrutiny of the law since spouses may generally charge each other
with nonsexual physical abuses. Indeed, there has been a growing recognition of the need to bring the problems of spousal abuse into the
mainstream of the law.

In addition, the refusal of legal redress against coercive or
abusive sexual relations is not needed to guard the privacy of voluntary marital sex against third parties, particularly the government.
To allow one spouse to claim this right as a shield for the abuse of
the other is an untenable perversion of its purpose. [10]

While the issue has not reached the courts in this country, the
high court of Israel has held, under that country's Women's Equality
Act, that the marriage license does not alter one's right to choose
when and whether to have sexual relations with one's spouse and that
it is unconstitutional to deny a married woman the right to file rape
charges against her husband. [11] Under our ERA, marriage between
the parties would still be a legitimate factor in weighing the merits
of a particular rape charge, but there is no satisfactory rationale
for refusing to entertain a complaint altogether. At the very least,
states may be required to eliminate the spousal exception for those
couples who are no longer living together, whether by private choice
or under a court decree, in order to mitigate the impact of this rule
on women.

Policy Recommendations

While the courts have used the doctrine of "unique physical characteristics" to sustain traditional rape statutes against ERA challenges, state legislatures have the option of extending both the protections and penalties of rape laws to both sexes. Under such an approach, all victims of unwanted sexual aggression or of sexual advances they are incompetent to handle because of age or mental capa-

city are provided with a uniform measure of protection. In addition, sex neutralization eliminates the need for the detailed physiological delineations required by the "unique physical characteristics" doctrine. Freed of these constraints, statutory definitions of rape can focus on relevant sex-neutral considerations, such as the degree of force, the nature of the sexual contact, and the age and mental capacity of the victim. Thus, for example, an act of forcible penetration might be treated more severely than mere touching—regardless of the sex of the parties involved, the locus of penetration, or the characterization of the act as homosexual or heterosexual—because penetration is per se a more intrusive form of assault and more likely to cause physical injury than simple contact or harassment.

Protection of women from rape would not be jeopardized by this sex-neutralization and consolidation process. Indeed, comprehensive legislative reform may rid rape laws of the sexist trappings now encumbering them. For example, if opinions in all cases of sexual assault were to be harmonized under one statutory scheme, the impact of judicial precedent developed under traditional rape provisions that perpetuates sex stereotyping of rape victims would be minimized. In addition, consolidation would encourage the reform of restrictive evidentiary rules that derive from this same sex stereotyping. Moreover, since most people probably would agree that homosexual rape is as serious a crime as heterosexual rape, it would be appropriate to set common penalties for both.

In addition to sex-neutralizing classifications of perpetrators and victims, these classifications should be reviewed to see if they are truly responsive to the needs of the victim-community. In particular, spousal exclusions and the scope of statutory rape laws should be reevaluated. Whether or not the ERA mandates the modification of spousal exclusions, it is wise, in light of current data concerning physical abuse in the home, to permit persons allegedly raped by their spouses to bring a charge. Questions of proof or false claims can be handled as in any other offense, and protection will have been extended to many individuals in need of public support for their complaints.

As noted in the section on ERA impact, states that have statutory rape laws punishing sexual contact per se may retain these laws only in a form that does not distinguish among perpetrators and victims on the basis of sex unless the legal age limit is such that only prepubescent female victims are covered. Because these statutes punish sexual contact of a voluntary nature, it is also important for states to review the scope of such provisions to determine if their underlying rationale—the protection of young people from sexual advances to which they are too immature to give meaningful consent—is truly being served. In states where the legal age of nonconsent still extends to 16 and beyond, the strict liability of statutory rape laws is an inappropriate standard for the voluntary sexual liaison of two older youths. Moreover, the inevitable focus on a more mature complainant's sexual history undercuts the impact of other cases in which the youth and sexual immaturity of the victim should compel extreme concern. It is probably best for states to amend their laws by limiting statutory rape to sexual contact with very young children, perhaps below the age of 14 or even 12, for whom meaningful consent is impossible. Older youths still can be protected against undue sexual advances by related provisions proscribing nonconsensual sexual activity or specially penalizing sexual contact with a minor by a family member, a guardian, or some other person in a position of authority.[12] States that choose to continue covering the middle and older teenage range should, at the very least, limit liability to defendants who are several years older than the complainant.

The critical issue of enforcement must also be addressed. Because of the high incidence of unreported rapes and unsuccessful rape prosecutions, there is little to be gained from sex neutralization and consolidation of sexual assault statutes unless steps also are taken to remove barriers to effective enforcement. Of primary concern is the elimination or amendment of strict evidentiary rules peculiar to rape cases.

In the area of prior sexual conduct and reputation evidence, a number of states have enacted legislation that avoids an absolute bar against the use of such evidence by the defense yet guards the complainant against highly prejudicial or humiliating cross-examination in the courtroom. These enactments generally provide for an in camera review (that is, before the judge alone) of prior conduct evidence, followed by a judicial order as to its admissibility and the manner in which it may be presented to the jury.[13] Similarly, lowering the maximum penalty for rape to conform to that for other felonies should remove an obstacle to jury willingness to convict when the facts warrant it and thereby improve rape law enforcement.

Innovative forms of affirmative legislation should also concern policy makers considering the enforcement of rape laws. In particular, new legislation or regulations should focus on increasing the number of female law enforcement personnel, particularly in rape control units; providing sensitivity training for all personnel with whom rape victims routinely come in contact; and establishing rape crisis centers for counseling and medical attention.

State Reform Efforts

States that have reconsidered their rape statutes in an effort to remove sex bias generally have enacted two types of change: reworking the statutory definitions of rape and the evidentiary standards for rape prosecutions. Some states also have revamped investigatory mechanisms in an attempt to make them more sensitive to rape victims.

Since 1970, a large number of states have amended the common law definitions of forcible and statutory rape through the use of sex-neutral phraseology, thereby treating sexual aggression by and against both males and females in a uniform fashion. Presently, 18 states* have both forcible and statutory rape provisions that are facially neutral as to the actor and the victim (see Table 4.1). Fourteen of these treat forcible and statutory rape in a single, consolidated format, with the ages of the actor and victim as one among a number of factors determining the degree of seriousness of the crime.[†] Four other states (Illinois, Kansas, Louisiana, and Utah) have sex neutralized only their statutory rape provisions, while a fifth (Maryland) has sex neutralized its forcible rape provisions but still retains a sex-based definition of statutory rape. In enacting sex-neutral terminology, a few states have retained the term "rape,"[‡] but most have adopted new generic terms to describe all criminal sexual aggression, such as "sexual battery" or "criminal sexual conduct."[14]

Some states have retained separate provisions for heterosexual vaginal rape and enacted complementary statutes to reach other kinds of heterosexual or homosexual assaults. These statutes, often derivatives of the Model Penal Code, commonly prohibit "deviate sexual intercourse" or "sodomy," defined as any sexual aggression or penetration other than that of the penis penetrating the vagina.[15]

Reforms concerning the spousal exclusion also have been adopted in a number of states, with a view to limiting the scope of the exception to ongoing and viable marriages. The most common approach has been to define "spouse" as a legal husband or wife unless the couple is living apart or one spouse has filed for separate maintenance or divorce.[16] A few states now have laws that contain no reference to or exceptions for spouses.[17]

---

*Arkansas, Colorado, Florida, Indiana, Kentucky, Maine, Massachusetts, Michigan, Minnesota, Montana, Nebraska, New Hampshire, New Mexico, North Dakota, Ohio, Pennsylvania, South Dakota, and Washington. Massachusetts law still has sex-based provisions regarding administering drugs to a female for purposes of seduction and having intercourse with a feebleminded or insane female, but its general rape provisions have been sex neutralized (see Table 4.1 for citations).

[†]Arkansas, Colorado, Florida, Kentucky, Maine, Michigan, Minnesota, Montana, Nebraska, New Hampshire, New Mexico, North Dakota, Ohio, and South Dakota.

[‡]Massachusetts, Ohio, Pennsylvania, and Washington, for example, still retain the term "rape" but with a sex-neutralized definition.

In addition to the efforts to sex neutralize and treat statutory rape as other forms of criminal sexual conduct, the primary focus since 1970 has been on lowering the age range for victims. Over half the states now set the statutory age of consent at 15 or lower, at least for the more serious degrees of statutory rape, and many provide that the actor must be a number of years older than the complaining witness.[18]

In addition to changes in statutory definitions of sexual assault, approximately half of the states have undertaken significant reform of the evidentiary rules peculiar to rape cases. The most common reforms have been restrictions on the use of evidence concerning a rape victim's past sexual behavior or reputation for chastity to impeach credibility or rebut a claim of nonconsent.[19] Nineteen states have enacted provisions requiring that such evidence first be offered to the judge in camera so that (s)he can make a legal determination of its relevance and potential prejudicial nature outside the presence of the jury.[20] Some of these states also permit only evidence of specific sexual behavior between the complainant and the defendant* or other specific sexual contact that would account for the presence of semen, pregnancy, or disease at issue in the trial.[†] A few states (Colorado, Florida, and North Dakota) exempt evidence of prior sexual conduct or contact between the parties from the pretrial screening requirements. The use of evidence of reputation for chastity to impeach the complaining witness' credibility, rather than to rebut nonconsent, has been completely disallowed in some jurisdictions as irrelevant or unnecessarily prejudicial per se.[‡] California and Nevada have explicit provisions forbidding instructions to the jury concerning a rape victim's "unchaste character" or judicial implications about the credibility or likelihood of consent based on past sexual behavior.[21] Both South Carolina and Virginia have an unusual pretrial proceeding allowing out-of-court deposition from the victim designed to protect her from humiliation.[22]

On the issue of standard of proof, Connecticut, Florida, Iowa, Michigan, New Mexico, Pennsylvania, New York, and Washington have repealed, or enacted affirmative disallowances of, special corroboration requirements for the testimony of forcible rape victims.[23]

---

*California (to rebut nonconsent), Iowa (other behavior admissible if within past year), Indiana, Michigan, Montana, Nebraska, Oregon (to rebut nonconsent), and Pennsylvania and Washington (both states make past behavior with defendant admissible on issue of consent).

†Indiana, Michigan, and Montana.

‡Florida, Nevada (only as rebuttal to prosecution evidence), Oregon, and Washington.

Colorado and Nevada prohibit instructing the jury that the victim's testimony should be strictly scrutinized solely because of the nature of the charge or difficulty of proof.[24] Michigan, Ohio, and Pennsylvania specifically prohibit in their reform provisions any requirement that rape victims show actual physical resistance in order to prove the use of force.[25]

In an effort to improve the pretrial treatment of rape victims as well as the quality of rape reporting and prosecution, California,[26] Massachusetts,[27] and Minnesota[28] have enacted affirmative legislation establishing special educational and administrative programs for rape assistance. These include counseling of rape victims and the training of personnel with whom victims come in contact to develop heightened sensitivity. The California and Massachusetts provisions specifically encourage utilization of more policewomen in rape enforcement. The Minnesota enactment and reform enactments in both Nevada and Ohio also provide that medical expenses incurred by the victim be absorbed by the state as a cost of prosecution.[29]

One of the best models of rape law reform is an act that went into effect in Michigan in 1975. The new Michigan act represents a major departure from the law's traditional treatment of rape and provides a good model for other states willing to undertake a serious program of sex neutralization and consolidation of their sexual assault statutes and reform of their evidentiary standards.

All sexual aggression is treated under a single statutory scheme titled "criminal sexual conduct." The neutral terms "actor," "victim," and "person" are used throughout to designate relevant parties. A primary drawback of these otherwise broad definitions is an exclusion of acts between married persons unless they are living apart and a legal separation or divorce is pending.

The crime is divided into three degrees of seriousness, based on such variables as the age and mental capacity of the victim, the level of force, and the nature of the sexual contact (touching or penetration), without regard to gender or any other biological differentiations. "Sexual penetration," which constitutes the most serious degree of sexual misconduct, is broadly defined to cover not only traditional heterosexual intercourse but also oral and anal intercourse and the intrusion of any object into the genital or anal openings. "Sexual contact," which constitutes the second degree of sexual misconduct, is also broadly defined to cover contact with not only the primary genital area but also the groin, inner thigh, buttock, or breast.

Statutory rape is merged into the general nonconsensual rape provisions. Under the first two degrees, a victim of statutory rape must be under the age of 13 unless the perpetrator is a relative or member of the victim's household or is in some other position of authority. Only under the least serious degree are persons between the ages of 13 and 16 protected against voluntary sexual conduct, and actual penetration is an essential element of the crime. These distinctions should be further refined by a requirement that a defendant in a case involving nonforceable conduct with a teenage complainant be at least three or four years older than the victim.

The Michigan law also remedies many of the traditional disparities in the evidentiary rules and standards for rape prosecutions. Special corroboration requirements and the need to prove resistance are affirmatively disallowed, although cautionary instructions or remarks to the jury alluding to the victim's sexual reputation are not.

The Michigan law permits restrictive use of evidence of the victim's sexual conduct or reputation with regard to consent. Such evidence is admissible only if it relates to past sexual contact with the defendant or to a specific instance of sexual activity that could account for the source of semen, pregnancy, or disease at issue in the trial. The act requires the defendant to make an offer of proof to the court within ten days of arraignment if such evidence is going to be presented. Finally, the act provides that the judge rule on the offer of proof in a closed pretrial hearing to determine its relevance to the case and to balance its prejudicial nature against its probative value.

The Michigan law does not specify under what circumstances, if any, evidence of the victim's sexual conduct or reputation is admissible with regard to his or her general credibility. Such an omission raises the possibility that this evidence will be allowed in court without adequate restrictions. The California Evidence Code, recently amended by an enactment entitled Robbins' Rape Evidence Law, provides that a defendant must make a special motion during trial with an offer of proof of the relevance of prior sexual conduct to the credibility of the witness. The court can then order a special hearing outside the presence of the jury to determine its relevance and to stipulate what evidence, if any, will be admitted and the nature of the questioning. Neither law adds the desirable restriction that this type of motion should be entertained only if the complaining witness first raises the issue with testimony concerning his or her prior sexual history or reputation.

The model statute laid out below is based primarily on the Michigan statute, with recommended changes and additions, including partial incorporation of the California Evidence Code.*

---

*The text is excerpted from the Michigan law, and the numbering is altered accordingly; underscored words are amendments or additions, and brackets indicate deletions.

Model Rape Statute

Definitions

(a) "Actor" means a person accused of criminal sexual conduct.

(b) "Intimate parts" includes the primary genital area, groin, inner thigh, buttock, or breast of a human being.

(c) "Mentally defective" means that a person suffers from a mental disease or defect which renders that person temporarily or permanently incapable of appraising the nature of his or her conduct.

(d) "Mentally incapacitated" means that a person is rendered temporarily incapable of appraising or controlling his or her conduct due to the influence of a narcotic, anesthetic, or other substance administered to that person without his or her consent, or due to any other act committed upon that person without his or her consent.

(e) "Physically helpless" means that a person is unconscious, asleep, or for any other reason is physically unable to communicate unwillingness to an act.

(f) "Personal injury" means bodily injury, disfigurement, mental anguish, chronic pain, pregnancy, disease, or loss or impairment of a sexual or reproductive organ.

(g) "Sexual contact" includes the intentional touching of the victim's or actor's intimate parts or the intentional touching of the clothing covering the immediate area of the victim's or actor's intimate parts, if that intentional touching can reasonably be construed as being for the purpose of sexual arousal or gratification.

(h) "Sexual penetration" means sexual intercourse, cunnilingus, fellatio, anal intercourse, or any other intrusion, however slight, of any part of a person's body or of any object into the genital or anal openings of another person's body, but emission of semen is not required.

(i) "Victim" means the person alleging to have been subjected to criminal sexual conduct.

First Degree Criminal Sexual Conduct

(a) A person is guilty of criminal sexual conduct in the first degree if he or she engages in sexual penetration with another person and if any of the following circumstances exists:

(1) That other person is under 13 years of age.

(2) The other person is at least 13 but less than 16 years of age and the actor is a member of the same household as the victim, the actor is related to the victim by blood or affinity to the fourth degree of the victim, or the actor is in a position of authority over the victim and used this authority to coerce the victim to submit.

(3) Sexual penetration occurs under circumstances involving the commission of any other felony.

(4) The actor is aided or abetted by one or more other persons and either of the following circumstances exists:

(i) The actor knows or has reason to know that victim is mentally defective, mentally incapacitated or physically helpless.

(ii) The actor uses force or coercion to accomplish the sexual penetration. Force or coercion includes but is not limited to any of the circumstances listed in subdivision (6) (i) to (v).

(5) The actor is armed with a weapon or any article used or fashioned in a manner to lead the victim to reasonably believe it to be a weapon.

(6) The actor causes personal injury to the victim and force or coercion is used to accomplish sexual penetration. Force or coercion includes but is not limited to any of the following circumstances:

(i) When the actor overcomes the victim through the actual application of physical force or physical violence.

(ii) When the actor coerces the victim to submit by threatening to use force or violence on the victim, and the victim believes that the actor has the present ability to execute these threats.

(iii) When the actor coerces the victim to submit by threatening to retaliate in the future against the victim, or any other person, and the victim believes that the actor has the ability to execute this threat. As used in this subdivision, "to retaliate" includes threats of physical punishment, kidnapping or extortion.

(iv) When the actor engages in the medical treatment or examination of the victim in a manner or for purposes which are medically recognized as unethical or unacceptable.

(v) When the actor, through concealment or by the element of surprise, is able to overcome the victim.

(7) The actor causes personal injury to the victim, and the actor knows or has reason to know that the victim is mentally defective, mentally incapacitated, or physically helpless.

(b) Criminal sexual conduct in the first degree is a felony punishable by imprisonment in the state prison for [life or for any term of years] not more than 20 years.

Second Degree Criminal Sexual Conduct

(a) A person is guilty of criminal sexual conduct in the second degree if the person engages in sexual contact with another person and if any of the following circumstances exists:

(1) That other person is under 13 years of age.

(2) That other person is at least 13 but less than 16 years of age and the actor is a member of the same household as the victim, or is related by blood or affinity to the fourth degree to the victim, or is in a position of authority over the victim and the actor used this authority to coerce the victim to submit.

(3) Sexual contact occurs under circumstances involving the commission of any other felony.

(4) The actor is aided or abetted by 1 or more other persons and either of the following circumstances exists:

(i) The actor knows or has reason to know that the victim is mentally defective, mentally incapacitated or physically helpless.

(ii) The actor uses force or coercion to accomplish the sexual contact. Force or coercion includes but is not limited to any of the circumstances listed in First Degree Criminal Sexual Conduct (6) (i) to (v).

(5) The actor is armed with a weapon, or any article used or fashioned in a manner to lead a person to reasonably believe it to be a weapon.

(6) The actor causes personal injury to the victim and force or coercion is used to accomplish the sexual contact. Force or coercion includes but is not limited to any of the circumstances listed in First Degree Criminal Sexual Conduct (6) (i) to (v).

(7) The actor causes personal injury to the victim and the actor knows or has reason to know that the victim is mentally defective, mentally incapacitated, or physically helpless.

(b) Criminal sexual conduct in the second degree is a felony punishable by imprisonment for not more than [15 years] ten years.

Third Degree Criminal Sexual Conduct

(a) A person is guilty of criminal sexual conduct in the third degree if the person engages in sexual penetration with another person and if any of the following circumstances exist:

(1) That other person is at least 13 years of age and under 16 years of age, and the defendant is at least four years older.

(2) Force or coercion is used to accomplish sexual penetration. Force or coercion includes but is not limited to any of the circumstances listed in First Degree Criminal Sexual Conduct (6) (i) to (v).

(3) The actor knows or has reason to know that the victim is mentally defective, mentally incapacitated or physically helpless.

(b) Criminal sexual conduct in the third degree is a felony punishable by imprisonment for not more than [15 years] ten years.

Second or Subsequent Offenses

(a) If a person is convicted of a second or subsequent offense under First, Second, or Third Degree Criminal Sexual Conduct, the sentence imposed under those sections for the second or subsequent offense shall provide for a mandatory minimum sentence of at least five years.

(b) For purposes of this section, an offense is considered a second or subsequent offense, if, prior to conviction of the second or subsequent offense, the actor has at any time been convicted under First, Second, or Third Degree Criminal Sexual Conduct, or under any similar statute of the United States or any state for a criminal sexual offense including rape, carnal knowledge, indecent liberties, gross indecency, or an attempt to commit such an offense.

Assault with Intent to Commit Criminal Sexual Conduct

(a) Assault with intent to commit criminal sexual conduct involving sexual penetration shall be a felony punishable by imprisonment for not more than ten years.

(b) Assault with intent to commit criminal sexual conduct in the second degree is a felony punishable by imprisonment for not more than five years.

Corroboration of Victim's Testimony

The testimony of a victim need not be corroborated in prosecutions under sections above.

Resistance

A victim need not resist the actor in prosecution under sections above.

In Any Criminal Prosecution for the Crime of Rape

For violation of sections above or for an attempt to commit or an assault with intent to commit any such crime, the jury shall not be instructed that it may be inferred that a female who has previously consented to sexual intercourse with persons other than the defendant would be therefore more likely to consent to sexual intercourse again.

A jury shall not be instructed that prior sexual conduct in and of itself of the complaining witness may be considered in determining the credibility of the witness.

Unchaste Character

The term shall not be used by any court in any criminal case in which the defendant is charged with a violation of sections above or attempt to commit or assault with intent to commit any crime defined above in any instruction to the jury.

Admissibility of Evidence on Issue of Fact

(a) Evidence of specific instances of the victim's sexual conduct, opinion evidence of the victim's sexual conduct, and reputation evidence of the victim's sexual conduct shall not be admitted under sections above unless and only to the extent that the judge finds that the following proposed evidence is material to a fact at issue in the case and that its inflammatory or prejudicial nature does not outweigh its probative value:

(1) Evidence of the victim's past sexual conduct with the actor.

(2) Evidence of specific instances of sexual activity showing the source of origin of semen, pregnancy, or disease.

(b) If the defendant proposes to offer evidence described in subsection (a) (1) or (2), the defendant within [ten] 30 days after the arraignment on the information shall file a written motion and offer of proof. The court may order an in camera hearing to determine whether the proposed evidence is admissible under subsection (a). If new information is discovered during the course of the trial that may make the evidence described in subsection (a) (1) or (2) admissible, the judge may order an in camera hearing to determine whether the proposed evidence is admissible under subsection (a).

Admissibility of Evidence on Issue of Credibility

(a) In any prosecution under sections above, if evidence of sexual conduct of the complaining witness is offered to attack the credibility of the complaining witness, the following procedure shall be followed:

(1) A written motion shall be made by the defendant to the court and prosecutor stating that the defense has an offer of proof of the relevancy of evidence of the sexual conduct of the complaining witness proposed to be presented and its relevancy in attacking the credibility of the complaining witness.

(2) The written motion shall be accompanied by an affidavit in which the offer of proof shall be stated.

(3) If the court finds that the offer of proof is sufficient, the court shall order a hearing out of the presence of the jury, if any, and at such hearing allow the questioning of the complaining witness regarding the offer of proof made by the defendant.

(4) At the conclusion of the hearing, if the court finds that evidence proposed to be offered by the defendant regarding the sexual conduct of the complaining witness is relevant, the court may make an order stating what evidence may be introduced by the defendant and the nature of the questions to be permitted. The defendant may then offer evidence pursuant to the order of the court.
(b) The court shall entertain a motion under this section only upon a finding by the court that the complaining witness first put his or her sexual conduct or character into issue.

Suppression of Names and Details

Upon the request of the counsel or the victim or the actor in a prosecution under sections above, the magistrate before whom any person is brought on a charge of having committed such offense shall order that the names of the victim and actor and details of the alleged offense be suppressed until such time as the actor is arraigned on the information, the charge is dismissed, or the case otherwise concluded, whichever occurs first.

Married Persons

Alternative I: A person does not commit sexual assault under this act if the victim is his or her legal spouse, unless the couple are living apart [and] or one of them has filed for separate maintenance or divorce.
Alternative II: Nothing in this act shall preclude the bringing of a charge of sexual assault by an individual against a person who is his or her legal spouse.

PROSTITUTION

Background

With the exception of a few Nevada counties that have exercised a local option to legalize it,[30] prostitution is a criminal offense in every jurisdiction. Traditionally, prostitution was defined as an act that could be committed only by women, while men who paid for or were paid for sexual activity were not penalized.[31] This disparity in treatment was a legal embodiment of stereotypes about men's and women's proper social and sexual roles and of the view that a woman's sexual "wares" were a commodity for men to purchase at will. In recent years, many jurisdictions have amended their prostitution laws to cover the activity of both male and female prostitutes in both heterosexual and homosexual encounters.* However, less than half the states explicitly penalize the patrons of prostitution, and many of those that do impose less stringent penalties against patrons than prostitutes (see Table 4.2).[32] In addition, even when male prostitutes and patrons are covered by statutes, selective enforcement still tends to center on the activities of female prostitutes.

Litigation under the equal protection clause of the Fourteenth Amendment challenging statutes or selective enforcement practices that treat prostitutes differently from patrons has not been generally successful.[33] The traditional view of prostitution as a "female occupation" has led to judicial acceptance of the state's choice to deter prostitution-related activities by prosecuting the predominantly female seller class rather than the predominantly male buyer class.

In addition to the disparate treatment of female prostitutes as compared to male prostitutes or patrons, there are other serious problems with the drafting of prostitution laws. Almost half of the states still criminalize the status of being a prostitute instead of or in addition to proscribing acts of providing sexual services for money. Frequently, the status of being a prostitute has been incorporated into a state's general prohibitions against vagrancy, loitering, or disorderly conduct. In Arizona, for example, "a lewd and dissolute person who lives in and about houses of ill fame" is defined as a "vagrant" and is subject to arrest.[34] In California, "every person who . . . willfully resides in a house of ill fame is guilty of a misdemeanor," and that person's "common repute" may be received as competent evidence of character.[35] Another common variation is a provision making it unlawful to "remain in" or "reside in" any one of a long list of locations "for purposes of prostitution." By penalizing a "type" or "status" of person, such provisions may be vulnerable to the charges of undue vagueness and unlawful "preventive detention" under which so many general loitering or vagrancy ordinances have been invalidated in recent years.[36] In addition, 40 jurisdictions have laws prohibiting so-

---

*Eight of these jurisdictions—Arkansas, California, Connecticut, Idaho, Maine, Montana, Oklahoma, and Pennsylvania—explicitly cover homosexual prostitution either by statutory definition or through clearly developed legislative history or case law. The remaining 20 jurisdictions use neutral language, such as "sexual conduct," or a combination of terms, such as "sexual intercourse or deviate sexual conduct," indicating that both homosexual and heterosexual behavior are included. In addition, 19 states that do not cover paid homosexual acts in their prostitution laws have general proscriptions against sodomy, whether or not it is performed for a fee.

TABLE 4.2

State Prostitution Law Reforms

State	Statute	Origin of Law (post-1960 reforms)	Conduct Proscribed	Homosexual Included[a]	Status[b]	Neutrality[c]	Patron[d]
Alabama	Ala. Code (1958) Vagrancy: tit. 14, § 437		A vagrant is . . . any person who is a prostitute.		x	nf	
Alaska	Alaska Stat. (1962) Prost: § 11.40.210–230		The giving or receiving of her body by a female for sexual intercourse for hire is unlawful. It is illegal to engage in prostitution or to procure or to solicit.			df	
Arizona	Ariz. Rev. Stat. Ann. (1956) Vagrancy: § 13–991 Prost: § 13–589		A lewd and dissolute person who lives in and about houses of ill fame is a vagrant. As is a person who resides in a house of ill fame.		x	nf	
Arkansas	Ark. Stat. Ann. (Supp. 1975) Vagrancy: § 41–2914 Prost: § 41–3001, § 41–3002 Patron: § 41–3003	Acts 1975, No. 280, §§ 2914, 3001, 3002, 3003	It is illegal for any person in return for or in expectation of a fee to engage or offer or agree to engage in sexual activity with another person.	en	x	nf	Same penalty m, f
California	Cal. Penal Code (West 1970) Prost: § 647(b) Vagrancy: § 315	Prost: Stats. 1970, ch. 43, § 1; Stats. 1971, ch. 1581	Every person who solicits or engages in an act of prostitution is breaking the law. "Prostitution" includes any lewd act for consideration.	en	x	nf	
Colorado	Colo. Rev. Stat. Ann. (Supp. 1971) Prost: §§ 40–7–201, –202 Patron: § 40–7–205	Prost: L. 1971, at 451, § 1 Patron: repealed and reenacted by L. 1971, at 452, § 1	Anyone who performs, offers, or agrees to perform act of sexual intercourse or any act of deviate sexual intercourse for money or solicits another for prostitution is guilty of a misdemeanor.	nf		nf	Lesser penalty m, f

State	Citation	Session Laws	Description				Penalty
Connecticut	Conn. Gen. Stat. Ann. (Rev. to 1975) Prost: § 53a-82 Patron: § 53a-83	Acts 1969, No. 828, §§ 82, 83	Anyone who engages or offers to engage in sexual conduct for a fee is committing a crime.	en		en	Same penalty m, f
Delaware	Del. Code Ann. (Rev. 1974) (1975 Cum. Supp.) Prost: tit. 11, § 1342 Patron: tit. 11, § 1343	Prost: 11 Del. Laws, ch. 1953, § 1342 Patron: 58 Del. Laws, ch. 497, § 1	Prostitution is engaging, agreeing, or offering to engage in sexual conduct with another person in return for a fee. Sex of the parties is no defense.	nf		en	Lesser penalty m, f
District of Columbia	D.C. Code Ann. (1967) Prost: § 22-2701		Unlawful to invite, entice, persuade, or to address, to invite, entice, or persuade for the purpose of prostitution, or any other immoral or lewd purpose.	nf		nf	
Florida	Fla. Stat. Ann. (1965) Prost: § 796.07 Patron: § 796.07(3)(b)		Prostitution is a giving of the body for sexual intercourse for hire. It is unlawful to engage in prostitution or to solicit.			nf	Same penalty m, f
Georgia	Ga. Code Ann. (1972) Prost. § 26-2012	L. 1968, at 1249, 1301	A person commits prostitution when one performs or offers to perform acts of sexual intercourse for money.			en	
Hawaii	Hawaii Rev. Stat. (1968) Prost and Patron: §§ 768-51, -52		Any man or woman who solicits or procures one to commit an act of prostitution with him- or herself, or any man or woman who engages in prostitution is committing a misdemeanor.	en		en	Same penalty m, f
Idaho	Idaho Code Ann. (1947) Prost: § 18-5613	L. 1972, ch. 381, § 19, as amended by L. 1973, ch. 15, § 1	A person is guilty of prostitution if he or she is an inmate of a house of prostitution or engages in sexual activity as a business or solicits a patron.	en	x	en	

(continued)

69

TABLE 4.2 (continued)

State	Statute	Origin of Law (post-1960 reforms)	Conduct Proscribed	Homosexual Included[a]	Status[b]	Neutrality[c]	Patron[d]
Illinois	Ill. Ann. Stat. (Smith-Hurd 1972) Prost: ch. 11, §§ 14,15 Patron: ch. 11, § 18	Prost: Acts 1961, No. 11-14 Patron: Acts 1961, No. 11-18	Any person who for money commits or agrees to commit an act of sexual intercourse or deviate sexual conduct or any person who solicits for purposes of prostitution is committing an illegal act.	nf		nf	Lesser penalty m, f
Indiana	Ind. Ann. Stat. (1975) Prost: § 35-30-1-1	Acts 1975, ch. 325, at 1772	Any person who frequents or lives in a house of ill fame or commits or offers to commit sexual intercourse or sodomy for hire is guilty of prostitution.	nf	x	nf	
Iowa	Iowa Code Ann. (1946) Prost: §§ 724.1, 724.2		Any person who occupies a house of ill fame or leads a life of a prostitute or any person who shall solicit another to have carnal knowledge is committing a crime.	nf	x	nf	
Kansas	Kan. Stat. Ann. (1974) Prost: § 21-3512 Patron: § 21-3515	Patron and Prost: L. 1969, ch. 180	Prostitution is performing an act of sexual intercourse or offering or agreeing to perform an unlawful sexual act or sexual intercourse for hire.	nf		nf	Lesser penalty m, f
Kentucky	Ky. Rev. Stat. Ann. (Supp. 1974) Prost: § 529.020	Acts 1974, ch. 406, § 251	Prostitution is when he engages or agrees or offers to engage in sexual conduct with another person in return for a fee.	nf		nf	
Louisiana	La. Rev. Stat. Ann. (1974) Prost: § 14:82 Vagrancy: § 14:282		Prostitution is the practice by a female of indiscriminate sexual intercourse with males for compensation.	nf	x	df	
Maine	Me. Rev. Stat. Ann. (1975 Supp.) Prost: tit. 17A, §§ 851, 853	L. 1975, ch. 499, § 1	Prostitution is engaging or agreeing or offering to engage in sexual intercourse or sexual act in return for pecuniary benefit.	en		nf	

State	Statute	Amendment	Description				
Mary-land	Md. Ann. Code (1957) Prost: art. 27, §§ 15, 16		It is illegal to engage in prostitution or lewdness or to solicit for purpose of prostitution. Prostitution is sexual intercourse for hire.	nf		nf	
Massa-chusetts	Mass. Gen. Laws Ann. (1970) Vagrancy: ch. 272, § 53		Lewdness--unnatural sexual practice. "Common nightwalkers, both male and female, disorderly persons, lewd, wanton and lascivious persons in speech and behavior, prostitutes, disturbers of the peace . . . may be punished by . . . "	nf	x	nf	
Michi-gan	Mich. Comp. Laws Ann. (1970) Prost: § 750.448 Patron: § 750.449a	As amended by Acts 1969, No. 243, § 1	It is unlawful for any person, male or female, 17 years of age or older, to solicit any person to commit prostitution or to do any other lewd or immoral act.	en		nf	Same penalty m only
Minne-sota	Minn. Stat. Ann. (1964) Prost: § 609.32, subd. 4(1) Patron: § 609.32 subd. 4(4)	L. 1967, ch. 507, § 9, as amended by L. 1974, ch. 507, § 2	Prostitution is engaging or offering or agreeing to engage for hire in sexual intercourse or sodomy.	nf		nf	Same penalty m, f
Missis-sippi	Miss. Code Ann. (1972) Prost: § 97-29-49		It is unlawful to engage in prostitution or to solicit for purposes of prostitution.	nf		nf	
Mis-souri	Mo. Ann. Stat. (1953) Prost: § 563.080		Any person(s) . . . camping or traveling in a city or near a highway for purposes of prostitution.	nf	x	nf	
Mon-tana	Mont. Rev. Codes Ann. (1947) (1967) Supp. to Crim. Code) Prost and Patron: § 94-5-602	L. 1975, ch. 80, § 1	Prostitution if person engages, agrees, or offers to engage in sexual intercourse with another person for compensation. Sexual intercourse defined to include homosexual conduct.	en		nf	Same penalty m, f
Neb-raska	Neb. Rev. Stat. (1964) Vagrancy: § 28-1119		The vagrancy statute includes all prostitutes.	nf		nf	

(continued)

71

TABLE 4.2 (continued)

State	Statute	Origin of Law (post–1960 reforms)	Conduct Proscribed	Homosexual Included[a]	Status[b]	Neutrality[c]	Patron[d]
Nevada	Nev. Rev. Stat. (1973) Vagrancy: § 207.030(b)		Vagrant defined to include every person who solicits any act of prostitution.	nf		nf	
New Hampshire	N.H. Rev. Stat. Ann., as amended (Supp. 5, 1971) Prost: § 645:2, I(a) Patron: § 645:2, I(b)	L. 1971, ch. 518, § 1	Prostitution is soliciting or engaging in sexual intercourse or deviate sexual relations for consideration.	nf		en	Same penalty m, f
New Jersey	N.J. Rev. Stat. Ann. (1969) Prost: §§ 2A-170-5, -133-2		Any person who practices prostitution or solicits its unlawful sexual intercourse or any other unlawful, indecent, lewd, or lascivious act is disorderly. Any person who solicits or engages in prostitution is acting unlawfully.	nf		nf	
New Mexico	N.M. Stat. Ann. (1953) Prost: §§ 40A-9-11, -13 Patron: § 40A-9-12	L. 1963, ch. 303, §§ 9-11 to -13	Engaging or offering to engage in prostitution, or knowingly soliciting for prostitution is illegal. Prostitution is knowingly engaging or offering to engage in sexual intercourse for hire.	nf		nf	Lesser penalty m, f
New York	N.Y. Penal Law (McKinney 1967) Prost: §§ 230.00, 230.10, 240.37 Patron: § 230.05	L. 1965, ch. 1030; L. 1976, ch. 344	Prostitution is engaging in sexual conduct with another person for a fee. Loitering for purposes of engaging in a prostitution offense is also unlawful.	nf	x	en	Lesser penalty m, f
North Carolina	N.C. Gen. Stat. (1969) Prost: §§ 14-203, -204		Prostitution is offering of a body for sexual intercourse for hire or indiscriminate sexual intercourse without hire. To engage in prostitution; to solicit for prostitution; to occupy places for purposes of prostitution; to receive person into place for purposes of prostitution.		x	nf	

State	Citation	Session Law	Provision				
North Dakota	N.D. Cent. Code (1975 Supp.) Prost: § 12.1-29-03	L. 1973, ch. 116, § 28	A person is guilty of prostitution if he: (1) is an inmate of a house of prostitution or otherwise engaged in sexual activity as a business; (2) solicits another person with the intention of being hired to engage in sexual activity.	nf	x	nf	
Ohio	Ohio Rev. Code Ann. (Page 1975) Prost: § 2907.25	L. 1972, H.B. 511	No person shall engage in sexual activity for hire. No person shall solicit another to engage in sexual activity for hire.	nf		nf	
Oklahoma	Okla. Stat. Ann. (1958) Prost: tit. 21, §§ 1029, 1030		Prostitution is the giving or receiving of a body for sexual intercourse for hire, or indiscriminate sexual intercourse without hire. Engaging in or soliciting for prostitution is illegal.			nf	
Oregon	Ore. Rev. Stat. (1974) Prost: § 167.002 Prost and Patron: § 167.007	Prost: L. 1971, ch. 743, § 249 Prost and Patron: L. 1971, ch. 743, § 250; L. 1973, ch. 52, § 1	Prostitution is a male or female who engages in sexual conduct for a fee. A person commits the crime of prostitution if (1) he engages in sexual conduct in return for a fee; (2) he pays or offers or agrees to pay a fee to engage in sexual conduct.	nf		en	Same penalty m, f
Pennsylvania	Pa. Stat. Ann. (1973) Prost and Patron: tit. 18, § 5902	Acts 1972, No. 334, § 1	A person is guilty of prostitution if he or she is an inmate of a house of prostitution or otherwise engages in sexual activity as a business or loiters in or within view of any public place for the purpose of being hired to engage in sexual activity; includes homosexual relations.	en	x	en	Lesser penalty m, f

(continued)

TABLE 4.2 (continued)

State	Statute	Origin of Law (post-1960 reforms)	Conduct Proscribed	Homosexual Included[a]	Status[b]	Neutrality[c]	Patron[d]
Rhode Island	R.I. Gen. Laws Ann. (1965) Vagrancy: § 11-45-1 Prost: § 11-34-5		Unlawful to loiter . . . in a public or private place for purpose of inducing, enticing, soliciting, or procuring another to commit lewdness, fornication, unlawful sexual intercourse . . . or to commit, induce, entice, or solicit a person to commit any such act; or to receive or offer or agree to receive any person . . . for purposes of committing such acts. A common prostitute is a vagrant.		x	nf	
South Carolina	S.C. Code Ann. (1962) Prost: § 16-409		It is unlawful to engage in prostitution or solicit for purposes of it or remain in place for purposes of prostitution or receive a person into place for purposes of lewdness or prostitution.				
South Dakota	S.D. Comp. Laws Ann. (1967) Prost: § 22-23-1		Every person who for purposes of prostitution or lewdness resorts to, uses, occupies, or inhabits a house of ill fame or leads a life of prostitution or lewdness.	nf	x	nf	
Tennessee	Tenn. Code Ann. (1956) (1975 Repl. Vol.) Prost: §§ 39-3501, -3502		Prostitution is giving or receiving of a body for sexual intercourse for hire or not for hire if indiscriminate. It is unlawful to engage, procure, or solicit for prostitution; enter or remain in place, vehicle, building, and the like, for purposes of prostitution; or permit any person to do same.		x	nf	

State	Citation	Session Law	Description				
Texas	Tex. Penal Code (1974) Prost and Patron: art. 43.02	Acts 1973, ch. 399	Offering, agreeing to engage, or engaging in sexual conduct in return for a fee payable to the actor or soliciting another in a public place to engage with him in sexual conduct for hire.	nf		en	Same penalty m, f
Utah	Utah Code Ann. (1953) Prost: § 76-10-1302	L. 1973, ch. 196	Prostitution is engaging or offering or agreeing to engage in any sexual activity with another person for a fee, or being an inmate of a house of prostitution, or loitering in or near public place for purpose of being hired to engage in sexual activity.	nf	x	nf	Lesser penalty m, f
Vermont	Vt. Stat. Ann. (1958) Prost: tit. 13, § 2631		Prostitution is sexual intercourse for hire or indiscriminate sexual intercourse not for hire. Engaging in prostitution or soliciting is illegal; also occupying place or receiving person into place for purposes of prostitution.		x	df	
Virginia	Va. Code Ann. (1950) (1975 Repl. Vol.) Prost: § 18.2-346 Patron: § 18.2-347	Acts 1975, chs. 14, 15	Any person who commits fornication or adultery for money or offers to commit or does any act in furtherance thereof or is residing in a bawdy house is committing a misdemeanor.	nf	x	nf	Same penalty m, f
Washington	Wash. Rev. Code Ann. (1975 Sp. Pamphlet) Prost: §§ 9A.88.030, 9A.88.50	L. 1975 (1st Ex. Sess.), ch. 260	Engaging or agreeing or offering to engage in sexual conduct with another person for a fee. Sex of parties is no defense.	nf		en	
West Virginia	W. Va. Code Ann. (1966) Prost: § 61-8-5(b)		Any person who shall engage in prostitution or who shall solicit an act of prostitution or resides in structures for purposes of prostitution or receives a person for purposes of prostitution.		x	nf	

(continued)

75

TABLE 4.2 (continued)

State	Statute	Origin of Law (post-1960 reforms)	Conduct Proscribed	Homosexual Included[a]	Status[b]	Neutrality[c]	Patron[d]
Wisconsin	Wis. Stat. Ann. (1958) Prost: § 944.30 Patron: § 944.31		Any female who has or offers nonmarital sexual intercourse for value, or is an inmate of a place of prostitution is acting illegally.		x	df	Lesser penalty m only
Wyoming	Wyo. Stat. Ann. (1957) Prost: §§ 6-90, -94		Prostitution is sexual intercourse for hire, or indiscriminate sexual intercourse without hire. It is unlawful to engage in sexual intercourse for hire or aid and abet any female who frequents a house of ill fame or commits fornication for hire. Any female who frequents houses of ill fame or who commits fornication for hire shall be deemed a prostitute.		x	df	

[a]The following states, which do not cover homosexual acts for a fee in their prostitution laws, have general provisions proscribing sodomy or "acts against nature," with or without a fee: Alabama, Alaska, Arizona, Louisiana, Massachusetts, Mississippi, Missouri, Nebraska, New Mexico, North Carolina, Rhode Island, South Carolina, Tennessee, Vermont, Virginia, West Virginia, Wisconsin, and Wyoming. Some of the states that include homosexual acts in the prostitution law have separate sodomy statutes as well. California has recently amended its sodomy law to remove criminal sanctions from consensual sodomy and oral copulation between adults. Cal. Penal Code § 286 (1970), as amended by Stats. 1975, ch. 71.

[b]Arkansas, Missouri, New York, North Carolina, South Carolina, South Dakota, Tennessee, Vermont, and West Virginia have status provisions that include the language "for purposes of prostitution." The remaining states simply criminalize being in a certain location or being a vagrant, without limiting such provisions with a "purposes" clause.

[c]This category classifies laws that refer to prostitutes as "he or she" as explicitly neutral; laws that refer to prostitutes as "any person" as neutral on their face; and laws that use "she" or "female" as discriminatory on their face.

[d]This category notes not only whether a particular jurisdiction has a patron law but also whether this law applies to both males and females and whether the penalty is equal to or less than that for prostitutes.

Note: en—explicitly neutral; f—female; df—discriminatory on its face; m—male; nf—neutral on its face.

Source: Compiled by the authors.

licitation or negotiation for purposes of prostitution.* Such laws en-
croach on First Amendment free speech rights and, as statutes that
criminalize mere words or gestures, may raise issues of vagueness
in violation of the due process clause.

Two types of prostitution-related laws permit serious invasions
of privacy. One is a general prohibition against all "indiscriminate"
sexual behavior, whether or not money is exchanged, which still exists
in at least five states.[37] The second is laws requiring venereal disease tests for those who are suspected of, arrested for, or convicted
of prostitution or related offenses, variations of which are found in
at least 12 states.[†] Indeed, any state regulation of consensual adult
sexual behavior not directly harmful to others raises serious questions
of constitutional rights of individual privacy.[39]

In recent years, there has been a growing movement in favor
of the decriminalization of prostitution because of the issues of privacy, equal protection, and due process and the inevitable victimiza-
tion of female prostitutes by law enforcement. While state legislatures
have yet to act affirmatively on this question, numerous national groups
have issued policy statements and are actively involved in lobbying
and litigation efforts to this end.

In February 1976, the American Bar Association House of Delegates rejected by only two votes a recommendation that state legislatures repeal all laws prohibiting commercial sexual conduct between
consenting adults in private. The formal recommendation, prepared
by the Section of Individual Rights and Responsibilities of the ABA,
notes that:

---

*The statutes of District of Columbia, Iowa, and Nevada penalize
negotiations for purposes of prostitution without any mention of actual
engagement in sexual activity. Thirty-seven other states also penal-
ize negotiation or solicitation as part of more extended proscriptions
against prostitution-related activities: Alaska, Arkansas, California,
Colorado, Connecticut, Delaware, Florida, Georgia, Hawaii, Idaho,
Illinois, Indiana, Kansas, Kentucky, Maine, Maryland, Michigan,
Minnesota, Mississippi, Montana, New Hampshire, New Mexico,
North Carolina, North Dakota, Ohio, Oklahoma, Rhode Island, South
Carolina, Tennessee, Texas, Utah, Vermont, Virginia, Washington,
West Virginia, and Wisconsin.
†Connecticut, Idaho, Michigan, Nevada, New Jersey, North Caro-
lina, Oklahoma, South Dakota, Vermont, Virginia, West Virginia, and
Wyoming. Perhaps the most extreme of these is found in New Jersey,
where a "prostitute or lewd person . . . may be required to submit to
examination at any time."[38]

> Evolving concepts of equal protection and the right of pri-
> vacy, concern about victimless crimes, and revitalization
> of the women's movement have all contributed to an increas-
> ing interest in studying, challenging, and dismantling pros-
> titution laws. Constitutional challenges to prostitution
> laws have been brought in several states and the District
> of Columbia and the question promises to remain before
> the courts for years to come. [40]

The recommendation then goes on to list numerous groups and organizations that have already gone on record supporting decriminalization.

Impact of the ERA

Explicit Discrimination

Under the equal rights amendment, states are required to prove
that any sex-based distinction in their prostitution laws is dictated by
physical characteristics peculiar to only one sex and closely related
to the purpose of the statute. It is unlikely that such an argument can
be successfully sustained. Members of either sex can solicit, procure,
or engage in sexual activity for hire; neither does the sex of a partici-
pant have any bearing on the state interests advanced for regulating
such activities (for example, curbing unseemly street activities; protecting people from sexual exploitation; controlling the spread of venereal diseases; upholding social morals; or limiting collateral criminal behavior). Thus, once a state decides to prohibit heterosexual
and/or homosexual activity for hire, the drawing of lines based on the
sex of the perpetrator violates the ERA. State interests in the alleged
convenience or efficiency of criminalizing activities of only female
prostitutes are not sufficient justification to overcome the ERA's
strict prohibition of sex-based classifications.

Neutral Rules

The critical issue of equality in the area of prostitution is not
whether a statute has a sex-neutral definition of "prostitute." Rather,
the severe problems are posed by ostensibly neutral rules that result
in the disparate treatment of female prostitutes. One example is the
statutory coverage of only heterosexual activity. Because heterosexual prostitutes are far more likely to be female, such a law subjects
more women than men to arrest for prostitution. More important,
in states with statutes penalizing only the seller of sex, and even in

those jurisdictions where patrons are theoretically subject to prosecution, different penalties and selective enforcement tactics often result in a highly disparate impact of the law on the predominantly female class of prostitutes. The impact of these disparities is clearly inconsistent with the principle of the ERA. The amendment may require states to impose equal statutory penalties on patrons and prostitutes and on heterosexual and homosexual prostitutes. Evenhanded enforcement of the laws against these different groups also may be required to soften the disparate impact of current practices on women.

Policy Recommendations

Mounting pressure to take prostitution out of the ambit of criminal law enforcement has gained momentum from the ERA's absolute equality standard because of the overriding impact that any regulation of prostitution inevitably has on women as a class. Another important impetus for decriminalization has been the sense that prostitution laws invade zones of individual privacy, particularly where they involve consensual intimate behavior between adults not directly harmful to others. Under this analysis, of course, coercing another person into prostitution or taking advantage of the sexual immaturity of a child, both of which offend a significant public interest, could still be prohibited.

In addition, those statutes that prohibit mere solicitation or the status of being a prostitute are objectionable on policy grounds because of their vagueness and consequent use to detain persons before any act is actually committed. Such laws should be eliminated from state and local criminal codes even if prohibitions against actual acts of prostitution are retained.

If serious consideration is to be given to the repeal of criminal prostitution laws because of the constitutional problems they pose and because of changing public policy in this area, care should be taken to distinguish between outright decriminalization and legalization. The latter term often is used to describe the implementation of a regulatory licensing/ inspection regime over prostitutes. By its very nature, any such regime might well result in even greater harassment of women and even deeper incursions into the realm of private sexual behavior. Moreover, the legalization of prostitution might give tacit sanction to the use of economic coercion to force women, especially poor women, into prostitution against their will.

In those jurisdictions where decriminalization of consensual sexual activity for money is not yet a politically viable option, steps should be taken to conform existing prostitution laws to constitutional standards of equality and due process and to encourage evenhanded en-

forcement of these laws. Short of decriminalization of prostitution,
careful statutory drafting aimed at sex neutralization and emphasis
on behavior rather than status is recommended.

Both homosexual and heterosexual activity should be prohibited
in a common scheme, with explicit language stating that the sex of
the parties involved is immaterial and that prostitutes and patrons
are subject to the same penalties. Provisions that penalize promiscuous sexual activity in general, without regard to the exchange of
money, and those that penalize status, reputation, or residence should
be repealed, as should those that prohibit solicitation without proof
of actual sexual activity. In those jurisdictions where the public is
concerned about the promotion of prostitution and its various corollary
forms of crime or corruption, it would be appropriate to impose more
severe penalties and enforcement efforts rather than maintaining
discriminatory definitions. In addition, equality-minded reformers
should keep in mind that miscellaneous local ordinances, as well as
state criminal codes, may be the source of prostitution-related laws
and also should be checked for sex-discriminatory language and impact.
Finally, sexist interpretation and enforcement of seemingly neutral
statutory provisions must be sought out and challenged by appropriate
means, including litigation.

State Reform Efforts

Both the constitutional and public policy problems with prostitution laws have been the impetus for increasing law reform in recent
years. As early as 1962, the American Law Institute's Proposed Official Draft of the Model Penal Code included a section dealing with
prostitution and related offenses that not only completely neutralized
the definition of prostitution in terms of the sex of the perpetrator but
also included a sex-neutral penalty for patrons and procurers.[41]
Every state with laws now covering both male and female prostitutes
and patrons as well as heterosexual and homosexual conduct has
adopted those reforms since that time. Most reform activity has occurred in the past five years, often as part of major criminal code revisions.* Support for the ERA and the other forces to eliminate sex
discrimination have played a significant role in this reform movement.

Since 1970, 18 states have enacted amendments sex neutralizing
their definition of prostitution, and 11 have criminalized the activities

---

*Prostitution reforms were part of widespread criminal law revi-
sions resulting in the publication of new criminal codes in Arkansas,
Kansas, Kentucky, Maine, Montana, New York, North Dakota, Ohio,
Oregon, Pennsylvania, Texas, Utah, Virginia, and Washington.

of patrons. With the exception of Virginia, all states that sex neutralized their definition of prostitution since 1970 also used language encompassing homosexual activity, either by referring specifically to sodomy or employing an overall neutral term such as "sexual conduct" or "sexual activity." A fuller description of these recent amendments and the current prostitution laws of all the states can be found in Table 4.2.

The Michigan legislature, in 1973, and the Maryland legislature, more recently, considered proposals to decriminalize prostitution as part of a general effort to eliminate sex discrimination from their laws.[42] They were not successful, however.

Short of decriminalization, Connecticut's recent statutory amendments are the best example of thoughtfully drafted reforms in this area. Provisions penalizing promiscuous sexual activity in general and allowing convictions based solely on the reputation of the individual or on the premises in question were eliminated. Sex-neutral language replaced sex-based definitions; homosexual activity was explicitly covered; and the penalties for patrons and prostitutes were equalized. In addition, an affirmative statement on the irrelevance of the sex of the parties involved was included. Pimps and promoters of prostitution were given more severe penalties than patrons and prostitutes. The new scheme not only makes more rational distinctions between the various kinds of prostitution-related activities and more reasoned judgments about their relative seriousness to the public well-being but also mitigates the disparate impact that prostitution laws traditionally have had on women. The text of the Connecticut law follows:

Model Prostitution Law

Prostitution: Class A Misdemeanor

(a) A person is guilty of prostitution when such person engages or agrees or offers to engage in sexual conduct with another person in return for a fee.

(b) Prostitution is a class A misdemeanor.

Patronizing a Prostitute: Class A Misdemeanor

(a) A person is guilty of patronizing a prostitute when:

(1) Pursuant to a prior understanding, he pays a fee to another person as compensation for such person or a third person having engaged in sexual conduct with him; or

(2) he pays or agrees to pay a fee to another person pursuant to an understanding that in return therefor such person or a third person will engage in sexual conduct with him; or

(3) he solicits or requests another person to engage in sexual conduct with him in return for a fee.

(b) Patronizing a prostitute is a class A misdemeanor.

Sex of Parties Immaterial

In any prosecution for prostitution or patronizing a prostitute, the sex of the two parties or prospective parties to the sexual conduct engaged in, contemplated or solicited is immaterial, and it shall be no defense that:

(a) Such persons were of the same sex; or

(b) the person who received, agreed to receive or solicited a fee was a male and the person who paid or agreed or offered to pay such fee was a female.

Promoting Prostitution: Definitions

(a) A person "advances prostitution" when, acting other than as a prostitute or as a patron thereof, he knowingly causes or aids a person to commit or engage in prostitution, procures or solicits patrons for prostitution, provides persons or premises for prostitution purposes, operates or assists in the operation of a house of prostitution or a prostitution enterprise, or engages in any other conduct designed to institute, aid or facilitate an act or enterprise of prostitution.

(b) A person "profits from prostitution" when acting other than as a prostitute receiving compensation for personally rendered prostitution services, he accepts or receives money or other property pursuant to an agreement or understanding with any person whereby he participates or is to participate in the proceeds of prostitution activity.

Promoting Prostitution in the First Degree: Class B Felony

(a) A person is guilty of promoting prostitution in the first degree when he knowingly:

(1) Advances prostitution by compelling a person by force or intimidation to engage in prostitution, or profits from coercive conduct by another; or

(2) advances or profits from prostitution of a person less than sixteen years old.

(b) Promoting prostitution in the first degree is a class B felony.

Promoting Prostitution in the Second Degree: Class C Felony

(a) A person is guilty of promoting prostitution in the second degree when he knowingly:

(1) Advances or profits from prostitution by managing, supervising, controlling or owning, either alone or in association with others, a house of prostitution or a prostitution business or enterprise involving prostitution activity by two or more prostitutes; or

(2) advances or profits from prostitution of a person less than eighteen years old.

(b) Promoting prostitution in the second degree is a class C felony.

Promoting Prostitution in the Third Degree: Class D Felony

(a) A person is guilty of promoting prostitution in the third degree when he knowingly advances or profits from prostitution.

(b) Promoting prostitution in the third degree is a class D felony.

Permitting Prostitution: Class A Misdemeanor

(a) A person is guilty of permitting prostitution when, having possession or control of premises which he knows are being used for prostitution purposes, he fails to make reasonable effort to halt or abate such use.

(b) Permitting prostitution is a class A misdemeanor.

SENTENCING

Background

Sex discrimination in the correctional system begins with the disparate nature of sentencing laws under which male and female offenders are incarcerated. The primary source of disparity in treatment based on sex has been the existence in a number of jurisdictions of statutes that mandate indeterminate sentences for women while men receive set minimum and maximum terms.[43] This theory of dual sentencing embodies the sex-stereotypical presumption that women, including women offenders, are more malleable than men and thus more amenable to reform and rehabilitation. In practice, this means that a woman offender remains in custody until the prison administration finds that she has indeed been "corrected" while a man who has been imprisoned "does time" for some set period, the possibility for his reform being considered more tenuous.[44] Under such a dual scheme, a woman may be incarcerated for a longer period of time than a man convicted of the same offense. On the other hand, she has an opportunity to be paroled much earlier because, unlike her male counterpart, she faces no minimum sentence.

A second source of disparity in the sentencing of male and female offenders is state statutory schemes that treat males as adults
at a younger age than females for purposes of criminal sanctions,
thus exposing them to different types of sentences and custodial facilities. This issue is discussed in the juvenile justice section later
in this chapter.

Finally, traditional perspectives on men and women offenders
bring sex-based attitudes into the sentencing process even in those
jurisdictions where the statutes are neutral on their face. Such attitudes are revealed both in the decisions of judges and others who have
discretion over the length of incarceration and in the administrative
policies of parole boards concerning eligibility, timing, and conditions of parole. [45] Some of these stereotypes result in shorter prison
sentences for women, on the average, than for men convicted of similar offenses. [46]

Sex-based statutory differentials in sentencing have been challenged under the equal protection clause in recent years. As a result,
sentencing statutes in Connecticut, New Jersey, and Pennsylvania
have been declared unconstitutional. [47]

Impact of the ERA

The ERA would prohibit sex-based statutory or administrative
policies in sentencing and parole. For example, in Commonwealth v.
Butler, the Pennsylvania Supreme Court held that a sentencing scheme
that provided minimum as well as maximum sentences for men but
only maximums for women was unconstitutional under the equal rights
amendment to that state's constitution. [48] Finding that the statute for
women was an exception carved out of the earlier sex-neutral provision
under which men were sentenced, the court struck down the sex-based
exception, leaving men and women both subject to the general statute
requiring that both a minimum and a maximum sentence be imposed.

Generally, the ERA requires that men and women be subject
to the same sentencing standards, whether indeterminate or fixed,
and that individual decisions be made on the basis of relevant sex-
neutral characteristics, such as the severity of the crime, prior
criminal record, and so on. Similarly, parole standards must be uniform across sex lines.

Policy Recommendations

Under the ERA, the explicit sex discrimination in sentencing
laws must be eliminated. However, a more subtle discrimination,
harmful to both sexes, lies in judges' consideration of different fac-

tors when sentencing men and women. Efforts should be made to counter the stereotypes that skew this exercise of discretion. It would be wise for the states to specifically forbid, in statutes or regulations, sex-stereotyped decision making in both the sentencing and parole processes. This could be implemented most effectively by promulgating a list of non-sex-based factors to be considered in making sentencing decisions. Such regulations could be accompanied by training sessions to make judges and others aware of the extent to which their actions are influenced by improper sex bias.

The sex discrimination questions, however, are only one aspect of more general dissatisfaction with current sentencing practices. Class and racial as well as sex inequities have been documented, and a number of suggestions for making sentencing decisions more rational, including appellate review, have been discussed. A debate concerning the merits of indeterminate sentencing for both men and women is also going on, with recent comment suggesting that the uncertainty and arbitrariness to which a prisoner is subject under an indeterminate system effectively precludes rehabilitation. [49] Moreover, the reform of state statutes to provide minimum and maximum terms rather than indeterminate sentences would avoid the traditional result of encouraging women to act in an immature fashion, like "good little girls," to earn release. The general sentencing law of Pennsylvania is typical; states may wish to add more varied types of dispositions and sentences to their statutes. [50]

Whatever the resolution of these larger issues about appropriate sanctions for criminal behavior, the laws should be applied in an even-handed way to the men and women who come before the courts.

State Reform Efforts

Several states have taken legislative action to correct sex discrimination in the sentencing process. Arkansas and Kansas have repealed differential sentencing laws for women within the last several years. [51] In addition, Maine has repealed its statutes setting sex-differential age limits for confinement under indeterminate reformatory sentences. [52] Maine and Connecticut recently have sex neutralized their statutes governing escape from prison. [53] Pennsylvania amended its sentencing law for women after it was held unconstitutional in 1968; the amended law was struck down under the state ERA in 1974. [54]

The states have not yet tackled the difficult enforcement issue of judicial discretion in sentencing.

PRISONS

Background

Several factors in addition to sentencing practices operate to create widespread disparities in the treatment of men and women in adult penal institutions. One is the rigid segregation of inmates into single-sex institutions. A second is the extremely small number of incarcerated women compared to men. A third is the sex-stereotyped penological theories concerning women, which gave rise to the physical structure and programming peculiar to women's prisons. [55]

In 1971, only 5 percent of incarcerated adults were women. [56] No state has more than one prison for women, and some board convicted women in neighboring states. Women are thus more likely to be located at longer distances from their homes, which makes visits from family and friends as well as the use of community resources in rehabilitation difficult. [57] The range of work, job training, and educational opportunities is far smaller in women's prisons than in the larger and more diverse male prison systems. The small number of women may also account for the lack of classification of female inmates according to crime, age, or rehabilitative needs and the consequent inability to gear programming to individual inmates. [58]

Sex stereotyping exacerbates the impact of the numerical disproportion of men and women. Female inmates are generally seen as less dangerous than their male counterparts, and their institutions are therefore often less physically harsh. However, this view of women as wayward children also has severe drawbacks. Rules and procedures are not regularized in an effort to prepare women to live in a legalistic society; rather, women's prisons tend to be administered in a paternalistic fashion in which arbitrariness and favoritism dictate many decisions. [59] Too often, female prisoners are not trained to reenter society as adults with marketable job skills but rather are exposed only to a limited range of vocational training considered "appropriate" for them in terms of traditional female roles. [60]

Discrimination also exists in employment opportunities for prisoners. Programs that enable inmates to develop occupational skills, such as furlough and work release, are frequently not available to women on the same basis as they are to men. [61] One Washington, D.C., study found that only 4 percent of eligible women as compared to 29 percent of eligible men received furloughs and that only 9 percent of women as compared to 30 percent of men were given work releases. [62] Reasons given by prison officers for the discrepancy are, first, that the small numbers of women make the cost of administering the programs, particularly the cost of providing separate housing for the women on work release, too high and, second, that rehabilitative programming is less important to women than men because they do not have to support dependents.[63] As in vocational training, the employment services that do exist for female inmates are oriented toward domestic work or careers considered suitable for women, such as cosmetology.

The foregoing comments apply mainly to state and federal prisons. The situation in county jails, in which a large percentage of women are incarcerated, is somewhat different. Women in jails are commonly segregated in a separate wing, where there may be only one or two inmates at any given time. As a result, such incarceration is often the equivalent of solitary confinement. Even where there are substantial numbers of women, facilities such as libraries, legal research materials, and visiting rooms are often available to women on a much more restricted basis than they are to men. Not even the limited opportunities for work, training, or exercise, which male inmates of jails may have, are available to most jailed women.[64]

Women in prisons and jails suffer from other restrictive rules as well. Prison prohibitions on visits from children or visits involving contact greatly handicap an incarcerated parent attempting to maintain a relationship with a child. Even where visitation is permitted for both male and female prisoners on the same basis, the impact of any restriction is greater on women, who are much more likely to be single parents.[65]

The problems of inadequate prison medical care are also severe for women. Denial of access to outside specialists, particularly gynecologists and obstetricians, can cause great hardship. Pregnant women face a patchwork of arbitrary and often oppressive policies concerning abortion, prenatal care, postpartum care, child custody, and sterilization.[66]

Traditionally, there have been far fewer cases challenging institutional conditions brought by women inmates than by men. Nevertheless, the number of lawsuits raising constitutional questions concerning women's prisons has risen dramatically over the past several years. Suits have challenged a range of practices, including discriminatory booking procedures,[67] lack of access to legal research materials,[68] denial of equal access to vocational education and work release programs,[69] and lack of adequate medical care.[70] Several suits have attacked the whole panoply of deprivations at an institution. As a result of Garnes v. Taylor,[71] a comprehensive suit against conditions at Washington, D.C.'s Women's Detention Center, new procedures for the transfer of women to the federal prison in West Virginia are being implemented, and a decision is forthcoming on the issues of medical care, communications and visiting, access to community programs, and conditions of incarceration.

A recent New Mexico case raised an equal protection challenge to conditions for women sentenced to the New Mexico penitentiary, an all-female institution on the grounds of the male prison. [72] The court found unconstitutional the denial to women of many opportunities available to the men and ordered defendants to give plaintiffs wider vocational training, opportunity to get better paying jobs, equal access to legal materials, and equal opportunity to earn "good time." The court denied several claims, however, because of the defendants' security reasons for disallowing women from certain programs in the male prison.

Employment discrimination in the hiring of prison personnel is another pervasive problem. [73] The general practice is that men's prisons do not employ women in any supervisory jobs involving inmates while women's prisons tend to employ women as supervisory personnel but men as top administrators. Both the American Correctional Association and the National Advisory Commission on Criminal Justice Standards and Goals have recognized that these staffing patterns are both illegal and inadvisable and have recommended that staff of both sexes be utilized in order to obtain the best rehabilitative environment in prisons without violating each inmate's right to privacy. [74] Several cases have been brought on constitution agrounds and under Title VII challenging rules that bar women from various jobs in prisons and state institutions. [75]

Impact of the ERA

Under the equal rights amendment, distinctions in the treatment and housing of prisoners on the basis of sex must end. This means that correctional institutions no longer can be segregated on the basis of sex. Even if present facilities for women were equal in educational and employment opportunities to those for men or if present facilities for men were equal in their structural comforts to those for women, a dual system of "separate but equal" correctional facilities would still violate the equality principle. [76] Of course, as the background section (above) documents, facilities are not now equal and are not likely to become equal under a dual system because of the disproportionately small number of women offenders and because of prevailing sex stereotypes. Thus, as a leading commentary on the ERA concludes:

> The only feasible means of resolving the many disparities and inequities found today in any survey of conditions in men's and women's prisons is to physically integrate the institutions. Such an approach is not only consistent with

the theory of the Equal Rights Amendment, but, as will
be seen, represents the only practical solution to the
many inequalities found in women's prisons today. [77]

Under such a system, prisoners can be classified and assigned to institutions or particular programs on the basis of sex-neutral factors,
such as security risk, geographical location of their homes, job training goals, and personal characteristics. Similarly, staff will have to
be hired and assigned on a sex-neutral basis.

Even under the ERA, however, the principle of equality must
be harmonized with other constitutional guarantees. The right of privacy and the Eighth Amendment's guarantee of freedom from cruel
and unusual punishment both can be respected without a sacrifice of
the sex equality mandated by the ERA. Segreation of the sexes for
private functions need not impair the benefits gained from the sex
integration of the institution. [78] The careful design of staffing patterns
and programs in integrated institutions would insure women's equal
access to available benefits without jeopardizing their safety or privacy rights.* In a sex-integrated institution, most of the daily activities, such as vocational training, education, recreation, and work,
can be shared by members of both sexes and supervised by personnel
of either sex. The need for same-sex staff in more sensitive matters,
such as bathing or body searches, would not justify complete segregation of either staff or inmates. Of course, in local and county jails,
where inmates spend a large percentage of their time in cells and
where intake procedures occur frequently, it would be reasonable to
require at least one staff member of each sex to be present at all
times. [79]

Policy Recommendations

In the matter of prison reform, more needs to be accomplished
than mere sex integration. Studies and experience have shown the de-

---

*In situations in which a small number of women will be intro-
duced into a largely male prison population, steps will have to be
taken to avoid the negative impact of the disparity in numbers; for
example, women should not be introduced into maximum security institutions, if at all, until integration procedures have been successfully established elsewhere. In some instances, the adjustment can
be eased by grouping the women with a similarly sized group of men
within the institution for programming purposes in order to enhance
their psychological and physical security.

grading and counterproductive effects the prison environment has on efforts to train and rehabilitate convicted persons. The use of smaller institutions, halfway houses, community resources, and other models for the attainment of correctional goals is highly advisable.[80] These programs are particularly suited to many women prisoners, whose convictions tend to be for nonviolent and property-related crimes. The ERA requires only that whatever forms these changes take, they must include a commitment to complete sex equality in the treatment of prisoners and the administration of institutions and programs.

Reform must not be restricted to the sex neutralization of statutory language, however. Such amendments theoretically open up certain opportunities within present penological structures for equal treatment of men and women, but they should be accompanied by explicit legislative history or statutory language calling for the implementation of sex-neutral practices throughout the corrections system and backed up with affirmative programs for change in staffing, facilities, programs, and services.

Many or even most discriminatory aspects of a penal system may derive from administrative practices and regulations and inadequate appropriations for women's programs. Therefore, to effectively reach these practices, reform must go beyond the elimination of statutory discrimination. In integrating prisoners, for example, careful oversight through regulations is essential in order to prevent abuses and insure reasonable standards of privacy and safety for all involved. On the question of staffing, facially discriminatory statutes must be amended, affirmative action programs instituted, and specific guidelines established for the identification of persons with counseling, vocational, and physical skills, sensitivity to the needs of inmates of both sexes, and capability of handling security problems. Since emotions run high on the subject of prisons, reform is politically difficult, and legislators may be discouraged from even investigating present conditions. As the process of ERA conformance goes on, however, these obstacles will have to be overcome if change is to be more than cosmetic.

Moreover, statutory reform should provide the commissioner of corrections with guidance for the lengthy process of transition that such change entails. Additional legislative guidelines or the establishment of a skilled task force to oversee an orderly pattern of experimentation and implementation of equality, beginning with the lowest security facilities, is advisable.

State Reform Efforts

To date, only minimal changes have been made in sex-based policies governing penal institutions. Primarily, these have been terminological changes sex neutralizing statutory references to staffing of facilities or to work and training assignments for inmates. In Kentucky, for example, a statute referring to prison guards as "men" was amended to read "person,"[81] and special references to the selection of women for certain staff positions in Iowa's correctional system recently were deleted by that state's legislature.[82] Two states modified work release or work assignment provisions. Maryland changed the word "wife" to "spouse" in a statute authorizing the design of an "extended work release program" for prisoners sentenced for nonsupport. This reflects changing law on the duty of spousal support.[83] Iowa modified the definition of suitable work for inmates in a work release program open to members of both sexes. Formerly, the program included housekeeping for female prisoners; now, it includes child care and housekeeping for prisoners of either sex who have children in their homes.[84] The Iowa bill also sex neutralized a provision allowing able-bodied inmates over 16 years of age to be assigned physical labor.[85]

In a few jurisdictions, more far-reaching steps have been taken to incorporate an equality standard into the correctional system. In 1974, for example, California passed legislation requiring equal availability of facilities, programs, services, and privileges to male and female inmates of county facilities by 1979.[86] However, the state's ability to accomplish this goal has been hindered by the passage of a 1975 statute prohibiting the imposition of any requirement to integrate male and female prisoners for participation in educational, recreational, or work programs.[87] Comprehensive legislation on equality in programming also has been introduced in recent years in Colorado, Minnesota, and New York.[88]

As of 1973, the federal government and three states have started the integration of minimum security institutions, in which all activities are integrated but separate sleeping and bathroom facilities are provided for each sex.[89] In addition, Iowa has authorized sex integration of its special "correctional release center." The center, located at the prison honor farm, receives inmates who are within 90 days of discharge or parole "for intensive training to assist the inmate in the transition to civilian living."[90]

A comprehensive bill introduced unsuccessfully before the Minnesota legislature in 1973 provides a good model for the kinds of statutory reform necessary to initiate the sex integration of inmates. The primary reform is an affirmative statement that it shall be the policy of the state to afford all inmates equal opportunities for treatment, rehabilitation, education, and vocational training, regardless of sex, and that access to the services of a particular facility should not be barred by sex.[91] The body of the bill amends existing statutes dealing with issues such as staffing, work programs, transfers, and probation so that all the rules are uniformly applicable to all institutions and all sex-based designations for the various state correctional institutions, including juvenile facilities, are eliminated. At the county jail level, the bill provides that the supervisor may be male or female but that the associate supervisor should be of the opposite sex because of the special privacy needs particular to small custodial facilities. [92] While the Minnesota bill was a significant step beyond the simple elimination of sex-based statutory references because of its explicit mandate for equality, including sex integration, it provided the commissioner of corrections with little practical guidance for the transitional process.

JUVENILE JUSTICE

Background

Many of the sex discrimination problems discussed in the sections on adult sentencing and prisons also are found in the juvenile justice system. The analysis presented here presumes that the reader is familiar with the previous discussion.

There are three types of sex-based discrimination in juvenile law: age differentials in statutes concerning juvenile court jurisdiction and the disposition and confinement of juveniles; sex segregation of institutions and supervision for boys and girls; and sex-based differences in definitions of delinquency and average length of sentences.

Age Differentials[93]

As of 1970, four states—Illinois, New York, Oklahoma, and Texas—had statutes that set a lower maximum age limit for juvenile court jurisdiction over males than over females. [94] Kentucky provided detention facilities for boys under 17 and girls under 18. [95] Three states—Colorado, New Mexico, and Ohio—had statutes that provided harsher treatment for males brought to juvenile court than for females by permitting the incarceration of males in more restrictive institutions. [96] Until 1974, New York authorized confinement of females beyond the age at which males could be held. [97] In contrast, Oklahoma required females to be released at age 18 and allowed males to be confined until age 21. [98]

Various assumptions underlie these disparate provisions. Boys are expected to commit more serious offenses at younger ages and to require harsher treatment than girls, yet girls are expected to require protective supervision for a longer time, perhaps because of fears

about illicit sexual activity and pregnancy out of wedlock. The reversal of the usual age rules in Oklahoma may be based on the same rational as marital age distinctions—that girls mature earlier than boys
and, because they are expected to become wives and mothers, do not
need to spend as much time preparing for adulthood as boys do. Whatever the rationale, such distinctions ignore individual differences by
relying on overbroad sex-based averages and stereotypes. A New
York statute permitting juvenile court jurisdiction over females beyond the maximum age limit for males was held unconstitutional by
the Court of Appeals of New York. [99]

Sex Segregation in Confinement and Supervision

Juvenile institutions, like adult institutions, are, for the most
part, sex segregated. [100] The employment discrimination in juvenile
institutions is also similar to that in adult prisons; that is, men supervise boys and women supervise girls.

Not surprisingly, the sex segregation of institutions for boys
and girls produces the same disparities in programming and resource
allocation as are found in adult prisons, although the larger proportion of girls to the total incarcerated juvenile population may ease
the impact of the size and distance factors. Sex stereotyping in counseling and job training programs is pervasive and particularly damaging during adolescence, when people are absorbing motions about
what work and roles are appropriate for them. Segregation of both
inmates and staff also has deleterious effects on the development of
social attitudes toward the opposite sex and of skills crucial to healthy
adulthood. [101] A court in Pennsylvania upheld the sex segregation
of staff at the youth detention facility there because all staff supervised
intimate bodily functions of the inmates. [102] A Wisconsin court upheld the use of sex as a criterion in hiring child care workers for a
juvenile institution, but in the context of a scheme designed to maintain a sexually balanced staff, which would provide role models, personal counseling, and privacy for juveniles of both sexes. [103]

Differential Definitions of Delinquency
and Length of Sentences

Different arrest and delinquency standards have been applied to
girls and boys, as evidenced by the fact that 70 percent of female
youth are detained for status offenses, such as truancy, incorrigibil-
ity, or promiscuity, while only 23 percent of male youth are detained
for such offenses. [104] This phenomenon is accentuated in some states
by the assignment of referees to hear juvenile cases on the basis of
the sex of the offender, thus creating two systems with different stan-

dards for the adjudication of delinquency and for the correlation of seriousness of offense and penalty.[105] Most of this discrimination occurs because of the wide discretion allowed juvenile authorities under facially sex-neutral but vague statutes. These laws, which would not satisfy due process standards if applied to adults, are based on the theory that the state operates toward minors as parens patriae in a primarily corrective or educative rather than punitive manner. As long as juveniles can be incarcerated for offenses that would not be crimes if committed by adults and the double standard of acceptable male and female adolescent behavior is prevalent, there will be a tendency for girls to be incarcerated for behavior tolerated in boys.

In addition, although girls are, on the average, institutionalized for less serious conduct than boys, they often are incarcerated for longer periods of time. National statistics from 1964 and two studies conducted since that time have shown girls averaging between 2 and 2.7 months longer than boys in juvenile institutions.[106] This difference results in part from judges' discretionary power to sentence male juveniles to state prison under the adult criminal code and girls to indeterminate sentences in the reformatory under the juvenile code.[107] Parole standards also are applied differently to boys and girls. Presumably because of paternalistic attitudes on the part of the authorities and perhaps also because of an attempt to prevent them from getting pregnant, girls are incarcerated longer.[108]

Impact of the ERA

Explicit Discrimination

The ERA prohibits statutory age differentials based on sex. The Supreme Court of Illinois held that a statute providing that 17-year-old male offenders be treated as adults while 17-year-old females were subject to the juvenile court act violated the equal rights provision in that state's constitution.[109] The ERA also prohibits sex segregation in confinement and supervision and the sex stereotyping in programs and behavior standards that inevitably follows. The ostensible goal of juvenile institutions—to correct deviant patterns of behavior before they are firmly established—makes the elimination of sex segregation particularly important. As in adult institutions, considerations of privacy and freedom from cruel and unusual punishment will have to be harmonized with the principle of equality as they are applied to institutional life. Segregation of sleeping areas, bathing and toilet facilities, and all areas where disrobing occurs and of staff who supervise these areas and facilities will protect the inmates' privacy; all other activities and staff must be integrated.[110]

Neutral Rules

Juvenile court acts that are neutral on their face often have a severely disparate impact on women because stereotypes about appropriate male and female adolescent behavior infect the decision-making process in juvenile court. As noted above, far more girls than boys are detained for conduct that would not be criminal if committed by an adult. Sex-based standards for release not found in the statutes and based on moral considerations concerning sexual activity also disadvantage girls. Nonsexist state interests do not justify the application of juvenile court laws in a sex-stereotyped way, and such practices may violate the ERA because of their disparate impact. In order to break with this sex-discriminatory history, states may be required to make the laws defining delinquent behavior more specific; to educate judges and other authorities about the sexism inherent in their decisions; and to require that the same standard of impermissible behavior be applied to all juveniles regardless of sex.

Policy Recommendations

The equalization of jurisdictional and sentencing statutes and the sex integration of juvenile institutions, supervision, programs, and court and counseling personnel required by the ERA will help to break down the double standard of morality applied to juveniles. In addition, legislatures should initiate studies of juvenile commitment and release processes to identify areas where affirmative programs to eliminate sex stereotyping and differential treatment can be undertaken.

Other reforms that have been suggested are: (1) repealing laws permitting institutionalization of juveniles for being "in need of supervision" or for other status offenses; (2) stating more explicitly the behavior that is prohibited; and (3) passing laws setting a maximum fixed term of six months or one year for juvenile offenses, with a provision for recommitment at the end of that term. [111]

As in adult corrections, statutory change is only the beginning of necessary reform, particularly in the area of the sex integration of facilities and programs. After amending laws that create sex-segregated homes, farms, or juvenile institutions, states must support these amended statutes with appropriations permitting the necessary renovations and consolidation of institutions to occur promptly. There must be a commitment in the statutes and in the administrative follow-up to programs and rehabilitation that combat sex stereotypes and encourage children of both sexes to reach their fullest potential as individuals. The ERA should hasten the process of reform by requiring attention to the integration of programs. Hopefully, the process will involve a full-scale reexamination of current modes of treatment and incarceration.

There is a growing body of legal commentary and litigation concerning these and related matters of juvenile justice that is beyond the scope of this book. Reformers, however, should consider correcting sex-discriminatory aspects of the system in the context of broader changes suggested in available literature.[112]

State Reform Efforts

As is true in the adult prison system, efforts to correct the sex discrimination in the juvenile justice system have been few and have avoided the central problems. This is particularly unfortunate because adolescence is a crucial time to break a cycle of destructive behavior.

Efforts at change have been most successful in connection with jurisdictional age differentials partially because these are set forth in statutes, and are therefore included in computer-based studies and legislative packages, whereas other aspects of the juvenile system are largely controlled by administrative policies and regulations. Since 1970, at least six states have taken either legislative or judicial steps to eliminate disparities in jurisdictional age. Illinois, New York, and Texas have sex neutralized their juvenile court jurisdictional provisions by applying the lower age limitation to both males and females,[113] while Oklahoma, after a series of challenges in state and federal courts, has equalized its jurisdictional age at the higher end.[114] Kentucky has eliminated an age/sex distinction in its statute creating juvenile institutions; the statue now covers both males and females to age 18.[115] New Mexico has amended a provision once applicable only to young male offenders to permit both males and females under 23 who are sentenced to incarceration for more than six months to be sent to the state reformatory, a medium security institution.[116]

Little has been done to integrate programs and facilities, however.[117]

5

DOMESTIC RELATIONS

INTRODUCTION

Traditionally, marriage has been a patriarchal institution. Under the common law, a woman's legal and social identity merged into that of her husband at marriage. In return for his duty to support her, he gained rights of management over the household and over her property and income, a claim to her household and sexual services, and custody of their children. Divorce was rarely available to end an unsuccessful marriage. The more onerous aspects of patriarchal authority over married women were removed in the last century, freeing married women to manage their own assets, carry on business, contract and sue in their own behalf, work outside the home, and be granted child custody, for example. In addition, divorce has become more available in recent decades. However, the move from a patriarchal to a partnership model of marriage, in which women have full rights equal to those of men, has not yet been completed. Particularly for those women who have chosen the traditional role of homemaker, the sex-biased social, legal, and financial ramifications of marriage continue to deny them equal rights and opportunities.

The legal relationship between parents and children born out of wedlock has also had a history of sex-based doctrines, though here the mother, rather than the father, traditionally has been assigned the sole or primary legal control. As a rule, the father of a child born out of wedlock had no rights or responsibilities under the common law. Most states codified these rules, and only in recent years has there been a move to review their discriminatory impact on both parents and their children.

This chapter treats three major aspects of marriage that are undergoing significant change as a result of the move toward the part-

nership model: the merger of spousal identity, the financial relationship between spouses, and the nonfinancial aspects of marriage dissolution. It also treats the subject of the legal relationships between
parents and children born out of wedlock, a fourth focus of change
toward sex equality in the law of domestic relations.

The first six sections cover issues raised by the traditional
merger of a woman's identity with her husband's at marriage: legal
ages of majority and marriage, names, children's names, domicile,
children's domicile, and consortium. Sex differentials in the age at
which boys and girls are allowed to marry or at which they are defined as adults under the law reflect all the larger sex role distinctions and definitions of identity in marriage. As a general rule, girls
have been permitted to begin their life's work of marriage and childbearing at a younger age than boys, who, in order to prepare to support a family, have been encouraged to pursue education and training
before marrying. Among the remnants of the patriarchal structure
of marriage are the customs and laws dictating that a married woman
use her husband's surname and take his domicile and, similarly, that
the children of the marriage take their father's name and domicile.
In addition, if a married woman is negligently injured by a third party,
her husband has a right to sue for loss of her services, but in some
states she has no comparable claim against third-party interference
with her husband's marital duties and affection.

The next five sections deal with the financial aspects of marriage: liability for family expenses during marriage, spousal support
and alimony, child support, marital property, and probate. While
women traditionally have received no legal recognition for their economic role in the family, the reality in most marriages is that both
partners perform important economic roles, contrary to the sex-
based doctrines in the law. In many, perhaps most, ongoing marriages, spouses pool their energies and resources, and they both exercise economic decision-making power and share in the property and
income the family acquires. The situations with which the law must
deal, however, are those in which the marriage has dissolved by
death or divorce or in which the parties no longer agree on the terms
of their relationship with each other or with their children. When
these problems occur in families in which one spouse has an outside
job and the other cares for the home and children, the law must step
in to equalize the parties' bargaining power if the non-wage-earning
spouse is to receive fair treatment.

There are four major ways in which the law can require a wage-
earning or property-holding spouse to compensate the other spouse
for the performance of housework and child care: obligating the wage-
earner to pay for certain purchases made by the non-wage-earner,
giving spouses ownership rights to each other's income, actually trans-

ferring income from one spouse to the other, and transferring ownership and management of property from one spouse to the other.
These transfers can be required during an ongoing marriage or can
be postponed until the dissolution of the marriage by death, divorce,
or extended separation. The value of laws requiring transfer of obligations, ownership rights, income, or property from one spouse to
the other depends upon the availability of a legal remedy during marriage, the factors the court takes into account in determining the
amount of transfer, the availability of enforcement against an uncoop-
erative spouse, and the existence of a community property or a common law property system of ownership. In each section, the historical legal doctrines and current statutory provisions are described
and analyzed. Throughout, the community property and common law
property systems of ownership are distinguished and compared.

The following two sections deal with the nonfinancial aspects of
marriage dissolution: divorce grounds and child custody. Once a
rarity, divorce now has become an event experienced by millions of
people in our society. The law has been forced to respond to this
change in social reality by reevaluating divorce grounds, not only in
terms of the sex bias traditionally embodied in many "fault" grounds
for divorce but also in terms of the proper role of fault in determining
whether to grant a divorce and how to assign spousal rights and obligations after the divorce. The rise in the divorce rate and the changing role of women generally have also prompted review of the traditional statutory and judicial standards controlling the assignment of
child custody when parents separate. From the common law rule
that a father had an absolute right to custody, tradition has swung in
the opposite direction in the last several decades to a presumption
that it is in the child's best interest, particularly if he or she is
young, to live with the mother. Now, the sex biases underlying both
of these standards have been called into question, and the law is in
transition as it begins to adopt a sex-neutral rule.

The remaining section reviews a number of legal issues arising from a tradition of sex bias regarding the relationship of parents
and out-of-wedlock children. These include child custody, termination of parental rights, adoption, and inheritance between parents
and children. The issues of names and domicile for children born
out of wedlock are treated in the separate sections covering those
general topics. As in the area of relationships within marriage, the
law concerning children born out of wedlock has made a significant
but as yet incomplete move in recent years toward sex equality.
This movement has been the result of changing marriage patterns,
growing acceptance of the principle of sex equality generally, and the
related move toward the elimination of discrimination based on the
birth status of an individual, as supported by a number of important
United States Supreme Court decisions.

AGE OF MAJORITY

Background

Traditional age of marriage laws generally allowed girls to marry at 16 with parental consent and at 18 without, while boys could marry at 18 if their parents concurred and 21 if not. These differentials grew out of the social expectation that women marry earlier than men and that they need not pursue education beyond high school or learn a skill or trade because they would not have to work outside the home to support themselves or their families. Boys, on the other hand, were not permitted to assume the obligations of a family until they were educated or trained to earn a living. At present, 23 states have unequal marriage ages for men and women. *

The second common age differential by sex was found in laws governing the age at which an individual is considered an adult under the law. By 1976, all states had set the same age of majority for males and females. In Stanton v. Stanton,[1] the United States Supreme Court ruled that, in the context of child support, the Utah law that set the age of majority at 21 for males and 18 for females was in violation of the equal protection clause of the Fourteenth Amendment because it was based on outmoded stereotypes concerning appropriate male and female roles, similar to those that lay behind marriage age differentials.

———————————————

*These are (the numbers in parentheses are the ages of marriage as of 1972 for men, without and with parental consent, followed by the parallel ages for women): Alabama (m: 21/17, f: 18/14); Alaska (m: 19/18, f: 18/16); Arkansas (m: 21/18, f: 18/16); Delaware (m: 19/18, f: 19/16); Florida (m: 21/18, f: 21/16); Georgia (m: 19/18, f: 19/16); Iowa (m: 19/18, f: 18/16); Louisiana (m: 21/18, f: 21/16); Michigan (m: 18/no provision, f: 18/16); Mississippi (m: 21/17, f: 21/15); Nebraska (m: 19/18, f: 19/16); Nevada (m: 21/18, f: 18/16); New Jersey (m: 21/18, f: 18/16); New York (m: 21/16, f: 18/16); North Carolina (m: 18/16, f: 18/16/12-18 if pregnant); Ohio (m: 21/18, f: 21/16); Rhode Island (m: 21/18, f: 21/16); South Carolina (m: 18/16, f: 18/14); South Dakota (m: 18/18, f: 18/16); Utah (m: 21/16, f: 18/14); West Virginia (m: 18/18, f: 18/16); and Wyoming (m: 18/16, f: 18/15). Some of these ages have changed since 1972, but these states still have unequal ages.

Impact of the ERA

The equal rights amendment requires that the age at which a state permits an individual to marry or defines an individual as an adult be the same for both men and women. The laws of all the states that now set the same age of majority for males and females comply with the principle of the amendment.

Policy Recommendations

As the Supreme Court recognized in Stanton and as the legislative trend clearly demonstrates, the stereotypes about role differentiation that rationalize statutory age differentials no longer have a place in the law. Women are pursuing higher education in greater and greater numbers; members of both sexes are deferring marriage and the decision to have children; and women are entering and remaining in the labor market at ever-increasing rates.[2] Since men and women mature physically long before marriage is socially acceptable, no difference along sex lines is warranted on that basis. Moreover, there is no policy justification for sex-based marriage age laws. Decisions about marriage should be left to individual judgment once the state has set a generally applicable minimum limit.

State Reform Efforts

The solution chosen by most states to the problem of differential ages of marriage has been to allow persons over 18 to marry without parental consent and those over 16 to marry with parental consent. Since the end of 1972, 17 states have equalized marriage ages by legislative action.[3] A recent amendment to a Montana law permitting underage marriage with judicial consent requires the court to find that the underage party is capable of assuming the responsibilities of marriage and that marriage will serve his or her best interest before granting approval. The law states explicitly that pregnancy alone does not establish that the best interest of the underage party will be served by marriage.[4] The Illinois law on judicial consent to marriages of 15-year-olds requires the court to find that the woman is pregnant or has given birth, that the male has acknowledged in court or in writing that he is the father of the child, that the parties are entering the marriage in good faith and not solely to legitimize the child, and that marriage is in the best interest of the parties and the child.[5]

Arkansas and Utah were the last states to bring their age of majority laws into conformity with the principle of sex equality; they both did so in 1975 by equalizing the age of majority at 18.[6]

NAMES

Background

Traditionally, women have adopted the surnames of their husbands upon marriage to replace their own birth-given surnames. While this practice was and still continues to be largely a matter of custom rather than law, it has had a significant impact on women's legal and social status, representing in a public and symbolic fashion the merger of a wife's identity into her husband's. In addition, the custom has become so commonplace that a multiplicity of policies and regulations embody an expectation that women will behave in this way, making it difficult for a woman to follow her own desires concerning name change or name retention without running into legal snares.

The common law rule regarding name change is straightforward: any individual is free to adopt a name by consistent usage, so long as there is no intent to deceive or defraud others. No court procedure is required, and no regard is given to whether the name is a birth-given name, one acquired at marriage, or a name picked randomly by an individual. This rule, which originated in the common law of England, still prevails today in most jurisdictions in this country.[7] The majority of states, however, also have enacted elaborate statutory procedures for name change[8] that presume a woman's adoption of her husband's name upon marriage. The result of these statutory enactments has been to discourage official acceptance of the simpler and less costly method of name change and to perpetuate the misconception that a married woman is required by law to use her husband's surname. Moreover, some states even provide, as a matter of statute, that a name change by a married man results automatically in a name change for his wife and children, that a married woman cannot change her name at all, or that she cannot change it without her husband's consent. In response to the growing move by women to retain or resume their birth-given names and by couples to adopt hyphenated names after marriage, however, state courts are beginning to rule that these statutes neither abrogate the common law rule of name change nor dictate women's name choice.

Voter Registration Laws

The issue of a woman's right to use the name of her choice often arises in connection with various state registration and licensing procedures. For example, voter registration officials who believe that the use of the husband's surname is a legal requirement have refused to allow women to vote using their chosen names. The process often is set in motion by arbitrary mechanisms such as the regular reporting of newspaper wedding announcements to local election boards.[9] The resulting disenfranchisement of women who refuse to comply with such requirements has been a major focus of litigation concerning a woman's freedom to choose her own name.

An early decision upholding women's rights in this area was State ex rel. Krupa v. Green,[10] in which a woman who had retained and voted under her birth-given name after marriage sought to run for a judgeship under that name. An Ohio court held that the custom of a woman taking her husband's name at marriage was not compelled by law and that the practice of requiring reregistration by all married women could not be justified for women who did not actually change their names upon marriage. Since that time, state courts in Maryland,[11] Connecticut,[12] Kansas,[13] Tennessee,[14] and Massachusetts[15] and federal courts in Arkansas[16] and Kentucky[17] have ruled similarly regarding voting registration statutes, based on the common law rule and constitutional protections.

Motor Vehicle Registration and Driver's Licenses

Driver's license and motor vehicle registration procedures also have created problems for women who do not use their husbands' names. In Forbush v. Wallace,[18] the United States Supreme Court affirmed without opinion a lower court finding that a requirement for a woman to use her husband's surname on a driver's license was not a denial of equal protection. In that case, however, the plaintiff did not contest that the common law of Alabama required her to assume her husband's surname at marriage. The case has therefore not generally been followed in those states that recognize name change at marriage as a matter of choice. Pennsylvania, for instance, has issued an Attorney General's Opinion since Forbush explicitly stating that a married woman can change her operator's license or vehicle registration or retain it in her birth-given name.[19]

Passports

Passport issuance is an area in which women have had problems resuming their birth-given names after having adopted their husbands'

surnames for a time. Although technically a federal matter, passport policies have been affected by the application of state law presumptions about women's names. The Passport Agency usually has
allowed immediate issuance of a passport in a newly adopted name if
the name is changed by repute upon marriage or widowhood, by repute
or by court order upon divorce, or by court order in the absence of
a change in marital status. In the case of other changes by repute,
however, the agency generally requires use of an "also known as"
(a.k.a.) designation until the new name has been used exclusively for
ten years. [20] In January 1974, the agency changed its policy concerning women who had resumed their own names by the time of passport
application after having once used their husbands' surnames. They
now must show one year of consistent and exclusive use of such
names in order to use them to obtain passports. [21] Women who have
consistently retained their own names during marriage should be able
to get passports in such names with no problems.

Divorce

The majority of states have some statutory provision allowing
an order permitting a divorced person to resume use of a birth-given
or prior surname to be incorporated into a divorce decree. Such provisions usually do not apply to a man who adopted a new surname
upon marriage and wishes to change it upon divorce. In addition,
these laws often deny women in certain situations the right to a name-
change order or give discretion to the trial judge in these instances.
The most common exclusions are women who are defendants or who
are judged at fault in the divorce action, [22] who are the recipients of
alimony, [23] or, most often, who have minor children of that marriage. [24]
Some statutes also provide that a woman may be ordered not to use a
husband's surname upon divorce, regardless of her wishes. [25]
Courts in Illinois, California, New Jersey, and Vermont have
rules in favor of women's right to resume their prior surnames upon
divorce—in Illinois, regardless of whether permission to do so was
given in the decree, [26] and in California, New Jersey, and Vermont,
despite the presence of minor children. [27]

General Name-Change Statutes

Although most state statutory provisions for name change have
long been facially neutral as to the sex of the applicant, discrimination against married women has been prevalent in the judicial interpretation of these laws. Many name change statutes require that
some "good cause" be shown why a person's name should be changed
or simply give the court discretion in granting requests. While most

name changes are granted as a matter of course, these discretionary powers frequently have been exercised to deny married women a change of name. However, a trend has been emerging in higher state courts to limit such judicial leeway to search for fraudulent intent only and to find denials of women's petitions on other or unstated grounds as an abuse of judicial discretion.[28] Confusion in the community and possible impact on minor children both have been explicitly rejected as reasons to deny a married woman's petition for a court-sanctioned name change.[29]

Impact of the ERA

Explicit Discrimination

The equal rights amendment requires the repeal or amendment of all sex-based statutory name provisions. This includes general name-change provisions that exclude married women as well as those that single women out for different treatment, such as requiring a husband's consent or, conversely, automatically changing a woman's name in conjunction with a name change by her husband. Special registration and licensing provisions that incorporate presumptions about whether a woman's name has been changed at marriage are also invalid under the ERA.[30] To the extent that a state chooses to legislate about name-change standards and procedures beyond the common law rule, these statutory enactments must treat individuals seeking to change or retain their name without regard to their sex.

Neutral Rules

The ERA also requires strict scrutiny of facially neutral name-change standards that impact women disproportionately. For example, a rule that prohibits a name change by the custodian of minor children or requires the consent of the other parent inevitably will fall more heavily on women. Not only are women the vast majority of single-parent child custodians but also they are the most likely to have undergone a name change at marriage, thus requiring a second change to resume a birth-given name or take on a new married name following divorce. Under the ERA, states must show that such a facially neutral rule is closely related to a compelling state interest. If another rule could be devised that would have a less drastic impact on women and nonetheless satisfy the state interest, then the first rule could not stand. To continue this example, a rule balancing the interests of the child and the custodial parent rather than an absolute standard arbitrarily weighted against that parent is an appropriate option under a strict equality standard.

Policy Recommendations

In addition to efforts to eliminate provisions in state laws suggesting or requiring that married women use their husbands' surnames,
some states have considered affirmative legislation setting forth the
law on names. Three major types of laws have been proposed or
adopted: laws requiring couples to register name choices upon marriage; laws affirmatively allowing name changes upon divorce; and
laws codifying the common law right to use the name of one's choice.

The proposed marriage registration laws are problematic for
several reasons. By singling out marriage as a name-changing event,
they are in accord with current social reality, and their procedural
formality could potentially result in couples considering more carefully the various options and implications of name choice. However,
they also lend additional social and legal support to the patriarchal
history of name change for women. In addition, unless they are carefully drafted, they may be interpreted to restrict or replace common
law rights to name change.[31] Thus, women who registered in their
husbands' names at marriage might be prevented from resuming a
premarriage surname during or after the marriage unless they resort
to costly formal procedures. Finally, some of the proposals restrict
a couple's choice of names to specific options,[32] usually relating to
current family names and precluding the choice of an altogether new
common surname or, at times, a hyphenated combination of existing
surnames. If a state chooses to enact an affirmative registration law,
explicit provisions should be included stating that the choice of names
is not limited and that the registration procedures are in no way in
derogation of the common law of name change.

Name change upon divorce is another area in which states may
enact affirmative legislation. Three types of reform provisions aimed
at eliminating sex discrimination and facilitating desired name changes
should be considered: those specifically allowing either spouse to
resume a prior surname upon divorce; those eliminating judicial discretion in granting divorce-related name changes; and those eliminating explicit exceptions to the right to resume a prior surname. A
straightforward model combining all three elements is the Wisconsin
statute, recently amended to read: "The court, upon granting a divorce . . . shall allow . . . either spouse, upon request, to resume
. . . a former legal surname, if any."[33] This provision removes any
discretion from the judge in determining the appropriateness of the
name change and eliminates any requirement of consent from the other
spouse. An additional safeguard would be an affirmative clause stating
that the provision does not abrogate common law rights of name change,
so that the statute provides a convenient method for change without
limiting other options.

Perhaps the most effective step a state can take both to eliminate all traces of sex discrimination in the law of name change and to accommodate individual name choice in the most economical fashion is simply codification of the common law of names. Such codification need not, and probably should not, be tied exclusively to marriage or divorce laws. Rather, it should stand as a general statement of the right of an individual to freedom of name choice by consistent usage, in the absence of an intent to defraud others. Other provisions affirmatively upholding the right of an individual to use a chosen name in a particular situation, such as marriage, divorce, or specific registration situations, could then be added to relevant statutes to supplement and clarify the general rule, especially where custom has been to the contrary. For example, the Federal Reserve Board has issued regulations to implement the Equal Credit Opportunity Act stating:

> A creditor shall not prohibit an applicant from opening or maintaining an account in a birth-given first name and surname or a birth-given first name and a combined surname.[34]

The Massachusetts legislature has extended the same right to all individuals in a statute in its Fair Labor Practices Code, which makes it illegal

> [f]or any person responsible for recording the name of or establishing the personal identification of an individual for any purpose, including that of extending credit, to require such individual to use, because of such individual's sex or marital status, any surname other than the one by which such individual is generally known.[35]

State Reform Efforts

As documented in the discussion above, the recent trend toward sex equality in name choice has resulted largely from opinions by state courts and attorneys general. At times, however, these opinions have prompted legislative reforms, and a few states have initiated legislative action independent of judicial pressure.

At least three states have undertaken fairly comprehensive revision of their statutory name provisions in an effort to eliminate sex bias. Iowa amended both its vehicle[36] and voter registration[37] laws in 1974 to eliminate references to marriage as a name-changing event and thus remove any presumption that women must use their husbands' surnames for these or other purposes. The Iowa legislature

already had passed other reforms in 1972 clarifying the right of a
married woman to use the state's statutory name-change procedures
in the same manner and for the same purposes as any other individual[38]
and providing that a husband's statutory name change "may," rather
than "shall," result in a name change for the wife.[39] The Massachusetts legislature has enacted reforms clarifying the right of members
of either sex to retain a prior surname upon marriage and making it
an unlawful practice for any person responsible for recording the
name or identification of an individual, as in processing a credit application, to require the use of a particular surname based on that
individual's sex or marital status.[40] Prompted by litigation, the legislature also amended its voter registration statute to allow registration
by married persons under a retained surname.[41] Oregon passed a
comprehensive bill in 1975 providing that statutory name changes generally should be granted, unless inconsistent with the public interest,
that either person in a marriage may retain a prior surname, and
that a court must decree a name change upon divorce to any spouse
who requests such a change.[42]

While less comprehensive in scope, reforms geared to particular name-changing events also have been passed in other states.
Alaska, Michigan, Minnesota, New York, Washington, and Wisconsin
have enacted legislation regarding name change upon divorce. The
Alaska and Minnesota amendments sex neutralize their divorce statutes
to allow either spouse to resume a prior surname;[43] the Michigan
amendment eliminates prior limitations of a woman's right to change
her name upon divorce;[44] and the New York, Washington, and Wisconsin amendments eliminate judicial discretion in granting name
changes upon divorce.[45] In addition, Hawaii enacted a new provision
permitting an individual, upon marriage, to retain a present surname,
take a spouse's surname, or use a hyphenated combination of the two;[46]
Kentucky passed an amendment clarifying a married woman's right to
use statutory name-change procedures in the same way that anyone
else can;[47] Michigan eliminated a provision under which a woman's
name changed automatically when her husband underwent a statutory
name change;[48] and New Mexico removed a presumption of name
change for women upon marriage from its voter registration law.[49]

CHILDREN'S NAMES

Background

Long-standing custom as well as official policy generally have
dictated that children's surnames reflect both the child's "legitimacy"

status and the married father's dominance over his family's identity. A child of married parents is almost always given his or her father's surname as a matter of state regulation or policy. Parental desire to give a child some other name, such as a hyphenated combination of the parents' surnames, still meets with official opposition from state health departments and vital statistics bureaus. If the parents divorce or become separated, the father's opposition to a request by the mother that the child be permitted to use the mother's birth-given name or the name of her second husband often succeeds in blocking change.

In contrast, a child of unmarried parents traditionally has been given the mother's surname.[50] Under these circumstances, a mother generally is prevented from choosing a different surname for the child, including that of the putative father or another surname of her choice.

Recently, however, more and more women have chosen to retain their own surnames after marriage, giving rise to an interest in naming their children so as to reflect the identity of both the mother and the father. There also has been growing interest in greater freedom of choice of surname for the child of unmarried parents, compatible with the general elimination of prejudice and discrimination on the basis of birth status.

Most of the case law on children's names has involved conflicts between the wishes of a child's parents. Recent cases concerning name changes upon divorce generally have rejected the common law view that a father has a protected property right in having his progeny bear his name.[51] Courts have continued, however, to prefer retention of the father's name in a large number of cases, allegedly based on factual showings of the projected harm that would arise from the child not bearing the father's name.[52]

Impact of the ERA

Explicit Discrimination

For both married persons and unmarried persons whose parenthood has been legally established, the equal rights amendment prohibits rules governing the naming of a child at birth that favor the surname of one parent or grant decision-making power concerning names to only one sex. In addition, the ERA requires the elimination of any rule arbitrarily favoring the continued use of the father's or mother's name for the children throughout their minority.

Neutral Rules

Neutral rules, such as the "best interest of the child," have begun to develop as standards for deciding questions about children's names and are discussed below. Any sex-based presumptions that may develop in the application of such facially neutral standards must be repudiated under the ERA. Thus, a court could not presume that retention of the father's surname is always in the child's "best interest," regardless of the circumstances.

Policy Recommendations

These ERA standards are compatible with other existing and developing doctrines of the law of names. They promote the goal of prohibiting governmental interference with individual and family choices about such matters. They are also consistent with the common law right of persons to choose any name they please, in the absence of fraud, and the right that should logically follow—to give a child any name the parents choose. Finally, they support the principle that no one has a right to prevent another from using a name on the ground that the association suggested by the identity of name would be embarrassing.[53]

As long as the parents agree on a name or name change for their child, they should be free to make that decision as a matter of course. Minors of sufficient age and maturity should be allowed to make changes on their own or to object to a change desired by one or both parents.[54] In the case of a child born out of wedlock, the child is generally in the custody and control of the mother at birth. Her identity is automatically known at time, while the father's may not be legally ascertained until later. Therefore, until paternity is legally established and the parents assume equal rights and responsibilities, it is appropriate for the mother to exercise name choice. She should be free to involve the putative father in the naming decision, of course, but she should not be required to do so. A provision for change of a child's name, by usage or more formal procedures, once paternity is established, mitigates the impact of this rule on fathers who become actively involved with their children at a later date.[55] If unmarried persons of established parenthood disagree, the same principles that apply to married couples should control.

Parents sometimes may have an unresolvable conflict about a proposed name or name change, as when a divorced mother proposes to change her child's surname to her own or to that of the child's step-father. In such a case, sex-neutral factors stressing the best interest of the child should be the basis for the final decision. Such factors may include which parent has custody, the presence of other children in the family with another surname, the social difficulty the children may encounter in the use of a particular name, and the value of retaining a tie to the noncustodial parent.

State Reform Efforts

There has been little or no statutory action in recent years to eliminate sex bias in the law concerning children's names. Other than the case law discussed above, most change in the area of children's names has resulted from opinions of state attorneys general. While many of these opinions embody the principle of sex equality, their impact would be enhanced by legislative action explicitly setting forth statutory guidelines for children's names.

In Connecticut, the attorney general, after reviewing the common law of names, held that the administrative convenience of requiring a newborn to bear his or her father's surname is not sufficient justification for impinging on the right of parents to name their child as they wish.[56] The opinion states that the parents may give the child the mother's name or a combination of their names. An opinion of the attorney general of Massachusetts[57] and Pennsylvania Health Department regulations have reached the same conclusion.[58] The Pennsylvania regulations also state that, if the parents are separated or divorced at the time of the birth of the child, the custodial parent has the right to name the child.[59] On the issue of naming a child born out of wedlock, both the Wisconsin Attorney General's Opinion and these same Pennsylvania Health Department regulations explicitly give the unmarried mother the right to give her child any surname she chooses.[60]

DOMICILE

Background

Under the common law, the husband was the head of the household and, as such, had the authority to choose the marital abode. If his choice was reasonable, his wife was obliged to follow him wherever he went and live under whatever circumstances he chose. Only if the marital unit was broken by hostility was a married woman allowed to establish a separate domicile.[61] This basic rule, modified somewhat, is still the law in many states.[62] The doctrine has two legal consequences. First, a wife who refuses to live with her husband thereby gives him the right to obtain a divorce on grounds of desertion. Second, the domicile, residence, or settlement of married women is determined by that of their husbands instead of by the rules used to determine domicile, residence, or settlement for men and single women. These consequences are discussed separately below.

Desertion Laws

At present, at least theoretically, divorce on grounds of desertion is more readily available to men than to women. In general, in order to get a divorce on grounds of desertion, a man needs to show only that his wife refuses to live with him and that his choice of abode is reasonable. A woman cannot get a divorce on this ground unless her husband does not want her to live with him; he has no obligation to accept her choice of dwelling. The discriminatory impact on women of this discrepancy varies with the availability of alternative divorce grounds, particularly "no-fault" grounds or those based on a one-year voluntary separation. [63]

Civil Rights and Obligations

As Professor Kanowitz has explained, [64]

[A [domicile is the place where a person lives and has his true permanent home, to which whenever he is absent, he has the intention of returning. The question of a person's domicile is largely one of intent. [65]

Adult women who are unmarried and adult men, regardless of their marital status, have the legal right to establish or change a former domicile freely. This type of domicile—not surprisingly called a "domicile of choice" —can be acquired by those who are authorized to do so by actually residing in a particular locality and, at the same time, intending to remain there. [66]

The state interest in determining the strength of a person's attachment to a locality for the purpose of granting certain privileges or assigning certain responsibilities is served both by domicile laws and by laws using the related concepts of residence (commonly used for voting, for example) and settlement (used for allocating welfare payment responsibility among governmental units). [67] In most states, the rules concerning married women's residence and settlement are similar to those concerning domicile.

The special rules governing married women's domicile, settlement, and residence result in sex-based differences in eligibility for
resident tuition at state schools, jury duty, voter registration, venue
in law suits, tax liability, and jurisdiction over estates. For example, suppose that a woman who is domiciled in state X marries a man
who is domiciled in state Y, but she is temporarily residing in state
X for the purpose of attending school. Under the sex-discriminatory
laws currently in force in many states, she would lose her status as
a domiciliary and a permanent resident of state X, even though she
never left the state, and would acquire the domicile of her husband.
As a result, she might lose her right to lower resident tuition at state
X colleges and her rights to vote in state and local elections, serve
on a jury, or hold office in state X. [68]

At present, five states have laws declaring that the domicile of
a person shall not be denied or abridged on the basis of sex and that
a married person may establish his or her own domicile on the same
basis as all other adults. [69] In addition, New Jersey has a law declaring that the domicile of a married woman is established similarly to
any other person for the purposes of voting, office holding, probate,
jury service, and taxes. [70] Delaware and Hawaii have unusual provisions giving women who marry out-of-state domiciliaries the right to
retain their in-state domicile. [71] At least 15 states now permit married women to establish their residence for voting purposes on the same
basis as all other adults. [72] A number of these as well as several
others have changed their rules about residence for other purposes,
such as office holding, name change, or lower tuition for state schools. [73]

Impact of the ERA

Any legal doctrine establishing the domicile, residence, or settlement of women in a different fashion from that of similarly situated
men violates the ERA. Thus, any conclusive or rebuttable presumptions that the domicile, residence, or settlement of a married woman
follows that of her husband must be eliminated. In addition, the discriminatory interpretation of desertion grounds for divorce or any
rights and obligations of a civil nature based on a sex-biased definition of domicile, settlement, or residence requires revision under
the ERA. The assignment of domicile for these purposes could be
amended in two ways to comply with the ERA. The special rules governing domicile for married women could be eliminated, subjecting
them to the same standards now applicable to married men and all
unmarried persons, or the special presumptions for women could be
extended to apply to any married person. (In practice, the extension
to men of the conclusive presumption that now applies to married wo-

men would produce an insoluble conflict in the case of a disagreement over domicile between two spouses.)

Policy Recommendations

Desertion Laws

Under the ERA, the issue of desertion laws that rely on a sex-based determination of domicile can be solved in one of two ways. The first is to allow either spouse to obtain a divorce on desertion grounds if the other refuses to live in the same location. While this alternative might make divorce more available to women than it is under existing desertion standards, it poses problems of proof as to which spouse has actually refused cohabitation, since either is obligated to follow the other to a new location under a sex-neutral domicile law. The better solution is to limit desertion to those situations in which one spouse has not only refused to live in the house selected by the other but also has refused to share his or her own house with the other. In general, this alternative would make divorce less available to men on desertion grounds than it is now.

Civil Rights and Obligations

The state interest in assigning civil rights and obligations to a person based on the strength of that person's attachment to the locality is best served by an individualized rule rather than a conclusive presumption, which, in many cases, may be contrary to the facts. Eliminating the presumption that a married woman has the same domicile as her husband does not mean that married people will stop living together. Most will continue to do so. It only means that the fact of marriage alone is not sufficient to establish domicile, residence, or settlement. Rather, the legal status of a married woman's separate domicile is to be determined by sex-neutral factors tending to show an intention to reside in a particular place indefinitely, such as are now applied to unmarried individuals. The same sex-neutral factors apply to a person newly arrived in a state, in which case marriage to a local resident or domiciliary is obviously a factor tending to show intent, as is the individual's obtaining employment in the locality or creating other ties to the area.* In this way, married women are

---

*For certain purposes, such as the collection of residency-based taxes, a state might wish to establish a rebuttable presumption that the domicile, residence, or settlement of one spouse is also that of

able to protect their interests in a locale, whether separate from or the same as their husbands', on the basis of their actual intent and behavior rather than being subject to an arbitrary presumption about their domicile based on their sex and marital status.

These changes in state domicile laws can be accomplished by affirmative statutory language such as the following:

The right of any person to become a resident domiciled in the state of _____ shall not be denied or abridged because of sex or marital status. The domicile of one spouse does not fix by operation of law the domicile of the other spouse, which shall be determined by reference to the same factors as in the case of any other individual capable of having an independent domicile.

Neither spouse has a right superior to the other spouse in the choice and establishment of a marital domicile. The refusal of a spouse to follow the other spouse who has chosen or established a new domicile does not of itself constitute desertion or abandonment as a ground, bar, or defense in any divorce action.

State Reform Efforts

A number of states have amended their laws concerning domicile, residence, or settlement in the last six years to eliminate special rules or presumptions concerning married women. Oregon and Maryland have passed laws stating explicitly that the domicile of a married person is not determined on the basis of sex or marital status and that he or she can establish a domicile independent of his or her spouse.[74] Ohio has repealed a law stating that the domicile of a married woman is presumed to be that of her husband.[75]

Other states have made more limited changes. Arizona, Connecticut, Florida, and Montana have sex neutralized the law governing the determination of residence for voting.[76] New Mexico has amended its voting law to bring its terminology into line with the sex neutralization of its substance in 1969.[77] Arizona has also amended the law on residence for venue; Florida has changed the law on residence for name change; Iowa has sex neutralized the definition of settlement for poor relief purposes; and Wisconsin has eliminated the special rule for married women in the provisions governing the determination of resident status for tuition at state schools.[78]

the other, thereby putting the burden on an individual to prove otherwise in the rare case where spouses maintain separate domiciles or residences.

CHILDREN'S DOMICILE

Background

Under the common law, a child of married parents takes the domicile of the mother. In general, when parents separate, the child takes the domicile of the custodial parent.[79] If the parent with whom the child is domiciled dies, the child assumes the domicile of the other parent. However, some courts have held that the child takes the domicile of the father even though he or she lives with the mother or with neither parent.[80] These doctrines originally derived from the father's status as head of the household, entitled to the child's custody and services and obliged to support and educate him or her. Problems arise when such sex-based doctrines result in the legal designation of a child's domicile in which he or she has never actually lived or is not presently living.* These rules may cause confusion and unnecessary complication in legal proceedings in which the domicile of the child is determinative. For instance, adoption jurisdiction and judicial power with respect to guardianship and custody may be curtailed because of artificial domicile designations.[81] They also may frustrate the purposes of the doctrine of domicile, such as providing the child with the protection of the jurisdiction best able to enter and enforce decrees concerning his or her welfare and permitting the state to offer privileges to persons believed to have a permanent connection to it. For example, a rule assigning domicile in a non-residence state may deprive a child of the benefit of lower tuition rates or admission standards at schools in the state of residence.

Impact of the ERA

The equal rights amendment, as well as other forces for the reform of family law, eliminates rules rooted in patriarchal tradition, requiring instead the use of rules derived from a model of shared parental rights and responsibilities. Under the ERA, statutory or judicial rules favoring the assignment to a child of one parent's domicile over the other's on the basis of sex are invalid. A rule assigning

---

*While this discussion refers generally to domicile, the same questions arise in the determination of legal residence and settlement for minors, which are the terms used in a number of contexts, particularly welfare and education, to refer to a person's attachment to a locale. See the section on domicile above.

domicile based on actual residence or a "best interest of the child" standard, for example, meets the sex equality requirement of the ERA without altering the common law result in a majority of cases.

Policy Recommendations

In general, the legal and social interests underlying the assignment of domicile to minors are satisfied by a sex-neutral rule based on the domicile of the parent, parents, or other legal guardian with whom the child lives. Under most circumstances, the resulting domicile reflects the child's actual residence in and attachment to a particular locale and appropriately entitles the minor to the rights and privileges dependent upon domicile. In a case where a parent or parents of the child retain a domicile in a state other than the one in which they temporarily reside with the child—for example, in order to attend school or serve in the military—the domicile of the parents should still apply to the minor since it reflects the long-term intentions of the family unit. *

The determination of the child's domicile when the parents live together but have separate domiciles requires additional guidelines. If one parent's domicile coincides with the child's residence, that domicile should be ascribed to the child because it is desirable for actual residence, parental domicile, and the child's domicile to coincide. When neither parent is domiciled in the place of temporary residence, the parental domicile with which the child has the most extensive ties should apply, subject to a "best interest of the child" standard. This rule is most consistent with the purpose of domicile— the allocation of rights and responsibilities on the basis of actual ties to a particular location—and also accords with the interest of children in having a common domicile with their parents.

State Reform Efforts

At least five states have taken steps in the past few years to eliminate sex bias in statutes concerning children's domicile and to

---

*Determination of an individual's domicile is a factual matter; evidence tending to show intent to reside in a location indefinitely or to return there is the basis for decision. For a minor, the intent of the parents to return with the child to a particular jurisdiction in which one or both of them is domiciled ordinarily will be determinative. Therefore, since it does not distort the common experience, this practice should be embodied in a rule of law.

develop sex-neutral guidelines. [82] In general, these reforms establish
rules basing a child's domicile (or legal residence or settlement, as
it is called in some contexts) on the domicile of the parents, if they
live together, or of the custodial parent.

CONSORTIUM

Background

Consortium is the right of one spouse to the other's services
or support, companionship, affection, and sexual attentions. Under
the common law, only the husband could sue for loss of consortium
when a third party negligently injured his spouse. The wife had no
cause of action for loss of her husband's consortium because a married woman was unable to bring suit in her own name, because she
had no right to her husband's services, and because, upon marriage,
her identity became part of a legal unity represented by the husband.

Logically, the Married Women's Property Acts (see p. 160-61)
should have changed this situation by extending the right to sue for
loss of consortium to married women or by eliminating the husband's
cause of action. [83] This equalization did not happen in most states
until the 1950s, however, following the influential decision in Hitaffer
v. Argonne Company. [84] Hitaffer held that a married woman has a
cause of action for loss of her husband's consortium since both law
and society now recognize that a married woman has an interest in
the marriage relationship and in any interference with that relationship equal to that of her husband. The position taken by the Washington, D.C., Court of Appeals in the Hitaffer case now prevails in 38
states and the District of Columbia, [85] as a result of judicial decision
in 30 of these and legislative action in 9. Of the remaining 12 states,
6 follow the common law and do not allow married women to sue for
loss of their husbands' consortium, [86] while 6 have abolished such actions for spouses of both sexes. [87]

Impact of the ERA

Under the equal rights amendment, a state may not recognize
either a statutory or common law right for a husband to sue for loss
of his wife's consortium, while denying that right to a wife. Those
few states that have not already sex neutralized their consortium doctrines may either extend the right to sue for loss of consortium to
married women or abolish the action altogether. The supreme courts

of two states that have ERAs in their state constitutions recently have held sex-based consortium doctrines unconstitutional and ruled that the form of action, available only to men, should be extended to married women whose husbands are injured by third parties.[88]

Policy Recommendations

The early common law action by a husband for loss of his wife's consortium was founded at least in part on the notion that a married woman was the property of her husband and owed him household as well as sexual services. The reaction of some states to the passage of the Married Women's Property Acts at the end of the last century was to abolish the husband's right to recover for negligent interference with his wife's services since such a right undercuts the emancipation of married women by treating them as property. Today, however, the trend has been to sex neutralize the form of action by extending it to married women, based on the presently accepted mutual rights of both spouses to the nonremunerated services, attentions, and affections of the other. Such extension is also in keeping with the public policy of assessing actual losses from negligent injuries against the tort-feasor involved. Therefore, those states that have abolished their consortium doctrines should enact a sex-neutral law. In those few states where the right to sue for loss of consortium is still available to husbands only, the legislature should take steps to establish equal rights for spouses of both sexes.

Moreover, even in the 30 states in which the courts have invalidated sex-based consortium doctrines, a direct affirmative statement that all married persons have the same rights irrespective of their sex is recommended as a method for reform. Such a statutory statement clarifies both the emancipation of married women from their common law status and the extension to them of the right to sue instead of relying on the courts to resolve the issue.

State Reform Efforts

As noted in the background section, sex-based consortium doctrines are largely a thing of the past, with only six states restricting the form of action to married men,[89] although 30 states remain in which the sex-neutral doctrine has not been incorporated into law. Eleven states have sex neutralized their consortium doctrines in the last six years, but in all of these states except Oklahoma the change occurred in the courts rather than the legislatures.[90] The Pennsylvania and Alaska cases were decided on the basis of the state ERAs.[91]

LIABILITY FOR FAMILY EXPENSES DURING
MARRIAGE

Background

The laws of all states establish economic responsibilities between spouses and between parents and children. However, these laws have almost no legal significance during an ongoing marriage since, as a rule, the courts will not intervene to settle disputes about the adequacy of support between spouses who are still living together. [92] The only support-related laws that are realistically enforceable during marriage are "necessaries" laws, which require one spouse to pay a merchant for necessaries, such as food, clothing, and shelter, purchased by the other, either for personal use or for their children.

Under the common law, this obligation was entirely sex-based. The wife could legally obligate her husband for both her own and the children's needs, but the husband could not so obligate his wife. The husband was liable whether or not he had given his consent to the purchase, except when the items were not necessaries, as defined by reference to the family's standard of living, when he had already supplied his wife or children with the items themselves or the means to purchase them, or when the parties were living apart through no fault of the husband. [93]

As early as 1935, many states had adopted modern "family expense" statutes to replace the common law necessaries doctrine. [94] Typically, these statutes extended to both spouses the obligation to pay for certain necessary family items purchased by either of them; they also often extended the definition of necessaries to include any item actually used by the family. [95] A fair number of these statutes retained some sex-based provisions, however, such as limitations on the items for which a wife could be held liable, requirements for creditors to proceed against the husband first, [96] or enforcement of the wife's obligation only after an underlying, sex-based support law had failed or a husband was disabled. [97] As of 1976, 11 states had family expense provisions with sex-based limitations such as these;[98] 26 states still retained completely sex-based common law standards for necessaries obligations;[99] ten states had enacted completely sex-neutral obligations for family expenses;[100] and two others had sex-neutral general support provisions with no special remedies for necessaries[101] (see Table 5.1).

Impact of the ERA

The ERA requires that all necessaries laws and family expense statutes apply equally to both spouses. This can be accomplished

either by repeal or by estension to women of equal responsibility to
pay for family necessaries. Equalization of obligations under the
ERA means that both spouses are obligated for the same range of
purchases, under the same conditions, with no assignment of primary
or secondary liability based on sex. However, as is true of the support obligation generally, a person's liability for necessaries still
would depend on his or her economic circumstances, family obligations,
and abilities.

Policy Recommendations

As discussed in the section on support and alimony below, it is
generally accepted that family members should be obligated to support
one another in accordance with their respective needs and capacities.
Shared liability to creditors for the purchase of necessary family items,
such as food, clothing, shelter, education, and medical care, is an
appropriate way to enforce this obligation. Therefore, the sex neutralization of necessaries laws is preferable to repeal.

Sex-based procedural limitations, such as provisions requiring
a creditor to execute for necessaries against a husband first, reflect
an underlying concern for protecting homemakers from unmanageable
debt liabilities. This concern is a commendable one and should be
retained in sex-neutral terms in modern family expense statutes by
way of language that places the primary economic burden for family
expenses on the wage-earning spouse. For example, a clause can be
added to a family expense statute requiring execution for such debts
against a wage-earner spouse first. Only if no property of a wage-
earner can be found should a creditor be allowed access to the separate property of a non-wage-earner spouse. Homemakers can be protected further by limiting judgment, even under these circumstances,
to those debts for which the homemaker actually contracted or which
can be shown to have actually gone to the support of the family.

As a practical matter, however, these laws, whether sex-based
or sex neutral, do not function primarily to facilitate economic partnership within marriage but rather to create an additional remedy for
creditors. If credit is extended to one spouse and that spouse subsequently defaults, the creditor may then use a necessaries law or family
expense statute to seek payment from the other spouse. These laws
do little to increase the overall economic security or creditworthiness
of a low-wage-earning or non-wage-earning spouse. Few creditors
are inclined to extend credit to a spouse when it is clear at the outset
that the only prospect of payment is a suit against the other spouse,
especially when the suit is based on a statutory obligation hedged with
conditions and restrictions. Instead, most creditors continue to require

TABLE 5.1

State Spousal Support Laws: During Marriage

State	Statute	Criminal Offense of Nonsupport	Sex Neutrality	Civil Family Law	Sex Neutrality	Support of Poor Law	Sex Neutrality
Alabama	Ala. Code (1959)	Tit. 34, § 90	Husband required to support wife in necessitous circumstances				
Alaska	Alaska Stat. (1962)	§ 11.35.010	Husband required to support wife in necessitous circumstances			§ 47.35.010	x Each required to support the other in necessitous circumstances
Arizona	Ariz. Rev. Stat. Ann. (1956)	§ 13-802 to -803	Husband required to support wife	§ 25-215	Husband required to support wife in necessitous circumstances	§ 46-295	
Arkansas	Ark. Stat. Ann. (1962)	§ 41-2405	x				
California	Cal. Civ. Code Ann. (1970)			§§ 5100, 5131, 5132	x		
	Cal. Penal Code Ann. (1970)	§ 270a	Husband required to support wife				
Colorado	Colo. Rev. Stat. Ann. (1974)	§ 14-6-101(1)	x	§ 14-6-110	x		
Connecticut	Conn. Gen. Stat. Ann. (1975)	§ 53-304(a)	Husband required to support wife	§ 46-10	Husband required to support wife	§ 17-320	x
Delaware	Del. Code Ann. (1975)	Ch. 13, § 521	x Each required to support the other in necessitous circumstances	Ch. 13, § 502	x	Ch. 13, s. 503	x

TABLE 5.1 (continued)

State	Citation		Citation		Citation	
Florida	Fla. Stat. Ann. (1965)	§ 856.04	Husband required to support wife			
Georgia	Ga. Code Ann.				Husband required to support wife	§ 23-2302 (1971)	x
Hawaii	Hawaii Rev. Stat. (1968)	§ 575-1	Husband required to support wife in necessitous circumstances	§ 573-7	Husband required to support wife		
Idaho	Idaho Code (1948)	§ 18-401	Husband required to support wife	§ 32-901	Husband required to support wife; wife required to support husband only if he is unable		
Illinois	Ill. Ann. Stat. (Smith-Hurd 1959)	Ch. 68, § 24	x Each required to support the other in necessitous circumstances				
Indiana	Ind. Stat. Ann. (1972)	§ 35-14-5-1 to -3	Husband required to support wife in necessitous circumstances	§ 31-1-9-10	x	§ 31-2-21-1	x Each required to support the other in necessitous circumstances
Iowa	Iowa Code Ann. (1969)	§ 731.1	Husband required to support wife	§ 252A.3	Husband required to support wife		
Kansas	Kan. Stat. Ann. (1974)	§ 21-3605, 3606	x Each required to support the other in necessitous circumstances				
Kentucky	Ky. Rev. Stat. (1975 Repl. Vol.)	§ 530.050	x				
Louisiana	La. Rev. Stat. (1974)	§ 14.74	Husband required to support wife in necessitous circumstances	Ch. 5, art. 119	x		
	La. Civ. Code (1952)						

(continued)

TABLE 5.1 (continued)

State	Statute	Criminal Offense of Nonsupport	Sex Neutrality	Civil Family Law	Sex Neutrality	Support of Poor Law	Sex Neutrality
Maine	Me. Rev. Stat. Ann. (1965)			Tit. 19, § 442, 443	x Each required to support the other in necessitous circumstances	§ 22-3452	x
Maryland	Md. Ann. Code (1976 Repl. vol.)	Art. 27, § 88(a)	Husband required to support wife				
Massachusetts	Mass. Gen. Laws Ann.	Ch. 273, § 1 (1970)	Husband required to support wife	Ch. 209, § 32 (1968)	Husband required to support wife in necessitous circumstances		
Michigan	Mich. Stat. Ann. (1974)	§ 28.358	Husband required to support wife	§ 25.222 (1)	Husband required to support wife in necessitous circumstances	§ 16.122	x
	Mich. Comp. Laws Ann. (1967)	§ 750.161		§ 552.451			
Minnesota	Minn. Stat. Ann. (1964)	§ 609.375	Husband required to support wife in necessitous circumstances				
Mississippi	Miss. Code Ann. (1973)			Duty of support based on case law: see, for example, Wilson v. Wilson	Husband required to support wife		
Missouri	Mo. Ann. Stat. (1953)	§ 559.353	Husband required to support wife				

State	Statute	§		§		§	
Montana	Mont. Rev. Codes Ann. (1949 Repl. vol.)	§ 94-301	Husband required to support wife in necessitous circumstances	§ 36-103	x	§ 71-235	x
Nebraska	Neb. Rev. Stat. (1965 Repl. vol.)	§ 28-449	Husband required to support wife				
Nevada	Nev. Rev. Stat.	§ 201.020 (1963)	Husband required to support wife in necessitous circumstances	§ 123.110 (1973)	Husband required to support wife; wife required to support husband only if he is unable		
New Hampshire	N.H. Rev. Stat. Ann. (1968)	§ 460:23	Husband required to support wife	§ 458:31	x	§ 167:3	x
New Jersey	N.J. Rev. Stat. (1940)	§ 2A:100-2	Husband required to support wife in necessitous circumstances			§ 44-140	x Each required to support the other in necessitous circumstances
New Mexico	N.M. Stat. Ann. (1953)	§ 40A-6-2 (1972 Repl. vol.)	x Each required to support the other in necessitous circumstances	§ 57-2-1	x		
New York	N.Y. Dom. Rel. Law (McKinney 1965)			§ 32	Husband required to support wife; wife required to support husband only if he is unable		
North Carolina	N.C. Gen. Stat. (1969 Repl. vol.)	§ 14-322	Husband required to support wife in necessitous circumstances				

(continued)

125

TABLE 5.1 (continued)

State	Statute	Criminal Offense of Nonsupport	Sex Neutrality	Civil Family Law	Sex Neutrality	Support of Poor Law	Sex Neutrality
North Dakota	N.D. Cent. Code (1971 Repl. vol.)	§ 14-07-16	Husband required to Support wife in necessitous circumstances	§ 14-08-01	Husband required to support wife		
Ohio	Ohio Rev. Code Ann. (Page 1972)			§ 3103.03	Husband required to support wife; wife required to support husband only if he is unable		
Oklahoma	Okla. Stat. Ann. (1966)	Tit. 21, § 853	Husband required to support wife in necessitous circumstances	Tit. 32, § 1	x		
Oregon	Ore. Rev. Stat. (1975)			§ 108.040	x		
Pennsylvania	Cons. Pa. Stat. Ann. (1972)	Tit. 18, § 4321	Husband required to support wife in necessitous circumstances				
	Pa. Stat. Ann. (1968)			Tit. 48, § 131	Husband required to support wife	Tit. 62, § 1973	x
Rhode Island	R.I. Gen. Laws Ann. (1969 Repl. vol.)			§ 15-11-5	Husband required to support wife		
South Carolina	S.C. Code Ann. (1962)	§ 20-303	Husband required to support wife	§ 15-1228	Husband required to support wife		
South Dakota	S.D. Comp. Laws Ann. (1969)	§ 25-7-4	Husband required to support wife in necessitous circumstances	§ 25-7-1, -5	Husband required to support wife; wife required to support husband only if he is unable	§ 25-7-6	x

State	Citation	§	Provision	§	Provision	
Tennessee	Tenn. Code Ann. (1975 Repl. vol.)	§ 39-201	Husband required to support wife			
Texas	Tex. Fam. Code (1975)			§ 4.02	Husband required to support wife; wife required to support husband only if he is unable	
Utah	Utah Code Ann. (1953)	§ 76-15-1	Husband required to support wife in necessitous circumstances	§ 78-45-3, -4	Husband required to support wife; wife required to support husband only if he is unable	
Vermont	Vt. Stat. Ann. (1974)	Tit. 15, § 202	x Each required to support the other in necessitous circumstances	Tit. 33, § 931 Tit. 15, § 291	x	
Virginia	Va. Code Ann. (1975 Repl. vol.)	§ 20-61	x Each required to support the other in necessitous circumstances			
Washington	Wash. Rev. Code Ann. (1961)	§ 26.20.030	x	§ 26.16.205	x	
West Virginia	W. Va. Code Ann. (1966)	§ 48-8-1	Husband required to support wife in necessitous circumstances	§ 48-2-28	Husband required to support wife	
Wisconsin	Wis. Stat. Ann. (1957)	§ 52.05, 52.055	Husband required to support wife in necessitous circumstances	§ 52.01	Husband required to support wife	§ 52.01, 52.03 x
Wyoming	Wyo. Stat. Ann. (1957)	§ 20-71	Husband required to support wife in necessitous circumstances			

Source: Compiled by the authors.

127

a low-wage-earning or non-wage-earning spouse—usually the wife—to
get explicit authorization from the primary wage-earner, in the form
of a signature on the credit application itself, before extending credit
even for basic family purchases.

Of course, the broader the scope of purchases allowed under
the statute and the easier the procedures established for creditors to
secure the liability of a spouse who has not actually signed for a purchase, the more effective necessaries laws are in enhancing the
economic status and security of a homemaker spouse. Only in a community property jurisdiction, however, where each spouse has an ongoing right to obligate the income and property of the other, is the
non-wage-earning spouse really protected during the marriage. Separate property jurisdictions, in reviewing their necessaries laws and
other policies concerning the income and property of married people,
may wish to supplement these laws with more far-reaching provisions
establishing an affirmative right of each spouse to half of the other's
income. These laws, as they exist in community property jurisdictions, are discussed in the section on marital property below.

State Reform Efforts

The earliest move toward sex equality in assigning liability to
spouses for family expenses during marriage occurred around the
turn of the century, in conjunction with the widespread enactment of
Married Women's Property Acts by the states. Of the ten states that
now have wholly sex-neutral provisions, one enacted this reform since
1970 as part of its sex neutralization efforts.[102] New Mexico, which
had a sex-based family expense provision, repealed its law in 1973.[103]
See Table 5.1 for state law citations.

SPOUSAL SUPPORT AND ALIMONY DURING
SEPARATION AND UPON DIVORCE

Background

Under the common law, spousal support obligations were entirely sex-based. The husband had sole responsibility for the support
of his wife. In return, he had an absolute right to his wife's services,
either within his home or outside it, which included the right to collect
her wages from her employer. He also had a legal right to control
all of his wife's property. Furthermore, until the late nineteenth and
early twentieth centuries, divorce, which would permit separated

spouses to remarry, was not readily available. Therefore, unless
the marriage was annulled, the husband's obligations to his wife and
his rights over her income and property continued until their marriage
was dissolved by death.

Today, in all states the wife has the right to control both her income and her property, and absolute divorce is available. The spousal
support obligation has been embodied in as many as six different types
of state laws in addition to the necessaries and family expense laws
already described. These are criminal laws, poor laws, general
civil family laws, laws governing legal separation or separate maintenance, laws providing for alimony or maintenance pending divorce
proceedings, and alimony provisions in the divorce laws themselves.
At present, the laws of only six states* impose no obligations on the
wife or exwife for the support of her husband or former husband. At
the same time, reform of sex-based laws has been uneven, so that
only 11 states[†] impose identical obligations on marital partners and
expartners of both sexes.

On their face, laws that use sex as a basis for allocating spousal
support and alimony obligations appear to discriminate against men
(see Table 5.2).[‡] In fact, although these laws do discriminate against
men, they discriminate much more harshly against women. First, the
number of men who are discriminated against by these laws is quite
small. Support and alimony generally are available only to women
who are unable to support themselves through outside employment,
either because of long years spent out of the labor market as a homemaker, physical or emotional disability, or the demands of child
care. Therefore, the men who actually suffer from the discriminatory
impact of sex-based laws are the relatively few men who are disabled
or who perform the homemaker role, not the vast majority of men
who are employed and earn adequate incomes to support themselves.

Second, many states also consider fault on the part of the spouse
seeking alimony as a key factor in deciding whether to award alimony
and in determining the size of the award. This factor disfavors potential recipients of alimony because, while fault cannot very readily be
used to increase alimony awards in cases in which the court believes

---

*Alabama, Georgia, Mississippi, South Carolina, Tennessee,
and Wyoming. Alabama's alimony law was recently ruled unconstitutional because it does not provide for awards to men.[104]

†California, Colorado, Delaware, Illinois, Kansas, Kentucky,
New Mexico, Oregon, Texas, Virginia, and Washington.

‡Sex-based alimony refers to laws that make some distinctions
between alimony for husbands and alimony for wives. Some of these
laws use different standards based on sex and others provide alimony
only for wives.

TABLE 5.2

State Spousal Support and Alimony Laws: Upon Divorce

State	Statute	Upon Legal Separation*	Sex Neutrality	Pending Divorce	Sex Neutrality	Upon Divorce	Sex Neutrality
Alabama	Ala. Code (1959)	Tit. 34, § 36	x	Tit. 34, § 30	Husband required to support wife	Tit. 34, §§ 32–33	Husband required to support wife
Alaska	Alaska Stat. (1962)			§ 09-55-200	Husband required to support wife	§ 09.55.210 (1973)	x
Arizona	Ariz. Rev. Stat. Ann. (1956)	§ 25-319	x	§ 25-315	x	§ 25-319	x
Arkansas	Ark. Stat. Ann. (1976)			§§ 34-1210, -1213	Husband required to support wife	§ 34-1211	Husband required to support wife
California	Cal. Civ. Code Ann. (1970)	§ 4801	x	§ 4357	x	§ 4801	x
Colorado	Colo. Rev. Stat. Ann. (1974)	§ 14-10-114	x	§ 14-10-108	x	§ 14-10-114	x
Connecticut	Conn. Gen. Stat. Ann. (1975)	§ 46-52	x	§ 46-50	x	§ 46-52	x
Delaware	Del. Code Ann. (1975)			Tit. 13, § 1509	x	Tit. 13, § 1512	x
Florida	Fla. Stat. Ann. (1965)			§ 61.071	x	§ 61.08, as amended by L. 1971, ch. 71-241, § 10	x
Georgia	Ga. Code Ann. (1969)	§ 30-213	Husband required to support wife	§§ 30-202, -206	Husband required to support wife	§ 30-209	Husband required to support wife

State	Code						
Hawaii	Hawaii Rev. Stat. (1968)			§ 580-9		§ 580-47	x
Idaho	Idaho Code (1948) (1963 Repl. vol.)			§ 32-704	Husband required to support wife	§ 32-706	Husband required to support wife
Illinois	Ill. Ann. Stat. (Smith-Hurd 1959)	Ch. 68, § 22	x	Ch. 40, § 16	x	Ch. 40, § 19	x
Indiana	Ind. Stat. Ann. (Burns 1972)			§ 31-1-11.5-7	x Alimony restricted to cases in which a spouse is physically or mentally incapacitated	§ 31-1-11.5-9	x
Iowa	Iowa Code (1971)			§ 598.11	x	§ 598.21, as amended by Acts 1970, ch. 1266, § 25	x
Kansas	Kan. Stat. Ann. (1974)	§ 60-1610(c)	x	§ 60-1607(c)	x	§ 60-1610(c)	x
Kentucky	Ky. Rev. Stat. Ann. (1975)	§ 403.200	x	§ 403.160	x	§ 403.200	x
Louisiana	La. Civ. Code Ann. (1952)	Art. 160	Husband required to support wife	Art. 148	Husband required to support wife	Art. 160	Husband required to support wife
Maine	Me. Rev. Stat. Ann. (1965)	Tit. 19, § 581	Husband required to support wife	Tit. 19, § 693	Husband required to support wife	Tit. 19, § 721	Husband required to support wife
Maryland	Md. Ann. Code (1976 Repl. vol.)	Art. 16, § 25	Husband required to support wife	Art. 16, § 5	x	Art. 16, § 3	x

(continued)

131

TABLE 5.2 (continued)

State	Statute	Upon Legal Separation*	Sex Neutrality	Pending Divorce	Sex Neutrality	Upon Divorce	Sex Neutrality
Massachusetts	Mass. Gen. Laws Ann. (1968)	Ch. 208, § 20	Husband required to support wife	Ch. 208, § 17	x	Ch. 208, § 34	x
Michigan	Mich. Comp. Laws Ann. (1967)	§ 552.23	x	§ 552.13	x	§ 552.23	x
Minnesota	Minn. Stat. Ann. (1964)			§ 518.62	x	§ 518.55	x
Mississippi	Miss. Code Ann. (1973)			§ 93-5-17	x	§ 93-5-23	Husband required to support wife
Missouri	Mo. Ann. Stat. (1953)	§ 452.335	x	§ 452.315	x	§ 452.335	x
Montana	Mont. Rev. Codes Ann. (1949 Repl. vol.)	§ 48-322	x	§ 48-318	x	§ 48-322	x
Nebraska	Neb. Rev. Stat. (1965 Repl. vol.)	§ 42-368	x	§ 42-357	x	§ 42-365	x
Nevada	Nev. Rev. Stat. (1975)	§ 125.190	Husband required to support wife	§ 125.040	Husband required to support wife	§ 125.150	Husband required to support wife
New Hampshire	N.H. Rev. Stat. Ann. (1968)	§ 458.31	Different standards of support required of husband and wife	§ 458:16	x	§ 458:19	Husband required to support wife
New Jersey	N.J. Rev. Stat. (1940)	§ 2A:34-23	x	§ 2A:34-23	x	§ 2A:34-23, as amended by L. 1971, ch. 212, § 8	x

State	Citation							
New Mexico	N.M. Stat. Ann. (1953)	§ 22-7-2	x	§ 22-7-6(a)	x	§ 22-7-6, as amended by L. 1973, ch. 319, § 7	x
New York	N.Y. Dom. Rel. Law (McKinney) (1963)	§ 236	Husband required to support wife	§ 236	Husband required to support wife	§ 236, as amended by L. 1968, ch. 699	Husband required to support wife
North Carolina	N.C. Gen. Stat. (1969 Repl. vol.)	§ 50-16.1	x	§ 50-16.3	x	§ 50-16.2	x
North Dakota	N.D. Cent. Code (1971 Repl. vol.)	§ 14-06-03	x	§ 14-05-23	x	§ 14-05-24	x
Ohio	Ohio Rev. Code Ann. (Page 1972)					§ 3105.18	x
Oklahoma	Okla. Stat. Ann. (1966)	Tit. 12, § 1284	x	Tit. 12, § 1276	x	Tit. 12, § 1278, as amended by L. 1975, ch. 350, § 1	x
Oregon	Ore. Rev. Stat. (1975)	§ 107.105	x	§ 107.095	x	§ 107.105	x
Pennsylvania	Pa. Stat. Ann. (1968)	Tit. 23, § 47	Husband required to support wife	Tit. 23, § 46	x		
Rhode Island	R.I. Gen. Laws Ann. (1969 Repl. vol.)	§ 15-5-9	x	§ 15-5-16, -18	Husband required to support wife	§ 15-5-6	Husband required to support wife
South Carolina	S.C. Code Ann. (1962)	§ 20-113-1	Husband required to support wife	§ 20-112	Husband required to support wife	§ 20-113	Husband required to support wife

(continued)

133

TABLE 5.2 (continued)

State	Statute	Upon Legal Separation*	Sex Neutrality	Pending Divorce	Sex Neutrality	Upon Divorce	Sex Neutrality
South Dakota	S.D. Comp. Laws Ann. (1969)	§ 25-4-39	Husband required to support wife	§ 25-4-38	Husband required to support wife	§ 25-4-41	Husband required to support wife
Tennessee	Tenn. Code Ann. (1975 Repl. vol.)	§ 36-820	Husband required to support wife			§ 36-820	Husband required to support wife
Texas	Tex. Fam. Code (1975)			§ 3.59	Different standards of support required of husband and wife		
Utah	Utah Code Ann. (1953)	§ 30-4-1	Husband required to support wife	§ 30-3-3	x	§ 30-3-5	x
Vermont	Vt. Stat. Ann. (1974)	Tit. 15, § 556	x	Tit. 15, § 204	x	Tit. 15, § 754	x
Virginia	Va. Code Ann. (1975 Repl. vol.)	§ 20-107	x	§ 20-103	x	§ 20-107	x
Washington	Wash. Rev. Code Ann. (1961)	§ 26.09.090	x	§ 26.09.060	x	§ 26.09.050	x
West Virginia	W. Va. Code Ann. (1966)	§ 48-2-28	Husband required to support wife	§ 48-2-13	x	§ 48-2-15	x
Wisconsin	Wis. Stat. Ann. (1957)	§ 247.26	x	§ 247.23	x	§ 247.26	x
Wyoming	Wyo. Stat. Ann. (1957)	§ 20-36	Husband required to support wife	§ 20-58	Husband required to support wife	§ 20-63	Husband required to support wife

*This column includes statutory provisions for support or alimony in all situations of spousal separation without divorce, whether labeled divorce from bed and board, separate maintenance, or legal separation.

Source: Compiled by the authors.

the payor spouse is at fault, it easily can be used to decrease awards in cases in which the court believes the recipient spouse is at fault. *
As the former group consists largely of women, the use of the fault factor has a far greater negative impact on women than men. More- over, a number of states withdraw the right to alimony when a divorced spouse remarries, regardless of the circumstances.

A third factor affecting the real impact of alimony laws is the fact that many courts use a set percentage of the provider's salary— usually one-quarter to one-third—as a rule of thumb in limiting the amount of both spousal and child support that they will award. In these states, support laws operate primarily to decrease welfare costs rather than to provide meaningful economic protection to family mem- bers.

Finally, support awards are so poorly enforced that most separ- ated and divorced women are forced to choose either to work outside the home or to accept welfare, even in those unusual situations in which the amount of support awarded might theoretically meet their needs. For example, a study by the Committee on the Homemaker of the National Commission for the Observance of International Wo- men's Year showed that only 14 percent of divorced wives were awarded alimony in 1975 and that only 46 percent of these collect it regularly. [105] Census Bureau data indicate that the median income of women living on alimony, pensions, and annuities combined is only $1,151 annually. Only 3.33 percent of all women receive any income from these sources, although 8 percent of all women are di- vorced and 12.3 percent are widowed. [106]

Impact of the ERA

Explicit Discrimination

The ERA requires that all laws concerning spousal support and alimony be sex neutral. Technically, this could be accomplished

---

*Delaware's law is particularly egregious. It authorizes alimony awards to respondents in divorce actions, not petitioners, and only in divorces sought on grounds of mental illness or incompatability. Thus, a financially dependent spouse must choose between receiving support and seeking a divorce. Even the respondent is absolutely barred from receiving support if the other spouse seeks a divorce on the ground of voluntary separation or misconduct of the respondent. The clause concerning the statute's purposes makes the intent of the legislature clear. Among the purposes listed is "not to award alimony to petitioners who seek divorce for any reason and reject the respon- dent as a spouse."

either by the repeal of existing sex-based laws or by the extension
of these laws to cover male recipients and female providers. However, the legislative history of the ERA makes quite clear the intent
of Congress that these laws should be extended,[107] and the repeal of
spousal support laws seems highly unlikely.

Neutral Rules

Stringent limitations on spousal support and alimony obligations,
judicial bias against dependent spouses, the use of fault as a factor,
and inadequate enforcement have a disparate impact on women, who
are the majority of recipients of support and alimony. Therefore,
an argument can be made that the ERA requires the states to adopt
more generous alimony and support laws, to restrict judicial discretion, to adopt more effective enforcement procedures, and to pursue
enforcement of the laws more vigorously.

Policy Recommendations

In addition to sex neutralizing the language of existing sex-based
support and alimony laws, states should give serious consideration to
the adoption of specific guidelines for judges regarding the factors to
be taken into account in setting support and alimony awards. Determination of the factors to be considered in regulating intrafamily economic relationships is appropriately a legislative rather than a judicial function. Judges may have widely varying notions of what would
be equitable in a particular situation and often are influenced in their
awards by personal biases against certain life choices. The legislatures, by enacting guidelines, can more broadly consider the values
of the people of their states, weigh the different interests involved,
and develop a general framework to promote more consistent results
from case to case and among different geographical areas within the
state. In addition, guidelines give fair notice to citizens of the obligations and rights of marital partners and, in most cases, provide
better protection to spouses who are not employed outside the home.
Specific legislative guidelines also prevent judges from interpreting
facially sex-neutral statutes with a conscious or unconscious sex
bias because they force judges to articulate the reasons for their decisions, which, in turn, enables appellate courts to review lower
court decisions more effectively.

A careful policy review of support and alimony laws must also
include reevaluation of a state's statutory provisions for the enforcement of awards.[108] The economic consequences of the high default
rate currently existing among spouses with family support obligations

is devastating, particularly for women. Whatever reforms are
enacted to redefine support obligations in line with modern family dynamics, these changes will not have the intended beneficial impact on
homemakers unless enforcement mechanisms are developed to give
teeth to the underlying support rights.

In most states, arrears in support can be collected by executing
against the property of the obligor, and, in some states, garnishment
of wages or other assets is available. Most states also allow obligors
to be jailed for contempt for failure to pay court-ordered awards.
This remedy may be of little practical value to a needy spouse in the
short run, however, although it may have some deterrent effect over
the long run. In addition to remedies available against a payor spouse
residing in the same state as the payee, every state has some variation of the Uniform Reciprocal Enforcement of Support Act (URESA).[109]
Under this act, a recipient of support can file a complaint in the state
of residence and have it forwarded for adjudication and collection to
the jurisdiction where the obligor-spouse is located.

These common methods of enforcement, however, are available
only after arrearages have built up as a result of a pattern of default.
More valuable to support recipients are devices aimed at avoiding default altogether. These include requiring the posting of security or
bond with the court to guarantee payment at the time the award is first
made, requiring the obligor to pay directly to the court or some other
official collection agency that monitors the payment schedule, and in-
stituting involuntary wage assignments for support obligations so that
support is deducted automatically from the obligor's paycheck.[110]
Unfortunately, such affirmative devices are not widely available under
current state statutes or enforcement programs. This is the result
of official disregard for support enforcement generally, in part due
to an underlying presumption that an obligor will pay regularly, making it unnecessary for the state to interfere until default occurs. This
disregard and the presumption underlying it should be repudiated in
light of the existing abysmal record of payment. Finally, states
should consider the adoption of provisions that explicitly provide for
the vesting of support rights as soon as each payment becomes due,
thus guaranteeing immediate or eventual payment in full. This protects the recipient from the constant threat that support payments
will be reduced retroactively, a common phenomenon when an obligor-
spouse is charged with large arrearages.

State Reform Efforts

As mentioned above in the background section, there are several
types of laws that govern the economic relations of separated or di-

vorced spouses, and in 11 states these laws are entirely sex neutral. Of the remaining states, 6 impose spousal support obligations only on men, and 33 have a mixture of sex-based and sex-neutral laws. Of this latter group, 23 have sex-neutral alimony laws,* and one has no alimony for spouses of either sex.† See Table 5.2 for citations to these support and alimony laws.

Although it is not clear when the various states first began to equalize spousal support obligations, the evidence suggests that most reforms have been fairly recent. A review of the legislative history shows that five of the states with entirely sex-neutral laws had both sex-based support and alimony laws prior to 1968[111] and that an additional 14 states have sex neutralized their alimony laws since 1968.[112] Two other states that formerly imposed support obligations only on husbands also recently reformed their laws to impose mutual obligations on both spouses.[113]

An even more significant development has been the recent adoption by 13 states[114] of detailed factors to guide courts in making alimony or maintenance awards and by seven states[115] of more limited lists of factors. The Uniform Marriage and Divorce Act (UMDA) has been quite influential in divorce law reform generally because of its innovative provisions concerning no-fault divorce. Although only four states have adopted its provisions concerning spousal maintenance verbatim,‡ other states have relied on its provisions in drafting their own lists of factors.

Many of the factors used in both the detailed and limited factor states are simply codifications of the types of standards that many judges have already begun to use to determine alimony awards. Typical factors include: the duration of the marriage and the age of the parties,** the physical and emotional condition of the parties and the standard of living established during the marriage,*** the prop-

---

*Five of these have only one sex-based law: Alaska, Connecticut, Indiana, Montana, and Wisconsin. The remaining 18 are: Arizona, Florida, Hawaii, Iowa, Maryland, Massachusetts, Michigan, Minnesota, Missouri, Nebraska, New Jersey, North Carolina, North Dakota, Ohio, Oklahoma, Utah, Vermont, and West Virginia.

†Pennsylvania only provides for alimony pending divorce.

‡One weakness of the UMDA factor list is its failure to take into account the contribution of the homemaker in making support awards. See discussion in the text below.

**All 13 detailed-factor states, New Jersey, and New York.

***All 13 detailed-factor states except Oregon and Nebraska, plus North Carolina (condition of the parties and standard of living), Wyoming, Nevada, and Hawaii (condition left by the divorce), and Iowa (physical condition).

erty and other financial resources of the parties, * needs (Connecticut, Massachusetts, and Virginia) and obligations (Massachusetts, Virginia, Washington, and Ohio) of the parties, the employability of the spouse seeking maintenance,[†] and the desirability of requiring the custodial parent to seek employment outside the home.[‡]

In the process of codifying and reviewing traditional alimony standards, however, all 13 states with detailed factors also have made significant changes in those standards. Two areas are particularly noteworthy. The first concerns the need to give additional guidance to judges in the process of evaluating the earning capacity of the parties. Such guidance is necessary to avoid forcing homemakers to take low-wage, low-status jobs rather than giving them the opportunity to upgrade their skills to a level commensurate with their abilities or with what they might have achieved had not marriage interrupted their schooling or employment. This concern has been expressed in a variety of ways in all 13 detailed factor states. Nine states refer to the educational levels of the parties (Ohio and Virginia), to the opportunity of the parties to obtain training or education (Virginia), or to the time necessary to acquire sufficient education or training to enable the party seeking maintenance to find appropriate employment (UMDA states, Arizona, and Washington). The most specific provision is that of Washington, which defines appropriate employment as "employment appropriate to his skill, interests, style of life and other attendant circumstances." Other states have dealt with this concern by directing the court to consider such factors as occupation, vocational skills and employability (Connecticut and Massachusetts), work experience and earning capacity (Oregon), and the relative earning abilities of the parties (Ohio). One problem with these statutes is that they may be interpreted to direct the court to compare the immediate job prospects of the man and woman rather than to focus on the disparity between her current and potential capacity and the need to order payment of maintenance so that she can get the training necessary to fulfill that potential.

---

*All 13 detailed-factor states except Nebraska. That state refers instead to the circumstances of the parties and their contributions to the marriage. In addition, all nine of the limited-factor states (including Nevada and Wyoming) direct the court to consider one or more of the following factors: need, ability to pay, financial resources, capacity of the wife for self-support, earnings, earning capacity, or pecuniary condition of the parties.

[†]All 13 detailed-factor states.

[‡]All of the detailed-factor states except Washington, Massachusetts, and Virginia. [116]

Two states have taken a different approach to the situation of the homemaker by expressly directing courts to consider the contribution of a homemaking spouse. The Ohio provision simply lists the contribution of a spouse as homemaker among the factors to be considered. The Nebraska provision is more specific: courts are to consider "a history of the contributions to the marriage of each party, including contributions to the care and education of the children and interruption of personal careers and educational opportunities." These provisions ensure that the homemaker's past uncompensated services will be taken into account in equalizing the parties' economic situations after divorce.

The second area in which several states have significantly changed traditional standards for the award of alimony concerns the broadening of the types of financial information courts are to consider. Two states, Ohio and Massachusetts, have adopted provisions directing judges' attention to the spouses' future expectations of and opportunities for financial gain.* Similarly, Arizona attempts to promote financial equity by directing courts to consider excessive or abnormal expenditures, and the destruction, concealment, or fraudulent disposition of community, joint tenancy, and other property held in common. Both types of provisions probably benefit homemakers more often than wage-earning spouses since wage-earners are more likely to have future opportunities for financial gain—for example, in the form of retirement benefits—and to have been in a position to misuse community financial resources.

The major weakness of the UMDA is that it is premised on the idea that past contributions to the marriage should be reflected in property division only, not in an award of maintenance. Thus, the property division factors include the "contribution of each spouse to acquisition of the marital property, including contribution of a spouse as homemaker," while the maintenance provisions not only exclude this factor but also limit maintenance awards to situations in which the spouse seeking maintenance

---

*The Ohio provision concerning future financial opportunities is more specific, providing that courts must consider both the retirement benefits of the parties and their expectations and inheritance. The Massachusetts provision may be more far-reaching, however, directing courts to consider the parties' opportunities for the future acquisition of capital assets and income. Massachusetts also has a provision directing consideration of each party's contribution to the acquisition, preservation, or appreciation in value of their respective estates. This might possibly be used to bring in issues similar to those that must be considered under the Arizona provision concerning misuse of community resources, which is discussed below.

lacks sufficient property to provide for his reasonable needs, and
is unable to support himself through appropriate employment or is
the custodian of a child whose condition or circumstances make it
appropriate that the custodian not be required to seek employment
outside the home.

If a couple does not have much property, the major asset in their
marriage is probably the earning capacities of the spouses. Excluding
the contribution of the homemaking spouse in ordering maintenance
payments ignores this reality. Furthermore, the terms "reasonable
needs" and "appropriate employment" are not defined. Depending on
judicial construction, these provisions may be used either to channel
former homemakers into undesirable jobs or to recognize the validity
of a former homemaker's desire to develop skills and obtain employment in the field of his or her choice.

If the specific factors listed in each state are considered as a
whole, fairly significant differences in emphasis are evident. Overall, the laws of Ohio, Washington, and Nebraska convey the greatest
sense of concern for spouses who have not previously been wage-
earners. This becomes more striking when these laws are compared
with the laws more closely modeled on the UMDA. The former laws
do not burden non-wage-earning spouses by preferring property awards
to maintenance awards, and they either articulate more factors or expressly take the contributions of the homemaking spouse into account.
The remaining states fall somewhere between these two models.[117]

It should be noted, however, that the UMDA is still more favorable to non-wage-earning spouses than most other divorce laws, especially some fairly recent laws that attempt to diminish as much as
possible the legal and economic interdependence of former marital
partners. Several states that have not adopted detailed guidelines
for the award of alimony have, nonetheless, adopted fairly stringent
limitations on alimony awards. For example, Indiana's divorce law
provides:

> The court may make no provision for maintenance except
> that when the court finds a spouse to be physically or men-
> tally incapacitated to the extent that the ability of such in-
> capacitated spouse to support himself or herself is mate-
> rially affected, the court may make provision for the main-
> tenance of said spouse during any such incapacity, subject
> to further order of the court.

Hawaii's law reflects a similar distrust of the dependent spouse,
for, in addition to the customary right of either party to move for a
new hearing on the basis of a change in circumstances, it provides:

Upon the motion of the party against whom an order was
entered supported by an affidavit setting forth in particular that the other party, although able and capable of substantially rehabilitating himself or herself financially,
has wilfully failed to do so, the moving party, may, in the
discretion of the court and upon adequate notice to the non-
moving party, be granted a hearing [concerning reduction
or elimination of maintenance payments, pursuant to a
standard directing the court to consider all proper circumstances. Substantial arrears in support payments are
not a bar to such a reduction hearing].

Somewhat less stringent provisions designed to encourage non-
wage-earning spouses to return to the labor market following divorce
have been adopted in Florida and New Hampshire. Florida has two
separate categories, rehabilitative alimony and permanent alimony,
the implication of the former being that it is transitional in nature.
New Hampshire provides that alimony may only be awarded for three
years, after which time it may be "renewed, modified, or extended
if justice requires for periods of not more than three years at a time."
    Finally, states still vary considerably on whether or not fault
is to be explicitly considered in the determination of economic matters during divorce proceedings. Of the thirteen detailed factor
states, five expressly direct that marital fault is not to be considered,
four direct that it is to be considered, and four are ambiguous. *
    Problems with support enforcement, unfortunately, have not
yet received the level of state attention that is needed. The passage
by Congress in 1975 of amendments to the Social Security Act hopefully will spur state activity in the area of child support and eventually
encourage increased enforcement of spousal support.[118] These amendments, known as the Child Support Enforcement Program, provide
for the establishment of an interstate parent locater service, which is

---

*Fault is not to be considered in Montana, Colorado, Delaware,
Arizona, and Washington. But note the inconsistency in Delaware
law: only a respondent in a divorce action can get alimony, so that
the desire to end a marriage apparently has become a new type of
fault disqualification. Fault is to be considered in Massachusetts
(conduct of the parties during marriage), Connecticut (the causes of
the dissolution), Missouri (the conduct of the party seeking maintenance during the marriage), and Virginia (fault is a bar to alimony).
Ambiguous provisions are found in Kentucky (no explicit provision),
Nebraska (contributions to the marriage), Oregon (other matters the
court deems relevant), and Ohio (all relevant factors).

aimed primarily at securing support obligations from absent parents of children receiving public assistance but is also available to nonwelfare recipients. The act also provides for wage garnishment for federal employees with outstanding child support obligations. Under these amendments, states are required to establish their own organizational units to administer the new Child Support Enforcement Program, including their own state parent locater service. A high level of federal reimbursement for the administrative costs incurred by the states as well as special incentive payments for localities collecting child support in public assistance cases should act as catalysts in state and local development of enforcement efforts that relate to the new federal system. As of June 1976, 18 states had already keyed into the federal parent locater service with requests for assistance.[119]

The efficacy of these state efforts in alleviating the impact of arrearages and defaults on those spouses and children who rely on support awards will depend on a number of factors. The most important ones are whether the state and local units actually take responsibility for collecting outstanding awards in those cases in which support recipients have assigned their support rights to the state in order to collect public assistance; whether state and federal parent locater services are actually made available to nonwelfare recipients of support awards; whether these enforcement services are extended to cover spousal as well as child support awards; and, finally, whether sufficient regard is given to the overall welfare of the family unit in deciding whether custodial parents must cooperate in finding and collecting support from an absent parent in order to collect public assistance.

A final development concerning the adequacy and enforcement of support has been the enactment in some states of provisions requiring financial disclosure by the parties to spousal and child support awards. The most comprehensive of these was passed in New York in 1975.[120] It provides that in all proceedings concerning alimony or support, "there shall be compulsory disclosure by both parties of their respective financial status." It goes on to detail that the "sworn statement of net worth" must include "all income and assets of whatsoever kind and nature and wherever situated and . . . a list of all assets transferred in any manner during the preceding three years, or the length of the marriage, whichever is shorter." An Iowa provision, enacted in 1970,[121] is also fairly detailed in outlining the disclosures to be made but applies to a respondent in a support case only if the respondent resists the application for support or if the court specifically orders such disclosure. Thus, the spouse petitioning for support does not have a certain way of obtaining information about the assets of the other. A Nebraska provision, enacted in 1972, requires disclosure only from the applicant, giving the court discretion about whether the respondent must make a detailed disclosure of assets.[122] Two other states, Michigan and Vermont, which have had general disclosure provisions for a number of years, recently amended these provisions to reflect the sex neutralization of their underlying support obligations.[123] Finally, a few states have adopted the UMDA provision that permits the court to issue a preliminary injunction against transferring or otherwise disposing of or concealing property when a temporary award of maintenance or support is issued, so that the obligor cannot defeat the award by concealing assets.[124]

A model statute setting forth appropriate guidelines for alimony determinations based upon a number of innovative state laws follows.*

Model Guidelines for the Award of Alimony

In a proceeding for dissolution of marriage, legal separation, declaration of invalidity,[†] or in a proceeding for maintenance following dissolution of the marriage by a court which lacked personal jurisdiction over the absent spouse, the court may grant a maintenance order for either spouse.[‡] The maintenance order shall be in such amounts and for such periods of time as the court deems just, without regard to marital misconduct, after considering all relevant factors including but not limited to:

(a) the standard of living established during the marriage;
(b) the duration of the marriage;
(c) the ages and the physical and emotional conditions of the parties;**
(d) the extent to which it would be inappropriate for a party, because he will be custodian of a minor child of the marriage, to seek employment outside the home;***

---

*Language from the UMDA is underscored; state provisions are footnoted to the appropriate state.

†Washington. This provision is for states with annulment, as well as divorce and legal separation, in their relevant statute.

‡At this point, significant UMDA language requiring prior findings about employability, availability of property as a source of support, and the needs of children for the full-time care of a custodian has been omitted.

**The Ohio version has been used because it expressly compares both parties. UMDA considers all these factors about the spouse seeking maintenance only, thereby encouraging sexist stereotypes, instead of using a more equitable comparison of the complete situations of each party.

***This is Ohio's language.

(e) the time necessary to acquire sufficient education or training to enable the party seeking maintenance to find employment appropriate to his skill, interests, style of life, and other attendant circumstances;*

(f) the history of the contributions to the marriage by each party, including property brought to the marriage by either party, contributions to the care and education of the children, and interruption of personal careers or educational opportunities;[†]

(g) the financial conditions, resources, and property rights of each party including their retirement benefits, expectancies and inheritances, assets and liabilities, marital property apportioned to each party, and the extent to which a provision for support of a child living with the party includes a sum for that party as custodian;[‡]

(h) the respective work experience, educational levels, and earning capacities of the parties;** and

(i) excessive or abnormal expenditures, destruction, concealment or fraudulent disposition of community, joint tenancy, and other property held in common. ***

CHILD SUPPORT DURING MARRIAGE AND UPON DIVORCE[††]

Background

Under the common law, child support obligations, like spousal support obligations, were entirely sex-based. Men had the sole legal obligation to support their children and the concomitant right to control all the earnings and property of their wives and children. These laws have been substantially changed. At present, child support laws in 33 states apply equally to both parents.[†††] Thirteen other states

---

*This is Washington's version

[†]This is Nebraska's provision, with the addition of Ohio factor (10).

[‡]This provision is based on language from Oregon, Ohio, and the UMDA.

**This provision is modeled on Oregon law, with the addition of educational levels from Ohio. See also Virginia on educational levels.

***This provision is from Arizona.

[††]This chapter treats the support of children of married parents. The legal status of children born out of wedlock is discussed below.

[†††]Alabama, Arizona, Arkansas, Colorado, Delaware, Florida, Hawaii, Idaho, Illinois, Indiana, Kansas, Kentucky, Louisiana, Maine,

have at least one statute, either in the marriage or in the divorce context, which imposes equal financial responsibilities on both parents. *
In two states, a mother is liable to support her children only when the
father is unable to do so. † In two other states, only the father is
charged statutorily with the support of his children. ‡ See Tables
5.3 and 5.4 for citations to these laws.

The patterns of sex discrimination in the area of child support
are similar to those in the area of spousal support, that is, they are
more unfair to women than to men. Laws imposing heavier responsibilities on fathers than on mothers do discriminate against men, but
it is only a small group of men—those who have custody of their children and whose separated or divorced spouses are employed and earning an income large enough to include child support payments. Even
under a sex-neutral law, if the mother is unemployed or is making
an inadequate income, a father with child custody has no right to
child support contributions from her because the obligation is allo-
cated on the basis of income and earning capacity. And if the mother
rather than the father has custody, she is probably already contributing half or more of the children's support, simply because court-
ordered support payments are almost universally too small to cover
the expenses of child rearing. In addition, enforcement of child support awards is very poor. One of the few reliable studies found that
after one year, only 38 percent of fathers were complying with child
support orders and 42 percent were making no payment whatsoever.
These default rates continued to rise with the passage of time. [125]
Another source of sex discrimination in many cases is the failure to
take the value of the custodial parent's unpaid contributions into account in allocating financial responsibilities between parents. Instead,
income or earning capacity is the sole factor. As a result, the actual
contribution to child rearing made by the custodial parent is discount-
ed. ** In fact, unfair financial burdens on custodial parents, rather

---

Maryland, Massachusetts, Minnesota, Mississippi, Montana, Nevada,
New Hampshire, New Mexico, North Carolina, North Dakota, Tennes-
see, Texas, Utah, Vermont, Virginia, Washington, West Virginia,
Wisconsin, and Wyoming.

*Alaska, California, Connecticut, Georgia, Iowa, Missouri, New
Jersey, New York, Ohio, Oklahoma, Oregon, Pennsylvania, and South
Dakota.

†Rhode Island and South Carolina.

‡Michigan and Nebraska.

**This form of discrimination does not operate in cases in which
the children are so young or so numerous that outside employment
for the mother is precluded and in which the father's income is suffi-

TABLE 5.3

State Child Support Laws: During Marriage

State	Statute	Criminal Offense of Nonsupport	Sex Neutrality	Civil Family Law	Sex Neutrality	Support of Poor Law	Sex Neutrality
Alabama	Ala. Code (1959)	Tit. 34, § 90	x				
Alaska	Alaska Stat. (1962)	§ 11.35.010	x	§ 25.20.030	x	§ 47.35.010	Father required to support child; mother required only if he is unable
Arizona	Ariz. Rev. Stat. Ann. (1956)	§ 13-801	x			§ 46-295	x
Arkansas	Ark. Stat. Ann. (1962)	§ 41-2405	x				
California	Cal. Civ. Code Ann. (1970)			§ 196	Father required to support child; mother required only if he is unable		
	Cal. Penal Code Ann. (1970)	§ 270	x				
Colorado	Colo. Rev. Stat. Ann. (1974)	§ 14-6-101(1)	x	§ 14-6-110	x	§§ 30-17-107, -108	Father required to support child; mother required only if he is unable
Connecticut	Conn. Gen. Stat. Ann. (1975)	§ 53-304(a)	x	§ 46-10	Father required to support child		
Delaware	Del. Code Ann. (1975)	Ch. 13, § 521	x	Ch. 13, § 501(a),	x	Ch. 13, § 503	x
Florida	Fla. Stat. Ann. (1965)	§ 856.04	x	(c), 701			

(continued)

TABLE 5.3 (continued)

State	Statute	Criminal Offense of Nonsupport	Sex Neutrality	Civil Family Law	Sex Neutrality	Support of Poor Law	Sex Neutrality
Georgia	Ga. Code Ann.			§ 74-105 (1973)	Father required to support child	§ 23-2302 (1971)	x
Hawaii	Hawaii Rev. Stat. (1968)	§ 575-1	x				
Idaho	Idaho Code (1948)	§ 18-401	x	§ 32-1003	x		
Illinois	Ill. Ann. Stat. (Smith-Hurd (1959)	Ch. 68, § 24	x	Ch. 68, § 23a	x	Ch. 68, § 24	x
Indiana	Ind. Stat. Ann. (1972)	§ 35-14-5-1 to -3	x	§ 31-1-9-10	x	§ 31-2-21-1	x
Iowa	Iowa Code Ann. (1969)	§ 731.1	Father required to support child; mother required only if he is unable	§ 252A.3	Father required to support child; mother required only if he is unable	§ 252.2	x
Kansas	Kan. Stat. Ann. (1974)	§ 21-3605	x				
Kentucky	Ky. Rev. Stat. (1975 Repl. vol.)	§ 530.050	x	§ 405.020	x		
Louisiana	La. Rev. Stat. (1974)	§ 14.74	x; Both parents required to support child in necessitous circumstances	La. Civ. Code (1952) Ch. 5, art. 227	x		
Maine	Me. Rev. Stat. Ann. (1965)	Tit. 19, § 481	x; Both parents required to support child in necessitous circumstances	Tit. 19, § 214, 442, 443	Father required to support child	§ 22-4467, -3452	x
Maryland	Md. Ann. Code (1976 Repl. vol.)	Art. 27, § 88 (b)	x	Art. 72A, § 1	x		

148

State	Statute						
Massachusetts	Mass. Gen. Laws Ann.	Ch. 273, § 1 (1970)	x			Ch. 273, § 23 (1958)	x
Michigan	Mich. Stat. Ann. (1974) Mich. Comp. Laws Ann. (1967)	§ 28.358 § 750.161	Father required to support child	§ 25.221 § 552.333	x	§ 16.122	x
Minnesota	Minn. Stat. Ann. (1964)	§ 609.375	x				
Mississippi	Miss. Code Ann. (1973)	§ 97-5-3	x			§ 43-31-25	x
Missouri	Mo. Ann. Stat. (1953)	§ 559.353	x				
Montana	Mont. Rev. Codes Ann. (1949 Repl. vol.)	§ 94-304	x	§ 61-114	Both parents required to support child in necessitous circumstances — x	§ 71-235	x
Nebraska	Neb. Rev. Stat. (1965 Repl. vol.)	§ 28-449	Father required to support child				
Nevada	Nev. Rev. Stat. (1963)	§ 201.020	x				
New Hampshire	N.H. Rev. Stat. Ann. (1968)	§ 460:23, -24	x	§ 458:35	x	§ 167:2	
New Jersey	N.J. Rev. Stat. (1940)	§ 2A:100-2	x			§ 44-140	Father required to support child; mother required only if he is unable
New Mexico	N.M. Stat. Ann.	§ 40A-6-2 (1972 Repl. vol.)	x			§ 13-1-45 (1953)	x
New York	N.Y. Penal Law (1967) N.Y. Dom. Rel. Law (McKinney 1965)	§ 260.05	x	§ 32	Father required to support child; mother required only if he is unable		

(continued)

149

TABLE 5.3 (continued)

State	Statute	Criminal Offense of Nonsupport	Sex Neutrality	Civil Family Law	Sex Neutrality	Support of Poor Law	Sex Neutrality
North Carolina	N.C. Gen. Stat. (1969 Repl. vol.)	§ 14-322	x	§ 50-13.4	Father required to support child; mother required only if he is unable		
North Dakota	N.D. Cent. Code (1971 Repl. vol.)	§ 14-07-15, -709-22	x Both parents required to support child in necessitous circumstances	§ 14-08-01	Father required to support child	§ 50-01-19	x
Ohio	Ohio Rev. Code Ann. (Page 1972)	§ 3113.06, 3113.99	x	§ 3103.03	Father required to support child; mother required only if he is unable	§ 3113.06	x
Oklahoma	Okla. Stat. Ann. (1966)	Tit. 21, § 852	x	Tit. 10, § 4-5	Father required to support child; mother required only if he is unable	Tit. 10, § 12	x
Oregon	Ore. Rev. Stat. (1975)	§ 163.555	x	§ 108.040	x	§ 108.110, 109.040	x
Pennsylvania	Cons. Pa. Stat. Ann. (1972)	Tit. 18, § 4321	Father required to support child				
Rhode Island	Pa. Stat. Ann. (1968) R.I. Gen. Laws Ann. (1969 Repl. vol.)	§ 15-9-3	x	Tit. 48, § 131 § 15-11-5, -6	Father required to support child x	Tit. 62, § 1973 § 40-5-13	x x
South Carolina	S.C. Code Ann. (1962)	§ 20-303	Father required to support child	§ 15-1228, -1229	Father required to support child; mother required only if he is unable		

150

State	Statute	§	Father required to support child; mother required only if he is unable	§	Father required to support child; mother required only if he is unable	§	Father required to support child; mother required only if he is unable
South Dakota	S.D. Comp. Laws Ann. (1969)	§ 25-7-18		§ 25-7-7		§ 25-7-6	x
Tennessee	Tenn. Code Ann. (1975 Repl. vol.)	§ 39-202	x				
Texas	Tex. Penal Code (1975) Tex. Fam. Code (1975)	§ 25.05	x	§ 4.02	x		
Utah	Utah Code Ann. (1953)	§ 76-15-1	x	§ 78-45-3, -4	x		
Vermont	Vt. Stat. Ann. (1974)	Tit. 15, § 202	Both parents required to support child in necessitous circumstances / x	Tit. 33, § 931 Tit. 15, § 291	x		
Virginia	Va. Code Ann. (1975 Repl. vol.)	§ 20-61	Both parents required to support child in necessitous circumstances / x				
Washington	Wash. Rev. Code Ann. (1961)	§ 26.20.030	x	§ 26.16.205	x	§ 74.20.010 et seq.	x
West Virginia	W. Va. Code Ann. (1966)	§ 48-8-1	Both parents required to support child in necessitous circumstances / x				
Wisconsin	Wis. Stat. Ann. (1957)	§ 52.05, 52.055	Both parents required to support child in necessitous circumstances / x	§ 52.01	x	§ 52.01, 52.03	x
Wyoming	Wyo. Stat. Ann. (1957)	§ 20-71	x	§ 14-18	x	§ 14-18	x

Source: Compiled by the author.

151

TABLE 5.4

State Child Support Laws: Upon Divorce

State	Statute	Upon Legal Separation*	Sex Neutrality	Pending Divorce	Sex Neutrality	Upon Divorce	Sex Neutrality
Alaska	Alaska Stat. (1962)			§ 09.55.200	x	§ 09.55.210	x
Arizona	Ariz. Rev. Stat. Ann. (1956)	§ 25-320	x	§ 25-315	x	§ 25-320	x
Arkansas	Ark. Stat. Ann. (1976)			§ 31-1211	x	§ 34-1211	x
California	Cal. Civ. Code Ann. (1970)			§ 4357	x	§ 4700	x
Colorado	Colo. Rev. Stat. Ann. (1974)	§ 14-10-115	x	§ 14-10-108	x	§ 14-10-115	x
Connecticut	Conn. Gen. Stat. Ann. (1975)	§ 46-57	x	§ 46-50	x	§ 46-57	x
Florida	Fla. Stat. Ann. (1965)			§ 61.13	x	§ 61.13	x
Georgia	Ga. Code Ann. (1969)	§ 30-213	Father required to support child	§ 30-206	Father required to support child	§ 30-207	Father required to support child
Hawaii	Hawaii Rev. Stat. (1968)			§ 580-11	x	§ 580-47	x
Idaho	Idaho Code (1948) (1963 Repl. vol.)			§ 32-704	Father required to support child	§ 32-706	Father required to support child

State	Statute	Father required to support child	Father required to support child		Different standards of support required of father and mother
Illinois	Ill. Ann. Stat. (Smith-Hurd 1959)			Ch. 40, § 19	x
Indiana	Ind. Stat. Ann. (Burns 1972)		§ 31-1-11.5-7 — x	§ 31-1-11.5-12	x
Iowa	Iowa Code (1971)		§ 598.11 — x	§ 598.21	x
Kansas	Kan. Stat. Ann. (1974)	§ 60-1610(a) — x	§ 60-1607(c) — x	§ 60-1610(a)	x
Kentucky	Ky. Rev. Stat. Ann. (1975 Repl. vol.)	§ 403.210 — x	§ 403.160 — x	§ 403.210	x
Maine	Me. Rev. Stat. Ann. (1965)	Tit. 19, § 581	Tit. 19, § 693	Tit. 19, § 752	x
Maryland	Md. Ann. Code (1976 Repl. vol.)	Art. 16, § 25 — x	Art. 16, § 5A — x	Art. 16, § 5A	x
Massachusetts	Mass. Gen. Laws Ann. (1968)	Ch. 208, § 20 — x		Ch. 208, § 28	x
Minnesota	Minn. Stat. Ann. (1964)		§ 518.62 — x	§ 518.17, 518.57	x
Mississippi	Miss. Code Ann. (1973)		§ 93-5-17 — x	§ 93-5-23	x
Missouri	Mo. Ann. Stat. (1953)	§ 452.340 — x	§ 452.315 — x	§ 452.340	x
Montana	Mont. Rev. Codes Ann. (1949 Repl. vol.)	§ 48-323 — x	§ 48-318 — x	§ 48-323	x
Nebraska	Neb. Rev. Stat. (1965 Repl. vol.)	§ 42-364 — x	§ 42-357 — x	§ 42-364	x

(continued)

TABLE 5.4 (continued)

State	Statute	Upon Legal Separation*	Sex Neutrality	Pending Divorce	Sex Neutrality	Upon Divorce	Sex Neutrality
Nevada	Nev. Rev. Stat. (1975)	§ 125.190	Father required to support child	§ 125.040	Father required to support child	§ 125.150	Father required to support child
New Hampshire	N.H. Rev. Stat. Ann. (1968)	§ 458:31	Different standards of support required of father and mother	§ 458:16	x	§ 458:17	x
New Jersey	N.J. Rev. Stat. (1940)			§ 2A:34-23	x	§ 2A:34-23	x
New Mexico	N.M. Stat. Ann. (1953)			§ 22-7-6(a)	x	§ 22-7-6	x
New York	N.Y. Dom. Rel. Law (McKinney (1963)	§ 240	x	§ 240	x	§ 240	x
North Carolina	N.C. Gen. Stat. (1969 Repl. vol.)	§ 50-13.5	x	§ 50-13.5	x	§ 50-13.4	x
North Dakota	N.D. Cent. Code (1971 Repl. vol.)	§ 14-06-03	x	§ 14-05-23	x	§ 14-05-24	x
Ohio	Ohio Rev. Code Ann. (Page 1972)					§ 3105.21, 3109.05	x
Oklahoma	Okla. Stat. Ann. (1966)	Tit. 12, § 1277	x			Tit. 12, § 1277	x
Oregon	Ore. Rev. Stat. (1975)	§ 107.105	x	§ 107.095	x	§ 107.10	x
Pennsylvania	Pa. Stat. Ann. (1968)					Tit. 23 § 55	x

State						
Rhode Island	R.I. Gen. Laws Ann. (1969 Repl. vol.)	§ 15-5-16	x	§ 15-5-16, -18	x	§ 15-5-16	x
South Carolina	S.C. Code Ann. (1962)			§ 20-115	x	§ 20-115	x
South Dakota	S.D. Comp. Laws Ann. (1969)	§ 25-4-39	Father required to support child	§ 25-4-38	Father required to support child	§ 25-4-41	Father required to support child
Tennessee	Tenn. Code Ann. (1975 Repl. vol.)	§ 36-820	Father required to support child			§ 36-820	Father required to support child
Texas	Tex. Fam. Code (1975)			§ 3.59	Different standards of support required of father and mother		
Utah	Utah Code Ann. (1953)	§ 30-4-3	Father required to support child	§ 30-3-3	x	§ 30-3-5	x
Vermont	Vt. Stat. Ann. (1974)	Tit. 15, § 557	x	Tit. 15, § 204	x	Tit. 15, §§ 557, 760	x
Virginia	Va. Code Ann. (1975 Repl. vol.)	§ 20-107	x	§ 20-103	x	§ 20-107	x
Washington	Wash. Rev. Code Ann. (1961)	§ 26.09.090	x	§ 26.09.060	x	§ 26.09.050	x
West Virginia	W. Va. Code Ann. (1966)	§ 48-2-28	x	§ 48-2-13	x	§ 48-2-15	x
Wisconsin	Wis. Stat. Ann. (1957)	§ 247.26	x	§§ 247.23	x	§ 247.26	x
Wyoming	Wyo. Stat. Ann. (1957)	§ 20-36	Father required to support child	§ 20-58 § 20-60	x	§ 20-61	x

*This column includes statutory provisions for child support in all situations of spousal separation without divorce, whether labeled divorce from bed and board, separate maintenance, or legal separation.

Source: Compiled by the authors.

155

than on parents charged with support, are the most striking
feature of state child support systems. Under present child custody
patterns, then, it is most often women, not men, who suffer from
the egregious forms of discrimination in this area of the law.

Impact of the ERA

Explicit Discrimination

The ERA requires that all laws concerning child support be sex
neutral. Each state will be expected to replace sex-based laws with
laws allocating child support responsibilities on the basis of the respective financial situations, personal obligations, and child custody
responsibilities of the parents.* Several state courts, considering
ERA challenges to sex-based child support laws, already have ruled
that mathematically equal contributions are not required by the ERA. [126]
These rulings are consistent with the ERA's legislative history in
Congress and with the practice in states that already have sex-neutral
laws as a result of legislative reforms.

Neutral Rules

The considerations in this area are the same as those discussed
above in the section on alimony and spousal support.

Policy Recommendations

The social policy considerations underlying law reform of child
support obligations closely parallel those discussed above in the section on spousal support and alimony. First, serious thought should be
given by the states to the adoption of specific statutory guidelines
setting forth the factors to be considered in the allocation of child
support responsibilities between parents. The adoption of specific

---

cient to permit the court to award sufficient support to cover the entire cost of child rearing.

*As discussed in the alimony section above, it is a technical pos-
sibility that conformance to the ERA could be accomplished by the repeal of child support laws rather than the extension of child support
obligations to both parents on an equal basis. The legislative history
of the ERA and the existence of sex-neutral laws in almost all states
make this possibility extremely remote.

guidelines provides an opportunity to review child support law in contexts other than divorce—for example, in situations where the parents
are separated or unmarried. The resulting broad reexamination of
child support laws should include efforts to coordinate guidelines in
this area with those for spousal support during marriage, alimony,
and property division upon separation or divorce, since all of these
types of financial transfers are interrelated.

New guidelines also should include an explicit statement of legislative intent that the uncompensated contributions of a custodial
parent in the form of child care and housekeeping services be eval-
uated and taken into account in the allocation of child support responsibilities between parents. The enactment of specific guidelines requiring comparison of the financial needs and obligations of both parents
and evaluation of child care and housekeeping services would mitigate
the current problem of child support awards that are inadequate to
cover even half the expenses of child rearing.

The second major area of concern for policy makers is that of
inadequate enforcement of court awards. The issues that states
should consider in formulating more effective enforcement techniques
are discussed above in the section on spousal support and alimony.

State Reform Efforts

It appears that the trend toward sex-neutral child support laws
began somewhat earlier than the trend toward sex-neutral spousal support and alimony laws and is thus more advanced. As mentioned
above, a substantial majority of states have adopted sex-neutral laws
governing child support, not only upon divorce but also during marriage and upon separation (see Tables 5.3 and 5.4). On the other
hand, although a number of states have also adopted detailed factors
for determining child support, these guidelines are generally not as
innovative as those in the area of spousal support. The child support
guidelines, rather than breaking new ground, consist largely of codifications of preexisting, judge-made child support rules. In addition,
no states appear to have extended the use of detailed factors into the
area of child support during an ongoing marriage.

Since 1971, seven states have adopted the Uniform Marriage
and Divorce Act guidelines for child support,[127] which provide:

> In a proceeding for dissolution of marriage, legal separa-
> tion, maintenance, or child support, the court may order
> either or both parents owing a duty of support to a child
> to pay an amount reasonable or necessary for his support,
> without regard to marital misconduct, after considering
> all relevant factors including:

(1) the financial resources of the child;

(2) the financial resources of the custodial parent;

(3) the standard of living the child would have enjoyed
had the marriage not been dissolved;

(4) the physical and emotional condition of the child and
his educational needs; and

(5) the financial resources and needs of the noncustodial
parent.

Two of these states, Indiana and Ohio, apparently felt that the UMDA's
language concerning the child's educational and medical needs was
not specific enough. Indiana has supplemented the UMDA with the following provision:

Such child support order may also include, where appropriate:

(1) sums for the child's education in schools and at institutions of higher learning, taking into account the
child's attitude and ability and the ability of the parent
or parents to meet these expenses; and

(2) special medical, hospital or dental expenses necessary to serve the best interests of the child.

Similarly, Ohio added to the UMDA's list "the educational needs of
the child and the educational opportunities which would have been
available to him had the circumstances requiring a court order for his
support not arisen." In addition, both Ohio and Arizona have modified
UMDA factor number two to include the custodial parent's needs.
Arizona also inserted the following provision as an additional factor
in determining the amount of both spousal maintenance and child support awards: "excessive or abnormal expenditures, destruction, concealment or fraudulent disposition of community, joint tenancy and
other property held in common." Finally, Missouri chose to reject
the UMDA's sex neutrality by adding as the first factor to be considered
"the father's primary responsibility for support of his child."

Connecticut and North Carolina also have adopted detailed factors for the award of child support.[128] The North Carolina provision
closely parallels the standards of the UMDA but has not directly incorporated the textual language and format of that act. The Connecticut provision spells out the underlying standards of the needs and capacities of the parties in a more explicit list of factors than those of the
UMDA states or North Carolina:

Upon or subsequent to the annulment or dissolution of any
marriage or the entry of a decree of legal separation, or

divorce, the parents of a minor child of the marriage,
which child is in need of maintenance, shall maintain
such child according to their respective abilities. In determining whether a child is in need of maintenance, and,
if in need, the respective abilities of the parents to provide such maintenance and the amount thereof, the court
shall consider the age, health, station, occupation,
earning capacity, amount and sources of income, estate,
vocational skills and employability of each of the parents
and the age, health, station, occupation, educational
status and expectation, amount and sources of income,
vocational skills, employability, estate and needs of the
child.

In general, states that do not have specific guidelines either list
the financial resources of each parent as the only factor to be considered or simply list no factors at all. [129]

Another important trend has been the attempt by several states,
including some with detailed factors for the award of child support,
to coordinate child support awards with alimony and property division.
The Uniform Marriage and Divorce Act itself provides that one of the
circumstances to be considered in awarding maintenance is whether
"the spouse seeking maintenance . . . is the custodian of a child
whose condition or circumstances make it appropriate that the custodian not be required to seek employment outside the home." Of the
detailed factor provisions discussed directly above, the Arizona
and Ohio laws, which make the needs of the custodial parent one of
the child support factors, and the considerably more detailed Connecticut provision to the same effect are good examples of coordination.
Similarly, in a number of other states, contributions to the children's
welfare, the needs of the children, or parental obligations toward
children have been made factors in the determination of alimony and
property division. Nebraska's provision is the most specific, * stating that one factor in the award of alimony shall be

---

*Wyoming directs a court awarding alimony to consider "burdens
imposed on (property) for the benefit of the wife and children"; Hawaii directs the court awarding alimony to consider the "burdens imposed on either party for the benefit of the children of the parties";
and Oregon includes among factors for the award of spousal support
"the ages, health and dependency conditions of the children of the
parties." The spousal maintenance provisions of Montana, Ohio, and
Nebraska look to the contributions of the homemaking spouse, including child-rearing responsibilities.

a history of contributions to the marriage by each party, including contributions to the care and education of the children, and interruption of personal careers or educational opportunities, and the ability of the supported party to engage in gainful employment without interfering with the interests of any minor children in the custody of such party.

It should be noted that these efforts at coordination produce quite different effects, depending on their emphasis. Provisions such as Nebraska's mandate a direct comparison of the situations of each parent with regard to the children. In contrast, the provisions of the UMDA contain an implicit bias against support awards to the custodial parent by failing to mention the custodial parent's nonfinancial contribution to the children's welfare, by excluding the custodial parent's needs from the factors used to determine child support, and by generally preferring property division to monetary transfers. States that wish to adopt a comparative approach rather than an approach that disfavors spousal and child support awards should follow the Nebraska model, amending it to include future contributions to the care of the children and interruption of personal careers and educational opportunities caused by the child custody provisions of the divorce decree, as well as past contributions and interruptions.

State law reform in the area of child support enforcement is treated in the section above on alimony and spousal support.

MARITAL PROPERTY

Background

During Marriage: Common Law States

Forty-two states and the District of Columbia* have a common law property system.[130] Under this sytem, the person in whose name title is held has all rights to the property until it is sold or given away.†

---

*Those that do not are Arizona, California, Idaho, Louisiana, Nevada, New Mexico, Texas, and Washington.

†This was not the case under the common law, when married women were severely limited in their ability to carry out any transactions concerning their property. Most of these legal disabilities were lifted by the Married Women's Property Acts passed in all the states

In other words, a spouse has no right to own or manage any of the other spouse's property, except the right to support, which is usually unenforceable as long as the spouses are living together.

Under this system, either spouse is free to make a gift to the other spouse by putting title in the other's name. A husband and wife are also free to hold property jointly. As any other two people, they can be tenants in common. Each then owns half of the property, which is subject to liability for his or her individual debts and can be sold without affecting the ownership of the other half. There are no automatic rights of survivorship for one tenant in common to the share of the other. Spouses also can hold property as joint tenants. This form of ownership differs from tenancy in common in that the survivor takes automatic title to the whole property, without probate, on the death of the other joint tenant.

In over 20 jurisdictions, husbands and wives also can hold property as tenants by the entirety. Tenancy by the entirety is a special form of property ownership restricted to married persons that arose under the common law and is based on the notion of marriage as an indivisible "unity" of two persons. "They are neither properly joint-tenants, nor tenants in common: for husband and wife being considered as one person in law, they cannot take the estate by moieties (half), but both as seised of the entirety."[132] Each tenant by the entirety has an undivided, one-half interest in the property. In many states, personal as well as real property can be held in this form.* Entire-

---

over the last half of the nineteenth century. Many archaic provisions are still on the books, however, and the Married Women's Property Acts[131] themselves introduced sex-based language by referring explicitly to the rights of married women rather than married persons. These remnants of the common law should be repealed, if they impose special procedures on married women or classify them with minors and incompetents in assessing the legal significance of their acts. Affirmative legislation passed to create equal status for women can remain on the books, although it is preferable to sex neutralize the language of such provisions. States that undertake to clean up their codes by repealing traditional statutes concerning the status of married women must take care that the repeal of a statute modifying or abrogating common law doctrines concerning the rights and status of married women does not thereby revive those doctrines.

*Both real and personal property may be held by the entireties in Alaska, Arkansas, Delaware, District of Columbia, Florida, Hawaii, Maryland, Massachusetts, Mississippi, Missouri, Oklahoma, Pennsylvania, Tennessee, Vermont, and Virginia. Some commentators also include Kentucky and Rhode Island, although case law reveals few or

ties property is jointly managed and controlled by husband and wife
in the majority of jurisdictions today. Both spouses must join in any
action concerning the property, and profits and possession are mutually
enjoyed. The separate debts of one spouse generally cannot be satisfied from the property unless the debtor survives the nondebtor. [133]
Only Massachusetts, Michigan, and North Carolina retain the common
law rule that the husband manages and controls the entire property. [134]
In most of the entireties jurisdictions, a separated spouse cannot
force a partition of or adjudication of rights to entireties property.
Only divorce or the death of a spouse dissolves the special mutuality
of ownership.

Entireties ownership is intended to protect property for the
marital unit by insulating it from the claims of separate creditors or
from the mismanagement by either spouse operating alone. Many of
the features of this form of ownership making it protective of the
marital unit are also beneficial to wage-earning spouses. First,
the property is protected from their separate creditors. Second, by
holding the house and some assets by the entirety, wage-earners can
satisfy a desire to assure some measure of security to their spouses,
particularly full-time custodians of young children, without completely
relinquishing control. At the same time, non-wage-earning spouses
benefit from tenancy by the entirety by gaining ownership and control
of property that, in most instances, would otherwise belong to the
wage-earner alone.

In states in which there is joint control and exemption from liability for separate debts, both spouses are ensured enjoyment of the
property during the marriage. The survivorship rights assures passage of the property without the complexities or costs that may accompany probate. A non-wage-earning spouse or one who has custody of
the children is protected during separation from being forced either
to purchase the other half of the property or to find new housing at a
time of financial insecurity. In most states, the interest in having
married persons hold their property by the entirety is furthered by
a rebuttable presumption that all property jointly owned by the spouses
is held by the entirety. [135]

There are some circumstances under which tenancy by the entirety may not benefit married persons, however. In the three states
with husband management, the assets of the wife may be depleted
without her consent, and her right to half of the property on divorce
or all the property if she survives may be effectively nullifed. The
inability to force partition during separation may sometimes make it

---

no instances of personal assets actually being held in this form in
those jurisdictions.

difficult for a married person to obtain assets that would be extremely useful during the transition period.[136] Long judicial experience with sex-based tenancy law also has burdened the change to sex neutrality with anachronisms. In many states, sex-based presumptions about property ownership, carry-overs from the common law,[137] are still used by the courts.

Despite these drawbacks, a common law state in which a large percentage of marital assets are held by the entirety approximates, to some extent, the community property system, in which joint ownership of virtually all property acquired during marriage is mandated by law.

During Marriage: Community Property States

Eight states have a community rather than common law property system, derived from French and Spanish law. In these states, almost all property acquired after the marriage, including the earnings of either spouse, belongs to both spouses as a "community."[138] The community property doctrine is usually said to create a vested right for each spouse to an undivided, one-half share of the total community. The contrast with a separate property system is most apparent in the typical case of a wife earning much less than her husband or working as a homemaker without wages, for, under the community property system, she is considered an owner of half of their combined wealth and income, including his salary.

The practical value of her rights within an intact marriage, however, depends upon the legal assignment of the right to manage this community. In six of the eight states, the community is jointly managed.[139] In Texas, commingled community property is jointly managed, but a spouse has sole management over anything he or she would have owned if single, so long as it is kept separately from community assets. Only in Louisiana does the husband have the right, which he once had in all eight states, to the sole management of the community, including his wife's wages.[140] Management is a comprehensive term, usually encompassing the right to obligate, alienate, give away, or bequeath the property. In the six joint-management states, with certain limitations, either spouse may manage the community personal property and obligate it for debts for the benefit of the community.[141] Both spouses must generally join in any transactions concerning community real property. In these states, non-wage-earning spouses are able to get credit on the same basis as the wage-earners since both have equal legal rights to the wage-earner's income. This result is guaranteed by regulations promulgated by the Federal Reserve Board pursuant to the Equal Credit Opportunity Act of 1974.[142] Generally, when spouses in a community property state separate but do not divorce, the separate earnings of each spouse are removed from the community and therefore from community management. [143]

Upon Divorce: Common Law States

In ten* of the common law states, the courts do not have the power to transfer property from one spouse to the other upon divorce. Property owned separately remains the property of the person who has title. [†] Jointly owned property is partitioned and the proceeds divided equally between the spouses. The courts in the remaining common law states are not so severely restricted. In the District of Columbia and Tennessee, they can divide jointly held property equitably, giving one or the other spouse more than half if warranted. [144] In the three states with explicitly sex-based property division laws, the courts also can transfer the separate property of the husband to the wife. [145] Seven states permit the court to divide all the property, separate and joint, that the spouses have acquired during the marriage. [146] The remaining 21 subject all the property, however held and whenever acquired, to the jurisdiction of the court. [147]

Traditionally, the decisions about how to divide joint property and whether to transfer the separate property of one spouse to the other have been left to the unfettered discretion of the court. [148] The most common use of this power to make equitable property divisions was as an adjunct to alimony or support awards. [149] Fault generally played a large part in these determinations: an innocent spouse might be awarded the family home or assets of the other spouse, while an adulterer was expressly barred from receiving anything. [150]

In recent years, divorce courts in a number of states have begun to look at a broad range of factors in distributing property. [151] Fault is still a significant factor in most of these jurisdictions. [152] In other states, statutes have been amended over the last several years to require the courts to consider a set of comprehensive clearly delineated factors in making property divisions on divorce. These reforms are discussed below in the section on state law reform.

---

*Alabama, Florida, Georgia, Maryland, Mississippi, New York, Pennsylvania, Rhode Island, South Carolina, and Virginia.

[†]This rule can work extreme hardship on dependent spouses, particularly in relation to the family home that he or she will be forced to purchase or vacate. The situation is somewhat mitigated to the extent that these states permit and encourage both personalty and real estate to be held in tenancy by the entirety, which is divided equally on divorce.

Upon Divorce: Community Property States

All the community property states require a division of the community assets upon divorce. In two of the eight states, the community must be equally divided between the spouses;[153] in the others, the courts are empowered to divide the community property equitably, with the expectation that the spouses will receive substantially equal shares.[154] As in the common law states, the courts have had discretion in these decisions, but, as a rule, fault and financial contribution have been the decisive factors.[155] In six of the eight states, the courts do not have statutory power to transfer the separate property of either spouse to the other.[156] As in the common law states, the laws on property division have been amended in recent years. These changes are discussed below in the state law reform section.

Impact of the ERA

Explicit Discrimination

The equal rights amendment prohibits all sex-based rules concerning marital property, such as those governing the management of property during marriage and the division of assets on divorce. Sex-based judicial doctrines, which arose under the common law, must be recast in sex-neutral terms. Two Pennsylvania presumptions of this type have been challenged under the state ERA. The Pennsylvania Supreme Court held unconstitutional the presumption that a husband's contribution to the purchase price of entireties property was a gift while a wife's created a trust in her favor.[157] The court held that all spousal contributions to jointly held property are to be presumed gifts unless proven otherwise. In another case, the same court rejected a presumption that, in the absence of the wife's proof of contribution to the purchase price, the husband owns the household goods.[158] The court held that since both spouses make a contribution to the household, financial or unremunerated, the household goods should be presumed to be jointly owned. This sex-neutral rule complies with the equality principle and the partnership theory of marriage. (It also would be permissible under the ERA to presume that all interspousal contributions toward jointly held property are not gifts to the other spouse or to abolish the presumptions altogether and judge each case on its merits.)

Common law states with sex-differential rules concerning the liability of entireties property for the separate debts of a spouse must amend those provisions. Similarly, in those states that now give husbands sole management over entireties or community property, both spouses must be given equal management rights.

States with sex-based statutes or judicial precedent concerning property division at divorce also must amend their laws to comply with the ERA. The property of both spouses must be equally subject to division under sex-neutral standards. Sex-neutral rules for property distribution based on the actual circumstances of the parties must be substituted for sex-based ones. For example, in a case under the state ERA in Texas, the court upheld an unequal distribution of community property in favor of the wife because the lower court had based its decision on sex-neutral factors such as her lower earning capacity. [159]

Neutral Rules

A strong argument can be made that property laws in the common law states and in Texas violate the equal rights principle because of their disparate impact on women. In these states, the wage-earner has no legal obligation to share the ownership or control of the property he or she earns with the non-wage-earning spouse during the ongoing marriage. The problem is most severe in those states that do not permit the courts to divide the property equitably, regardless of title, at the time of divorce. Women predominate among non-wage-earning spouses in this country, and even those women who work outside the home earn, on the average, far less than their husbands because of the discrimination they face in the labor market. Therefore, a system of property ownership that relies on title or direct financial contributions to property acquisition has a disproportionate impact on women. Only a partnership model of management, control, and legal ownership during marriage and on divorce, such as is found in most of the community property states, conforms fully to the demands of the equality principle. At the minimum, states must mitigate the impact of a separate property system by providing for the equitable distribution of all assets of the spouses at the time of divorce.

Policy Recommendations

During Marriage: Common Law States

Common law states have two options for reform: the adoption of a community property approach or the modification of existing common law doctrines to reduce current sex-related inequities. With regard to the control of income during an ongoing marriage, the community property option would automatically grant each spouse equal rights to the income of the other. The comparable common law reform would be the enactment of laws permitting spouses to make legally enforceable contracts requiring one spouse to give the other a portion of his or her income.[160] With regard to rights to share property, the options are legally mandated joint control or a system of optional sharing based on antenuptial or other interspousal contracts and various forms of joint ownership, such as tenancy by the entirety. With regard to both income and property, the adoption of a community property system in effect creates a presumption in favor of joint ownership but allows spouses to contract out of such a system, while the retention of a common law property system with expanded interspousal contract rights in effect creates a presumption against joint ownership but allows spouses to establish joint ownership by mutual agreement.*

The adoption of a community property system, though politically and practically a difficult step, has much to recommend it. It accords with popular ideology about the institution of marriage and constitutes a long overdue societal recognition of the concrete value of the home-making and child care services non-wage-earning spouses provide. It also improves the position of non-wage-earning spouses vis-a-vis third parties, without requiring judicial intervention in an ongoing marriage, because it enables both spouses to get independent credit on the basis of the community property and either spouse's earning record. A community property system places the burden of seeking legal advice on couples who wish to depart from community principles rather than on those who wish to adopt a more egalitarian marital structure. Since few spouses are likely to have the information and legal assistance necessary to adopt formal contracts about their economic relations, with the exception of joint ownership of real estate, the presumption of the community property system would more effectively equalize marital property ownership for the majority of couples than would the common law system. Finally, since even common law states are beginning to adopt quasi-community-property concepts for divorce purposes, there are now, in many states, fewer changes necessary to achieve a complete community property system.

The difficulties of the community property model should not be underestimated, however. Women who now work outside the home and wish to maintain independent control of their own property and income would have more difficulty in doing so under a community property system. More generally, the philosophical desirability of in-

---

*At present, no common law state permits spouses to make enforceable contracts about shares in each other's income in exchange for the performance of other marital duties. In other words, rather than establishing a presumption against joint legal control of income, all common law states in fact prohibit such joint legal control.

creasing the economic interdependence of spouses, as opposed to encouraging each to be as economically independent as possible, can be
questioned. Community property law is also quite complicated. To
the extent that the real problem is not legal rights to economic control but the practical and psychological difficulties of actually sharing
the income or property earned by another person, the costs of switch-
ing from one property system to another might not seem to be worth
the gains.

Finally, in the area of property ownership, tenancy by the entirety has both advantages and disadvantages as compared to community ownership. The major disadvantage to a non-wage-earning spouse
is that it is optional rather than automatic, although it is relatively
easy to create a tenancy by the entirety if both spouses wish to do so.
On the other hand, in at least some jurisdictions, tenancy by the entirety has the advantage of superior protection against separate debts
and, in all 20 entireties jurisdictions, has the advantage of the surviving spouse's succession to full ownership of the property without
probate, as contrasted to the community property spouse's right in
probate to only one-half of the community upon the death of the other.

Common law states may wish to make a thorough study of the
laws presently in effect and their practical application and then evolve
their own systems, borrowing some concepts from the community
property states, keeping some of the old laws, and creating new structures where appropriate.* If a complete community property system
is rejected, the adoption or modification of laws permitting tenancy
by the entirety ownership† and the passage of laws permitting the en-

---

*Technically, there is no reason why the option of tenancy by the
entirety ownership cannot be combined with a community property system, although no state presently has both. Such a combination would
provide maximum protection for the property of a family unit and for
non-wage-earning spouses, while being flexible enough to accommodate
a variety of family economic situations and needs.

†Some special form of property ownership during marriage is important because of the absence of effective alternatives to protect a
dependent spouse. Most states have a variety of laws on the books to
increase this protection, such as an exemption of the homestead from
creditors up to a certain dollar amount; a rule that neither spouse can
sell the home without the consent of the other, irrespective of title;
and tax- and probate-related benefits for the surviving spouse vis-a-
vis the homestead. However, these protections are woefully inadequate in light of the current value of homes. Even were they modern-
ized and the protected values brought up to reasonable amounts, as
they should be, they do not meet the needs of most families. The pro-

forcement of interspousal contracts about income transfers should be given serious consideration.

In particular, a statute concerning entireties ownership should include these features:

1. Property held jointly by married persons is presumed to be held by the entirety, though it may be held in other forms of joint ownership if expressly provided.

2. Personal as well as real property can be held by the entirety.

3. Survivorship rights attach to property held in this manner.

4. Only the contingent survivorship interest of a debtor spouse is subject to liability for that person's debts. This leaves the lifetime interests of both spouses and the survivorship interest of the nondebtor spouse protected.

5. Property held by the entirety is jointly managed. Any transaction, encumbrance, or conveyance concerning the property must be joined in by both spouses. Profits and possession are mutually and indivisibly enjoyed. *

6. The creation of an agency relationship in one spouse by the other will not be assumed from the existence of the marriage or the seeming acquiescence of that spouse in the actions of the other concerning the property. The agency must be affirmatively proven.

---

tections often do not cover personal property, which is crucial to the functioning of the family. For citations and further discussion of these laws, see the section on probate below.

*If a state wants to approximate the community property system through the use of the entireties doctrine, this feature of the estate can be varied. For instance, property held by the entirety could be subject to liability for debts incurred by one spouse for family necessaries. This would be similar to the rule in the community states that one spouse can obligate the community for "community" debts. It also would avoid the need for the signatures of both spouses in order to use such property for those purchases and might encourage more spouses to use this form of ownership. Of course, this variation raises problems about the definition of necessaries because creditors would push the courts to broaden that category. It also reduces greatly the long-term protection against dissipation of the estate usually afforded to the non-wage-earner spouse by entireties ownership. It would, however, give the non-wage-earner access to credit for family purchases up to the amount of property held by the entireties.

7. The courts may adjudicate the rights of the spouses in entireties property when they have been separated for an extended period and have not secured or do not plan to secure a divorce.* Either
spouse may seek and obtain an accounting of profits received from
entireties property at any time during the continuance of the estate or
following a joint conveyance.

The method chosen by the Pennsylvania Supreme Court of sex
neutralizing the gift and household goods presumptions is another good
model for reform. [161] Household goods should be presumed to be
jointly owned. Similarly, contributions to jointly held property or
transfers of title to one's spouse should be presumed to be gifts,
subject to the contributing spouse's right to rebut the presumption. [†]

During Marriage: Community Property States

The community property states already have the basis for an
equitable property system during marriage, at least in those states
with joint management. It would be preferable for Louisiana and
Texas to modify their laws to permit either spouse to obligate their
community income and to jointly and severally manage the personal
property acquired by either spouse. The current Texas law is unwise
because it permits the spouse who earns more income to prevent the
other spouse from acquiring any rights to it simply by keeping it separate. As a result, non-wage-earning spouses in Texas, as in the common law states, have no guaranteed right to a share of income during
marriage and consequently no ability to obtain credit.

---

*Under these circumstances, the normal rules concerning parti-
tion may be unduly rigid. A few jurisdictions now permit levies
against entireties property to satisfy an absent spouse's spousal or
child support obligations or permit the assignment of title or possession of the family home to one spouse, usually the custodial parent,
during separation. This power should be expanded so that upon a petition requesting the adjudication of rights to the property due to the
lengthy separation of the parties, the court will have broad equitable
powers to partition the property, award possession or uneven distribution of the rents and profits, or take other appropriate action.
†To rebut the presumption, the contributor or other challenger
should be required to show that the other spouse knew and agreed
that a gift was not intended or, if this raises overly difficult questions
of proof, that the contributor communicated to the titleholder that a
gift was not intended.

One improvement of marital property law in the community property states might be the creation of a procedure for spouses to assert their ownership and control of the property during the marriage. This might be accomplished by a law giving a spouse the right to an accounting and, if necessary, to court action in order to assure access to property and assets during the ongoing marriage.

Upon Divorce: Common Law and Community Property States

There are sound policy reasons why property division should assume a central role in the determinations made on the dissolution of marriage. If marriage is a partnership to which both spouses contribute and from which both draw, the assets should be divided equitably between husband and wife if divorce occurs. The main asset taken by the earner from the marriage, his or her earning potential, will never be fully shared by the homemaker spouse, as the poor enforcement record on alimony and child support decrees shows. Property division is one way to assure the non-wage-earning spouse some assets at the critical time of divorce.

In many instances, the precedents established earlier, even under facially neutral laws, must be repudiated. Requiring judges to refer to a set of particular factors adopted by the legislature will facilitate this process. The factors should be comprehensive and should weigh both the past contributions of wage-earners and homemakers and their future needs and contributions, based on the child care obligations of either or both parents and their respective earning abilities. The Uniform Marriage and Divorce Act, which has been the basis for many recent reforms, is a good starting point for drafting such a list of factors.

In addition, the property division required at divorce should include all assets and income owned or acquired by either spouse, regardless of legal title. In community property states, this can be accomplished by dividing community assets. In common law states, however, it will require the adoption of a statute specifying that all property is subject to division.

The underlying presumption should be that property acquired during the marriage be divided equally. The courts should begin by looking at the property earned or acquired during the marriage, including income earned during that time by property acquired before the marriage. This is appropriate, as these assets usually represent the effort of the marital unit and also reflect the standard of living under which the family has been living prior to divorce. However, in many cases, the courts will have to reach other property, such as that acquired by gift or bequest or acquired before the marriage, in order to make an equitable division. If, for example, one spouse has wasted or destroyed assets of the marital unit, other property should be distributed; or, if one spouse has received substantial assets as a gift or inheritance that increased the family standard of living, they also should be subject to division. In many other situations as well, the court may conclude that a transfer of such additional property, not directly a product of the marriage, is necessary in order to carry out the statutory mandate.

The Uniform Marriage and Divorce Act is again a useful model. It provides two property division alternatives: one subjects all property to distribution in accordance with carefully drafted specific standards; the other, drafted for community property states, relies on their existing system of property categorization, while adopting more specific standards for divorce-related distribution. The details of each option are discussed below in the section on state law reform activity.

State Reform Efforts

During Marriage: Common Law States

In recent years, efforts have been made to remove the remaining explicit statutory discriminations concerning property ownership and control during an ongoing marriage. In addition, significant reform concerning equitable property division on divorce has occurred. Two of the three states in which husbands control tenancy by the entirety property have enacted reform in recent years. In 1973, legislation was passed in Massachusetts that not only equalized management rights but also eliminated the presumption that all real property held jointly by husband and wife is entireties property. Now, conveyances to a husband and wife jointly, unless otherwise indicated, are presumed to create a joint tenancy in which there are equal management rights. [162]

During Marriage: Community Property States

Until the last several years, husband management was the rule in all of the community property states. Reforms enacted since 1969 have equalized management of the community in Arizona, California, Idaho, Nevada, New Mexico, and Washington. [163] In Texas, the new rule is that assets actually commingled are to be jointly managed. [164] The laws vary somewhat in their delineation of the powers one spouse may exercise without joinder of the other, but in all the states, trans-

actions concerning real property must now be joined in by both
spouses. *

Upon Divorce: Common Law States

The major focus of reform efforts in marital property has been
the law regarding property distribution at the time of divorce. Almost half the common law states have amended their property division
statutes over the last six years. The changes mark a new attitude
toward the role of property division in divorce—that is, that, where
possible, an appropriate distribution of marital assets should be a
major element in the resolution of the divided family's economic situation.

The UMDA's provisions on property division have been the primary model for reform. Of the 12 states that have enacted comprehensive changes geared toward equitable distribution, Colorado, Delaware, Indiana, Kentucky, Maine, Missouri, and Montana have enacted
some variation of the UMDA provisions.[165] The legislatures in Hawaii, Minnesota, and Ohio and the courts in Michigan and New Jersey
have adopted property division standards with similar coverage and
content.[166] These statutes and court decisions all impose an affirmative duty on the courts to distribute the property of the spouses, in
some cases limited to property acquired during the marriage. The
courts are instructed to make their determinations based on a comprehensive list of statutory factors designed to focus attention on the
parties' past contributions to the marital unit and their future needs
and expectations.

The extent of reform does vary from state to state within this
group, however. As mentioned above, the UMDA includes two property division alternatives.[167] The first provides, in pertinent part:

> In a proceeding for dissolution of the marriage, legal sep-
> aration, or disposition of property following a decree of
> dissolution of the marriage or legal dissolution by a court

---

*In California, Washington, and Nevada, both spouses also must
take part in transactions concerning household goods. Neither alone
can give away community property without receiving consideration.
In Arizona and Nevada, both spouses must join in the creation of any
suretyship or indemnity relationship. In Nevada and Washington,
both spouses must join in transactions concerning the assets of a
jointly managed business; in California and Nevada, if one spouse is
operating a community business, that person can act alone, subject
to a requirement that he or she act in good faith.

which lacked personal jurisdiction over the absent spouse,
or lacked jurisdiction to dispose of the property, the court,
without regard to marital misconduct, shall, and in a proceeding for legal separation, may, finally equitably apportion between the parties the property and assets belonging
to either or both however and whenever acquired, and
whether the title thereto is in the name of the husband or
wife or both. In making appointment the court shall consider the duration of the marriage, any prior marriage of
either party, any antenuptial agreement of the parties, the
age, health, station, occupation, amount and sources of
income, vocational skills, employability, estate, liabilities,
and needs of each of the parties, custodial provisions,
whether the apportionment is in lieu of or in addition to
maintenance and the opportunity of each for future acquisition of capital assets and income. The court shall also
consider the contribution or dissipation of each party in the
acquisition, preservation, depreciation, or appreciation in
value of the respective estates, and as the contribution of
a spouse as a homemaker or to the family unit.

The second, which is designed for community property states committed to their existing system of characterizing property as community or separate, has identical language concerning the situations in
which the court has jurisdiction, and then states:

[T]he court shall assign each spouse's separate property
to that spouse. It also shall divide community property,
without regard to marital misconduct, in just proportions
after considering all relevant factors including:

(1) contribution of each spouse to acquisition of the
marital property, including contribution of a spouse
as homemaker;
(2) value of the property set apart to each spouse;
(3) duration of the marriage; and
(4) economic circumstances of each spouse when the
division of property is to become effective, including
the desirability of awarding the family home or the
right to live therein for a reasonable period to the
spouse having custody of any children.

These provisions can readily be analyzed in terms of two basic
issues: the property subject to allocation by the court and the factors
to be used by the court to allocate property. With regard to both issues, although the two provisions have a similar thrust, the first al-

ternative is more sweeping than the second. Thus far, most states have chosen the narrower approach to the issue of what property is subject to distribution, while about half have chosen a broad list of factors determining distribution and half, a narrower list.

On the question of the property subject to distribution, Montana is the only common law state that has adopted the common law alternative of the UMDA, although Indiana also subjects all separate properties to distribution.* The remainder of the common law UMDA states have altered the UMDA to exclude from distribution property acquired by either spouse before marriage or acquired during marriage by gift, devise, bequest, or inheritance. Delaware accomplished this goal by adopting a modified version of the common law alternative; Kentucky and Maine adopted variations of the community property alternative. †

Regarding the factors used as a basis for distribution, both Delaware and Montana have adopted the common law alternative, and Kentucky has adopted the factors set forth in the community property alternative. The remaining four states have adopted the community property list, except for the duration of the marriage factor. In addition, Missouri has added fault; Colorado, the increase or decrease in the value of the separate property of each; and Indiana, the earnings or earning ability of the spouses and the actions of either that led to waste of the property.

The failure of most states to include separately owned property in the division and the choice of the more limited community property list of factors represent a continuation of the traditional stance on these issues. In states that otherwise have a separate property regime, this approach is inadequate to correct the existing economic

---

*Although the Indiana statute covers all property, it also requires its origin—for example, as a gift or bequest—to be considered in making the division.

†In addition to excluding from distribution property acquired by either spouse before marriage or acquired during marriage by gift, devise, bequest, or inheritance, Delaware excludes property received in exchange for property acquired prior to marriage. Kentucky excludes any property acquired after a decree of legal separation, while Colorado includes property acquired until the divorce decree. Kentucky also excludes the increase in value of property acquired before marriage to the extent that such increase did not result from the efforts of the parties during marriage. Maine's definition is similar to that of Kentucky. In all of the states, property can be excluded by agreement of the spouses, and the presumption that particular property is marital property can be overcome with appropriate proof.

balance between wage-earning spouses and homemakers and is contrary to the UMDA recommendations for these states.

Of the five non-UMDA reform states, three have factors quite similar to the UMDA's common law alternative, Michigan and New Jersey by court opinion[168] and Ohio by statute. Hawaii and Minnesota have narrower laws. Hawaii's refers to the merits of the parties, their relative abilities, the condition in which each is left by the divorce, and the burdens imposed concerning children. Minnesota has an even more limited provision that refers to the nature and determination of issues (presumably fault), the amount of alimony, the manner in which the property was acquired, and the parties' contributions thereto.

On the question of the property subject to distribution by the court at divorce, three of the non-UMDA reform states subject all property owned by the spouses to equitable distribution, and two limit distribution to property acquired by the spouses during marriage, except by gift, devise, bequest, or inheritance.* In addition, in 1969, North Carolina gave statutory authority to the courts to transfer title to property at divorce,[169] and, in 1972, Nebraska amended its provision about court authority over property at divorce to allow courts to award disposition of property if they find that a voluntary property settlement is unconscionable.[170]

A number of other states have recently removed specific sex-discriminatory provisions from their laws concerning property division at divorce. Connecticut previously allowed awards only from the husband's estate to the wife; now the court may assign to either spouse any or all of the estate of the other spouse.[171] Vermont repealed a section that barred an adulterous wife from receiving any property.[172] Wisconsin previously permitted the courts to award the husband's property to the wife if she was not adulterous; now there is sex-neutral equitable division, and the adultery of either is a bar.[173] Oklahoma has also enacted sex-neutral fault considerations. If both spouses are at fault, the law permits the court to divide marital property equitably; if only one is at fault, that person's separate property also is subject to transfer by the court for child support.[174]

Upon Divorce: Community Property States

The property division laws in a number of community property states have been amended recently as well. The Texas law was amende

---

*Hawaii, Michigan, and Ohio subject all property owned by the spouses to equitable distribution. Minnesota and New Jersey use the more limited approach. See p. 175 for a discussion of the parties' power to exclude property from distribution by mutual agreement.

in 1969 to permit equitable division and to give the courts the power
to transfer title from one spouse to the other.[175] Washington adopted
the UMDA in 1973 but went further than the community property alternative to give the court power over the separate property of the spouses
as well.[176] Arizona amended its law in 1973 to provide for equitable
distribution of the community at divorce, without regard to fault, but
has not spelled out statutory factors for the courts to consider, except waste of the community assets by one spouse.[177] California
previously relied on fault as a major consideration but rejected it
with the statutory change to mandatory 50-50 division in 1969.[178]
A 1973 amendment in New Mexico permits either spouse to request
the court to restrain the use or disposition of property pending divorce.[179]

ECONOMIC RIGHTS UPON THE DEATH
OF A SPOUSE

Background

Surviving Share

Non-wage-earning spouses have more economic rights as surviving spouses than they have either during an ongoing marriage or
after separation or divorce. The common law doctrine of dower
guarantees a widow the use for her life of one-third of all the real
property her husband owned at any time during the marriage. The
husband had a lesser right called curtesy, conditioned on the birth
of children to the marriage.[180] Eight common law states still have
a sex-based law of this type; five of them give surviving spouses different shares on the basis of sex,[181] and three guarantee a share
only to widows.[182]

Thirty-four of the common law jurisdictions have moved away
from this sex-based model and expressly guarantee the same share
of an estate to a surviving spouse of either sex. Most states have
accomplished this sex neutrality not by extending the traditional dower
doctrine to men but by enacting a simpler and more meaningful form
of protection for all surviving spouses. In 25 states, the surviving
spouse is now guaranteed outright ownership of a share of all property,
both real and personal, owned by the decedent at death if he or she
elects against the will.[183] These usually are referred to as "elective"
or "nonbarrable" statutory share provisions. Only in the District of
Columbia and New Jersey is the surviving spouse entitled to only a
traditional dower share, a life estate in the real property owned by

the other during the marriage.[184] In seven other states, the statutory share law was superimposed on the common law right, and some of the dower characteristics remain.[185] For example, Connecticut gives the survivor a share of all real and personal property owned at the time of death, but only as a life estate. In West Virginia, the share is given in outright ownership but is limited to the real property owned by the decedent during the marriage. Georgia is the only state that provides no guaranteed share for surviving spouses of either sex.[186]

In the eight community property states, a surviving spouse inherits half of the community property outright, and each spouse has a right to will the other half of the community property and any separate property he or she may own to whomever he or she chooses.[187]

As most of these protections attach only to the assets in the estate upon a spouse's death, it is possible for one spouse to deprive the other of any real share by transferring assets to third parties before death. This problem arises particularly in the common law states, where spouses manage all their separate property, and in Louisiana, where the husband has an exclusive right to manage the community during his lifetime. Some jurisdictions have enacted protections to preserve a surviving share from this kind of depletion by including in the estate certain types of lifetime transfers.[188] This assures the survivor a fair portion of assets accumulated through the joint effort of both spouses although held in the name of the decedent alone.

Short of this type of drastic attempt to disinherit, a number of accepted practices in estate planning are based on a distrust of the financial abilities of women and may be detrimental to their interests as surviving spouses. For example, a person can leave all or most of his estate to his wife for her life, stipulating that the principal is to pass directly to the children upon her death. This has tax advantages but may force that widow to choose between the enjoyment of a life estate in a large amount of money and outright ownership and power to control the disposition of a much smaller share if she elects against the will.

One example of an estate planning technique that undercuts the guarantee of a surviving spouse's share in community property states is known as a "widow's election." Even though it may be used by both men and women, it is so called because it is more often men who have large estates and who use it to avoid excessive taxes. Under such a provision, a husband can leave his wife a life estate in all or most of the community property and provide that she must elect to take either outright ownership of the share of the estate guaranteed by law or the larger life estate. If she takes the life estate, she may avoid the necessity of selling property—in order to divide the property among the various heirs—and she also gains the benefit of having the

property taxes only once—when it passes at her death to the subsequent
heirs designated in the will—instead of twice—once when it passes
from her husband to her and once when it passes from her to her
heirs. On the other hand, as the holder of a life estate instead of an
absolute title to the property, she loses the right to dispose freely
of the property, including the right to will it. In many cases, the
husband will compound the problem by placing the share provided
under the will in trust, so that his widow is not even free to manage
the money during her lifetime.

In seven of the eight community property states, one spouse can
put the other to an election without an explicit statement to that effect.
If the husband's will disposes of all or part of the community property
in a manner indicating that he believed it to be his separate property
and did not expect his wife to take her half interest in addition to what
he left her, the widow is put to the election.[189]

Allowances, Exemptions, and Taxes

In addition to a surviving share, surviving spouses, particularly
widows, often have a variety of other rights against a deceased spouse's
estate. For example, many jurisdictions provide a fixed or discretionary allowance from the estate during probate to relieve the immediate needs of a surviving spouse and family. Most states also have
some form of homestead exemption shielding the homestead from execution in a sale held to satisfy the debts of the estate.[190]

There are also several common types of differential tax treatment of widows and widowers. In many states, the statutorily pre-
scribed allowance from the estate for a widow during the probate period is exempt from the taxable estate of the deceased husband.[191]
Some states allow a widow but not a widower an annual property tax
exemption.[192] The particular forms of relief vary from state to
state, but the effect of all of them is to exempt from taxation certain
property that passes to the widow or that she owns while treating the
widower on the same basis as other taxpayers. While directly beneficial to women, differential tax treatment affects the pattern of marital property ownership by discouraging property ownership by married women.

In addition to these explicit sex-based tax differentiations, which
at least facially benefit women, other provisions that are neutral on
their face have a detrimental impact on women as a class. For example, in many states, inheritance taxes are assessed against that
portion of an estate not contributed by the surviving spouse.[193] Proof
of the fact of contribution must be shown by the survivor. For women
who have spent all or most of their married lives working in the home,
direct financial contribution to the estate may be hard or impossible

to prove. Even for the woman who has worked in the family business
or farm that comprises the corps of the estate, documentation of financial contribution may be difficult to produce.

Impact of the ERA

Explicit Discrimination

The equal rights amendment prohibits differential treatment of
surviving spouses regarding a guaranteed share in a deceased spouse's
estate on the basis of sex. The amendment also proscribes special
homestead or other tax exemptions currently available to surviving
spouses of only one sex. Under the ERA, states are free to extend
sex-based guarantees to members of both sexes, repeal such provisions, or institute new, sex-neutral standards applicable to all surviving spouses.

Neutral Rules

Under the ERA, a neutral rule that has a discriminatory impact
on members of one sex is subject to strict scrutiny. Thus, for example, a rule exempting from taxation the portion of an estate for which
a surviving spouse can prove contribution impacts women disproportionately because they predominate among non-wage-earning spouses,
for whom proof of contribution is difficult. Such a rule must be
shown to be necessary for and closely related to a compelling state
interest. If a less drastic rule that preserves the state interest can
be formulated, then this change is required under a strict scrutiny
standard.

Policy Recommendations

Surviving Share

In a comprehensive reform of probate law, a basic policy decision must be made concerning protections for surviving spouses.
One alternative is a sex-neutral version of the common law doctrine
of dower. Under a dower system, a survivor is entitled to the use of
a fixed share of any real property that has come into the decedent's
possession at any time during the marriage. To protect this potential interest, a spouse must join in the transfer or conveyance of any
real property by the other spouse throughout the marriage, thus consenting to its removal from the estate and, consequently, from even-

tual inheritance by the survivor. This requirement of spousal joinder in every conveyance forces some degree of joint decision making, approximating a community property system for real estate. Therefore, some separate property states that still have the common law doctrines in effect may decide to retain them in sex-neutral form. However, other policy reasons, particularly the goal of avoiding excessive encumbrances against the free flow of property, dictate against this method of protecting a surviving spouse.

An alternative to the common law rights of survivorship is a statutory right to elect against the will outright ownership of a fixed portion of both the real and personal property in the estate. This alternative is in line with the broader reform of probate laws over the past several years, particularly with the growing acceptance of the principles of the Uniform Probate Code. The statutory share (the "nonbarrable" or "elective" share) is generally calculated from the value of the decedent's estate at death, augmented in some instances by the value of those lifetime transfers of assets that are essentially "will substitutes" to third parties.

This method of protecting surviving spouses is preferable to the common law alternative for several reasons. For one, the statutory share is based on an estate that includes the personal as well as real property of the deceased, thus offering a more realistic protection in light of the wide range of forms of property ownership today. In addition, the protection attaches at the point of death rather than directly interfering with inter vivos transfers of separate property by an individual. This removes undue restrictions on alienability of land as well as the underlying inducements to forgery and fraud engendered by the common law requirement of spousal consent.

Among the sex-neutral statutes providing a nonbarrable share for surviving spouses, the Uniform Probate Code is a well-designed model for reform.[194] The Uniform Probate Code guarantees an elective share of one-third of the estate, regardless of the provisions in a will. That percentage is based on the "augmented" estate, calculated by adding the value of certain lifetime transfers by the decedent. These include transfers made by the decedent during the marriage that are essentially "will substitutes" to third parties as well as wealth received by the survivor from the decedent.[195] This protects retroactively against exhaustion of the estate during the decedent's lifetime and the resulting defeat of the survivor's rights. It does not restrict the alienability of any separate property of the deceased spouse during his or her lifetime, however. A second beneficial feature of the Uniform Probate Code is that a spouse who elects to take a nonbarrable share against the will does not automatically forfeit special gifts or bequests under the will itself. Rather, these gifts are charged against the elective share. Overall, the code represents

an appropriate model for guaranteeing some security after the loss
of a spouse and for recognizing the indirect as well as direct contributions of the survivor to the accumulation of the decedent's estate.

Allowances, Exemptions, and Taxes

In the area of special allowances and tax exemptions that are
now available only to widows, social policy reasons dictate against
the repeal of the protections that now exist. Such laws originated in
an effort to minimize the financial distress a widow suffered after the
death of the husband upon whom she was dependent. The assumption
of the dependency of all women and the financial self-sufficiency of
all men that underlies these laws is outdated. The statutes discriminate against needy widowers by depriving them of the exemption and
against women who contribute to the finances of the household by making their estates less valuable to their spouses. The better solution
is to extend these benefits to widowers, either as an automatic right
or one based on a neutral standard of need for survivors of both sexes.

Regarding benefits directly associated with the period of transition following a spouse's death—such as an allowance for expenses
during probate of the estate or the protection of the homestead from
debts or taxes related to settlement of the estate—an automatic right
for any surviving spouse is an appropriate state option. This not only
correlates with the real needs of the vast majority of surviving spouses,
for whom the transition period to self-sufficiency is a difficult one,
but also avoids the expense and time associated with assigning such
benefits on an individualized basis of need. These social policy rationales are not appropriate to the long-term benefits that some
states traditionally have assigned to widows, such as lifetime property
tax exemptions. Here, the options of repeal or enactment of sex-
neutral standards of need might also be reasonable alternatives.

States that currently assess inheritance taxes only on the portion of the estate to which the surviving spouse cannot prove financial
contribution should consider a revision of their standards to those
having a less drastic impact on women who work in the home or in
family run commercial or agricultural businesses. A recommended
approach to reform in this area is the infusion of the "contribution"
standard with a conclusive presumption, for purposes of inheritance
taxation, that not less than one-half of the property passing to a surviving spouse was contributed by that person. This policy is not only
more favorable to women but also represents a more realistic appraisal of both the financial and nonfinancial partnership aspects of
most marriage units. [196]

State Reform Efforts

The reform efforts of most states have already brought them into compliance with the minimum requirements of the ERA. Only eight states explicitly treat widows and widowers differentially in their laws concerning elective shares or dower and curtesy.[197] Many recent reforms protecting against the disinheritance of a surviving spouse have gone even further, in line with the above recommendations and the model of the Uniform Probate Code's "augmented" share. In contrast, however, the special tax and allowance laws generally have not been sex neutralized.

Of the 20 common law jurisdictions that have a sex-neutral non-barrable share for surviving spouses, ten have enacted these reforms in the last five years. Eight of these have enacted the elective share provisions of the Uniform Probate Code[198] (see note 194 to this chapter for text), while two others have enacted other elective share models.[199] Of the common law states with sex-neutral versions of traditional dower rights, two have enacted these reforms in recent years.[200]

All the community property states have sex-neutral laws giving the surviving spouse a one-half interest in the community assets.[201] In 1975, New Mexico corrected a related discriminatory provision that gave the husband greater power to dispose of the community than the wife.[202] Subsidiary provisions also have been sex neutralized in other community property states in recent years. California, for example, has extended to both spouses the liability for the other's separate debts up to the amount of the survivor's interest in the community; formerly, only the wife bore that liability.[203] Another California amendment eliminated probate whenever the deceased spouse wills all the community property to the survivor, a benefit previously enjoyed only by widows.[204] Provisions in Washington[205] and Arizona[206] preventing the elective share of a widow from reaching certain of her husband's partnership rights have been extended to limit the share of a widower as well.

Miscellaneous probate statutes unrelated to the surviving share also have been amended with an eye to sex neutralization. A Kentucky statute governing the right of a minor parent to appoint a guardian by will has been extended to women on the same basis as men.[207] New Mexico has passed a bill giving both parents a preferred right to be appointed guardian of a child's estate,[208] where before the father alone had been preferred. Hawaii has provided that marriage automatically revokes the will of a woman as well as that of a man;[209] Arizona has instead abolished the rule for men.[210]

As noted above, few changes have occurred in state property and inheritance tax exemptions for widows. Arizona[211] and Pennsylvania[212] have extended property tax exemptions to widowers, and similar proposals have been considered but not enacted in other states.[213]

GROUNDS FOR DIVORCE OR ANNULMENT

Background

The most common fault grounds for divorce are facially sex neutral. They include nonsupport, desertion, adultery, cruel and barbarous treatment, and indignities to the person. However, they may be discriminatory in effect because they have been construed in the light of other discriminatory doctrines, such as domicile or support laws.* Only a few grounds for divorce or annulment apply solely to one sex or the other. The most common are age, when the minimum age of marriage differs for men and women;[†] pregancy by a man other than the husband at the time of marriage;[214] and nonsupport by the husband.[215] Other examples of sex-based divorce or annulment grounds include: a husband's vagrancy,[216] a wife's refusal to move with the husband to another state and her absence for two years,[217] a wife's having been a notorious prostitute before marriage,[218] a husband's having been a notoriously licentious person before marriage without her knowledge,[219] and a husband's indignities to his wife's person.[220]

Impact of the ERA

Explicit Discrimination

Differences between the rights of husbands and wives to claim grounds for divorce or annulment are invalid under the ERA. The elimination of sex-based grounds may be accomplished by repeal or extension of the ground to either spouse.

---

*For a discussion of the relationship of sex-based domicile rules and the desertion ground, see the section on domicile above. Sex-neutral divorce laws that make nonsupport a ground must be read with the general state law on support, which is often sex-based. See the section on alimony and spousal support above.

†See the section on age of majority above. Generally, age is a ground for divorce in Rhode Island and annulment elsewhere, unless the underaged party ratifies the marriage by continued cohabitation after reaching the age of consent.

Neutral Rules

Care must be taken in the reform of divorce grounds to ensure that, while facially neutral, the laws do not in fact impact wives unfairly. This can occur if related sex-discriminatory laws, such as those regarding domicile or support, are incorporated into facially neutral divorce grounds. In addition, women will suffer from the accumulated effects of past discrimination if a state removes all fault grounds, which often function as an economic bargaining tool for non-wage-earners, without enacting equitable property division and maintenance laws.

Policy Recommendations

Other than nonage or nonsupport, traditional sex-based grounds for divorce are generally anachronisms or duplications of other sex-neutral provisions. Rarely used, they probably can be repealed without harm to divorce law. Legitimate concern for a spouse's desertion or cruelty are covered in most states by other sex-neutral provisions.* Since a wife's pregnancy by another is not precisely covered by other grounds, this ground can be either extended to permit a wife to divorce a husband who has impregnated another woman prior to the marriage or repealed as anachronistic.[221] Inequality in annulment on the ground of age will be eliminated effectively by related reform equalizing the age at which men and women are permitted to marry, making it unnecessary to alter sex-neutral annulment statutes. Finally, as support obligations in the family become more equitably determined by individual ability rather than sex, states can decide whether to amend nonsupport grounds to apply to either spouse or repeal them.

Apart from the elimination of sex discrimination, a central policy issue in the area of divorce law reform has been the adoption of nonadversary grounds for divorce by the majority of jurisdictions in recent years.† The ability of many persons to travel to a jurisdic-

---

*In Tennessee, for example, either spouse may obtain a divorce for desertion or absence for one year, and there is a ground of "cruel treatment" that could cover "indignities to the person," a sex-based provision available only to wives.

†The states in which a no-fault ground is the sole or primary ground for divorce are Arizona, California, Colorado, Delaware, Florida, Hawaii, Iowa, Indiana, Kentucky, Michigan, Missouri, Nebraska, Oregon, and Washington. The states in which a no-fault ground has been added to the list of grounds are Alabama, Connecticut,

tion where divorces are readily available and the willingness of divorcing parties in stricter jurisdictions to allege or fail to contest more or less fictional grounds for divorce have largely subverted the purpose of fault-based grounds.[223] Recognizing these facts as well as the unreasonableness of permitting divorce for only limited and specific reasons, many models for legislative reform now recommend evaluating the overall health of the marriage rather than assigning guilt to one spouse. The UMDA, for example, provides only one ground for divorce, "irretrievable breakdown" of the marriage, irrespective of the relative fault of the parties involved.[224]

The move toward no-fault divorce must not, however, ignore the economic needs of the parties to a divorce, particularly those of a low- or non-wage-earning spouse. Unfortunately, many states have adopted no-fault grounds in recent years without considering their impact on income and property transfers between spouses. For many, the ability to contest a divorce premised on fault grounds has provided critical leverage in securing a better "voluntary" financial settlement, due to the threat of considerable additional expense and delay associated with a contested divorce. This type of bargaining has been especially important for spouses in states where courts are not statutorily charged with the duty to divide the property equitably at divorce.* States undertaking divorce law reforms that include the adoption of no-fault grounds should take care to incorporate explicit statutory provisions for equitable division of property and maintenance payments, such as those found in the UMDA, including judicial consideration of the homemaker's contribution to the family welfare.[225]

Georgia, Idaho, Maine, Minnesota, Montana, New Hampshire, New Mexico, North Dakota, Ohio, Texas, and Vermont. The states that do not have a no-fault ground per se but include a one-year voluntary separation among the grounds for divorce are Louisiana (if pursuant to a judgment of separation from bed and board, or two years if not pursuant to such a judgment), Maryland, Nevada, New York (the separation must be pursuant to a written separation agreement or a decree or judgment of separation), North Carolina, Virginia, and Wisconsin; the District of Columbia also allows divorce on the one-year voluntary separation ground.[222]

†The coupling of no-fault grounds with adequate financial protections is particularly critical in a jurisdiction such as Pennsylvania, where there is currently no provision for alimony. For a discussion of property division on divorce, see the section on marital property above.

State Reform Efforts

The major trend in divorce law reform in recent years has been the adoption of no-fault divorce grounds by a large number of states to either replace or supplement traditional fault grounds.[226] An indirect benefit of this trend has been the related repeal of many sex-based fault grounds. In particular, a number of states have eliminated sex-based nonsupport grounds in the process of adopting standards based on no-fault factors, such as whether a marriage is "irretrievably broken" or the dissolution is "irreconcilable."[227] In addition, at least one state that has retained fault grounds recently amended its provision to delete sex-based grounds relating to the wife's pregnancy by another man and prostitution prior to the marriage and reworded a subsection on voluntary separation to place the underlying obligations of support equally on both parties.[228]

CHILD CUSTODY

Background

Under the common law, the father was the natural guardian of his children and was entitled to custody in cases of spousal separation or divorce.[229] Later, when legal rules concerning the husband's role as head of the household became less rigid, statutory and judicial presumptions that children of "tender years" should be in their mother's custody were developed.

At present, only a few states have statutory provisions regarding child custody that set standards explicitly preferring one parent over the other on the basis of sex.[230] However, there is still fairly widespread judicial acceptance of maternal preference rules, such as the "tender years" doctrine.[231] Even in those jurisdictions where there has been statutory or judicial adoption of a modern and facially neutral "best interest of the child" standard, judges may nonetheless continue to determine custody in a sex-biased manner because of their personal views about proper sex roles in the family.

While women seeking child custody may fare better on the average under such indefinite standards, open-ended judicial discretion often has disfavored women who have deviated from a traditional homemaker's role by seeking education and employment outside the home.[232] Women who choose an untraditional life-style, particularly one involving extramarital sexual activity, also have fared poorly under such standards, regardless of the quality of their relationship with their children.[233] In contrast, similar behavior by fathers seeking custody

may be regarded by courts as insignificant, expected, or, in the case
of employment- or education-related activities, exemplary. Judicial
reliance on sex-stereotypical "double standards" has a particularly
egregious impact in those jurisdictions where statutory or case law
permits fault factors in the divorce to affect custody.[234]

In recent years, however, courts in a number of jurisdictions
have explicitly rejected or at least modified sex-stereotypical rules
for resolving child custody disputes, and both courts and legislatures
have begun to develop more detailed standards for evaluating the actual relationship between parent and child.[235]

Impact of the ERA

Explicit Discrimination

The equal rights principle does not permit sex-based or sex-
stereotypical rules of law to control or guide judicial determinations
of custody. Nor does the ERA require the adoption of particular standards by state courts or legislatures. Rather, rules must be articulated that are both neutral on their face and based on sex-neutral concepts of parental care. For example, it is appropriate under the
ERA to consider the closeness and stability of a child's attachment
to a parent or to favor continuity of a pattern of care but not to presume that a parent of one sex or the other had been the primary care-
taker or should automatically assume this role in the future.

Courts may consider such factors as parental life-style or parental sexual activity that may have a negative impact on the child, the
arrangements either parent would make for daily care of the child,
and each parent's previous and present relationship with the child.
In each instance, however, the issues considered must be shown to
be related to the child's welfare and must be applied across the board
to parents of both sexes seeking child custody. Whenever a particular
standard is applied only to parents of one sex or is interpreted differently depending on the sex of the parent involved, the ERA prohibits
its use as a factor.[236]

Neutral Rules

Facially neutral standards that have a disparate impact on one
sex are subject to strict scrutiny under the ERA. For example, if a
state adopted a policy of considering the income of each parent as a
factor in determining the best custodian, women—particularly those
who had spent a substantial part of their time in the past in homemaking and child care—would be unduly disadvantaged. The ERA requires

that such a standard be scrutinized to see if it is in fact closely related to the purpose of a child custody determination and if it is a
necessary factor or rather one that could be replaced with another
having a less drastic impact on one sex.

Policy Recommendations

Determination of child custody when there is a dispute between
the natural parents is a serious and complicated matter, which should
be neither reduced to arbitrary rules nor left to the unfettered discretion of individual judges. The trend by states in recent years to reject rigid sex-based rules and to adopt standards geared to individual
determinations of the child's best interest is a wise one, not just in
terms of constitutional equality but also in terms of focusing custody
determination on the most relevant and critical issue, the welfare of
the child. However, the best interest rule is insufficient to overcome
the exercise of arbitrary judicial discretion without clear legislative
enumeration of the factors to be considered.

The UMDA provides a good model of a child custody statute that
begins with the underlying standard of the child's best interest but
goes on to specify several fundamental factors the court should consider: the wishes of both the parents and the child; the interrelationship of the child with the parents, siblings, and others significantly
affecting the child's best interest; the child's present adjustment to
home, school, and community; and the mental and physical health of
all individuals involved. To a large degree, these factors simply
codify those considerations currently being used by the courts in custody cases in most states. However, the codification provides written grounds for appeal in those cases where a party feels the judge
has exercised discretion unfairly.

The UMDA also includes a sentence that expressly forbids judicial consideration of parental conduct in determining custody, so
long as that conduct does not affect the parent's relationship with the
child. Thus, marital misconduct or the sexual behavior of a parent
would not become an issue in a custody dispute as a matter of course,
as it does now in a number of jurisdictions. This explicit exclusion of
parental conduct evidence is preferable to those statutes that explicitly
allow marital fault to preclude or hamper a custody claim or leave
this question open to individual judicial discretion.

One final provision, which the UMDA does not contain, but which
has been adopted by a number of states following the UMDA's lead in
enumerating statutory factors, is also advisable: an affirmative
statement that the court shall not use any presumption favoring the
parent of one sex in determining the child's best interest. This as-

sures that the court must be able to enunciate nonsexist reasons for the application of facially neutral statutory rules in each particular case.

State Reform Efforts

The most far-reaching reform of custody laws in recent years has been the enactment by a number of states of comprehensive, sex-neutral statutory guidelines for judicial determination of custody rights. Eight states have enacted guidelines modeled on provisions of the UMDA, discussed above in the policy section. Of these, Colorado and Delaware have adopted the UMDA model outright.[237] Indiana, Missouri, Montana, Ohio, and Washington have enacted the UMDA guidelines covering the wishes of both the child and parent; the interrelationship of the child with the parents, siblings, and others significantly affecting the child's best interests; the child's present adjustment to home, school, and community; and the mental and physical health of all concerned.[238] They do not, however, include the final UMDA provision excluding evidence of parental conduct that does not affect the parent's relationship with the child. Arizona falls into this same group except that it also does not include the mental and physical health of the parties as a factor to be considered.[239]

Three other states, Florida, Minnesota, and Nebraska, have enacted detailed factors that do not explicitly parallel UMDA language.[2] The Nebraska statute treats issues similar to those of the UMDA but focuses solely on the child, looking specifically at the child's wishes, the relationship of the child to each parent, and the general health, welfare, and social behavior of the child. Florida and Minnesota have enacted identical provisions covering many of the same considerations as the UMDA model, but they utilize more subjective terminology emphasizing the "love, affection, and other emotional ties" existing between parent and child and the "moral fitness" of the parent. They also look at the capacity of the parent to provide materially for the child, a factor that could jeopardize maternal custody if no consideration is given to support from the noncustodial parent as an additional resource.

In addition, five of these eleven states and three others have adopted affirmative statutory provisions since 1968 specifically forbidding custodial preference based solely on the sex of the parent.[241]

OUT-OF-WEDLOCK CHILDREN

Background

Traditionally, under common law, a child born to parents not married to one another was filius nullius—child of nobody—and had few legal rights in relation to either parent. Under modern law, legal differences between parent-child relationships based on marital status are still commonly found in such areas as support, inheritance, adoption, custody and visitation, surnames, birth certificates, social insurance and employment-related benefits, and citizenship.[242] The issue of sex discrimination in relation to out-of-wedlock children arises in two ways. First, there is discrimination against unwed fathers in the sense that the law disfavors the establishment of a legal relationship between unwed fathers and their children, while most states presently accord similar legal treatment to all relationships between mothers and children, regardless of the mother's marital status. Second, there is discrimination against unwed mothers and their children, not in the establishment of a legal relationship between them but in the sense that they are accorded unfair treatment both by the government and by private institutions, such as employers, landlords, and creditors.

While legal differences between father-child relationships in which paternity has been established and those in which it has not or cannot be established are inevitable, the legal restrictions on father-child relationships are not now limited to relationships in which the father is in fact unidentifiable. Thus, many of the barriers preventing a legal status between a father and child equal to that between a mother and child go beyond those necessitated by biological factors. The differential treatment of the parent-child relationship based on the sex of the parent results in direct and indirect forms of discrimination affecting the rights of both children and their biological parents. In other words, legitimate or illegitimate status depends solely on the marital status of the parents, not on the actual family situation and the existing relationship between the father and the child.

There has been growing concern in recent years for the legal position of children born out of wedlock. A number of United States Supreme Court decisions have improved the status of these children by casting grave constitutional doubt on statutory distinctions based on "illegitimacy." While the court has not focused on the sex discrimination aspect of these cases, almost all revolve to some degree around the lack of legal recognition of parenthood between father and child. Several of these cases have resulted in the invalidation of statutory restrictions prohibiting or limiting the collection of benefits by a child through the biological father. [243] In addition, in <u>Stanley</u> v. <u>Illinois</u>, decided in 1972, the court ruled, on due process and equal protection grounds, that an unwed father who had cared for his children over an extended period of time must be accorded the same legal protection of his parental status as married parents and unwed mothers. In this case, the court held that to deprive such a father of custody, the state of Illinois must demonstrate that he was "unfit," rather than presuming him to be "unfit" and requiring him to take affirmative action to protect his right to custody of his children. [244] At the same time, although the Supreme Court has not yet directly ruled on the issue, lower federal courts have begun to question the constitutionality of discrimination against women based solely on the fact of unwed motherhood. [245]

Impact of the ERA

Explicit Discrimination

The basic premise of the equal rights amendment—that there be no legislative classification based on sex—has a major impact on the law concerning parents' and children's rights and obligations. Simply stated, it requires that there be no differences in the legal treatment of parent-child relationships based on the sex of either the parent or the child, except where the unique physical characteristics of one sex make a sex-based difference in legal rights or duties unavoidable. In other words, sex differentiation in the law concerning parents and children must be reduced to the biological minimum.

The only biological difference between parents relevant to their legal rights and duties concerns their relative identifiability: the natural mother is necessarily present at the birth of the child and is therefore easily identifiable in almost all cases, whereas the identity of the father may be difficult to ascertain or demonstrate. This difference makes it permissible under the ERA to require a legal procedure for ascertaining paternity before applying certain parental rights and obligations to a particular male while applying these same rights and obligations to the mother without such a procedure. However, once the identity of the father has been ascertained, the rights and obligations in the parent-child relationship must be the same for both mother and father.

Neutral Rules

The ERA's mandate that neutral rules not be used as a subterfuge for sex discrimination provides an additional basis for the scru-

tiny of rules with a harsh impact on either unwed mothers or unwed
fathers. Because of the long tradition of sexist presumptions in this
area of law, which have had negative consequences for both unwed
parents and their children, states should review the factual justification for any rules that make it inordinately difficult for unwed fathers
or their children to establish parenthood or penalize women because
they are not married to the fathers of their children. In the sections
below on policy considerations and state law reform, specific provisions of law and the problems they present are discussed.

Policy Recommendations

Assuming that sex-based differences in the treatment of parent-
child relationships must be minimized, the relevant social policy considerations revolve around two questions: (1) what procedures should
the legislature establish for determinations of paternity, and (2) how
should the rights and obligations of children and their natural parents
be defined?

Many of the complicated issues raised by these questions have
been carefully analyzed by a special committee of the National Conference of Commissioners on Uniform State Law, first appointed in
1969. As a result of the committee's efforts, the Uniform Parentage
Act (UPA), a comprehensive model law on the legal rights of parents
and children born out of wedlock, was approved by the conference in
1973. This act sets out a clear procedure for establishing parentage
and enunciates standards for the attachment or termination of rights
in various contexts. Since the UPA represents such an advance in
legal thinking about the relationship between parents and children born
out of wedlock and is not yet widely known, this section discusses its
provisions in some detail, drawing in part upon the commentary of
the commissioners.

The principle of the UPA, set out in its first two provisions, is
that the "parent and child relationship," defined as the legal relationship existing between a child and his natural or adoptive parents with
regard to rights, privileges, duties, and obligations, extends equally
to every child and to every parent, regardless of the marital status
of the parents. The remainder of the act is concerned with the procedural network for establishing the identification of persons in whom
these rights and obligations exist. As the prefatory notes of the act
explain, with relationship to out-of-wedlock children, those persons
are the fathers. (To cover the rare case in which there may be uncertainty as to the mother, the present act permits a declaratory action on the question of maternal descent.)

In order to identify the father, the Act first sets up a network of presumptions which cover cases in which proof
of external circumstances (in the simplest case, marriage
between the mother and a man) indicate a particular man
to be the probable father. While perhaps no one state now
includes all these presumptions in its law, the presumptions
are based on existing presumptions of "legitimacy" in state
laws and do not represent a serious departure. Novel is
that they have been collected under one roof. All presumptions of paternity are rebuttable in appropriate circumstances.

The ascertainment of paternity when no external circumstances presumptively point to a particular man as the father
is the next major function of the Act.   Noteworthy is the
pre-trial procedure envisaged by the Act which, the Committee expects, will greatly reduce the current high cost
and inefficiency of paternity litigation.

Under section 4(a) of the UPA, a man is presumed to be the
natural father of a child if:

(1) he and the child's natural mother are or have been
married to each other and the child is born during the marriage, or within 300 days after the marriage is terminated
by death, annulment, declaration of invalidity, or divorce,
or after a decree of separation is entered by a court;
(2) before the child's birth, he and the child's natural
mother have attempted to marry each other by a marriage
solemnized in apparent compliance with law, although the
attempted marriage is or could be declared invalid, and,
(i) if the attempted marriage could be declared invalid only by a court, the child is born during the attempted marriage, or within 300 days after its termination by death, annulment, declaration of invalidity,
or divorce; or
(ii) if the attempted marriage is invalid without a
court order, the child is born within 300 days after
the termination of cohabitation;
(3) after the child's birth, he and the child's natural
mother have married, or attempted to marry, each
other by a marriage solemnized in apparent compliance
with law, although the attempted marriage is or could
be declared invalid, and
(i) he has acknowledged his paternity of the child
in writing filed with the [appropriate court or Vital
Statistics Bureau];

(ii) with his consent, he is named as the child's father on the child's birth certificate; or

(iii) he is obligated to support the child under a written voluntary promise or by court order;

(4) while the child is under the age of majority, he receives the child into his home and openly holds out the child as his natural child; or

(5) he acknowledges his paternity of the child in a writing filed with the [appropriate court or Vital Statistics Bureau], which shall promptly inform the mother of the filing of the acknowledgment, and she does not dispute the acknowledgment within a reasonable time after being informed thereof, in a writing filed with the [appropriate court or Vital Statistics Bureau]. If another man is presumed under this section to be the child's father, acknowledgment may be effected only with the written consent of the presumed father or after the presumption has been rebutted.

A presumption may be rebutted only by clear and convincing evidence or by a court decree establishing another man's paternity. If two or more presumptions create a conflict, the one founded on weightier considerations of policy and logic controls.

The UPA's use of presumptions for determining the rights of parents and children not covered by the traditional presumption of legitimacy within marriage has several advantages. First, it favors findings of parenthood in a wide category of situations, since the presumption itself operates as legal evidence of parenthood in the absence of other evidence to the contrary. Second, it decreases the number of adjudications of parentage that must be made. An adjudication is required only if there is no male who is a presumed father or if there is more than one person of the same sex as to whom a presumption of parentage exists. Third, it goes quite far toward eliminating unnecessary distinctions between children on the basis of their parents' marital status by recognizing that the legal fact of marriage to a child's mother is only one of several factors tending to corroborate a biological father–child relationship.* Fourth, by also giving

---

*There should be a presumption regarding the naming of a man as the father on a child's birth certificate with his and the natural mother's consent apart from a marriage or marriage-like relationship. At present, this factor is only one of a number of subsidiary factors under subsection (3) of section 4(a) related to the presumption of marriage. Since the birth certificate offers documentary proof and is a factor already used for determining paternity in a number of

men the right to challenge these more flexible presumptions of parenthood, it lifts the traditional burden on the mother and child to establish paternity. Unlike the laws of many states, the UPA allows fathers,
as well as mothers, children, and the state itself, to initiate proceedings concerning parenthood.

Moreover, because challenges to presumptions based on marriage or on a relationship between parents resembling marriage are
restricted to a smaller circle of contestants and to a shorter time period than challenges to other circumstantial presumptions, it is more
difficult for a man in such a situation to deny parenthood.* The UPA
suggests a three-year statute of limitations for bringing parentage actions, which is intended to "serve as an admonition that paternity actions should be brought promptly." However, the act provides that a
minor child has up to three years after reaching majority to initiate
an action, effectively giving the child a 21-year statute of limitations.

According to the UPA, this extended statute of limitations does
not affect laws relating to distribution, heirship, or the closing of a
decedent's estate. The UPA should be modified to make it clear that
this proviso is consistent with the Uniform Probate Code provisions
relevant to out-of-wedlock children. [246] The Uniform Probate Code
permits parenthood to be established in probate or intestacy proceedings by "clear and convincing evidence," even in cases where parenthood has not been established during the deceased child's or deceased
parent's lifetime. The high burden of proof helps prevent fraudulent
claims while recognizing that, as a matter of public policy, a child
born out of wedlock should not be disinherited when appropriate proof
of parentage is available.†

-----

states, it should rate as a presumption on its own. More important,
the addition of a putative father's name to the birth certificate is popu-
larly believed to be a legally effective method of acknowledging paternity. In addition, a state might wish to add, as a proviso to presumption number five, that all acknowledgments filed with the appropriate
institution, whether or not they establish a presumption of parenthood,
shall be kept on record and shall entitle that person to notice of proceedings set out in the act until such time as the court establishes
another man's paternity.

*In the interest of the child, the act also provides, as a general
rule, that agreements between alleged or presumed parents, which
have not been approved by the court, will not bar an action under these
sections.

†In 1975, the commissioners expressed a deference to the use
of UPA standards for inheritance in those states that enact both the
UPA and the Uniform Probate Code. However, incorporation of the

The potential for conflict between parents prompts the UPA's express provision that neither the mother nor the father can represent the child in an action to determine parentage; rather, minor children are to be represented by their guardian or a court-appointed representative. To avoid another obvious form of conflict, an amendment should be added to prohibit representation of the child by a state agency that has initiated the proceedings against the wishes of a parent in an effort to get support payments. Indeed, at this or some other appropriate point in the UPA, explicit statutory language should be added giving authority to a natural parent, custodian, or guardian to seek a court order halting parentage proceedings begun by third parties when such proceedings may not be in the best interests of the minor child. *

The UPA requires that notice be given to the natural mother and each man presumed or alleged to be the natural father and provides for confidential hearings of an informal nature as an initial step in determining the existence or nonexistence of a father-child relationship. At such a hearing, witnesses can be ordered to testify under oath, and immunity against criminal prosecution can be extended to witnesses in order to compel their testimony.

Relevant medical testimony, not always compellable in court proceedings because of the confidentiality between patient and doctor, is not so privileged under the UPA. The paternity-related evidence admissible at such a preliminary hearing is set out in section 12 of the act:

Uniform Probate Code standards set out in section 2-109 is preferable. The only two states that have thus far enacted both acts—Montana and North Dakota—have chosen to incorporate the Uniform Probate Code standards as suggested above.

*In their commentary, the commissioners suggest that states may wish to adopt a provision requiring an appropriate state agency to bring an action to determine the existence of a father-child relationship if the child had no presumed father and there had been no action to determine parenthood or institute adoption proceedings within a year of birth. The desirability of compulsory state parentage determinations is brought into serious question, however, by the constitutional right to privacy as well as by the possible adverse social consequences of extensive state intervention into family decision making concerning such fundamental questions. This is especially true in the absence of concrete signs of family pathology. The presumptions and time limitations established by the act seem a better way to protect both children's and parents' rights.

§ 12.   [Evidence Relating to Paternity]

Evidence relating to paternity may include:

    (1) evidence of sexual intercourse between the mother and alleged father at any possible time of conception;

    (2) an expert's opinion concerning the statistical probability of the alleged father's paternity based upon the duration of the mother's pregnancy;

    (3) blood test results, weighted in accordance with evidence, if available, of the statistical probability of the alleged father's paternity;

    (4) medical or anthropological evidence relating to the alleged father's paternity of the child based on tests performed by experts. If a man has been identified as a possible father of the child, the court may, and upon request of a party shall, require the child, the mother, the man to submit to appropriate tests; and

    (5) all other evidence relevant to the issue of paternity of the child.

Section 14 prohibits the admission of testimony, however, relating to sexual access to the mother by an unidentified man, unless offered by the mother. In addition, an alleged father can offer evidence only about sexual access by an identified man not present at the hearing it that man has made available to the court blood tests that do not exclude the possibility of his paternity. According to the commissioners' commentary, these limitations were added because of "the problem of perjured testimony concerning alleged sexual access to the mother offered by other men on behalf of the alleged father. (The act is not clear about whether this limitation applies only at a formal action or at the pretrial hearings as well. That it is placed after the section of pretrial recommendations and deals generally with the evidentiary rules applicable to a formal trial supports the former interpretation. The section does not explicitly limit the rule to the trial stage, however. It should be made clearly applicable to both stages.)

    Following a pretrial hearing, the judge or referee is directed, in section 13, to recommend an appropriate settlement based on the probability of establishing a father-child relationship and on the interest of the child in a judicial declaration of such a relationship. These recommendations may include:

    (1) that the action be dismissed with or without prejudice;

    (2) that the matter be compromised by an agreement among the alleged father, the mother, and the child, in which the father and child relationship is not determined

but in which a defined economic obligation is undertaken
by the alleged father in favor of the child and, if appropriate, in favor of the mother, subject to approval by the
judge [or referee] conducting the hearing. In reviewing
the obligation undertaken by the alleged father in a compromise agreement, the judge [or referee] conducting
the hearing shall consider the best interest of the child,
in the light of the factors enumerated in Section 15(e), dis-
counted by the improbability, as it appears to him, of establishing the alleged father's paternity or nonpaternity of
the child in a trial of the action. In the best interest of
the child, the court may order that the alleged father's
identity be kept confidential. In that case, the court may
designate a person or agency to receive from the alleged
father and disburse on behalf of the child all amounts paid
by the alleged father in fulfillment of obligations imposed
on him; and

(3) that the alleged father voluntarily acknowledge his
paternity of the child.

If any of the parties, including a temporary guardian, refuses to accept a recommended settlement, the judge then sets the case down
for a formal trial. According to section 14, a trial on the question
of parentage should be without a jury, unless required by a state's
constitution, because of the emotional atmosphere in cases of this nature.

Once a parentage proceeding has been concluded, the order of
the court concerning the existence or nonexistence of a father-child
relationship is determinative for all purposes. Besides declaring
parentage, this order also may contain relevant provisions regarding
support obligations, custody and guardianship, visitation rights, modification of a birth certificate, or any other matter in the best interest
of the child.

Section 15 sets out a good list of sex-neutral criteria for determining the allocation of child support obligations:

(1) the needs of the child;
(2) the standard of living and circumstances of the parents;
(3) the relative financial means of the parents;
(4) the earning ability of the parents;
(5) the need and capacity of the child for education, including higher education;
(6) the age of the child;
(7) the financial resources and the earning ability of the
child;

(8) the responsibility of the parents for the support of others; and

(9) the value of services contributed by the custodial parent.

States that already have enacted their own set of sex-neutral guidelines may wish to modify the UPA provision to conform to their existing law. Section 15 also states that an order may direct a father to pay the reasonable expenses of the mother's pregnancy and confinement. In order to be clearly sex neutral, this should be changed to allow for the allocation of an "appropriate share, based on the respective standards of living, circumstances, relative financial means, earning abilities and obligations of the parents." The court may order that support payments be made directly to the mother (which should be changed to read "custodial parent"). Willful failure to obey a support order is civil contempt of court.

In addition to proceedings to determine parentage, the UPA also is concerned with proceedings in which a mother proposes to relinquish a child for adoption. Section 24 of the act sets out the rules and procedures by which a natural father or possible natural father is given notice of the adoption and an opportunity to be heard. This allows a father to have parentage adjudicated at that point, if it has not been previously determined, to seek custody and child support, or to otherwise block the adoption proceedings. Under section 24, any man whose parental rights have not been terminated previously or determined not to exist by a court must be given notice of an adoption proceeding if he is:

(1) a presumed father under Section 4(a), (2) a father whose relationship to the child has been determined by a court, or (3) a father as to whom the child is a legitimate child under prior law of this State or under the law of another jurisdiction.

Men in any of these three categories may appear at the hearing and assert their custodial interests. The UPA also grants them all the rights provided for fathers under the maintenance or termination of parent-child relationships, preferably the Revised Uniform Adoption Act drafted by the same authors. Under the latter act, standards of parental neglect are applied to determine if a parent's rights should be terminated, with the additional proviso that the parental rights of a noncustodial parent may be terminated if he or she is withholding consent to adoption contrary to the best interests of the child.[247]

In the event that there is no man in any of these categories, the mother or other interested party can ask the court to terminate the parental rights of the unknown natural father so that the adoption may proceed. Prior to a termination of rights, however, the UPA instructs the court to make an effort to identify the natural father by questioning the mother and other appropriate persons and, at the discretion of the court, by posting notice of the proceeding in a manner likely to notify the father.

With regard to the rights of women involved in parentage or adoption proceedings under the UPA, two privacy issues should be considered: (1) should a court be allowed to inquire about a woman's social and sexual relationships in order to determine a father's identity, and (2) should notice by publication, including the mother's name, be required in adoption proceedings?

As a general matter, it is undesirable for the government to intrude in family decision making, and the long history of governmental persecution of unwed mothers and children makes procedures for compelling the mother's testimony particularly unwise. A putative father who wishes to establish an active relationship with his child can reasonably be expected to file a formal declaration of parentage or take other steps to insure that his interest in the child is known.

Unfortunately, many states already have the power to force women to disclose the identity of their children's fathers. In fact, the federal government currently conditions a state's participation in programs for Aid to Families with Dependent Children on the existence of state mechanisms to locate putative fathers and seek support payments from them. Under these circumstances, it is recommended that attention be focused on efforts to protect women from unnecessary prying as much as possible and to invoke a "best interest of the child" standard as a bar to parentage determinations that would endanger a child. The UPA provisions limiting the admissibility of evidence concerning a mother's sexual relationships are a step in this direction. In addition, the commissioners recommend that publication of adoption proceedings should be done only at the discretion of the court, since it is highly probable that in most cases publication will not lead to identification of the father but may lead to substantial embarrassment of the mother and may even deter adoption proceedings in the best interests of a child. *

---

*States desiring to minimize the mother's embarrassment may wish to add the following language, which is based on Wisconsin's law concerning notice in cases of this nature: If notice is given by publication or public posting, the name of the mother shall be included only if the court, following a hearing on the need for inclusion of the mother's name, determines that such inclusion is essential to give effective notice to the natural father and that the need for such inclusion outweighs the mother's right to privacy.

In addition to reviewing laws concerned with the treatment of unwed fathers and their children, it is advisable that states review their statutes, agency regulations and practices, and judicial decisions to eliminate discrimination against women on the basis of unwed motherhood or against families that consist of unwed mothers and their children. Since the biological fact of unwed motherhood is usually obvious whereas unwed fatherhood is usually easy to conceal, apparently neutral rules penalizing unwed parenthood, in practice, fall almost exclusively on women. An affirmative statement in a state's laws prohibiting discrimination on the basis of sex in employment, credit, education, insurance, and/or housing is an appropriate tool to combat such discriminatory rules.

State Reform Efforts

Most state laws concerning children born out of wedlock are a patchwork of incomplete approaches to the problems of ascertaining parentage and defining and enforcing rights and obligations between unwed parents and their children. A state-by-state description of the legal doctrines concerning out-of-wedlock children is beyond the scope of this report. However, a number of states recently have passed legislation that moves toward legal equality among children, regardless of their birth status, and significantly diminishes sex distinctions in the treatment of unwed parents. Five states have adopted some version of the UPA, and 10 states have adopted one of the two alternative provisions concerning illegitimacy in the Uniform Probate Code.[248] At least six states have developed their own relatively comprehensive statutes concerning the rights of unwed parents and children in the context of adoption, establishment of parenthood, and parenthood termination and/or inheritance. Some of the more interesting provisions adopted in recent years are discussed below.[249]

The five states that have adopted the UPA are California, Hawaii, Montana, North Dakota, and Washington.[250] Although all have made some changes in adopting the UPA, North Dakota and Montana have adhered most closely to its overall format, while Hawaii, California, and Washington have each made substantial changes in a number of provisions.[251] All five, however, have made a significant break with traditional state law on parentage determination. This section briefly discusses only significant changes relating to sex discrimination, including alterations of the UPA's (1) presumptions of paternity, (2) statute of limitations for bringing parentage actions, (3) assignment of state powers vis-a-vis parentage determinations, (4) privacy protections, and (5) provisions governing adoption proceedings.

In the area of presumptions, the two major variations from the UPA are California's deletion of the procedure for written declarations of paternity—which significantly narrows the scope of the act and the ability of putative fathers to use its provisions—and changes in Montana and Washington—which make it easier to rebut a presumption of paternity in the former state and more difficult in the latter. *

Washington, Hawaii, Montana, and California have changed the UPA's time limits for bringing actions. California has omitted certain UPA time limits on actions to declare the nonexistence of parentage. The most important change in Hawaii and Montana is the elimination of the provision permitting children to bring actions within three years of their majority. In contrast, Washington places no time limits on the bringing of actions by any party except the state, which is subject to a limit of five years after the birth of the child or after the last contribution to the child's support by the father. Washington's change has several consequences. Under the UPA, there are some situations in which the mere passage of time serves either to establish paternity or to foreclose a determination of paternity. By largely eliminating time limits, resolution is less likely to occur automatically in Washington. At the same time, however, Washington's higher burden of proof for challenging a presumption of parentage tends to preserve the UPA's bias in favor of parentage establishment. Furthermore, the elimination of time limits allows parenthood determinations after the death of either the child or the father, thereby facilitating inheritance between parents and children.

Montana, California, Washington, and Hawaii have modified the UPA in various ways to increase the power of the state, either by authorizing or requiring the state to bring actions to establish paternity in nonsupport cases or by setting forth procedures for the arrest of a nonsupporting parent. On the other hand, California and Washington omit the UPA provision permitting a state agency to be appointed temporary guardian of the child during a parentage proceeding, thus decreasing the state's influence over the determination of the "best interests of the child."

California and Washington have cut back on the UPA's protections of the privacy rights of unwed mothers by omitting certain limitations on testimony concerning the mother's sexual activities.

Hawaii and Washington have significantly modified the UPA's adoption provisions by decreasing the burden placed on the courts and

---

*Montana lightens the burden of proof to rebut a presumption by requiring only "a preponderance of the evidence" rather than a standard of "clear and convincing evidence." Washington, on the other hand, requires "clear, cogent and convincing evidence."

the mother to identify and notify an absent putative father. In Hawaii,
if there is no presumed father, adjudicated father, or father as to
whom the child is legitimate under prior law or the law of another
state, the court determines whether any identified putative father has
exercised parental rights, duties, and concerns. If he has not, his
rights are terminated; if he has, he receives notice of the proceeding.
This is a stricter test for putative fathers since it adds a subjective
behavioral standard for the right of notification. Washington's law
has a similar effect. While it includes extensive provisions providing
for published notice to unknown fathers and personal notice to all identified putative fathers, it does not provide for the court's necessarily
prior inquiry of the mother concerning the identity and whereabouts
of possible fathers. Therefore, its coercive impact is less than the
UPA's.

In addition to these UPA states, at least six others have substantially reduced the burdens on parent-child relationships outside marriage without adopting a comprehensive system based on presumptions.
Of these states, four have adopted procedures by which unwed parents
can assert parenthood by a formal or informal out-of-court declaration, which entitles them to notice of adoption or parenthood termination proceedings and, in one or two states, entitles them or their children to other rights as well.[252] Three states—Wisconsin, Oregon,
and Michigan—explicitly authorize putative fathers to bring actions
for the establishment of parentage.[253] In fact, these states permit
such actions by a broader group of men than does the UPA, the only
criteria being that the men declare themselves to be the natural fathers of the children and that the actions be brought within the requisite time limits. Once paternity is adjudicated, all three states permit the father to seek custody and child support.

Another protection provided by a number of these states is a
system for giving notice of adoption or parenthood termination proceedings to both identified and unidentified putative fathers. In some
states, the notice provisions are broader than those of the UPA.
Michigan, which has a strict mandate to make reasonable efforts to
identify and locate parents, requires notice to all putative parents
whose identity and whereabouts are known.[254] Wisconsin, Oregon,
and Minnesota require notice to a father whose parentage has been
adjudicated, and Colorado, Michigan, Minnesota, and Wisconsin also
require notice to a parent who has filed a declaration of parental interest.[255] In addition, some of the states entitle a man to notice if:

---

*Colorado, Maine, Michigan, Minnesota, Oregon, and Wiscon-
sin. While additional states may have made changes, these six are
illustrative of major trends.

he has supported (Colorado—or paid medical bills—Maine, Minnesota, and Oregon) or attempted to support the child (Maine and Oregon); he lives or has lived with the mother and/or the child in a familial relationship (Maine, Minnesota, Oregon—during 60 days prior to proceeding—and Wisconsin) or has attempted to establish such a relationship with the child (Maine); or he has been named on the child's birth certificate (Colorado—with consent—Maine and Minnesota—without regard to consent).

With regard to unidentified fathers, four of these states allow the court to attempt to identify possible fathers or to make inquiry of the mother concerning the father's identity,[256] and four states also require notice by publication to unidentified or unlocatable fathers.[257]

Once a putative father has appeared and begun to participate in adoption or parentage termination proceedings, the states studied differ in the extent to which putative fathers may prevent adoption or parenthood termination. The biological fact that the natural mother is always present at the birth of the child engenders a difference in the legal rights of the mother and father. Of necessity, a mother always begins as the presumed custodian. In contrast, unless the mother agrees to a transfer of custody, the father must first show parenthood and then show that a transfer of custody to him is in the child's best interest. However, the situation in which a mother is relinquishing custody to adoptive parents or other custodians admits of a wider variety of legal standards.

All of the six non-UPA states studied have more or less inclusive provisions for dispensing with the consent of a parent in certain circumstances: if the parent (1) is not entitled to notice under the law, (2) has received notice and fails to appear at the hearing, (3) does not contest the adoption or termination of parental rights, (4) has waived notice of the hearing or the right to consent to an adoption, (5) has voluntarily relinquished parental rights or previously had parental rights terminated, or (6) cannot be located or his identity is unknown.[258]

Among these states, Wisconsin and Minnesota are at one extreme. Both states apply customary standards of parental neglect to parents of both sexes in determining whether a parent's consent to adoption or parenthood termination is necessary.[259] In other words, unless a noncustodial parent has abandoned the child for a considerable period of time or mistreated the child in some way, the court may not terminate that parent's right to veto an adoption. The other four states give fewer rights to the putative father. Oregon and Maine require that the father both seek custody and show that he is fit and able to assume custody.[260] Colorado applies customary standards of parental neglect to fathers who have established certain connections to the child but terminates the rights of other putative fathers without

notice or a hearing. [261] The first is fathers who have provided care
to either mother or child or who have had custody of the child. Their
rights can be terminated only in accordance with general parental
neglect standards. The second group of fathers, who have not previously been involved with their children, must seek custody and satisf
a "best interest of the child" standard. If the father is successful
and if the parental rights of the mother have been terminated, the
court "shall enter an order granting custody to the putative father
and legitimating the child for all purposes."[263] Michigan law also
provides that

> At the request of the mother, her formal execution of a
> release or consent shall be delayed until after court de-
> termination of the status of the putative father's request
> for custody of the child. [264]

Under traditional parentage law, time limits on the initiation
of parentage and support actions are often unduly restrictive. Five
of the non-UPA states studied have broken away from the traditional
approach. Colorado, Michigan, and Wisconsin each limit actions to
within either five or six years after the child's birth, [265] but these
limits do not apply if the father has taken certain actions: in Colorado
and Michigan, if he has acknowledged paternity in writing or furnishec
support; and in Wisconsin, if he has cohabited with the child's mother.
In Colorado, these actions on the part of the father remove the time
limit completely; in Michigan, support extends the time limit, and
acknowledgment eliminates it; and in Wisconsin, the time limit is
five years after the parents separate. Minnesota and Maine have no
time limit on the initiation of proceedings, but both limit the amount
of time for which support recovery can be obtained: in Maine to six
years immediately preceding the action, and in Minnesota to four
years. [266]

Some non-UPA states have improved their laws in the area of
inheritance rights between unwed fathers and their children in the absence of a will. Ten states have adopted the Uniform Probate Code
provisions on intestate succession between unwed fathers and their
children. In addition, to these ten, at least one of the non-UPA
states studied allows parentage to be established for inheritance purposes by informal acknowledgment, [267] four by written, out-of-court
acknowledgment, [268] and five by formal acknowledgment in court or
parenthood adjudication during the lifetime of the decedent. [269]

States considering ERA conformance legislation in the area of
illegitimacy can learn a number of lessons from the reform efforts
discussed above. The most important lesson is the need for the complete elimination of sex-based distinctions in parental rights, so that

the adjudicated father has rights equal to those of the natural mother in relationship to their child. Once the ERA is adopted, courts will construe legislation to promote this result, but it is preferable for reform legislation to state specifically that adjudication of parentage in any context legitimates a child for all purposes and that an adjudicated father has the same right to seek custody and child support as the mother. In adopting such legislation, states have an opportunity to develop sex-neutral standards that protect the best interests of the child.

Several of the non-UPA states discussed above have taken steps in this direction, but none has done so as clearly or completely as is desirable. States should carefully reexamine their laws in all relevant areas, including inheritance, adoption, termination of parental rights, paternity adjudication, and birth and name registration, rather than proceeding in a piecemeal fashion.

Another lesson that can be drawn is the importance of explicit language covering both the rights of each party in an adoption or parentage proceeding and the standard to be used in the required determination. For example, Colorado has provisions for parental consent but no clear provisions concerning notice to the parents, while Maine permits a putative father to seek custody but does not give the court any standards to guide its deliberation.

Finally, states should seriously consider adopting broad provisions enabling putative fathers to assert their paternity either by initiating a parentage action or filing a formal declaration of paternity. In the case of adoption or termination of parental rights, some form of inquiry into the identity and whereabouts of a putative father may be desirable, but only if the provisions clearly prohibit coercion of the mother's testimony either by the court or by other state officials. Likewise, children should be entitled to file their own actions for the ascertainment of parentage. Of course, appropriate safeguards for the interests of other parties, including time limit, appointment of counsel, and appointment of a temporary guardian for the child, also should be developed. Without procedures by which the father or the child can initiate proceedings, state law may run afoul of both strict equality principles as well as the due process clause of the Fourteenth Amendment. The Uniform Parentage Act is still the best starting place for reform because of its comprehensiveness and overall consistency.

6

EMPLOYMENT AND
EMPLOYMENT-RELATED
BENEFITS

INTRODUCTION

Employment, because of the economic independence and security it brings, continues to be a vital focus of the movement toward legal equality between the sexes, especially as more and more women enter the labor market. By 1974, more than half of the women 18 to 64 years of age had full-time employment, and the number rises each year. Close to half of all married women now work, while one out of ten women workers is head of a family.

This chapter focuses on the public aspects of employment, covering those areas where the government is itself a regulator of employment conditions in the private sector, an employer, or the administrator of employee-related social insurance programs. In all of these roles, the government—federal, state, and local—has a history of bias against women workers that reflects the traditional biases of society at large. These biases are based on the assumptions that women are dependent on men, that their proper role is homemaking, and that, when they do work, their attachment to the labor force is weak, their income is not essential to the financial security of their families, and their fragility and limited abilities require special "protections" in the work force.

The manifestations of discrimination in the public sector closely parallel those in the private employment sector. Government policies have worked against equality for women by sex segregating civil service job classifications, denying women fair opportunities for training and promotion, and undercutting the worth of women's incomes to their spouses and children through inequitable dependent and survivor benefits upon their unemployment, disability, retirement, or death. All employers, both private and public, are now bound by the federal

statutory prohibitions against sex discrimination in the terms and
conditions of employment found in Title VII of the Civil Rights Act of
1964. The government, in its role as employer or regulator of employment conditions, however, also is bound by constitutional standards of equality because its policies entail "state action." Thus,
its involvement in the employment field will require scrutiny under
the ERA.

LABOR LAWS APPLIED TO WOMEN ONLY

Background

In the late nineteenth and early twentieth centuries, almost
every state enacted labor laws limiting occupations that were open to
women and regulating the conditions under which they worked. Although often called "protective," these laws have in practice discriminated against women by making it difficult for them to obtain desirable
and high-paying jobs for which they are fully qualified. These labor
laws have served as an obstacle to promotions and supervisory positions in particular. Recent research into the origins of these laws
reveals that they were based on stereotypes about women's transient
and secondary role in the labor market and their weak physical condition as well as on the desire of male workers to reduce competition
for higher paying jobs.[1] The value of the laws is also questionable
because they are characterized by uneven coverage, wide variation
from state to state, and, ironically, exemptions for situations in
which protection would seem most appropriate. For example, domestic workers and workers in canneries and other businesses involved
in seasonal food production are often exempt from the hours and night-
work laws. These exemptions are not based on the ability of these
workers to obtain decent conditions for themselves but on the convenience for employers of having workers available for long hours. Moreover, the exclusion of men from coverage under the small number of
truly beneficial laws is discriminatory.

Labor laws for women generally fall into three broad categories:
(1) laws excluding women from certain jobs, (2) laws regulating hours
or conditions of work or prohibiting the lifting of weights over a certain limit, and (3) laws providing supposed benefits, such as minimum
wages, rest periods, or mealtimes. Federal antidiscrimination laws
have had a major impact on these three categories of state law.

Women workers began to challenge restrictive and exclusionary
state labor laws in court after the passage of Title VII of the Civil
Rights Act of 1964, which prohibits sex discrimination in employment.[2]

These challenges demonstrated clearly the negative effect of most sex-
based protective laws on women's wages, employment and promotional
opportunities, and working conditions. The discriminatory impact of
the exclusionary laws is clear. The restrictive hours and weight-
lifting laws are also discriminatory since they operate to deny many
women premium pay and jobs requiring overtime, although they may
help those women who want to limit their work time because of home
responsibilities. Even the "benefit" laws may discriminate against
members of both sexes. Frequently, for example, employers penalize women workers for their legally mandated rest period by docking
their pay or putting them on special schedules that exclude them from
higher paying jobs.[3] On the other hand, male workers are sometimes
the victims of discrimination because they are denied certain benefits
guaranteed to women by law. This is less common, however, because unions often have bargained for broad guarantees for members
of both sexes and because, by the 1960s, most of the truly beneficial
laws, particularly the minimum wage laws, had been extended to men
by the legislatures.[4]

In order to assess the ERA's impact on employment laws, it is
necessary first to describe the effect Title VII already has had on exclusionary, restrictive, and benefit laws.

The Equal Employment Opportunity Commission (EEOC), which
interprets and enforces Title VII, has issued guidelines declaring that
protective state labor laws contravene the federal statute. The guidelines state that restrictive or exclusionary laws do not take into account the "capacities, preferences, and abilities of individual females
and, therefore, discriminate on the basis of sex." The commission
ruled that such laws are superseded by the federal law and cannot be
used by an employer covered by the federal statute to justify differential treatment of women workers. In practice, this sweeping theoretical "invalidation" has resulted in three different kinds of practical
action and, therefore, a very uneven state of the labor laws: discriminatory laws may have been repealed or extended to men by the state
legislatures; they may have been challenged and specifically held invalid under Title VII by the courts, while still remaining on the books;
or they may have remained on the books, unenforced or tacitly enforced because no one has challenged them. This section discusses
all three states of present law in describing the impact of Title VII,
but a more extensive treatment of specifically legislative action can
be found in the section on state reform efforts below.

As a result of Title VII and women's insistence on equality, 20
exclusionary laws have been repealed since 1964.[5] With regard to
restrictive laws, courts generally have followed the principles of the
EEOC guidelines in deciding cases challenging sex-based labor laws
regulating hours or weight lifting. The first major decision came in

the case of <u>Rosenfeld</u> v. <u>Southern Pacific Co.</u>, decided by a federal
district court in 1968 and affirmed by the Court of Appeals in 1971,
invalidating a California weight-lifting statute.[6] Most other restrictive laws have met a similar fate. For example, weight-lifting laws
have been invalidated in at least four cases and have been repealed in
almost all the states that once had them.[7] Three that remain on the
books have been invalidated.* Similarly, the maximum hours laws
of at least nine states have been struck down by the courts under Title
VII.[8] In response to this clear mandate, 21 states have repealed
their laws† and the attorneys general of 23 jurisdictions‡ have ruled
that the maximum hours laws do not apply to employees covered by
Title VII.[9] Eighteen** of these laws remain on the books.[10] Four
states have repealed the related laws prohibiting women from working
at night, and the two that remain are not enforced.*** Several states
also have removed statutes that disqualify women from employment
for a certain period before and after childbirth.[11] (See Table 6.1 for
sex-based state labor laws still on the books.)

The EEOC guidelines on benefit laws state that employers who
follow state laws requiring a minimum wage, rest, or meal periods

---

*California, Massachusetts, and Ohio. Citations to these and
all other sex-based state labor laws still on the books, including those
not now enforced, are found in Table 6.1

†The states, with the year of repeal, are: Arizona (1970), Colorado (1971), Connecticut (1974), Delaware (1965), Kentucky (1974),
Maryland (1969), Michigan (1975), Minnesota (1974), Missouri (1972),
Montana (1971), Nebraska (1969), Nevada (1975), New Jersey (1971),
New York (1970), North Dakota (1973), Oregon (1971), Rhode Island
(1974), South Carolina (1973), South Dakota (1973), Vermont (1970),
and Virginia (1974).

‡Arkansas, California, Connecticut, District of Columbia, Illinois, Kansas, Kentucky, Maine, Massachusetts, Michigan, Minnesota, Mississippi, Missouri, New Hampshire, North Dakota, Oklahoma,
Pennsylvania, Rhode Island, South Dakota, Tennessee, Texas (voluntary overtime law held invalid), Washington, and Wisconsin.

**The jurisdictions in which the laws remain either in statutes or
regulations are: Arkansas, California, District of Columbia, Illinois,
Kansas, Louisiana, Maine, Massachusetts, Mississippi, New Hampshire (modified by administrative ruling making overtime voluntary),
New Mexico (law can be waived by employee), Ohio, Oklahoma, Pennsylvania, Tennessee, Texas, Utah (voluntary overtime), and Wisconsin.

***The law is not enforced in Ohio and is only enforced for those
who request it in New Hampshire.

TABLE 6.1

State Labor Laws for Women Only

State	Statute	Minimum Wage	Overtime Pay	Seats (s), Meals (m), Rest Period (r), (misc.)	Maximum Hours	Night Work	Occupational Exclusions: Mines (m), Alcohol (a), (misc.)	Weight Lifting	Barbers, Cosmetologists
Alabama	Ala. Code (1958)			Tit. 26, § 337 (s)[a]					Tit. 46, § 64 (a)(1)
Arkansas	Ark. Stat. Ann. (1947)[a]		§ 81-601[b]	§ 81-410(m), § 81-609(m), § 81-620(s), § 81-407(misc.)	* § 81-622		§ 52-612(m)		
California	Cal. Labor Code (1971)		* § 1350	§ 1253; see § 1173	* § 1350, 1350.5	* § 1350		* § 1251	
Colorado	Colo. Rev. Stat. Ann.	§ 8-6-101 to -919 (1974)	§ 8-6-101 (1974)	§ 8-11-118(r)(1974) see § 8-6-101, -104 (1974)		§ 1350			§ 15-1-15(3) (1963)
Connecticut	Conn. Gen. Stat. Ann.						§ 30-90 (1969) (a) (1972)		§ 20-250(4) (1969)[c]
District of Columbia	D.C. Code Ann. (1968)			§ 36-310(s), § 36-303(r), § 36-304(m)*	* § 36-301, -302	§ 36-206, -302			
Georgia	Ga. Code (1974)			§ 54-401(s)					
Idaho	Idaho Code (1948)		§ 44-1107[d]	§ 44-1108(s)					
Illinois	Ill. Rev. Stat. (1969)				Ch. 48, § 5[e]		Ch. 93, § 129(m)		

212

State	Citation					
Indiana	Ind. Ann. Stat. (1974)					§ 25-8-1-2(3)
Kansas	Kan. Stat. Ann. (1964)	§ 44-639, -643[f]		*§ 44-640, -643	§ 44-640, -543	
Kentucky	Ky. Rev. Stat. (1972)					§ 317A.010
Louisiana	La. Rev. Stat. Ann. (1964)	§ 23-358, -354[f]	§ 23:292(s) § 23:293(s) § 23:312(m) § 23:333(r)	*§ 23:311, 23:332	§ 26:88(8), 285(8)(a)	Tit. 37, § 492g
Maine	Me. Rev. Stat. Ann. (1974)		Tit. 26, § 735(s)	*Tit. 26, §§ 731-34		
Maryland	Md. Ann. Code (1971)		Art. 43, § 200 (misc.)			h
Massachusetts	Mass. Gen. Laws Ann. (1971)			*Ch. 149, § 56		*Ch. 149, §§ 53, 53A
Michigan	Mich. Comp. Laws Ann. (1967)		§ 408.1011 (1967) (misc.)			§ 750.556 (1968) § 338.752 (1967)
Minnesota	Minn. Stat. (1970)					§ 155.02[i]
Mississippi	Miss. Code Ann. (1972)			§ 71-1-33		
Missouri	Mo. Ann. Stat. (1965)		§ 292.170(s)[j]			
Nebraska	Neb. Rev. Stat. (1971)	Neb. Const. art. XV, § 8[k]				§ 71-210 to -224

(continued)

TABLE 6.1 (continued)

State	Statute	Minimum Wage	Overtime Pay	Seats (s), Meals (m), Rest Period (r), (misc.)	Maximum Hours	Night Work	Occupational Exclusions: Mines (m), Alcohol (a), (misc.)	Weight Lifting	Barbers, Cosmetologists
Nevada	Nev. Rev. Stat. (1973)								§ 644.020
New Hampshire	N.H. Rev. Stat. Ann. (1966)			§ 277:8(s)	§ 275:15, [1] 275:16	§ 275:17[1]			§ 313:2
New Jersey	N.J. Stat. Ann.			§ 34:2-29(s) (1965)					§ 45:4-30 (1963)
New Mexico	N.M. Stat. Ann. (1974)			§ 59-5-4(m) § 59-5-10(s)	§ 59-5-1, -2, -5, -6, -7, -13m				
New York	N.Y. Labor Law (1965) N.Y. Gen. Bus. Code (McKinney 1968)			§ 203-b(s)[n]					§ 401(5), 431 (4)
Ohio	Ohio Rev. Code Ann. (1973)			§ 4107.42	* § 4107.42, 4107.46, 4017.47	* § 4107.42	* § 4107.43 (a)(m) (misc.)	o	§ 4713.01
Oklahoma	Ok. Stat. Ann.			Tit. 40, § 83, 86(s) (1954)	* Tit. 40, § 81 (1954)			o	Tit. 50, § 71 (1971)
Oregon	Ore. Rev. Stat. (1975)								§ 67.010(f)

State	Code						
Pennsylvania	Pa. Stat.		* Tit. 43, §108(s), Tit. 43, §110(m), Tit. 43, §111, 112 (misc.) (1964)	* Tit. 43, §103, 107, 126 (1964)	* Tit. 43, §105	Tit. 52, §70-272(m) (1966)[p], Tit. 47, §4-493(25) (misc.) (1969)	
Rhode Island	R.I. Gen. Laws Ann.		* §28-3-14(m) (1969)		q	§3-8-2(a) (1969)	§5-10-1 (1957)
South Carolina	S.C. Code Ann. (1962)		§40-256(s)				
Tennessee	Tenn. Code Ann.			* §50-718 (1966)			§62-308 (1955)
Texas	Tex. Rev. Civ. Stat.	* Art. 5172(a)(4) (1962)	Art. 5172a(s), Art. 5173-5178 (misc.) (1962)	* Art. 5172 (1962)			Art. 8401; 8407a, §4; 8451a (1967)[r]
Utah	Utah Code Ann. (1974)	§34-22-8, -13	* §34-22-9	§34-22-14[s]	k	§34-22-1(m)	§58-11-12[t]
Vermont	Vt. Stat. Ann. (1975)						Tit. 26, §566[u]
West Virginia	W.Va. Code Ann. (1973)		§21-3-11(s)				
Wisconsin	Wis. Stat. Ann. (1974)	§104.02 v	§103.16(s)	* §103.01, 103.02			
Wyoming	Wyo. Stat. Ann. (1967)	Tit. 27, §27-220, -218	Tit. 27, §27-219(s), §27-218(r), §27-233(s)			w	

(continued)

215

TABLE 6.1 (continued)

* Indicates that the law or laws cited have been invalidated by court or attorney general opinion as conflicting with Title VII. In the District of Columbia, * applies only to (m). (State Labor Laws, supra note 7, is the source of this information.)

a When all provisions cited are in the same code volume, that year is given in the "statute" column; if not, the year of each volume is given after the specific section cited.

b This law has been extended to all employees by a court decision: Potlatch Forests v. Hays, Inc., 465 F.2d 1081 (8th Cir. 1972).

c This law was held unconstitutional in Tuozzoli v. Killian, 386 F. Supp. 9 (1974).

d This law was repealed by implication in Idaho Trailer Coach Ass'n v. Brown, 95 Idaho 910, 523 P.2d 42 (1974).

e This law was invalidated and is enforced only for employers of fewer than 15 employees.

f This law is inoperative; no wage rates have been set.

g This law was held unconstitutional in Pavone v. Louisiana State Bd. of Barber Examiners, 364 F. Supp. 961 (E.D. La. 1973), aff'd, 505 F.2d 1022 (5th Cir. 1974)

h A Maryland statute requiring cosmetologists to use different methods to shampoo men's and women's hair was held to violate the Maryland ERA. Maryland State Bd. of Barber Examiners v. Kuhn, 270 Md. 496, 312 A.2d 216 (1973).

i This was held a violation of equal protection in Minnesota Bd. of Barber Examiners v. Laurance, 218 N.W.2d 692 (1974).

j This was extended to all employees by Mo. Op. Att'y Gen. No. 287 (1973).

k This constitutional provision authorizes laws regulating the hours and conditions of women's and children's employment and securing them a proper minimum wage.

l This night-work law can be waived by agreement of the employer and employee under N.H. Rev. Stat. Ann. § 275.17a (1966). The Labor Department reports that the maximum hours law is also enforced only for those who request it.

m The law can be waived by the employee.

n See N.Y. Op. Att'y Gen. No. 47 (1972).

o The Labor Department reports that a weight-lifting law that is not enforced is still on the books.

p This was superseded by an opinion of the attorney general based on the state ERA.

q The Labor Department reports that transportation must be assured if women work at night.

r Held a violation of equal protection in Bolton v. Texas Bd. of Barber Examiners, 350 F. Supp. 494 (1972), aff'd, 409 U.S. 807 (1972). See also Tex. Op. Att'y Gen. No. M-1270 (1972).

s This section provides voluntary overtime for women.

t Statutory definition of cosmetology was held unconstitutional in Leitham v. McGinn, 524 P.2d 323 (1974).

u See Vt. Op. Att'y Gen. No. 85 (1972).

v The Labor Department reports that a sex-based overtime pay law is in effect in Wisconsin.

w The Labor Department reports that a prohibition on women working in mines is currently in effect in Wyoming.

Source: Compiled by the authors.

for women only violate Title VII. If an employer can show that business necessity precludes the extension of these benefits to members
of both sexes, they are not to be provided to members of either sex. [12]

The EEOC's lead has been followed by the courts and legislatures in connection with these benefit laws, as with the restrictive
and exclusionary ones. Challenges to these provisions have decreased
considerably because, in part, these laws already have been extended
to men legislatively. For example, 38 jurisdictions now have minimum wage laws for men and women;* 25 jurisidctions have sex-neutral
overtime pay laws;[†] and 19 state meal, rest, or seating requirement
laws cover workers of both sexes.[‡] Thirteen states have repealed
some of their sex-based benefit laws[14] and those in four other jurisdictions (District of Columbia, Maine, Ohio, and Pennsylvania) have
been declared invalid. One federal court, faced with a challenge to
an overtime pay law for women, extended the coverage of the law to
men rather than striking it down, but another federal court refused to
do so. [15] In addition, men often have been able to obtain equivalent
benefits through union contracts.

This review of actions, repeals, and invalidations since 1964
demonstrates the profound impact that the mandate for equal employment opportunity for women has had on sex-based state labor laws.
Decisions by federal agencies and courts, followed in many jurisdictions by state fair employment practices laws, have broadened the opportunities open to women workers and reduced drastically the number of laws that require attention under the ERA.

---

*These are: Alaska, Arkansas, California, Connecticut, Dela-
ware, District of Columbia, Georgia, Hawaii, Idaho, Illinois, Indiana,
Kentucky, Maine, Maryland, Massachusetts, Michigan, Minnesota,
Montana, Nebraska, Nevada, New Hampshire, New Jersey, New Mexico, New York, North Carolina, North Dakota, Ohio, Oklahoma, Oregon, Pennsylvania, Rhode Island, South Dakota, Texas, Vermont, Virginia, Washington, West Virginia, Wyoming. This change occurred
even before Title VII. Only Arkansas, California, Minnesota, and
Washington have amended their laws to cover men within the last several years. Arizona, however, has repealed its minimum wage law
for women recently. [13]

[†]Alaska, Connecticut, District of Columbia, Hawaii, Kentucky,
Maine, Maryland, Massachusetts, Michigan, Minnesota, Montana,
Nevada, New Hampshire, New Jersey, New Mexico, New York, North
Carolina, North Dakota, Ohio, Oregon, Pennsylvania, Rhode Island,
Vermont, Washington, and West Virginia.

[‡]Meal period: Illinois, Kentucky, Massachusetts, Nebraska,
Nevada, New Hampshire, New York, North Dakota, Oregon, and Wash-
ington; rest period: Kentucky, Nevada, North Dakota, Oregon, and
Washington; and seats: Florida, Massachusetts, Montana, and Oregon.

A number of states still have discriminatory laws on the books that have not been sex neutralized in the process of Title VII litigation and reform because they were not specifically invalidated by the courts or repealed (or extended) by the legislatures. They therefore have an anomolous status and, though theoretically invalid, remain unchallenged and tacitly enforced.

Some of these laws, however, have been limited in their scope by legislative amendments rather than repeal or extension. With respect to exclusionary laws, five states (Arkansas, Connecticut, Illinois, Louisiana, and Rhode Island) still prohibit women from holding jobs in mines or establishments selling alcoholic beverages.[16] A Utah law permits women to work in mines unless the Industrial Commission finds, after investigation and public hearing, that such work is detrimental to their health and safety.[17]

Regarding restrictive laws, the Michigan weight-lifting law, the only weight-lifting law still enforced, prohibits giving a woman a task disproportionate to her strength.[18] Though still sex-based, such a law has a less detrimental effect than a blanket rule prohibiting women from lifting items over a certain weight. Only one sex-based maximum hours law (New Mexico) has not been declared invalid, and it permits a woman to work overtime for premium pay if she signs an agreement to that effect. Illinois and Ohio, however, enforce their maximum hours law for employers with fewer than 15 employees, who are not covered by Title VII, even though the invalidation of a law under Title VII usually has resulted in the cessation of enforcement for anyone.[19] Night-work prohibitions exist in three jurisdictions (District of Columbia, Kansas, and New Hampshire); in one of these, the law can be waived by agreement of the employer and employee subject to approval by the Industrial Commission.[20] Two other states (Utah and Rhode Island) permit night work for women but require that the employer provide transportation.[21]

In the area of benefit laws, five states have minimum wage laws that apply only to women; two of these are inoperative, however, as no rates have been set under them.* Three states (Colorado, Wyoming, and Wisconsin) have sex-based overtime pay laws that have not been declared invalid; 21 jurisdictions[†] have sex-based meal, rest period, or seating laws that are still in effect.

---

*Colorado, Utah, Wisconsin, Kansas, and Louisiana—the last two being inoperative.

[†]Alabama, Arkansas, California, Colorado, District of Columbia, Georgia, Idaho, Louisiana, Nevada, New Hampshire, New Jersey, New Mexico, New York, Oklahoma, Rhode Island, South Carolina, Texas, Utah, West Virginia, Wisconsin, and Wyoming.

While successful Title VII litigation usually has the effect of ceasing the enforcement of sex-discriminatory laws for all employers, Title VII's literal jurisdiction does not include employers with fewer than 15 employees. The Illinois and Ohio maximum hours laws are good examples of the very literal enforcement of Title VII.

Statutes regulating the training, licensing, and permitted activities of barbers and cosmetologists, though not enacted as protective laws for women only, contain similar kinds of sex-discriminatory provisions. The most common form of discrimination is a prohibition against cosmetologists serving male customers, while barbers can serve either men or women. Some of the statutes contain an explicit prohibition; others refer to cosmetologists working in beauty parlors "patronized by women and children" and thus accomplish the same result by indirection.* Twenty-two states have some variety of discriminatory law concerning these two occupations. Seven of these[†] have been held unconstitutional by courts or state attorneys general on equal protection or state ERA grounds.

Impact of the ERA

The impact of the equal rights amendment on state labor laws that apply to women only has been seriously misunderstood in much of the public discussion surrounding the ratification of the amendment. These laws, and changes in them that have occurred over the past decade, have been cited by opponents of the amendment as an example of the benefits women will lose under the ERA. This argument is either a misconception or a deliberate choice to ignore the facts. First, the large majority of these sex-based laws have functioned to constrict the opportunities and compensation of women workers, and the few beneficial laws have been notoriously unenforced. Second,

---

*Those states that forbid cosmetologists from serving male clients are Colorado, Indiana, Michigan, Nebraska, Nevada, New Jersey, New York, and Rhode Island. Kentucky, New Hampshire, Ohio, Oklahoma, and Tennessee have laws that refer to shops patronized mainly by women or work done principally on women. In addition, the laws on the licensing of barbers in Alabama and Oregon refer explicitly to "male customers." To the extent that both men and women can work as either cosmetologists or barbers, without sex-based restrictions, such laws are not really "protective" of the worker but are restrictions on the sex of the customer alone.

[†]These are laws in Connecticut, Louisiana, Maryland, Minnesota, Texas, Utah, and Vermont.

and more important, the changes in recent years have been brought
about by Title VII and comparable state fair employment practices
laws, not the ERA. Moreover, these changes will continue even
without the ERA. Third, despite some small number of unwise results, most of these changes have been helpful to women. Last, it
seems clear that concerted activity in the legislatures to assure intelligent compliance with the ERA will help working women in both
the short and long run. In fact, the ERA will bring to the already
partially completed process of reform a clear legislative history to
guide the course of conformance and a mandate for adopting laws to
meet the genuine needs of workers of both sexes. Moreover, it will
extend Title VII's protection to employers with less than 15 employees.

Explicit Discrimination

A state can comply with the amendment either by extending
present laws to apply to members of both sexes or by repealing them.
However, it would cripple industry to extend maximum hours or
weight-lifting laws to men, and it would be a loss for women to repeal
the laws on meal or rest periods where they are enforced. Obviously,
the restrictive laws should be repealed and the beneficial ones extended to all workers. This is the conclusion Congress drew when it
explicitly addressed the impact of the ERA on sex-based state labor
laws. The Senate Majority Report on the amendment states:

> Ratification of the Equal Rights Amendment will result in
> equal treatment for men and women with respect to the
> labor laws of the States, as in other legal matters. This
> will mean that such restrictive discriminatory labor laws
> as those which bar women entirely from certain occupa-
> tions will be invalid. But those laws which confer a real
> benefit, which offer real protection, will, it is expected,
> be extended to protect both men and women. Examples
> of laws which may be expanded include laws providing for
> rest periods or minimum wage benefits or health and safety
> protections. Men are now sometimes denied the very real
> benefits these laws offer. As Professor Leo Kanowitz
> pointed out to your Committee at its Hearings in September
> 1970: "The fears of some opponents of the [Equal Rights
> A]mendment that its adoption would mullify laws that pres-
> ently protect women only are thus unfounded—since the
> equality of treatment required by the [A]mendment can be
> achieved by extending the benefits of those laws to men
> rather than by removing them for women." The Associa-

tion of the Bar of the City of New York pointed out in discussing laws requiring rest periods for women only, that
they "may be extended to both sexes without burden or
disruption." . . .

The question of whether laws found unconstitutional under the Equal Rights Amendment will be struck down or extended to cover both men and women, is a question which
extends beyond the area of labor legislation. Of course,
the legislatures of the several States will have the primary
responsibility for revising those laws which conflict with
the Equal Rights Amendment. Indeed, the purpose of delaying the effective date of the Equal Rights Amendment
for two years after ratification is to allow legislatures—
particularly those which meet only in alternate years—and
agencies an opportunity to review and revise their laws
and regulations. As stated above, the Committee expects
that any labor law, or other legislation, which is truly protective will be extended to both sexes, while laws which
are restrictive will become null and void.[22]

While characterization of a law as benefit or burden is generally
straightforward, there are instances in which a law may benefit some
workers and burden others. In such a situation, a sex-neutral alternative to current law is permissible under the ERA. For example,
the substitution of a voluntary overtime provision for all workers to
replace maximum hours laws for women is clearly a reform that complies with the amendment.

The ERA prohibits sex distinctions in the statutory regulation
of the professions. Under two state ERAs, laws subjecting cosmetologists to different rules when cutting men's and women's hair have been
declared unconstitutional. Moreover, the courts have stated that cosmetologists may serve customers of both sexes, subject to state licensing requirements.[23] Other laws that limit the sex of the customers
barbers or cosmetologists may serve must be amended since they are
not based on any unique physical characteristic of men or women.
Reference to men's beards in the statutory enumeration of tasks a profession may perform may be permissible under the amendment but
is hardly necessary.

Neutral Rules

Explicitly sex-based labor laws do not pose neutral rule issues.
Nor will such laws, when neutralized, present problems because they
would not have a disparate impact on women. However, some facially
neutral cosmetologist laws that have replaced laws explicitly limiting

the sex of the professional or the customers, may indeed have a disparate impact on women. The discriminatory impact results from the traditional and continuing pattern of sex segregation of patrons. Cosmetologists, the majority of whom are women, are more highly trained and have a wider range of skills than barbers; yet this social pattern prompts men who would patronize them to go to barbers instead, thus benefiting the predominantly male profession of barbers. Neutral statutes alone may not solve this problem. Joint licensure or consolidation of the two professions may be necessary to overcome the pattern.

Policy Recommendations

Sound policy reasons support the revisions in sex-based labor laws required by Title VII and the ERA. As Congress itself realized in passing the amendment, the ERA provides a mandate to consolidate the changes brought about by Title VII into an intelligent and comprehensive state labor code. Such changes can bring true protections for workers of both sexes who need them and the elimination of restrictions that hamper women's ability to obtain jobs for which they are qualified. The fact that Congress clearly considered the ERA's impact on sex-based labor laws provides strong impetus for adoption of the principles and policies endorsed at the time. Because of its explicit legislative history, the ERA provides an even firmer basis for legislatures and courts to enact and enforce consistent changes along these lines than does Title VII. Both congressional intent and policy considerations thus lead to the same conclusion: meal, rest, and minimum wage requirements should be extended to all workers.

Comprehensive reform of state labor laws requires more than the repeal or neutralization of existing laws, however; it should include the formulation of provisions governing terms and conditions of employment that meet the needs of some workers without imposing rigid rules on all of them. This can be done either by the legislature or by a commission with the power to hold public hearings and issue regulations. Wherever the drafting occurs, careful consideration should be given to the enactment of provisions permitting voluntary overtime, protecting a worker from job tasks disproportionate to his or her strength or requiring mechanical aids in heavy lifting, permitting refusal of night work for good cause, including child care responsibilities, requiring seats in certain jobs, and mandating rest and meal periods, to name a few.

Whether the promulgation of the substantive standards is done by the legislature or an agency, enforcement of the laws must be improved so that workers in fact obtain the rights to which they are en-

titled. Enforcement should not be left to employers and male-dominated unions. Meaningful penalties should accompany sex neutralization of the laws, as well as the right of both the aggrieved employees
and the state agency to pursue enforcement. An aggressive division
within the state labor department would be an appropriate body to perform the enforcement function and to investigate conditions and formulate functional statutes or regulations to replace currently sex-based
laws. Because a smaller percentage of women workers are unionized
and because women work in the lowest paid jobs with the least favorable terms and conditions of employment, state law probably will continue to play a much larger role for women workers than for their
male counterparts. It is therefore appropriate that the division in
charge of enforcing laws in this area consist of persons concerned
and knowledgeable about the disadvantaged position of women workers.

The related question of sex discrimination in the statutory regulation of certain professions should also be addressed in the fashion
noted above. States may want to consider one licensing procedure
for the combined professions. If two professions are retained, it
should be made clear that with either license an operator may perform many of the same activities on customers of either sex.

State Reform Efforts

As discussed above, the bulk of the legislative activity concerning labor laws for women has been a result of action under Title VII
and state fair employment practices laws. The ERA has been an additional factor in states reviewing their labor laws as part of compliance with a state equal rights provision, such as Maryland and
Washington. Other states that have looked comprehensively at their
sex-based labor statutes include Connecticut, Kentucky, Massachusetts, Michigan, Nevada, and North Dakota. Most other states have
eliminated the restrictive laws invalidated by Title VII but have not
done any comprehensive review of their laws. Regardless of whether
these labor laws have been theoretically invalidated by Title VII or
effectively invalidated by court action, states must make a comprehensive effort to conform their laws to the Title VII equality principle.
Sex-discriminatory laws must not be retained on the books because,
if unchallenged, they can be tacitly enforced, and even if challenged
successfully, jurisdictional limitations of Title VII may still permit
them to be selectively enforced. A review of state legislative repeals
and efforts to amend state exclusionary, restrictive, and beneficial
labor laws follows.

Most of the exclusionary laws concerning women, which prohibited
them from working in or around mines, in establishments that serve

alcohol, or "in dangerous or unhealthy" professions have been repealed in recent years. Ten states have repealed rules against women working or supervising work in a mine or quarry. Five states
have repealed prohibitions of women serving alcoholic beverages,
and three states have repealed five other miscellaneous prohibitions.[24]
In addition, a Pennsylvania statute excluding women from boxing and
wrestling was declared unconstitutional under the state ERA by the
state attorney general.[25] At least 12 states have replaced laws setting different minimum ages for the employment of boys and girls or
barring girls under a certain age from employment with provisions
fixing a uniform minimum age for the employment of all persons.[26]
Five states have eliminated the ban on cosmetologists serving men.[27]

Maximum hours laws were the most common sex-based protective labor laws. Of such laws in effect in 1969, 39 of 42 applied only
to women.[28] As noted above, in the last five years, 17 of these laws
have been repealed. Prohibitions against night work for women have
been repealed in four states. Three states* have exempted employees
from coverage of the maximum hours law if they receive premium
pay for overtime under the Fair Labor Standards Act. Four states†
have amended their laws to provide voluntary overtime for women.
Washington's new sex-neutral regulations do not prohibit mandatory
overtime but do permit an employee to appeal to the department if he
or she objects to employer overtime rules.[29] New Hampshire has
solved the night-work problem in an innovative way. Persons refusing to work the third shift for good cause, which includes child care
responsibilities, are eligible to receive unemployment compensation.[30]
Several states also have repealed outdated limitations on the hours
during which female minors can work.[31]

Weight-lifting laws, the other common form of restrictive law,
have been repealed in nine states.[32] Four state laws prohibiting employment for a certain period before and after childbirth have been
repealed recently.[33] A new Consolidated Work Order in Oregon prohibits requiring any employee to lift "excessive weights."[34] The
Washington weight-lifting rule states that lifting requirements must
be made known to prospective employees and that proper instructions
on lifting techniques must be provided.[35]

With regard to benefit laws, almost all minimum wage laws
have been amended to include men as well as women (see p. 217).
Seating, rest, and mealtime requirements in ten states have been ex-

---

*North Carolina (1967), Tennessee (1969), and Virginia (1966).
†New Hampshire (1967), New Mexico (1969), Texas (1971), and
Utah (1973). The Texas law has been invalidated by Title VII. All
of these laws are sex based.

tended to workers of both sexes. The Washington regulations, which are typical, give workers a thirty-minute lunch break no less than two hours nor more than five hours after the beginning of the shift. All workers receive rest breaks of at least ten minutes for each four hours of shift, and no employee is required to work more than three hours without such a break.[36] In a number of other states these laws have been repealed.[37] Although in some instances women workers will continue to receive these benefits as a result of labor contracts, it is far preferable to extend the benefits to men by law, so that unorganized workers also have safeguards, then to permit the labor department to make warranted exemptions.

Several states have sex neutralized miscellaneous regulations. Maryland has amended a health regulation stating that female employees who work where food is being prepared for canning must wear clean aprons or dresses to require that all employees engaged in such work wear clean apparel.[38] An Iowa statute requiring women working in contact with food to wear hairnets and men to wear caps has been retained as a sex-neutral requirement that employees shall use effective hair restraints to prevent the contamination of food.[39] In Washington, employers who require their workers to wear uniforms or specific styles and colors of clothing must provide the required apparel and adequate storage for clothing worn to and from work.[40]

PUBLIC EMPLOYMENT

Background

States are required by federal[41] and often by state civil rights laws to provide equal opportunity in public employment to both sexes. However, while some of the more blatant forms of sex discrimination are being eliminated, the status of women in state employment remains abysmally low.[42] While a proportionately higher percentage of government jobs than private sector jobs are held by women, most women in the public sector continue to occupy the lowest job rungs.[43] Many states still use sex-differentiated job titles,[44] thus communicating sex stereotypes to supervisors and prospective employees alike. In other states, while statutory job titles have been neutralized, discriminatory administrative policies exclude women from many jobs and prevent equal treatment on the jobs they have.[45] In still other states, the law is neutral on its face, but bias in personnel decisions limits women's ability to move up to better jobs. In addition, women suffer as relative latecomers to a "last-hired, first-fired" system and face difficulties in meeting rigid job progression requirements.

Discrimination has been particularly egregious in jobs requiring certain physical aptitudes and abilities, such as law enforcement and various types of skilled and unskilled labor positions.* While women have at times been totally excluded from such job categories, discrimination also takes the form of stringent physical tests and height and weight limits unrelated to job performance, which screen out otherwise capable female applicants.

Veterans Preference Programs

In addition to statutes and policies explicitly restricting the job opportunities of women in public employment, veterans preference programs in most states have resulted indirectly in a constriction of job opportunities for women. These programs generally are implemented by awarding veterans an automatic bonus on state civil service examinations, thus boosting them ahead of other equally or more qualified candidates. In at least two states (Minnesota and New Jersey), there is an absolute preference for a veteran over any other candidate. Massachusett's system of absolute preference for veterans was recently held by a three-judge federal court to violate women's equal protection rights under the Fourteenth Amendment.[47]

The number of women who are veterans and can take advantage of these preference programs is extremely small. This is due in large part to sex discrimination in the military, which derives from the explicit statutory exclusion of women from certain jobs and a wholly sex-segregated system of enlistment and promotion.[48] As a result, women as a class bear the brunt of the varied policies that treat veterans preferentially in the civil service system.

Public Employee Pensions

Pensions are another major area in which sex discrimination in public employment occurs. Public employees commonly receive pensions as a fringe benefit. The source of sex discrimination in this area is the assumption that the employees are men and their surviving beneficiaries are dependent women. Frequently, statutory language refers to the employee as "he" and the surviving beneficiary as

---

*There have been numerous Title VII lawsuits against police departments, and rules barring women have been struck down in several. In addition, a lawsuit recently was filed against the federal Law Enforcement Assistance Administration for failure to act against several city and state police departments that receive agency funds and allegedly discriminate against women in their employment policies.[46]

"his widow." In addition, many statutes have procedural provisions
that require a woman's spouse to prove actual dependency in order
to qualify for a pension based on her employment but conclusively
presume that a man's spouse is dependent and therefore eligible for
pension benefits.[49] This extra procedural burden undercuts the value
of a working woman's contribution to her family in the form of income-
replacing fringe benefits.

This sex role stereotyping is aggravated by the use of sex-based
rating tables in calculating benefits.* Under an annuity model, a woman pensioner often receives lower periodic payments than a similarly situated man or has been required to make larger monthly contributions while working on the theory that the payout period will be
longer, on the average, for a woman. Male retirees suffer a greater
reduction in current benefits than women when they elect a "survivor's
option" because of the addition of a female life expectancy. This tends
to discourage male employees from electing such an option, thereby
leaving many women survivors without adequate income when their
husbands die. In recent challenges to differential pension benefits,
courts consistently have struck down sex-based differentials in contributions and payout rates as prohibited sex discrimination under both
Title VII and the Fourteenth Amendment.[50]

In addition, some public employee retirement plans set different
ages at which men and women may retire with full pension benefits
or at which retirement is mandatory. In contrast to the annuity-based
plans, which assume a longer lifespan for women workers, these programs generally discriminate by allowing women to retire earlier with
full benefits and by setting lower mandatory retirement ages for women. The first practice is unfair to men, while the second unfairly
banishes women from the labor market at an earlier age than men.
EEOC guidelines prohibit pension or retirement plans that establish
different optional or compulsory retirement ages based on sex, or
which differentiate in benefits on the basis of sex.[51] Recent court
decisions have found that retirement plans that favor one sex by calculating eligibility for full benefits on the basis of earlier retirement
or shorter length of service violate Title VII.[52]

Impact of the ERA

Explicit Discrimination

The ERA requires the sex neutralization of all public job classifications and other status references that specifically designate or ex-

---

*Rules that set a different periodic payment for men and women
under state pension or annuity plans generally are not found in statutes but in implementing regulations.

clude one sex. It also requires the elimination or amendment of all
regulations or policies that prefer one sex over the other at any stage
of the employment process, including recruitment, hiring, assignments, training, promotions, salary, benefits, and all other conditions of employment. While public employees presently have a cause
of action for job-related sex discrimination under federal civil rights
statutes, the ERA provides a stricter standard for the review of their
claims.

Under the ERA, both the substantive and procedural sex bias in
public employee pension programs must be eliminated. Sex neutralization of statutory references to employees and their beneficiaries
is required. In addition, permitting members of one sex to qualify
presumptively for a benefit while requiring others to prove dependency
in order to qualify is a direct violation of the equality standard. Such
procedural shortcuts must be either eliminated or applied to both sexes
equally. Sex-based rating tables and payment calculations must be
replaced under the ERA with a sex-neutral system assigning risk
classes on non-sex-based lines or making no distinctions in payout
based on personal characteristics of the recipients. (For a discussion of the theoretical principles that compel this result and related
legal developments, see the section on insurance in Chapter 8.)

Neutral Rules

Neutral rules, such as tests and physical requirements that exclude a large percentage of women from certain job classifications,
are subject to strict scrutiny under the ERA because of their disparate impact on applicants of one sex. Unless the state could prove a
close and necessary relationship between the test and successful job
performance, such requirements would have to be eliminated or revised to meet that standard. Thus, for example, height and weight
requirements that traditionaly have been a bar to women applicants
for law enforcement jobs would have to be reviewed and in many cases
revised under an equality principle.

While veterans preference programs clearly have a disparate
impact on women in public employment, the discrimination is of an
indirect rather than explicit nature. They are another form of neutral rule that requires strict scrutiny under the ERA. Not only do
they have a severely adverse impact on the employment of women but
also they serve to perpetuate prior and continuing sex discrimination
in the armed forces. Although the goals of these programs—to ease
reentry into civilian life and reward the veteran for his service—are
valid and possibly even compelling ones, there are other methods for
achieving them that impact women less heavily. Implementation of
the equality principle will entail a careful reconsideration of these pro-

grams, with an eye to developing alternative policies to mitigate their effect on women.

Policy Recommendations

Opening up all job classifications in the public sector to both men and women, eliminating discriminatory policies in the terms and conditions of these jobs, and carefully reforming neutral rules that have a severely disparate impact on women—all of which will occur through implementation of the equal rights principle—will go a long way toward alleviating the sex-linked barriers women traditionally have faced in public employment. The simple elimination of overt barriers, however, will not be adequate in itself to remedy long-standing patterns of discrimination. States also must be prepared to enact and implement legislation aimed at overcoming the effects of past practices.* To realize equal employment opportunity, this legislation should focus on programs to encourage the recruitment, hiring, training, and upgrading of women employees.

An important component of this effort is the development of more flexible work hours or the reorganization of some job slots into part-time positions, enabling workers with family commitments to compete for public jobs.

Veterans Preference

There clearly are valid public policy reasons for the enactment of special legislation to benefit veterans seeking employment in the public sector. The traditional barriers to women's full participation in the military, with its attendant vocational and financial benefits, as well as general discrimination in public employment, however, create a conflict between veterans preference laws and statutes aimed at removing roadblocks to employment opportunity for women. Thus, it is critical that government support for veterans be designed so that it is least likely to hamper women's opportunities. Government programs that are not job-specific but provide financial assistance to veterans for education or housing, for example, can help ease their transition into civilian life and improve their economic situation without posing any direct threat to women seeking public employment. To the extent that job-specific preferences are retained, they should be limited.

---

*The principle of affirmative action is to institute positive, concrete procedures that will both identify and correct employment practices that perpetuate patterns of discrimination and compensate for the damage they have done in the past. [53]

The most common form of job-related preference is a bonus point system. If a state chooses to use such a system, bonus points for veterans' examination scores should not exceed three to five points. Any larger bonus may simply have the effect of an absolute preference because of the relatively close range of scoring on many civil service tests.[54] In addition, bonus points should be limited to the initial re-entry job or to a definite period after service, perhaps up to three years excluding full-time school, so that the bonus can ease transition without carrying an indefinite and thus unfair preference. Other alternatives include limiting the bonus points to those job classifications for which the veteran has received in-service training or experience or applying service time to a veteran's seniority rating, rather than boosting his entry score.* By adopting one of these less extreme but still effective means of supporting veterans' reentry into the job market, a state can avoid the nearly complete bar of women from civil service competition that is occurring in some localities.[55]

Public Employee Pensions

As noted above, the ERA requires that the state apply the same policies to male and female workers and their survivors in the area of pension benefits. The remaining question is what that policy should be, particularly in relation to survivor's benefits. The wiser course, and the one most in keeping with the legislative intent of Congress, is simply to eliminate all requirements for proof of dependency for surviving spouses, allowing an automatic assignment of benefits whenever survivorship rights arise.[56] The primary reason for this approach is that pension benefits are properly seen as part of a worker's compensation. A rule that denies survivor's benefits merely because the surviving spouse earns as much or more than the deceased worker implies that the full value of a worker's wages depends in part on whether he or she is the primary or secondary wage earner rather than on the quantity or quality of his or her work. Since women are more likely than men to be secondary earners, such a rule overwhelm-

---

*Another alternative that has been proposed in a number of states is the extension of veterans preference to spouses, which has the advantage of increasing women's governmental employment opportunities. The disadvantage is that the choice of which women are given the increased opportunities is somewhat arbitrary in that it is based not on a woman's individual capacities or service but on that of her spouse. However, since spouses of service personnel also have sacrificed for their country in most cases—for example, by enduring extended separations from their spouses—the benefit is not wholly irrational.

ingly discounts the financial contribution of women to their families
and discriminates against two-earner families. In addition, granting
survivor's benefits to all spouses without proof of individual need will
eliminate the administrative costs associated with determinations of
eligibility.

State Reform Efforts

A number of states have taken steps to sex neutralize statutory
references to public employees and officials, often as part of omnibus
bills aimed at sex neutralizing state codes as a whole. Iowa, for example, has enacted an omnibus bill eliminating gender references in
statutes concerning rights and obligations of public employees, particularly military personnel and public officials.[57] References to military and law enforcement personnel also have been sex neutralized in
Arizona,[58] Connecticut,[59] Kentucky,[60] New York,[61] Virginia,[62] and
Washington.[63] Similarly, Indiana,[64] Kentucky,[65] and Virginia[66]
have sex neutralized references to public positions involving highways,
agriculture, mines, and general engineering and maintenance once
limited to men.

Some states have gone beyond changes in statutory terminology
to enact innovative affirmative legislation. California, for example,
now requires all state agencies to submit affirmative action programs
to the Fair Employment Practices Commission and requires each
state agency, department, office, and commission to publish annual
employment statistics.[67] The State Personnel Board, which administers the state civil service system, has been empowered to develop
guidelines for offsite training for state employees.[68]

Other states have taken similar steps. Connecticut now requires
state agencies and departments to develop affirmative action plans
for their units; these efforts are overseen by the Commission on Human Rights and Opportunities.[69] Hawaii has adopted a resolution requesting the governor to establish a statewide affirmative action plan
for state employees.[70] Maryland has passed a law providing that sex
cannot be a qualification for state employment competitive examinations nor a basis for job discrimination.[71]

In response to an extensive study on the status of women in state
employment[72] and pressure to implement the principle of the ERA,
the Ohio State Highway Patrol and the Ohio National Guard have re-
examined their recruiting and selection processes and have begun to
change them in order to encourage women's participation.[73] The
California legislature has passed a bill mandating the California Highway Patrol to study the feasibility of employing women through the use
of an experimental training program.[74]

Reform legislation recognizing the special employment needs
of workers with family responsibilities has been enacted in Illinois
and Maryland. The Illinois act authorizes the director of state personnel to designate up to 10 percent of the jobs in any state agency
under the governor's control as "flexible hours" or part-time positions.[75] The Maryland laws explicitly encourage a policy of part-
time employment and provide for it in the state merit system,[76] and,
within limits, prohibit the denial of promotional opportunities to state
employees because they are currently on sick or maternity leave.[77]
California has passed a special provision forbidding school districts
to refuse to hire, employ, or train pregnant employees or discriminate against them in the terms or conditions of employment. The
enactment also states that a temporarily disabled employee shall not
be terminated under an employment policy providing insufficient or
no leave if such a policy has a disparate impact on employees of one
sex and is not justified by necessity of the public schools.[78]

Veterans Preference Programs

A few states with veterans preference programs have taken
legislative steps to minimize their adverse impact on women in public employment. In Washington, a preference is now available to both
veterans and their spouses, with no condition of survivorship; formerly, only widows were entitled to benefits.[79] California[80] and
Minnesota[81] now extend preference to widows of veterans but still
exclude widowers and all spouses during the veteran's lifetime. As
noted earlier, an absolute preference system in Massachusetts was
held to be a violation of the Fourteenth Amendment by a federal district court in 1976.[82] Since that time, the Massachusetts Attorney
General's Office has been considering new legislation to comply with
the court's ruling.

Public Employee Pensions

Sex neutralization of statutory terminology has been the most
common reform adopted to correct sex discrimination in the area of
public employee pensions. Broad terminological changes have been
enacted in Maryland, [83] Arizona, [84] Kentucky, [85] Iowa, [86] New Mexico, [87] Washington, [88] and to a lesser extent in Virginia, [89] Connecticut,
Hawaii, [91] and the District of Columbia. [92] In the area of dependency,
most states that automatically gave the widow benefits but required
proof of dependency from the widower have eliminated that requirement, expanding the group of people entitled to public employee pensions. Such changes were made in Illinois, [93] Washington, [94] and
Kentucky. [95] States that traditionally required both widows and widow-

ers to prove dependency but applied a more stringent standard to
widowers generally have chosen to apply the more lenient widow's
test to surviving spouses of both sexes. For example, the Minnesota
Teacher's Retirement Act was amended in 1974 to eliminate the requirement that, in order to receive benefits, a widower must be either
65 and dependent upon the teacher for more than half of his support
or totally and permanently disabled. The revised act requires only
that a widow or widower had been living with and dependent upon the
teacher at the time of the teacher's death and did not remarry since.[96]
In states that previously excluded widowers from benefits entirely,
benefits generally have been extended to them on the same basis as
they are paid to widows. For example, the class of persons eligible
to receive the pension of a resident of the Iowa soldiers' home was
expanded from dependent wives and children to dependent spouses
and children. (The standards for admission to the home differ from
the pension provision. Formerly, the widow of a veteran could enter
the home if the veteran would have been eligible during his lifetime.
Now, any surviving spouse is eligible if the veteran would have been.)[97]

    Connecticut has solved the problem of unequal benefits by equal-
izing the retirement benefits and retirement age for men and women.
Formerly, women could retire with full benefits five years earlier
than men.[98]

UNEMPLOYMENT COMPENSATION

Background

    Unemployment compensation laws, which exist in all the states,
provide state-run plans to compensate individuals for wage loss during periods of involuntary unemployment. Generally, as a prerequi-
site to obtaining benefits, an individual must have worked a certain
number of weeks in the previous quarter and earned a certain minimum
amount, must make a claim for benefits, register at an employment
office, be able to work, and be available for and actively seeking suitable work.[99] Unemployment insurance laws treat the various reasons
for leaving work differently, depending on the cause, its motivation,
and whether the worker intends to return to the work force in the immediate future. The most favored category is "good cause," which
encompasses those reasons for leaving a job that do not disqualify
the worker from receiving unemployment compensation. In 28 states,
good cause is limited to work-related reasons only, such as a layoff

or unsafe working conditions.* Other jurisdictions define good cause
to include personal circumstances necessitating leave from employment as well. Generally, those reasons for leaving work that do not
fit into a jurisdiction's definition of good cause are classified as disqualifying "voluntary leaves" for which the worker is held to some
standard of reeligibility before unemployment benefits are available.†

Several features of the unemployment compensation laws discriminate on the basis of sex. The most common are special provisions concerning pregnancy and childbirth. A second set of discriminatory provisions are those that declare workers who leave employment for family-related reasons ineligible for benefits until they have
complied with special reeligibility rules. Third, statutes that provide supplemental benefits for dependents of unemployed workers often are interpreted in such a way that women workers rarely receive
them. Finally, domestic work and employment by a family member
are routinely excluded from coverage under unemployment compensation laws.

Pregnancy and Maternity

Special disqualifications concerning pregnancy include automatic
disqualification for a certain time before and/or after childbirth, regardless of the claimant's ability to work, availability for work, or
reason for unemployment;‡ disqualification when unemployment is "due

---

*States that restrict good cause for leaving work to reasons con-
nected to or attributable to the employer are: Alabama, Arizona, Arkansas, Colorado, Connecticut, Delaware, Florida, Georgia, Indiana,
Iowa, Louisiana, Maine, Massachusetts, Michigan, Minnesota, Mississippi, Missouri, Montana, New Hampshire (by regulation), New
Jersey, New Mexico, North Carolina, Oklahoma, Tennessee, Texas,
Vermont, West Virginia, and Wisconsin.

†"Voluntary leaving" may be work-related, such as provoking
one's discharge by repeatedly arriving late for work without good
cause, or personal in nature, such as leaving work to return to school.
In a few states, as a result of so-called protective labor laws, what
may be good cause for a woman worker to leave or refuse work is
considered voluntary leaving for a man. The most common of these
is the refusal of night work.[100]

‡The jurisdictions with time limits are Colorado, District of
Columbia, Kansas, Montana, New Jersey, Rhode Island, and Texas.
The time limits range from 30 days to four months before childbirth
and from 30 days to two months after. In some instances, the time
limit operates as a presumption of disability that an individual can re-

to" or "because of" preganancy;* disqualification from the time of
leaving work until the claimant has worked a certain amount of time
or earned a certain amount of money after the child is born;[†] disqualification following childbirth until the claimant presents proof of
ability to work not required of other temporarily disabled workers;[‡]
and disqualification for several weeks following the end of a pregnancy-related disability to give the employer time to rehire the
claimant, a disqualification not imposed on other temporarily disabled
workers (see Table 6.2).** These special rules derive from several
assumptions: that it is reasonable for an employer to fire a woman
because she is pregnant, that a pregnant woman's attachment to the
labor force must be tested by more stringent standards than that of
other workers, and that all pregnancies and deliveries are disabling
for several weeks or months before or after birth.

In Turner v. Dep't of Employment Security,[103] the United
States Supreme Court held that Utah's automatic denial of benefits to
a pregnant claimant for 12 weeks before the expected date of childbirth and 6 weeks after childbirth violated the due process clause of
the Fourteenth Amendment because it established an irrebuttable presumption concerning her availability for work. This reasoning clearly
would apply to any other irrebuttable time limit or reemployment qualification imposed only on pregnant unemployment claimants. Statutory

---

but rather than an absolute rule. See Table 6.2 for citations to the
laws and a more detailed explanation of provisions.

*See, for example, the law of Nevada in Table 6.2. Section
612.440(2) can be interpreted to cover both voluntary separations during pregnancy and employer-mandated separations within 60 days prior
to childbirth.[101]

[†]See the laws of Colorado, Indiana, Minnesota, and West Virginia in Table 6.2. The laws of Colorado and West Virginia can be
interpreted to cover the situations described in the above note and also
separations for some other reason occurring during pregnancy. The
Indiana and Minnesota provisions explicitly apply only to voluntary departures from employment.

In some states, this provision is not applicable if the claimant
applied for or accepted a leave of absence. See the laws of Indiana
and Minnesota in Table 6.2. Compare the laws of Arkansas and Louisiana, which do not have the post-leave work requirement but do provide that leave due to pregnancy is not disqualifying if the woman has
taken a leave of absence.

[‡]See the laws of Delaware, Maryland, Nevada, Ohio, and West
Virginia. Although there could be an equivalent requirement imposed
on other temporarily disabled workers, there is no evidence of one
in the regulations or case law of these five states.[102]

**Alabama (3 weeks) and Tennessee (21 days).

TABLE 6.2

State Unemployment Insurance Laws' Special Provisions Relating to Pregnancy

State	Statute and Legislative History	Current Provision	Former Provision (if relevant)
Alabama	Ala. Code tit. 26, § 214(B)(1) (1958)	If leave of absence due to pregnancy extends beyond tenth week after pregnancy, benefits may not be denied if claimant gave three weeks' notice of desire to return, is able to work, and has not refused reinstatement to a suitable job.	
Arkansas	Ark. Stat. Ann. § 81-1106(a) (1960)	Not disqualified if separated voluntarily due to pregnancy, obtains leave of absence, and applies for but does not receive reinstatement.	Disqualified from date of separation until she has obtained 30 days' paid work; not applicable if she obtains leave of absence and applies for but does not receive reinstatement after leave.
Colorado	Colo. Rev. Stat. § 82-4-8(7)(a), (1)(c), (d) (1963)	Prior to childbirth: if leaving is voluntary, disqualified until termination of pregnancy; if involuntary, not disqualified until 30 days before birth, unless by reasonable rule of employer. After childbirth: disqualified until she has had 13 weeks' work; if sole support of child or invalid husband, eligible 30 days after.	
Delaware	Del. Code Ann. tit. 19, § 3315(8) (1975), as amended by 58 Del Laws, ch. 518 (1972)	Disqualified for any week she is unable to work or is unavailable for work because of pregnancy; doctor's certificate required to establish availability after childbirth.	

District of Columbia	D.C. Code Ann. § 46-310(h) (1967)	Disqualified six weeks before and six weeks after birth.	
Indiana	Ind. Ann. Stat. § 22-4-15-2 (1974), as amended by Acts 1974, No. 110, § 4	Disqualified from time of separation until she works ten weeks with a weekly salary at least equal to the weekly benefit amount—but only if she fails to apply for or accept leave under employer's plan.	Qualification in last clause added in 1974.
Iowa	Iowa Code Ann. § 96.5(1)(d) (1972), as amended by Acts 1975, ch. 92, §§ 5-11	Pregnancy treated like any other illness or disability: not disqualified from unemployment if she has a doctor's certificate of ability to work and if she makes herself available to the employer.	
Kansas	Kan. Stat. Ann. § 44-705(c) (1973)	Unavailable for work 90 days before and 30 days after birth.	
Louisiana	La. Rev. Stat. Ann. § 23:1601(b) (1964), as amended by Acts 1974, No. 394, § 1	An otherwise eligible claimant who on account of pregnancy has been required to leave her employment because of employer policy or doctor's advice is not disqualified if application has been made for a leave of absence, if such is available.	Disqualified 12 weeks before and 6 weeks after birth.
Maryland	Md. Ann. Code art. 95A, § 6(f) (1957), as amended by L. 1973, ch. 652	Disqualified while disabled due to pregnancy but eligible during pregnancy if able to work as certified by physician.	Disqualified for the four months before to two months after; doctor's certificate may be required to establish dates; eligible in first five months if able to work.
Minnesota	Minn. Stat. Ann. § 268.09(2) (1959), as amended by L. 1973, ch. 599	Disqualified from date of separation until she has had six weeks' insured work only if she fails to take advantage of maternity leave rights provided by law.	Last clause added in 1973.

(continued)

237

TABLE 6.2 (continued)

State	Statute and Legislative History	Current Provision	Former Provision (if relevant)
Montana	Mont. Rev. Codes Ann. § 87-106(h) (1947)	Disqualified if she leaves her job due to pregnancy; ineligible for two months before and after childbirth unless she presents medical evidence of ability to work at her most recent employment.	
Nevada	Nev. Rev. Stat. § 612.435, 612.440 (1), (2) (1973), as amended by L. 1973, at 1361-62, § 14	Disqualified for benefits when unemployed due to pregnancy and from week of separation unless proof of ability to work is submitted.	Unemployment deemed to be due to pregnancy if within 60 days of expected confinement.
New Jersey	N.J. Stat. Ann. § 43:21-4(c) (1) (1962)	Unavailable for work four weeks before and four weeks after childbirth (but eligible for disability benefits instead).	
Ohio	Ohio Rev. Code Ann. § 4141.29(D)(2)(c), (G) (1969)	Disqualified from date of separation until medical evidence of ability to work and work with former employer no longer available (if she has moved so that return with former employer is unreasonable because of distance, her disqualification lasts until she has earned the lesser of one-half her average weekly wage or $60).	
Oregon	Ore. Rev. Stat. § 657.155(2) (1969) (1974 Repl. vol.); former § 657.160 repealed by L. 1973, ch. 398, § 3	Presumed unable to work if unemployed because of a disability, including pregnancy, until administrator determines she is able to work.	Presumed unable to work if unemployed "due to" pregnancy until administrator determines she is able to work.

State	Citation	Provision
Rhode Island	By regulation	Rebuttable presumption of inability to work from four months before to six weeks after child-birth.
South Dakota	S.D. Comp. Laws Ann. § 61-6-3 (1967), as amended by L. 1974, ch. 329	Person separated from employment due to temporary disability, including pregnancy, is eligible when "able to work and available for work." Disqualified from voluntary leaving until 30 days after confinement or from involuntary dismissal due to pregnancy within 60 days before until 30 days after.
Tennessee	Tenn. Code Ann. § 50-1324A (1955) (1966 Repl. Vol.)	Disqualified from date of separation until 21 days after she is able to work.
Texas	By policy, subsequently upheld by judicial decision (Vick v. TEC, U.S. App., 5th Cir., June 12, 1975)	Unavailable for work from date of separation (three months if laid off) until six weeks after childbirth.
Utah	Utah Code Ann. § 35-4-5(h) (1974) Invalidated by the U.S. Supreme Court, Nov. 16, 1975.	Disqualification for 12 weeks before and 6 weeks after childbirth and for any other week of unemployment due to pregnancy.
West Virginia	W.Va. Code Ann. § 21A-6-3(7)(a) (1970)	Disqualified from time of separation until she has worked 30 days in covered employment; with medical evidence of ability to work, no more than six weeks after childbirth if voluntarily left and no more than six weeks before and after birth if laid off.

Source: Adapted from a chart by Margaret Dahm, in U.S. Department of Labor, Benefit Series Service—Unemployment Insurance, Rep. No. 304 (September 1975, International Women's Year Special Supplement).

unemployment compensation provisions concerning pregnancy also
have been found unconstitutional on Fourteenth Amendment grounds
by state courts in Iowa, Maryland, Michigan, Washington, and Wisconsin[104] and by federal courts in Connecticut, Maryland, Michigan,
and Ohio.[105] And in the wake of Turner, the attorney general of
Tennessee has issued an official opinion declaring that state's pregnancy provision unconstitutional.[106]

An interesting case recently was decided in California that
unites the issues of unfair treatment of pregnant workers, eligibility
for unemployment benefits, and the general existence of sex discrimination in the workplace. In Prescod v. Calif. Unemployment Insurance Appl Bd.,[107] a California Court of Appeals found that a woman
had good cause, for unemployment compensation purposes, when she
left her job on the grounds of sex discrimination. Her employer initially had refused to reinstate her after a maternity leave and subsequently denied her promotion opportunities.

Marital and Domestic Obligations: "Voluntary Leaving"

A common form of discrimination in the definition of "good
cause" or "voluntary leaving" is the disfavoring of leaves necessitated
by changes in marital or domestic circumstances, such as marriage,
moving with a spouse to a new residence, or a temporary need to care
for a sick relative. Under present social patterns, women are more
likely than men to leave work for domestic reasons. There are 15
states* that have special provisions governing the eligibility for unemployment compensation of persons who leave work for such reasons.
In only one of these states, Arkansas, have leaves compelled by marital or domestic obligations been statutorily recognized as good cause,
and that provision is limited to circumstances in which a worker follows a spouse to a new location.[108] However, in one other state,
California, the law defining domestic reasons for leaving as good
cause only if the worker is the sole or major support of his or her
family was invalidated by the supreme court. This provision was
held to be unconstitutional sex discrimination because, although neutral on its face, it has a severely disparate impact on women.[109]
In fact, the court noted that 99 percent of the persons disqualified under this provision in 1971 were women. The court held that the state
had shown no compelling interest supporting the treatment of domestic reasons less favorably than other non-job-related good causes for

---

*Arkansas, California, Colorado, Idaho, Kansas, Kentucky,
Mississippi, Nevada, New York, Ohio, Oklahoma, Oregon, Pennsylvania, Utah, and West Virginia.

leaving and noted that the normal requirement that a person be able
and available for work in order to collect unemployment compensation
would effectively prevent undeserved payment to women occupied with
family care. (The court applied the strict scrutiny test because the
statute, in addition to creating a sex classification, impinged on constitutionally protected decision making concerning family and repro-
duction.)

In the rest of the jurisdictions, domestic causes of absence
from the labor market are not held to be good cause and thus disqualify the worker from receiving benefits for some specified period of
time. Of the 14 states that explicitly penalize domestic reasons for
leaving work, four treat such reasons less stringently than other voluntary leaves,[110] two treat them more stringently,[111] five treat
them equally,[112] and the remaining four treat them differently from
other voluntary leaves, with the comparative stringency depending on
the particular facts of the case.[113]

Dependency Benefits

The definition of dependency for purposes of supplemental dependency payments raises another issue of sex-based disrcimination
in unemployment laws. Eleven states provide extra payment or raise
the maximum weekly benefit ceiling for persons with dependents.[114]
A dependent generally is defined in these laws to include a child under 16 or 18 or an older child with a physical or mental incapacity
preventing wage earning. Connecticut also specifically includes a
nonworking spouse as a dependent.

Two types of discrimination arise in the definition and determination of dependency. First, most states require that the claimant
provide at least half of the support of a dependent or at least half of
the family income in order to qualify for an allowance.[115] Women
are more likely to provide less than half of their children's or family's
support than men because of their lower average earnings.[116] Second,
some states interpret even a sex-neutral dependency standard with
a presumption that the husband is the primary wage earner.[117] As a
result, even in those families in which the wife earns more than the
husband, she may have difficulty claiming supplemental benefits. *

---

*In Rhode Island, a federal district court has invalidated provi-
sions requiring women but not similarly situated men to prove the dependency of their children and to show total support in order to claim
supplemental benefits. The provisions also denied dependency benefits to any woman whose children's father was under a court order to
support them, even if the woman in fact supplied total support.[118]

Domestic Workers and Family Employees

A final issue raised by the unemployment compensation laws
is the impact on women of certain statutory exclusions from coverage.
All the states traditionally have excluded from benefits workers who
are employed by family members and domestic workers. Both of
these categories are composed mainly of women, at least in part because of the history of sex discrimination and sex role stereotyping
in the labor market. While the original reasons for these particular
classes of exclusion are not completely clear, they are consistent
with a general tradition of the denial of government benefits and protections to workers in these areas, including minimum wage, social security, and worker's compensation.

The exclusion of employees of family members probably stems
from the view that such jobs are often simply make-work or structured
to accommodate fluctuating needs peculiar to family members rather
than to respond to external market factors. This view is exacerbated
by the fact that many persons, particularly women, who work in family
run businesses receive no direct salary for their labor and therefore
might not be able to document their claims for benefits.

The exclusion of domestic workers signifies a general disdain
for traditional "woman's work" as well as a practical recognition that
domestic workers often are employed on a daily basis by several employers, so that no one employer may become legally responsible to
document the work history and initiate coverage under such protective
systems as unemployment compensation. Several states now cover
domestic work if the employer pays more than a certain amount per
quarter or per year.[119] With the extension of the federal minimum
wage and social security law to this work, unemployment compensation also may expand to cover it in the near future.*

Impact of the ERA

Explicit Discrimination

Under the equal rights amendment, statutes concerning pregnancy and childbirth are subject to strict scrutiny to assure that the

---

*Private household workers were brought under the Federal Fair
Labor Standards Act by the 1974 amendments to that legislation. Under the amendments, household workers who earn $50 from any em-
ployer in a calendar quarter or who work a total of at least eight hours
a week in one or more households are covered by the minimum wage
standards.[120]

legislation is closely related to a compelling state interest in the unique aspects of these physical conditions and that the uniqueness rubric is not being used to shield sex discrimination. In most legislative contexts, pregnancy is of concern because it causes temporary disability or may be the basis of a request for work leave, but it is no different for those purposes than other physical disabilities or reasons for taking a leave. For the purposes of unemployment compensation laws, specifically, which are to provide financial assistance to persons who become unemployed through no fault of their own and to encourage employers to maintain full employment capacity and refrain from firing workers without good cause, a pregnant woman is no different from any person with a temporary disability. From this perspective, the common types of pregnancy rules found in these laws are impermissible.

Most of the disqualifications for marital and domestic reasons are not explicitly sex-based, but their impact on women is disproportionate. This issue is discussed below in the section on neutral rules. However, there may be regulations or policies in some states that explicitly treat men and women differently in determining eligibility for unemployment benefits after leaving work for marital or domestic reasons. Such policies are invalid under the ERA. In Washington, for example, which has a state ERA, the practice of finding good cause for a woman but not a man to leave work in order to follow her or his spouse to a new location recently was overturned by the Washington Supreme Court.[121]

While the major discrimination in dependency requirements involves neutral rules with a disparate impact on women (to be discussed below), some states use sex-based presumptions that male workers are the primary supporters of their wives and children or hold women to a higher standard of proof as to their dependents. Under the ERA, sex-based presumptions or procedural shortcuts for one sex are not allowed.

Neutral Rules

Pregnancy and maternity policies that apply to leaves associated with preparing for a new baby or with child care after birth have a disparate impact on women because they are by tradition the primary caretakers of young children. Under the ERA, a woman or a man who wishes to take time off to prepare for a new baby or to care for a child should be treated at least as favorably, in terms of the stringency of requalification standards once the leave period is over, as a person requesting temporary leave from the labor force for any other personal reason.

Provisions requiring a worker who becomes reavailable for employment after a domestic-related leave to resume bona fide employ-

ment or work for a specified period before requalifying for unemployment benefits have a disparate impact on women. At present, it is
women who are most likely to leave employment temporarily to tend
to a sick child or to follow a spouse who is transferred by his employer or the armed services. Under the ERA, a facially neutral
marital or domestic disqualification challenged because of its disparate impact on women is strictly scrutinized. The issue is whether
there is a strong state interest served by the rule that could not be
carried out by a provision with a less drastic impact on the affected
class.

Provisions for dependency benefits based on whether the unemployed worker's income provides the "major support" or some other
percentage of income of the spouse or children seeking to claim dependency are usually sex neutral on their face. In practice, however,
they fall more heavily on women workers as a class due to their lower
average earnings. Because of their disparate impact on one sex,
percentage-of-income standards are called into question under the
ERA. The burden is on the state to show the necessity for such standards and to prove that alternatives having a less drastic impact on
women workers are not available.

The exclusion of domestic workers and family employees from
unemployment compensation has an obvious and disparate impact on
women, who generally fill the ranks of these two classes of employees. [122] While individual states are, to an extent, free to establish
unemployment coverage according to their own priorities, a choice
to exclude a particular category of employment that creates an extreme hardship on members of one sex is subject to strict scrutiny
under the equal rights principle. The response that it is simply im-
practical to cover domestic workers or family employees because of
their sporadic employment history, the large number of short-term
employers, or the difficulty of documenting the validity of claims for
compensation is not sufficient to justify exclusions that impact women so severely. Under the ERA, administrative inconvenience is not
a sufficient rationale for governmental policies that have an unfair
impact on workers of one sex; some more compelling interest must
be shown to warrant such exclusions.

Policy Recommendations

Pregnancy and Maternity

Apart from the constitutional and other legal impediments to
treating pregnancy differently from other physical conditions that are
disabling or other personal circumstances that prompt leaves from

work, other social considerations support more equitable treatment of pregnancy within state unemployment systems. It is increasingly common for women with children to work: 37 percent of mothers of children under 6 and 54 percent of mothers of children 6 to 17 were in the labor force in 1974.[123] These women should not be penalized by overbroad regulations based on stereotypes about the incompatability of motherhood and employment outside the home. In addition, there is a consensus among doctors that a woman's capacity to work at any time during her pregnancy or after childbirth depends on a variety of factors, including her health and the nature of her job.[124] In any event, no arbitrary time limit is needed since leaves due to pregnancy- and childbirth-related disabilities can be governed by the same rules as other temporary disabilities.

Of course, if a particular woman is physically unable to do any job or is informed by her doctor that she should not continue to work, then she is not available for work as required by law, and she should be ineligible for unemployment compensation for the duration of her disability. However, if a pregnant woman cannot perform her present job because of its physical demands but is willing and able to do lighter work, she should be eligible for compensation on the same basis as other partially disabled workers in that state.[125] For those periods when a pregnant worker is, in fact, disabled and thereby ineligible for unemployment compensation, the state or private employer should provide adequate income replacement through an employee disability insurance program.

Domestic and Marital Obligations

As noted above, each state determines eligibility for unemployment compensation based on whether the reason for leaving work constitutes good cause under that state's unemployment rules and regulations. Currently, a number of states do not recognize domestic or marital obligations as good cause for leaving work, and some place more severe restrictions on reeligibility after such leaves than after other personal leaves. The underlying presumption is no longer valid that marriage, a move to accompany a spouse to a new job, or a leave to care for a member of the family, particularly if a woman is involved, signals an intention to permanently abandon the labor force. A growing number of women, including those with families, are entering the labor force and attempting to build a long-term attachment to it. The existence of sex discrimination in the market hampers this growth, as do state policies such as those discussed here, which simply drive one more wedge between women's reasonable employment goals and the traditional sex roles concerning family obligations.

Those states that do not now recognize any personal reasons for quitting work as good cause should reconsider the policy of accept-

ing only job-related reasons. At least, serious thought should be
given to eliminating strict reeligibility requirements for persons attempting to reenter the job market after a voluntary leave compelled
by severe illness or death in the immediate family or a family relocation.* In those states that currently recognize some necessary personal reasons as good cause, domestic obligations of a compelling
nature should be included in this category by statute. Giving discretion to individual hearing officers may well perpetuate erroneous presumptions about married women's lack of long-term employment
goals.

Whatever the state policy on eligibility after a personal leave,
there is no justification for treating domestic leaves more strictly
than other personal leaves. Since anyone collecting unemployment
compensation must, by definition, be available for and actively seeking work, the state interest in compensating only those who are still
part of the labor market is adequately served by the application of a
uniform eligibility rule to everyone who leaves work voluntarily, without singling out those motivated by marital or domestic reasons for
stricter treatment.†

Dependency Benefits

Under the ERA, if a state offers supplemental dependency benefits to unemployed workers, standards for eligibility must be the same
for both men and women, that is, free of sex-based presumptions.
However, the substance of those neutral standards raises separate
public policy considerations. The issue is whether to eliminate or
extend to men special proof-of-dependency requirements traditionally
applied only to women. Because such requirements, even if sex
neutral, have a disparate impact on women, the wiser solution is to
adopt a presumption of dependency for the spouse and children of
both male and female unemployed workers.

---

*California, Idaho, Nevada, Pennsylvania, and Utah allow persons
who leave work for domestic reasons but who are the sole or major
support of their families to qualify for unemployment compensation.
While such exceptions mitigate the severity of the usual disqualifications particularly for female-headed families, women as a class do
not benefit in proportion to their numbers because of their lower average incomes.

†The Ohio Task Force concluded on the basis of testimony by
Professor Hugh Ross of Case Western Reserve Law School, Cleveland,
Ohio, that Ohio's strict reeligibility provision could be eliminated
without danger of malingering.[126]

As a result of a tradition of sex discrimination in the labor market, women workers are paid less than men even within similar work classifications, and many women are still segregated into lower paying positions. A state that offers supplemental dependency benefits using a "major support," "sole support," or high "percentage of income" formula only widens the current disparity between the average incomes of men and women. In addition, such a policy unfairly discounts the significance of women's contributions to their families' economic security and fails to come to grips with current economic realities. In most families in which both spouses work, the income of both is essential for the maintenance of their standard of living. * Whatever the exact ratio of their separate incomes, they are mutually dependent, and their children are, in turn, dependent on both parents. Therefore, to allow supplemental benefits only when the spouse who earns a majority of the family income becomes unemployed not only impacts women disproportionately but also ignores the financial interdependence of two-earner families.

In addition, since supplemental benefits frequently bear little relationship to the actual costs of supporting a family, states might wish to allow two unemployed wage earners in a family to claim benefits for the same dependents, regardless of the proportion of income each contributes. [128] Alternatively, if duplication of benefits is not acceptable, states might choose to allow supplemental benefits to whichever spouse becomes unemployed first.

Domestic Workers and Family Employees

Apart from serious constitutional questions concerning the continued validity of excluding domestic workers and family employees from unemployment compensation coverage, social considerations also dictate a review of state policy in this area. In 1973, the median income of full-time private household workers was only $2,069 annually. [129] Of these, 98 percent are women, [130] many of whom are forced into this lowest rung of employment because of a history of economic, sexual, and racial oppression that has left them without adequate skills and education for job mobility. [†] Many are heads-of-

---

*The number of husband-wife families in which the wife works has more than doubled since 1952. In 1973, the wife was a wage earner in over 50 percent of these families, with white wives earning close to one-fourth of the family income and black wives earning nearly one-third. [127]

†As of March 1973, over 20 percent of all minority women over age 35 who were wage earners were private household workers. Only

household and the sole support of their families. While these workers
certainly would seem to be both worthy and in need of unemployment
compensation when they are laid off through no fault of their own or
when they attempt to reenter the labor market after a leave to care for
a family member, they traditionally have been disregarded by unemployment and other income replacement programs.

While less is known statistically about family employees, it is
a well-accepted truth that women often work for years as office administrators, bookkeepers, or salespersons in small family-run enterprises without accruing employment-related benefits. Unfortunately, many women work for their spouses and other relatives without remuneration and thus have no accurate documentation of their
work histories. Exclusion from coverage under certain social insurance programs and fringe benefits exacerbates this tendency on the
part of both the public and their employers to view these workers as
volunteers or as persons not truly committed to the labor market.
To the extent that persons who are employed by family members do
so for compensation, their work histories should be documented,
and they should be entitled to income replacement programs, such
as state unemployment insurance, when their jobs run out, so long
as they are willing and able to take other suitable employment.

State Reform Efforts*

Pregnancy and Maternity

Since 1971, at least 30 states have taken legislative action to
remedy the discriminatory treatment of pregnancy in unemployment
insurance programs. Of the 19 states that have repealed special

----

about 6 percent of those under 35 have this occupation, however, because of the rise of educational level and the reduction of discrimination.[131]

*A substantial number of reforms in unemployment compensation
laws have been achieved in the past four years. Some of the impetus
for the change in unemployment compensation programs stems from
activities of the U.S. Department of Labor Manpower Administration.
Beginning in December 1970, the administration encouraged state employment security bureaus to change policies and to request changes
in legislation that discriminates on the basis of sex. Memoranda sent
to all such bureaus advised them of legal developments, identified
specific types of laws as discriminatory, and recommended changes
in each of the areas discussed in this chapter.[132]

pregnancy provisions, 15 originally had included rigid time limits before and/or after birth.[133] Oklahoma has both repealed its previous time limits and enacted an affirmative provision stating that, "Nothing in this act shall prohibit pregnant women, who otherwise qualify for benefits under this title, from receiving said benefits for the full number of weeks to which they are entitled."[134] In addition, six states* have replaced time limits with provisions disqualifying women from benefits only while they are actually disabled due to pregnancy and requiring proof of ability to work (usually a doctor's certificate) to reestablish eligibility (see Table 6.2 for the new provisions). Of these, the provisions passed in Oregon and South Dakota are preferable because they explicitly cover pregnancy-related disabilities on the same basis as other temporary physical disabilities.

Four other states (Arkansas, Indiana, Louisiana, and Minnesota) have amended their laws so that a woman who has taken a maternity leave and been denied reinstatement is not disqualified from unemployment benefits (see Table 6.2). Arkansas accomplished this change by repealing its restrictive reemployment requirement and retaining a previously enacted provision that a woman not reinstated after a voluntary pregnancy leave is not disqualified from unemployment benefits. In this form, the law protects a woman taking a voluntary leave without implying that she can be forced to take a leave while she is still willing and able to work. The Indiana, Louisiana, and Minnesota provisions also protect a woman who takes a voluntary leave.

Domestic and Marital Obligations

Nine states recently have repealed laws establishing special reeligibility rules for departures from work for marital and domestic reasons. Eight of these states still disqualify a worker for such departures but treat reeligibility no less favorably than reeligibility for any other kind of voluntary leaving.[136] One state, Arkansas, repealed its reeligibility provision[137] and now treats departure to accompany a spouse to a new location as good cause for leaving if the individual shows availability for employment in the new locale.[138]

Dependency Benefits

In the last few years, four states have changed their dependency provisions. A new Illinois provision gives dependency benefits to the

---

*Delaware, Iowa,[135] Maryland, Nevada, Oregon, and South Dakota.

first parent to become unemployed if that parent provides at least one-quarter of the support of a dependent and if both parents together provide more than half of that dependent's support.[139] Similarly, in Maryland, a claimant who provides "partial" support (rather than "whole" or "main") can now get dependency benefits, but only one person can receive benefits for a given dependent.[140] The Maryland reform also deleted a presumption that the male head-of-household provides the primary support of his children. Rhode Island has repealed provisions requiring women but not similarly situated men to prove the total dependency of their children on them and denying dependency benefits to a woman in the case of the mere existence of a support order against her child's father.[141] The amended provision requires all claimants to establish a claim for dependency allowances to the director's satisfaction.[142]

Domestic Workers and Family Employees

There has not been widespread state reform in extending coverage to domestic workers and family employees. The biggest boon for domestic workers has been their coverage for the past two years under a temporary federal program of special unemployment assistance, which makes private household workers eligible for benefits as long as they meet general state criteria for wages and length of service.[143] A few states also have adopted coverage for domestic workers who meet certain income levels for the year.[144]

DISABILITY INSURANCE

Background

Five states and Puerto Rico have state disability insurance programs. These programs make cash benefits payable to workers who suffer wage loss due to nonoccupational disease or injury. They fill the gap between unemployment insurance, for those who are able to work but are unemployed through no fault of their own, and worker's compensation, for those who are disabled by work-connected disease or injury. The California, New Jersey, and Rhode Island programs are coordinated with the state unemployment compensation system;[145] the New York program is integrated with the worker's compensation plan;[146] and the Puerto Rico and Hawaii programs are run by separate government divisions.[147] All plans are funded by employee contributions,[148] with additional employer contributions in Hawaii, New Jersey, New York, and Puerto Rico.[149]

In California, Hawaii, New Jersey, and Puerto Rico, the state plan automatically covers workers unless an employee substitutes a private plan with terms as favorable to the employee as the state one.[150] In New York, the law provides that the employer must provide some plan, whether it is the state fund itself or a private one at least as favorable.[151] Rhode Island does not use private plans at all; everyone is under the state-administered program.[152]

The primary source of discrimination against women in these programs is their differential treatment of pregnancy. In California, for example, benefits are payable to women disabled because of complications or illness arising from pregnancy, but women cannot get benefits for disability due to normal pregnancy and childbirth.[153] In New Jersey, women can receive disability payments for pregnancy for a limited time only—four weeks before and four weeks after the termination of pregnancy—a period when they are ineligible for unemployment compensation.[154] Other disabilities are reimbursed on the basis of the actual time a worker is out because of sickness, up to 26 weeks for any given period of disability. In Rhode Island, workers can receive a lump sum payment not to exceed $250 for the time they are disabled due to pregnancy. Individuals unemployed because of sickness resulting from miscarriage or abortion are entitled to regular benefits,[155] 55 percent of weekly wages for up to 26 weeks. In Puerto Rico and New York, no payments are made to women disabled because of pregnancy until they have completed two weeks of work subsequent to the termination of the pregnancy.[156] Only Hawaii covers women disabled from pregnancy or termination of pregnancy on the same basis as those disabled from any other cause.[157]

The exclusion in the California plan of disability arising from normal pregnancy and childbirth was challenged on equal protection grounds and found constitutional by the United States Supreme Court in Geduldig v. Aiello.[158] The Court, applying a loose standard of scrutiny and relying heavily on certain unique features of the California plan, held that the distinction between pregnancy and other disabilities was reasonable in light of the state's interest in maintaining a comprehensive, self-sufficient plan within the reach of lower paid employee contributors. The Court went on, in Gilbert v. General Electric,[159] to hold that it is legal under Title VII of the Civil Rights Act of 1964 to exclude disability resulting from normal pregnancy from employer disability insurance programs, absent a showing of invidious sex discrimination. It is possible that this showing can be made with proof of a history of explicit discrimination in disability and other social benefit laws as well as with testimony by persons administering such programs. One final form of attack may be available for those state plans that distinguish between single and married women in providing maternity- or pregnancy-related disability payments. Such distinctions are subject to challenge under the constitutional right to privacy in childbearing choices, as developed by the United States Supreme Court in recent years.[160]

Until 1973, Rhode Island's disability insurance program also discriminated against women in determining eligibility for dependency allowances.* The statute required a woman but not a man to prove sole support of a child and denied a woman the dependency allowance if the child's father was subject to a support order, even if she in fact totally supported the child.[161] This provision was found to be unconstitutional in <u>Bowen</u> v. <u>Hackett</u>.[162]

Impact of the ERA

Explicit Discrimination

Under the strict equality standard of the ERA, the result in <u>Aiello</u> would not stand. The ERA subjects any classification involving a unique physical characteristic to strict scrutiny to determine whether the classification is closely related to a state interest. For purposes of the goals of a program, such as that reviewed in <u>Aiello</u>, pregnancy is no different from all other temporary disabilities. Since there is nothing unique about pregnancy that warrants its necessary exclusion from disability plans, a state's choice to exclude it as a special category is invalid under the ERA.

The ERA also prohibits state use of eligibility standards that embody sex-based presumptions. A state that awards supplemental benefits for dependents, for example, cannot require a woman to prove her support of a family member, while merely assuming that a man in the same circumstances is the primary provider for a spouse or child.

Neutral Rules

Any supplemental dependency benefits awarded only to "major" or "sole" supporters of a family member have a disparate impact on women, who have lower average earnings than men. The impact of

---

*New Jersey, Hawaii, and California do not increase temporary disability benefits for persons with dependents. For a fuller discussion of the disparate impact that proof-of-dependency requirements may have on one sex, even if sex neutralized, see the unemployment compensation section above.

the ERA on such benefits is discussed in the section on unemployment compensation above.

Policy Recommendations

There has been a growing effort in recent years to alter the treatment of pregnant women who are part of the labor force and to reform laws that traditionally have undercut their ability to choose the combined option of bearing children and maintaining a long-term connection with the job market. The exclusion of pregnancy-related disability from state-run employee disability programs is an obstacle to such progress without any justifiable social rationale. In Aiello, the state of California argued that pregnancy-related disabilities should be excluded because their expense would jeopardize the availability of a broad-based disability program. Such a rationale is simplistic and indicative of an underlying sexist disregard for the needs of a large segment of the working population. In purely financial terms, the interests furthered by the noncoverage of pregnancy could as well have been handled by modifying the plan to spread the increased costs equitably over the entire employee population rather than letting the burden fall only on pregnant women. For example, the maximum employee contribution to the plan, which is fixed in higher income brackets, could have been raised, or the benefits could have been lowered across the board by a small amount, without seriously jeopardizing the overall goals of the plan. In this way, the exclusive burden felt by women employees and their families would be eliminated without sacrificing the state interest in cutting costs.

State Reform Efforts

Hawaii's Temporary Disability Insurance Law was amended in 1973 to provide treatment and coverage of pregnancy-related disability on a basis equal with any other nonoccupational disability.[163] Changes in temporary disability plans also have occurred in California and Rhode Island as a result of litigation challenging the constitutionality of discriminatory provisions. During the Aiello litigation,[164] California modified its plan to cover disability due to complications of pregnancy.[165] Following a court challenge to dependency requirements for women in both unemployment and temporary disability programs in Rhode Island,[166] the proof-of-dependency provisions were amended to apply to all claimants.[167]

Unfortunately, each of these modifications is problematic. The Aiello exclusion of normal disabilities of pregnancy does not meet the equal rights standard as discussed above. The discretion given to the director of the Rhode Island program to determine eligibility may still be used to set dependency requirements that, though facially neutral, impact female claimants disparately (see p. 250).

WORKER'S COMPENSATION

Background

The source of sex discrimination in worker's compensation laws is the assumption that the worker is male and the dependents are a female spouse and/or children. The terminology regarding death benefits reflects this expectation. In some states, for example, only widow beneficiaries are granted procedural advantages in applying for death benefits.* Other states award survivor's benefits only to dependent spouses but presume that wives are dependent if cohabiting with the worker (see Table 6.3 for 24 jurisdictions that automatically provide benefits to widows, while requiring widowers to be actually dependent and/or incapacitated).[169] On the other hand, a widower generally must prove his financial dependency before he is entitled to benefits, and often he receives benefits only if there are no children of the deceased worker.[170]

Although some statutes providing death benefits may appear sex neutral on their face, they incorporate biased provisions of other sections of the law in which they appear. For example, some states define a "widower" as someone who is incapacitated or an invalid, while the definition of "widow" includes no such limitation.[171] Other jurisdictions have sex-based provisions governing the termination of benefits, which provide a lump sum payment to a widow but not a widower upon remarriage[172] or set different criteria for termination.[173] Another state, whose provisions for death benefits at first glance appear sex neutral, provides benefits to the wife but not the husband in a common law marriage.[174]

Eight jurisdictions require factual proof of dependency for the receipt of death benefits by the surviving spouse (see Table 6.3).

---

*In Ohio a widow applying for the remainder of her husband's disability benefits can apply on behalf of her children as well; if the children are applying alone, a guardian is required. A widower is apparently denied the procedural benefit that the widow is permitted, and his children must have a guardian appointed.[168]

Failure to define dependency clearly leaves room for bias in discretionary decision making.[175] Although most states presume the dependency of the children, a few states require that the children be proven dependent in fact (see Table 6.3). This creates a possibility that the spouse with the lesser income may not be entitled to income replacement for the protection of his or her children.[176]

Discrimination also occurs in the payment of supplemental dependency grants in disability benefit plans. Some states increase the amount of compensation based on the number of dependents.* In other jurisdictions, the dependents are entitled to receive the compensation on the death of the disabled worker even if the death is not caused by the compensated injury.† Although most states conclusively presume that a minor child is dependent, a few fail to define dependency for purposes of increased compensation.[177] This presents a danger that the child may be considered dependent only upon the parent with the greater income, resulting in less compensation for a disabling injury to a secondary wage earner.[178]

Impact of the ERA

Explicit Discrimination

Any statute permitting one sex to receive death or disability benefits that the other sex cannot receive or requiring one sex to prove eligibility for dependency benefits while awarding benefits to the other sex automatically or pursuant to a presumption of dependency is invalid under the ERA.

Neutral Rules

The use of a standard for eligibility that, though neutral on its face, has a disparate impact on women is subject to strict scrutiny under the ERA. Supplemental dependency benefits requiring proof of "major" or "sole" support impact women workers unfairly because of their lower average earnings. The effect of the ERA on such standards is discussed in the section on unemployment compensation above.

---

*Four states with this provision have a sex-based definition of dependency. See Table 6.3.

†Five states with this provision have a sex-based definition of dependency. See Table 6.3.

TABLE 6.3

State Dependency and Survivorship Rights Reforms

State	Statutes	Death Benefits for Surviving Spouse[a]	Disability Benefits for Dependents and/or Survivors[b]	Amendments Sex Neutralizing Dependency Standards (since 1970)
Alabama	Ala. Code tit. 26 (1958)	§§ 280–287	§ 279–280	Yes
Alaska	Alaska Stat. (1975)	Sex-neutral presumption § 23.30.215	Sex-neutral survivorship § 23.30.195	Yes
Arizona	Ariz. Rev. Stat. Ann. (1971)	Sex-neutral presumption § 23–1046	Sex-neutral survivorship	Yes
Arkansas	Ark. Stat. Ann. (1960)	Sex-neutral presumption §§ 81–1310(b), –1302, –1315		No
California	Cal. Labor Code (West 1971)	Sex-based definitions § 4701, 3501		No
Colorado	Colo. Rev. Stat. Ann. (1974)	Sex-neutral proof §§ 8–50–101, –111		Yes
Connecticut	Conn. Gen. Stat. Ann. (1972)	Sex-neutral presumption § 31–306		No
Delaware	Del. Code Ann. tit. 19 (1974)	Sex-neutral presumption § 2330		Yes
District of Columbia	D.C. Code Encycl. Ann. (1968)	Sex-neutral presumption § 36–501, para. 21	§ 36–501	No
Florida	Fla. Stat. Ann. (1966)	Sex-based throughout § 440.16, 440.02	Sex-neutral survivorship	Yes
Georgia	Ga. Code Ann. (1952)	Sex-neutral proof §§ 114–413, –414		No
Hawaii	Hawaii Rev. Stat. (1968)	Sex-based presumption § 386–41, –42	§ 386–34, –42	Yes
Idaho	Idaho Code (1973)	Sex-neutral presumption §§ 72–413, –410 Sex-based presumption	Sex-neutral survivorship § 72–408, –410 Sex-based dependency supplement	No

State	Citation	Provision	Provision	Statute benefits
Illinois	Ill. Ann. Stat. tit. 48 (Smith-Hurd 1969)	§ 138.7 Sex-neutral presumption		Yes
Indiana	Ind. Ann. Stat. (Burns 1974)	§ 22-3-3-17, -19 Sex-based presumption		No
Iowa	Iowa Code Ann. (1949)	§§ 85.31, 85.42 Sex-neutral presumption		No
Kansas	Kan. Stat. Ann. (1973)	§ 44-510b Sex-neutral proof		Yes
Kentucky	Ky. Rev. Stat. Ann. (1972)	§ 342.070, 342.075 Sex-neutral presumption		Yes
Louisiana	La. Rev. Stat. Ann. tit. 23 (West 1964)	§ 1231, 1251 Sex-neutral presumption		Yes
Maine	Me. Rev. Stat. Ann. tit. 39 (1965)	§ 58 Sex-based presumption[c]		No
Maryland	Md. Ann. Code art. 101 (1964)	§ 36 Sex-neutral proof	§ 36 Sex-neutral survivorship	Yes
Massachusetts	Mass. Gen. Laws Ann. ch. 152 (1958)	§§ 31-32 Sex-based presumption	§§ 35A-36 Sex-based dependency supplement and survivorship	No
Michigan	Mich. Stat. Ann. (1975)	§ 17.237 (321), (331) Sex-based presumption	§ 17.237 (351), (331) Sex-based dependency supplement	No
Minnesota	Minn. Stat. Ann. (1972)	§ 176.111 Sex-based throughout		No
Mississippi	Miss. Code Ann. (1972)	§ 71-3-25 Sex-based definitions		No
Missouri	Mo. Ann. Stat. (Vernon 1972)	§ 287.240 Sex-based presumption		No
Montana	Mont. Rev. Codes Ann. (1949)	§ 92-704.1, -413 Sex-neutral presumption		No

(continued)

TABLE 6.3 (continued)

State	Statutes	Death Benefits for Surviving Spouse[a]	Disability Benefits for Dependents and/or Survivors[b]	Amendments Sex Neutralizing Dependency Standards (since 1970)
Nebraska	Neb. Rev. Stat. (1943)	§ 48-122 / Sex-neutral proof		No
Nevada	Nev. Rev. Stat. (1975)	§ 616.615, 616.510 / Sex-neutral presumption		No
New Hampshire	N.H. Rev. Stat. Ann. (1966)	§ 281.22 / Sex-neutral proof		No
New Jersey	N.J. Stat. Ann. (1965)	§ 34:15-13 / Sex-based presumption	§ 34:15-12, -13	No
New Mexico	N.M. Stat. Ann. (1953)	§ 59-10-18.7, -12.10 / Sex-neutral presumption	Sex-based survivorship	Yes
New York	N.Y. Workmen's Comp. Law (McKinney 1965)	§ 16 / Sex-based definitions	Sex-based survivorship	No
North Carolina	N.C. Gen. Stat. (1972)	§ 97-38, -39 / Sex-based definitions	§ 97-37, -39	No
North Dakota	N.D. Cent. Code (1960)	§ 65-05-17 / Sex-based definitions	§ 65-05-09 / Sex-neutral dependency supplement	No
Ohio	Ohio Rev. Code Ann. (1973)	§ 4123.54, 4123.59 / Sex-based presumption	§ 4123.57	No
Oklahoma	Okla. Stat. Ann. tit. 85 (1970)	§ 22 / Sex-neutral presumption	Sex-based survivorship	Yes
Oregon	Ore. Rev. Stat. (1975)	§ 656.204 / Sex-neutral presumption	§ 656.208	No
Pennsylvania	Pa. Stat. Ann. tit. 77 (1952)	§ 561, 562 / Sex-based presumption	Sex-neutral survivorship / § 541, 562	No
Rhode Island	R.I. Gen. Laws Ann. (1956)	§ 28-33-12, -13 / Sex-based presumption	Sex-based survivorship	No

State	Code citation			
South Carolina	S.C. Code Ann. (1962)	§ 72-161, -17, -18 Sex-based presumption		No
South Dakota	S.D. Comp. Laws Ann. (1967)	§ 62-4-12 Sex-neutral presumption	§ 62-4-4, 1-2 Sex-neutral survivorship	Yes
Tennessee	Tenn. Code Ann. (1955)	§ 50-1010, -1013 Sex-based presumption	§ 50-1008, -1013 Sex-based dependency supplement	No
Texas	Tex. Rev. Civ. Stat. art. 8306 (Vernon 1967)	§§ 8-8a Sex-neutral presumption		No
Utah	Utah Code Ann. (1953)	§ 35-1-68, -71 Sex-based throughout	§ 35-1-67, 37-1-71 Sex-based dependency Supplement § 642	No
Vermont	Vt. Stat. Ann. tit. 21 (1967)	§§ 632-635 Sex-based presumption	Sex-neutral dependency supplement	No
Virginia	Va. Code Ann. (1950)	§ 65.1-65, -66 Sex-neutral proof		Yes
Washington	Wash. Rev. Code Ann. (1962)	§ 51.32.050 Sex-neutral presumption		Yes
West Virginia	W.Va. Code Ann. (1973)	§ 23-4-10 Sex-neutral presumption	§ 23-4-6, -10 Sex-neutral survivorship	Yes
Wisconsin	Wis. Stat. Ann. (1973)	§ 102.46, 102.51 Sex-neutral presumption		No
Wyoming	Wyo. Stat. Ann. (1957)	§ 27-87 Sex-based definitions		No

[a] This column designates whether a state has (1) a sex-neutral presumption of eligibility for death benefits for surviving spouses; (2) a sex-neutral test of eligibility for "dependent" spouses; (3) a sex-based presumption of eligibility favoring widows; or (4) sex-based definitions (for example, the pairing of "surviving wife" with "dependent husband" or "dependent wife" with "incapacitated husband") controlling eligibility of surviving spouses.

[b] This column only includes those states that provide special dependent's supplements or survivorship rights to the family members of a disabled worker. Those states that are blank simply provide a set percentage of wages to the disabled worker, regardless of dependents, which discontinues at that worker's death.

[c] In Maine, case law has created a presumption of dependency in a widow. See Moriarty's Case, 126 Me. 358, 138 A. 555 (1927).

Source: Compiled by the authors.

Policy Recommendations

The sex discrimination problems in current worker's compensation laws can be solved in one of two ways. The special presumptions of eligibility that apply to one sex can be extended to give automatic eligibility to members of both sexes, or the more stringent requirements of proof required of one sex can be applied to both. There are social policy reasons why the former is the wiser course.

The accrual of benefit rights to a worker in the event of his or her disability or death is quite properly viewed as part of that person's compensation. It is a form of income replacement or insurance to which all workers contribute and is as much a part of their remuneration as a weekly pay check.[179] Therefore, a worker should be entitled to this income replacement when he or she is disabled from job-related injuries or dies regardless of need on the part of the family or surviving spouse. By limiting benefits to spouses or children of only those workers who can prove need, the law in effect arbitrarily reduces the wages of workers who are not the sole or major support of their families.

Moreover, such a sex-neutral policy impacts women disproportionately because it is their families who receive benefits less often under proof standards. It is therefore wise to eliminate the sex discrimination in current provisions by removing special need requirements for the spouses and children of workers and handling the claims of all family member beneficiaries on an automatic basis.

State Reform Efforts

A number of states have revised their worker's compensation statutes in recent years to eliminate sex discrimination. Some of these reforms have been straightforward terminological changes, replacing sex-based terms, such as "wife," "husband," "widow," and "widower," with sex-neutral substitutes, such as "spouse," "surviving spouse," and "dependent."[180] These changes remove the underlying presumption that workers are male and their beneficiaries and dependents are female.[181] In some states, sex neutralization also has involved substantive changes in the standards for determining when benefits are to be extended or terminated.

In the past 5 years, 14 states have eliminated bias in the granting of survivor's or supplemental dependency benefits by extending these benefits automatically to spouses of both sexes.[182] This has been done either by creating a conclusive presumption of the dependency of all spouses or by including spouses of both sexes in the statutory enumeration of prospective beneficiaries automatically entitled to death benefits.* These changes meant the elimination of special dependency requirements for widowers and special requirements that a widower be an invalid or incapable of self-support in order to claim survivor's benefits.

Four other states have sex neutralized their dependency requirements for surviving spouses, not by repealing dependency standards but by enforcing them equally for spouses of both sexes. In both Florida and Virginia, all surviving spouses must now show that they were living with and dependent upon the deceased at the time the injury was incurred and are not remarried.[184] Kansas[185] and Maryland[186] also have neutralized their death benefits by requiring some proof of dependency for surviving spouses of either sex.

---

*Eliminating all references to "dependency" and relying rather on rights accruing automatically to "survivors" is a preferable approach to statutory language in these cases. Even where a state legislature intends to eliminate any special tests for dependency, use of the term implies that some qualification other than survivorship might be imposed in individual cases. The Washington provision, which simply refers to "surviving spouses" as beneficiaries, is a good example of a straightforward statute that avoids any ambiguities raised by a latent dependency standard.[183]

7

CIVIL RIGHTS AND
PUBLIC OBLIGATIONS

JURY SERVICE

Background

Women traditionally have been excluded from significant involvement as jurors in our legal system, and the ingrained tradition of predominantly male juries has been harmful in a number of ways. It has denied women a basic right of citizenship for decades after they were accorded the right to vote. Juries from which women are absent cannot offer litigants a verdict delivered by a fair cross-section of the community. In addition, the laws and practices that exclude women from juries discriminate against men with regard to exemptions, length, and frequency of jury service. The lack of women jurors also has a differential impact on the treatment of male and female litigants. A recent study indicates that female jurors tend to favor women while male jurors favor men, for example, by giving them lighter sentences or higher awards of damages.[1]

The laws that govern jury service for women are based on the stereotypes that women's duty to home and family precludes civic responsibilities outside the home and, to a lesser degree, that jury duty is too coarse for the sensibilities of most women. These views are embodied in a number of different discriminatory selection policies. The principal ones are "absolute exclusion of women from jury duty;[2] exclusion of women from jury duty unless they register their willingness to serve;[3] an optional exemption that a woman may exercise solely on the basis of being a woman;[4] child care exemptions for women only, which are apparently automatic on a showing of child custody;[5] and child care exemptions that are sex neutral on their face but discriminatory in effect because they are almost exclusively granted to women. [6]

All the absolute exclusions and registration requirements have been changed in recent years, and only three states now have categorical exemptions for women. Sex-based and facially neutral child care exemptions, on the other hand, have been increasing in number as the absolute exclusions disappear. Thirteen states* now have child care exemptions, and variations are found in several other states as well. [7]

A state statute requiring affirmative registration by women who wished to serve on juries was held unconstitutional by the United States Supreme Court in 1975. In Taylor v. Louisiana, the Court held that a criminal defendant's Sixth Amendment right to trial by an impartial jury selected from a cross-section of the community was violated by excluding women from the jury venires. [8] Although the opinion was not based on the constitutional rights of the women as jurors, it signals the end of statutes and practices that preclude the effective participation of women on juries. (The Court did state that statistics from the U.S. Department of Labor "certainly put to rest the suggestion that all women should be exempt from jury service based solely on their sex and the presumed role in the home.")[9]

Impact of the ERA

Explicit Discrimination

Under the equal rights amendment, all exemptions based on sex are unconstitutional. The ERA provides a stronger standard than the Taylor holding, which requires proof of a lack of a fair cross-section in the jury venire and applies only to criminal cases. The ERA also prohibits sex-based child care exemptions and, at a minimum, requires the substitution of exemptions based on the function of child care rather than on the sex of the person performing the function. It is also permissible under the ERA to subsume the child care hardship under a general hardship standard or eliminate it altogether.

---

*These are Connecticut, Florida, Georgia, Massachusetts, Montana, New Jersey, New York, Oklahoma, South Carolina, Texas, Utah, Virginia, and Wyoming. In Rhode Island and Nebraska, women are not called to serve as jurors unless it is first determined that the "accommodations and facilities" are such as to allow the presence of women. In addition, Alabama specifically permits women to apply to the court to be excused for good cause but does not offer the same option to men.

<u>Neutral Rules</u>

In addition to explicitly sex-based statutes, sex-neutral laws and exemptions may have a disparate impact on one sex. Sex-neutral child care exemptions are likely to have such an impact because many more women than men have primary care of small children. In addition, such laws may be administered by personnel who exempt women with children more readily than men. Similarly, if there is no specific child care provision, the general hardship exemption may be administered more leniently toward women with children than persons claiming hardship on other bases. As these policies serve no legitimate function, states may be required under the ERA to take steps to insure the application of the same standards to men and women claiming exemptions under a sex-neutral provision.

Policy Recommendations

The requirement of the ERA that all exemptions be framed in sex-neutral language is a desirable first step toward the elimination of sex stereotyping from the process of jury selection. More must be done, however, to assure that there are significant numbers of women in the jury venire and that the obligation to serve falls equally on men and women without imposing an unfair burden on persons caring for young children.

If a sex-neutral child care exemption is retained, it should be drawn narrowly to excuse only those for whom the type of jury service for which they are being called is a genuine hardship. A person should be required to appear personally to claim the exemption, and the standards should be at least as stringent as those applied in other exemption categories. Preferably, child care responsibilities should be incorporated into a general hardship or other sex-neutral exemption category and implemented through guidelines or other directives to assure that this does not result in loosening the standards for the application of the exemption. Likewise, sex neutrality must be assured in states where court personnel exercise administrative discretion to exempt people. The types of exemptions, the nature of their enforcement, and the onerousness of the various types of jury service are all factors that must be researched in a particular state or county in order for reformers to decide on the best type of legislation or judicial rule making.

State Reform Efforts

Absolute exclusion of women from jury duty, which existed in three states until the late 1960s, was eliminated by judicial mandate in one state and repealed in the two remaining states.[10] Affirmative registration requirements, which existed in two states at the beginning of the 1960s, were repealed in both—in Louisiana, during the pendency of both civil litigation and criminal appeals challenging its validity.[11] Of five state laws establishing categorical exemptions for women, two—New York's and Georgia's—were repealed in 1975.[12]

As legislatures have come to see the discriminatory nature of the various types of exemptions based solely on sex, child care exemptions have sometimes been substituted. There also has been a tendency for child care exemptions previously available only to women to be extended to men. For example, when Massachusetts first declared women eligible for jury service in 1949, it exempted women nurses, women hospital assistants, women members of religious orders, mothers or other women with custody of a child, and women who would be "embarrassed" by the nature of the prosecution.[13] The occupational exemptions were extended to men in 1969[14] and the child custody exemptions in 1973.[15] ("Embarrassment" may still excuse only women.)[16] Similarly, child care exemptions for women only were first created in Virginia in 1971[17] and then extended to a parent of either sex who personally cares for a child in 1973.[18] Oklahoma also has recently extended its child care exemptions to male parents.[19] The six states that have sex-neutral child care exemptions require a person seeking an exemption to show that he or she cares for the child "directly"[20] or "personally,"[21] while the sex-based statutes generally required only that the women have legal custody of the child. In Oklahoma, a parent also must show that his or her absence will result in hardship.[22]

Both Florida and Louisiana formerly required women to register in order to be called for jury service. Florida replaced its earlier system with child care exemptions for women only in 1967.[23] Louisiana repealed the registration requirement and adopted a new constitutional article, implemented by a state supreme court rule, guaranteeing all citizens the opportunity to serve on juries and forbidding exclusion from jury service "on account of race, color, religion, sex, national origin, or economic status." The listed exemptions do not include child care.[24]

BOARDS AND COMMISSIONS

Background

Historically, women have been underrepresented on the various boards and commissions established in many states to oversee or make policy for state institutions or to regulate certain professions.

Discrimination against women both in politics and in employment has
contributed to this pattern since appointments are commonly based
on political or professional credentials. In particular, policy-making
boards have been closed to women; moreover, the small number of
commissions to which women have been appointed are those concerned
with subjects traditionally considered of interest to women, such as
libraries or hospitals.[25]

Early efforts to assure the representation of women on certain
boards and commissions often took the form of quotas[26] requiring a
minimum number of women to be appointed to a board or commission.
While this does ensure at least token representation, the impact of
quotas is not necessarily "benevolent." Such quotas often apply only
to the boards considered appropriate for women, those dealing with
community services, for example; as such, they perpetuate the idea
of separate spheres for men and women. Quotas also may foster the
ideas that it is not necessary to have the input of women on boards and
commissions unless mandated by law and that the use of male nouns
and pronouns regarding these boards really indicates a sex-based
limitation. In any case, such boards generally have remained exclusively male. Finally, the quotas are usually quite small and, in
many cases, may serve to limit rather than increase the numbers of
women appointed.

Impact of the ERA

Explicit Discrimination

To end this discrimination, the equal rights amendment requires that boards and commissions be open to women as well as men.
To achieve this goal, states must investigate both their statutes and
their practices concerning board appointments.

Terminology changes are a first step toward sex neutralizing
laws relating to boards and commissions. Such changes will have
little substantive impact where it is already clear that both men and
women are eligible for particular boards, but they will be a clear
statement of new policy in those cases in which terminology seems
to have become a factor in the limitation of certain positions to men.
This might be emphasized by stating that "men and women" rather
than "persons" are eligible for board positions.

Explicit sex-based quotas also must be repealed under the ERA
and be replaced with sex-neutral language concerning board or commission members. Even quotas not based on explicit statutory language but on well-established tradition that a particular seat is a
"woman's" seat or a "man's" seat must be repudiated under the ERA.

Neutral Rules

Even sex-neutral statutes may have a disparate impact on women because of the failure of those who make the appointments to choose women for more than a small fraction of the positions. Such discriminatory patterns are due in part to the tradition of appointing political colleagues to these posts and in part to the underrepresentation of women in the occupations typically regulated by state boards, such as ophthalmology or pharmacy. Legitimate state interests are not furthered by such patterns, and the ERA may require states to publicize vacancies to women and others who would not otherwise be considered for appointment and to review their selection process to be sure it provides safeguards against "business as usual."

Policy Recommendations

Whether or not the ERA requires states to go beyond repealing sex-based quotas and sex neutralizing terminology, it is advisable that states take affirmative steps to increase the number of women in these positions. Appointments to boards often involve considerable power and prestige, and it is appropriate that the states make an effort to reverse established patterns of appointment. Affirmative action programs can increase the number of women on boards by opening the process of scrutiny and participation. This would bring names of appropriate people to state attention and probably would lead to an improvement in the quality of appointments as well as the elimination of some positions that perform no useful function and are a drain on the state's resources.

State Reform Efforts

At least two states have repealed sex-based quota requirements from their codes.[27] Three others have enacted legislation eliminating sex-based language.[28] As a reminder of the requirements of sex equality, statutes no longer refer to every appointee as male. In addition, affirmative action programs have been developed by some states. Hawaii introduced four bills in 1974 to encourage the appointment of women to boards and commissions. These bills offer a good cross-section of possible affirmative actions that could be taken. The bills do the following: (1) request the administration to take affirmative action to increase the number of women on boards and commissions,[29] (2) urge the establishment of a temporary commission to study boards and commissions,[30] (3) request the governor to appoint more women to boards and commissions,[31] and (4) request the presence of more women on boards and commissions and require proof concerning each male appointment that no qualified women applied.[32] Such affirmative action is a good way to make the statutory reform of sex-based terminology more meaningful. California has enacted a law requiring the governor to prepare and maintain a public registry on state boards and commissions, including such information as the names of appointees, their terms of office, and vacancies.[33] This is an excellent accompaniment to a statute requesting the appointment of more women; such a requirement will make it easier for women's groups or any group outside the mainstream of political life to submit names and to lobby for the appointment of qualified individuals at the appropriate time.

8

ANTIDISCRIMINATION
LAWS

INTRODUCTION

A large number of states have enacted antidiscrimination laws covering a variety of substantive areas. The most frequently treated areas are credit, including real property, credit cards, business loans, and other personal property transactions; housing, including the sale, rental, and advertisement of housing; public accommodations, including establishments providing food, board, and recreation; employment, including hiring, firing, promotions, terms, and conditions; and insurance, including availability, scope of coverage, and rate setting of policies for disability, health, and life insurance. A number of states also have passed laws forbidding discrimination in education, including obligations on the part of school administrators to take affirmative action to provide equal opportunity.

The relationship of the ERA to these different areas varies with the amount of state involvement in the area. Public educational institutions are governed by the ERA because they are state action. In insurance, states generally require that all policies offered for sale within the state be approved by a state insurance department for compliance with standards of fairness, and this level of regulation may trigger the application of constitutional standards. Discriminatory practices in the other areas treated here generally are not traceable to direct state involvement, but they have come under scrutiny by ERA reformers because discrimination by private institutions often undermines the efforts of women to attain true equality. New civil rights legislation concerning private conduct has therefore accompanied ERA reform in many states.

Another factor in widespread state adoption of antidiscrimination laws is the passage of significant federal legislation in these areas over the past several years. One of the areas of greatest advancement by means of antidiscrimination affirmative legislation in the past decade has been employment. Title VII of the Civil Rights Act of 1964[1] and the Equal Pay Act of 1963[2] cover a broad range of employment practices and afford a remedy for the aggrieved individual in federal court. Much has been written about these laws elsewhere, and because they and the state laws that parallel them largely predate current ERA-related reform, this report does not attempt to discuss either policy or reform efforts in the private employment area.[3]

Other federal laws have been amended in the last four years. Title IX of the Education Amendments of 1972[4] makes it unlawful for any federally assisted educational program to discriminate on the basis of sex in its activities, including curriculum, admissions, employment, extracurricular programs, and athletics. Regulations to implement the law, which is administratively enforced, went into effect in July 1975. In October 1974, the Equal Credit Opportunity Act[5] was enacted, prohibiting discrimination on the basis of sex or marital status in any credit transaction. It covers the action of retail stores, credit card companies, banks, and other lending institutions. The regulations to implement the act embody a fairly strong definition of equality, although they do not disturb state marital property laws that may lead to the denial of equal credit opportunity to women. A private civil action in federal court is available under the act, and punitive damages can be collected.

The area of housing and home financing also received congressional attention in 1974. The Fair Housing Act[6] was amended to include sex in the prohibition against discrimination in the sale, financing, and rental of housing. The National Housing Act[7] was amended to include a provision prohibiting sex discrimination in federally related mortgage lending and requiring lenders to consider the combined income of both spouses applying for a mortgage.

Many of the antidiscrimination laws on the federal as well as the state level simply extend preexisting civil rights laws to encompass discrimination on the basis of sex and sometimes marital status. Others tackle new areas, such as credit and insurance, which have recently been identified as sources of widespread discrimination against women.

The sections in this chapter treat credit, housing, public accommodations, insurance, and education. Some of these areas already are affected by the ERA, and all of them are critical components in presenting a complete picture of recent law reform in the states.

CREDIT

Credit transactions of all types, from revolving charge accounts to business loans and mortgages, are one of the areas pervaded by sex discrimination. Typical practices documented by credit studies include discounting all or part of a wife's income for a joint husband/wife credit application, denying married women separate credit in their own names based on their individual creditworthiness, and denying credit to single, separated, or divorced women who otherwise meet relevant standards of creditworthiness.[8]

Until recently, consumer protection statutes treating credit focused primarily on interest rate ceilings, financial disclosures, and credit bureau misconduct. With the growing consciousness concerning the disparate treatment of women in the credit market and wider acceptance of equal rights principles, however, a large number of jurisdictions, including the federal government, have passed laws prohibiting sex discrimination in credit in recent years. The most far-reaching new legislation is the Federal Equal Credit Opportunity Act, a 1974 amendment to the Consumer Credit Protection Act.[9] This act covers a broad scope of credit transactions, prohibiting discrimination by any creditor or agent of a creditor against any applicant on the basis of sex or marital status. It provides for both administrative and private court actions, allowing damages of up to $500,000 in class action challenges to creditors' practices in addition to attorneys' fees. The act is being implemented with extensive regulations that provide, among other protections, that an applicant can demand a statement of reasons for the refusal of credit, that separate accounts cannot be denied on the basis of sex or marital status, and that part-time income and income from child support or alimony must be counted if there is reasonable certainty of continuity.[10]

Well over half the states and the District of Columbia also have enacted varying degrees of protection for women in the credit area, the most recent laws being modeled on the new Federal Act. These laws fall into four main categories: (1) general credit provisions covering all forms of credit transactions, (2) consumer credit provisions expressly excluding home financing, (3) home financing provisions, and (4) public accommodations provisions explicitly or implicitly extending to credit-granting institutions. In addition, a number of jurisdictions have enacted prohibitions not only of discrimination based on sex but also of discrimination based on the marital status of the credit consumer. This is an important complement to a sex standard since studies of credit discrimination indicate that it is often the marital status of a woman, as well as her sex, that triggers disparate treatment in the credit market. The most common pattern has been the enactment of public accommodation or general credit provisions to cover retail credit matters in conjunction with separate provisions for home finance. At present, 17 states and the District of Columbia have enacted such statutory combinations to cover the full range of credit transactions; seven of these jurisdictions protect against both sex and marital status discrimination (see Table 8.1 for a state–by–state description of current laws).

Most state credit laws are enforced by state civil rights agencies or by state departments that regulate banking and real estate practices. These are generally preexisting agencies assigned additional responsibilities by recent sex discrimination amendments; hence, while administrative remedies are generally available to women cost-free, they may involve the time lag often associated with administrative backlogs. About half the jurisdictions provide for private court actions by individuals as an alternative to administrative relief. In some states, attorney's fees and/or court costs may be awarded to successful complainants. [11]

Due to differences in coverage, definitions, and enforcement mechanisms, the potential of these state laws to eliminate credit discrimination varies extensively. The California credit provision is a good example of a promising statutory scheme. This law specifically provides that credit cannot be denied to an individual if another individual of different marital status or sex with the same property and earnings would have been granted credit. By defining earnings to include spousal and child support, pensions, and social security disability and survivorship benefits, the statute protects women frequently denied credit on the basis of narrow criteria of creditworthiness. Finally, this statute provides strong enforcement mechanisms by allowing class actions, punitive damages of up to $100,000, attorney's fees and court costs for the aggrieved party in a successful action, and a $2,500–per–day fine for the intentional violation of a court injunction by the credit-granting institution.

Perhaps the biggest barrier to equal credit for women is state property laws that define the legal rights and obligations of married persons because both federal and state fair credit provisions generally defer to them. Two areas of concern are laws defining property ownership by married people and the duty of spousal support. Both impact married women disproportionately because of the legal and social tradition of the husband as family breadwinner and financial manager. (See Chapter 5 for further discussion of the effects of property and support laws on married women's creditworthiness.)[12] Frequently, creditors, who prefer to grant credit to the husband because of stereotyped views about women's economic unreliability, use these state laws as an excuse even though the laws in fact do not have the claimed result.* Therefore, it is important that those who draft credit re-

---

*For example, in those states where married couples can own property together in a special form known as tenancy by the entirety, realtors and mortgage institutions may insist that a married woman

TABLE 8.1

State Credit Law Reforms

State	Credit Laws	Protected Status	Date	Enforcement
Alabama	Public Accommodations Alaska Stat. § 18.80.230 (1962)	Sex, marital status, change in marital status, pregnancy, parenthood	1972	Administrative remedy, private action, attorney's fees
	Home Finance Alaska Stat. § 18.80.250 (1962)	Sex, marital status		
Arizona	None			
Arkansas	General Credit Acts 1975, No. 566	Sex, marital status	3/26/73	Private action
California	General Credit Cal. Civ. Code § 1812.30 (West 1972)	Sex, married woman's separate property	10/1/73	Private action
Colorado	Home Finance Colo. Rev. Stat. Ann. § 69-7-5 (1963)	Sex, marital status	6/14/73	Administrative remedy, private action, attorney's fees
	Consumer Credit Colo. Rev. Stat. Ann. para. 73-1-109 (1963)	Sex, marital status	6/7/73	
Connecticut	General Credit Conn. Gen. Stat. Ann. § 36-437 (1958)	Sex, marital status	6/13/73	Administrative remedy, attorney's fees
Delaware	Public Accommodations Del. Code Ann. tit. 6, § 4504 (1974)	Sex, marital status	5/10/72	Administrative remedy
	Home Finance Del. Code Ann. tit. 6, § 4603 (1974)	Sex, marital status		
District of Columbia	General Credit D.C. Rules and Regs. tit. 34 (1973)	Sex, marital status	11/16/73	Administrative remedy, attorney's fees
Florida	General Credit Fla. Stat. Ann. § 725.07 (1969)	Sex, marital status	10/1/73	Private action, attorney's fees
Georgia	None			

(continued)

273

TABLE 8.1 (continued)

State	Credit Laws	Protected Status	Date	Enforcement
Hawaii	Home Finance Hawaii Rev. Stat. § 515-5 (1968)	Sex	1971	Administrative remedy, private action
Idaho	Home Finance Idaho Code § 67-5909 (1973)	Sex	1969	Administrative remedy, private action
Illinois	Credit Cards Ill. Ann. Stat. ch. 121½, § 385.1 (Smith-Hurd 1973)	Sex, marital status	1973	None
Indiana	Public Accommodations Ind. Ann. Stat. § 22-9-1-2 (Burns 1974)	Sex	1971	Administrative remedy
	Home Finance and General Credit Ind. Ann. Stat. § 22-9-1-2 (Burns 1974	Sex	P.A. and Home Fin. 1974 General Cr.	
Iowa	Public Accommodations Iowa Code Ann. § 601A.7 (1975)	Sex	7/1/74	Administrative remedy
	Home Finance Iowa Code Ann. § 601A.9 (1975)	Sex, marital status		
Kansas	Public Accommodations Kan. Stat. Ann. § 44-1009(c) (1973)	Sex	1972	Administrative remedy
	Home Finance Kan. Stat. Ann. § 44-1017 (1973)	Sex		
Kentucky	Home Finance Ky. Rev. Stat. § 344.370 (1973)	Sex	6/21/74	Administrative remedy, private action, attorney's fees
Louisiana	General Credit La. Rev. Stat. Ann. § 9:3581-5 (1950)	Sex, marital status	1975	None
Maine	Home Finance Me. Rev. Stat. Ann. tit. 5, § 4582	Sex	7/1/72	Administrative remedy, private action
	General Credit Me. Rev. Stat. Ann. tit. 5, § 4595, et seq. (1964)	Sex, marital status		

274

State	Statute	Basis	Effective date	Remedy
Maryland	Home Finance Md. Ann. Code art. 49B, § 23(a) (1972)	Sex, marital status	7/1/73	Administrative remedy
	Consumer Credit Md. Ann. Code art. 83, §§ 128(e), 153C(b) (1975)	Sex, marital status		
Massachusetts	Public Accommodations Mass. Ann. Laws ch. 272, § 92A (1975)	Sex, marital status	1973	Administrative remedy, private action, attorney's fees
	Home Finance Mass. Ann. Laws ch. 151B, § 4 (3B) (1965)	Sex, marital status		
	General Credit Mass. Ann. Laws ch. 151B, § 4(14) (1965)	Sex, marital status		
Michigan	Home Finance Mich. Comp. Laws Ann. § 564.102 et seq. (1967), as amended by Acts 1975, No. 183	Sex, marital status	1975	Administrative remedy
Minnesota	Home Finance Minn. Stat. Ann. § 363.03.2(3) (1966)	Sex, marital status	8/1/73	Administrative remedy, attorney's fees
	General Credit Minn. Stat. Ann. § 363.03.8-7 (1966)	Sex		
Mississippi	None			
Missouri	None			
Montana	Public Accommodations Mont. Rev. Codes Ann. § 64-306(2) (1947)	Sex, marital status	6/16/75	Administrative remedy, private action, attorney's fees
	Home Finance Mont. Rev. Codes Ann. § 64-306(4) (1947)	Sex, marital status		
Nebraska	None			
Nevada	None			

(continued)

TABLE 8.1 (continued)

State	Credit Laws	Protected Status	Date	Enforcement
New Hampshire*	Public Accommodations N.H. Rev. Stat. Ann. § 354A:8 IV (1966)	Sex, marital status	Sex: 1971; m.s.: 1975	Administrative remedy
New Jersey	Public Accommodations N.J. Stat. Ann. § 10.5-4(f) (1960)	Sex, marital status	1973	Administrative remedy
	Home Finance N.J. Stat. Ann. § 10.5-12(i) (1960)	Sex, marital status	1972	
New Mexico	Public Accommodations N.M. Stat. Ann. § 4-33-7(F) (1953)	Sex	1973	Administrative remedy
	Home Finance N.M. Stat. Ann. § 4-33-7(H) (1953)	Sex		
New York	General Credit N.Y. Exec. Law § 296-a (McKinney 1972)	Sex, marital status	1974	Administrative remedy, private action
North Carolina	None			
North Dakota	None			
Ohio	Home Finance Ohio Rev. Code Ann. § 4112.02(H) (Page 1965)	Sex	2/18/73	Administrative remedy, private action
Oklahoma	None			
Oregon	Public Accommodations Ore. Rev. Stat. § 30.670, 30.675 (1974)	Sex, marital status	10/73	Private action, attorney's fees
Pennsylvania	Public Accommodations Pa. Stat. Ann. tit. 43, § 955 (1964)	Sex	1969	Administrative remedy, private action
	Home Finance Pa. Stat. Ann. tit. 43, § 952 (1964)	Sex		

276

State	Statute	Coverage	Date	Remedy
Rhode Island	General Credit R.I. Gen. Laws Ann. § 34-37-4.1 (1956)	Sex, marital status	5/11/73	Administrative remedy, private action
South Carolina	None			
South Dakota	Public Accommodations S.D. Comp. Laws Ann. §§ 20-13-23, -24 (1967)	Sex	1972	Administrative remedy
	Home Finance S.D. Comp. Laws Ann. § 20-13-21 (1967)	Sex		
Texas	General Credit Tex. Rev. Civ. Stat. Ann. art. 5069-2.07 (1971)	Sex	8/27/73	Administrative remedy, private action, court costs
Utah	Public Accommodations Utah Code Ann. § 13-7-3 (1953)	Sex	5/8/73	Private action
Vermont	General Credit Vt. Stat. Ann. tit. 8, § 1211 (1971)	Sex, marital status	7/1/74	Private action
Virginia	Home Finance Va. Code Ann. § 36-90 (1970)	Sex	1973	Administrative remedy, private action
	General Credit Va. Code Ann. § 59.1-21.19 (1970)	Sex	1975	
Washington	General Credit Wash. Rev. Code Ann. § 49.60.224	Sex, marital status	6/7/73	Administrative remedy, private action, attorney's fees
West Virginia*	Public Accommodations W.Va. Code Ann. § 5-11-9(f) (1971)	Sex	1971	Administrative remedy
Wisconsin	General Credit Wis. Stat. Ann. § 138.20 (1974)	Sex, marital status	8/4/73	
Wyoming	None			

*New Hampshire and West Virginia have public accommodations statutes, but credit does not fall under the scope of the statute.

Source: Compiled by the authors.

forms carefully examine alleged conflicts between equal credit opportunity and other state laws.

One type of state law that has been harmonized with the Federal Act is "multiple agreement" laws, which forbid the extension of certain open-ended credit accounts to either a husband or wife separately. While designed to protect family consumers against the higher finance charges resulting from smaller separate accounts,[13] they have in fact exacerbated the tendency for married women's credit histories to be subsumed under those of their husbands. Under the Federal Equal Credit Opportunity Act, married persons are free to demand separate credit histories and accounts even though higher financing charges may result.

The federal government has taken a lead in the credit area by detailing unlawful practices and providing meaningful remedies. It is appropriate for the states to follow by explicitly resolving conflicts between state law and equal credit opportunity.

HOUSING

Background

The real estate and home-financing industries traditionally have followed many explicitly sex-discriminatory practices, including sex-stereotyped advertising, the refusal to sell or rent to women, disparate terms and conditions of property transactions for women and men, and the denial or discounting of credit to women customers. In addition, many industry practices, while not explicitly sex discriminatory, impact women more severely because of the interplay of various social factors. Perhaps the most critical of these are policies barring families with children from housing, particularly single-parent families, because the vast majority of single parents in this country are women.* Similarly, the discounting of sources of income related to dependent children, such as Aid to Families with Dependent Children

---

who desires to buy property in her own name must include her husband in the deed and mortgage, on the erroneous assumption that a married woman has to own property as a tenancy by the entirety.

*According to the U.S. Census Bureau, of the 8.438 million children under 18 living with only one parent in March 1970, approximately 91 percent were living with their mothers and only about 9 percent with their fathers. The percentage differences become even more extreme as the age of the child decreases.[14]

or child support, results in a disparate impact on women in the housing market.

State Reform Efforts

At present, 24 states and the District of Columbia have enacted
laws that prohibit sex discrimination in both real estate transactions
and home finance. Of these, 17 also prohibit discrimination on the
basis of marital status.* In addition, 12 other states prohibit sex
discrimination in either housing or home finance but not both; some
of these also cover marital status (see Table 8.2).

Some state legislatures have attempted to curb more subtle
forms of discrimination against women with express protections for
certain characteristics in addition to sex and marital status. Alaska,
for instance, amended its fair housing law in June 1975 to proscribe
discrimination in housing based on changes in marital status, pregnancy, or parenthood; these additions also became part of their credit
provisions at the end of October 1975.[15] The District of Columbia
dealt with the same problems by simply defining "marital status" in
its human rights law to include the statuses of being "married, single,
divorced, separated, or widowed, and the usual conditions associated
therewith, including pregnancy or parenthood."[16] Minnesota includes
in its fair housing and credit law a prohibition of discrimination against
recipients of public assistance.[17]

While discrimination based on parenthood or marital status may
be more effectively prohibited by a specific statute, the doctrine of
"disparate impact" provides some protection against such discrimination in states whose laws explicitly prohibit only sex-based discrimination. Maryland, for example, has implemented its fair housing
legislation with strict housing finance guidelines directing the Maryland Commission on Human Relations to scrutinize all standards with
a disparate effect upon a particular class of applicants.[18]

Spurred by the growth of political interest in equal rights for
women generally and the adoption of ERAs in some states specifically,
90 percent of these state enactments have been adopted within the past
five years. Although there are wide variations in the scope of prohibited acts found in current state statutes, many of these laws are
patterned on the Federal Civil Rights Act of 1968,[19] which originally
prohibited racial discrimination in a broad range of real estate practices and recently has been amended to include sex discrimination.

---

*Three of these prohibit marital status discrimination in housing
only and one in home finance only.

TABLE 8.2

State Housing and Finance Law Reforms

State	Fair Housing and Housing Finance Laws	Sex	Marital Status	Other	Effective Date	Court Enforcement of Investigative Powers	Orders	Other Agency Powers
Alaska	Housing Alaska Stat. § 18.80.240 (1962) Finance § 18.80.250 (1962)	x	x	Changes in marital status, pregnancy, parenthood	Sex: 8/4/72 Others: 6/3/75	x	By complainant	May intervene in private civil actions
California	Housing Cal. Health and Safety Code § 35700 (1973) Finance Cal. Civ. Code § 1812.30 (1972)	x	x		Housing: 1976 Finance: 1973			
Colorado	Housing Colo. Rev. Stat. Ann. § 69-7-5 (1963) Finance Same as above	x	x		Sex: 1959 Marital status: 6/14/73	x	x	Initiate own complaints
Connecticut	Housing Conn. Gen. Stat. Ann. § 53-35 (1958) Finance § 36-437 (1958)	x	x		Sex: 1973 Marital status: 1974			Initiate own complaints
Delaware	Housing Del. Code Ann. tit. 6, § 4603 (1974) Finance Same as above	x	x		5/10/72	x		

State	Citation		Changes in marital status, pregnancy, parenthood, sexual orientation	Date		Comments
District of Columbia	Housing D.C. Rules and Reg. § 34-13.1 (1973); Finance Same as above	x	x	1973	x	Initiate own complaints, may refer to real estate commission
Florida	Housing Finance only Fla. Stat. Ann. § 725.07 (1973)	x	x	10/1/73	x	Initiate own complaints
Hawaii	Housing Hawaii Rev. Stat. § 515-3 (1968); Finance § 515-5 (1968)	x	x	Sex: 1971 Marital status: 5/17/75	x	Initiate own complaints
Idaho	Housing Idaho Code § 67-5909 (1973); Finance Same as above	x		1969	x	Initiate own complaints, refer findings to county prosecutor
Indiana	Housing only Ind. Ann. Stat. § 22:9-2 (1974)	x	x	1971	x	Cannot initiate own complaints; refer to real estate licenser
Iowa	Housing Iowa Code Ann. § 601A.8 (1975); Finance § 601A.9 (1975)	x	x	7/1/74	x	Initiate own complaints
Kansas	Housing Kan. Stat. Ann. § 44-1016 (1973); Finance § 44-1017 (1973)	x		7/1/72	x	Initiate own complaints; "pattern and practice" suit by attorney general

(continued)

281

TABLE 8.2 (continued)

State	Fair Housing and Housing Finance Laws	Sex	Marital Status	Other	Effective Date	Court Enforcement of Investigative Powers	Orders	Other Agency Powers
Kentucky	Finance only Ky. Rev. Stat. § 344.370 (1973)	x			6/21/74	x	x	Initiate own complaints
Louisiana	Finance only La. Rev. Stat. § 9:3581-5 (1975)	x	x		1975			
Maine	Housing Me. Rev. Stat. Ann. tit. 5, § 4582 (1964) Finance Same as above	x			7/1/72			File court action on complainant's behalf; class actions allowed
Maryland	Housing Md. Ann. Code art. 49B, § 22 (1972) Finance Art. 49B, § 23a (1972)	x	x		Sex: 7/1/72 Marital status: 7/1/74	x	x	
Massachusetts	Housing Mass. Ann. Laws ch. 151B, § 4 (1971) Finance Ch. 151B, § 4 (14) (1971)	x	x	Housing: children Finance: receives federal assistance	Sex: 1971 Marital status: 5/17/73		By complainant	
Michigan	Housing Mich. Comp. Laws § 564.102 (1967), as amended by Acts 1975, No. 183 Finance Same	x	x		6/29/75	x	x	Initiate own complaints

State	Statute			Public assistance				
Minnesota	Housing Minn. Stat. Ann. § 363.03 (1, 2) (1966) Finance § 363.03.2(3) (1966)	x	x		8/1/73	x		
Montana	Housing Mont. Rev. Codes Ann. § 64-306(3) (1947) Finance § 64-306(4) (1947)	x	x		Housing: 7/1/74 Finance: 6/16/75	x	x	Initiate own complaints
Nevada	Housing only Finance repealed Nev. Rev. Stat. § 118.100 (1973)	x			7/1/73			Initiate own complaints
New Hampshire	Housing only N.H. Rev. Stat. Ann. § 354-A:8(v) (Supp. 1973)	x	x		Sex: 1971 Marital status: 5/3/75		x	
New Jersey	Housing N.J. Stat. Ann. § 10:5-12(g), (h) (1960) Finance § 10:5-12(l) (1960)	x	x		6/70		x	
New Mexico	Housing N.M. Stat. Ann. § 4-33-7(G) (1953) Finance § 4-33-7(H) (1953)	x			6/16/73	x	x	

(continued)

TABLE 8.2 (continued)

State	Fair Housing and Housing Finance Laws	Sex	Marital Status	Other	Effective Date	Court Enforcement of Investigative Powers	Orders	Other Agency Powers
New York	Housing N.Y. Exec. Law § 296(5) (McKinney 1972) Finance § 296a (McKinney 1972)	x	x	Childbearing potential	3/5/74	x	x	Initiate own complaints; attorney general also may enforce act; Human Rights Appeal Board
Ohio	Housing Ohio Rev. Code Ann. § 4112.02(H) (Page 1965) Finance Same	x			12/18/73	x	x	Commission may appeal judicial reversal of order
Oregon	Housing Ore. Rev. Stat. § 659.033 (1974) Finance § 30.670 (1973) or § 659.045	x	x		10/5/73		x	Class actions
Pennsylvania	Housing Pa. Stat. Ann. tit. 43, § 955 (1964) Finance Same as above	x			1969	x	x	Initiate own complaints; refer to real estate licenser
Rhode Island	Finance R.I. Gen. Laws Ann. § 34-37-4.1 (1956)	x	x		1973			

State	Statute			Date	
South Dakota	Housing S.D. Comp. Laws Ann. § 20-13-20 (1967) Finance § 20-13-21 (1967)	x		1972	x
Texas	Finance only Tex. Rev. Civ. Stat. Ann. art. 5069-2.07 (Supp. 1974)	x		8/27/73	x
Utah	Finance only Utah Code Ann. § 13-7-3 (Supp. 1973)	x		5/8/73	
Vermont	Finance only Vt. Stat. Ann. tit. 8, § 1211 (1970)	x	x	7/1/74	
Virginia	Housing Va. Code Ann. § 36-88 (1970) Finance § 36-90 (1970)	x		6/1/73 New procedure: 6/1/75	Refer violation to attorney general
Washington	Housing Wash. Rev. Code Ann. § 49.60.222 (Supp. 1973) Finance § 49.60.224 (Supp. 1973)	x	x	Sex: 6/6/73 Marital status: 1975	
Wisconsin	Finance only Wis. Stat. Ann. § 138.20 (Supp. 1973)	x	x	8/4/73	

Source: Compiled by the authors.

285

With the exception of Indiana, which does not delineate specific prohibited acts, all state statutes prohibiting sex discrimination in real
estate transactions copy the Federal Act's basic guarantee of freedom from discrimination in the purchase or rental of a residential
unit or undeveloped land; in the terms, conditions, and privileges in
connection with such purchase or rental; and in the provision of services or facilities. Most also contain the other prohibitions found in
the Federal Act· advertisements that indicate discriminatory practices, failure to negotiate or transmit bona fide offers in good faith,
representations that dwellings are not available when in fact they are,
the use of applications or inquiries that indicate a discriminatory intent, and the exclusion of persons from access to multiple listing services or real estate brokers' organizations. Blockbusting and restrictive covenants also are prohibited by a number of statutes, although
these are more apt to be relevant in racial discrimination cases than
in the sexual context.

Most state laws that cover financing, as well as sales and rentals, include a provision similar to that found in the Federal Act prohibiting the denial of credit or the imposition of different terms and
conditions on financial assistance in connection with the purchase,
repair, or construction of a dwelling on the basis of sex. Most also
prohibit inquiries that indicate an intention to discriminate.

The state laws, like the Federal Act, seem generally concerned
with the impact of the prohibited behavior rather than with the intent
of the perpetrator. Typical of this attitude is a passage from a decision of the Maryland Commission on Human Relations:

> In considering whether or not Respondent is guilty of any
> act proscribed by the Maryland statute, we keep in mind
> that Complainant need not show overt, deliberate, obvious
> racial discrimination. . . . What the law prohibits is dis-
> criminatory conduct. . . . A deliberately discriminatory
> motivation is not essential to a finding of guilt, if the con-
> duct has the prohibited effect.[20]

In addition, the majority of states do not require that the proscribed
basis of discrimination, such as sex or marital status, be proven the
sole cause of the denial of equal opportunity; it is sufficient that such
unlawful bias was a factor in the overall decision. (An exception is
the state of Connecticut, which uses the stricter standard requiring
proof that the sex or marital status of the party is the sole cause for
the discriminatory treatment in a credit transaction.)

Almost every state has legislated exceptions to limit their otherwise broad proscriptions against discriminatory conduct. The most
common exception is rental property with only a small number of

units, one of which is occupied by the owner or members of the owner's family. Others permit single-sex accommodations* or sales or rentals to "singles" or "married couples" only.[†] Other frequent exceptions are made for charitable or religious institutions. More amorphous, and thus potentially more threatening as loopholes for discrimination, are those statutory exceptions based on "business necessity" or "reasonable grounds." Montana, for example, recently revised its state fair housing law to allow for "reasonable distinctions based on sex."[21] While the revision specifies that exceptions are to be strictly construed, landlords may file petitions requesting exemption from the antidiscrimination law. The District of Columbia, which has one of the most comprehensive and far-reaching human rights laws in the country, recognizes exceptions for "business necessity."[22] No categorical exemptions are available, however; "necessity" must be proved in each individual case. The statute also makes clear that the "necessity" standard is not satisfied by mere preference or by the use of comparative or stereotypical characterizations.

Enforcement

Several types of remedies are important to effective enforcement of fair housing laws: (1) preliminary injunctive relief to preserve the status quo pending resolution of a discrimination charge;[23] (2) court enforcement of an agency's order;[24] (3) agency power to initiate its own complaints;[‡] (4) affirmative action to remedy discrimination;[25] (5) monetary damages, both compensatory and punitive, available from both the administrative agency and the court;[26] and (6) private court actions, preferably with provision for court-awarded attorney's fees (see Table 8.3).[27] Those interested in effective enforcement should scrutinize their state laws carefully to see if the remedies provided are sufficient to encourage victims of discrimination to press charges and to discourage landlords, realtors, and bankers from persisting in discriminatory practices.

Because of the ineffectiveness of many administrative remedies and inadequate agency staffing and appropriations, it is especially important that fair housing and housing finance laws authorize private civil court actions and the award of attorney's fees and costs.[28]

---

*For example, Colorado, Connecticut, Iowa, New Jersey, Oregon, and Virginia.

[†]Alaska and Connecticut (marital status is defined in the statute as not including unrelated man and woman living together).

[‡]Agencies in Colorado and the District of Columbia have this power.

PUBLIC ACCOMMODATIONS

While many places of public accommodation, such as hotels, bars, and clubs, traditionally have been closed to women, this area of sex discrimination has been ignored by federal and state law.* In recent years, however, 21 states with statutes prohibiting discrimination in public accommodations on the basis of race, religion, and national origin have extended their laws to cover sex; six of these statutes cover marital status as well. Like state prohibitions of discrimination in housing and credit transactions, laws banning discrimination in public accommodations generally are enforced by state civil rights agencies, although some jurisdictions also provide a private right of action for complainants as an alternative to administrative relief, and some impose criminal sanctions as well (see Table 8.4).

A number of states have interpreted "public accommodation" quite broadly to include, in addition to retail, food, and boarding establishments, banking and commercial institutions,[29] schools,[30] and health facilities.[31] Utah includes all enterprises regulated by the state, such as licensed insurers and public utilities, businesses subject to the Uniform Consumer Credit Code, and all establishments selling liquor. Such a broad reading of "public accommodation" is particularly critical in states without separate laws prohibiting discrimination in credit or insurance. It is also important that state enactments prohibit discriminatory advertising as well as discriminatory treatment on the premises. At present, 11 states[†] have done so by statute.

Existing public accommodations statutes commonly have several types of exemptions. Some of these standard exemptions are not problematic because they either fall outside the ordinary meaning of "public accommodation" or involve behavior protected by the Constitution. For example, five states exclude bathrooms and bathing facilities from sex integration requirements.[32] If such an exemption is narrowly applied (for example, separate locker rooms accompanying a shared swimming pool), it is acceptable under the constitutionally protected right of privacy regarding disrobing and bodily functions. Iowa's exclusion of religious institutions if the sex-based distinction stems from religious beliefs[33] is consistent with the First Amendment protection of the free exercise of religious beliefs. The exclu-

---

*Title II of the Civil Rights Act of 1964, which bars discrimination in public accommodations, has never been amended to prohibit discrimination based on sex.

†Alaska, Colorado, Delaware, Iowa, Maine, Montana, New Hampshire, New York, Pennsylvania, South Dakota, and West Virginia.

TABLE 8.3

State Enforcement and Remedial Powers of Housing Law

State	Injunctive Relief Through Agency Action	Affirmative Action	Monetary Damages	Cease and Desist	Private Action by Complainant	Costs or Attorney Fees
Alaska	Immediate	Order sale or rental	Actual damages	x	x Judicial review and enforcement	x
California	After "probable cause" finding	Order sale or rental	Up to $1,000	x	x	
Colorado	After "probable cause" finding	Order sale or rental	"Financial assistance"	x	x Judicial review	
Connecticut	After "probable cause" finding		Actual damages		x Judicial review only	x
Delaware	After "probable cause" finding		Compensatory relief	x	Judicial review only	
District of Columbia	Immediate	Posting, compliance reporting	Compensatory relief	x	x Judicial review	x
Florida					x	x
Hawaii	Immediate	Order sale or rental, posting, compliance reporting, ads	"Damages"—$500 assumed	x	Mandamus and judicial review	x
Idaho	Immediate				x	
Indiana		Posting, compliance reporting	Compensatory relief	x	Judicial review only	

(continued)

289

TABLE 8.3 (continued)

State	Injunctive Relief Through Agency Action	Affirmative Action	Monetary Damages	Cease and Desist	Private Action by Complainant	Costs or Attorney Fees
Iowa	Immediate	Posting, compliance reporting, "affirmative action"		x	Judicial review only	
Kansas		Posting, compliance reporting, "affirmative action"		x	Judicial review and en- forcement	
Kentucky	Immediate	Posting, compliance reporting		x	x Mandamus	x
Louisiana					Unclear	
Maine		Through court only	Through court only	Through court only	x	
Maryland	Immediate	"Affirmative action"		x		
Massachusetts	After "probable cause"	"Affirmative action"	Actual damages	x	Judicial review and en- forcement only	x
Michigan	Immediate	"Affirmative action"	Through court only	x	Judicial review	
Minnesota	Immediate	Order sale or rental, "affirmative action"	Compensatory and punitive	x	Judicial review only	x
Montana	Immediate	Posting, compliance reporting, "reasonable measures"		x	x Judicial review	x
Nevada	After agency finding of dis- crimination			x	x	x

290

New Hampshire		"Affirmative action"		x	Judicial review only	
New Jersey		Compliance reporting, "affirmative action"		x	Judicial review only	
New Mexico	Immediate	Posting, compliance reporting, "affirmative action"	Actual damages		Judicial review only	
New York	After agency finding of violation	"Affirmative action," order granting of credit	Compensatory damages	x	Judicial review	
Ohio		"Affirmative action"		x	Judicial review	
Oregon			If order violated	x	Judicial review	x
Pennsylvania	Immediate	"Affirmative action"		x	Enforcement	
Rhode Island						
South Dakota		"Affirmative action"		x	Judicial review only	
Texas			Only in court	x	x	Court costs
Vermont					Unclear	
Virginia	Immediate		Only in court	x	x	
Washington			Compensatory relief	x	x	x
Wisconsin			Civil fine			

Source: Compiled by the authors.

291

TABLE 8.4

State Public Accommodations Law Reforms

State	Public Accommodations Laws	Protected Status	Date	Enforcement
Alaska	Alaska Stat. § 18.80.230 (1962)	Sex	1972	Administrative remedy, criminal penalty
Colorado	Colo. Rev. Stat. Ann. § 25-1-1 (1963)	Sex	1969	
Connecticut	Conn. Gen. Stat. Ann. § 53-35 (1958)	Sex, marital status	1973	Criminal penalty
		marital status	1974	
Delaware	Del. Code Ann. tit. 6, § 4604 (1974)	Sex, marital status	1971	Administrative remedy
Indiana	Ind. Ann. Stat. § 22;9-2 (1974)	Sex	1971	Administrative remedy
Iowa	Iowa Code Ann. § 601A.7 (1975)	Sex	1970	Administrative remedy
Kansas	Kan. Stat. Ann. § 44-1016 (1972)	Sex		Administrative remedy
Maine	Me. Rev. Stat. Ann. tit. 5, § 4592 (1964)	Sex	1964	Administrative remedy
Maryland	Md. Ann. Code art. 49B, § 11 (1972)	Marital status	1974	Administrative remedy
Massachusetts	Mass. Ann. Laws ch. 272, § 92A (1975)	Sex	1971	Administrative remedy, criminal penalty
Minnesota	Minn. Stat. Ann. § 363.03(3) (1966)	Sex, marital status (educational institutions only)	1973	Administrative remedy
Montana	Mont. Rev. Codes Ann. § 64-306(2) (1947)	Sex	1971	Administrative remedy, criminal penalty
Nebraska	Neb. Rev. Stat. § 20-122 (1970)	"All persons"	1969	Administrative remedy
New Hampshire	N.H. Rev. Stat. Ann. § 354A:8 IV (1966)	Sex, marital status	1971	Administrative remedy
			1975	
New Jersey	N.J. Stat. Ann. § 10-5-12(f) (1960) and § 10-5-4 (1960)	Sex, marital status	1970	Administrative remedy
New Mexico	N.M. Stat. Ann. § 4-33-7(F) (1953)	Sex	1973	Administrative remedy
New York	N.Y. Exec. Law § 296.2(a) (McKinney 1972)	Sex	1972	Administrative remedy
Oregon	Ore. Rev. Stat. § 659.037 (1974)	Sex, marital status	1973	Administrative remedy
Pennsylvania	Pa. Stat. Ann. tit. 43, § 952 (1964)	Sex	1969	Administrative remedy
South Dakota	S.D. Comp. Laws Ann. §§ 20-13-23, -24 (1967)	Sex	1972	Administrative remedy
Utah	Utah Code Ann. § 13-7-3 (1953)	Sex	1973	Attorney general and private action
West Virginia	W.Va. Code Ann. § 5-11-9(f) (1971)	Sex	1971	Administrative remedy

Source: Compiled by the authors.

sion of private clubs by several states[34] also may be consistent in theory with the First Amendment protection of freedom of association. In practice, however, difficult questions arise because, while some recreational or dining facilities are organized as membership associations, the qualifications and responsibilities of "members" are slight. The activities of such associations are much like businesses open to the public, the private club format often being simply a ruse to circumvent civil rights laws. Several of the state laws address this problem. Three have language expressly requiring the club to be "in its nature distinctly private," and a fourth requires the club to be "in its nature private."[35] Two statutes expressly state that even a bona fide club's activities are subject to the law when they are open to the public.[36] The other nine statutes, while not explicit on this point, also could be construed to prohibit discrimination by truly private groups in their public activities.[37]

A second group of exemptions, however, represents a more significant dent in the comprehensiveness of public accommodations statutes. The exclusion of single-sex residences by three states[38] and of boarding houses by four others[39] may be local compromises that do not seriously interfere with equal opportunity. However, Delaware extends its boarding house exclusion to units that have up to ten rooms and are not necessarily owner-occupied, so that small motels might be exempt. Connecticut permits the denial of sleeping accommodations to unmarried couples, thereby narrowing that state's statutory prohibition of marital status discrimination. Indiana exempts religious institutions, without specifying that the permissible sex distinction must derive from religious beliefs, and private schools, although many private educational institutions, like other privately owned businesses, solicit business from and offer services to the general public. Other exemptions are more puzzling. Delaware excludes barbershops and hairdressers. A 1973 New Jersey case also approved discrimination by beauty parlors and barbershops by defining them as places that are "in their nature" restricted to one sex, although no authority for such a justification is written in the New Jersey statute.[40]

Finally, three states give their enforcement agencies broad discretion to grant other exemptions from their antidiscrimination provisions. Montana, for example, allows its commission to approve exemptions based on "reasonable grounds." New York's enforcement agency may approve sex discrimination for "bona fide considerations of public policy." In Colorado, sex discrimination may be lawful without prior approval if it has a "bona fide relationship to the goods, services . . . of a place of public accommodation." To avoid the potentially crippling effect of such exemptions on the overall impact of a public accommodations law, it is crucial that equal rights advocates either fight to omit such open-ended language from reform legislation or watch carefully to assure that these standards are narrowly construed.

INSURANCE

Background

Common insurance industry practices include discrimination
on the basis of sex in the availability of policies, scope of coverage,
and rate setting. In addition, state statutes often protect female but
not male beneficiaries by exempting their proceeds from tax and debt
liability. Availability problems, deriving from discriminatory underwriting standards, are especially acute in the field of income replacement insurance. A woman who works outside the home often is denied
such insurance altogether, made to wait a longer period than a man to
receive coverage, or offered only partial coverage for a shorter period of time than a man. This is particularly true if she does not have
a high-level position. Homemakers generally are unable to insure the
value of their work to their families.

Significant problems also arise in obtaining coverage for conditions related to pregnancy. Both health and disability insurance policies commonly exclude normal childbirth and complications of childbirth, unless a disproportionately expensive family coverage option
is selected.* In employment-related health insurance, therefore,
single female employees often are provided less coverage than wives
of male employees. Pregnancies of dependent female children generally are excluded even under a family plan. Despite such exclusions,
which sometimes cover all disorders of the "female organs," women
often pay extraordinarily high rates for health and disability plans.

Men pay higher premiums for life insurance than women because
sex-classified actuarial data show that the average woman lives longer
than the average man. However, women usually get a rate reduction

------

*The high cost of a family plan derives from the fact that it is
based on a unit of two children and two adults. The insurance industry has refused to separate the cost of insuring pregnancy-related
conditions from the additional expense of providing health care services to a spouse and two children. There is no reason why the treatment of pregnancy-related conditions cannot be included in the standard coverage for an individual. Newborn (or newly adopted) children
could be given automatic coverage on the parent's policy for 60 days,
during which time the parent could purchase family coverage.

equivalent to only three years even though, on the average, they actually live six to eight years longer.* Another consequence of sex-
based averaging in actuarial estimates of life expectancy is that women receive lower annuity payments at retirement even though they
have made equal contributions with men during their working years.

The overall effect of these forms of discrimination is to prevent
women from obtaining routine economic protection, both for their own
support and medical needs and for those of their dependents and survivors.

Impact of the ERA

The ERA will reach these practices because, as in other areas
of the law, state statutes that now explicitly grant different rights or
opportunities to men and women must be sex neutralized and because
a state's broad involvement in insurance regulation makes the state
and any companies whose policies it approves vulnerable to constitutional attack. (Even if insurance contracts are held not to be "state
action," states still can utilize their regulatory power to prohibit sex
discrimination in insurance. These points are discussed in detail
below.)

Special Tax, Credit, and Inheritance Provisions

Some states establish by statute special tax exemptions, exemptions from attachment by creditors, and provisions for inheritance to
protect life insurance proceeds. Revision is required because these
statutes often use only female references for beneficiaries and male
references for policyholders, assuming that women are always the
dependent spouses and apparently leaving unprotected any proceeds
a widower may receive from his wife's policy. Such laws deny men
certain financial benefits when they receive insurance proceeds and
deny families the full value of women's contribution to their financial
security. Since financial dependency within marriage is often mutual,
both spouses merit protection under the insurance laws. These statutes should be redrafted to extend benefits to both sexes.

---

*This apparent advantage for women also is offset by the fact that
life insurance policies provided as a fringe benefit for high level employees are less likely to be available to women since women are con-
centrated in low-level jobs.

Sex-Based Rating

A second group of sex-based insurance laws are those permitting sex-based rate setting. This practice is almost universal in the fields of life and annuity insurance and also appears in other types of insurance, such as auto liability, but generally not pursuant to explicit statutory language. Sex-based rating for life insurance and annuities has until recently been perceived as fair because it is based on actuarial differences in the life expectancy of the sexes rather than on the unproven social or moral judgments underlying many other sex-based laws. However, a classification based on average facts denies rights and opportunities to members of the group who do not share the common characteristic. Such arbitrary classification methods clearly would not be tolerated by this society if they were premised on racial rather than sexual averaging. The ERA requires that only individual differences that cut across sex categories, and therefore are themselves sex neutral, form the basis for legislative line drawing. Because the overlap of the longevity of men and women is considerable, [41] sex-averaging necessarily groups a sizable number of long-lived men with all other men, imposing an unfairly high life insurance rate on them, while it groups short-lived women with all other women, unfairly reducing their annuity payouts.

Although insurance rate making necessarily requires some form of averaging, the ERA would permit sex-based classification only if a unique physical characteristic found in all or some members of one sex but not in the other were shown to be a definitive cause of an invariable difference in the longevity of men and women. However, no such factor has been identified. In addition, so many variables in lifestyle and environment affect mortality that physiological processes alone could probably never be used to predict life-spans accurately. [42]

State Action and the Equality Principle

Apart from the explicit statutory provisions discussed above, state law tolerates rather than mandates most kinds of discrimination suffered by women in the insurance market. While the mere licensing or registration of insurance companies would probably not bring constitutional restrictions on discriminatory state action to bear on otherwise private insurance practices, state insurance regulation generally goes far beyond that. [43] Indeed, the state often officially sanctions the content, terms, and rates of all insurance contracts offered for sale within state borders. Thus, in those states where insurance policies are available only to certain classes of women or are available only on discriminatory terms, both the state departments of insurance and insurance companies themselves may become the objects of equal rights litigation. [44]

Beyond what may be required by the constitutional doctrine of "state action" under the ERA, states should, as a matter of policy, attempt consistent enforcement and implementation of the equal rights principle throughout their regulatory activity. It is inequitable for a state to permit its regulatory agencies to perpetuate discrimination in the private sector while prohibiting discrimination in the various insurance programs provided by the public sector. Moreover, state efforts to eliminate sex discrimination by private insurers would solve the current dilemma of employers who face federal liability under the Equal Pay Act of 1963 and Title VII of the Civil Rights Act of 1964 for extending discriminatory insurance benefits to their employees yet cannot find private coverage that meets an equality standard.[45]

As to annuities and life insurance plans, there has been disagreement among the federal agencies that enforce fair employment laws about what constitutes equal treatment. Several of the agencies permit an employer to choose between equal contributions and equal benefits. The Equal Employment Opportunities Commission now requires equal periodic benefit payments to similarly situated male and female employees,[46] which necessitates, given the use of sex-based tables, unequal contributions for men and women. A plan based on unisex tables would yield equal benefits for equal contributions. It also would discourage the development of a "black market" of sex-based policies that might arise if only certain insurance policies were required to comply with a strict equality standard.[47]

The same reasoning applies to employee health and disability policies. Most individuals insure themselves and their families against major medical costs through plans connected with their employment. The most pervasive form of discrimination in these insurance plans concerns coverage for pregnancy-related costs and disabilities, whether the pregnancy is terminated by abortion or birth. Under the ERA, any classification involving a unique physical characteristic, such as pregnancy, must be strictly scrutinized to determine its relationship to a compelling state interest in order to prevent such classifications from serving as a subterfuge for sex discrimination. In terms of the goals of these plans—insuring against medical expenses and loss of income during a period of physical disability—the costs imposed by pregnancy-related disability do not differ from those imposed by other conditions covered by these forms of insurance. A number of state civil rights laws and court decisions support the idea that it is impermissible sex discrimination to treat pregnancy differently from other temporary disabilities, although the United States Supreme Court has recently held that Title VII does not presently affect such practices.[48] States could ease the difficulty faced by employers attempting to find insurance that complies with this rule by disapproving private plans that discriminate against women in their health and disability coverage. * Such proscription of discriminatory policies should not be restricted to employment-related policies but should extend to all companies regulated by the state.

State Reform Efforts

A number of states have enacted prohibitions of common forms of discrimination against women or are currently considering them. Many of these are general antidiscrimination provisions covering the whole area of insurance, while others address specific discriminatory practices.

General Antidiscrimination Laws

At least six states now prohibit sex discrimination generally in insurance transactions: Illinois,[49] Massachusetts,[50] New York,[51] Pennsylvania,[52] Utah,[53] and Washington.[54] All of these, along with a number of legislative proposals offered in other states, prohibit a company from failing or refusing to issue or renew any policy on the basis of sex. (In Oregon and California, the insurance departments have published proposed regulations that prohibit some forms of sex discrimination under the authority of existing state law.)[55] Illinois, New York, Washington, and Pennsylvania also prohibit discrimination on the basis of marital status. (It should be noted, however, that these four states, while prohibiting discrimination in the issuance of insurance contracts, still permit rating based on sex-classified risk.)

A number of states have no statutes directed specifically at sex discrimination but do prohibit unfair practices in the issuance of insurance, including differential terms, conditions, or premiums for persons "of the same class and hazards." Such statutes are found in Arizona,[56] Georgia,[57] Ohio,[58] Montana,[59] South Carolina,[60] South Dakota,[61] Vermont,[62] Virginia,[63] and Wisconsin.[64] Correspondence with a number of these states' insurance departments indicates that these prohibitions have not been interpreted to include sex-based differentials because men and women are not seen as members of the same class.[65]

In addition, 21 states have statutes prohibiting sex discrimination in public accommodations (see the section on state public accommodation laws above). Since insurance companies do business in the

---

*Five states and Puerto Rico establish statewide disability insurance plans by statute. For a discussion of the discrimination in these plans and recent changes, see Chapter 6.

public sector, these statutes should apply to them, yet, with a few exceptions, they have not been widely used to equalize insurance practices, and a pattern of enacting separate insurance laws has developed. Thus, further legislative reform is advisable in these states.

Special Tax, Credit, and Inheritance Provisions

Arizona has amended a statutory exemption of life insurance proceeds from execution, attachment, or judicial sale.[66] Formerly applicable only to proceeds paid to a wife from a policy on the life of a deceased husband, the new statute extends the exemptions to proceeds paid to a husband from a policy on the life of a deceased wife. Maryland similarly amended its general insurance contracts law so that the exemption of insurance proceeds from creditors' claims now applies to policies payable to either spouse.[67] An unsuccessful Minnesota bill[68] would have repealed the automatic right of an insured to remove his wife as his life insurance beneficiary upon divorce. The bill attempted to treat this situation as all others, in which the right to change beneficiaries is dependent upon such a power being reserved in the policy or upon consent of the beneficiary.

Sex-Classified Rates

The issue of sex-segregated schedules for life insurance and annuity premiums and payment has not been widely addressed by antidiscrimination laws. While unisex rating has been proposed as an effective and feasible solution to the discrimination inherent in sex-segregated rating systems, reform efforts up to this point have been directed at simply prohibiting arbitrary distinctions in rates and requiring that they be based on "credible supporting data" or be "actuarially reasonable." Often the statute explicitly exempts sex-based tables; even where it does not do so, sex-based rating has not been considered violative of antidiscrimination statutes.* Recent proposals in New York and Oregon to equalize premium ratings and new Illinois insurance regulations also retained the exception for sex-based ac-

---

*The claim that sex-based tables reflect "actuarial reality" gives them an undeserved air of immutability. Actuarial tables merely estimate risk on the basis of the average experience of those included in the group. As long as the insurance companies group people on a basis that has some consistent predictive value, the group experience will always seem to bear out the rates. Since there are usually a variety of factors that have a consistent predictive value, there are therefore a variety of "actuarial realities."

tuarial data.[69] A recent Maryland proposal, however, would have
eliminated any reference to sex in calculating net premiums and
present values of life insurance policies.[70]

Excessive rates for disability insurance for women are being
attacked in Gilpin v. Schenk, pending in federal court in New York.[71]
Of particular interest is the fact, discovered by the plaintiffs in Gilpin, that New York insurance companies were using risk experience
data from 1933 to determine women's premiums. The case provides
a good example of challenging sex discrimination that may appear to
be statutorily sanctioned by challenging the factual basis underlying
the actuarial tables themselves. However, although life insurance
and annuity rates that reflect actuarial reality would be an improvement over many current practices, they are not a permissible substitute under the ERA for unisex rates, and much remains to be done
to accomplish equality in this area through affirmative state legislation.

Health and Disability Insurance Coverage

A number of states have taken action in this area. Statutes in
Colorado,[72] Illinois,[73] Minnesota,[74] Oregon,[75] Pennsylvania,[76]
Maine,[77] and Maryland,[78] for example, all require that benefits for
maternity be available to both married and unmarried policyholders.*
Colorado requires that maternity care be offered to both married and
unmarried women in nonfamily contracts. These statutes also provide that dependents' health insurance benefits must be the same for
married and unmarried policyholders. In addition, the Minnesota,
Maine, and Maryland laws provide that maternity benefits must be
available to dependent minor females under family plans. Finally,

---

*Bills to prohibit discrimination in eligibility for pregnancy-
related benefits were also introduced in the 1975 legislative sessions
in Massachusetts (S.1862—Commerce and Labor Committee), New
Jersey (S.3246—Dodd et al., referred to Committee for Institutions
and Health and Welfare), and New York (A.7319—Miller, referred to
Health Committee). These laws would have required the availability
to unmarried persons of family policies that include this coverage.
They did not solve the inequity resulting from the availability of this
coverage only in policies intended for a four-person unit. While these
bills did not pass their respective legislatures, a few states, such as
Massachusetts and Colorado, have passed laws that are neutral in
regard to sex and marital status and that provide coverage for newborn infants and adopted children in policies with provisions for dependents or family members.[79]

Maryland has prohibited such practices as placing a below-cost limitation on maternity benefits by requiring that pregnancy-related payments be provided on the same basis as other medical claims.

No statute requires the inclusion of full maternity benefits in every health insurance policy rather than the addition of separate riders. The Colorado, Illinois, Minnesota, and Oregon laws go the furthest in equalizing the treatment of married and unmarried women. They provide that the child of an unmarried woman who has not chosen dependent family coverage must be covered to the same extent as the child of a married woman who has chosen such coverage. (A 1974 Minnesota insurance bill, S.F. 2963, which was not enacted, would have equalized the right of unmarried parents of both sexes to obtain insurance for their children by extending equal coverage to the illegitimate child of an insured person who is its adjudicated or acknowledged parent.)

California has enacted new legislation[80] prohibiting any limitations on health insurance coverage of sterilization based on the reason for the sterilization and on the coverage of or deductibles for involuntary complications of pregnancy in health insurance plans that provide maternity benefits, unless the provisions apply generally to all benefits paid under such plans. An Idaho statute[81] now requires that pregnancy benefits be continued for 12 months following the termination of a group plan for any covered person who is already pregnant at the time of termination. Finally, a new Rhode Island "catastrophic health insurance plan,"[82] funded by the state, includes maternity benefits as one of the minimum standards for a qualified plan.[83]

Colorado now requires all health insurance policies that provide coverage on an expense-incurred basis for disability due to sickness and accidents to provide similar coverage for complications related to pregnancy or childbirth; it also requires that complications of pregnancy and childbirth be treated in the same manner as any similar sickness or disease under individual, group service, or indemnity contracts.[84] A Montana statute prohibits public and private employers from terminating employment due to pregnancy, refusing to grant a leave of absence for pregnancy, denying an employee who is disabled due to pregnancy any compensation or leave benefits to which she is entitled, or requiring an employee to take a mandatory leave for an unreasonable length of time.[85] The statute also provides equitable remedies for any employee so injured.

A new rule promulgated by the Illinois Insurance Department prohibits the establishment of different conditions or benefits based on an individual's sex, sexual preference, or marital status. This includes prohibitions of restrictive benefit periods or definitions of disability for women and of the treatment of pregnancy complications differently from any other illness.[86]

A number of the general "unfair practices" statutes discussed
earlier also may have implications for maternity coverage. It can
be argued that disabilities arising from pregnancy and childbirth
must receive the same treatment as all other temporary disabilities,
for the purposes of sick leave and temporary disability insurance,
since they are the same type of hazard as all other medical and surgi-
cal procedures and must be treated accordingly.[87]

Finally, Minnesota has attacked a more subtle form of discrimination extremely damaging to women in its supplemental disability insurance plan for auto accidents. The plan provides coverage for the
loss of services and substitute services reimbursement if the injured
party is one who normally has the full-time responsibility for the care
and maintenance of a home, with or without children. The policy will
pay for the reasonable value of such work or the reasonable expenses
incurred in procuring a substitute, whichever is greater, up to a
maximum of $15 a day.[88] In line with this concept, the new Ohio law
requires the availability of income disability insurance to homemakers.[89]

Attention has only recently been drawn to the multifaceted discrimination women suffer in connection with insurance. State statutes
prohibiting discrimination in underwriting and coverage are beginning
to be enacted. Sex-based rating and some discriminatory practices
have not yet been outlawed. Their inclusion in affirmative legislation is essential to avoid extensive litigation and to reach the whole
range of discriminatory practices women face.

EDUCATION*

Overview

Public and private educational institutions have long been characterized by discrimination against women and girls. Every dimension of the educational process—from school admissions and employment to the scope and perspective of curricula—is marred by sex
biases that hamper women's development in psychological, intellectual, physical, and economic terms. In patterns of the employment

---

*Education is critical in its overall impact on the quality of life
for women. Because of the extensive attention paid to sex discrimination in education by others, however, this section will be brief. Only
equal opportunity in school athletics will be discussed at length because of its particular difficulties.[90]

of teachers and training of students, schools reflect the general societal attitude that women are best suited for domestic, clerical, and
other supportive roles while men are expected to excel in physical
and intellectual activities and to pursue high vocational or professional
aspirations. Women educators, for example, are consistently chan-
neled into the ranks of grade school teachers or held at low-level in-
structorships in institutions of higher education, while men dominate
supervisory positions and university professorships. As students,
women have been segregated into separate schools or programs, held
to higher admission standards or subjected to sex-based quotas,
barred from scholarships, restricted in their choice of academic and
vocational training, and limited by inadequate career counseling. In
addition, female students, teachers, and sometimes other school employees have been discriminated against on the basis of pregnancy,
parenthood, or marital status. [91]

To the extent that schools are publicly operated or involve sufficient state action, the ERA will reach and invalidate sex discriminatory practices, including the sex segregation of institutions, facilities,
and programs. [92] In addition, the process of ERA reform provides
states with an opportunity to take affirmative steps to mitigate the effects of past discrimination. A number of states already have begun
to implement equal rights in education; some of the reforms and
changes that seem particularly promising are discussed below.

Several states have enacted comprehensive prohibitions of sex
discrimination in their public school systems, bringing state law to
bear on some of the activities affected by Title IX of the Education
Amendments of 1972. [93] Some of the state laws are broadly worded,
prohibiting discrimination "against any pupil in this state . . . in admission to or in obtaining any advantages, privileges, or courses of
study." [94] Other comprehensive sex discrimination provisions are
more detailed, specifying nondiscrimination in admissions, in required enrollments in courses, and in career counseling as well as
prohibiting curricula, textbooks, or activities that "reflect adversely"
on persons because of sex (or race). Illinois prohibits discrimination
in employment or appointment to any position in a school district,
discrimination against students in admission to courses and athletic
programs, and segregation of schools. [95] Some of these state laws
expressly provide for private court actions. [96]

Other states have enacted legislation remedying problems in
specific areas, including the prohibition of discrimination in scholar-
ship, loan, and grant programs, [97] in the state university, [98] and in
athletic programs. [99] In addition, affirmative legislation has been
enacted. For example, some states require educational agencies
to commit themselves to increasing the number of women and minorities at all levels of responsibility, [100] and others provide funds for

continuing education programs that aid older women returning to school after a period as homemakers.[101]

The problem of teaching materials that disparage or ignore women has been tackled in several states by requiring the development of curricula that give proper emphasis to the history, culture, and achievements of women and minorities and by establishing programs in women's studies.[102] Guidelines for the review and reform of sexist texts and curricula have been developed in California, for example, to implement a state law requiring the elimination of sex stereotypes from textbooks.[103] A related curriculum development that should help young men and women make intelligent life-style choices is the addition of instruction in family law,[104] family finances, marriage law, and family health.[105]

School Athletics

Impact of the ERA

The most difficult subject in the education area, as well as the most controversial, is equality of athletic education and competition for both sexes. While discrimination in other areas of education can be remedied by fairly clear-cut programs of sex integration and affirmative action, equalization of opportunity in athletics raises more severe doctrinal questions under the ERA. Because of its problematic nature and its less extensive coverage in other materials, the issue of equality in school athletics will be treated at length in this chapter.

To evaluate the impact of the ERA on school athletics, it first must be ascertained whether unique physical characteristics of the sexes cause differences in men's and women's athletic ability that would justify complete or partial sex segregation. There is little doubt that there are large differences between the sexes in average athletic performance and physical potential for athletic achievement.[106] It is not yet known how much of these differences can be attributed to socialization factors, such as training and interest in athletics, and how much to physical factors, such as bone structure, hormone levels, height, weight, and the proportion of fat to muscle in body weight. Furthermore, it appears that the physical differences between women and men are average differences only (that is, some women have a lower proportion of body weight that is fat than some men, although on the average men's proportion is around 15 percent and women's proportion is around 25 percent).[107] It also appears that the physical differences can be reduced by training. For example, the ability of swimmers of both sexes to use oxygen efficiently, and hence to have greater endurance, is greatly enhanced by early training. Finally, athletic performance is obviously not entirely based

on physical ability. Many other individual factors, such as determination to win, sense of timing, and skill play a large role in athletic
competitions.

For these reasons, it would be impossible to show that all differences in average athletic ability and performance between men and
women are caused by unique physical characteristics. The most that
is clear at present about physical explanations for sex differences in
this area is that average physical differences between the sexes (for
example, in height and weight) do play a role. However, it is possible that unique physical characteristics will be found that give members of one sex a biological advantage over members of the other sex
in a given sport. These might be characteristics unique to one sex
that increase the risk of injury or decrease athletic potential.

If characteristics were found that affect the risk of injury, sex
segregation would be permitted only under certain highly improbable
conditions. First, there would have to be no alternative less drastic
than sex segregation to protect individuals from the effects of the
sex-based handicap. For example, a state could not cite an alleged
vulnerability of female breast tissue to injury as a justification for
sex segregation because equipment has been developed that protects
women's breasts from injury.[108] Likewise, even if it were found
that women's bone structure is more fragile, sex segregation would
not be permitted if height and weight classifications within a sex-integrated team structure would serve to protect women athletes. Second, the state could not prevent females from taking risks with their
own bodies that male athletes are allowed to take merely because the
characteristic creating the risk in women is sex-linked and in men is
individual. Third, if some but not all members of one sex have a
sex-linked characteristic, sex segregation could be justified only if
there were no viable method of testing individuals for actual suscepti-
bility to injury.

Similar standards would apply to a unique physical characteristic
that diminished athletic aptitude. Sex segregation would not be permissible if there were a practical method of determining the presence
of the characteristic in a particular individual and its impact on athletic potential. Similarly, such a trait could not be used to justify
sex segregation if other physical characteristics not unique to one sex
could be shown to have an equal or greater effect on athletic ability.
It also would have to be demonstrated that sex segregation is the only
available method for ensuring equitable competition.

It is therefore unlikely that a system of sex segregation, ration-
alized by unique physical characteristics, would be approved under
the ERA. Moreover, such a system does not prevent members of
the same sex with different biological aptitudes from competing with
each other. Hence, any state interest in protecting biologically disad-

vantaged individuals from competition with biologically advantaged
individuals would not be served by sex segregation.

If it is found that unique physical characteristics are an adequate rationale for sex-segregated teams, other factors will determine the ERA's impact. One is the extent to which sex-neutral rules
can be promulgated to enable members of both sexes to compete
against each other on an equal basis and to provide high school students
of both sexes with equal athletic opportunities. If it is shown that the
physical differences between the sexes that affect athletic potential
are average differences rather than characteristics unique to each
sex, such rules are the obvious alternative. Rules based on such factors as height, weight, and the ratio of height to weight would group
individuals according to athletic potential, regardless of sex, thus
ensuring equitable competition. While it would be necessary to allow
individuals to compete in higher categories if they had the ability to
do so, individuals would not be permitted to compete below their size
category. Thus, a system of neutral rules would eliminate male
domination of all athletic opportunities and preserve the principle of
sex-integrated competition. Only those boys and girls with equal
physical potential would be competing against each other.

The viability of such a system would depend on a number of
factors. The rules would have to be sophisticated enough to account
for true differentiations in athletic potential. For example, tall women might lose the chance for fair competition if a simple height requirement pushed them into a category beyond their overall potential
for a sport such as basketball. The rules also would have to be scrutinized to be sure the standards were neither too high nor too low to
allow both sexes equal opportunities in competition. It is possible
that more teams than are presently provided would have to be established to fully implement the principle of equal opportunity. This
would entail additional expense but would have the benefit of extending
athletic opportunities to a wider cross-section of the school population.[109]

Under any system of athletic competition, the extent to which
past and present sex discrimination is responsible for differences
between men's and women's average athletic ability and interest would
have to be taken into account. Women's athletic opportunities cannot
be equal to those of men unless affirmative action is taken to alleviate
the deleterious effects of past denial of equal access to athletic facilities, financial and social support, training, and competitive opportunities. Consequently, the maintenance of some all-female teams might
be temporarily justified in order to allow girls to develop their athletic skills. It would, however, be difficult to justify preventing individual girls with exceptional ability from competing on otherwise
all-male teams in order to provide better opportunities to their sex

as a group because this would be contrary to the underlying principles of the ERA. In the long run, such policies are probably harmful to the cause of women's athletics because exceptional athletes play a vital role in expanding horizons for all athletes and inspiring other women to compete to the best of their ability.

In the last few years, a number of equal protection cases have been brought by exceptional female athletes to challenge their exclusion from all-male teams in various noncontact sports.[110] Interests asserted in these cases by the schools and athletic associations to justify discrimination include: tradition, cost control, the prevention of physical and psychological damage to participants of both sexes, the protection and development of girls' athletic programs, and the ensurance of equitable competition.[111] About half of these cases have been decided favorably to plaintiffs.[112] In three of the cases in which relief was denied, a substantial girls' athletic program did exist, a factor relied on in the courts' decisions.[113]

In addition, female athletes have, on several occasions, obtained settlements that included the elimination of a ban on coeducational competition.[114] In New Haven, Connecticut, women high school students and teachers recently obtained a favorable settlement in a suit challenging "a systematic pattern of sex discrimination" in the funding of varsity sports.[115] The settlement provides that teams will be established for women in all sports sanctioned by the Connecticut Interscholastic Athletic Conference for which there is sufficient demand. Apparently, the settlement does not prevent women from seeking admission to all-male teams when there is insufficient demand for the establishment of a separate women's team.

School athletics also are affected by the recent federal enactment of Title IX of the Education Amendments. This provides that, with certain exceptions, "No person in the United States shall, on the basis of sex, be excluded from participation in, be denied the benefits of, or be subjected to discrimination under any education program or activity receiving federal financial assistance."[116] It is still unclear what the impact of Title IX will actually be on athletic opportunities because HEW has significantly undercut the guarantee of equality with regulations permitting schools to maintain sex-segregated teams in contact sports.[117] In addition, there is no requirement for affirmative action, equal spending, or nondiscrimination in the treatment of separate teams.

As yet, only some of the consequences of applying equal rights principles to school athletics are clear. It is evident that the amendment will enable exceptional women athletes to compete with the best athletes in their communities, regardless of sex. Further, it appears that the amendment provides a variety of effective tools for the attainment of equal athletic opportunity for women. There are many acceptable routes to equitable competition and equal opportunity: the development of sex-neutral rules, the requirement of equal per capita expenditures, the exploration of the role of unique physical characteristics in determining athletic potential, and the creation and implementation of meaningful affirmative action programs.

State Reform Efforts

Because of the growing influence of the equality principle in sports, a number of states have undertaken legislative reform of school athletic programs. California,[118] for example, has enacted broad changes that provide for equal participation in public school sports for both sexes. Kentucky has passed a narrower bill requiring secondary schools with basketball teams for boys to maintain an equivalent program for girls or else forfeit all interscholastic competition for one year.[119] Kansas recently passed an affirmative action measure appropriating special funds to support women's athletics at its state colleges and universities.[120]

CHAPTER 1

1. American Civil Liberties Union, The Equal Rights Amendment: A Lifetime Guarantee (New York: ACLU, n.d.), p. 4.

2. George Vold, "Group Conflict Theory as Explanation of Crime," in Deviance, Conflict, and Criminality, ed. R. Serge Denisoff and Charles H. McCaghy (Chicago, New York, San Francisco, and London: Rand McNally, 1973), p. 80.

3. Ibid., p. 81.

4. Dale Rogers Marshall and Janell Anderson, "Implementation and the Equal Rights Amendment," in Impact ERA: Limitations and Possibilities, ed. The Equal Rights Amendment Project of the California Commission on the Status of Women (Millbrae, Calif.: Les Femmes, 1976), pp. 51-56. These devices are discussed at length by Marshall and Anderson.

5. Ruth B. Cowan, "Legal Barriers to Social Change: The Case of Higher Education," ibid., pp. 158-83. Ruth Cowan's analysis of the reasons why present antidiscrimination law has not achieved equality in education provides concrete examples of legislative and administrative barriers to enforcement and compliance.

6. Ibid., pp. 168-74.

7. Mary C. Dunlap, "The Equal Rights Amendment and the Courts," in Impact ERA, p. 30.

8. Eloise C. Snyder, "Legal Change and Social Values," in Impact ERA, p. 149.

9. Charles Elkins, "Social Order and the Equal Rights Amendment," in Impact ERA, pp. 218-19.

10. Kate Millet, Sexual Politics (New York: Avon, 1971), pp. 121-22.

11. Ibid., p. 166.

12. Ibid., pp. 166-67.

13. John Horton, "Order and Conflict Theories of Social Problems as Competing Ideologies," American Journal of Sociology 71 (1966). Horton describes the two opposing views of society and social change in detail, with special reference to minority groups.

14. Elkins, pp. 220-21.

CHAPTER 2

1. For a more detailed discussion of the failure of women to gain equality of legal status through the Civil War Amendments, see B. Babcock, A. Freedman, E. Norton, and S. Ross, Sex Discrimination and the Law: Causes and Remedies 1-19 (1975).

2. 335 U.S. 464 (1948).

3. 368 U.S. 57 (1961).

4. Reed v. Reed, 404 U.S. 71 (1971).

5. The equal protection doctrine as applied to sex discrimination is treated more extensively in A. Bingaman, A Commentary on the Effect of the Equal Rights Amendment on State Laws and Institutions 4-21 (1975).

6. Frontiero v. Richardson, 411 U.S. 677 (1972).

7. Geduldig v. Aiello, 417 U.S. 484 (1974).

8. This history is set out in S. Rep. No. 92-689, 92d Cong., 2d Sess. 4-6 (1972) [hereafter cited as S. Rep. No. 92-689].

9. Id. at 11.

10. Id.

11. Id. at 12.

12. Brown, Emerson, Falk, and Freedman, The Equal Rights Amendment: A Constitutional Basis for Equal Rights for Women, 80 Yale L. J. 871, 892 (1971) [hereafter cited as Brown].

13. S. Rep. No. 92-689, supra note 8, at 12.

14. See, for example, Commonwealth v. Pennsylvania Interscholastic Athletic Ass'n, 334 A.2d 839 (Cmwlth. Ct. 1975), in which a state ERA was held to prohibit an athletic regulation excluding girls from certain public school interscholastic sports teams.

15. Brown, supra note 12, at 900.

16. 44 U.S.L.W. 4789 (U.S. June 6, 1976).

17. Id. at 4792.

18. See Singer v. Hara, 11 Wash. App. 247, 522 P.2d 1187 (1974), which upheld Washington's statutory prohibition of same-sex marriage.

19. In Frank v. Frank, 62 D. and C. 2d 102 (1973), a Pennsylvania county court declined to decide whether provisions allowing only a wife to obtain a divorce from bed and board together with alimony pendente lite were violative of the ERA, as such provisions were validated by the agreement and waiver flowing from a marriage contract. In subsequent opinions, however, the Supreme Court of Pennsylvania has not hesitated to subject the various rights and obligations of marriage, including traditionally sex-based support obligations, to an absolute standard of review under the ERA. See, for example, Henderson v. Henderson, 458 Pa. 97, 327 A.2d 60 (1974).

20. In Montana, for example, two ERA cases of substantial import—involving child custody standards and the award of alimony and attorney's fees—were avoided by the supreme court because of counsel's failure to raise the constitutional challenge to these statutory schemes in a proper manner at trial See Gilbert v. Gilbert, 533 P.2d 1079 (1975); and Clontz v. Clontz, 531 P.2d 1004 (1975).

21. Maryland courts particularly have insisted that a party must be seeking a benefit under a statute rather than be required to assume an obligation under it in order to challenge it. See Minner v. Minner, 19 Md. App. 154, 310 A.2d 208 (1973); and Colburn v. Colburn, 20 Md. App. 246, 316 A.2d 283 (1974). While there is some dubious precedent for this position, it probably represents judicial unwillingness to strike down important (albeit sex-based) legal obligations and a desire to see the legislature solve this problem.

22. S. Rep. No. 92-689, supra note 8.

23. This standard has become more common, and it appears to be the one the United States Supreme Court will apply in most facial sex discrimination cases. See cases cited note 25 infra.

24. See, for example, Sail'er Inn v. Kirby, 5 Cal. 3d 1, 485 P.2d 529 (Sup. Ct. 1971).

25. See Kahn v. Shevin, 416 U.S. 351 (1974). In most other cases, the Court has applied the "heightened rationality" test. See Weinberger v. Wiesenfeld, 95 S. Ct. 1225 (1975).

26. See, for example, Dandridge v. Williams, 397 U.S. 471 (1970).

27. It should be noted that while Colorado recognizes a "strict scrutiny" standard in sex discrimination cases, its ERA has been interpreted to apply only when sex is the sole basis for a statutory provision or scheme. See People v. Green, 183 Col. 25, 514 P.2d 769 (Sup. Ct. 1973).

28. In dicta, the Connecticut Supreme Court recently indicated that the Connecticut ERA mandates a "strict scrutiny" standard. Page v. Welfare Comm'r, 44 U.S.L.W. 2426, _____ A.2d _____ (Feb. 24, 1976).

29. See, for example, People v. Ellis, 57 Ill. 2d 127, 311 N.E.2d 98 (1974), in which the Illinois Supreme Court declared, at 101:

> In contrast to the Federal Constitution, which, thus far, does not contain the Equal Rights Amendment, the Constitution of 1970 contains section 18 of article I, and in view of its explicit language, and the debates, we find inescapable the conclusion that it was intended to supplement and expand the guaranties of the equal protection provision of the Bill of Rights and requires us to hold that a classification based on sex is a "suspect classification" which to be held valid must withstand "strict judicial scrutiny."

30. 458 Pa. 97, 327 A.2d 60 (1974).

31. 457 Pa. 90, 320 A.2d 139 (1974).

32. 458 Pa. 289, 328 A.2d 851 (1974).

33. People v. Green, 183 Col. 25, 514 P.2d 769 (1973); People v. Medrano, 24 Ill. App. 3d 429, 321 N.E.2d 97 (1974); Brooks v. Maryland, 24 Md. App. 334, 330 A.2d 760 (1975); and Finley v. State of Texas, 527 S.W.2d 553 (Ct. Crim. App. 1975).

34. A more lengthy discussion of the general rules for judicial application of the ERA can be found in Brown, supra note 12, at 912-20.

35. In no reported criminal case has a court extended criminal liability to a previously uncovered class through ERA interpretation. In only one reported case has a court chosen to strike down sex-based liability altogether, resulting in the complete overturning of a defendant's conviction. People v. Yocum, 31 Ill. App. 3d 586, 335 N.E.2d 183 (1975) (conviction for aggravated incest between father and stepdaughter overturned because statute did not prohibit sexual conduct between mother and adopted or stepson).

36. 458 Pa. 289, 328 A.2d 851 (1974).

37. The concurring opinion of Justice Pomeroy in Butler, id. at 303, contains a more detailed description of why striking down the exception for

female offenders was the correct judicial response to the unconstitutional statutory discrimination between male and female offenders.

    38. 24 Ill. App. 3d 671, 321 N.E.2d 312 (1974).

    39. 57 Ill. 2d 127, 311 N.E.2d 98 (1974).

    40. See, for example, Scanlon v. Crim, 500 S.W.2d 554 (Tex. Ct. Civ.
App. 1973) (extending the action for common law breach of marriage promise
to men); Einstein Medical Center v. Gold, 66 D. and C. 2d 347 (Phila. Co.
1975) (extending concept of responsibility for "necessaries" to wives); and
Hopkins v. Blanco, 457 Pa. 90, 320 A.2d 139 (1974), and Schreiner v. Fruit,
519 P.2d 462 (Alaska Sup. Ct. 1974) (extending right to sue for loss of consortium to wives).

    41. Cragun v. Hawaii and Kashimoto, Civil No. 43175 (1st Cir. Ct.
1975), cited in 1 Women L. Rep. 1.162 (Mar. 1, 1975).

    42. 513 S.W.2d 229 (1974).

    43. 511 S.W.2d 111 (1975).

    44. DiFlorido v. DiFlorido, 331 A.2d 174 (1975).

    45. Tan v. Tan, 3 Ill. App. 3d 671, 279 N.E.2d 486 (1972).

    46. Com. ex rel. Buonocore v. Buonocore, 340 A.2d 579 (Super. Ct.
1975).

    47. Panico v. Robinson, 23 Ill. App. 3d 848, 320 N.E.2d 101 (1974).

    48. Ayers v. Employment Security Dep't, 85 Wash. 2d 500, 536 P.2d
610 (1975).

    49. Hanson v. Hutt, 83 Wash. 2d 195, 517 P.2d 599 (1973).

    50. Commonwealth v. Pennsylvania Interscholastic Athletic Ass'n, 334
A.2d 839 (Cmwlth. Ct. 1975); Darrin v. Gould, 85 Wash. 2d 859, 540 P.2d
885 (Sup. Ct. 1975); and Mora v. St. Vrain Valley Sch. Dist., Civil No. 75-
3182-1 (Boulder Co., Colo. Dist. Ct., filed Dec. 3, 1975). In a fourth case,
involving a public school regulation forbidding long hair for male students,
the Court of Civil Appeals in Houston, Texas, set out an interpretation of the
state ERA incorporating a "suspect classification" analysis, but it refrained
from applying any judicial standard to the regulation on the ground that the
court should not interfere in the daily rule making of the schools. Mercer v.
Board of Trustees, North Forest Ind. Sch. Dist., Civil No. 1302 (Houston,
Tex. Ct. Civ. App., filed June 2, 1976).

    51. Texas Woman's Univ. v. Chayklintaste, 521 S.W.2d 949 (Ct. Civ.
App. 1975).

CHAPTER 3

    1. The methodology behind the work of the Ohio Task Force for the Im-
plementation of the Equal Rights Amendment is set forth in their final report
to the governor and the attorney general in July 1975, which is cited in the
bibliography at the end of this book. For another state's approach to establishing a broad-based commission for ERA conformance, see the Special
Study Commission on the Equal Rights Amendment, First Interim Report to
the Commonwealth of Massachusetts, October 19, 1976.

CHAPTER 4

1. For an extensive discussion of the legal history of rape, see The National Legal Data Center, Inc., The Historical Scales of Justice Attempting to Reach a Balance: The Weight of Rape (1975).

2. Indeed, at times, women attempting to report rape incidents are themselves charged by the police with crimes such as assault or prostitution. See, for example, Mack v. Reilly, Civil No. 74–299 (D.N.J., filed 1972), brought by the Women's Rights Litigation Clinic, Rutgers–Newark. That this skeptical attitude concerning the credibility of victims is widespread is suggested by the following passage from the President's Commission on Law Enforcement and Administration of Justice, Task Force Report: Crime and Its Impact—An Assessment 25 (1967): "In the case of forcible rape some police departments regularly conclude that as many as 50% of the complaints received were not offenses." For other examples of police attitudes toward rape victims, see Salerno, Rape and the Police Department, 8 New York Magazine, June 23, 1975, at 40.

3. According to the Summary Chart Form on Forcible Rape, included in the National Legal Data Center, Inc., National Legislative Review (June 1975), seven jurisdictions—Connecticut, Delaware, District of Columbia, Georgia, Massachusetts, Rhode Island, and Vermont—still retain special corroboration requirements for rape prosecutions. See also The Rape Corroboration Requirement: Repeal Not Reform, 81 Yale L.J. 1364 (1972).

4. National Legal Data Center, id. Twelve states have made substantial reforms limiting the use of evidence concerning a victim's prior sexual conduct or reputation for chastity. See note 20 infra for a listing of these legislative changes.

5. For discussion of the history of rape penalties and the issues they raise, see B. Babcock, A. Freedman, E. Norton, and S. Ross, Sex Discrimination and the Law: Causes and Remedies 863–69 (1975) [hereafter cited as Babcock].

6. See, for example, Ala. Code tit. 14, §§ 395, 397–98 (1959); Alaska Stat. §§ 11, 15, 130 (1962); Idaho Code § 18–6104 (1948); Iowa Code Ann. tit. 35, § 698.1 (1950); Mich. Comp. Laws Ann. § 750.520b(B) (1968).

7. See, for example, the discussion included in Brown, Emerson, Falk, and Freedman, The Equal Rights Amendment: A Constitutional Basis for Equal Rights for Women, 80 Yale L.J. 871, 955–62 (1971).

8. People v. Medrano, 321 N.E.2d 97, 24 Ill. App. 3d 429 (1974) (sex-based rape law does not violate equal protection; sociological and physiological reasons, including vulnerability to pregnancy, justify sex-based law); Brooks v. State, 330 A.2d 670, 24 Md. App. 334 (Ct. Spec. App. 1975) (court upheld sex-based rape law; limitation to male actions reasonable because only males can act as principals in first degree rape and to women as victims because women are subject to possibility of pregnancy); and Finley v. Texas, 527 S.W.2d 553 (Ct. Crim. App. 1975) (rape law fits within unique physical characteristics exception of equality principle).

9. Finley v. Texas, 527 S.W.2d 553, 556 (1975).

10. For a presentation of these and other views on the issue of spousal exceptions, see District of Columbia City Council, Memorandum of the Report of the Public Safety Committee Task Force on Rape 48–50 (July 9, 1973). There is a growing concern for the variety of physical abuses, including rape, that a spouse may experience within marriage. See, for example, Women in Transition, A Feminist Handbook on Separation and Divorce 413 et seq. (1975).

11. See Norton, Impact of the Equal Rights Amendment, 3 Human Rights L. Rev. 125, 137 (1973).

12. See, for example, N.M. Stat. Ann. §§ 40A–9–20 et seq. (1975), which only provides for statutory rape of a child under 13 unless the perpetrator is in a position of authority over the child. "Position of authority" is defined to include a parent, relative, household member, teacher, employer, or other person who, by reason of position, is able to exercise undue influence over a child up to 16 years of age.

13. Professors Anthony Amsterdam and Barbara Babcock prepared a memorandum for the American Civil Liberties Union of Northern California in 1974, which proposes such a hearing system and discusses the desirability of balancing defense interests with those of rape complainants. The memorandum is reprinted in Babcock, supra note 5, at 840–43.

14. See, for example, Florida (sexual battery); Michigan (criminal sexual conduct); Montana (sexual intercourse or assault); Nebraska (sexual assault); and New Mexico (criminal sexual penetration or contact).

15. See, for example, Delaware law, which has a sex-based forcible rape law and sex-neutral provisions covering sexual assault and sodomy; Hawaii, which has a sex-based forcible rape law and a sex-neutral provision for "deviate sexual intercourse" with the same penalties and parallel definitions; Kentucky, which has facially neutral rape and sodomy laws but defines rape as sexual intercourse in its "ordinary sense"; Texas, which has a traditional sex-based rape law in conjunction with statutes prohibiting forcible "deviate sexual intercourse" and "sexual abuse"; and Utah, which retains distinct but largely parallel provisions for rape and forcible sodomy.

16. See, for example, Ky. Rev. Stat. Ann. § 510.010(3) (1975), which uses the term "marriage" to describe persons living together as man and wife, regardless of their legal relationship, and excludes spouses living apart under judicial decree; Mich. Comp. Laws Ann. § 750.520(1) (1968), under which a spouse can commit prohibited sexual assault if the spouses are living apart and one has filed for separate maintenance or divorce; Nev. Rev. Stat. § 200.373 (1973), which allows a husband to be convicted of the rape of his wife if he is an accomplice or accessory to the rape by a third person or if at the time of the incident the couple were living apart and one of them had filed an action for separate maintenance or divorce; N.M. Stat. Ann. § 40A–9–20 (1953), as amended by L. 1975, ch. 109, § 1, which excludes from "spouse" one who is living apart from one's husband or wife or one who has filed for separate maintenance or divorce; and Utah Code Ann. § 76–5–407 (1953), as added by L. 1973, ch. 196, which provides that for purposes of the sexual offense laws persons living apart under a decree of judicial separation are not married.

17. See, for example, the laws of Florida and Nebraska. Hawaii's law does not contain a spousal exclusion. It does, however, provide that rape in the first degree and sodomy in the first degree can be established only if the "female" ("other person" in the sodomy law) "is not, upon the occasion, the assailant's voluntary social companion who had within the previous 12 months permitted him sexual contact unless the assailant recklessly inflicts serious bodily injury on the victim or the victim is under fourteen."

18. See Arkansas (statutory rape under 11/carnal abuse up to 16); Colorado (under 15/actor four years older); Connecticut (under 14); Florida (11 or under); Georgia (under 14); Hawaii (under 14); Indiana (under 12); Kentucky (under 12); Louisiana (under 12); Maine (under 14); Maryland (under 14); Michigan (under 13); Minnesota (under 13); Mississippi (under 12); New Hampshire (under 13); New Jersey (under 12/actor over 16); New Mexico (under 13); North Carolina (under 12/actor over 16); North Dakota (under 15); Ohio (under 13 or actor four years older); Oklahoma (under 14 unless actor over 18); Pennsylvania (under 14); Utah (under 14); Virginia (under 13); and Washington (under 11).

19. See, for example, Okla. Stat. Ann. tit. 22, § 750 (1958), as added by L. 1975, ch. 19, § 1.

20. Cal. Evid. Code § 782 (West 1966), as added by Stats. 1974, ch. 569, § 1; Colo. Rev. Stat. Ann. § 18-3-407 (1973), as repealed and reenacted by L. 1975, at 630, § 1; Fla. Stat. Ann. § 794.022 (1965), as amended by L. 1974, ch. 74-121; Hawaii Rev. Stat. § 37-707 (1968), as amended by L. 1974, ch. 83; Ind. Ann. Stat. Ann. §§ 35-1-32.5.1 et seq. (Burns 1975), as added by Acts 1975, ch. 322; Iowa Code Ann. § 782 (1950), as added by Acts 1974, ch. 1271; Mich. Comp. Laws Ann. § 750.520j (1968), as amended by Acts 1974, No. 266; Mont. Rev. Codes Ann. § 94-5-503 (Supp. 1975), as amended by L. 1975, chs. 2, 129; Neb. Rev. Stat. § 28-408.05 (1975), as amended by L. 1975, L.B. 23, § 9; Nev. Rev. Stat. §§ 48.2, 50.4 (1968), as amended by Acts 1975, at 600; N.M. Stat. Ann. § 40A-9-26 (1953), as amended by L. 1975, ch. 109, § 7; N.Y. Crim. Proc. Code § 60-42 (McKinney 1965), as added by L. 1975, ch. 230, § 1; N.D. Cent. Code §§ 12.1-20-14, -15 (1976), as added by L. 1975, ch. 118; Ore. Rev. Stat. § 163.475 (1975), as amended by L. 1975, ch. 743, § 2; Pa. Stat. Ann. tit. 18, § 3104 (1973), as amended by Acts 1976, No. 53, § 1; S.D. Comp. Laws Ann. § 22-45-1 (1969), as added by L. 1975, ch. 169, § 3; Tenn. Code Ann. § 40-2445 (1975), as added by L. 1975, ch. 44, § 1; Tex. Penal Code § 21.13 (1974), as added by Acts 1975, ch. 203, § 3; and Wash. Rev. Code § 9.79 (1961), as amended by L. 1975 (1st Ex. Sess.), ch. 14.

21. Cal. Penal Code §§ 1127d-e (West 1970), as amended by Stats. 1974, chs. 1092-93; and Nev. Rev. Stat. § 175.186 (1968), as amended by Acts 1975, at 1132.

22. South Carolina has had this procedure since 1909. S.C. Code Ann. §§ 16-73 et seq. (1962); and Va. Code Ann. § 18.2-67 (1950), as amended by Acts 1960, ch. 358, Acts 1975, chs. 14, 15, 606.

23. Conn. Gen. Stat. Ann. § 53a-68 (1975), as repealed by Acts 1969, No. 828, § 69, No. 74-131; Fla. Stat. Ann. § 794.022 (1965), as added by L.

1974, ch. 74-121; Iowa Code Ann. § 782.4 (1950), as repealed and reenacted by Acts 1974, ch. 1271, § 1; Mich. Comp. Laws § 750.520(h) (1968), as amended by Acts 1974, No. 266; N.M. Stat. Ann. § 40A-9-25 (1953), as amended by L. 1975, ch. 109, § 6; N.Y. Penal Law § 130.16 (McKinney 1975), as added by L. 1974, ch. 14, § 1 (under this new enactment corroboration no longer is required unless incapacity to consent is at issue); Pa. Stat. Ann. tit. 18, § 3106 (1973), as amended by Acts 1976, No. 53, § 2; and Wash. Rev. Code ch. 9, § 79 (1963), as amended by L. 1975 (1st Ex. Sess.), ch. 14, § 2.

24. Colo. Rev. Stat. Ann. § 18-3-408 (1973), as repealed and reenacted by L. 1975, at 631, § 1.

25. Mich. Comp. Laws Ann. § 750.520(i) (1968), as amended by Acts 1974, No. 266; Ohio Rev. Code Ann. § 2907.03 (1975), as added by L. 1972, H.B. 511, provides that coercion as opposed to force is sufficient for the lesser offense of "sexual battery"; and Pa. Stat. Ann. tit. 18, § 3107 (1973), as amended by Acts 1976, No. 53, § 2, does not prohibit the defendant from introducing evidence that the victim consented to the conduct.

26. A. Con. Res. 217 calls upon the Commission on Police Officer Standards and Training (POST) to develop training courses for law enforcement personnel relative to the proper investigation of rape cases; A. Con. Res. 218 requests POST to implement a program for training specialists to investigate rape cases and for developing special rape investigation units; A. Con. Res. 219 calls upon local law enforcement agencies to implement an affirmative assignment program to place more policewomen in positions that will enable them to respond to cases of reported rape.

27. Mass. Ann. Laws ch. 6, § 118 (1973), as amended by Stats. 1974, ch. 581. The Massachusetts act provides that municipal police training schools must provide training for members of rape prevention and prosecution units. This law is designed to improve the quality of reporting, counseling, and prosecution.

28. Minn. Stat. Ann. § 241.51 (1972), as added by L. 1974, ch. 578. The Minnesota statute provides for voluntary counseling of victims as well as payment of costs of medical treatment. However, most of its provisions are discretionary in nature or lack a source of funding.

29. Nev. Rev. Stat. § 449.244 (1975); and Ohio Rev. Code Ann. § 2907.28 (1975).

30. See Nev. Rev. Stat. § 244.345(8) (1975).

31. Alaska, Louisiana, and Wisconsin still refer specifically to "females" in their statutes defining prostitution. Tennessee, Vermont, and Wyoming, while not specifically stating that only a female can commit acts of prostitution, have provisions, such as those prohibiting the procurement of prostitutes, which refer only to "females," thereby suggesting a sexist interpretation of the entire prostitution-related section of the code. Also, even if the terminology is facially neutral, law enforcement personnel and courts may continue to interpret such statutes with a traditional bias against only female prostitution unless case law or legislative history supports an explicitly sex-neutral policy. Virginia, for example, has a history of sexist judicial interpretation of a statute that uses the term "any person." Trent v. Commonwealth

181 Va. 338, 25 S. E. 2d 350 (1943). Oklahoma, on the other hand, which has a traditionally phrased statute, extends coverage to male and female prostitutes alike under its case law. Landrum v. State, 96 Okla. Crim. 356, 255 P. 2d 525 (1953).

32. In addition, some other jurisdictions have provisions that could be interpreted to cover patrons, although their language may have been originally drafted to criminalize the actions of pimps and procurers. See, for example, the Mississippi prostitution law, which criminalizes prostitution and solicitation for purposes of prostitution as well as penalizing those who "participate in the doing of the prohibited acts." One other state, Idaho, used to have a patron statute but repealed this provision in 1973.

33. Constitutional challenges to prostitution laws and to the use of selective enforcement strategies impacting women disparately have been numerous in recent years. Perhaps the most comprehensive collection of litigation can be located in the Docket of the Sexual Privacy Project of the American Civil Liberties Union, 22 E. 40th St., New York, New York 10016. One of the strongest judicial statements sustaining an equal protection challenge is U. S. v. Moses, 41 U. S. L. W. 2298 (D. C. Super. Ct. Nov. 3, 1972), in which the selective enforcement techniques of the District of Columbia Police Department were held to violate both due process and equal protection. That decision was recently overturned, however, by the D. C. Court of Appeals, Civ. No. 7042 (May 22, 1975). A similar challenge is pending in Alameda County, California, in the case of Riemer v. Jensen (available from ACLU docket). That suit charges that the prostitution law violates exercise of speech and sexual privacy and that selective enforcement against female prostitutes rather than male patrons through the use of male decoy police violates equal protection. Still at a pretrial stage, the Riemer suit has resulted in a preliminary injunction requiring the police department to reach at least 25 percent parity in the number of hours decoys of both sexes are employed.

See generally Rosenbleet and Pariente, Prostitution of the Criminal Law, 11 Am. Crim. L. Rev. 373 (1973), and Haft, Hustling for Rights, 1 Civ. Lib. Rev. 8 (1974), for discussions of constitutional problems raised by prostitution laws.

34. Ariz. Rev. Stat. Ann. § 13-991 (1956).

35. Cal. Penal Code § 315 (West 1970).

36. See, for example, Papachristou v. City of Jacksonville, 405 U. S. 156 (1972), in which the United States Supreme Court declared a Florida vagrancy statute unconstitutional. Due process was denied, the Court held, because the law was being used to prosecute suspicions about future illegality rather than actual or ongoing activities. It may be argued that the conditional clause, "for purposes of prostitution," removes what would otherwise be status-oriented crime, such as "loitering" or "residing in," from constitutional challenge. However, unless proof of actual activities is required for conviction, such provisions still suffer from vagueness and have a propensity to penalize future or merely suspected activities.

37. See, for example, the prostitution laws of North Carolina, Oklahoma, Tennessee, Vermont, and Wyoming.

38. N.J. Rev. Stat. Ann. § 2A:26:4-32 (1969).

39. The constitutional right of privacy in intimate sexual matters has been recognized in a line of Supreme Court cases over the past decade. See, for example, Griswold v. Connecticut, 381 U.S. 479 (1965); Eisenstadt v. Baird, 405 U.S. 438 (1972); and Roe v. Wade, 410 U.S. 113 (1973). But see Doe v. Commonwealth Attorney of the City of Richmond, 403 F. Supp. 1199 (E.D. Va.), aff'd per curiam, 96 S. Ct. 1489 (1976), in which a three-judge federal court, in upholding the constitutionality of a Virginia statute criminalizing consensual sodomy, stated that the constitutional right of privacy is limited to the marital relationship and matters of family life.

The significance for constitutional law of the Supreme Court's affirmation of the lower court decision, without opinion, is not clear. It does suggest, at least, that constitutional protection of private homosexual activity will be more difficult to establish than similar protection for heterosexual behavior. In addition, one federal appellate court has held that the essentially private nature of activities entitled to constitutional protection is lost when participants invite others to view or record sexual behavior, whether within the marital context or not. Lovisi v. Slayton, 44 U.S.L.W. 2542 (4th Cir. 1976), aff'ing 363 F. Supp. 620 (E.D. Va. 1973).

40. American Bar Association, Section of Individual Rights and Responsibilities, Report to the House of Delegates 3 (February 1976).

41. Model Penal Code § 251.2 (Prop. Off. Draft 1962). The Model Penal Code provides a lesser penalty for patrons than prostitutes, however, as well as perpetuating traditional language creating a status crime of loitering "for purposes of" prostitution.

42. Michigan H.B. 4907 (1973); and Maryland S.B. 574 (1975). Oregon H.B. 2636 (1975) proposed reducing prostitution to a violation punishable only by a fine and resulting in a sealed record, but the bill did not pass.

43. See, for example, Conn. Gen. Stat. Ann. § 18-65 (1972), as amended by Acts 1975, No. 75-633, § 1; Iowa Code Ann. §§ 245.6, 245.7 (1969); Md. Ann. Code art. 27, § 689(e) (1976); and Mass. Gen. Laws Ann. ch. 279, § 18 (1968), as amended by Stats. 1972, ch. 293, § 3. A New Jersey statute permitting indeterminate sentencing for women is still on the books, although it has been declared unconstitutional. N.J. Stat. Ann. § 30:4-155 (1964).

44. Temin, Discriminatory Sentencing of Women Offenders: The Argument for ERA in a Nutshell, 11 Am. Crim. L. Rev. 355, 358 (1973). See also Iowa Code Ann. § 24.51 (1969).

45. See U.S. v. Maples, 501 F.2d 985 (4th Cir. 1974), in which the trial court sentenced a man for 15 years and a woman for 10 years for the same crime, explicitly taking the sex of the offenders into account. The court of appeals reversed and remanded, holding that sex is an impermissible basis for a disparity in sentences. For differences in policies for fixing date and terms of parole for male and female inmates by boards of sentence and parole, see Equal Rights Amendment Project of the California Commission on the Status of Women, ERA Conformance· An Analysis of California State Codes 167 (1975).

46. One in every six persons arrested is a woman; one in every 34 incarcerated is a woman. Crisman, "Position Paper on Women in Prisons,"

June 10, 1976, at 1 (unpublished paper of ACLU National Prison Project, 1346 Connecticut Ave., N.W., Suite 1031, Washington, D.C. 20036) [hereafter cited as Crisman]. This is due in large part to the types of offenses committed, but to some extent it also is due to the bias of judges against sending single parents to jail and to their belief that female participation in serious crime is induced by attachment to a man.

47. See U.S. ex rel. Robinson v. York, 281 F. Supp. 8 (D. Conn. 1968); Liberti v. York, 28 Conn. Supp. 9, 246 A.2d 106 (1968); State v. Chambers, 63 N.J. 287, 307 A.2d 78 (1973); and Com. v. Stauffer, 214 Pa. Super. 113, 251 A.2d 718 (1969). Com. v. Daniel, 430 Pa. 642, 243 A.2d 400 (1968), held the Pa. Muncy Act, Pa. Stat. Ann. tit. 61, § 566 (1964), unconstitutional because it allowed women to be imprisoned longer than the maximum for men for the same crime. After the decision, the statute was amended and subsequently has been challenged under the state ERA. See discussion below.

48. 458 Pa. 289, 328 A.2d 851 (1974).

49. See, for example, Dershowitz, Let the Punishment Fit the Crime, New York Times Magazine, Dec. 28, 1975, § 6 at 7; McGee, A New Look at Federal Sentencing: Part II, Federal Probation, Sept. 1974, at 3–11; and Schreiber, Indeterminate Therapeutic Incarceration of Dangerous Criminals: Perspectives—Problems, 56 Va. L. Rev. 602 (1970). Other material is available from the National Prison Project, 1346 Connecticut Ave. N.W., Washington, D.C. 20036.

50. Pa. Stat. Ann. tit. 19, § 1057(6) (1964):

> Whenever any person, convicted in any court of this Commonwealth of any crime punishable by imprisonment in a State penitentiary, shall be sentenced to imprisonment therefor in any penitentiary or other institution of this State, or in any county or municipal institution, the court, instead of pronouncing upon such convict a definite or fixed term of imprisonment, shall pronounce upon such convict a sentence of imprisonment for an indefinite term: Stating in such sentence the minimum and maximum limits thereof; and the maximum limit shall never exceed the maximum time now or hereafter prescribed as a penalty for such offense; and the minimum limit shall never exceed one-half of the maximum sentence prescribed by any court.
>
> Whenever any person is convicted of any crime punishable by simple imprisonment, the court, may in its discretion, pronounce a sentence either for a fixed term or for an indefinite term, as may seem proper under the circumstances of the case, but in no case to exceed the maximum term prescribed by law as a penalty for such offense.

51. Ark. Stat. Ann. § 46–804 (1947), as amended by Acts 1971, No. 195, § 1; and Kan. Stat. Ann. § 21–4601 (1974), as repealed by L. 1969, ch. 180, § 21–4601.

52. Until recently, Maine permitted the confinement of men from ages 15 to 36 and women from 16 to 40 in reformatories with indeterminate sen-

tences not to exceed three years. Me. Rev. Stat. Ann. §§ 34–802, –853 (1965), as repealed by L. 1975, ch. 499, §§ 65, 67. These statutes were amended to permit men and women not older than 26 to be sentenced under these provisions. In 1975 a new criminal code was enacted that eliminated indeterminate sentencing for both men and women.

53. These statutes and the former escape law for women, Me. Rev. Stat. Ann. §§ 34–710, –751, –859 (1965), were repealed by L. 1975, ch. 499, although §§ 710 and 751 had been upheld by the court in Wark v. State, 266 A.2d 62 (1970), on the theory that a higher sentence for escape by men was justified by the greater risk of violence presumed to be involved. A new sex-neutral escape provision was enacted by the 1975 law. Me. Rev. Stat. Ann. § 17–755 (Supp. 1975). Conn. Gen. Stat. Ann. § 18–66 (Supp. 1972) and §§ 53a–169, –170 (1958), which contained different escape provisions for men and women, were amended by Acts 1973, No. 73–639, §§ 12, 14, 15. Section 18–66 was repealed, and ss 53a–169, –170 now apply to both men and women.

54. See Com. v. Butler, 458 Pa. 289, 328 A.2d 851 (1974), for a history of the Muncy Act.

55. See Note, The Sexual Segregation of American Prisons, 82 Yale L.J. 1229 (1973) [hereafter cited as Sexual Segregation], for an extensive discussion of traditional and current policies concerning women in prison. It is important to note that for many women prisoners the effects of sex discrimination are compounded by the problems of race discrimination. Singer, Women and the Correctional Process, 11 Am. Crim. L. Rev. 295 (1973) [hereafter cited as Singer], notes that in a 1971 study of the Women's Detention Center in Washington, D.C., the percentage of black women increased at every step in the judicial and correctional process from 73 percent of first bookings at the Women's Detention Center to 97 percent of cases receiving a sentence of three months or longer.

56. American Bar Association Commission on Correctional Facilities and Services, Women in Detention and Statewide Jail Standards, 7 Clearinghouse Bulletin 1 (March 1974) [hereafter cited as ABA Commission].

57. Sexual Segregation, supra note 55, at 1232nn.11, 13, 1233n.14. See generally A Report by the Ohio Task Force for the Implementation of the ERA 44 (1975) [hereafter cited as Ohio Task Force Report]; Pennsylvania Program for Women and Girl Offenders, Proposed Pennsylvania Criminal Justice Goals and Standards for Women 58–61 (1975) [hereafter cited as Pa. Program]; Crisman, supra note 46, at 1–2; and Haft, Women in Prison: Discriminatory Practices and Some Legal Solutions, 8 Clearinghouse Rev. 1 (May 1974) [hereafter cited as Haft]. Singer, supra note 55, at 307, points out that as of 1973 the Federal Bureau of Prisons operated eight halfway houses, none of which were for women.

58. Sexual Segregation, supra note 55, at 1234n.24; Singer, supra note 55, at 300–01; and Pa. Program, id. The Pennsylvania Program study also found that women inmates generally had less access to legal resources and the courts than men.

59. See generally Women's Prison Association, Study in Neglect: A Report on Women Prisoners (1972) (available from the Women's Prison Ass'n,

110 2d Ave., New York, N.Y.) [hereafter cited as Women's Prison Association Report]; and Sexual Segregation, supra note 55, at 1241.

60. Crisman, supra note 46, at 2; also Haft, supra note 57, at 3-4; and Singer, supra note 55, at 301.

61. Of nine reformatories and penitentiaries in the federal prison system, six all-male institutions provide work release, but the Federal Reformatory for Women at Alderson, Virginia, has no such program. This pattern of exclusion from work release programs is repeated in many state and county prison systems. Note, Denial of Work Release Program to Women: A Violation of Equal Protection, 47 S. Cal. L. Rev. 1453 (1974) [hereafter cited as Denial of Work Release]. A number of suits successfully challenging sex discrimination in training and employment programs on equal protection grounds have been settled or have not been reported. For a fuller discussion of the litigation in this area see Crisman, supra note 46.

62. Crisman, supra note 46, at 2-3. This small percentage of women participated in these programs despite the fact that 80 percent of the women were convicted of misdemeanors and that a majority of their offenses involved property and victimless crimes. The study also revealed that "men released on furloughs were placed in job and job training projects as well as higher education programs. Placements included jobs in government, construction, retailing and auto mechanics. No women prisoners were placed in these programs."

63. Denial of Work Release, supra note 61, at 1459-62, 1480-83.

64. See ABA Commission, supra note 56, at 13, 20; Women's Prison Association Report, supra note 59; Haft, supra note 57, at 3; and Singer, supra note 55, at 300.

65. For discussion of these issues, see Haft, supra note 57, at 4; Crisman, supra note 46, at 3, 9-10. The Crisman paper includes references to pending litigation on these points.

66. Haft, supra note 57; and Crisman, supra note 46, at 8-9.

67. Keenon v. Conlisk, 507 F.2d 1259 (7th Cir. 1974).

68. Smith v. Bounds, Civil No. 74-2378 (4th Cir., filed Sept. 30, 1975).

69. Dawson v. Carberry, Civil No. C-71-1916 (N.D. Cal., filed 1971) (judge ordered the defendants to develop a work furlough program for women); and Taylor v. Whitmore, Civil No. C-73-0415 SC (N.D. Cal., filed Sept. 1974) (case dismissed when defendants provided a halfway house facility for women).

70. See the Appendix on Pending Litigation in Crisman, supra note 46.

71. Civil No. CA 159-72 (D.D.C., filed 1972).

72. Barefield v. Leach, Civil No. 10282 (D.N.M. Dec. 18, 1974).

73. For a revealing study of sex-based patterns in the staffing of the Bureau of Corrections in one state, see Pennsylvania Program for Women and Girl Offenders, Report on the Employment of Personnel by Race and Sex in Pennsylvania's Criminal Justice Agencies (1975).

74. As the ABA Commission, supra note 56, at 26, states:

[T]he recommendation of the National Advisory Commission on Criminal Justice Standards and Goals is that "male and female institutions of adaptable design and comparable populations should be converted to coeducational facilities" with use of "staff of both sexes who have interest, ability, and training in coping with the problems of both male and female offenders." Standard 11.6, Report on Corrections (1973). Many years before, the American Correctional Association emphasized the value of male staff in women's institutions (a principle that appears equally valid for female staff in male institutions):

> The majority of employees of a women's institution will be women; however, male staff is strongly advised in appropriate areas such as teaching, casework, religion, psychiatry, psychology, and medicine as well as in the more traditional areas of maintenance and farm. Careful selection of male employees is essential, however. This trend toward a more normal environment for both staff and inmates in the institution community is believed to be necessary for a good treatment program. [ACA Manual of Correctional Standards, ch. 34 on Facilities and Programs for Women, p. 564 (1966)].

It should be noted that the foregoing principles were enunciated in the context of major state institutions, rather than local detention facilities.

The NAC has set the following rule: "Staff members of both sexes should be utilized to meet privacy requirements and make the institution as normal as possible." Commentary, Standard 9.6.

75. See, for example, Reynolds v. Wise, 375 F. Supp. 145 (N.D. Tex. 1974), prohibiting sex discrimination under Title VII; Stonecipher v. Wisconsin Dep't of Industry, Labor, and Human Relations, 12 E.P.D. para. 10,979 (Dane Co. May 28, 1976), upholding sex integration of staff at a juvenile facility under the state human relations law; in re Long, 127 Cal. Rptr. 732 (Ct. App. 3d Dist. 1976), approving female staff at a male juvenile facility, though not in jobs overseeing living quarters; but see Long v. California State Personnel Bd., 41 Cal. App. 3d 1000, 116 Cal. Rptr. 562 (1974), denying placement of a female minister in that same male institution both on equal protection grounds and under Title VII. In Robertson v. Hall, filed Oct. 1974, ACLU Women's Rights Project Docket No. WR 6221 (D. Mass.), a temporary restraining order barring the exclusion of applicants under 5 ft. 7 in. for jobs as correction officers in the Massachusetts Department of Correction was granted. The case was subsequently dismissed as moot following the amendment of the statute to eliminate the height requirement. See also Flanagan v. Hall, Civil No. CA 74-644 (Plymouth Super. Ct., filed Nov. 1974), ACLU Women's Rights Project Docket No. WR 6227, in which male correction officers are challenging the assignment of female correction officers to male institutions; and Lancaster v. California State Personnel Bd. and Dep't of Corrections, ACLU Women's Rights Project Docket No. WR 6228 (S.D. Cal.), a

Title VII suit filed by a female parole officer for back pay and seniority rights. For further information on these cases contact the ACLU Women's Rights Project.

76. Sexual Segregation, supra note 55, at 1262nn.164-67, contains excerpts from the Hearings before Subcommittee 4 of the House Committee on the Judiciary, 92d Cong., 1st Sess. (1971), on the federal ERA supporting this position.

77. A..Bingaman, A Commentary on the Effect of the Equal Rights Amendment on State Laws and Institutions 67 (1975) [hereafter cited as Bingaman]. See also Haft, supra note 57, at 5.

78. But see the brief of the American Civil Liberties Union amicus curiae in in re Long, 127 Cal. Rptr. 732 (Ct. App. 3d Dist. 1976), on appeal to the California Supreme Court, for the view that no sex-specific right of privacy permits inmates in a male juvenile facility to claim a constitutional violation based on the presence of females supervising the living quarters.

79. As the ABA Commission, supra note 56, at 21-27, points out, provisions for the supervision of women inmates and minors by women are common in state laws. Indeed, the ABA group observes that the provision for female supervision of women and the requirement for their presence are the most commonly recurring standards concerning women in prisons. For example, the Illinois and Pennsylvania state jail standards require that "a matron must be on duty, awake and alert at all times" whenever there is a female prisoner. Other state standards quoted in the ABA bulletin state that only matrons are permitted to have keys to areas where females are detained, that matrons attend all visits to women, and even that they supervise all meals of female prisoners. The presence of matrons has been thought to guard against exploitation by male inmates or staff while giving maximum privacy in close confinement situations. The standards of all the states mentioned in the ABA Bulletin (Michigan, Illinois, Pennsylvania, New York, and California) also provide for searches of female prisoners by matrons to protect bodily privacy.

80. This recommendation is supported by many commentators, including Singer, supra note 55, at 306-07; Haft, supra note 57, at 5; and Crisman, supra note 46. The Crisman paper discusses legal theories that may be used to bolster an argument for this policy in litigation. See also Pa. Program, supra note 57.

81. Ky. Rev. Stat. Ann. §§ 441.150, 441.170 (1973), as amended by Acts 1974, ch. 386, §§ 101-02. The commentary accompanying the distribution of this bill to assembly members described this change as terminological only, signifying perhaps that hiring practices were not specifically to be changed as a result of this amendment.

82. Iowa Code § 245.2 (1973), as amended by Acts 1974, ch. 1093, § 40; and Iowa Code § 338.4 (1949), as amended by Acts 1974, ch. 1093, § 51.

83. Md. Ann. Code art. 27, § 700E(a), (b) (1957), as amended by Acts 1974, ch. 304.

84. Iowa Code § 247A.2 (1973), as amended by Acts 1974, ch. 1093, § 43.

85. Iowa Code s 356.16 (1973), as amended by Acts 1974, ch. 1093, § 53.

86. Cal. Penal Code § 4029 (1970), as added by Stats. 1974, ch. 1416, § 1. The text of this bill and commentary can be found in The Equal Rights Amendment Project of the Commission on the Status of Women, ERA Conformance: An Analysis of the California State Codes 164–66 (1975).

87. Cal. Penal Code §§ 4001, 4021 (1970), as amended by Stats. 1975, ch. 592. The bill, originally introduced as A.B. 372 (1975) by Assemblyman Gary Hart, would have eliminated the prohibition on sex-integrated county jail programs, but it was amended before passage.

88. Colorado H.B. 1445 (1975); Minnesota S.F. 2940, § 1 (1973); New York A.2835 (Reg. Sess. 1975–76). In 1975, the commissioner of the Department of Corrections in South Carolina appointed an agencywide Task Force on Women Employees and Women Offenders to study the "status, role, function and future of women employees and/or offenders . . . in relation to the Civil Rights Act, Equal Employment Act, recommendations of the National Advisory Commission on Criminal Justice Standards and other laws/standards which might affect such persons." National Resource Center on Women Offenders, 1 The Woman Offender Report, Nov./Dec. 1975, at 7.

89. The federal institutions in Ft. Worth, Texas, and in Lexington, Kentucky, and the state correctional institutions in Muncy, Pennsylvania, and in Framingham, Massachusetts, are all sex integrated. In both Massachusetts and Pennsylvania, a handful of men were transferred to a women's prison; in Muncy, the first group of men consisted of four individuals carefully screened by the Department of Corrections. Florida, Mississippi, and New Mexico, among others, have separate units for each sex within the same institution. Sexual Segregation, supra note 55, at 1231n.4.

90. Iowa Code §§ 246A.1, 246A.3 (1973), as amended by Acts 1974, ch. 1093, §§ 41–42.

91. S.F. 2940 (1973) provides at § 1:

[PUBLIC POLICY.] It is the policy of this state that all inmates of all state correctional institutions shall be afforded equal opportunities for treatment, rehabilitation, education and vocational training, including on the job training opportunities, regardless of sex.

It is the policy of this state that the commissioner of corrections shall make all expeditious and diligent effort in the most economic manner feasible to afford to each inmate equal access to all services provided by all state correctional institutions.

It is the policy of this state that no treatment, rehabilitation, educational or vocational training opportunity available at any state correctional institution shall be denied any inmate of any state correctional institution on the basis of sex.

92. Section 641.38 provides:

[ASSOCIATE SUPERVISOR AND ASSISTANT SUPERVISOR.] In any such county, the sheriff, with the approval of a majority of the judges of the district court therein, shall appoint a competent [woman] person to act as [matron] associate supervisor in the jail, who shall be a deputy sheriff and qualify as such before performing [her] his duties as [matron] associate supervisor and [the matron] shall act under the direction of the sheriff [and shall have exclusive charge of all female prisoners confined in the jail and shall engage in no other occupation or employment]. If the sheriff is a male the associate supervisor shall be a female. If the sheriff is a female the associate supervisor shall be a male. The associate supervisor shall have exclusive charge of all prisoners of his own sex confined in the jail and shall engage in no other occupation or employment. When the average number of [female] prisoners of the same sex as the associate supervisor confined in the jail [during the preceding six months] shall have been ten or more during the preceding six months, an assistant [matron] supervisor may be appointed in like manner, who shall have like duties as the [matron] associate supervisor and shall engaᵦ in no other business or occupation. When in any such county and [such] assistant [matron] supervisor shall be appointed, the assistant [matron] supervisor shall perform [her] his duties as such during the night-time and occupy the quarters provided for [such matron] the associate supervisor in the county jail, and it shall be the duty of [such matron] the associate supervisor or assistant [matron] supervisor to perform such duties in charge of the [female] prisoners confined in the jail as the sheriff may by order direct.

93. In preparing this subsection, the authors relied heavily on Davis and Chaires, Sex Discrimination in Juvenile Law, 7 Ga. L. Rev. 494 (1973).
94. Ill. Ann. Stat. ch. 37, § 2-2 (1965) (male 17, female 18); N.Y. Judiciary Law §§ 712(b), 718 (McKinney 1975) (both male 16, female 18); Okla. Stat. Ann. tit. 10, § 1101 (1968) (male 16, female 18); Tex. Rev. Civ. Stat. Ann. art. 2338-1 (1971), as repealed by Acts 1973, ch. 544, § 3 (male 17, female 18). See note 113 infra for later developments with regard to these laws.
95. Ky. Rev. Stat. Ann. § 201.080 (1972), as amended by Acts 1974, ch. 386, § 40.
96. See Colo. Rev. Stat. Ann. § 19-8-116 (1973), which establishes, in addition to the state boys school, a training school for boys at the state reformatory where boys over 16 may be incarcerated if, in the opinion of the court, it would be in the best interest of the child and the public that he be placed there. The predecessor provision provided for such incarceration if the boy had run away from the boys school or if his conduct had been dangerous or disruptive. Colo. Rev. Stat. Ann. § 22-8-16 (1973). There is no similar provision for girls. N.M. Stat. Ann. § 42-7-5 (1953) authorizes the confinement of male offenders under the age of 23 who receive sentences of imprisonment in excess of six months in the state reformatory, a medium

security institution. See note 116 infra for its subsequent history. Ohio Rev. Code Ann. § 2151.355(E) (Page 1968 Repl. Vol.), as amended by L. 1974, H.B. 1067, provides that a male child 16 years of age or older who has committed an offense that would be a felony if committed by an adult may be placed in "a maximum security institution operated by the Ohio youth commission for the training and rehabilitation of such delinquent children." An earlier version, Ohio Rev. Code Ann. § 2151.35(E) (1968), which permitted incarceration in the adult prison, was invalidated on due process grounds because the juvenile was denied the procedural protections adults received, such as trial by jury, yet was placed in the adult facility. State v. Fisher, 245 N.E.2d 358 (Ct. App. 1969).

97. In New York, males can be held without consent until age 18; females until age 20. N.Y. Judiciary Law § 756(c) (McKinney 1975), as amended by L. 1974, ch. 937, § 8.

98. Okla. Stat. Ann. tit. 10, § 1139(b) (1966).

99. Patricia A. v. City of New York, 31 N.Y.2d 83, 289 N.E.2d 432, 335 N.Y.S.2d 33 (1972).

100. Bingaman, supra note 77, at 66. The federal youth centers in Morgantown, West Virginia, and Pleasanton, California, have become sex integrated.

101. Ohio Task Force Report, supra note 57, at 13. See also Rogers, "For Her Own Protection . . . ": Conditions of Incarceration for Female Juvenile Offenders in the State of Connecticut, 7 Law & Soc. Rev. 223 (1972) [hereafter cited as Rogers].

102. City of Philadelphia v. Pennsylvania Human Relations Comm'n, 300 A.2d 97 (Pa. Com. Ct. 1973).

103. Stonecipher v. Wisconsin Dep't of Indus., Labor, and Human Relations, 12 E.P.D. para. 10,979 (Dane Co. May 28, 1976). Compare Futrell v. Ahrens, 44 U.S.L.W. 2123 (N.M. Sup. Ct. October 20, 1975), concerning a state university regulation prohibiting visitation in dormitory bedrooms by persons of the opposite sex.

104. ABA Commission, supra note 56, at 7-8, reports:

	Status Offenses	Felony Offenses	Misdemeanor Offenses	Drug Offenses
Males	23%	49%	22%	6%
Females	70%	7%	17%	6%

In a 4-year longitudinal study in one major eastern state (all juvenile courts), [the National Assessment of Juvenile Corrections at the University of Michigan] was able to identify white females as most likely to be detained for status offenses (62% of all white girls detained) and non-white males as least likely to be detained on status offenses (12% of all non-white boys detained).

See also Rogers, supra note 101, at 225, reporting Connecticut statistics indicating that 18 percent of the boys and 80 percent of the girls were committed for offenses that would not be criminal if committed by adults; and Lerman, Child Convicts, 8 Transaction 35 (1971), reporting that more than 80 percent of girls incarcerated in a state institution in New Jersey were "criminals without crimes," having been committed for such offenses as running away from home; being incorrigible, ungovernable, and beyond control of parents; being truant; being promiscuous; engaging in sexual relations and becoming pregnant. For further information see Singer, supra note 55, at 298n.18.

105. Ohio Rev. Code Ann. § 2151.15 (Page 1968).

106. In 1964, the nationwide median length of stay in institutions for girls was 10.7 months; for boys it was 8.2 months. U.S. Department of Health, Education and Welfare, Children's Bureau, Statistics on Public Institutions for Delinquent Children—1964 (1965). In the early 1970s, girls in Connecticut spent an average of seven months, while boys stayed for an average of five. Rogers, supra note 101, at 226–27. In New York, girls averaged 12-month stays, while boys averaged 9.3 months. Gold, Equal Protection for Juvenile Girls in Need of Supervision in New York State, 46 N.Y.L.F. 57 (1971).

107. See, for example, New York's Youthful Offenders Act, N.Y. Code Crim. Proc. § 913–m (McKinney 1958).

108. See Rogers, supra note 101, at 227.

109. People v. Ellis, 57 Ill. 2d 127, 311 N.E.2d 98 (1974). Now, both males and females 17 or older are treated as adults for purposes of criminal prosecution.

110. The reasoning used in City of Philadelphia v. Pennsylvania Human Relations Comm'n, discussed above, would not stand under the ERA. Such casual acceptance of governmental assertions about the need for all staff to be sex segregated because of the supervision of personal bodily functions would be replaced with a requirement that only the staff persons with those particular responsibilities be of the same sex as the juveniles while all other jobs be open to members of both sexes. The government also would be precluded from allocating tasks in such a way that all or most personnel had to supervise personal bodily functions, as this could be a tactic to maintain a sex-segregated staffing pattern. For the view that privacy rights are not a defense for the sex segregation of staff in a juvenile institution, see the brief amici curiae of the American Civil Liberties Union of Northern California in the case of in re Long and Jones, available from the ACLU Foundation of Northern California, 814 Mission St., 3d Fl., San Fran., Ca. 94103.

111. See Bingaman, supra note 77, at 60–66. As to the latter reform, she suggests that a maximum term of six months is more likely to be effective than a term of one year in view of the relatively short sentences served by most juvenile offenders.

112. The failings of incarceration, the absence of due process rights, and the extreme vagueness of status offense statutes, recommendations about juveniles' right to treatment, and other reforms are discussed in several articles in A Symposium: Juveniles and the Law, 12 Am. Crim. L. Rev. 1 (1974). This collection also includes a bibliography on the juvenile justice system in general and juvenile court procedures, treatment and institutions, and the abuse of children.

113. Ill. Ann. Stat. ch. 37, § 702-2 (1972), and Tex. Fam. Code § 51.02.
(1975), as amended by Acts 1972, ch. 20, § 3, both set the jurisdictional age
limit at 17 for both girls and boys instead of 18 for girls and 17 for boys. In
Texas, liability of both girls and boys extends to age 18 for acts committed
during the seventeenth year, however. Since the decision in Patricia A.,
the New York legislature has amended the Family Court Act to reflect this
decision. N.Y. Judiciary Law § 711 (McKinney 1975). Another New York
statute authorizing a peace officer to return a male under the age of 16 or a
female under the age of 18 who has left home to the parents or guardian apparently has not been challenged or amended. N.Y. Judiciary Law § 718
(McKinney 1975).

114. Okla. Stat. Ann. tit. 10, § 1101 (1968), as amended by L. 1972, ch.
122, § 1, was finally struck down in Lamb v. Brown, 456 F.2d 18 (10th Cir.
1972). The Court of Criminal Appeals relied on Lamb in Schaffer v. Green,
496 P.2d 375 (1972), which invalidated Okla. Stat. Ann. tit. 10, § 1101A
(1968), a statute that extended juvenile court jurisdiction over all children in
cases involving nondelinquent conduct to age 18 but maintained the age/sex
distinction for delinquency. Okla. Stat. Ann. tit. 10, § 1101 (1968), as
amended by L. 1972, ch. 122, § 1, raised the age to 18 for both sexes.

115. Ky. Rev. Stat. Ann. § 201.080 (1972), as amended by Acts 1974,
ch. 386, § 40.

116. N.M. Stat. Ann. § 42-7-5 (1972 Repl. Vol.), as amended by L.
1973, ch. 139, § 2.

117. See, for example, Iowa Code Ann. § 242.15 (1969), as amended by
Acts 1967, ch. 209, § 332 (allowing girls as well as boys in state juvenile institutions to work in state parks or forestry or soil conservation camps).

CHAPTER 5

1. 421 U.S. 7 (1975).

2. As the Supreme Court said in Stanton, id. at 14–15:

No longer is the female destined solely for the home and the rearing of the family, and only the male for the marketplace and the
world of ideas. (citation omitted) Women's activities and responsibilities are increasing and expanding. Coeducation is a fact, not
a rarity. The presence of women in business, in the professions,
in government, and indeed in all walks of life where education is
a desirable, if not always a necessary antecedent, is apparent.

3. The states that had sex-neutral laws before 1972 are (the numbers
in parentheses are the age of marriage without parental consent followed by
the age with consent): Cal. Civ. Code § 4101 (1970) (18/under 18); Conn. Gen.
Stat. Ann. §§ 46-5f, -5g (1960) (18/16); Idaho Code § 36-202 (1963) (18/16);
Kan. Stat. Ann. § 23-106 (1974) (18/under 18); Me. Rev. Stat. Ann. tit. 19,
§ 62 (1964) (18/16); Pa. Stat. Ann. tit. 48, § 1-5 (1965) (18/16); Tenn. Code

Ann. § 36–408 (1955) (18/16); and Wash. Rev. Code Ann. § 26.04.010 (1961) (18/17).

Montana had a sex–neutral law with 19/18 age limits prior to 1972. It was repealed in 1975 and replaced by a sex–neutral law with different age limits and other new provisions. Those states that have sex–neutralized their laws since 1972 are: Ariz. Rev. Stat. Ann. § 25–102 (1956), as repealed and reenacted by L. 1974, ch. 181, § 2 (18/16); Colo. Rev. Stat. § 90–1–6 (1973), as amended by L. 1973, ch. 290, § 1 (18/16); Hawaii Rev. Stat. § 572–1 (1968), as amended by L. 1972, ch. 182, § 1, ch. 192, § 1; Hawaii Rev. Stat. § 572–2 (1968), as amended by L. 1972, ch. 2, § 34, ch. 192, § 1; Ill. Rev. Stat. ch. 89, §§ 3, 3.1, 6 (1969), as amended by Acts 1974, No. 78–1297, § 26; Ind. Ann. Stat. § 31–1–1–1 (1973), as amended by Acts 1974, ch. 131, § 1; Ind. Ann. Stat. § 31–1–1–4 (1973), as amended by Acts 1973, ch. 295, § 1 (18/17); Ky. Rev. Stat. §§ 402.020, 402.030, 402.210, 402.260 (1971), as amended by Acts 1974, ch. 386, §§ 90–91, 93–94 (18/under 18); Md. Ann. Code art. 62, § 9 (1972 Repl. Vol.), as amended by Acts 1973, ch. 651, § 29 (18/16); Mass. Gen. Laws Ann. ch. 207, § 33 (1958), as amended by L. 1971, ch. 255, § 2; Minn. Stat. Ann. § 517.02 (1969), as amended by L. 1973, ch. 725, § 72 (18/16); Mo. Ann. Stat. § 451.090 (Supp. 1975), as amended by L. 1974 (2d Ex. Sess.), at 975, § 1 (18/15); N.H. Rev. Stat. Ann. § 457:5 (1968 Repl. Vol.), as amended by L. 1973, ch. 72, § 35 (18/under 18); N.M. Stat. Ann. §§ 57–1–5, –6, as amended by L. 1975, ch. 32, §§ 1–2 (18/16); N.D. Cent. Code § 14–03–02 (Supp. 1975), as amended by L. 1975, ch. 126, § 2 (18/16); Ore. Rev. Stat. §§ 106.010, 106.060 (1975), as amended by L. 1975, ch. 583, §§ 1–2 (18/17); Okla. Stat. tit. 43, § 3 (1961), as amended by L. 1975, ch. 39, § 1 (18/16); Tex. Fam. Code §§ 1.51, 1.52 (1975), as amended by Acts 1973, ch. 577, § 7 (18/16); Va. Code Ann. §§ 20–48, –49 (1960), as amended by Acts 1975, ch. 644 (18/18); Vt. Stat. Ann. tit. 18, § 5142 (1968 Repl. Vol.), as amended by L. 1973, No. 201, § 11 (18/16); and Wis. Stat. Ann. § 245.02 (1967), as amended by L. 1975, ch. 94, § 73 (18/16). Montana, as noted above, amended its law in 1975, but the prior law was also sex neutral. Mont. Rev. Code Ann. § 48–306 (1961), as added by L. 1975, ch. 536, § 6 (18/below 18 with judicial consent), replacing § 48–143, as repealed by L. 1975, ch. 536, § 45 (19/18).

At the same time that the Wyoming legislature passed a sex–based marriage age law, prohibiting marriage for a male under 18 and a female under 16, with certain exceptions (Wyo. Stat. Ann. § 20–2.1 [1959]), as added by L. 1975, ch. 61, § 1), it also passed a bill allowing either parent to consent to the marriage of a minor child; formerly, the father, if living, had the superior right (Wyo. Stat. Ann. § 20–8.1 [1959], as amended by L. 1975, ch. 61, § 1).

4. Mont. Rev. Codes Ann. § 43–308 (1961), as added by L. 1975, ch. 536, § 8.

5. Ill. Stat. Ann. ch. 89, § 3 (1966), as amended by Acts 1969, No. 76–1057, § 1.

6. Ark. Stat. Ann. § 57–103 (1971 Repl. Vol.), as amended by Acts 1975, No. 892, § 1; and Utah Code Ann. § 15–2–1 (1973 Repl. Vol.), as

amended by L. 1975, ch. 39, § 1. Arkansas has maintained the age of majority at 21 for alcoholic beverages, and Utah permits courts in divorce actions
to order support to age 21 for both males and females.

7. For an extensive discussion of the common law of names, see Stuart
v. Board of Supervisors for Howard Co. 266 Md. 440, 447-48, 295 A.2d 223,
227 (1972).

8. The only state that enacted a statute explicitly requiring married
women to use their husbands' names was Hawaii. Hawaii Rev. Stat. § 574-1
(1968). In 1975, the 1st Circuit Court of Hawaii declared this statute invalid
as it applied to voter registration. Cragun v. Hawaii and Kashimoto, Civil
No. 43175 (1st Cir. Ct. 1975). The law was repealed in 1975 and replaced
with a provision permitting an individual, at marriage, to declare one's own
name, that of the spouse, or a hyphenated combination of the two to be one's
present surname. L. 1975, ch. 114, § 1.

9. See, for example, Ill. Rev. Stat. ch. 46, § 4-16 (1969), which provides:

> County clerk may . . . treat . . . information procured from his
> death and marriage records on file in his office as an application
> to erase from the register any name concerning which he may so
> have information that the voter is no longer qualified to vote under
> the name, and give notice thereof.

Registrars in other states have sometimes erased women's registrations upon
marriage without explicit statutory authority.

10. 114 Ohio App. 497, 177 N.E.2d 616 (1961).

11. Stuart v. Board of Supervisors of Elections for Howard Co., 266
Md. 440, 295 A.2d 223 (1972).

12. Custer v. Bonadies, 30 Conn. Supp. 385, 318 A.2d 639 (Super. Ct.
1974).

13. Gallop v. Shanahan (unreported), Civil No. 120,456 (Shawnee Co.
Dist. Ct. 1972).

14. Dunn v. Palermo, 522 S.W.2d 679 (D. Tenn. 1975).

15. Sheppard v. Clark; Anthes v. Board of Registrars; and Susan Pettey
v. Board of Registrars (all unreported). See the American Civil Liberties
Union, Women's Rights Project Docket Nos. WR 8211, 8212 (1974).

16. Walker et al. v. Jackson, 391 F. Supp. 1395 (E.D. Ark. 1975).
The Arkansas federal court further held unconstitutional that section of the
state constitution requiring the name of a woman voter to be prefixed by "Miss"
or "Mrs." on her affidavit of registration. An opposite result was reached
by a California Court of Appeal in Allyn v. Allison, 34 Cal. App. 3d 448,
110 Cal. Rptr. 77 (1973), where the court upheld the election code requirement that a woman insert a "Miss" or "Mrs." before her name when regis-
tering.

17. Gay v. Board of Registration Commissioners, 466 F.2d 879 (6th
Cir. 1972). In Minnesota, the secretary of state, in response to pending litigation, issued a directive permitting women to use their birth names to register and vote.

18. 405 U.S. 970 (1972), aff'g mem., 341 F. Supp. 217 (M.D. Ala. 1971).

19. Pa. Op. Att'y Gen. No. 62 (1973), reported at 3 Pa. Bull. 2155.

20. This requirement is set forth in § 4(b)(1)(a) of the internal regulations of the Passport Office, issued pursuant to 22 C.F.R. § 51.24 (1974). The agency also requires some documentation before the a.k.a. passport will be issued.

21. In re Lawson, reported in the American Civil Liberties Union, Women's Rights Project Docket No. WR 8205 (1974). The case was dismissed in January 1974, after the Passport Office reversed its policy. For a helpful briefing of the issues women may face in exercising their right to use their chosen names on their passports, see the correspondence in the case of Andrea Kruger, available from the Connecticut Women's Educational and Legal Fund, Inc., 614 Orange Street, New Haven, Conn. 06511.

22. See, for example, Minn. Stat. Ann. § 518.27 (1969), as repealed and reenacted by L. 1974, ch. 107, § 17 (woman as the defendant); and Okla. Stat. tit. 12, § 1278 (1951) (woman at fault).

23. See, for example, Wis. Stat. Ann. § 247.20 (1957).

24. See, for example, Ark. Stat. Ann. § 24–1216 (1947); Ky. Rev. Stat. § 403.230 (1970); Mich. Comp. Laws § 552.391 (1970), as repealed and reenacted by Acts 1975, No. 40, § 1; S.D. Comp. Laws Ann. § 25-4-47 (1967) (if custodial parent); and Wis. Stat. Ann. § 247.20 (1957) (if custodial parent). In Egner v. Egner, Coon v. Coon, and Walls v. Walls, 133 N.J. Super. 403, 337 A.2d 46 (App. Div. 1975), the court held it an abuse of discretion to deny resumption of the maiden name to women with unemancipated children under the New Jersey statute (N.J. Stat. Ann. § 2A:34–21 [1952]).

25. See, for example, N.J. Stat. Ann. § 2A:34–21 (1952); and Wash. Rev. Code Ann. § 26.09.150 (1961). In addition to denying equal protection to women, such provisions are in derogation of the common law principle that there is no property right in a personal name allowing its "owner" to prevent its use by another.

26. Reinken v. Reinken, 351 Ill. 409, 184 N.E. 639 (1933).

27. In re Banks, 42 Cal. App. 631, 117 Cal. Rptr. 37 (1974): Egner v. Egner (Coon v. Coon, Walls v. Walls), 133 N.J. Super. 403, 337 A.2d 46 (App. Div. 1975); and Elwell v. Elwell, 313 A.2d 395 (Vt. 1973).

28. See, for example, Application of Lawrence, 133 N.J. Super. 408, 337 A.2d 49 (App. Div. 1975); Marshall v. State of Florida, 301 So. 2d 477 (Dist. Ct. App. 1974); Petition of Hauptly, 312 N.E. 2d 857 (Ind. 1974); in re Reben, 342 A.2d 688 (Me. 1975); Kruzel v. Podell, 67 Wis. 2d 138, 226 N.W.2d 458 (1975); in re Judith Natale, 44 U.S.L.W. 2070 (Mo. Ct. App. July 29, 1975); Application of Halligan, 46 A.D.2d 170, 371 N.Y.S.2d 458 (App. Div. 1974), rev'g 76 Misc. 2d 190, 350 N.Y.S.2d 63 (Sup. Ct. 1973).

In Lawrence and Reben, the court noted that the petitioner was applying with her husband's consent, raising at least some threat that such a petition might be denied during an ongoing marriage for lack of consent. Any requirement of consent abrogates the common law right to name change, and such a requirement with regard to married women only would be in clear violation

of an equality principle. In <u>Reben</u>, the court also stated that the Maine statute was a replacement of the common law procedure of name change rather
than an alternative.

29. See, for example, Application of Lawrence, 133 N.J. Super. 408,
337 A.2d 49 (App. Div. 1975) (confusion and children); Petition of Hauptly,
312 N.E.2d 857 (Ind. 1974) (children); Kruzel v. Podell, 67 Wis. 2d 138,
226 N.W.2d 458 (1975) (future children); in re Banks (Cal. Ct. App., 1st
App. Dist. Div. 4 Oct. 24 1974) (children), reported in the American Civil
Liberties Union, Women's Rights Project Docket No. WR 8006 (1974).

30. State equal rights provisions have been the basis for attorney general opinions or court decisions invalidating requirements that married women register in their husbands' surnames in Hawaii, Illinois, Pennsylvania,
and Texas. See Cragun v. Hawaii and Kashimoto, Civil No. 43175 (1st Cir.
Ct. 1975); <u>Pa. Op. Att'y Gen.</u> No. 72 (1973), reported at 3 Pa. Bull. 2657;
<u>Ill. Op. Att'y Gen.</u> No. 5-695 (1974); and <u>Tex. Op. Att'y Gen.</u> No. H-432
(1974).

31. See, for example, in re Reben, 342 A.2d 688 (1975), in which the
Supreme Judicial Court of Maine held that a statutory name-change procedure
superceded the common law.

32. See, for example, S.F. 2987, introduced in the Minnesota Senate
1973 legislative session, which gave the contracting parties to a marriage
three options regarding names: the family name of the man, the family name
of the woman, or the retention by each party of his or her family name prior
to marriage. The parties' choice had to be designated on the marriage license, as well as the name to be taken by their children should prior family
names be retained. The section further provided that a person who had previously taken a spouse's name at marriage could not retain that name as a
family name upon a subsequent marriage. For those marriages that predated
the amendment, provision was made for any person who had adopted the name
of a spouse to apply to resume his or her own family name.

The Wisconsin State Assembly also considered, but did not adopt, a
proposal concerning the selection of surnames at marriage in their 1973 session (A.B. 23, § 144). This proposal was similar to the Minnesota model in
requiring an affirmative selection of a "legal" surname at marriage, but it
added the options of a hyphenated surname or the retention of any former legal
surname, whether birth-given or otherwise acquired. Again, the choice of
completely new names was not offered.

33. <u>Wis. Stat. Ann.</u> § 247.20 (1957), <u>as amended by</u> L. 1975, ch. 94,
§ 78.

34. 12 <u>C.F.R.</u> § 202.4(e) (1976).

35. <u>Mass. Gen. Laws Ann.</u> ch. 151B, § 4(15) (1965), <u>as amended by</u>
Stats. 1975, ch. 367, § 3.

36. <u>Iowa Code Ann.</u> §§ 106.5(5) (1949), 321.41 (1966), <u>as amended by</u>
Acts 1974, ch. 1093, §§ 24, 49, respectively.

37. <u>Iowa Code Ann.</u> § 48.6 (1973), <u>as amended by</u> Acts 1974, ch. 1093,
§ 16.

38. <u>Iowa Code Ann.</u> § 674.1 (1946), <u>as repealed and reenacted by</u> Acts
1972, ch. 1129, § 1.

39. Iowa Code Ann. § 674.12 (1946), as amended by Acts 1972, ch. 1129, § 13.

40. Mass. Gen. Laws Ann. ch. 151B, § 4(15)(1965), as amended by Stats. 1975, ch. 367, § 3.

41. Mass. Gen. Laws Ann. ch. 51, § 2 (1971), as amended by Stats. 1975, ch. 367, § 1; and Mass. Gen. Laws Ann. ch. 51, § 36 (1971), as amended by Stats. 1975, ch. 367, § 2.

42. Ore. Rev. Stat. §§ 33.410, 107.105 (1974), as amended by L. 1975, ch. 733, § 1.

43. Alaska Stat. § 09.55.210(7) (1962), as amended by Acts 1974, ch. 127, §§ 72–73; and Minn. Stat. Ann. § 518.27 (1969), as amended by L. 1974, ch. 101, § 17.

44. Mich. Stat. Ann. § 552.391 (1970), as amended by Acts 1975, No. 40, § 1.

45. N.Y. Dom. Rel. Law § 240–a (1964), as amended by L. 1973, ch. 642, § 1. Under a new Dissolution of Marriage Act, Washington has amended its code to provide that a court "shall order a former name restored" upon request by a woman whose marriage is dissolved but has retained an old provision allowing the court discretion to order the woman to assume a name other than that of the husband at the husband's request. Wash. Rev. Code § 26.09.150 (1961), as added by L. 1973 (1st Ex. Sess.), ch. 157, § 15.

46. Hawaii Rev. Stat. § 574–1 (1968), as amended by L. 1975, ch. 115, § 1.

47. Ky. Rev. Stat. § 401.010 (1972), as repealed and reenacted by Acts 1974, ch. 66, § 1, Acts 1974, ch. 386, § 88.

48. Mich. Comp. Laws § 711.1 (1970), as amended by Acts 1975, No. 47.

49. N.M. Stat. Ann. § 3–4–5–C(1) (1953), as amended by L. 1973, ch. 51, § 1.

50. See Pennsylvania Department of Health, "Important Notice to Pennsylvania Hospitals and Physicians," May 17, 1967 (unpublished memorandum). In some jurisdictions, while a mother is not allowed to give an out-of-wedlock child the surname of the putative father, she is allowed to put his name on the birth certificate. Some states also provide procedures for change of a child's name once paternity is determined or the parents marry each other.

51. Under this standard, the father forfeited that right only when he had been guilty of conduct so destructive of the familial relationship that it would harm the child to continue the association by name. See cases cited in Laks v. Laks, 25 Ariz. App. 58, 540 P.2d 1277 (1975); and Application of Lone, 134 N.J. Super. 213, 338 A.2d 883 (1975).

52. See, for example, Laks v. Laks, 25 Ariz. App. 58, 540 P.2d 1277 (1975); Hall v. Hall, 351 A.2d 917 (Md. Ct. Spec. App. 1976); Robinson v. Hansel, ____ Minn. ____, 223 N.W.2d 138 (1974); and Tolbert v. Tolbert, 131 Ga. App. 388, 206 S.E.2d 63 (1974). In those cases that do grant the petition for change of name, the father's opposition is often disallowed on procedural grounds rather than on the merits. See, for example, Fulgham v.

Paul, 229 Ga. 463, 192 S.E.2d 376 (1972); in re Thomas, 404 S.W.2d 199
(Mo. 1966); Webber v. Parker, 246 La. 886, 167 So. 2d 519 (1964); but see
Clinton v. Morrow, 220 Ark. 377, 247 S.W.2d 1015 (1952).

53. See, for example, 74 Wis. Op. Att'y Gen. 118 (1974); Petition of
Falcucci, 355 Pa. 588, 50 A.2d 200 (1947).

54. See cases cited in Hall v. Hall, 351 A.2d 917 (Md. Ct. Spec. App.
1976); and Laks v. Laks, 25 Ariz. App. 58, 540 P.2d 1277 (1975).

55. See, for example, Pa. Stat. Ann. tit. 35, § 450.603 (1964), which
allows children to obtain a birth certificate with a new surname when their
names have been changed by court order and, if they were born out of wedlock,
when paternity has been adjudicated, when the parents marry, or when their
names have been changed by usage.

56. Conn. Op. Att'y Gen. (Jan. 23, 1975).

57. Mass. Op. Att'y Gen. No. 74-75-29 (1974). Apparently the Massachusetts opinion has aroused the opposition of the City and Town Clerks Associations, and a bill has been proposed that would permit the recording of the
surname of a legitimate child only as the legal surname of the husband (H.B.
684, Lombardi, 1976 session).

58. 28 Pa. Code §§ 1.1 et seq. (1975).

59. 28 Pa. Code § 1.7 (1975).

60. 74 Wis. Op. Att'y Gen. 118 (1974); and 28 Pa. Code § 1.6 (1975).

61. This rule is a result of the fact that, at common law, the legal
existence of a married woman was suspended. See 1 W. Blackstone, Commentaries on the Laws of England 442 (Cooley ed. 1884) [hereafter cited as
Blackstone]: "By marriage, the husband and wife are one person in law,
that is the very being or existence of the woman is suspended during the marriage, or at least is incorporated and consolidated into that of the husband."

62. See, for example, in re Daggett, 255 N.Y. 243 (1931); and Tate v.
Tate, 149 W.Va. 591, 142 S.E.2d 751 (1965). Many states, including those
that have completed or considered comprehensive statutory reform to eliminate sex discrimination, still have some form of sex-based domicile, residence, or settlement rules. These include: Iowa—see, for example, Mitchell
v. Mitchell, 193 Iowa 153, 185 N.W. 62 (1921) (stating the rule that a husband,
as head of the household, has a right to choose the domicile); Kentucky—see,
for example, Dunning v. Dunning, 325 S.W.2d 315 (1959) (interpreting Ky.
Rev. Stat. § 403.020(2)(a) (1972), which makes desertion a ground for divorce);
Minnesota—see, for example, Lemke v. Lemke, 259 Minn. 548, 108 N.W.2d
344 (1961) (husband has the right to fix the domicile of the family); Minn.
Stat. Ann. § 200.02 (1962); Op. Att'y Gen. No. 409-J-2 (1952); but see Keppel
v. Donovan, 326 F. Supp. 15 (1970), aff'd 405 U.S. 1034 (1970); Montana—
see, for example, Crenshaw v. Crenshaw, 120 Mont. 190, 182 P.2d 477
(1947) (husband has authority to establish the matrimonial and family domicile); Vermont—see, for example, Whitcomb v. Whitcomb, 115 Vt. 331, 58
A.2d 814 (1948) (stating that if a husband provides a suitable home and she
is properly supported and treated, his wife must live with him); Washington—
see, for example, Buchholz v. Buchholz, 63 Wash. 213 115 P.88 (1911) (husband ordinarily fixes family domicile; wife can establish separate domicile

only if he deserts her or there is a mutual abandonment of the marriage relationship); in re Bale, 63 Wash. 2d 83, 385 P.2d 545 (1963); but see Ayer v. Employment Security Dep't, 536 P.2d 610, 85 Wash. 2d 500 (1975) (the court reversed a denial of unemployment benefits to a man who left a job to follow his wife to a new job location, holding that the decision on job location must be made by both spouses, not on the basis of an arbitrary domicile rule); and Wisconsin—see, for example, 61 Op. Att'y Gen. 365 (1972); 18 Op. Att'y Gen. 359 (1929); 17 Op. Att'y Gen. 489 (1928); Ashland Co. v. Bayfield Co., 244 Wis. 210, 214, 12 N.W.2d 34, 36 (1943) (a married woman cannot establish a legal settlement for poor relief purposes apart from her husband, if he has settlement within the state).

63. In those 33 states and the District of Columbia that have either a "no-fault" or a one-year voluntary separation ground for divorce, either in addition to or instead of a desertion ground, the impact of sex-based domicile on divorce is probably minor. See the section on divorce grounds below for a catalog of these states. In the remaining states, the discrimination is significant to the extent that divorce is not readily available to a woman on other grounds, such as some version of cruelty, abusive treatment, incompatability, or indignities, which may be liberally interpreted. See Note, The Administration of Divorce: A Philadelphia Study, 101 U. Pa. L. Rev. 1204 (1953), in C. Foote, R. Levy, and F. Sander, Cases and Materials on Family Law 683 (1966).

64. L. Kanowitz, Women and the Law 46-47 (1969) [hereafter cited as Kanowitz].

65. Peirce v. Peirce, 379 Ill. 185, 39 N.E.2d 990 (1942).

66. H. Goodrich, Handbook of the Conflict of Laws 40 (4th ed. E.F. Scoles 1964).

67. Aside from sex discrimination, another area of constitutional concern regarding domicile, residency, or settlement requirements is the length of time required by states to establish such a status after moving to a new location. In recent years, the Supreme Court has struck down lengthy durational residency requirements on the ground that they penalize the exercise of the fundamental constitutional right to travel without serving any compelling state interest. Unreasonable residency rules for receipt of welfare payments, eligibility to vote, and state reimbursement of hospitals for nonemergency medical care to indigent patients have been held unconstitutional. Shapiro v. Thompson, 384 U.S. 618 (1969); Dunn v. Blumstein, 405 U.S. 330 (1972); and Memorial Hospital v. Maricopa Co., 415 U.S. 250 (1974). See also Butler v. Breyer, 355 F. Supp. 405 (S.D. Ohio 1972). But see Sosna v. Iowa, 419 U.S. 393 (S.D. Ohio 1975), in which the court held that a one-year residency requirement for filing a divorce petition was constitutional because it served important state interests and did not unduly infringe petitioner's rights.

68. A state school rule automatically classifying a woman as an out-of-state domiciliary for tuition purposes on the basis of her husband's domicile was held unconstitutional in Samuel v. University of Pittsburgh, 375 F. Supp. 1119 (W.D. Pa. 1974). On the other hand, equal protection challenges

to the underlying policy of charging lower tuition rates to resident, as opposed
to nonresident, students generally have been unsuccessful. See Hooban v.
Boling, 503 F.2d 648 (6th Cir. 1974); and Montgomery v. Douglas, 398 F.
Supp. 1139 (D. Colo. 1974). In addition, a regulation that embodied the common law presumption by giving great weight to the marriage of a nonresident
female to a resident male in determining her residency classification for tuition purposes but requiring proof of residency from a nonresident male married to a resident female was upheld in Clarke v. Redeker, 259 F. Supp. 117
(S.D. Iowa 1966). While the court upheld the general rule that a woman's
residency follows that of her husband, it also held that the state tuition regulation created a rebuttable presumption. The court remanded for reconsideration the petition of the male complainant, who was married to a resident female.

    69. These are: Ark. Stat. Ann. §§ 34-1307 to -1309 (1962), as added
by Acts 1941, No. 355, §§ 7-9; Colo. Rev. Stat. Ann. § 14-2-210 (1973), as
added by L. 1969, at 824, § 1; Me. Rev. Stat. § 21-242(7) (1965), as added
by L. 1969, ch. 360, § 1; Md. Code Ann. art. 16, § 29 (1973 Repl. Vol.),
as added by L. 1976, ch. 690; and Ore. Rev. Stat. § 108.015 (1975), as
added by L. 1973, ch. 434, § 1.

    70. N.J. Rev. Stat. § 37:2-3 (1968), as added by L. 1927, ch. 168, § 1.
Cases decided within five years after this statute was passed gutted its meaning by grafting the common law rule onto the statutory interpretation. See,
for example, Carpino v. Carpino, 7 N.J. Misc. 1121, 148 A. 615 (1930).
Recent precedent may be more in line with the language of the law.

    71. Del. Code Ann. tit. 13, § 1702 (1953), as added by 40 Del. Laws,
ch. 209, § 2; and Hawaii Rev. Stat. § 572-4 (1968), as added by L. 1931, ch.
51, § 1. A woman loses the benefit of this statute if, after marriage, she
assumes the domicile of her husband. See Note, Women's Loss of Residency
by Marriage, 1947 Wis. L. Rev. 275.

    72. See, for example, Ariz. Rev. Stat. Ann. § 16-925 (1956), as amended
by L. 1973, ch. 172, § 57; Conn. Gen. Stat. Ann. § 9-12 (1956), as amended
by Acts 1973, No. 73-630, § 1; Cal. Elections Code § 14282 (1961) (sex-neutral definition of residence for voting); Fla. Stat. Ann. § 97.102 (1960), as
amended by L. 1973, ch. 73-333, § 31; Ill. Stat. Ann. ch. 46, § 3-1 (1965)
(sex-neutral definition of residence for voting); but see Stevenson v. Baker,
347 Ill. 304, 179 N.E. 842 (1932), which suggests that the wife's residence
follows that of her husband; Ind. Ann. Stat. § 3-1-21-3 (§ 29-4803) (1972),
as added by Acts 1945, ch. 208, § 189, interpreted by 1963 Ind. Op. Att'y
Gen. No. 15, at 67 (if wife does not live in a household with her husband,
she may establish a separate voting residence); Iowa Code § 47.4 (1973)
(sex-neutral definition of residence for voting); Mass. Gen. Laws Ann. ch.
51, § 1 (1971), as amended by L. 1966, ch. 109 (all married women, not
just those separated from their husbands, are now eligible to vote and register in the city or town where they reside); Mich. Comp. Laws Ann. § 168.492
(1967), as interpreted by 1961-62 Mich. Op. Att'y Gen. No. 4038, at 483
(only the period of the wife's residence in the state may be counted in determining her qualification as elector, in view of her right to have different resi-

dence from her husband); <u>Mont. Rev. Codes Ann.</u> § 23-3022(8) (Supp. 1975), <u>as amended by</u> L. 1975, ch. 164, § 1, L. 1975, ch. 177, § 1 (person's residence for voting is where (s)he resides); <u>N.M. Stat. Ann.</u> §§ 3-1-(B), (J) (1970 Repl. Vol.), <u>as amended by</u> L. 1973, ch. 70, § 1, L. 1969, ch. 240, § 6 (person's residence for voting is where his/her family abides or otherwise, if (s)he resides elsewhere and intends to remain there); <u>N.Y. Dom. Rel. Law</u> § 61 (McKinney 1964), <u>as added by</u> L. 1929, ch. 455 (domicile of married woman determined by same rules as any other person for purposes of voting and office holding); <u>N.D. Cent. Code</u> § 54-01-26(5) (1975 Repl. Vol.) (residence of husband is presumptively the residence of the wife except for voting purposes); <u>Ohio Rev. Code Ann.</u> § 3503.02(D) (1972 Repl. Vol.) (residency for election purposes is where the family of a married man or woman resides; when they are separated and live apart, it is the place where each individual resides); and <u>Wis. Stat. Ann.</u> § 246.15 (1970), <u>as added by</u> L. 1921, ch. 529 (general married women's rights act, giving women equal rights and privileges as to residence for voting among other things); sex-based settlement law for welfare purposes remains (<u>Wis. Stat. Ann.</u> § 46.10(3)(a) [1970]).

Minnesota has a provision that has been interpreted to mean that a woman married to a registered voter of Minnesota for the length of time necessary to become a voter and otherwise qualified to vote would be justified in stating her legal residence as that of her husband even though she does not actually live in Minnesota. <u>Minn. Stat. Ann.</u> § 200.02(25) (1962), <u>as interpreted by</u> Minn. Op. Att'y Gen. No. 490-J-2 (1952).

Many states have amended their voter qualification statutes in recent years to remove durational residency requirements and lower the voting age to 18. These new statutes are generally sex neutral and do not refer specifically to the determination of married women's eligibility to register. See, for example, <u>N.H. Rev. Stat. Ann.</u> § 54:1 (1970 Repl. Vol.).

73. These include: <u>Ariz. Rev. Stat. Ann.</u> § 12-401 (1956), <u>as amended by</u> L. 1973, ch. 172, § 16 (venue); <u>Fla. Stat. Ann.</u> § 97.091 (1960), <u>as amended by</u> L. 1971, ch. 71-307, § 1 (name change); <u>Iowa Code</u> § 252.16 (1969), <u>as amended by</u> Acts 1974, ch. 1093, §§ 46, 47 (settlement for welfare purposes); <u>N.Y. Dom. Rel. Law</u> § 61 (McKinney 1964), <u>as added by</u> L. 1929, ch. 455 (office holding); and <u>Wis. Stat. Ann.</u> § 36.27 (1966), <u>as amended by</u> L. 1973, ch. 335, § 7 (definition of resident for lower tuition at state schools).

74. <u>Md. Code Ann.</u> art. 16, § 29 (1973 Repl. Vol.), <u>as added by</u> L. 1976, ch. 690; and <u>Ore. Rev. Stat.</u> § 108.015 (1975), <u>as added by</u> L. 1973, ch. 434, § 1.

75. <u>Ohio Rev. Code Ann.</u> § 3103.02 (1972 Repl. Vol.), <u>as repealed by</u> L. 1973, H.B. 233, § 2. Alaska has also repealed a law imposing certain civil disabilities on married persons, which could be construed to mean that a married person may now establish his or her own domicile. <u>Alaska Stat.</u> § 25.15.110 (1962), <u>as amended by</u> L. 1974, ch. 127, § 99.

76. For citations see note 72 supra.

77. <u>N.M. Stat. Ann.</u> § 3-1-6(B) (1970 Repl. Vol.), <u>as amended by</u> L. 1973, ch. 70, § 1.

78. For citations see note 73 supra.

79. See, for example, Aeres v. Aeres (D.C. Ct. App. October 31, 1975), cited in 2 F.L.R. 2023 (1975).

80. See generally, H. Clark, Law of Domestic Relations 151-52 (1968) [hereafter cited as Clark]; See also Yarborough v. Yarborough, 290 U.S. 202 (1933). In a Delaware variation of the general rule, a child takes the father's domicile if he has a domicile within the state and the mother's if he does not have domicile within the state and she does. Del. Code Ann. tit. 13, §§ 1703-704 (1953).

81. Clark, supra note 80, at 606-10. However, in most cases, the child's physical presence within the state provides "subject matter" jurisdiction for purposes of protecting a neglected or abandoned child or determining legal custody. See, for example, Com. ex rel. Blank v. Rutledge, 234 Pa. Super. 339 (1975). The residence or domicile of the petitioners in adoption is usually adequate to satisfy adoption statutes.

82. Iowa Code § 252.16(5) (1969), as added by Acts 1974, ch. 1093, §§ 46-47 (minor's settlement for welfare based on that of custodial parent); Md. Ann. Code art. 72A, § 1A (1970 Repl. Vol.), as amended by Acts 1976, ch. 690 (child's domicile is that of parent or legal guardian); Ore. Rev. Stat. § 108.105 (1975), as amended by L. 1975, ch. 434, § 1 (child's domicile is that of parents or custodial parent); Tex. Fam. Code § 11.04 (1975), as amended by Acts 1975, ch. 476, § 3 (child's residence coincides with that of parent, guardian, or other adult with care and control of child for purposes of venue for court action); and Wash. Rev. Code § 72.33.020 (1962), as amended by L. 1973 (1st Ex. Sess.), ch. 154, § 101 (child's residence imputed from that of parents, custodial parent, or other guardian).

83. Some states began at that time to allow wives to sue for loss of consortium due to intentional interference with the marital relationship by adopting related actions such as that for alienation of affections, but these actions were more difficult to sustain, were infrequently used, and have since been abolished in most states. Examples of actions sustained for intentional or malicious injury to a wife's right of consortium can be found in cases in New Mexico—Birchfield v. Birchfield, 29 N.M. 19, 217 P. 616 (1923); and Murray v. Murray, 30 N.M. 557, 240 P. 303 (1925); North Dakota—King v. Hansom, 13 N.D. 85, 99 N.W. 1085 (1906); Gessner v. Horne, 22 N.D. 60, 132 N.W. 432 (1911); and Rott v. Gehring, 33 N.D. 294, 157 N.W. 413 (1916); and Vermont—Knapp v. Wing, 72 Vt. 334, 47 A. 1075 (1900).

84. 183 F.2d 811 (D.C. Cir. 1950).

85. Alabama—Swartz v. U.S. Steel Corp., 293 Ala. 439, 304 So. 2d 881 (1974), overruling Smith v. United Constr. Workers, 271 Ala. 42, 122 So. 2d 153 (1960); Alaska—Schreiner v. Fruit, 519 P. 2d 462 (1974); Arizona —City of Glendale v. Bradshaw, 108 Ariz. 582, 503 P. 2d 803 (1972); Arkansas—Missouri Pac. Transp. Co. v. Miller, 227 Ark. 351, 299 S.W.2d 41 (1957); California—Rodriguez v. Bethlehem Steel Corp., 12 Cal. 3d 382, 115 Cal. Rptr. 765, 525 P.2d 669 (1974); Colorado—Colo. Rev. Stat. Ann. § 14-2-209 (1973), as added by L. 1961, at 560, § 1; Delaware—Yonner v. Adams, 3 Storey 229, 167 A.2d 717 (Super. Ct. 1961); and Stenta v. Leblang, 185 A.2d 759 (1962); District of Columbia—Hitaffer v. Argonne, 87 U.S. App.

D.C. 57, 183 F.2d 811, cert. denied, 340 U.S. 852 (1950); Florida—Gates
v. Foley, 247 So. 2d 40 (1971), overruling Ripley v. Ewell, 61 So. 2d 420
(1952); Georgia—Brown v. Georgia-Tennessee Coaches Inc., 88 Ga. App.
519, 77 S.E.2d 24 (1953); Hightower v. Landrun, 109 Ga. App. 510, 136
S.E.2d 425 (1964); compare Louisville & Nashville R.R. Co. v. Lunsford,
216 Ga. 287, 116 S.E.2d 232 (1960); Hawaii—Nishi v. Hartwell, 473 P.2d
116 (1970); Idaho—Nichols v. Sonneman, 91 Ida. 199, 418 P.2d 562 (1966);
Illinois—Dini v. Naiditch, 20 Ill. 2d 406, 170 N.E.2d 881 (1960); Indiana—
Troue v. Marker, 253 Ind. 284, 252 N.E.2d 800 (1970), overruling Miller v.
Sparks, 136 Ind. App. 148,189 N.E.2d 720 (1963); and McVickers v. Chesa-
peake & Ohio R.R. Co., 194 F. Supp. 848 (E.D. Mich. 1969) (interpreting
Ind. law); Iowa—Acuff v. Schmidt, 248 Iowa 272, 78 N.W.2d 480 (1956); Kentucky—Kotsiris v. Ling, 451 S.W.2d 411 (1970); Maine—Me. Rev. Stat. Ann.
tit. 19, § 167-A (1965), as added by L. 1967, ch. 13; compare Potter v.
Schafter, 161, Me. 340, 211 A.2d 891 (1965) (in which the court refused to
create a cause of action for wives' loss of consortium, holding that legislative action was required); Maryland—Deems v. Western Maryland Ry. Co.,
247 Md. 95, 231 A.2d 514 (1967), overruling Coastal Tank Lines v. Canoles,
207 Md. 37,113 A.2d 82 (1955); Massachusetts—Diaz v. Eli Lilly Co., 73
A.S. 1263, 302 N.E.2d 555 (1973); Michigan—Montgomery v. Stephan, 359
Mich. 33, 101 N.W.2d 227 (1960); Minnesota—Thill v. Modern Erecting Co.,
284 Minn. 508, 170 N.W.2d 865 (1969), overruling Hartman v. Cold Spring
Granite Co., 247 Minn. 515, 77 N.W.2d 651 (1956); Mississippi—Miss. Code
Ann. § 93-3-1 (1972), as added by L. 1968, ch. 304, § 1; see also Tribble
v. Gregory, 288 So. 2d 13 (1974); Missouri—Novak v. Kansas City Transit
Co., 365 S.W.2d 539 (1963); and Manning v. Jones, 349 F.2d 992 (8th Cir.
1965); Montana—Duffy v. Lipsman-Fulkerson & Co., 200 F. Supp. 71 (1961);
and Dutton v. Hightower & Lubrecht Constr. Co., 214 F. Supp. 298 (1963);
Nebraska—Luther v. Maple, 250 F.2d 916 (8th Cir. 1958); Guyton v. Solo-
mon Dehydrating Co., 302 F.2d 283 (8th Cir.), cert. denied, 371 U.S. 817
(1962); and Cooney v. Moomaw, 109 F. Supp. 448 (D. Neb. 1953); Nevada—
General Elect. Co. v. Bush, 88 Nev. 360, 498 P.2d 366 (1972); New Hampshire—N.H. Rev. Stat. Ann. § 508:8-2 (1968), as added by L. 1967, ch. 218,
§ 1; New Jersey—Ekalo v. Constructive Service Corp. of America, 46 N.J.
82, 215 A.2d 1 (1966) (wife may sue if she joins claim with that of her husband; this may raise problems if the husband refuses); New York—Millington
v. S.E. Elevator Co., 22 N.Y.2d 498, 393 N.Y.S.2d 305, 239 N.E.2d 897
(1968), overruling Kronenbitter v. Washburn Wire Co., 4 N.Y.2d 524, 176
N.Y.S.2d 354, 151 N.E.2d 898 (1958); Ohio—Clem v. Brown, 3 Ohio Misc.
167, 207 N.E.2d 390 (1965); Oklahoma—Okla. Stat. Ann. tit. 32, § 15 (1958),
as amended by L. 1973, ch. 73, § 1; see Duncan v. Gen. Motors Corp., 499
F.2d 835 (10th Cir. 1974) (holding that Oklahoma's refusal to apply statute
retroactively violates U.S. Constitution); Oregon—Ore. Rev. Stat. § 108.010
(1973), as added by L. 1941, ch. 228, § 1; Pennsylvania—Hopkins v. Blanco,
457 Pa. 90 (1974) (decision based on commonwealth's ERA), overruling Neu-
berg v. Bobowicz, 401 Pa. 146, 162 A.2d 662 (1960); and Brown v. Glenside
Lumber & Coal Co., 429 Pa. 601, 240 A.2d 822 (1968); Rhode Island—Mari-

anni v. Nanni, 95 R.I. 153, 185 A.2d 119 (1962); South Carolina—S.C. Code
§ 10-2593 (1962), as added by L. 1969, at 615; South Dakota—Hoekstra v.
Helgeland, 78 S.D. 82, 98 N.W.2d 669 (1959); and Bitsos v. Red Owl Stores,
350 F. Supp. 850 (D.S.D. 1972); Tennessee—Tenn. Code Ann. § 25-109
(1955), as added by L. 1969, ch. 86, s 1; see Burroughs v. H.E. Jordan, Jr.,
224 Tenn. 418, 456 S.W.2d 652 (1970) (holding statute not retroactive); West
Virginia—W.Va. Code Ann. § 48-3-19-a (1966), as amended by L. 1969, ch.
51 (eliminating effect of Seagraves v. Legg, 147 W.Va. 331, 127 S.E.2d
605 [1962], on consortium for wives); and Wisconsin—Moran v. Quality
Aluminum Casting Co., 34 Wis. 2d 542, 150 N.W.2d 137 (1967) (conditions
relief on joinder with husband's claim).

    86. New Mexico, North Dakota, and Vermont distinguish between inten-
tional and negligent loss of consortium and allow a wife to recover only if
she is injured intentionally or maliciously. See note 83 supra. The states
that do not allow a wife to sue for loss of consortium are: Louisiana—Hollin-
quest v. Kansas City So. Ry. Co., 88 F. Supp. 905 (W.D. La. 1950); Rollins
v. Beaumont Port Arthur Bus Lines, 88 F. Supp. 908 (W.D. La. 1950); and
Talley v. Employer's Mut. Liab. Ins. Co., 248 La. 785, 181 So. 2d 783
(Ct. App. 1965); New Mexico—Roseberry v. Starkovitch, 73 N.M. 211, 387
P.2d 321 (1963); North Dakota—N.D. Cent. Code Ann. § 14-07-05 (1971)
(North Dakota courts have not actually dealt with the problem of negligently
caused loss of consortium. One commentator has suggested that they would
hold the common law distinction between husband and wife in this area no
longer tenable and would allow the wife to sue for loss of consortium. Recent
cases: Husband and Wife—Wife's Action for Loss of Consortium—Discrimination on the Basis of Sex, 44 N.D. L. Rev. 276 [1968]); Texas—Garrett v.
Reno Oil Co., 271 S.W.2d 764 (Ct. Civ. App. 1954); Vermont—Vt. Stat. Ann.
tit. 15, § 66 (1958); Baldwin v. State, 125 Vt. 317, 215 A.2d 492 (1965); and
Herbert v. Layman, 125 Vt. 481, 218 A.2d 706 (1966); and Wyoming—Bates
v. Donnafeld, 481 P.2d 347 (1971).

    87. Connecticut—Marri v. Stamford St. Ry. Co., 84 Conn. 9, 78 A.2d
582 (1911); and Lockwood v. Wilson H. Lee Co., 144 Conn. 155, 128 A.2d
330 (1956); Kansas—Kan. Stat. Ann. § 23-205 (1974), as construed in Clark
v. S.W. Greyhound Lines, 144 Kan. 344, 58 P.2d 1128 (1936); Criqui v.
Blaw-Knox Co., 208 F. Supp. 605 (1962), aff'd, 318 F.2d 811 (10th Cir. 1963)
(interpreting Kan. law); and Hoffman v. Dantel, 192 Kan. 406, 388 P.2d 615
(1964); North Carolina—Helmsteler v. Duke Power Co., 224 N.C. 821, 32
S.E.2d 611 (1945); Utah—Black v. United States, 263 F. Supp. 470 (1967);
Virginia—Va. Code Ann. § 55-36 (1974); Alsop v. Eastern A.L., 171 F. Supp.
180 (E.D. Va. 1959) (interpreting Va. law); Carey v. Foster, 221 F. Supp.
185 (E.D. Va. 1963), aff'd, 345 F.2d 772 (4th Cir. 1965) (interpreting Va.
Law); and Washington—Wash. Rev. Code Ann. §§ 26.16.150, 26.16.160
(1961); and Hawkins v. Front St. Cable Ry. Co., 3 Wash. 592, 28 P. 1021
(1891).

    88. Schreiner v. Fruit, 519 P.2d 462 (Alaska 1974); and Hopkins v.
Blanco, 457 Pa. 90 (1974).

    89. See note 86 supra.

90. Alabama, Arizona, California, Florida, Hawaii, Indiana, Kentucky, Massachusetts, Nevada, Oklahoma, and Pennsylvania. For the dates and citations of these changes, see note 85 supra. During the late 1960s, the law in eight states was changed as a result of litigation and in Maine, Mississippi, New Hampshire, South Carolina, Tennessee, and West Virginia by legislative change.

91. See note 88 supra.

92. State spousal and child support provisions, other than those specifically relating to liabilities for the purchase of family "necessaries," are discussed in the sections on support and alimony after separation or divorce and on child support. For a striking example of courts' refusal to enforce support requirements during an ongoing marriage, see McGuire v. McGuire, 157 Neb. 226, 59 N.W.2d 336 (1953).

93. For a more extensive discussion of the history of the necessaries doctrine, see Clark, supra note 80, at 189–92.

94. 3 C. Vernier, American Family Law § 160 (1935), cited by Clark, supra note 80, at 186n.59. Clark also notes, at 187, that family expense statutes concern the rights of creditors and not the obligations between husband and wife. In some states, a wife liable under a family expense statute would have a cause of action against her husband for reimbursement.

95. A typical provision is that of Illinois, first enacted in 1874: "The expenses of the family and of the education of the children shall be chargeable upon the property of both husband and wife, or of either of them, in favor of creditors therefore, and in relation thereto they may be sued jointly or separately." Ill. Ann. Stat. ch. 68, § 15 (Smith-Hurd 1959).

96. See, for example, Conn. Gen. Stat. Ann. § 46–10 (1960), which provides in part:

> [B]oth [husband and wife] shall also be liable when any article
> purchased by either has in fact gone to the support of the family.
> . . . It shall be the duty of the husband to support his family,
> and his property when found shall be first applied to satisfy any
> such joint liability; and the wife shall be entitled to an indemnity
> from the property of the husband for any property of her own
> that has been taken, or for any money that she has been compelled
> to pay, for the satisfaction of any such claim.

97. See, for example, Tex. Fam. Code § 4.02 (1975):

> Each spouse has the duty to support his or her minor children.
> The husband has the duty to support the wife, and the wife has
> the duty to support the husband when he is unable to support him-
> self. A spouse who fails to discharge a duty of support is liable
> to any person who provides necessaries to those to whom support
> is owed.

98. Ariz. Rev. Stat. Ann. § 25–215 (1956) (execute against husband first); Conn. Gen. Stat. Ann. § 46–10 (1960) (execute against husband first);

Mass. Gen. Laws Ann. ch. 209, § 7 (1969) (wife's liability limited); Minn.
Stat. Ann. § 519.05 (1969) (definition of necessaries for which wife liable
limited); Neb. Rev. Stat. § 42-201 (1974) (execute against husband first);
N.D. Cent. Code § 14-07-08(3) (1971) (see § 14-07-10, husband's special
liability); Ore. Rev. Stat. § 108.040 (1975) (different procedural limitations
for a wife's liability); Pa. Stat. Ann. tit. 48, § 116 (1965) (execute against
husband first); Tex. Fam. Code § 4.02 (1975) (wife's liability arises only if
husband unable to support himself); Vt. Stat. Ann. tit. 15, § 68 (1974) (only
wife's real estate liable); and W. Va. Code Ann. § 48-3-23 (1976) (execute
against husband first).

99.   Nine of these states have codified the common law doctrine of a
husband's liability for the wife's necessaries into specific statutory provisions:
Ga. Code Ann. §§ 30-206, -215 (1969), §§ 53-508, -510 (1974); Hawaii Rev.
Stat. § 573-7 (1968); Ky. Rev. Stat. § 404.040 (1972) (secondary liability for
wife possible); La. Civ. Code Ann. arts. 120, 1786 (West 1972); Md. Ann.
Code art. 45, § 21 (1971); Nev. Rev. Stat. § 123.090 (1975); Ohio Rev. Code
Ann. § 3103.03 (1972); Okla. Stat. tit. 32, § 10 (1958) (sex neutral for chil-
dren's necessaries); and S.C. Code Ann. §§ 20-206, -303 (1962).

The others impose the common law doctrine through interpretations of
support obligations by the courts or general Married Women's Property Act
provisions: Alabama—Green v. First National Bank, 49 Ala. App. 426, 272
So. 2d 895 (1971), aff'd 49 Ala. App. 749, 272 So. 2d 904 (1973); Arkansas—
general sex-based support provisions; Delaware—Parkinson v. Hammond, 35
Del. 145, 159 A. 572 (Super. Ct. 1910); but see Hyland v. Southwell, 329
A.2d 767 (Super. Ct. 1974); Florida—Holiday Hosp. Ass'n v. Schwarz, 166
So. 2d 493 (Ct. App. 1964); Idaho—Linton v. Linton, 78 Idaho 335, 303 P.2d
905 (1956); Indiana—Hickey v. Shoemaker, 132 Ind. App. 136, 167 N.E.2d
487 (1960); Kansas—Chipp v. Murray, 191 Kan. 73, 379 P.2d 279 (1963);
Maine—Brown v. Duryo, 121 Me. 226, 116 A. 451 (1922); Michigan—see an-
notations under Mich. Comp. Laws Ann. § 557.1 (1967); Mississippi—McLe-
more v. Riley's Hosp., 197 Miss. 317, 20 So. 2d 67 (1944); New Hampshire—
Tebbets v. Hapgood, 34 N.H. 420 (1857); New Jersey—Ricci v. Ricci, 96
N.J. Super. 214, 232 A.2d 709 (1967); but see Willery v. Fagan, 120 N.J.
Super. 416, 294 A.2d 624 (1972); New York—DeBrauwere v. DeBrauwere,
293 N.Y. 460, 96 N.E. 722 (1911); but see Pokress v. Pokress, 71 Misc.
2d 171, 335 N.Y.S.2d 861 (1972); North Carolina—see annotations under
N.C. Gen. Stat. § 52-2 (1966); Rhode Island—Lacombe v. Lacombe, 78 R.I.
118, 79 A.2d 760 (1951); Tennessee—see Tenn. Code Ann. § 47-17-105 (1964),
as amended by L. 1974 (Adj. Sess.), ch. 727, § 1; and Wisconsin—Seitz v.
Seitz, 36 Wis. 2d 282, 151 N.W.2d 86 (1967).

100.   Alaska Stat. §§ 25.16.050, 25.16.060, 25.16.100, 25.20.030 (Supp.
1975); Cal. Civ. Code § 5121 (1970); Colo. Rev. Stat. Ann. § 14-16-110 (1973);
Ill. Ann. Stat. ch. 68, § 15 (Smith-Hurd 1959); Iowa Code Ann. § 597.14
(1950); Mo. Rev. Stat. § 451.250 (1952); Mont. Rev. Codes Ann. § 36-109
(1961); S.D. Comp. Laws Ann. § 25-2-11 (1967); Utah Code Ann. § 30-2-9
(1969); Wash. Rev. Code Ann. § 26.16.205 (1961); and Wyo. Stat. Ann.
§ 20-22 (1959).

101. N.M. Stat. Ann. § 57-2-1 (1962 Repl. Vol.); and Va. Code Ann. § 20-61 (1975 Repl. Vol.).

102. Cal. Civ. Code § 5121 (West 1970), as amended by Stats. 1973, ch. 987, at 1900, § 10. California also sex neutralized its general spousal support provision. Cal. Civ. Code § 5132 (West 1970), as amended by Stats. 1973, ch. 987, at 1902, § 17. Virginia, which has no specific provision regarding necessaries, sex neutralized its general spousal support provision in 1975. Va. Code Ann. § 20-61 (1975 Repl. Vol.), as amended by Acts 1975, ch. 464.

103. N.M. Stat. Ann. § 57-2-3 (1962 Repl. Vol.), as repealed by L. 1973, ch. 320, § 14.

104. Abel v. Abel, Civil No. 198270 (Birmingham, Jefferson Co. Cir. Ct. Nov. 1976).

105. M. Griffiths, Recommendation of the Commission on the Homemaker to the National Commission on the Observance of International Women's Year, Jan. 12, 1976, at 3 [hereafter cited as Griffiths].

106. These Census Bureau data are cited by Blank and Rone, Enforcement of Interspousal Support Obligations: A Proposal, 2 Women's Rights L. Rep. 14n.8 (1975) [hereafter cited as Blank and Rone].

107. See Subcommittee No. 4 of the Commission on the Judiciary, Equal Rights for Men and Women, S. Rep. No. 92-689, 92d Cong., 2d Sess. 4 (1972).

108. For a comprehensive evaluation of existing support enforcement mechanisms and recommendations for change, see Blank and Rone, supra note 106, at 13.

109. The text of this act is found in 9 Uniform Laws Annotated (West 1971).

110. See, for example, Alaska Stat. § 09.55.210 (1973), which provides that the court may order parties to arrange with their employer for automatic payroll deductions to be forwarded by the employer directly to the clerk of court. The Uniform Marriage and Divorce Act (UMDA) provides in § 312 that a person obligated to pay support may be ordered to assign part of his or her periodic earnings or trust income to the person entitled to receive support. This assignment is binding on the employer or trustee, who must withhold the support obligation and send that amount directly to the person specified in the order. Section 311 of the UMDA allows the court to order payment of support directly to the court. The payment schedule is kept by court officials, who have a duty to notify an obligor of arrearages and can initiate contempt actions if prompt payment is not forthcoming. The individual receiving support also may initiate an action to collect arrearages.

111. Cal. Civ. Code § 4801 (1970), as amended by Stats. 1969, ch. 1608, § 8; Del. Code Ann. tit. 13, § 1512 (1975), as amended by 59 Del. Laws, ch. 350, § 1 (1974); Ind. Ann. Stat. § 31-1-11.5-9 (Burns 1972), as amended by Acts 1973, ch. 297, § 1, at 1585; Mont. Rev. Codes Ann. § 48-322 (1949 Repl. Vol.), as amended by L. 1975, ch. 536, § 22; and N.M. Stat. Ann. § 22-7-6 (1953), as amended by L. 1973, ch. 319, § 7.

112. Colo. Rev. Stat. Ann. § 14-10-14 (1974), as amended by L. 1971, at 526, § 1 (maintenance); Conn. Gen. Stat. Ann. § 46-52 (1975), as amended

by Acts 1973, No. 73-373, § 21; Fla. Stat. Ann. § 61.08 (1965), as amended by L. 1971, ch. 71-241, § 10; Ky. Rev. Stat. Ann. § 403.200 (1975 Repl. Vol.), as amended by Acts 1972, ch. 182, § 10 (maintenance); Md. Ann. Code art. 16, § 3 (1976 Repl. Vol.), as amended by Acts 1974, ch. 332; Mass. Gen. Laws ch. 208, § 34 (1968), as amended by Stats. 1974, ch. 565, Stats. 1975, ch. 400, §§ 33, 79; Mich. Comp. Laws § 552.23 (1967), as amended by Acts 1970, No. 182, § 1; Minn. Stat. Ann. § 518.55 (1964), as amended by L. 1969, ch. 1028, § 4; Mo. Rev. Stat. § 452.335 (1953), as amended by L. 1973, at 470, § 8; Neb. Rev. Stat. § 42-365 (1965 Repl. Vol.), as amended by L. 1972, L.B. 820, § 19; N.J. Rev. Stat. § 2A:34-23 (1940), as amended by L. 1971, ch. 212, § 8; Okla. Stat. Ann. tit. 12, § 1278 (1966), as amended by L. 1975, ch. 350, § 1; Vt. Stat. Ann. tit. 15, § 754 (1974), as amended by L. 1973 (Adj. Sess.), No. 201, § 10; and Wis. Stat. Ann. § 247.26 (1957), as amended by L. 1973, ch. 12, § 37.

113. Ore. Rev. Stat. § 107.105 (1975), as amended by L. 1971, ch. 280, § 13; and Wash. Rev. Code Ann. § 26.09.090 (1961), as amended by L. 1973 (Ex. Sess.), ch. 157, § 9 (separate maintenance).

114. Ariz. Rev. Stat. Ann. § 25-319 (1956), as amended by L. 1973, ch. 139, § 2; Colo. Rev. Stat. Ann. § 14-10-14 (1974), as amended by L. 1971, at 526, § 1; Conn. Gen. Stat. Ann. § 46-52 (1975), as amended by Acts 1973, No. 73-373, § 21; Del. Code Ann. tit. 13, § 1512 (1975), as amended by 59 Del. Laws, ch. 350, § 1 (1974); Ky. Rev. Stat. Ann. § 403.200 (1975 Repl. Vol.), as amended by Acts 1972, ch. 182, § 10; Mass. Gen. Laws ch. 208, § 34 (1968), as amended by Stats. 1974, ch. 565, Stats. 1975, ch. 400, §§ 33, 79; Mo. Rev. Stat. § 452.335 (1953), as amended by L. 1973, at 470, § 8; Mont. Rev. Codes Ann. § 48-322 (1949 Repl. Vol.), as amended by L. 1975, ch. 536, § 22; Neb. Rev. Stat. § 42-365 (1965 Repl. Vol.), as amended by L. 1972, L.B. 82, § 19; Ohio Rev. Code Ann. § 3105.18 (Page 1972), as amended by L. 1974, H.B. 233; Ore. Rev. Stat. § 107.105 (1975), as amended by L. 1971, ch. 280, § 13; Va. Code Ann. § 20-107 (1975 Repl. Vol.), as amended by Acts 1970, ch. 501; and Wash. Rev. Code Ann. § 26.09.050 (1961) as amended by L. 1973 (Ex. Sess.), ch. 157, § 9.

115. Ga. Code Ann. § 30-209 (1969), as amended by L. 1966, at 160 (sex-based); Hawaii Rev. Stat. § 580.47 (1968), as amended by L. 1967, ch. 76, § 5; Iowa Code Ann. § 598.21 (1971), as amended by Acts 1970, ch. 1266, § 22; N.Y. Dom. Rel. Law § 236 (McKinney 1965), as amended by L. 1968, ch. 699; N.J. Rev. Stat. § 2A:34-23 (1940), as amended by L. 1971, ch. 212, § 8; N.C. Gen. Stat. § 50-16.5 (1969 Repl. Vol.), as amended by L. 1967, ch. 1152, § 2; and W. Va. Code Ann. § 48-2-16 (1966), as amended by L. 1969, ch. 49. Nevada and Wyoming also have provisions laying out statutory factors for the award of alimony, but they are of older origin. Nevada's provision is still sex-based.

116. See also the provision in Hawaii concerning burdens on either party for the benefit of the children.

117. No states have yet used detailed factors for spousal support in circumstances other than divorce, annulment, and divorce from bed and board. Montana, however, in amending its general spousal support law to eliminate

sex bias, added a provision stating that "support" includes homemaking. Mont. Rev. Codes Ann. § 36-103 (1961 Repl. Vol.), as amended by L. 1975, ch. 293, § 1. This redefinition should be quite helpful in redressing the balance between wage-earning and non-wage-earning spouses.

118. P.L. 93-647 (1975); and P.L. 94-88 (1975).

119. See U.S. Office of Child Support Enforcement, Department of Health, Education and Welfare, First Annual Report to the Congress on the Child Support Program 36 (1976): Alabama, Delaware, Georgia, Illinois, Maine, Massachusetts, Michigan, Minnesota, New Hampshire, New Jersey, North Dakota, Oregon, Pennsylvania, Rhode Island, Tennessee, Texas, Vermont, and Washington.

120. N.Y. Dom. Rel. Law § 250 (McKinney 1965), as added by L. 1975, ch. 690, § 1.

121. Iowa Code Ann. § 598.13 (1950), as added by Acts 1970, ch. 1266, § 14.

122. Neb. Rev. Stat. § 42-359 (1974 Reissue), as added by L. 1972, L.B. 820, § 13.

123. Mich. Comp. Laws Ann. § 552.22 (1967), as amended by Acts 1970, No. 182, § 1; and Vt. Stat. Ann. tit. 15, § 754 (1974), as amended by L. 1973 (Adj. Sess.), No. 201, § 10.

124. See, for example, Wash. Rev. Code Ann. § 26.09.060 (1961), as added by L. 1973 (1st Ex. Sess.), ch. 157, § 6.

125. Eckhardt, Deviance, Visibility, and Legal Action: The Duty to Support, 15 Social Problems 470 (1968), cited in Blank and Rone, supra note 106, at 13-14. In another study, the Committee on the Homemaker of the National Commission on the Observance of International Women's Year found that of the 46 percent of mothers awarded child support following divorce, only 45 percent of this group was collecting it regularly. Griffiths, supra note 105, at 3.

126. Smith v. Smith, 13 Wash. App. 381, 534 P.2d 1022. (1975); and Friedman v. Friedman, 521 S.W.2d 111 (Tex. Ct. Civ. App. 1975).

127. Ariz. Rev. Stat. Ann. § 25-320 (1956), as amended by L. 1973, ch. 139, § 1; Colo. Rev. Stat. Ann. § 14-10-115 (1974), as amended by L. 1971, ch. 520; Ind. Ann. Stat. § 31-1-11.5-12 (Burns 1972), as amended by Acts 1973, ch. 297, at 1585; Ky. Rev. Stat. § 403.210 (1975 Repl. Vol.), as amended by Acts 1972, ch. 182, § 11; Mo. Rev. Stat. § 452.340 (1953), as amended by L. 1973, at 470, § 9; Mont. Rev. Codes Ann. § 48-323 (1949 Repl. Vol.), as amended by L. 1975, ch. 536, § 23; and Ohio Rev. Code Ann. § 3109.05 (Page 1972), as amended by L. 1974, H.B. 233.

128. Conn. Gen. Stat. Ann. § 46-57 (1960), as amended by Acts 1973, No. 73-373, § 26, Acts 1974, No. 74-169, § 14; and N.C. Gen. Stat. § 50.13.4 (1969 Repl. Vol.), as added by L. 1967, ch. 1153, § 2, as amended by L. 1969, ch. 895, § 17, L. 1975, ch. 814.

129. See, for example, the child support laws of Nebraska, Texas, and Vermont.

130. For further discussion of the history of the common law system, see B. Babcock, A. Freedman, E. Norton, and S. Ross, Sex Discrimination and the Law: Causes and Remedies 592-99 (1975) [hereafter cited as Bab-

cock]; I. Baxter, Marital Property preface (1973) [hereafter cited as Baxter]; and Johnston, Sex and Property: The Common Law Tradition, the Law School Curriculum, and Developments Toward Equality, 47 N.Y.U. L. Rev. 1033 (1972).

131. A few states have amended their Married Women's Property Acts in recent years. See, for example, Md. Code Ann. art. 45, § 14 (1971), as amended by Acts 1974, ch. 593, § 1 (concerning prenuptial debts of the spouses); and Kan. Stat. Ann. §§ 23-201 to -206 (1974), as amended by L. 1976, ch. 172, §§ 1-8. The affirmative provisions were amended and retained; the restrictive procedures were repealed.

132. Blackstone (4th ed. 1890), supra note 61, at 583. Tenancy by the entirety in real property is a recognized form of concurrent ownership between husband and wife in Alaska, Arkansas, Delaware, District of Columbia, Florida, Hawaii, Indiana, Kentucky, Maryland, Massachusetts, Michigan, Missouri, New Jersey, New York, North Carolina, Oklahoma, Oregon, Pennsylvania, Rhode Island, Tennessee, Vermont, Virginia, and Wyoming. Statutory references to entireties ownership still exist in Mississippi and in the Uniform Partnership Acts of Illinois and Utah, but actual use of this form of ownership seems to be negligible in those jurisdictions. 4A Powell on Real Property para. 621n.7 (1975) [hereafter cited as Powell], includes Wisconsin in its catalog of entireties jurisdictions, but in re Richardson's Estate, 229 Wis. 426, 282 N.W. 585 (1938), holds to the contrary. The status of tenancy by the entirety was in doubt in Montana until 1963, when it was definitively established, in Clark v. Clark, 143 Mont. 183, 387 P.2d 907 (1963), that entireties ownership was no longer available in that jurisdiction, since the legal fiction behind such ownership had been abolished. See Phipps, Tenancy by Entireties, 25 Temp. L.Q. 24 (1951) [hereafter cited as Phipps] for an in-depth discussion of both the common law and modern characteristics of entireties ownership.

133. See Baxter, supra note 130, at 9-22. In a few jurisdictions, each spouse may manage and collect the profits from his or her one-half interest in the property, but title cannot pass without the joinder of both. In Alaska, Arkansas, New Jersey, New York, and Oregon, except for the right of survivorship, the special incidents of entireties ownership have been revised to create tenancies in common: both spouses have equal rights to the possession, control, and income of the property during marriage, and their separate interests are generally subject to their separate debts, with some exceptions for homestead. Partition cannot be forced by separate creditors, however. Hawaii would also seem to fall into this pattern of treatment of entireties ownership. In re Dean's Trust, 47 Hawaii 629, 394 P.2d 432 (1964). Oklahoma has gone even farther in eroding the special incidents of entireties ownership, allowing a separate creditor to execute on entireties property by forcing a sale that can sever the property and destroy the right of survivorship of the nondebtor spouse. See Okla. Stat. tit. 60, § 74 (Cum. Supp. 1949); and Osborne, Co-ownership of Property in Oklahoma, 27 Okla. L. Rev. 585 (1974) [hereafter cited as Osborne]. See generally Powell, supra note 132, at para. 623. Two states, Kentucky and Tennessee, differ from this model in allow-

ing separate liens against a spouse's contingent survivorship right only, thus leaving the ultimate interests of a nondebtor spouse intact.

134. Phipps, supra note 171, at 29-31; see also Glendon, Tenancy by the Entirety in Massachusetts, 59 Mass. L.Q. 53 (1974) [hereafter cited as Glendon]. Massachusetts also retains the common law practice of charging the separate debts of the husband but not those of the wife against entireties property. In fact, even "joint and several" creditors can reach only the husband's interest, except in a mortgage situation where the husband and wife have conveyed a security interest in the estate. See Huber, Creditors' Rights in Tenancies by the Entireties, B.C. Ind. & Com. L. Rev. 197, 200 (1960). Recent suggestions in Tennessee cases that the common law control by husbands was reinstituted were repudiated by the state supreme court in Robinson v. Trousdale Co., _____ Tenn. _____, 516 S.W.2d 626 (1974). See, for example, Weaks v. Gress, 225 Tenn. 593, 474 S.W.2d 424 (1971).

135. A reversal of the common law presumption favoring entireties ownership has occurred in a few jurisdictions that have essentially sex-neutral entireties ownership. In Oklahoma, for example, there is a prevailing presumption favoring tenancy in common, regardless of the marital relationship of the concurrent owners. Osborne, supra note 133, at 592 et seq. A similar court-initiated change occurred in Alaska in 1963. In Carver v. Gilbert, 387 P.2d 928 (Alaska 1963), the court enunciated a policy preferring tenancy in common, unless a document expressly provided for a tenancy by the entirety with rights of survivorship, because of the obsolescence of the common law view of husband and wife as a single unit and the general preference for tenancy in common over forms of joint tenancy. Since that time, however, a statutory enactment of the common law presumption favoring entireties ownership by spouses of real property has supplanted the Carver decision. Alaska Stat. § 34.15.110 (1962), as amended by Acts 1970, ch. 211, § 1. Chapter 63 of the same laws, however, explicitly recognizes the validity of a conveyance by one spouse to himself and his spouse as tenants in common.

136. The inability of a separated spouse to force adjudication concerning entireties property is particularly burdensome in a jurisdiction such as Massachusetts, where the husband has control of the property during marriage and where a court cannot even grant possession of the family home to the wife before divorce. Dee v. Dee, 296 N.E.2d 521 (Mass. Ct. App. 1973). In Klein v. Mayo, 367 F. Supp. 583 (D. Mass. 1974), aff'd mem., 416 U.S. 953 (1974), the court denied an equal protection challenge to the entireties doctrine made by a separated woman who had been denied partition of the family home she held by the entireties with her husband. Although other forms of joint tenants are free to seek the partition of jointly held property, the court found no discrimination in this case since the husband also was prevented from securing a partitioning of interests short of final divorce. The court concluded that the inability to force a partition and the husband's exclusive right of possession during marriage were known consequences of the choice to hold the home by the entireties in Massachusetts and that the parties should have chosen another form of ownership at the outset if they disliked these features. Of course, whether the average married couple actually had

a realistic opportunity to choose joint tenancy or tenancy by the entirety prior to the statutory elimination of the presumption favoring entireties ownership in Massachusetts in 1973 is doubtful. See Glendon, supra note 134, at 58-59.

A number of states have created special exceptions to the rule concerning nonpartition of entireties prior to divorce. The new rules allow a court to award to a separated dependent spouse the use, occupancy, and in some cases title of, entireties property, particularly if it is the family home, in satisfaction of support obligations. See, for example, N.C. Gen. Stat. § 50-16.7 (1966), as amended by L. 1967, ch. 1152, § 2, L. 1969, ch. 541, § 5, ch. 895, § 18.

137. One such doctrine is the presumption that a contribution to the purchase of entireties property by a husband is a gift while a contribution by a wife creates a trust in her favor. This presumption arose out of the traditional view that marriage was a "confidential" relationship in which the wife could not freely bargain and in which the husband bore the responsibility of support. Thus, purchases from his assets were presumed to be in satisfaction of his obligation, while those of the wife, who had no support obligation or separate legal status, were protected for her benefit. In a number of other states where this presumption still exists, the courts have begun to place a heavy burden of proof on a wife trying to establish that a transfer to her husband or contribution to joint property was not a gift. See Moore v. McKelvey, 221 S.E. 2d 780 (S.C. 1976); and Olson v. Olson, 321, So. 2d 462 (Fla. Ct. App. 1975), where the court held that the wife's contribution toward a jointly held domicile must be shown to have been above and beyond the performance of ordinary marital duties in order for her to acquire a special equity in the property. For the more traditional view of the doctrine, see Skinner v. Skinner, 28 N.C. App. 412, 22 S.E. 2d 258 (1976); and Ingram v. Easley, 227 N.C. 442, 42 S.E. 2d 624 (1947). The presumption has been sex neutral in Missouri for a number of years. Hampton v. Niehaus, 329 S.W. 2d 794 (1959). For a fuller discussion of this presumption, see Starline, The Tenancy by the Entireties in Florida, 14 U. Fla. L. Rev. 111, 120-23 (1961); and Ramsey v. Ramsey, _____ Ark. _____, 531 S.W. 2d 28 (1976).

Another sex-based presumption was a Pennsylvania rule that the household goods belong to the husband unless the wife can show a financial contribution to their purchase price. The presumption was based on the view that the husband earned the money, bought the goods as part of his support duty, and therefore continued to own them on dissolution of the marriage. The rule has now been sex neutralized. See DiFlorido v. DiFlorido, 459 Pa. 641, 331 A.2d 174 (Sup. Ct. 1974), discussed further below.

138. The major exceptions are property inherited, received as a gift, or received in exchange for separate property, and, in most states, increments in the value of property acquired before the marriage.

139. See Ariz. Rev. Stat. Ann. § 25-214 (1956), as added by L. 1973, ch. 172, § 64; Cal. Civ. Code § 5125 (1970), as amended by Stats. 1973, ch. 987, § 14, Stats. 1974, ch. 546, § 14, ch. 1206, § 4; Idaho Code § 32-912 (1963), as amended by L. 1974, ch. 194, § 2; Nev. Rev. Stat. Ann. § 123.230

(1975), as amended by L. 1975, at 557, ch. 393; N.M. Stat. Ann. § 57–4A–8 (1953), as added by L. 1973, ch. 320, § 10, as amended by L. 1975, ch. 246, § 6; and Wash. Rev. Code § 26.16.030 (1961), as amended by L. 1972 (1st Ex. Sess.), ch. 108, § 3.

140. La. Civ. Code Ann., art. 2404 (1973). A wife in Louisiana now also has the right to obligate her wages, but the husband's wages and the remainder of the community are beyond her control. See La. Rev. Stat. Ann. § 9:3584 (1950), as amended by Acts 1975, No. 705, § 1.

141. Historically, the husband's separate property but not the wife's was liable for community debts not satisfied by the community property. The significance of the failure of most states to statutorily define "separate" and "community" debts in light of the Equal Credit Opportunity Act is discussed by A. Bingaman, A Commentary on the Effect of the Equal Rights Amendment on State Laws and Institutions (1975).

142. Regulation B, implementing the Act, is found at 12 C.F.R. §§ 202.1 et seq. (1976).

143. New Mexico is an exception. Both spouses' earnings remain community property upon separation unless there is an agreement to the contrary. N.M. Stat. Ann. § 57–4A–2 (1962). In this instance, Louisiana is similar to the other community states; upon separation, the wife's earnings become separate property, and she can manage them without limitation. In contrast to wages, designation of real property or of other personal property is permanent in all the states and applies to any subsequent form the property takes, for example, a sum of cash resulting from the sale of real property.

144. D.C. Code Encycl. § 16–910 (1966). No standards for division are included. The direct financial contribution of the parties is not the sole or decisive factor. King v. King, 286 A.2d 234 (D.C. Ct. App. 1972); and Sebold v. Sebold, 444 F.2d 864 (D.C. Cir. 1971). Tenn. Code Ann. § 36–825 (1955). Reasonable and just disposition is to be made of all jointly owned property.

145. North Dakota (N.D. Cent. Code § 14–05–24 [1971]) permits such equitable distribution of the real and personal property as is just. The separate property of the wife may not be touched. McLean v. McLean, 69 N.D. 665, 290 N.W. 913 (1940). In Arkansas (Ark. Stat. Ann. § 34–1214 [1962]), the wife gets one–third of personalty outright and one–third of realty for life if she gets the divorce. The grant is left to the discretion of the court if the husband is awarded the divorce. He has no similar right. Myers v. Myers, 226 Ark. 632, 294 S.W.2d 67 (1956); and Bowling v. Bowling, 237 Ark. 199, 372 S.W.2d 239 (1963). Joint property is divided on divorce. Ark. Stat. Ann. § 34–1215 (1961). The law in Vermont (Vt. Stat. Ann. tit. 15, §§ 751–52 [1974]) permits the court to apportion all the property of the spouses but states explicitly that the wife is entitled to her property even if she is at fault, unless the court has entered an order concerning it. A provision permitting the husband to be granted the estate of an adulterous wife was repealed in 1973. Vt. Stat. Ann. tit. 15, § 759 (1974), as repealed by L. 1973, No. 201, § 12.

146. The seven in which marital property is to be divided are: Colo. Rev. Stat. Ann. § 14–10–113(9) (1974); Del. Code Ann. tit. 13, § 1513 (1975);

Ky. Rev. Stat. Ann. § 403.190 (1972), as added by Acts 1972, ch. 182, § 9;
Me. Rev. Stat. Ann. tit. 19, § 722A (1965); Minn. Stat. Ann. §§ 518, 558
(1969); Mo. Ann. Stat. § 452-330 (Supp. 1976); and N.J. Stat. Ann. § 2A:34-
23 (1952).

147. Alaska Stat. § 09.55.210(6) (1962); Conn. Gen. Stat. Ann. § 46-51
(1960); Hawaii Rev. Stat. § 580-47 (1968); Ill. Ann. Stat. ch. 40, §§ 18-19
(Smith-Hurd 1976); Ind. Code § 31-1-11.5 (Burns 1975); Iowa Code Ann.
§ 598.21 (1950); Kan. Stat. Ann. § 60-1610 (1964); Mass. Gen. Laws Ann.
ch. 208, § 34 (1958); Mich. Comp. Laws Ann. §§ 552.19, 552.23 (1967) (separate
property is transferred only if marital property is inadequate); Mont. Rev.
Codes Ann. § 48-321 (1975); Neb. Rev. Stat. § 42-366 (1974); N.H. Rev.
Stat. Ann. § 458:19 (1968); N.C. Gen. Stat. § 50-16.7 (1966); Okla. Stat.
tit. 12, §§ 1275, 1278 (1965) (if both spouses are at fault, the court can divide all property equitably; if only one is at fault, separate property of that
spouse is divided for support of the children); Ohio Rev. Code Ann. § 3105.18
(Page 1972); Ore. Rev. Stat. § 105.105 (1975); S.D. Comp. Laws Ann.
§ 75-4-44 (1969); Utah Code Ann. § 30-3-5 (1969); W. Va. Code Ann. § 48-2-
21 (1966); Wis. Stat. Ann. § 247.26 (1957); and Wyo. Stat. Ann. § 20-63
(1957).

148. One situation in which the courts used these powers was to return
to the wife property she had purchased and put into her husband's name or
their names jointly. Consistent with the presumption that this was not a gift,
she was entitled to the property on divorce. See, for example, Ill. Ann.
Stat. ch. 40, § 18 (Smith-Hurd 1976); Alvarado v. Alvarado, 22 Ill. App.
3d 10, 316 N.E.2d 56 (1974); Gottemoller v. Gottemoller, _____ Ill. App.
3d _____, 346 N.E.2d 393 (1976) (the court held that the wife had not shown
special equity entitling her to the jointly owned property, despite her substantial contribution to the purchase price); N.D. Cent. Code § 14-05-24 (1971);
and McLean v. McLean, 69 N.D. 665, 290 N.W. 913 (1940). In the District
of Columbia, where marital property is equitably apportioned, the court may
award property with title held solely in the name of one spouse if the other
can show legal or equitable interest in it. Lyons v. Lyons, 295 A.2d 903
(Ct. App. 1972).

149. See, for example, Mass. Gen. Laws Ann. ch. 208, § 34 (1958);
N.C. Gen. Stat. § 50-16.7(b) (1966); and Tenn. Code Ann. § 36-820 (1955);
and W. Va. Code Ann. § 48-2-15 (1966).

150. See, for example, Vt. Stat. Ann. tit. 15, §§ 752, 759 (1974), as
repealed by L. 1973, No. 201, § 12; Ark. Stat. Ann. § 34-1214 (1962); and
Wis. Stat. Ann. § 247.26 (1957).

151. Alaska Stat. § 09.55.210 (1962); Groff v. Groff, 408 P.2d 998
(1965); and Nanover v. Nanover, 496 P.2d 644 (1972). N.H. Rev. Stat. Ann.
s 458:19 (1968); Heath v. Seymore, 110 N.H. 425, 270 A.2d 602 (1970); and
Comer v. Comer, 110 N.H. 505, 272 A.2d 586 (1970). N.D. Cent. Code
Ann. § 14-05-24 (Supp. 1975); and Ruff v. Ruff, 78 N.D. 775, 52 N.W.2d
107 (1952). S.C. Code Ann. § 20-113 (1962); Moyle v. Moyle, 262 S.C. 308,
204 S.E.2d 46 (1974); and Graham v. Graham, 253 S.C. 486, 171 S.E.2d
704 (1970). Tenn. Code Ann. § 36-825 (1955); Langford v. Langford, 220

Tenn. 600, 421 S.W.2d 632 (1967). Utah Code Ann. § 30-3-5 (1969); Martinett v. Martinett, 8 Utah 2d 202, 331 P.2d 821 (1958). Wyo. Stat. Ann.
§ 20-63 (Cum. Supp. 1975); and Storm v. Storm, 470 P.2d 367 (Wyo. 1970).

152. Alaska Stat. § 09.55.210(6) (1962); in re Harrington's Marriage,
199 N.W.2d 351 (Iowa 1972); in re William's Marriage, 199 N.W.2d 339
(Iowa 1972); Bennett v. Bennett, 208 Or. 524, 302 P.2d 1014 (1956); and
Beroud v. Beroud, 4 Or. App. 469, 478 P.2d 652 (1970).

153. Cal. Civ. Code s 4800 (1970); and La. Civ. Code arts. 2406, 2408
(1971). In California, quasi-community property, defined as property located
outside the state that would be community if acquired within the state, must
be divided equally as well.

154. See, for example, Shepard v. Shepard, 94 Idaho 734, 497 P.2d
321 (1972); Nelson v. Nelson, 436 S.W.2d 200 (Tex. Ct. Civ. App. 1969);
and Fletcher v. Fletcher, 516 P.2d 103 (Nev. Sup. Ct. 1973).

155. See, for example, former Idaho Code § 32-712(2) (1963), which was
construed to require that a spouse granted a divorce on grounds of extreme
cruelty or adultery be given at least one-half of the community property.
This provision was amended in 1965 to provide for equitable division, without
regard to fault. L. 1965, ch. 63, § 1.

156. Wash. Rev. Code Ann. § 26.09.080 (1961) and Nev. Rev. Stat.
§ 125.150 (1973) provide for distribution of separate property. The Nevada
law has sex-based standards for transfer of the separate property: all wives
but only husbands unable to support themselves are entitled to separate property of the other. Cases in Arizona suggest that separate property can be
reached there. Burton v. Burton, 23 Ariz. App. 159, 531 P.2d 204 (1975).

157. Butler v. Butler, _____ Pa. _____, 347 A.2d 477 (1975).

158. DiFlorido v. DiFlorido, 459 Pa. 641, 331 A.2d 174 (1974).

159. Cooper v. Cooper, 513 S.W.2d (Tex. Ct. Civ. App. 1974).

160. For further discussion of economic and other types of interspousal
contracts, see Babcock, supra note 130; and Weitzman, Legal Regulation of
Marriage: Tradition and Change, 62 Calif. L. Rev. 1169 (1974).

161. DiFlorido v. DiFlorido, 459 Pa. 641, 331 A.2d 174 (1974).

162. Mass. Gen. Laws Ann. ch. 184, § 7 (1958), as amended by Stats.
1973, ch. 210, § 1, provides:

> A conveyance or devise of land to a person and his spouse which
> expressly states that the grantees or devisees shall take jointly,
> or as joint tenants or in joint tenancy, or to them and the sur-
> vivor of them shall create an estate in joint tenancy and not a
> tenancy by the entirety. In a conveyance or devise to three or
> more persons, words creating a joint tenancy shall be construed
> as applying to all of the grantees, or divisees, regardless of
> marital status, unless a contrary intent appears from the tenor
> of the instrument.

Mass. Gen. Laws. Ann. ch. 209, § 3 (1958), as amended by Stats. 1975, ch.
558, § 3, treats transfers of real and personal property between husband and
wife in the same manner as transfers between single people.

In 1973, Rep. Peter Harrington introduced H.B. 853 to abolish the tenancy by the entirety altogether. The bill was sent to the Judicial Council for study and recommendation. It was filed again in 1974 and 1975, and most recently as H.B. 1954 (1976). H.B. 1954 would abolish tenancy by the entirety by changing the traditional presumption favoring entireties ownership within marriage to one favoring tenancy in common and providing that any attempt to create a tenancy by the entirety after a certain date would result instead in the creation of a joint tenancy.

163. Ariz. Rev. Stat. § 25-214 (1956), as amended by L. 1973, ch. 172, § 64; Cal. Civ. Code §§ 5105, 5125 (1970), as amended by Stats. 1973, ch. 987, § 4, at 1898; Idaho Code § 32-912 (1963), as amended by L. 1974, ch. 194, § 2, at 1502; Nev. Rev. Stat. § 12.230 (1975), as amended by Acts 1975, at 557; N.M. Stat. Ann. § 57-4A-8 (1953), as added by L. 1973, ch. 320, § 10, as amended by L. 1975, ch. 246, § 6; and Wash. Rev. Code § 26.16.030 (1961), as amended by L. 1972, ch. 108, § 3.

164. Tex. Fam. Code Ann. §§ 5.02, 5.22, 5.61 (1974), as added by Acts 1969, ch. 888, § 6.

165. Colo. Rev. Stat. Ann. § 14-10-113(9) (1974), as amended by L. 1973, at 553, 555, §§ 6, 7, 12, L. 1975, at 210, § 25; Del. Code Ann. tit. 13, § 1513 (1975), as added by 59 Del. Laws, ch. 350, § 1 (1974); Ind. Code § 31-1-11.5-11 (1975), as added by Acts 1973, ch. 297, § 1, at 1585; Ky. Rev. Stat. Ann. § 403.190 (1972), as added by Acts 1972, ch. 182, § 9; Me. Rev. Stat. Ann. § 19-722A (1965), as added by L. 1971, ch. 399, § 2, L. 1972, ch. 622, § 61-B; Mo. Rev. Stat. § 452-330 (Supp. 1976), as amended by L. 1973, at 470, § 7; and Mont. Rev. Codes Ann. § 48-321 (1975), as added by L. 1975, ch. 536, § 21.

166. Hawaii Rev. Stat. § 580-47 (1968), as amended by L. 1969, ch. 221, § 12; Mich. Comp. Laws Ann. §§ 552.19, 552.23 (1967), as amended by Acts 1970, No. 182, § 1, Acts 1971, No. 75, § 1 (this amendment also sex neutralized the terminology and added real estate to the property subject to division); Minn. Stat. Ann. § 518.58 (1969), as amended by L. 1974, ch. 107, § 122; N.J. Stat. Ann. § 2A:34-23 (1952), as amended by L. 1971, ch. 212, § 8; and Ohio Rev. Code Ann. § 3105.18 (Page 1972 Repl. Vol.), as amended by L. 1974, H.B. 233.

167. National Conference of Commissioners on Uniform State Laws, Uniform Marriage and Divorce Act [hereafter cited as UMDA] § 307 Alternatives A and B (1971).

168. See, for example, Schilleman v. Schilleman, 61 Mich. App. 446, 232 N.W.2d 737 (1975); but see Hutchins v. Hutchins, 36 Mich. App. 675, 194 N.W.2d 6 (1971), which, in addition to factors such as source of property, contribution toward acquisition, duration of marriage, and earning ability, lists "cause of the divorce." See, for example, Painter v. Painter, 118 N.J. Super. 33 287 A.2d 467 (1972).

169. N.C. Gen. Stat. § 50-16.7 (1966), as amended by L. 1969, ch. 895, § 27. This provision also allows the court to levy against profits or to assign to a wife, pending divorce, the possession of or title to entireties in order to meet support or alimony pendente lite obligations. Similar exceptions for

support purposes have been enacted in other entireties jurisdictions, where the husband does not have exclusive control rights but where mutuality rules prevent a dependent spouse from using entireties assets without the other spouse's permission. See, for example, Pa. Stat. tit. 48, § 133 (1965), providing that the court may execute against entireties property to enforce a support order in Pennsylvania.

170. Neb. Rev. Stat. § 42-366 (1974), as added by L. 1972, L.B. 820, § 20.

171. Conn. Gen. Stat. Ann. § 46-51 (1960), as added by Acts 1973, No. 73-373, § 20, as amended by Acts 1975, No. 75-331.

172. Vt. Stat. Ann. tit. 15, § 759 (1974), as repealed by L. 1973, No. 201, § 12.

173. Wis. Stat. Ann. § 247.26 (1957), as amended by L. 1971, ch. 220, §§ 12, 22, L. 1973, ch. 12, § 37.

174. Okla. Stat. Ann. tit. 12, §§ 1275, 1278 (1965), as amended by L. 1975, ch. 350, § 1.

175. Tex. Fam. Code § 3.63 (1975), as amended by Acts 1969, ch. 988, § 1.

176. Wash. Rev. Code Ann. § 26.09.080 (1961), as added by L. 1973 (1st Ex. Sess.), ch. 157, § 8.

177. Ariz. Rev. Stat. § 25-318 (1956), as amended by L. 1973, ch. 139, § 1.

178. Cal. Civ. Code § 4800 (1970), as added by Stats. 1969, ch. 1608, at 3333, § 8.

179. N.M. Stat. Ann. s 22-7-6 (1954), as amended by L. 1973, ch. 319, § 7.

180. Under these common law doctrines, a spouse has to consent to any transfer of real property by the other during their lifetimes—a means of protecting that spouse's potential survivorship interest. For a fuller discussion of the common law doctrines relating to probate and estates, see Babcock, supra note 130, at 614 et seq.

181. Ala. Code tit. 34, § 41 (1959); and Ala. Code tit. 61, § 18 (Supp. 1971); Ark. Stat. Ann. §§ 60-201 to -233 (1971); Hawaii Rev. Stat. §§ 733-1, -16 (1968); R.I. Gen. Laws Ann. §§ 33-4-1, -6-21, -22 (1970); and Tenn. Code Ann. §§ 30-601, -605, -606 (1966).

182. Mich. Stat. Ann. §§ 26.221, 27.3178(139), 27.3178(144) (1974); S.C. Code Ann. §§ 19-111, -155 (1962); and Utah Code Ann. §§ 74-4-3, -4 (1953). Utah has adopted the sex-neutral elective share provisions of the Uniform Probate Code, effective July 1977. Utah Code Ann. §§ 75-2-113, -201 (Supp. 1975), as enacted by L. 1975, ch. 150, § 3.

183. Alaska Stat. §§ 13.11.070 et seq. (1962), as enacted by Acts 1975, ch. 78, § 1; Colo. Rev. Stat. Ann. § 15-11-201 (1974), as enacted by L. 1973, at 1551, § 1, L. 1975, at 589, § 12; Del. Code Ann. tit. 12, § 901 (1975), as enacted by 59 Del. Laws, ch. 384, § 1 (1974); Fla. Stat. Ann. § 732.201 (1976), as enacted by L. 1975, ch. 75-220, §§ 12-13; Ill. Ann. Stat. ch. 3, §§ 2-8, -9 (Smith-Hurd 1961), as enacted by Acts 1975, No. 79-328; Ind. Ann. Stat. § 29-1-3-1(6-301) (Burns (1972); Kan. Stat. Ann. § 59-2233 (1964);

Ky. Rev. Stat. Ann. §§ 392.010, 392.020, 392.080 (1972); Me. Rev. Stat. Ann. 696. 18, § 1056 (1965); Md. Ann. Code art. 93, § 3–203 (1974); Minn. Stat. Ann. § 525.212 (1975); Miss. Code Ann. § 91–5–25 (1973); Mo. Ann. Stat. § 474.160 (1956); Mont. Rev. Codes Ann. § 91A–2–201, –212 (1964), as enacted by L. 1974, ch. 365; Neb. Rev. Stat. § 30.107 (1965); N.H. Rev. Stat. Ann. § 560:10 (1955), as amended by L. 1971, ch. 179, § 22; N.Y. Est. Powers & Trusts Law § 5–1.1 (McKinney 1967); N.C. Gen. Stat. § 30–1 (1966 Repl. Vol.); N.D. Cent. Code tit. 30.1–01–01 et seq. (Supp. 1975), as enacted by L. 1973, ch. 257, as amended by L. 1975, ch. 290; Okla. Stat. Ann. tit. 84, § 44 (1970); Ore. Rev. Stat. § 114.105 (1975); S.D. Comp. Laws Ann. § 29–1–5 (1967); Vt. Stat. Ann. tit. 14, §§ 402, 461–74 (1974); Wis. Stat. Ann. §§ 861.03, 861.05 (1971); and Wyo. Stat. Ann. § 2–47 (1959).

184. D.C. Code Encycl. Ann. §§ 19–102, –113 (1967); and N.J. Stat. Ann. § 3A:35–1, –2, 3A:37–1 (1953). The District of Columbia permits a surviving spouse to elect the intestate share, which he or she would receive if there were no will, instead of the dower share. The intestate law entitles him or her to fee ownership of a portion of the estate. See D.C. Code Encycl. §§ 19–112 to –114 (1967).

185. Conn. Gen. Stat. Ann. § 46–12 (1960); Iowa Code § 633.238 (1964); Mass. Gen. Laws Ann. ch. 189, § 1 (1969), ch. 191, § 15 (1969); Ohio Rev. Code Ann. §§ 2103.02, 2107.39 (1968); Pa. Stat. Ann. tit. 20, §§ 2102, 2105 (1975), as added by Acts 1972, No. 164; Va. Code Ann. §§ 64.1–16, –19, –29, –30 (1973); and W.Va. Code Ann. §§ 42–3–1, –1–8 (1966).

186. Ga. Code Ann. §§ 31–101 et seq. (1969), as repealed by L. 1969, at 123–24, §§ 102–11.

187. Ariz. Rev. Stat. Ann. §§ 14–2102, 3101 (Supp. 1973), as added by L. 1973, ch. 75, § 4; Cal. Prob. Code § 201.5 (West Supp. 1972); Idaho Code § 15–2–102(b)(1) (1948); La. Rev. Stat. Ann. art. 915 (1952); Nev. Rev. Stat. § 123.250 (1967); N.M. Stat. Ann. § 32A–2–102 (Supp. 1975), as enacted by L. 1975, ch. 257, § 2–102; Tex. Prob. Code § 45 (1956); and Wash. Rev. Code Ann. § 11.02.070 (1967). Arizona, Idaho, and New Mexico have adopted the Uniform Probate Code provisions relevant to a community property state, but only Idaho has enacted the "elective share" provisions. Idaho Code §§ 15–2–201, –202 (1948), as enacted by L. 1971, ch. 111.

188. The Uniform Probate Code, 8 Uniform Laws Ann. 287 (1972), for example, which is discussed in more detail in the policy recommendations section, augments the decedent's estate on which the surviving share is based by those lifetime transfers that are "will substitutes" to third parties.

189. See Wren, The Widow's Election in Community Property States, 7 Ariz. L. Rev. 1 (1965). Idaho, which has adopted the Uniform Probate Code, does not follow this rule.

190. Often these special allowances and exemptions are available only to widows. See, for example, Ohio Rev. Code Ann. § 2117.20 (1968), which provides an allowance to a widow and children for a year, set off from the decedent's estate; and Ohio Rev. Code Ann. § 2329.75 (1954), which exempts a widow and children from the sale of the homestead to satisfy the debts of the decedent.

191. See, for example, Vt. Stat. Ann. tit. 14, § 404 (1974).

192. See, for example, Fla. Stat. § 196.191(7) (1971). This provision was upheld by the United States Supreme Court in Kahn v. Shevin, 416 U.S. 351 (1974). Kahn, a widower living in Florida, challenged the annual $500 property tax exemption available only to widows in Florida as a violation of equal protection. The United States Supreme Court affirmed a finding by the Florida Supreme Court that the sex-based classification was valid because it had a fair and substantial relation to the legislative objective, which is to reduce the disparity between the economic capabilities of men and women that results from both overt discrimination and the socialization process.

193. See, for example, Ore. Rev. Stat. § 118.010(2)(a) (1974). The plight of one farm wife from Nebraska who was given no credit of contribution to the ranch she had worked on throughout her marriage is documented in National Commission on the Observance of International Women's Year, " . . . To Form a More Perfect Union . . . ": Justice for American Women 13-14 (1976).

194. Uniform Probate Code, 8 Uniform Laws Ann. 332-39 (1972). The text of the elective share provisions follows:

[Right to Elective Share.]

(a) If a married person domiciled in this state dies, the surviving spouse has a right of election to take an elective share of one-third of the augmented estate under the limitations and conditions hereinafter stated.

(b) If a married person not domiciled in this state dies, the right, if any, of the surviving spouse to take an elective share in property in this state is governed by the law of the decedent's domicile at death.

[Augmented Estate.]

The augmented estate means the estate reduced by funeral and administration expenses, homestead allowance, family allowances and exemptions, and enforceable claims, to which is added the sum of the following amounts:

(1) The value of property transferred by the decedent at any time during marriage, to or for the benefit of any person other than the surviving spouse, to the extent that the decedent did not receive adequate and full consideration in money or money's worth for the transfer, if the transfer is of any of the following types:

(i) any transfer under which the decedent retained at the time of his death the possession or enjoyment of, or right to income from, the property;

(ii) any transfer to the extent that the decedent retained at the time of his death a power, either alone or in conjunction with any other person, to revoke or to consume, invade or dispose of the principal for his own benefit;

(iii) any transfer whereby property is held at the time of decedent's death by decedent and another with right of survivorship;

(iv) any transfer made within two years of death of the decedent to the extent that the aggregate transfers to any one donee in either of the years exceed $3,000.

Any transfer is excluded if made with the written consent or joinder of the surviving spouse. Property is valued as of the decedent's death except that property given irrevocably to a donee during lifetime of the decedent is valued as of the date the donee came into possession or enjoyment if that occurs first. Nothing herein shall cause to be included in the augmented estate any life insurance, accident insurance, joint annuity, or pension payable to a person other than the surviving spouse.

(2) The value of property owned by the surviving spouse at the decedent's death, plus the value of property transferred by the spouse at any time during marriage to any person other than the decedent which would have been includible in the spouse's augmented estate if the surviving spouse had predeceased the decedent, to the extent the owned or transferred property is derived from the decedent by any means other than testate or intestate succession without a full consideration in money or money's worth. For purposes of this subsection:

(i) Property derived from the decedent includes, but is not limited to, any beneficial interest of the surviving spouse in a trust created by the decedent during his lifetime, any property appointed to the spouse by the decedent's exercise of a general or special power of appointment also exercisable in favor of others than the spouse, any proceeds of insurance (including accidental death benefits) on the life of the decedent attributable to premiums paid by him, any lump sum immediately payable and the commuted value of the proceeds of annuity contracts under which the decedent was the primary annuitant attributable to premiums paid by him, the commuted value of amounts payable after the decedent's death under any public or private pension, disability compensation, death benefit or retirement plan, exclusive of the Federal Social Security system, by reason of service performed or disabilities incurred by the decedent, and the value of the share of the surviving spouse resulting from rights in community property in this or any other state formerly owned with the decedent. Premiums paid by the decedent's employer, his partner, a partnership of which he was a member, or his creditors, are deemed to have been paid by the decedent.

(ii) Property owned by the spouse at the decedent's death is valued as of the date of death. Property transferred by the spouse is valued at the time the transfer became irrevocable, or at the decedent's death, whichever occurred first. Income earned by included property prior to the decedent's death is not treated as property derived from the decedent.

(iii) Property owned by the surviving spouse as of the decedent's death, or previously transferred by the surviving spouse, is presumed to have been derived from the decedent except to the extent that the surviving spouse establishes that it was derived from another source.

[Effect of Election on Benefits by Will or Statute.]

(a) The surviving spouse's election of his elective share does not affect the share of the surviving spouse under the provisions of the decedent's will or intestate succession unless the surviving spouse also expressly renounces in the petition for an elective share the benefit of all or any of the provisions. If any provision is so renounced, the property or other benefit which would otherwise have passed to the surviving spouse thereunder is treated, subject to contribution under subsection 2-207(b), as if the surviving spouse had predeceased the testator.

(b) A surviving spouse is entitled to homestead allowance, exempt property and family allowance whether or not he elects to take an elective share and whether or not he renounces the benefits conferred upon him by the will except that, if it clearly appears from the will that a provision therein made for the surviving spouse was intended to be in lieu of these rights, he is not so entitled if he does not renounce the provision so made for him in the will.

195. The official commentary to the Uniform Probate Code § 2-202, providing for the "augmented estate," lists two rationales for this approach: (1) to prevent the owner of wealth from making arrangements that transmit property to others by means other than probate to deliberately defeat the right of the surviving spouse to a share and (2) to prevent the surviving spouse from electing a share of the probate estate when the spouse has received a fair share of the total wealth of the decedent, either during the lifetime of the decedent or at death by life insurance, joint tenancy assets, and other nonprobate arrangements. Id. at 334.

196. This was the subject of an unsuccessful proposal before the Oregon legislature in 1975, H.B. 2608.

197. The states with sex-based laws as of 1976 are Alabama, Arkansas, Hawaii, Michigan, Rhode Island, South Carolina, Tennessee, and Utah. See notes 181 and 182 supra for citations. Utah has adopted the Uniform Probate Code, however, which will become effective in July 1977. The Michigan legislature considered a proposal in 1975 to extend dower rights to men, but it was not enacted. H.B. 4030 (1975).

198. The common law states that have adopted the Uniform Probate Code's elective share provisions since 1972 are Alaska (1972), Colorado (1973), Florida (1975), Montana (1974), Nebraska (1974), North Dakota (1973), South Dakota (1974), and Utah (1975). See notes 182 and 183 supra for citations.

199. Delaware and Illinois. See note 183 supra for citations.

200. Kentucky and Pennsylvania. See notes 183 and 185 supra for citations.

201. See note 187 supra. Arizona, Idaho, and New Mexico have adopted portions of the Uniform Probate Code, but only Idaho has enacted the elective share provisions. Idaho Code §§ 15-1-101 to -7-307 (1948), as added by L. 1971, ch. 111. Section 15-2-206(a) provides that when a survivor chooses the elective share, it does not affect the share due under the will or by intestate succession.

202. N.M. Stat. Ann. § 29-1-9 (1954), as repealed by L. 1975, ch. 257, § 9-1-1; and N.M. Stat. Ann. § 32A-2-102 (Supp. 1975), as enacted by L. 1975, ch. 257, § 2-102.

203. Cal. Prob. Code Ann. § 205 (West 1956), as amended by Stats. 1974, ch. 11, § 2, ch. 752, § 5.

204. Cal. Prob. Code Ann. § 202 (West 1956), as amended by Stats. 1974, ch. 11, § 2, ch. 752, § 5.

205. Wash. Rev. Code § 25.04.250 (1969), as amended by L. 1973 (1st Ex. Sess.), ch. 154, § 25. The new law reads: "A partner's right in specific partnership property is not subject to dower, curtesy or allowances to a surviving spouse, heirs, or next of kin."

206. Ariz. Rev. Stat. Ann. § 29-225 (1956), as amended by L. 1973, ch. 172, § 84.

207. Ky. Rev. Stat. Ann. § 394.030 (1972), as amended by Acts 1974, ch. 386, § 86. This provision creates an exception to the rule that a minor cannot execute a will.

208. N.M. Stat. Ann. § 32-1-2 (1953), as amended by L. 1973, ch. 60, § 2.

209. Hawaii Rev. Stat. § 536-11 (1968), as amended by L. 1973, ch. 102, § 1(a).

210. Ariz. Rev. Stat. Ann. § 14-2508 (Supp. 1973), as added by L. 1973, ch. 75, § 4, repealing § 14-134.

211. Ariz. Rev. Stat. Ann. § 42-271 (1956), as amended by L. 1973, ch. 172. Arizona has also extended to members of both sexes a provision allowing the widow of a holder of a license tap receipt to continue the business of the deceased. Ariz. Rev. Stat. Ann. § 42-1106 (1956), as amended by L. 1973, ch. 172.

212. Pa. Stat. Ann. tit. 72, § 4751-2 (1968), as amended by Acts 1973, No. 136, §§ 4-5.

213. See, for example, Missouri H.B. 1666 (1974), which would have extended special inheritance tax rates for widows to all surviving spouses. An Oregon proposal, H.B. 2608 (1975), would have created a conclusive presumption that not less than one-half of the property passing to the surviving spouse was contributed by that person, for purposes of inheritance taxation.

214. A ground for divorce in at least seven states: Alabama, Georgia, Mississippi, North Carolina, Oklahoma, Tennessee, and Wyoming; and for annulment in West Virginia. See, for example, N.C. Gen. Stat. § 50-5(3) (1966).

215. A ground for divorce in at least 12 states: Alabama, Alaska, Arkansas, Idaho, Maine, Massachusetts, North Dakota, Rhode Island, South Dakota,

Tennessee, Wisconsin, and Wyoming. See, for example, Alaska Stat. §
09.55.110 (1975).

216. See, for example, Wyo. Stat. Ann. § 20–38 (1959).

217. See, for example, Tenn. Code Ann. § 36–802 (1955).

218. See, for example, W. Va. Code Ann. § 48–21–1 (1976 Repl. Vol.)
(annulment).

219. See, for example, W. Va. Code Ann. § 48–21–1 (1976) (annulment).

220. See, for example, Tenn. Code Ann. § 36–802 (1975 Repl. Vol.).

221. See, for example, Va. Code Ann. § 20.89.1 (1950), which provides
for annulment for either a man or a woman who discovers that the other
spouse has parented a child by a third person prior to or within a few months
of the marriage.

222. The divorce laws for all 50 states plus the District of Columbia are
contained in the Reference File Binder of BNA's Family Law Reporter.

223. See Kanowitz, supra note 64, at 91–95; and Brown, Emerson, Falk,
and Freedman, Equal Rights Amendment: A Constitutional Basis for Equal
Rights for Women, 80 Yale L.J. 871, 949 (1971).

224. UMDA § 302.

225. Ibid., §§ 307–08.

226. See note 222 supra and p. 186.

227. See, for example, Ariz. Rev. Stat. Ann. § 25–312 (1956), as
amended by L. 1973, ch. 139, § 1; Cal. Civ. Code §§ 92, 105 (West 1954),
as amended by Stats. 1969, ch. 1608, at 3313, § 3; Colo. Rev. Stat. §
14–10–106 (1973), as repealed and reenacted by L. 1971, at 521, § 1; Del.
Code Ann. tit. 13, § 1522(9) (1975), as amended by 59 Del. Laws, ch. 350
(1974); Hawaii Rev. Stat. § 580–41(8) (Supp. 1975), as amended by L. 1970,
ch. 116, § 1, L. 1972, ch. 11, § 1; Ind. Ann. Stat. § 31–1–12–3 (1973), as
amended by Acts 1973, No. 297, § 1, at 1585; Mich. Stat. Ann. § 25.86
(1974), as amended by Acts 1971, No. 75; Neb. Rev. Stat. §§ 42–301 to –304
(1974), as repealed by L. 1972, L.B. 820; N.H. Rev. Stat. Ann. § 458.7(x)
(1968), as amended by L. 1971, § 445:1; N.M. Stat. Ann. § 22–7–1 (1953),
as amended by L. 1973, ch. 319, § 1; Wash. Rev. Code § 26.08.020(7) (1961),
as repealed by L. 1973 (1st Ex. Sess.), ch. 157, § 30.

228. Va. Code Ann. § 20–91 (1950), as amended by Acts 1973, ch. 644.

229. Clark, supra note 80, at 584. Under the common law, a father
could be deprived of custody only when he was shown to be corrupt or to be
endangering the child.

230. Ala. Code tit. 3, § 35 (1959) requires that in cases of abandonment
of the husband by the wife, he shall have custody of the children after they
are seven years of age; for younger children, the mother is presumably the
best parent regardless of the circumstances. Utah Code Ann. § 30–3–10
(1976) declares that there is a "natural presumption" that the mother is best
suited to care for young children.

231. See, for example, Cox v. Cox, 532 P.2d 994 (Utah Sup. Ct. 1975);
Klavans v. Klavans, 330 So. 2d 811 (Fla. Ct. App. 1976); Davidyan v. Davidyan, 229 Pa. Super. 495, 327 A.2d 139 (1974); Masek v. Masek, _____ S.D.
_____, 228 N.W.2d 334 (Sup. Ct. 1975); and White v. White, 215 Va. 765,
213 S.E.2d 766 (Sup. Ct. 1975).

232. See, for example, Anagnostopoulos v. Anagnostopoulos, 22 Ill. App. 3d 479, 317 N.E.2d 681 (1974), in which it is reported that the trial judge, in awarding custody of the ten-year-old daughter to the father, cited the facts that the mother rode a motorcycle, had continued her educational pursuits after the child was born, and intended to pursue a career in psychology; that she refused to spend a majority of her time maintaining the home; that she cursed; and that she had used marijuana on three occasions, among other reasons affecting his determination.

233. See, for example, Bunim v. Bunim, 298 N.Y. 391, 83 N.E.2d 848 (1949), in which the dissenting judge disputes the award of custody to the father, who has devoted little time to the children, as against an adulterous mother who has been a good and devoted parent, who has the deep affection of her children, and whose adultery was unknown to the children.

234. See, for example, Ga. Code Ann. § 30-127 (1969).

235. Several courts recently have modified their reliance on the "tender years" doctrine, while declining to overrule it altogether, by holding that it is but one factor to consider. See, for example, Jones v. Ard, 265 S.C. 423, 219 S.E.2d 358 (Sup. Ct. 1975); Lewis v. Lewis, 217 Kan. 366, 537 P.2d 204 (Sup. Ct. 1975); Goodman v. Goodman, 291 So. 2d 106 (Fla. Ct. App. 1974); Marcus v. Marcus, 24 Ill. App. 3d 401, 320 N.E.2d 581 (1974); and Cooke v. Cooke, 21 Md. App. 376, 319 A.2d 841 (1974). See also Burnside v. Burnside, _____ Va._____ , 222 S.E.2d 529 (1976), in which the Virginia Supreme Court upheld the tender years doctrine but found that it is not an "inflexible" rule. Other courts have held that the tender years doctrine is no longer valid under any circumstances because of its sex-based nature. See, for example, Drake v. Hohimer, 35 Ill. App. 3d 529, 341 N.E.2d 399 (1976); Scolman v. Scolman, 66 Wis. 2d 761, 226 N.W.2d 388 (Sup. Ct. 1975); Tye v. Tye, 532 S.W.2d 124 (Tex. Ct. Civ. App. 1975); Strom v. Strom, 226 N.W.2d 797 (Iowa Sup. Ct. 1975). See also Feldman v. Feldman, 45 App. Div. 2d 320, 358 N.Y.S.2d 507 (1974), in which the court recognized the right of a divorced woman to engage in private sexual activities without jeopardizing an award of child custody; Myers v. Myers, _____ Pa._____ , 360 A.2d 587 (Sup. Ct. 1976), in which the court reversed a transfer of custody from a mother to a father, holding that the mother's nonmarital relationship was just one fact to consider in assessing the child's best interests.

236. Courts in Illinois have not agreed on whether any maternal preference in child custody determinations is permissible under the state ERA. The cases show the difficulty the courts are having reconciling the equality principle with traditional child custody doctrines and the key role the facts of the particular case seem to play in determining the doctrinal result. See, for example, Randolph v. Dean, 27 Ill. App. 3d 913, 327 N.E.2d 473 (1975); Marcus v. Marcus, 24 Ill. App. 3d 401, 320 N.E.2d 581 (1974); Anagnostopoulos v. Anagnostopoulos, 22 Ill. App. 3d 479, 317 N.E.2d 681 (1974); and Garland v. Garland, 19 Ill. App. 3d 951, 312 N.E.2d 811 (1974). See also Cooke v. Cooke, 21 Md. App. 376, 319 A.2d 841 (Ct. Spec. App. 1974), where the court mentioned the ERA in holding the maternal preference permissible as a factor to be considered when all else was equal.

237. Colo. Rev. Stat. Ann. § 14-10-124 (1963), as added by L. 1971, at 529, § 1; Del. Code Ann. tit. 13, § 722 (Cum. Supp. 1975), as added by 59 Del. Laws, ch. 569, § 4 (1974).

238. Ind. Ann. Stat. § 31-1-11.5-21 (Burns 1973), as added by Acts 1973, ch. 297, § 1, at 1585 (Indiana also considers the age and sex of the child, however); Mo. Rev. Stat. § 452.375 (1952), as added by L. 1973, at 476; Mont. Rev. Codes Ann. § 21-138 (1967), as added by L. 1975, ch. 536, § 45; Ohio Rev. Code Ann. § 3109.04 (Page 1972 Repl. Vol.), as added by L. 1974, H.B. 233, 740, L. 1975, H.B. 1, H.B. 370; and Wash. Rev. Code Ann. § 26.09.190 (1961), as added by L. 1973 (Ex. Sess.), ch. 157, § 5.

239. Ariz. Rev. Stat. Ann. § 25.332 (1956), as added by L. 1973, ch. 139.

240. Fla. Stat. Ann. § 61.13 (1967), as amended by L. 1975, ch. 75-99, § 1; Minn. Stat. Ann. § 518.17 (1969), as amended by L. 1974, ch. 330, § 2 (this amendment added comprehensive factors, as well as deleting the traditional consideration of the child's age and sex); Neb. Rev. Stat. § 52-364 (1974 Reissue), as amended by L. 1974, L.B. 1015, § 4, at 1040.

241. Alaska Stat. § 09.55.205 (1973), as added by L. 1968, ch. 160, § 1; Del. Code Ann. tit. 13, § 722 (Cum. Supp. 1975), as added by 59 Del. Laws, ch. 569, § 4 (1974); Fla. Stat. Ann. § 61.13 (1967), as amended by L. 1971, ch. 71-241, § 15; Ind. Ann. Stat. § 31-1-11.5-21 (Burns 1973), as added by Acts 1973, ch. 297, § 1, at 1585; Minn. Stat. Ann. § 518.17 (1969), as amended by L. 1969, ch. 1030, § 1; Neb. Rev. Stat. § 42.364 (1974 Reissue), as amended by L. 1974, L.B. 1015, § 4, at 1040; N.H. Rev. Stat. Ann. § 458:17 (1968), as added by L. 1975, ch. 426, § 2; Tex. Fam. Code § 14.01(b) (Vernon 1973), as added by Acts 1973, ch. 543. See also N.Y. Dom. Rel. Law § 240 (1964) and Wis. Stat. Ann. § 247.24 (1957), which have affirmative provisions requiring equal consideration of parents of both sexes but are of apparently earlier vintage than those states listed above.

242. The most exhaustive study of the law and policy surrounding children born out of wedlock is H. Krause, Illegitimacy: Law and Policy (1971).

243. Gomez v. Perez, 409 U.S. 532 (1973) (child support); Weber v. Aetna Casualty Company, 406 U.S. 164 (1972) (worker's compensation); New Jersey Welfare Rights Organization v. Cahill, 411 U.S. 619 (1973) (AFDC benefits); Jimenez v. Weinberger, 417 U.S. 628 (1974) (disability); Beaty v. Weinberger, 478 F.2d 300 (5th Cir. 1973), aff'd 418 U.S. 901 (1974) (disability); Davis v. Richardson, 342 F. Supp. 588 (D. Conn. 1972), aff'd 409 U.S. 1069 (1972) (survivor's benefits); and Griffin v. Richardson, 346 F. Supp. 1226 (D. Md. 1972), aff'd 409 U.S. 1069 (1972) (survivor's benefits). In many of these cases, the mother of the child seeking benefits through the father initiated the action because of her need for extra income to raise the child. Thus, mothers of children born out of wedlock are often the indirect victims of discrimination against the fathers involved.

244. Following Stanley (405 U.S. 645 [1972]), the Court decided a Wisconsin case in which an unwed father contested an adoption decree entered without his consent. The Supreme Court vacated the lower court decision and remanded the case for proceedings in light of the Stanley decision. Rothstein

v. Lutheran Social Service, 405 U.S. 1051 (1972), vacating and remanding
State ex rel. Lewis v. Lutheran Social Service, 47 Wis. 2d 420, 178 N.W.2d
56 (1970). On remand, the Supreme Court of Wisconsin decided that the child
should remain with its adoptive parents.

245. See Andrews v. Drew School Dist., 507 F.2d 611 (5th Cir. 1975),
cert. granted, 423 U.S. 820 (1975), cert. dismissed as improvidently granted,
424 U.S. 903 (1976) (employment of teaching assistant who is mother of illegitimate child), and text accompanying note 91 of chapter 8.

246. An appropriate amendment is the addition after the clause concerning inheritance of the following language: "except as provided under [§ 2-109
of the Uniform Probate Code or other appropriate provision]." The text of
§ 2-109 is as follows:

Section 2-109. [Meaning of Child and Related Terms.]

If, for purposes of intestate succession, a relationship of parent and child must be established to determine succession by,
through, or from a person,

(1) an adopted person is the child of an adopting parent and not
of the natural parents except that adoption of a child by the spouse
of a natural parent has no effect on the relationship between the
child and that natural parent.

(2) In cases not covered by (1), a person born out of wedlock
is a child of the mother. That person is also a child of the father,
if:

(i) the natural parents participated in a marriage ceremony
before or after the birth of the child, even though the attempted
marriage is void; or

(ii) the paternity is established by an adjudication before the
death of the father or is established thereafter by clear and
convincing proof, except that the paternity established under
this subparagraph (ii) is ineffective to qualify the father or his
kindred to inherit from or through the child unless the father
has openly treated the child as his, and has not refused to support the child.

It should be noted, however, that the Uniform Probate Code disinherits
fathers of children born out of wedlock who have failed to acknowledge their
children. Under the ERA, such a proviso must be applied to unwed parents
of both sexes or omitted.

247. National Conference of Commissioners on Uniform State Laws, Revised Uniform Adoption Act § 19(c) (1969).

248. In section 2-109 of the Uniform Probate Code (1972), the commissioners recommend two alternate forms, one for those jurisdictions with the
UPA and one for states where the UPA is not in effect:

Section 2-109. [Meaning of Child and Related Terms.]

If, for purposes of intestate succession, a relationship of parent and child must be established to determine succession by, through, or from a person,

(1) an adopted person is the child of an adopting parent and not of the natural parents except that adoption of a child by the spouse of a natural parent has no effect on the relationship between the child and either natural parent.

(2) In cases not covered by Paragraph (1), a person is the child of its parents regardless of the marital status of its parents and the parent and child relationship may be established under the [Uniform Parentage Act].

Alternative subsection (2) for states that have not adopted the Uniform Parentage Act.

[(2) In cases not covered by Paragraph (1), a person born out of wedlock is a child of the mother. That person is also a child of the father, if:

(i) the natural parents participated in a marriage ceremony before or after the birth of the child, even though the attempted marriage is void; or

(ii) the paternity is established by an adjudication before the death of the father or is established thereafter by clear and convincing proof, but the paternity established under this subparagraph is ineffective to qualify the father or his kindred to inherit from or through the child unless the father has openly treated the child as his, and has not refused to support the child.]

Ten states, including two UPA states, have adopted some version of the latter alternative, setting out specific standards for inheritance between a child and a father outside of marriage. These are Alaska Stat. § 13.11.045 (1972), as added by L. 1972, ch. 78; Ariz. Rev. Stat. Ann. § 14-2109 (1975), as added by L. 1973, ch. 75; Colo. Rev. Stat. Ann. § 15-11-109 (1973), as added by L. 1973, ch. 451; Fla. Stat. Ann. § 732.108 (1976), as added by L. 1974, ch. 74-106; Idaho Code § 15-2-109 (1948), as added by L. 1971, ch. 111; Mont. Rev. Codes Ann. § 91A-2-109 (1947), as added by L. 1974, ch. 365; Neb. Rev. Stat. § 30-2309 (1943), as added by L. 1974, L.B. 354; N.M. Stat. Ann. § 32A-2-109 (1976), as added by L. 1975, ch. 257; N.D. Cent. Code § 30.1-04-09 (1975), as added by L. 1973, ch. 257; and Utah Code Ann. § 75-2-109 (1953), as added by L. 1975, ch. 150.

249. A number of states not discussed here have recently modified one or more of their laws concerning illegitimacy. See, for example, S.D. Comp. Laws Ann. § 25-6-1.1 (1969), as added by L. 1974, ch. 176. However, these changes are more limited than those treated in this section and, in most instances, tend toward minimal compliance with existing constitutional standards rather than actual equalization of treatment of all unwed parents and their chil-

dren. An example is Iowa's adoption law, which has been upheld by that state's supreme court against constitutional challenge in Catholic Charities of Dubuque, Iowa v. Zalesky, 232 N.W.2d 539 (1975). This law, which is one of the most extreme in its denial of rights to a noncustodial parent, provides that, in adoption cases involving unwed parents, "the parent having the care and providing for the wants of the child may give consent." Iowa Code Ann. § 238.28 (1971). In other words, an unmarried parent must both seek and obtain custody of the child prior to the initiation of adoption proceedings in order to have any right to contest the adoption. This provision applies to divorced parents, as well as to never-married parents, and does not even provide for notice to the noncustodial parent.

250. Cal. Civ. Code §§ 7000-18 (1970), as added by L. 1975, ch. 1244; Hawaii Rev. Laws §§ 584-1 to -26 (1967), as added by L. 1975, ch. 66; Mont. Rev. Codes Ann. §§ 61-301 to -327 (1947), as added by L. 1975, ch. 512; N.D. Cent. Code §§ 14-17-01 to -26 (1971 Repl. Vol.), as added by L. 1975, ch. 130; and Wash. Rev. Code Ann. §§ 26.2-26.21, 26.42-26.45, 4.28.185, 11.02.005, 11.04.081, 26.04.060, 26.32.030-26.32.085, 26.32.300-26.32.310, 26.37.010-26.37.015, 43,20.090, 51.08.030, 70.58.090-70.58.210 (1969), as amended by L. 1976, ch. 42.

251. The details of the state-by-state variations from the text of the UPA adopted by the commissioners are set forth in Uniform Parentage Act, 9 Uniform Laws Annotated 358-81 (West Supp. 1976).

252. Colo. Rev. Stat. § 19-1-103(21) (1974): "parent" is defined to include the natural parent of an illegitimate child who has affixed his name to the child's birth certificate, paid the medical costs of birth, supported the child, or "otherwise asserted his paternity in writing."

Mich. Comp. Laws Ann. § 710.33 (1968): notice must be filed prior to the birth of the child, which creates a rebuttable presumption of paternity and generates a right to notice of parentage-related proceedings. Mich. Comp. Laws Ann. §§ 710.34, 710.36 (1968): prebirth notice must be given to putative fathers, and fathers who have not received such notice at least 30 days prior to confinement must receive notice of any later adoption or parentage proceedings. These provisions were all added by Acts 1974, No. 296, § 1.

Minn. Stat. Ann. § 259.261 (1971), as added by L. 1974, ch. 66, § 10: formal affidavit is conclusive evidence of parenthood unless denied by other parent or interested party by the filing of a court action within 60 days.

Wis. Stat. Ann. §§ 48.025, 48.195 (1957), as added by L. 1973, ch. 263, §§ 2-3: declaration may be filed at any time entitling father to notice of parentage proceedings; declaration does not automatically extend parental rights, however, and can be challenged by mother in subsequent action.

253. Mich. Comp. Laws Ann. § 722.714(f) (1968); Ore. Rev. Stat. § 109.125 (1975 Repl. Vol.) (father can initiate proceedings before or after birth) and § 109.103 (1975 Repl. Vol.))either parent can initiate support or custody proceedings after paternity is established); and Wis. Stat. Ann. § 48.425(b) (1957), as added by L. 1973, ch. 263, s 8 (putative father may bring custody action).

254. Mich. Comp. Laws Ann. § 710.34 (notice before child's birth), § 710.36 (notice after birth) (1968), as added by Acts 1974, No. 296, § 1.

255. The notice provisions in the states other than Michigan are: Colo. Rev. Stat. §§ 19-4-107(1)(e)(II), 19-4-102 (1974); Minn. Stat. Ann. § 259.26 (1971), as amended by L. 1974, ch. 66, §§ 6-7; Ore. Rev. Stat. § 109.330 (1975 Repl. Vol.); and Wis. Stat. Ann. § 48.42 (1957), as added by L. 1973, ch. 263, §§ 5-6.

256. Colo. Rev. Stat. § 19-4-107(1)(e)(II) (1974): If either parent voluntarily relinquishes parental rights, the petition is supposed to contain both parents' names, if known.

Mich. Comp. Laws Ann. §§ 710.34, 710.36, 710.37 (1968), as added by Acts 1974, No. 296, § 1: court may receive evidence on the father's identity; woman who is pregnant out of wedlock may file a petition in probate court stating putative father's identity; a reasonable effort to locate the father may be made prior to the termination of parental rights.

Minn. Stat. Ann. § 259.26(2) (1975), as amended by L. 1974, ch. 66, § 7: a burden is placed on prospective adoptive parents to file an affidavit concerning their efforts to locate natural parents, including the names and addresses of known kin.

Wis. Stat. Ann. § 48.425 (1957), as added by L. 1973, ch. 263, § 7.

257. Colo. Rev. Stat. § 19-4-107(1)(e)(II) (1974); Minn. Stat. Ann. § 259.26(2) (1971), as added by L. 1974, ch. 66, § 7; Ore. Rev. Stat. § 109.330 (1975 Repl. Vol.); and Wis. Stat. Ann. § 48.42 (1957), as added by L. 1973, ch. 263, §§ 5-6.

258. Colo. Rev. Stat. §§ 10-1-103(21), 19-4-107 (1974): father has no rights unless, prior to adoption, he has paid support or medical expenses, affixed his name to the birth certificate, or otherwise asserted paternity in writing.

Me. Rev. Stat. Ann. tit. 19, § 532-C (1965), as amended by L. 1973, ch. 791, § 2: only mother need consent unless putative father is in birth record and whereabouts are known; is providing support or has attempted to do so; or is involved or has attempted to become involved in a family relationship with the child.

Mich. Comp. Laws Ann. § 710.37 (1968), as added by Acts 1974, No. 296, § 1: rights are terminated if, after reasonable efforts to locate him, putative father's identity or whereabouts remain unknown and he has made no provision for either mother or child; if his identity is known but not his whereabouts and he has provided no support for the mother, has shown no interest in the child, and has made no provision for the child's care within 90 days preceding the hearing.

Minn. Stat. Ann. § 259.261 (1971): putative parent not falling within certain categories of ongoing relationship with child must file an affidavit within 90 days of birth or 60 days of placement with prospective adoptive parents, whichever is sooner.

Ore. Rev. Stat. §§ 109.314-109.329 (1975 Repl. Vol.): no consent of putative parent is required unless he has married the mother or initiated filiation proceedings prior to adoption.

Wis. Stat. Ann. § 48.425 (1957), as added by L. 1973, ch. 263, § 7: termination of rights may occur if, after inquiry, court cannot identify natural father and at least 30 days have passed since birth.

259. Minn. Stat. Ann. §§ 256.24, 256.26, 256.261, 260.221 (1971), as added by L. 1974, ch. 66, §§ 1-4, 6-8; and Wis. Stat. Ann. §§ 48.425(2), 48.43 (1957), as amended by L. 1973, ch. 263, §§ 7-8. Technically, these states do not apply customary standards of parental neglect to all unwed fathers, since both allow the termination of the parental rights of putative fathers who do not appear and claim rights within a certain time period, who are not entitled to personal notice, or who have been determined by a court not to be the natural father. However, both states define the category of putative fathers entitled to notice quite broadly, and both enable such fathers to file declarations of parental rights. Therefore, these two states have been distinguished from others that limit the category of putative fathers entitled to assert their rights.

260. Ore. Rev. Stat. § 109.098 (1975 Repl. Vol.); and Me. Rev. Stat. Ann. tit. 19, § 532-C (1965), as amended by L. 1973, ch. 791, § 2 (father required to be "willing" and able to undertake parental responsibilities rather than "fit" and able).

261. Colo. Rev. Stat. § 19-1-103(21) (1974): customary standards, except that (1) termination of parental rights is more easily effected in stepparent adoptions and (2) a putative father who has not married the mother, asserted paternity in writing, paid support or medical costs, or affixed his name to the birth certificate is given no parental rights.

262. Mich. Comp. Laws Ann. §§ 710.31(3), 710.37, 710.39 (1968).

263. Mich. Comp. Laws Ann. § 710.39 (1968).

264. Mich. Comp. Laws Ann. § 710.31(3) (1968).

265. Colo. Rev. Stat. § 19-6-101 (1974); Mich. Comp. Laws Ann. § 722.714(b) (1968); and Wis. Stat. Ann. § 813.195 (1966).

266. Me. Rev. Stat. Ann. tit. 19, § 273 (1965); and Minn. Stat. Ann. § 257.255 (1975).

267. Me. Rev. Stat. Ann. tit. 18, § 1003 (1964).

268. Me. Rev. Stat. Ann. tit. 18, § 1003 (1964) (before notary public); Minn. Stat. Ann. § 525.172 (1975); Ore. Rev. Stat. § 112.105 (1973) (no witnesses needed); and Wis. Stat. Ann. § 852.05(1)(b) (1971), as amended by L. 1969, ch. 339, § 26 (witnesses needed).

269. Acknowledgment in court: Me. Rev. Stat. Ann. tit. 18, § 1003 (1964) (before justice of the peace); Mich. Comp. Laws Ann. § 702.83 (1968), as amended by Acts 1972, No. 235, § 1 (written acknowledgment recorded in office of county probate judge); and Wis. Stat. Ann. § 852.05(1)(b) (1971) (admitted in open court). Adjudication: Minn. Stat. Ann. § 525.172 (1975); Ore. Rev. Stat. § 112.105 (1973); and Wis. Stat. Ann. § 852.05(1)(b) (1971).

CHAPTER 6

1. An excellent discussion of the history of the controversy over sex-based state labor laws appears in B. Babcock, A. Freedman, E. Norton, and S. Ross, Sex Discrimination and the Law: Causes and Remedies 247-87 (1975) [hereafter cited as Babcock].

2. The Civil Rights Act of 1964 §§ 701–16, 42 U.S.C. §§ 2000e et seq. (1974).

3. Hearings on Section 805 of H.R. 16098 Before the Special Subcommittee on Education of the House Committee on Education and Labor, 91st Cong. 2d Sess., pt. 1, at 595 (1970) (testimony of Susan Ross). See Richards v. Griffith Rubber Mills, 300 F. Supp. 338 (D. Ore. 1969).

4. 29 C.F.R. § 1604.2(b) (1975).

5. Mining laws were repealed in: Ala. Code tit. 26, § 158, as amended by Acts 1971, at 3983; Ariz. Rev. Stat. Ann. § 23-261 (1971), as repealed by L. 1973, ch. 133, § 35, L. 1973, ch. 172, § 58; Colo. Rev. Stat. Ann. § 34-29-102 (1974), as repealed by L. 1971, at 1043, § 1; Ind. Ann. Stat. § 22-10-11-14 (1974), as amended by Acts 1955, ch. 168, § 97, at 342, Acts 1975, ch. 235, § 6 (now applies only to "young persons"); Ky. Rev. Stat. § 351.060, as amended by Acts 1964, ch. 386, § 64 (deleted requirement that mine commissioner be male); Mo. Ann. Stat. § 293.060 (1965), as repealed by L. 1975, H.B. No. 40, § 1; Md. Ann. Code art. 66C, §§ 489, 532 (1964), as repealed by Acts 1973 (1st Sp. Sess.), ch. 4, § 2; N.Y. Labor Laws §§ 174–76 (McKinney 1965), as repealed by L. 1973, ch. 377, § 11; N.Y. Labor Laws § 405 (McKinney 1965), as repealed by L. 1973, ch. 377, § 14; Okla. Stat. Ann. tit. 40, § 85 (1954), as amended by L. 1976, ch. 3, § 1; Wash. Rev. Code Ann. § 49.22.160 (mine inspector must be male), as amended by L. 1973 (1st Ex. Sess.), ch. 154, § 80 (now reads person); and Wyo. Stats. § 27-237 (1967), as repealed by L. 1959, ch. 100, § 1.

Laws banning women from serving alcoholic beverages were eliminated in the following states: Alaska Stat. § 04.01.040 (1962), as amended by Acts 1974; Ariz. Rev. Stat. Ann. § 4-244 (1956), as amended by L. 1973, ch. 172, § 8; Cal. Bus. and Prof. Code § 25656 (1964), as repealed by Stats. 1971, ch. 152, § 1 (a related statute prohibiting hostesses from soliciting drinks was amended to prohibit all persons from doing so. Cal. Bus. and Prof. Code § 25657 [1964], as amended by Stats. 1971, ch. 151, § 1); Conn. Gen. Stat. Ann. § 30-24b (1969), granting alcohol privileges to ladies in auxiliaries of certain clubs, was sex neutralized by Acts 1975, No. 75-193; and Ky. Rev. Stat. §§ 244.100, 244.320 (1971), as repealed by Acts 1974, ch. 80, § 1.

Miscellaneous prohibitions that were repealed are: Mich. Comp. Laws Ann. § 408.81 (1967) (women cannot work in factories with wheels and belts), as repealed and reenacted by Acts 1967, No. 195, § 1. New §§ 408.1011, 408.1028, 408.1029, 408.1031, and 408.1033 are safety provisions that apply to all employees; N.Y. Labor Law § 174 (canneries), § 175 (elevator operators), § 176 (messengers) (McKinney 1965), all repealed by L. 1973, ch. 377, § 11; Wash. Rev. Code Ann. § 49.12.190 (1962), as repealed by L. 1973, (2d Ex. Sess.), ch. 16, § 19 (certain jobs in telephone industry); and Wash. Rev. Code Ann. § 49.12.200 (1962), as amended by L. 1963, ch. 229, § 1 (prohibition on women serving in public office).

6. The Court of Appeals opinion is at 444 F.2d 1219 (9th Cir. 1971).

7. The cases invalidating the laws are: Manning v. General Motors Corp., 466 F.2d 812 (6th Cir. 1972), cert. denied, 410 U.S. 946 (1973); Jones Metal Products v. Walker, 29 Ohio St. 2d 173, 181 N.E.2d 1 (1972);

Ridinger v. General Motors Corp., 474 F.2d 949 (6th Cir. 1972); Rinehart
v. Westinghouse Electric Corp., 3 FEP Cases 851 (N.D. Ohio 1971); Local
246, Utility Workers Union v. Southern Cal. Edison Co., 320 F. Supp. 1242
(C.D. Cal. 1970); and Richards v. Griffith Rubber Mills, 300 F. Supp. 338
(D. Ore. 1969). The Labor Department reports that all but three of a dozen
laws on the books in 1964 have been repealed. U.S. Department of Labor,
Employment Standards Administration, Women's Bureau, State Labor Laws
in Transition: From Protection to Equal Status for Women 13 (Pamphlet No.
15, 1976) [hereafter cited as State Labor Laws]. This section relies frequently on information from this publication.

    8. See Manning v. General Motors Corp., 466 F.2d 812 (6th Cir.
1972), cert. denied, 410 U.S. 946 (1973); Jones Metal Products v. Walker,
29 Ohio St. 2d 173, 181 N.E.2d 1 (1972); Evans v. Sheraton Park Hotel, 5
FEP Cases 393 (D.D.C. 1972); Ridinger v. General Motors Corp., 325 F.
Supp. 1089 (S.D. Ohio 1971), 474 F.2d 949 (6th Cir. 1972); Kober v. Westinghouse Electric Corp., 325 F. Supp. 467 (W.D. Pa. 1971); Garneau v.
Raytheon Co., 323 F. Supp. 391 (D. Mass. 1971); General Electric Co. v.
Young, 3 FEP Cases 561 (W.D. Ky. 1971); Vogel v. Trans World Airlines,
346 F. Supp. 805 (W.D. Mo. 1971); Schaeffer v. San Diego Yellow Cabs, Inc.
(not reported) (S.D. Cal. 1970 or 1971); LeBlanc v. Southern Bell Tel. & Tel.
Co., 333 F. Supp. 602 (E.D. La. 1970); Local 246, Utility Workers Union
v. Southern Cal. Edison Co., 320 F. Supp. 1242 (C.D. Cal. 1970); and Cater-
pillar Tractor Co., v. Grabiec, 317 F. Supp. 1304 (S.D. Ill. 1970).

    9. Babcock, supra note 1, at 271n. 70. See also State Labor Laws,
supra note 7, at 13.

    10. See State Labor Laws, supra note 7, at 13.

    11. Conn. Gen. Stat. Ann. § 31-26 (1972), as repealed by Acts 1972,
No. 53, § 1; Mass. Gen. Laws Ann. ch. 149, § 155 (1971), as repealed by
Stats. 1974, ch. 345; Mo. Ann. Stat. § 290.060 (1965); as repealed by L.
1973, at 95, § 1; Vt. Stat. Ann. tit. 21, § 444 (1975), as repealed by L. 1969
(Adj. Sess.), No. 218, § 4. Massachusetts and Montana have passed laws
giving women employees a right to maternity leave. Mass. Gen. Laws Ann.
ch. 149, § 1050, as added by Stats. 1972, ch. 790, § 1; Mont. Rev. Codes
Ann. §§ 41-2601, -2606, as added by L. 1975, ch. 320, §§ 1-6. To the extent that this leave is for child rearing as opposed to childbearing purposes,
it should be equally available to parents of either sex. The provision for
leave during temporary disability due to childbirth should be as favorable as
other temporary disability rules.

    12. 29 C.F.R. § 1604.22(b) (1975).

    13. Ariz. Rev. Stat. Ann. §§ 23-311, -329 (1971), as amended by L.
1973, ch. 133, § 36 and L. 1973, ch. 172, § 111.

    14. Ariz. Rev. Stat. Ann. § 23-261 (1971), as repealed by L. 1973,
ch. 133, § 35; Conn. Gen. Stat. Ann. § 31-27 (1972), as repealed by Acts
1972, No. 74-185, § 5; Fla. Stat. § 450-091 (1966), as repealed by L. 1975,
ch. 75-195, § 4; Kan. Stat. § 44-111 (1964), as repealed by L. 1975, ch.
256, § 7; Mass. Gen. Laws ch. 149, § 99 (1971), as repealed by Stats. 1974,
ch. 372, § 1; Mich. Comp. Laws Ann. § 408.74 (1967), as repealed by Acts

1967, No. 282, § 18; Minn. Stat. Ann. § 182.44 (1966), as repealed by L.
1973, ch. 732, § 27; Neb. Rev. Stat. § 48-201 (1968), as repealed by L. 1969,
L.B. 398, § 1; R.I. Gen. Laws Ann. § 28-3-13 (1969), as repealed by L.
1975, ch. 205, § 1; S.D. Comp. Laws Ann. § 60-12-7 to -9 (1967), as amended
by L. 1973, ch. 303, §§ 3-5 (now refers to children); Tenn. Code Ann. § 50-
607 (1966), as repealed by L. 1972 (Adj. Sess.), ch. 561, § 24; Vt. Stat. Ann.
tit. 21, § 445 (1967), as repealed by L. 1969 (Adj. Sess.), No. 218, § 4; and
Va. Code Ann. § 40.1-34 (1970), as repealed by Acts 1974, ch. 272. Wash.
Rev. Code Ann. §§ 49.12.215, 49.12.220 (1961) were repealed by L. 1973
(2d Ex. Sess.), ch. 16, § 19, but the Industrial Welfare Committee, now empowered to issue regulations, has promulgated sex-neutral meal and rest requirements. See note 29 infra.

15. The case that extended the Arkansas law was Hays v. Potlatch Forests, 465 F.2d 1081 (8th Cir. 1972). But see State v. Fairfield Communities
Land Co., 13 FEP Cases 291 (1976), invalidating that same law. A court refused to extend the California minimum wage law to men in California Dep't
of Industrial Relations v. Homemakers, Inc., 509 F.2d 20 (9th Cir. 1974),
cert. denied, 96 S. Ct. 804 (1976). As a general matter, the courts are re-
luctant to extend laws in the absence of clear legislative history. As is discussed below, the existence of clear legislative history concerning the impact of the ERA on sex-based labor laws is one reason why the ERA will be a
very positive force in this area.

16. See also Mo. Ann. Stat. § 292.040 (1965), which prohibits women
from being asked to clean any mill gearing or machinery while it is in motion.

17. Utah Code Ann. § 34-22-1 (1974).

18. Mich. Comp. Laws Ann. § 750.556 (1968).

19. State Labor Laws, supra note 7, at 12.

20. The penalty provisions in the Kansas law were repealed by L. 1975,
ch. 256, § 7. The N.H. law may be relaxed by agreement pursuant to N.H.
Rev. Stat. Ann. § 275.17-a (1966).

21. See State Labor Laws, supra note 7, at 20.

22. Senate Committee on the Judiciary, Equal Rights for Men and Women, S. Rep. No. 92-689, 92d Cong., 2d Sess. 15 (1972) [hereafter cited as
S. Rep. No. 92-689].

23. Maryland State Bd. of Barber Examiners v. Kuhn, 270 Md. 496,
312 A.2d 216 (1973); and Panico v. Robinson, 23 Ill. App. 3d 848, 320
N.E.2d 101 (1974).

24. See note 5 supra.

25. Pa. Op. Att'y Gen. No. 41 (1973).

26. Ariz. Rev. Stat. § 23-235 (1971), as repealed and reenacted by L.
1972, ch. 40, § 5; Ga. Code Ann. § 54-303 (1974), as amended by L. 1974,
at 534; Ky. Rev. Stat. Ann. § 339.240 (1972), as repealed by Acts 1970, ch.
143, § 7; Md. Ann. Code art. 100, § 9 (1964), as amended by Acts 1969, ch.
501; art. 100, § 10, as amended by Acts 1968, ch. 105; art. 100, § 11, as
amended by Acts 1969, ch. 501, § 1; art. 100, §§ 26-34, as repealed by
Acts 1965, ch. 388; art. 91, § 6 (1969), as amended by Acts 1974, ch. 621;
Mass. Gen. Laws ch. 149, § 69 (1971), as amended by Stats. 1972, ch. 47;
ch. 149, §§ 71-73, as amended by Stats. 1972, ch. 47; Minn. Stat. Ann.

§ 181.41 (1966), as repealed by L. 1974, ch. 432, § 13; § 181.43 (1966), as repealed and reenacted by § 181A.04; Nev. Rev. Stat. § 609.220 (1971), as amended by Acts 1973, at 263; N.Y. Labor Law § 130 (McKinney 1965), as amended by L. 1972, ch. 351, § 1; § 133, as amended by L. 1973, ch. 377, § 5; Vt. Stat. Ann. tit. 21, § 439 (1967), as repealed by L. 1969 (Adj. Sess.), No. 218, § 4; Va. Code Ann. §§ 40.1-99, -100 (1970), as amended by Acts 1973, ch. 13; Wis. Stat. Ann. § 103.23 (1974), as amended by L. 1973, ch. 183, §§ 1, 2, 4; and Wash. Rev. Code Ann. § 26.28.060 (1961), as amended by L. 1973, ch. 154, § 39. An attorney general's opinion in Pennsylvania extended to girls an exception to the child labor law permitting boys 12 to 16 to be newspaper carriers. Pa. Op. Att'y Gen. No. 71 (1971).

27. Alaska Stat. § 08.28.320(10) (1973), as amended by Acts 1974, ch. 127, §§ 60-61; Ariz. Rev. Stat. Ann. § 32-50 (1956), as amended by L. 1973, ch. 172, § 89; Iowa Code Ann. §§ 157.1, 158.2 (1972), as repealed by Acts 1974, ch. 1093, § 95; Wash. Rev. Code Ann. § 18.18.010 (1961), as amended by L. 1965 (1st Ex. Sess.), ch. 3, § 1, L. 1973, ch. 148, § 16, L. 1973, ch. 154, § 21; and Wyo. Stat. Ann. § 33-167 (1959), as amended by L. 1969, ch. 176, §§ 1-2. Del. Code Ann. tit. 24, § 401 (1975) was amended by 59 Del. Laws, ch. 390 to remove the limitation on barbers cutting women's hair.

28. For a list of these states, see U.S. Department of Labor, Employment Standards Administration, Women's Bureau, Bull. No. 294, 1969 Handbook on Women Workers 271-73 (1969).

29. "State Adopts New Minimum Job Standards for Employees," Seattle Times, May 12, 1976, at F1. These rules were promulgated by the Industrial Welfare Committee, created in 1973 to regulate the terms and conditions of employment. Wash. Rev. Code Ann. §§ 49.12.005, 49.12.016, 49.12.035, 49.12.041, 49.12.170, as enacted by L. 1973 (2d Ex. Sess.), ch. 16. The committee issued temporary orders in 1975, which were considered too lenient. Final, tougher standards were instituted in May 1976. California also has given power to issue regulations on conditions of employment for both men and women to an industrial welfare commission. Cal. Labor Code § 1173, as enacted by Stats. 1973, ch. 1007, § 1. Orders issued by the commission in 1974 have been stayed by court order.

30. N.H. Rev. Stat. Ann. § 282:3(c) (1955), as amended by L. 1973, § 446:1; N.H. Rev. Stat. Ann. § 282:4 M(2) (1955), as amended by L. 1973, § 446:2.

31. Ariz. Rev. Stat. §§ 23-244, -244.01 (1971), as repealed and reenacted by L. 1972, ch. 40, § 5; Ark. Stat. Ann. § 81-608 (1947), as repealed by Acts 1963, No. 498, § 1; Ky. Rev. Stat. Ann. § 337.370 (1972), as repealed by Acts 1974, ch. 391, § 14; Mass. Gen. Laws ch. 149, § 67 (1971), as amended by Stats. 1973, ch. 925, § 55; Nev. Rev. Stat. § 609.240 (1971), as amended by Acts 1973, at 263; N.Y. Labor Law § 172 (McKinney 1965), as amended by L. 1973, ch. 377; Okla. Stat. Ann. tit. 40, § 76, as amended by L. 1975, ch. 151, § 1.

32. See note 7 supra.

33. See note 11 supra.

34. State Labor Laws, supra note 7, at 12.

35. See note 29 supra.

36. Ibid.

37. See note 14 supra.

38. Md. Ann. Code art. 43, § 200(1) (1971), as amended by Acts 1973, ch. 259.

39. Iowa Code § 170.19(6) (1973), as amended by Acts 1974, ch. 1083, § 28, Acts 1975, ch. 129, § 2. In 1974 the law was amended to require all employees whose hair did not extend below their ears to wear suitable hair covering and those whose hair did extend below their ears to wear hairnets. The more graceful provision now in effect was passed in 1975.

40. See note 29 supra.

41. The 1972 amendments to Title VII of the Civil Rights Act of 1964 extended coverage of the Act to state and federal governments in their capacity as employers. 42 U.S.C. §§ 2000e-2(a), 2000e-5(f)(1), 2000e-16 (1970), as amended by P.L. No. 92-261, 86 Stat. 103.

Title VII and the EEOC Guidelines of 1972 invalidate all laws and policies that exclude persons from job opportunities on the basis of sex except those few instances in which sex is a bona fide occupational qualification, for example, actress or model. Public employees have an additional remedy of a federal civil rights action under the Civil Rights Act of 1866, 42 U.S.C. § 1983.

42. See C. Samuels, The Forgotten Five Million: Women in Public Employment (1975), a recent comprehensive study of sex discrimination [hereafter cited as Samuels].

43. The Kentucky Commission on Human Rights, The Status of Women in Kentucky State Agencies (1972), reported that while women constituted 38.4 percent of full-time state employees, their average salary was almost $200 below the average monthly male salary; nearly four out of every ten women were in nonsupervisory clerical positions; and men outnumbered women 20 to one in the top six pay grades. Similar disparities were disclosed in a report prepared in September 1974 for the Civil Service Study Commission in Ohio. While 43 percent of state employees in Ohio are women, they comprise only 6 percent of the top ten pay grades, with no women in the top three grades. The average annual pay differential between men and women is more than $2,500. See Ad Hoc Women's Study Committee for Civil Service Law Revision to the Ohio Civil Service Study Commission, Memo, 1974 (appendix to A Report by the Ohio Task Force for the Implementation of the Equal Rights Amendment [July 1975] [hereafter cited as Ohio Task Force Report] on file at the State Library of Ohio) [hereafter cited as Civil Service Law Revision Memo].

44. See Samuels, supra note 42, at 20.

45. In addition to official discriminatory policies, women face a number of other pressures at work. See, for example, Williams v. Saxbe, _____ F. Supp. _____, 44 U.S.L.W. 2506 (D.D.C. April 20, 1976), in which the sexual harassment faced by women police officers in the District of Columbia Police Department was found to constitute sex discrimination.

46. National Black Police Ass'n v. Velde, 75 Civ. 144 (D.D.C. 1975).

47. Anthony v. The Commonwealth of Mass., _____ F. Supp. _____, 44 U.S.L.W. 2495 (1976). But see Branch v. DuBois, _____ F. Supp. _____, 45

U.S.L.W. 2188 (1976), upholding the Illinois veterans preference point system.

48. Until recently, the number of women permitted in the military was limited by regulation to 2 percent of all personnel. See 32 C.F.R. § 580.4(b). In Anthony v. The Commonwealth of Mass., _____ F. Supp._____, 44 U.S.L.W. 2495 (1976), the court noted that only 1.8 percent of all women appointed to the civil service division under review were veterans while 57 percent of the men were. Traditionally, women seeking military enlistment and appointment have been held to higher minimum age requirements, higher mental aptitude scores, and more strenuous physical requirements than men. In addition, married women and those with children under 18 were excluded.

49. Statutes of this type are similar to the regulations held invalid in Frontiero v. Richardson, 411 U.S. 677 (1973). Administrative convenience was not found to be a sufficiently strong state interest to require proof of actual dependency from husbands of female officers in order for them to receive "dependents'" privileges, while wives of male officers receive such benefits without question. For a more extensive discussion of dependency standards and their discriminatory effect, see the section on unemployment compensation below.

50. See, for example, Manhart v. City of Los Angeles Dep't of Water and Power, 387 F. Supp. 980 (C.D. Cal. 1975) (preliminary injunction issued against use of sex-segregated actuarial tables to require larger monthly retirement plan contributions by female employees; the use of such tables was found to constitute prohibited sex discrimination under the Equal Pay Act); Henderson v. State of Oregon, _____ F. Supp. _____, 11 FEP Cases 1218 (1975) (use of sex-segregated life expectancy tables to calculate lower monthly "refund annuity" payout to retired women public employees was held to violate Title VII); and Robertson v. Riley, Cause No. 4098, Vandenberg Circuit Ct. (Ind. 1975) (lower payout on pension/annuity plan for female teachers based on sex-segregated mortality tables was found to violate the equal protection clause of the Fourteenth Amendment).

The EEOC, which has jurisdiction over public and private plans, has concluded that equal periodic benefit payments are required to comply with Title VII. See 29 C.F.R. § 1604.9(f) (1974). Other federal agencies with jurisdiction over private pension plans, such as the Wage and Hour Division and the Office of Federal Contract Compliance in the Department of Labor, have lagged somewhat behind in their rule making, offering employers the option of making equal contributions or paying equal benefits for men and women. See, for example, 29 C.F.R. § 800.116(d) (1974); 41 C.F.R. § 60.20.3(c) (1974); and 39 Fed. Reg. 22231 (1974).

51. 29 C.F.R. § 160d.9(f) (1974).

52. See, for example, Rosen v. Public Service Electric and Gas Co., 477 F.2d 90 (3d Cir. 1973) (pension plan that preserves the traditional right of women working prior to 1967 to retire earlier with full benefits without creating an equivalent benefit for men who retired at that earlier age in the past violates Title VII); and Fitzpatrick v. Bitzer, 390 F. Supp. 278 (D. Conn. 1974), aff'd in part, rev'd in part on other grounds, 519 F.2d 559 (2d Cir.

1975) (State Retirement Act violates Title VII by discriminating in favor of
female employees as to the number of years of service required for eligibility
and computation of benefits; must use same age and same payout standards
without regard to sex).

53. For a more complete discussion of the development and implementation of an affirmative action plan for women in public employment as well
as the legal ramifications, see Samuels, supra note 42, at 149–80.

54. See, for example, letter of Massachusetts' Women's Lobby to Members of the Massachusetts General Court, April 8, 1976 (on file at Massachusetts Commission on the Status of Women), in which it is shown that a five-
to ten-point preference system would have an impact similar to an absolute
preference system because of the narrow spread of scores. The Women's
Lobby went on to urge the adoption of a time–limited point system.

55. Many of these recommendations are discussed in Ohio Task Force
Report, supra note 43, at 22–23. See also, Dybwad, Implementing Washington's ERA: Problems with Wholesale Legislative Revision, 49 Wash. L. Rev.
571, 591–52 (1974).

56. See S. Rep. No. 92–689, supra note 22, at 15.

57. Iowa Code Ann. § 29A.31 (1967), as amended by Acts 1974, ch.
1093, §§ 5–15, –17, –18, –40, –48, –57 (governor, secretary of state, state
militia, National Guard, commissioner of public safety, superintendent of
the women's reformatory, highway maintenance workers, sheriffs, and public assessors).

58. Ariz. Rev. Stat. §§ 11–441, –465, 13–1202, 26–122, –156, –159,
–161, –165, –171, –175 (1956), as amended by L. 1973, ch. 172 (sheriffs and
National Guard).

59. Conn. Gen. Stat. Ann. §§ 27–3, –4, –55, as amended by Acts 1974,
No. 74–321 (National Guard); Conn. Gen. Stat. Ann. § 23–20 (Supp. 1975), as
amended by Acts 1974, No. 74–83 (forest wardens and assistants); and Conn.
Gen. Stat. Ann. §§ 19–72a(b), 10–212a(a) (1975), as amended by Acts 1974,
Nos. 74–61, –86 (allow men to serve as public and school nurses).

60. Ky. Rev. Stat. §§ 37.170, 95.762, 441.150, 441.170 (1970), as
amended by Acts 1974, ch. 386, §§ 9, 22, 101, 102 (volunteer defense force,
police and fire departments, and prison guards).

61. N.Y. Mil. Law § 165 (1953), as amended by L. 1974, ch. 122, § 1
(opened up the New York Guard to women).

62. Va. Code Ann. §§ 2.1–116, –10–59, 19.1–308, –44–1, and 52–9.1
(1950), as amended by L. 1973, ch. 401 (National Guard and militia, police
officers and guards, and fire warden assistants).

63. Wash. Rev. Code § 38.04–030 (1964), as amended by L. 1973 (1st
Ex. Sess.), ch. 154, § 55 (to open the state militia to women). In addition,
Washington has corrected terminology in a provision allowing employees laid
off during budget reductions to be reinstated ahead of other job applicants in
order of seniority. Wash. Rev. Code § 41.08–040 (1972), as amended by L.
1973 (1st Ex. Sess.), ch. 154, § 60.

64. Ind. Rev. Code §§ 17–4–27.7–6, 8–9–5–5, 8–17–3–7, 8–21–9–12(k),
9–8–1–17, 14–2–7–17, 15–3–7–1, 15–3–7–12, 17–2–48–1 (1971), as amended by
Acts 1975, ch. 34.

65. Ky. Rev. Stat. §§ 220-270, 227.460 (1970), as amended by Acts 1974, ch. 386, §§ 48-49.

66. Va. Code Ann. §§ 3.1-36, -277, 65.1-65.1 (1950), as amended by Acts 1973, ch. 401.

67. Cal. Gov't Code § 19702.5 (1963), as amended by Stats. 1974, ch. 1395, § 1.

68. Cal. Gov't Code § 19451 (1963), as amended by Stats. 1971, ch. 1350, § 2.

69. Acts 1975, No. 75-536.

70. S.R. 9 (1974 Reg. Sess.).

71. Md. Ann. Code art. 64A, § 18(c)(d) (1972), as amended by L. 1975, ch. 272.

72. Civil Service Law Revision Memo, supra note 43.

73. Ohio State Highway Patrol on Hiring, Training, and Promotion, and the Ohio National Guard, presented to the Governor's Task Force for Equal Rights, Memos, 1974 (appendix to Ohio Task Force Report, supra note 43, on file at the State Library of Ohio).

74. Cal. Vehicle Code § 2266, as added by Stats. 1974, ch. 417, § 2.

75. This law was signed by the governor on August 26, 1975, as reporte in Rockford, Illinois, Register Republic, Aug. 28, 1975.

76. Md. Ann. Code art. 64A, § 50 (1972), as amended by Acts 1975, ch. 573, § 2 (states: maximum of 5 percent part-time employees).

77. Md. Ann. Code art. 100, § 77A (1972), as amended by Acts 1974, ch. 698.

78. Cal. Labor Code § 1420.2 (1971), as added by Stats. 1975, ch. 914.

79. Wash. Rev. Code § 73.16.010 (1963), as amended by L. 1973 (1st Ex. Sess.), ch. 154, § 107.

80. Cal. Gov't Code § 18973 (West 1963).

81. Minn. Stats. § 43.30 (1971). There was an unsuccessful attempt to sex neutralize this provision in 1974. S.F. 2974 (1974).

82. See note 54 supra.

83. Md. Ann. Code art. 77, § 208 (1975), as amended by Acts 1973, ch. 380 (teachers); art. 65, § 9(h) (1972), as amended by Acts 1973, ch. 383 (adjunct general); art. 88(B), § 31 (1969), as amended by Acts 1973, ch. 677, § 1 (police); art. 73(B), §§ 55-65 (1970), as amended by Acts 1973, ch. 2, § 2 (judges); art. 26, § 49-50c, as repealed and reenacted by Acts 1974, ch. 483 (judges); and art. 96½, §§ 4, 7, 47, 48 (1964), as amended by Acts 1973, ch. 224 (veterans).

84. Ariz. Rev. Stat. Ann. §§ 9-958, 962-63 (Supp. 1975), as amended by L. 1973, ch. 172, § 10 (firefighters); § 38-801 (1956), as amended by L. 1973, ch. 172, § 98 (judges); § 9-927 (Supp. 1975), as amended by L. 1973, ch. 172, § 9 (police); § 41-956 (1956), as amended by L. 1973, ch. 172, § 104 (ranger); and §§ 38-772-777 (1956), as amended by L. 1973, ch. 172, § 96 (highway patrol).

85. Ky. Rev. Stat. §§ 21.370, 21.420, 21.425, 21.520 (1971), as amended by Acts 1974, ch. 386, §§ 2-5 (judge, commissioners); § 26.660 (1971), as amended by Acts 1974, ch. 386, § 7 (police, judge); § 70.580 (1971

as amended by Acts 1974, ch. 386, § 11 (police officer); § 90.400 (1971), as amended by Acts 1974, ch. 386, § 13 (civil service); and § 95.101 (1971), as amended by Acts 1974, ch. 386, § 20 (city police, firefighters).

86. Iowa Code Ann. §§ 97A.6(8), (9), (13) (1946), as amended by Acts 1974, ch. 1093, §§ 20–22 (public safety, police officers); §§ 219.1, 219.4, 219.5 (1946), as amended by Acts 1974, ch. 1093, §§ 34–36 (soldiers' homes); and § 411.1(10) (1946), as amended by Acts 1974, ch. 1093, § 55 (police, firefighters).

87. N.M. Stat. Ann. §§ 5-5-24-1 to -4 (1953), as amended by L. 1973, ch. 71, § 1 (judges).

88. Wash. Rev. Code §§ 41.16.010, 41.16.100, 41.16.120, 41.16.140, 41.16.150, 41.16.160, 41.16.170 (1972), as amended by L. 1973 (1st Ex. Sess.), ch. 154, §§ 61–67; §§ 41.18.010, 41.18.040, 41.18.045, 41.18.080, 41.18.100 (1972), as amended by L. 1973 (1st Ex. Sess.), ch. 154, §§ 69–73; §§ 41.20.080, 41.20.085 (1972), as amended by L. 1973 (1st Ex. Sess.), ch. 181, §§ 5–6; §§ 41.24.160, 41.24.180 (1972), as amended by L. 1973, (1st Ex. Sess.), ch. 154, §§ 74–75; § 41.32.520 (1972), as amended by L. 1974 (1st Ex. Sess.), ch. 193, § 5; §§ 41.44.170, 41.44.210 (1972), as amended by L. 1973 (1st Ex. Sess.), ch. 154, §§ 78–79; § 51.12.080 (1962), as amended by L. 1973 (1st Ex. Sess.), ch. 154, § 92; and § 73.32.020 (1962), as amended by L. 1973 (1st Ex. Sess.), ch. 154, § 108.

89. Va. Code Ann. §§ 65.1-65 et seq. (1950), as amended by Acts 1973, ch. 401, § 1.

90. Conn. Gen. Stat. Rev. § 5-146 (1958), as amended by Acts 1974, No. 74-156, § 1 (state police).

91. Hawaii Rev. Stat. §§ 88-1, -85, -189 (1968), as amended by L. 1974, ch. 118, § 1 (municipal county pensions).

92. D.C. Code Ann. § 4-523(7) (1966), as amended by Bill No. 1-1-5002-A (veterans) (1975). See also the changes proposed in Montana in Omnibus Bill L.C. 0006 (1974).

93. Ill. Rev. Stat. ch. 108½, § 14-158 (1964), as amended by Acts 1969, No. 76-1251, § 1. But see ch. 108½, § 156, which creates a supplemental widow's annuity.

94. Wash. Rev. Code §§ 41.32.520 (1972), as amended by L. 1974 (1st Ex. Sess.), ch. 193, § 5.

95. Ky. Rev. Stat. § 161.520 (1971), as amended by Acts 1974, ch. 386, § 31. A proposed statute in Wisconsin would likewise have changed the law providing death benefits to cover wives and husbands regardless of dependency. A.B. 431 (1975).

96. Minn. Stat. Ann. § 354.05 (15) (1966), as amended by L. 1974, ch. 289, §§ 2-8.

97. Iowa Code § 219.15 (1969), as amended by Acts 1974, ch. 1093, § 36.

98. Conn. Gen. Stat. Ann. §§ 5-162, -163, -166 (1958), as amended by Acts 1975, No. 75-531.

99. See, for example, Ark. Stat. Ann. § 81-1105 (1960).

100. See, for example, Mass. Gen. Laws Ann. ch. 151A, § 25(c)(4) (1971) (no work between 12:00 and 6:00 a.m. is "suitable" for a woman). Spe-

cial night-work laws exempting women from accepting such work are illegal
under Title VII. See EEOC regulations at 29 C.F.R. § 1604.2(b)(1) (1975).
In New Hampshire, N.H. Rev. Stat. Ann. § 282:4(d) (1955), as added by L.
1971, ch. 156, § 37, replaces a law that disqualified all claimants who refused to work the night shift with an intelligent provision allowing both men
and women to refuse third-shift work in order to care for children.

101. Guerra v. Archie, 88 Nev. 172, 494 P. 2d 957 (1972).

102. For nonstatutory policy requiring closer examination of pregnant
claimants' availability for work, see, for example, Feehan v. Levine, 72
Civil No. 3717 (S.D.N.Y., filed July 1975). This suit challenges "Instructions
to Claims Examiners" requiring more stringent questioning of pregnant claimants and an application form asking claimants if they are pregnant. The
claims forms have been revised but still ask, "Will you require hospitalization
in the next 12 months?", which has the same impact as the previous forms.
These questions may be common in both state and interstate claims forms.
Conversation with plaintiff's attorney, Kathleen Peratis, Women's Rights Project, American Civil Liberties Union, Nov. 4, 1975.

103. Turner v. Employment Security Dep't and Board of Review of the
Industrial Commission of Utah, 423 U.S. 44 (1976), citing LaFleur v. Cleveland Board of Education, 414 U.S. 632 (1974).

104. Cunningham v. Iowa Employment Security Comm'n, No. 40676 (Johnson Co. Dist. Ct. August 31, 1973); Orner v. Board of Appeals, Employment
Security Admin. (Baltimore City Super. Ct. July 28, 1972); Rozankovich. v.
Kalamazoo Spring Corp. and Michigan Employment Security Comm'n (Ct.
App. 1972), reh'g denied, 44 Mich. App. 426, 205 N.W.2d 319 (1973); Hanson
v. Hutt, 83 Wash. 2d 195, 517 P.2d 599 (1973); Heier v. Department of Industry, Labor and Hum. Rel. and St. Vincent Hospital (Dane Co., Wis. Cir. Ct.
1973); and Maplewood Nursing Home of Sauk City v. D.L.H.R. (Wis. Cir. Ct.
1974), reported in CCH Unempl. Ins. Rptr. para. 8659.

105. Jordan v. Meskill, Civil No. 15671 (D. Conn. June 26, 1973), reported in CCH Unempl. Ins. Rptr. para. 21,420; Stickel v. Mason, Civil No.
72-1017-H (D. Md. April 27, 1973), reported in CCH Unempl. Ins. Rptr.
para. 21,421;IU, UAW v. Director & Michigan Employment Security Comm'n,
Civil No. 4-70066 (E.D. Mich. July 29, 1974), reported in CCH Unempl.
Ins. Rptr. para. 21,435; Lasko v. Garnes, Civil No. C72-1350 (N.D. Ohio Au
14, 1974), reported in CCH Unempl. Ins. Rptr. para. 21,421.

106. Tenn. Code. Ann. § 50-1324 (a) (1955) (1966 Repl. Vol.), provides
a 21-day waiting period before reeligibility following a period of pregnancy-
related disability to allow for recall by the woman's original employer. The
attorney general has declared this policy to be unconstitutional in light of
Turner in an official letter to J. D. Wallace, Commissioner of the Department
of Employment Security (June 21, 1976).

107. 127 Cal. Rptr. 540 (Ct. App. 1976).

108. Ark. Stat. Ann. § 81-1106(a) (1960) provides that departure to accompany a spouse to a new location is good cause for leaving work if the individual presents him/herself as available for employment in the new locale.

109. Boren v. Department of Employment Development, 130 Cal. Rptr.
683 (1976).

110. <u>Cal. Unep. Ins. Code</u> § 1264 (West 1972) provides that a worker who
leaves the market for domestic reasons must resume bona fide employment
before becoming reeligible for unemployment benefits; workers leaving for
other "voluntary" reasons, however, must resume work for a period of compensation equaling five times the weekly unemployment benefit amount. <u>Ohio</u>
<u>Rev. Code Ann.</u> § 4141.29(d)(2)(c) (Page 1973) requires that workers return-
ing from leaves prompted by domestic reasons earn wages of $60 or one-half
their average weekly wage, if less; workers returning from other "voluntary
leaves" must earn $360 or three times their weekly wage. <u>Ore. Rev. Stat.</u>
§ 657.176(3) (a,b,c) (1974) provides that remuneration equal to one week's
benefit amount must be earned by those returning from domestic-related
leaves while other workers must earn four weeks' benefit amount before establishing reeligibility.

111. <u>Kan. Stat. Ann.</u> § 44-706(a) (1973) provides that workers returning
from domestic-related leaves must earn eight times the benefit amount while
workers returning after other types of voluntary leave must simply wait six
weeks for reeligibility. By judicial interpretation, however, the more rigid
restrictions are applicable only if it is shown that the claimant intended to
withdraw from the labor market. Shelton v. Phalen, 214 Kansas 54, 519 P.2d
754 (1974). Similarly, <u>Utah Code Ann.</u> § 35-4-5-(i) (1974) requires workers
returning after domestic-related leaves to earn six times the weekly benefit
amount while others simply must wait five weeks.

112. <u>Idaho Code</u> § 72-1366(c)(d) (1973) (bona fide work with wages eight
times the weekly benefit amount); <u>Ky. Rev. Stat.</u> § 341.370(2)(b) (1972) (bona
fide work); <u>Miss. Code Ann.</u> § 71-5-513(i) (1972) (wages eight times the
weekly benefit amount); <u>N.Y. Labor Law</u> § 593(1)(b) (McKinney 1963) (three
days' work in each of four weeks; wages of $200); and <u>Pa. Stat. Ann.</u> tit. 43,
§ 802(2) (1964) (wages six times the weekly benefit amount).

113. <u>Colo. Rev. Stat. Ann.</u> § 82-4-8 (1973) (reeligibility varies with reason for leaving work; generally around 13 weeks of reemployment); <u>Nev. Rev.</u>
<u>Stat.</u> § 612.415 (1963) (domestic: bona fide employment; other: 15 weeks'
wait); <u>Okla. Stat.</u> tit. 40, § 214(g) (1954) (domestic: bona fide employment;
other: six weeks' wait); and <u>W.Va. Code Ann.</u> § 21A-6-3 (1973) (domestic:
30 days' insured work; other: six weeks' wait). Of course, the relative tight-
ness of the job market probably would determine whether securing bona fide
employment or waiting a specified number of weeks in order to establish reeligibility is the stricter standard. Also, in at least the state of Oklahoma,
conditions can be waived or modified on appeal, with a showing of "good cause"
for the absence and proof of availability.

114. <u>Alaska Stat.</u> § 23.20.350(b) (1962), <u>as amended by</u> Acts 1973, ch.
43; <u>Conn. Gen. Stat.</u> § 31.234 (1972); <u>Ill. Ann. Stat.</u> § 48-401(B) (Smith-Hurd
1966); <u>Ind. Ann. Stat.</u> § 22-4-12-2 (1974); <u>Md. Ann. Code</u> art. 95A, § 3(c)
(1957); <u>Mass. Gen. Laws</u> ch. 151A, § 29(c) (1932); <u>Mich. Comp. Laws Ann.</u>
§ 421.27(b)(2)(3) (1967); <u>D.C. Code Ann.</u> § 46-307(f) (1973); <u>Pa. Stat. Ann.</u>
tit. 43, § 804(e)(3) (1964), <u>as amended by</u> Acts 1968, No. 6, § 1; <u>Ohio Rev.</u>
<u>Code Ann.</u> § 4141.30(E) (Page 1973); and <u>R.I. Gen. Laws Ann.</u> § 28-44-6(B)
(1968).

115. See, for example, Ohio Rev. Code Ann. § 4141.30(e)(2) (Page 1973).
116. See U.S. Bureau of Labor Statistics, Department of Labor, Bull. No. 1880, U.S. Working Women: A Chartbook pt. 3 (1975).
117. Testimony of William T. Graessle, Assistant Director, Bureau of Unemployment Compensation, OBES, Columbus, Ohio, Feb. 7, 1975, Ohio Task Force Report, supra note 43, at 30. According to the Department of Labor, in 1972 states with dependency benefits paid them to 53.9 percent of male claimants but only 7.7 percent of female claimants. In 1972, 12 percent of all working wives contributed half or more of the family income. U.S. Department of Labor, Benefit Series Service, Unemployment Insurance, Rep. No. 304, at 9 (Sept. 1975, International Women's Year Special Supplement) [hereafter cited as Unemployment Insurance Rep.].
118. Bowen v. Hackett, 361 F. Supp. 854 (D.R.I. 1973).
119. Arkansas covers domestic workers in fraternities or sororities if there are more than three employees paid $500 per quarter. Ark. Stat. Ann. § 81-1103(6)(b) (1960), as amended by Acts 1973, Nos. 65, 329, 350. The District of Columbia covers domestic workers if paid more than $500 per calendar year. D.C. Code Encycl. § 46-301(b)(F) (1967), as amended by P.L. 92-211, § 3 (1971). Hawaii covers domestic workers if paid more than $225 per quarter. Hawaii Rev. Stat. § 383-7(2) (1968). New York includes domestic workers separately if paid $500 or more in a calendar year. N.Y. Labor Laws § 560(1) (McKinney 1965). Most states exclude domestic service workers in homes, college clubs, fraternities, or sororities. Several exclude only those who work in private homes: Alaska Stat. § 23.20.526(1) (1962); Del. Code Ann. tit. 19, § 3302(10)(d) (1974); Iowa Code Ann. § 96.19(g)(5) (1972); Me. Rev. Stat. Ann. tit. 26, § 1043(f)(5) (1964); N.J. Rev. Stat. § 42:21:19(7)(b) (1962); R.I. Gen. Laws Ann. § 28-42-8(2) (1968); Tenn. Code Ann. § 50-1309(6)(f) (1966); and Vt. Stat. Ann. tit. 21, § 1301(6)(c)(ii) (1967).
120. U.S. Department of Labor, Employment Standards Administration, Women's Bureau, Handbook on Women Workers 287 (1975) [hereafter cited as Handbook on Women Workers].
121. Ayers v. Employment Security Dep't, 85 Wash. 2d 500, 536 P.2d 610 (1975).
122. Approximately 98 percent of private household workers are women. Handbook on Women Workers, supra note 120, at 273.
123. U.S. Department of Labor, Employment Standards Administration, Women's Bureau, Highlights of Women's Employment and Education (May 1975).
124. See Brief of the IUE as Amicus Curiae, Appendix A at 1a-10a, La Fleur v. Cleveland Board of Education, 414 U.S. 632 (1974), in Babcock, supra note 1, at 325-30.
125. See, for example, Decision of Appeals Deputy No. 45445-AT-73 (North Carolina 1973), as reported in Unemployment Insurance Rep., supra note 117, at 43, and Rep. No. 386, at 21 (1974).
126. Ohio Task Force Report, supra note 43, at 29.
127. Handbook on Women Workers, supra note 120, at 137-39.
128. Several states—for example, Conn. Gen. Stat. § 31-234 (1958); Mass. Gen. Laws ch. 151A, § 29(c) (1932); and Pa. Stat. Ann. tit. 43,

§ 804(e)(3) (1964)—have provisions preventing the award of benefits to two individuals for the same dependents. Of course, in any state that requires the covered individual to provide more than 50 percent of the support of the dependent, it is unlikely that both parents could ever collect simultaneously for the same child, even without a specific prohibition against double collection.

129. U.S. Department of Commerce, Bureau of the Census, Current Population Reports, P-60, No. 93 (Advance Report).

130. Handbook on Women Workers, supra note 120, at 273.

131. Id. at 105–16.

132. Unemployment Insurance Rep., supra note 117.

133. Alaska Stat. § 23.20.380, para. 8 (1962), as repealed by Acts 1971, ch. 106, § 16; Conn. Gen. Stat. Rev. § 31–236(5) (1972) (two months before and two months after), as repealed by Acts 1973, No. 73–140; Ga. Code Ann. § 54–609(h) (1974), as repealed by L. 1974, at 101, 104; Hawaii Rev. Stat. § 385–7(6) (1968) (four months before and two months after), as repealed by L. 1973, ch. 159, § 1; Idaho Code § 72–1366(d) (1973) (12 weeks before and 6 weeks after), as repealed by L. 1975, ch. 47, § 1; Ill. Ann. Stat. ch. 48, § 420(C)(4) (Smith-Hurd 1966) (eight weeks before), as repealed by Acts 1975, No. 79, § 500; Me. Rev. Stat. Ann. tit. 26, § 1192(3) (1964) (disqualification for unemployment due to pregnancy), as repealed by L. 1971, ch. 538, §§ 23–27; Mass. Gen. Laws ch. 151A, § 27 (1965) (restrictive rules including a four-weeks-before-and-four-weeks-after rule), as repealed by Stats. 1973, ch. 1042; Mich. Comp. Laws Ann. § 421.28(1) (1967) (ten weeks before, six weeks after), as repealed by Acts 1974, No. 104, § 1; Mo. Rev. Stat. § 288.040(6) (1965) (three months before and four weeks after), as repealed by L. 1975, at 222; Neb. Rev. Stat. § 48–627(c) (1966) (12 weeks before), as repealed by L. 1972, L.B. 372; N.H. Rev. Stat. Ann. § 282:4(J) (1955, 1966 Repl. Vol.) (up to eight weeks before and eight weeks after), as repealed by L. 1973, 589; N.C. Gen. Stat. § 96–13(3) (1965) (three months before and three months after), as repealed by L. 1973, ch. 172, § 6; N.D. Cent. Code § 52–06–01(3)(b), (c) (1960), as repealed by L. 1973, ch. 391, § 24; Okla. Stat. tit. 40, § 215(h) (1954) (six weeks before and six weeks after), as repealed by L. 1975, ch. 40, § 1; Pa. Stat. Ann. tit. 43, §§ 801(d)(2), 802(b)(1) and (f) (1964) (inter alia, 30 days before and 30 days after; if laid off, 90 days before and 90 days after), as repealed by Acts 1974, No. 261, §§ 1–3; Vt. Stat. Ann. tit. 21, § 1344(4) (1967) (eight weeks before and four weeks after), as repealed by Acts 1973, No. 155 (Adj. Sess.), § 3; Wash. Rev. Code § 50.020.030 (1959) (17 weeks before and 6 weeks after)—the time limit was replaced with a less restrictive rule by L. 1973 (1st Ex. Sess.), ch. 167, § 2, which was then repealed by 1975 (1st Ex. Sess.), ch. 228, § 18; and Wis. Stat. Ann. § 108.04(1) (c) (1974) (at least ten weeks before and four weeks after), as repealed by L. 1973, ch. 247, § 9. Note: In this note and throughout, the dates shown for repealed sections of the codes are the dates of the last volume in which the authors have information that that section appeared.

134. Okla. Stat. tit. 40, § 215.1, as added by L. 1975, ch. 40, § 2.

135. In Iowa, the reform was accomplished by a state court's holding that a commission ruling establishing a presumption of unavailability for work

within three months prior to childbirth was unconstitutional. Cunningham v.
Iowa Employment Security Comm'n, No. 40676 (Johnson Co. Dist. Ct. Aug.
31, 1973). As a result, the preexisting statutory provision concerning temporary disabilities is now applied to pregnancy- and childbirth-related disabilities as well. Iowa Code Ann. § 96.5(1)(d) (1972), as amended by Acts 1975,
ch. 92, §§ 5-11.

136. Alaska Stat. § 23.20.380, para. 6 (1962), as repealed by Acts 1971, ch.
106, § 16; Hawaii Rev. Stat. § 383-29(3) (1968), as amended by L. 1973, ch.
53, § 1; Ill. Rev. Stat. ch. 48, § 420(c) (Smith-Hurd 1966), as replaced by
Acts 1975, No. 79-98, § 500; Ind. Ann. Stat. § 22-4-15-7 (1947), as repealed
by Acts 1971, ch. 355, § 47; Me. Rev. Stat. Ann. tit. 26, § 1193(1) (1964),
as amended by L. 1971, ch. 538, § 28; Minn. Stat. Ann. § 268.09(2) (1959),
as amended by L. 1973, ch. 599, § 9; Mont. Rev. Codes Ann. § 87-106(g),
(j), as repealed by L. 1971, ch. 415; N.D. Cent. Code § 52-06-01(3)(b) (1960),
as repealed by L. 1973, ch. 391, § 24.

137. Ark. Stat. Ann. § 81-1106(e) (1969), as repealed by Acts 1973, No.
329, § 6.

138. See Ark. Stat. Ann. § 81-1106(a) (1960).

139. Ill. Rev. Stat. ch. 48, § 401 (1969), as added by Acts 1975, No.
79-80. This provision is limited to parents who live together.

140. Md. Ann. Code art. 95A, § 3(c) (1957), as amended by Acts 1974,
ch. 708.

141. These provisions were invalidated in Bowen v. Hackett, 361 F.
Supp. 854 (D.R.I. 1973).

142. R.I. Gen. Laws Ann. § 28-44-6(B) (1968), as amended by L. 1973,
ch. 181, § 2.

143. The most recent enactment of such legislation is P.L. 94-566 (1976).

144. See Ark. Stat. Ann. § 81-1103(6)(b) (1960), as amended by Acts 1973,
Nos. 65, 329, 350 (covering domestic workers in fraternities or sororities if
there are more than three employees paid $500 per quarter); D.C. Code En-
cycl. § 46.301(b)(F) (1967), as amended by P.L. 92-211, § 3 (1971) (covering
domestic workers if paid more than $500 per year).

145. Cal. Unep. Ins. Code §§ 2601 et seq. (West 1972); N.J. Stat. Ann.
§§ 43:21-25 et seq. (1962); and R.I. Gen. Laws Ann. §§ 29-39-1 et seq. (1968).

146. N.Y. Workmen's Comp. Law §§ 200 et seq. (McKinney 1965).

147. Hawaii Rev. Stat. §§ 392-1 et seq. (1968); and P.R. Laws Ann. tit.
11, §§ 200 et seq. (1962).

148. Hawaii Rev. Stat. § 392-43 (1968); N.J. Stat. Ann. § 43:21-46 (1962),
as amended by L. 1968, ch. 406, § 1, L. 1970, ch. 324, § 2; N.Y. Workmen's
Comp. Law § 209 (McKinney 1965); P.R. Laws Ann. tit. 11, § 208 (1962);
Cal. Unep. Ins. Code § 2601 (West 1972); and R.I. Gen. Laws Ann. § 28-40-1
(1968).

149. Hawaii Rev. Stat. § 392-67 (1968); and N.J. Stat. Ann. § 43:21-46
(1962), as amended by L. 1968, ch. 406, § 1, L. 1970, ch. 324, § 1; N.Y.
Workmen's Comp. §§ 209-10 (McKinney 1965); and P.R. Gen. Laws Ann. tit.
11, § 208 (1962).

150. Cal. Unep. Ins. Code §§ 2601 et seq. (West 1972); Hawaii Rev. Stat. § 392-41 (1968); N.J. Stat. Ann. § 43:21-32 (1962); and P.R. Laws Ann. tit. 11, § 205 (1962), as amended by Stat. 1973, ch. 1212, § 273.

151. N.Y. Workmen's Comp. Law § 211 (McKinney 1965).

152. R.I. Gen. Laws Ann. § 28-39-1 (1968), as amended by L. 1971, ch. 95, § 1.

153. Cal. Unep. Ins. Code § 2626.2 (West 1972), as added by Stats. 1973, ch. 1026, § 3, Stats. 1973, ch. 1163, § 3.

154. N.J. Rev. Stat. § 43:21-39(e) (1962), as amended by L. 1967, ch. 30, § 9.

155. R.I. Gen. Laws Ann. § 28-41-8 (1968).

156. N.Y. Workmen's Comp. Law § 205(3) (McKinney 1965). The continuing validity of § 205(3) is put in question, however, by the ruling in State Division of Human Rights v. Crouse-Irving Memorial Hosp., 377 N.Y.S.2d 315 (4th Dep't 1975), in which the court ruled that the treatment of disability benefits for pregnancy must be the same as for any other nonoccupational disease.

157. Hawaii Rev. Stat. § 392-6(2) (1968).

158. 417 U.S. 484 (1974).

159. See, for example, Gilbert v. General Electric, 45 U.S.L.W. 4031 (Dec. 7, 1976).

160. See, for example, Eisenstadt v. Baird, 405 U.S. 438 (1972).

161. Former R.I. Gen. Laws Ann. § 28-41-5(c) (1968).

162. 361 F. Supp. 854 (D.R.I. 1973).

163. Hawaii Rev. Stat. § 392, as amended by L. 1973, ch. 60.

164. 417 U.S. 484 (1974).

165. Cal. Unep. Ins. Code § 2626.2 (West 1972), as added by Stats. 1973, ch. 1026, § 3, Stats. 1973, ch. 1163, § 3.

166. Bowen v. Hackett, 361 F. Supp. 854 (D.R.I. 1973).

167. See note 161 supra and accompanying text.

168. Ohio Rev. Code Ann. § 4123.60 (Page 1973).

169. See, for example, Ohio Rev. Code Ann. § 4123.59 (Page 1973); and Minn. Stat. Ann. § 176.111(1) (1966).

170. See, for example, Ohio Rev. Code Ann. § 4123.59 (Page 1973); Minn. Stat. Ann. § 176.111(3) (1966); and Vt. Stat. Ann. tit. 21, § 634 (1967) (definitions of dependency). Similar laws have been held violative of equal protection guaranteed by the due process clause of the Fifth Amendment. In Frontiero v. Richardson, 411 U.S. 677 (1973), the United States Supreme Court struck down a law providing medical and housing benefits to all wives of servicemen while requiring husbands of women officers to prove actual dependency. The Court held that the administrative convenience of presuming all wives to be dependent did not justify the discrimination against women officers and their spouses.

171. See, for example, Ark. Stat. Ann. § 81-1302 (1960). Another common provision is to require that the widower had been dependent on his deceased wife. S.C. Code Ann. § 72-17 (1962).

172. Ark. Stat. Ann. § 81-1315 (1960).

173. See, for example, Me. Rev. Stat. Ann. tit. 39, § 58 (1965), which
provides that a widow's benefits will terminate upon her remarriage as well
as her death but that a widower's benefits terminate only upon his death.
Mass. Gen. Laws Ann. ch. 152, § 31 (1958) allows a widow to continue receiving benefits beyond the stated maximum if she is in fact not fully self-support-
ing.

174. Ore. Rev. Stat. § 656.226 (1975). See also Del. Code Ann. § 2332
(1974), which provides for compensation payable to alien dependent widows.

175. See, for example, Moriarty's Case, 126 Me. 358, 138 A. 555 (1927),
which held that, for purposes of worker's compensation, the widow of a deceased employee is conclusively presumed to be dependent.

176. But see Colby v. Varney, 97 N.H. 130, 82 A.2d 604 (1951), where,
in determining whether a member of a household contributed more than the
cost of his or her own support, thereby entitling other members of the household to claim dependency, nonmonetary contributions were found to be relevant.
See also Toadvine v. Luffman, 14 Md. App. 333, 286 A.2d 790 (1972), where
the court held that a trier-of-fact could not properly find that a woman's earnings were not a consequential part of her children's maintenance and that the
children were totally dependent on the father when she had regularly contributed
close to 40 percent of the family's income.

177. N.D. Cent. Code § 65-05-09 (1960) provides

> an additional sum of five dollars per week for each dependent child
> under the age of eighteen years living or unborn at the date of the
> injury, or born during the period of disability, and for each child
> over eighteen years and incapable of self-support due to physical
> or mental disability and whose maintenance is the responsibility
> of the claimant.

Vt. Stat. Ann. tit. 21, § 642 (1967), provides "$5.00 a week for each depen-
dent under the age of 21 years."

178. But see Padilla v. Industrial Comm'n, 24 Ariz. App. 42, 535 P.2d
634 (1975), where the court defined the term "totally dependent" to mean those
persons totally dependent on the family unit. Therefore, where both parents
are employed and pool their incomes to support their household and children,
either parent is entitled to the additional per month dependency allowance provided by Ariz. Rev. Stat. Ann. § 23-1045 (1971).

179. See Wash. Rev. Code Ann. § 51.32.055 (1962), which declares that
the purpose of the title is to restore the injured worker as nearly as possible
to the condition of self-support of an able-bodied worker. 29 U.S.C.A. § 676
(1965), in establishing a commission to insure that the state worker's compensation laws provide an "adequate, prompt, and equitable system" of compensation, states that the purpose of the worker's compensation laws is to provide basic economic security as well as full protection from job-related injury. See also Note, Presumption of Dependence in Worker's Compensation
Death Benefits as a Denial of Equal Protection, 9 U. Mich. J. of L. Reform
138 (1975), which describes the purpose of worker's compensation as being
somewhere between that of tort recovery and social insurance.

180. See, for example, Hawaii Rev. Stat. § 386-54 (1968), as amended by L. 1974, ch. 157, § 1; Va. Code Ann. §§ 65.1-65 et seq. (1973 Repl. Vol.), as amended by Acts 1973, ch. 401; Ariz. Rev. Stat. Ann. § 23-1046A2 (1956), as amended by L. 1973, ch. 133, § 27; Fla. Stat. Ann. § 440.16 (1966), as amended by L. 1975, ch. 75-209, § 8.

181. Va. Code Ann. § 65.1-65.1 (1950, for example, which provides death benefits for the survivors of coal workers, now refers to the beneficiary as the "surviving spouse until death or remarriage" rather than simply the "widow."

182. Ala. Code tit. 26, § 280 (1958) (Cum. Supp. 1973), as amended by Acts 1973, No. 1062, § 15; Alaska Stat. §§ 23.30.195, 23.30.215 (1975), as amended by Acts 1974, ch. 127, §§ 87-89; Ariz. Rev. Stat. Ann. § 23-1046 (1971), as amended by L. 1971, ch. 173, § 17, L. 1973, ch. 133, § 27, L. 1974, ch. 184, § 17; Colo. Rev. Stat. Ann. § 8-50-101 (1974), as amended by L. 1975, at 298, § 17; Del. Code Ann. tit. 19, § 2330 (1974), as amended by 59 Del. Laws, ch. 454, § 14; Hawaii Rev. Stat. § 386.42 (1968), as amended by L. 1971, ch. 87, § 1, L. 1974, ch. 151, § 1; Ill. Ann. Stat. tit. 48, § 138.7 (Smith-Hurd 1969), as amended by Acts 1973, No. 78-358, § 1; Ky. Rev. Stat. Ann. § 342.075 (1972), as amended by Acts 1974, ch. 386, § 60; La. Rev. Stat. Ann. § 23:1251 (1964), as amended by Acts 1975, No. 583, § 13; N.M. Stat. Ann. § 59-10-12.10 (1953), as amended by L. 1973, ch. 47; Okla. Stat. Ann. tit. 85, § 22 (1970), as amended by L. 1972, ch. 219, § 1, L. 1975, ch. 371, § 1; S.D. Comp. Laws Ann. § 62-4-12 (1967), as amended by L. 1975, ch. 322, § 5; Wash. Rev. Code Ann. § 51.32.050 (1962), as amended by L. 1975, ch. 179, § 1 (1976); and W.Va. Code Ann. § 23-4-10 (1973), as amended by L. 1974, ch. 145.

183. See Wash. Rev. Code Ann. § 51.32.050 (1962), as amended by L. 1975, ch. 179, § 1 (1976).

184. Fla. Stat. Ann. § 440.02 (1966), as amended by L. 1974, ch. 74-197, § 1, formerly required a widower to have been living with the worker at the time of her death, dependent on her for support, and to be presently unmarried and incapacitated. While special proof of incapacitation for men has been eliminated by the reform amendment, it is still unclear what standard individuals of both sexes must now meet under the remaining sex-neutral and apparently unqualified "substantially dependent" standard. Similarly, under the former Virginia law, which set up "conclusive presumptions" about dependency, a husband not only had to prove dependency but also his inability to support himself. Under the amendment to Va. Code Ann. § 65.1-66 (1973 Repl. Vol.), as amended by L. 1973, chs. 401, 542, both spouses are now "presumed" dependent if living with each other at the time of the accident and "actually dependent" regardless of their ability of self-support. Ambiguity remains, however, about the meaning of "actually dependent" in the context of a statutory "conclusive presumption."

185. Kan. Stat. Ann. § 44-510b (1973), as amended by L. 1974, ch. 203, § 11, provides death benefits to those family members who are "wholly dependent" but, in the provision for computing the amount of benefits, refers to the "surviving legal spouse and/or wholly dependent child or children eligi-

ble for benefits under this section, " creating an ambiguity as to whether the spouse must be wholly dependent.

186. Md. Ann. Code art. 101, § 36(8), as amended by Acts 1973, ch. 218, provides that partly dependent persons shall receive compensation in proportion to the ratio of their weekly earnings to the average weekly wages of the deceased but that a spouse must be "wholly dependent" to receive full compensation.

CHAPTER 7

1. Nagel and Weitzman, Women as Litigants, 22 Hastings L.J. 171, 193 (1971).

2. This was a common practice before, and in some states long after, the Nineteenth Amendment was adopted in 1920. See B. Babcock, A. Freedman, E. Norton, and S. Ross, Sex Discrimination and the Law: Causes and Remedies 64-68 (1975), and text at note 10 infra.

3. See, for example, former La. Const. art. VII, § 41, replaced in 1974 by La. Const. art V, § 33.

4. Mo. Ann. Stat. § 494.031 (1949); R.I. Gen. Laws Ann. § 9-9-11 (1969); Tenn. Code Ann. § 22-101 (1955); and Ala. Code tit. 30, § 21 (1959).

5. Conn. Gen. Stat. Ann. § 51-218 (1958) (under 16 years of age); Fla. Stat. Ann. § 40-01(1) (1974) (pregnancy or a child under 18); Ga. Code Ann. § 59-112(b) (1965) (under 14); Tex. Rev. Civ. Stat. art. 2135(2) (1964) (under 10); Utah Code Ann. § 78-46-10(14) (1953) (minor children). In Wyoming, a woman is granted an exemption if she claims to have household duties or family obligations. Wyo. Stat. Ann. § 1-80 (1957). In South Carolina, mothers are not listed with other specifically exempted persons but are included in a provision permitting persons with "good and sufficient cause" to claim exemption. S.C. Code Ann. § 38-108 (1962) (under seven). Unlike other people in that category, they are not placed on the next jury list but have a continuing exemption. If in practice women are automatically given exemptions under this provision without showing cause, then the provision as applied is impermissibly discriminatory under the ERA.

6. Okla. Stat. Ann. tit. 38, § 28 (1953), as amended by L. 1975, ch. 302, § 28(a) (persons with custody of minor children if such person's absence would result in hardship); Mass. Gen. Laws Ann. ch. 234, § 1 (1959), as amended by Stats. 1973, ch. 582, § 1 (person having custody of and being responsible for the daily supervision of children under 16); Va. Code Ann. § 8-208.6(26) (1950), as amended by Acts 1973, ch. 439 (persons who have legal custody of and are directly and personally responsible for children under 16); N.J. Rev. Stat. § 2A-69-2(g) (1952) (service would interfere with the care of children); Mont. Rev. Codes Ann. § 93-1304(12) (1947) (person caring directly for one or more children); and N.Y. Judiciary Law § 507(7) (1975) (parent, guardian, or person who resides with child[ren] under 16 and is principally responsible for the care and supervision of such child[ren]).

7. R.I. Gen. Laws Ann. § 9-9-11 (1969); and Neb. Rev. Stat. § 25-1601.01 (1964). Ala. Code tit. 30, § 21 (1959).

8. 419 U.S. 522 (1975).

9. 95 S. Ct. 692, 700n.17 (1975). For different judicial opinions on the effect of Taylor on categorical exemptions for women, see Alessi v. Nadjari, 47 A.D.2d 189, 365 N.Y.S.2d 859 (1st Dep't 1975); People v. Tabb, 80 Misc. 2d 431, 364 N.Y.S.2d 357 (New York Co. 1975); and People v. Moore, 80 Misc. 2d 166, 364 N.Y.S.2d 113 (Nassau Co. 1975). See also New York Law Journal, Feb. 5, 1975, at 1. Contra People v. Moss, 80 Misc. 2d 633, 366 N.Y.S.2d 522 (Moss Co. 1975).

10. Alabama—exclusion of women held unconstitutional in White v. Crook, 251 F. Supp. 401 (1966); Mississippi—Miss. Code Ann. § 1762 (1943), as amended by L. 1968, ch. 335, § 1; and South Carolina—S.C. Code Ann. § 38-104 (1962), as amended by L. 1967, at 895.

11. Former La. Const. art. VII, § 41 and La. Code of Crim. Pro. art. 402, held unconstitutional by Taylor v. Louisiana, 419 U.S. 522 (1975); Fla. Stat. Ann. § 40.01(1) (1974), as amended by L. 1967, ch. 67-154, §§ 1-2.

12. Former N.Y. Judiciary Law § 507(7) (McKinney 1968) was repealed by L. 1975, ch. 4, § 1. Later that year § 507(7) became a sex-neutral exemption for anyone taking daily care of a child under 16. L. 1975, ch. 382, § 1. Ga. Code Ann. § 59-112(d)(6) (1965) was repealed by L. 1975, at 779.

13. Stats. 1949, ch. 347, § 1.

14. Stats. 1969, ch. 148, § 1.

15. Stats. 1973, ch. 582, § 1.

16. Mass. Gen. Laws Ann. ch. 234, § 1A (1973).

17. Acts 1971, ch. 263.

18. Acts 1973, ch. 439.

19. Okla. Stat. Ann. tit. 38, § 28 (1953), as amended by L. 1975, ch. 302, § 28(a).

20. Mont. Rev. Codes Ann. § 93-1304(12) (1947).

21. Va. Code Ann. § 8-208.6(26) (1950); and N.Y. Judiciary Law § 507(7) (1975).

22. Okla. Stat. Ann. tit. 38, § 28 (1953), as amended by L. 1975, ch. 302, § 28(a).

23. Fla. Stat. Ann. § 40.01(0) (1974), as amended by L. 1967, ch. 67-154, §§ 1-2.

24. La. S. Ct. R. 25, promulgated pursuant to La. Const. art. V, § 33 (1974).

25. See, for example, A Report by the Ohio Task Force for the Implementation of the ERA 51-52 (1975) [hereafter cited as Ohio Task Force Report].

26. See, for example, Pa. Stat. tit. 71, § 155 (1962); and Ohio Rev. Code § 3375.12 (1972), §§ 5153.05, 5153.08 (1970).

27. Conn. Gen. Stat. Ann. § 10-293 (1958), as amended by Acts 1974, No. 74-150, § 1. Sex-neutral language in Wash. Rev. Code § 28A.60.210 (1970), as amended by L. 1973 (1st Ex. Sess.), ch. 154, § 46, eliminated a spot expressly reserved for a woman on a special board of school district supervisors. On the other hand, the Ohio Task Force for the Implementation of the Equal Rights Amendment has recommended that the "number of mem-

bers of a board that are one sex shall never exceed the number of members of the opposite sex by more than one." Ohio Task Force Report, supra note 25, at 52. This proposal has some of the same problems as earlier versions of benevolent quotas and is an impermissible sex classification under the ERA.

28. Va. Code Ann. § 54-283 (1974) (State Board of Medicine); Iowa Code Ann. § 80.2 (1949), as amended by Acts 1974, ch. 1093, § 17 (Department of Public Safety); Ky. Rev. Stat. Ann. § 150.161 (1972), as amended by Acts 1974, ch. 386, § 28 (Department of Fish and Wildlife Resources); and Ky. Rev. Stat. Ann. § 246.150 (1972), as amended by Acts 1974, ch. 386, § 50 (Department of County Institutes).

29. S.R. 73 (1974).

30. H.B. 2478 (1974).

31. H.B. 233 (1974).

32. H.R. 192 (1974). This proposal goes the farthest to get women appointed to boards. However, the ERA does not require and policy reasons may argue against using such a method before discrimination has been proven to exist in a particular situation.

33. Cal. Gov't Code §§ 12033 et seq. (West 1963), as added by Stats. 1974, ch. 1453, § 2.

CHAPTER 8

1. 42 U.S.C. §§ 2000e et seq. (1969).

2. 29 U.S.C. § 206(d)(1)-(4) (1965), as amended by P.L. 88-38 (1963).

3. The text of federal and state fair employment practice laws can be found in 8 BNA Labor Rel. Rep. For a more general discussion of developments and policy in employment law, see B. Babcock, A. Freedman, E. Norton, and S. Ross, Sex Discrimination and the Law: Causes and Remedies, ch. 2 (1975). For issues relating to public employment, see Chapter 6 of this book.

4. 20 U.S.C. §§ 1681-86 (1974).

5. 15 U.S.C.A. §§ 1691 et seq. (1974), as amended by P.L. 93-495, §§ 701 et seq. (1974).

6. 42 U.S.C. § 3604 (1973), as amended by P.L. 93-383, § 808(b)(1) (1974).

7. 12 U.S.C. § 1735f-5 (1969), as amended by P.L. 93-383, § 808(a) (1974).

8. See, for example, Ohio Governor's Task Force on Credit for Women, Final Report: She Supports Her Children—and Can't Get a Loan . . . (Oct. 25, 1974); and Pennsylvania Commission on the Status of Women, Credit Report (Aug. 31, 1973).

9. 15 U.S.C.A. §§ 1691 et seq. (1974), as amended by P.L. 93-495, §§ 701 et seq.

10. Regulation B, implementing the Equal Credit Opportunity Act, is found at 12 C.F.R. §§ 202.1 et seq. (1976).

11. For further research and a critique of these laws, see Polikoff, Legislative Solutions to Sex Discrimination in Credit: An Appraisal, 2 Women's Rights L. Rep. 26 (1974).

12. See also Bingaman, Federal Credit Regulations and State Law, 1 Women L. Rep. 1.211 (May 15, 1975).

13. See, for example, the Uniform Consumer Credit Code § 3.509, which has been enacted in Colorado, Idaho, Indiana, Kansas, Oklahoma, Utah, and Wyoming. For further discussion concerning these laws, see Gates, Credit Discrimination Against Women: Causes and Solutions 27 Vand. L. Rev. 409, 415-17 (1974).

14. U.S. Bureau of the Census, Current Population Reports, Series P.20, No. 212, Marital Status and Family Status 20, table 5 (March 1970). Less startling but nonetheless unequal impact is created by patterns of discrimination against divorced people and widows or widowers. Statistically, among divorced men and women 24 years and older, men have a higher remarriage rate in every age group and in every time period after divorce than women. In 1970, the proportion of divorced men was 35 to every 1,000 married couples; the proportion for women was 60 per 1,000. U.S. Bureau of the Census, Current Population Reports, Series P-20, No. 223, 55, table 8 (1971). It is also important to note that not only do men die younger than women, on the average, but the remarriage rate for widowers in the 45-to-64-year-old bracket is four times that of the parallel group of widows. H. Carter and P. Glick, Marriage and Divorce: A Social and Economic Study 47-48 (1970). The discounting of certain sources of income among older people, such as pensions and public or private insurance funds, places a heavier burden on older women in the housing market, just as the discounting of alimony and child support as income impacts single mothers disproportionately.

15. Alaska Stat. § 18.80.240 (1962), as amended by Acts 1975, ch. 104.

16. D.C. Rules & Regs. tit. 34, § 13.1 (1973).

17. Minn. Stat. Ann. § 363.03 (1966).

18. The Housing Finance Guidelines of the Maryland Commission, adopted in March 1973 (after the enactment of a "sex" standard but prior to the addition of "marital status") provide that discrimination includes:

Any application of standards, terms or conditions . . . which has a disparate effect upon that applicant or class. The use of such standards, terms or conditions that have an adverse effect on the protected class must be validated as to their business risk. For example, standards that must be validated include: refusal to consider second income; refusal to consider stable income from overtime, bonuses and part-time work; use of isolated remotely past credit difficulties as absolute disqualification; rejection or under appraisal because of racial composition of neighborhood, the income level of racially mixed neighborhood, the age of the home or of homes in the neighborhood, an arbitrary minimum square footage requirement, the marital status of the applicant, or other restrictive financial practices, e.g., declining or refusing to make loan available for subsidized housing designed to assist low and moderate income families; establishing arbitrary cut off points

for borrower, income, loan amount or purchase price; rejection
on the basis that applicant has never previously owned a home;
requesting information from an applicant or a physician related
to the likelihood of pregnancy during the term of the loan; use of
a 20% upper limit on the mortgage payment to income ratio; use
of the 25% rule on an inflexible basis; use of an inflexible 33%
rule for total installment debt to income ratio.

Such guidelines are particularly critical in jurisdictions where the courts
are unwilling to strike down facially neutral policies.

19. 42 U.S.C. § 3604, as amended by P.L. 93-383, § 808(b)(1), 88
Stat. 729 (1974). The Housing and Community Development Act of 1974
amended the National Housing Act to prohibit sex discrimination in the financing of federally secured mortgages. 12 U.S.C. § 1735f-5 (1969), as amended
by P.L. 93-383, § 808 (a) (1974). For further discussion, see the section on
credit above.

20. Lord v. Malakoff, Maryland Comm'n on Human Relations Decision
No. H-71-0062 (1972), reported in Prentice-Hall Equal Housing Opportunity
Rep. para. 17,503.

21. Mont. Rev. Codes Ann. § 64-307, as amended by L. 1975, ch. 524.
Nature of service requires separate lavatory, dressing, bathing.

22. D.C. Rules & Regs. tit. 34, § 13.2 (1973).

23. See, for example, the laws of Alaska, Michigan, and Virginia,
which allow injunctive relief immediately upon the filing of a complaint.

24. See, for example, the laws of Kansas and Pennsylvania, which permit both the fair housing agency and the private complainant to seek court
enforcement of a favorable order.

25. See, for example, the statutes of Alaska, Colorado, and Hawaii for
the express authorization to order respondents to rent, sell, extend credit,
and the like. Clearly this is most valuable to a complainant, while other "affirmative action" remedies, such as requiring advertising that emphasizes
equal opportunity in housing, are geared more to the public interest. For
this latter type of provision, see, for example, the law of Hawaii and Katz
v. Massachusetts Comm'n Against Discrimination, 312 N.E.2d 182 (1974).

26. For examples of different types of provisions, see the laws of
Colorado, Delaware, Connecticut, Hawaii, Maine, and Minnesota. It is important for the statute to expressly authorize the award of monetary damages
by the agency, so that aggrieved individuals do not have to resort to an expensive court action. In states where the agency is not explicitly granted authority to award damages, the courts have divided on the question of whether or
not the agency has the discretion to do so. See, for example, Zahorian v.
Russell Fitt Real Estate Agency, 62 N.J. 399, 301 A.2d 754 (1973) (reading
a general statute to include such power); and Zamantakis v. Pennsylvania Human Relations Comm'n, 308 A.2d 612 (Com. Ct. 1973) (contra).

27. See the laws of Alaska and Kentucky for provisions for private court
actions and court-awarded attorney fees.

28. This view is developed in Note, 24 Cleveland State L. Rev. 79 (1975).

29. Mass. Ann. Laws ch. 272, § 92A (1975); Mont. Rev. Codes Ann. § 64-306(2) (1947); S.D. Comp. Laws Ann. §§ 20-13-23, -24 (1967). See also the discussion of public accommodations statutes in the credit section above.

30. Colo. Rev. Stat. Ann. § 25-1-1 (1963); Ind. Ann. Stat. § 22:9-2 (Burns 1974) (public schools only); Mont. Rev. Codes Ann. § 64-306(2) (1947); N.J. Stat. Ann. § 10-5-12(f) (1960) (excluding religious schools); and Pa. Stat. Ann. tit. 43, § 952 (1964).

31. Colo. Rev. Stat. Ann. § 23-1-1 (1963); and Mass. Ann. Laws ch. 272, § 92A (1975).

32. Ind. Ann. Stat. § 22:9-2 (1974); Mass. Ann. Laws ch. 272, § 92A (1975); Minn. Stat. Ann. § 363.03(3) (1966); Mont. Rev. Codes Ann. § 64-306(2) (1947); and N.M. Stat. Ann. § 4-33-7(f) (1953).

33. Iowa Code Ann. § 601A.7 (1975).

34. Kan. Stat. Ann. §§ 44-1001, -1002 (1973), as amended by L. 1974, ch. 209, § 1, exempts nonprofit fraternal associations or corporations from its public accommodations statutes; N.J. Stat. Ann. §§ 10-5-12(f) (1960); Ore. Rev. Stat. § 549.037 (1974); S.D. Comp. Laws Ann. §§ 20-13-23, -24 (1967); Utah Code Ann. § 13-7-3 (1953); and W. Va. Code Ann. § 5-11-9(f) (1971).

35. N.J. Stat. Ann. 10:1-5 (1960); Ore. Rev. Stat. § 30.675(2) (1975); Utah Code Ann. 13-7-2(a) (1973); and W. Va. Code Ann. 5-11-3(j) (1971).

36. S.D. Comp. Laws Ann. §§ 20-13-23, -24 (1967); and Utah Code Ann. § 13-7-3 (1953).

37. See, for example, Pennsylvania Human Relations Comm'n v. Loyal Order of Moose, Lodge No. 107, 294 A.2d 594, 448 Pa. 451 (1972), appeal dismissed, 409 U.S. 1052 (1972).

38. Conn. Gen. Stat. Ann. § 53-35 (1958); Mass. Ann Laws ch. 272, § 92A (1975); and N.Y. Exec. Laws § 296.2(a) (McKinney 1972).

39. Del. Code Ann. tit. 6, § 4604 (1974); Iowa Code Ann. § 601A.7 (1975); Utah Code § 13-703 (1953); and W. Va. Code Ann. § 5-11-9(f) (1971).

40. State v. Schwarcz, 123 N.J. Super. 482, 303 A.2d 610 (1973). The case was based on statutes regulating the licensing of barbers and cosmetologists, which expect a single-sex clientele in both barber shops and hairdressing salons. N.J. Stat. Ann. §§ 45:4-30, 45:A-5 (1963). For a discussion of these statutes, see the section on protective labor laws in Chapter 6.

41. See Bernstein and Williams, Title VII and the Problem of Sex Classifications in Pension Programs, 74 Col. L. Rev. 1202, 1221 (1974).

42. For a more detailed discussion of the impact of the ERA on sex-based rating practices, including the question of unique physical characteristics, see Brown and Freedman, Sex Averaging and the Equal Rights Amendment, 2 Women's Rights L. Rep. 35 (June 1975), in Equal Rights Amendment Project of the California Commission on the Status of Women, Impact ERA: Limitations and Possibilities 127 (1976) [hereafter cited as Brown and Freedman].

43. See, for example, Stern v. Massachusetts Indem. & Cas. Co., 365 F. Supp. 433 (E.D. Pa. 1973). But see Broderick v. Associated Hosp. Serv. of Phila., 536 F.2d 1 (3d Cir. 1976).

44. See, for example, Reichardt v. Payne, 396 F. Supp. 1010 (N.D. Cal. 1975), challenging sex-based discrimination in disability insurance policies. The court held that the actions of the insurance commissioner were state actions, though the sales of the individual insurance companies were not, but that a cause of action existed under 42 U.S.C. § 1985(3), on the theory that the companies had conspired to deprive plaintiffs of civil rights. Pending litigation includes: Gilpin v. Schenck, Civil No. 74-420 (S.D.N.Y., filed Jan. 24, 1975).

45. Under Title VII of the Civil Rights Act of 1964, employee insurance programs have been found to be "terms and conditions of employment," as to which there can be no discrimination on the basis of sex. 29 C.F.R. § 1604.9 (1975). Under the Equal Pay Act of 1963, employer contributions to insurance and annuity plans have been held to be compensation that must be equal for members of both sexes doing equal work. 29 C.F.R. § 800.116(d) (1974). The Office of Federal Contract Compliance and the Department of Health, Education and Welfare also have regulations on this subject in connection with their jurisdiction over federal contractors and federally assisted educational programs, respectively. See 41 C.F.R. § 60.20.3(c) (1974); and Fed. Reg. 22231 (1974).

46. In 1972, the EEOC declared that it would be an unlawful employment practice for an employer to have a pension or retirement plan that differentiates in benefits on the basis of sex. Greater cost for one sex was held to be no defense. 29 C.F.R. § 1604.9(e), (f) (1975). OFCC and HEW are considering regulations that would be consistent with the EEOC position. They also are considering proposals for the either/or option, and HEW has a third alternative that would mandate the use of unisex premium or rate tables. The EEOC guideline has been interpreted to require equal periodic benefits. EEOC Decision No. 72-1919, CCH EP Guide para. 6370 (1972); EEOC Decision No. 7- 118, CCH EP Guide para. 6431 (1974). The commission has suggested in this la- ter opinion that unisex tables are one way but not the only way in which the employer can achieve equality. See generally Halperin and Gross, Should Pension Benefits Depend on the Sex of the Recipient?, 62 AAUP Bulletin 43 (Spring 1976) [hereafter cited as Halperin and Gross].

47. This would occur particularly with employee groups consisting predominantly of members of one sex. For further discussion, see Halperin and Gross, id. at 2; and Brown and Freedman, supra note 42.

48. Gilbert v. General Electric, 45 U.S.L.W. 4031 (Dec. 7, 1976). For a discussion of the issues raised by states treating pregnancy disability less favorably than other temporary disabilities, see the section on unemployment insurance in Chapter 6.

49. Ill. Ins. Code R. 26.04.

50. Mass. Gen. Laws Ann. ch. 175, § 47c (1972), as added by L. 1974, ch. 668.

51. N.Y. Ins. Law § 40-e (McKinney 1966), as added by L. 1975, ch. 564, § 2.

52. Pa. Stat. Ann. tit. 40, ss 1171.1-1171.15 (1971), as added by Acts 1974, No. 205, §§ 1-16.

53. Utah Code Ann. §§ 13-7-2, -3 (1953).

54. Wash. Rev. Code Ann. §§ 49.60 et seq. (1962), as amended by L. 1973, ch. 141, § 1, ch. 214, § 1.

55. Ore. Ins. Comm'n R. IC (Proposed); and Cal. Ins. Regs. (Proposed) under Title 10 of NILS Cal. Admin. Register 71, No. 48-B, ch. 5, subch. 3, art. 15 (1971).

56. Ariz. Rev. Stat. Ann. § 20-448 (1956).

57. Ga. Code Ann. §§ 56-704(7), -507(a) (1970).

58. Substitute S.B. 425 (1976).

59. Mont. Rev. Codes Ann. § 40-3509 (1947).

60. S.C. Code Ann. § 37-1202(7)(b) (1962).

61. S.D. Comp. Laws Ann. § 58-33-12 (1967).

62. Vt. Stat. Ann. tit. 8, § 4724(7) (1971).

63. Va. Code Ann. § 38.1-52(7)(b) (1950).

64. Wis. Stat. Ann. § 20704(g)(2) (1957).

65. See, for example, Letter No. 500 from the South Carolina Department of Insurance, Nov. 13, 1974, by Howard Clark, Chief Insurance Commissioner and a letter from Virginia State Corporations Commission, Bureau of Insurance, by W. G. Flournoy, Nov. 12, 1974, in response to survey questionnaire sent by Ann Gaughan, then a third-year student at Rutgers-Camden Law School.

66. Ariz. Rev. Stat. § 33-1126(2) (1974), as amended by L. 1973, ch. 172.

67. Md. Ann. Code art. 48A-385 (1972), as amended by Acts 1973, ch. 7.

68. S.F. 2963 (Minn. 1973-74).

69. New York's proposed bill, A.8364 (1974), would have eliminated sex discrimination in premiums except where "actuarially reasonable." Similarly, Oregon's insurance department has held hearings on regulations to particularize the words of their insurance statutes. The proposed regulations on premiums state that distinctions based on sex are unfair except for those based on "credible supporting data." Ore. Ins. Comm'n R. IC (Proposed). The Illinois regulations permit rate differentiation on the basis of sex and marital status where it is based on "expected claim costs and expenses derived by applying sound actuarial principles to relevant and reasonably current company or intercompany studies, claim costs, and expense experience." NILS Off, Rules & Regs. of Ill. Ins. Dep't R. 26.04, § 4 (1976).

70. S.B. 282 (1973). This bill was not enacted.

71. Civil No. 74-420 (S.D.N.Y., filed Jan. 24, 1975).

72. Colo. Rev. Stat. §§ 10-16-138, -17-131 (1973), as added by L. 1975, at 91.

73. NILS Off. Rules & Regs. of Ill. Ins. Dep't R. 26.04, § 3a (1976).

74. Ore. Rev. Stat. § 743.037 (1973).

75. Minn. Stat. Ann. § 62A.041 (1968), as added by L. 1971, ch. 680, § 1, as amended by L. 1973, ch. 651, § 1.

76. Pa. Stat. Ann. tit. 40, § 1171.5(7) (1971).

77. Me. Rev. Stat. Ann. tit. 24, §§ 2318, 2741-42 (1974), as amended by L. 1975, ch. 276, § 1, L. 1975, ch. 428, § 1.

78. Md. Ann. Code art. 48A, §§ 354(G)–(H), 470(I), 477(J) (1957), as added by Acts 1975, chs. 682–83.

79. See, for example, Mass. Gen. Laws Ann. ch. 175, § 47c (1972), as added by Stats. 1974, ch. 785., § 1, as amended by L. 1975, ch. 196, § 1; and Colo. Rev. Stat. Ann. §§ 10-8-121, –16-134, –17-130 (1973), as added by L. 1975, at 90.

80. Sterilization prohibition: Cal. Ann. Ins. Code § 10121(a) (West 1972), as amended by Stats. 1975, ch. 944. Involuntary complications of pregnancy: Cal. Ann. Ins. Code §§ 10119.5, 11512.13 (West 1972), as added by Stats. 1975, ch. 944.

81. Idaho Code § 41–2214 (1961), as added by L. 1975, ch. 204, § 4.

82. R.I. Gen. Laws Ann. § 42–62–10(c)(2) (1970), as added by L. 1974, ch. 50, § 1.

83. Legislation proposed in Massachusetts and New York to require equal coverage for pregnancy in health insurance not enacted. Massachusetts —S. 1862 (introduced May 7, 1975, by Commerce and Labor Committee, referred to Ways and Means Committee; New York—S. 5567 (Donovan, April 23, 1975, referred to Insurance Committee); A. 7319 (H. J. Miller, Mar. 25, 1975, referred to Health Committee); A. 7513 (Reilly, Mar. 25, 1975, referred to Insurance Committee); and A. 7665 (Izard, Mar. 25, 1975, referred to Insurance Committee).

84. Colo. Rev. Stat. §§ 10-8-122, –16-137 (1973), as added by L. 1975, at 91.

85. Mont. Rev. Codes Ann. §§ 41–2601 et seq. (1967), as added by L. 1975, ch. 320.

86. NILS Off. Rules & Regs. of Ill. Ins. Dep't R. 24.06, § 3A (1976).

87. The Supreme Court's holdings in Geduldig v. Aiello, 417 U.S. 484 (1974), and Gilbert v. General Electric, 45 U.S.L.W. 4031 (December 7, 1976), concern federal (non-ERA) constitutional and Title VII requirements and do not control state policy on this subject. See, for example, Brooklyn Gas Company v. New York State Human Relations Commission (New York Ct. App. Dec. 20, 1976). For a more lengthy discussion of Aiello, see the section on disability in Chapter 6.

88. Minn. Stat. Ann. § 65B.44(5) (1971).

89. Substitute S.B. 425 (1976).

90. Some other resources on general issues of sex discrimination in education include:

Project on Equal Education Rights (PEER)
1029 Vermont Avenue, N.W., Suite 800
Washington, D.C. 20005

National Education Association (NEA)
1201 16th Street, N.W.
Washington, D.C. 20009

Project on the Status and Education of Women
Association of American Colleges (AAC)
1818 R Street, N.W.
Washington, D.C. 20009

NOW Education Task Force
3747 Huntington Street, N.W.
Washington, D.C. 20007

Citizens' Advisory Council on the Status of Women
Department of Labor Building, Room 1336
Washington, D.C. 20210

Education Law Center
605 Broad Street, Suite 800
Newark, N.J. 07012

National Foundation for the Improvement of Education
1156 15th Street, N.W., Suite 918
Washington, D.C. 20005

Education Commission of the States
300 Lincoln Tower
1860 Lincoln Street
Denver, Colo. 80203
This group has compiled a guide to state laws: A Handbook of
State Laws and Policies Affecting Equal Rights for Women in Education (1975).

91. See, for example, State ex rel. Idle v. Chamberlain, 175 N.E.2d
539 (Ohio 1961); Perry v. Granada Municipal Separate School Dist., 300 F.
Supp. 748 (1969); Ordway v. Hargraves, 323 F. Supp. 1155 (D. Mass. 1971)
(on admission of pregnant students to public schools); Frantz v. Stroud Union
School Dist. Bd. of School Directors, 41 D. & C. 2d 211 (1964) (restricting
married students to scholastic activities); Andrews v. Drew School Dist.,
507 F.2d 611 (5th Cir. 1975), cert. granted, 423 U.S. 820 (1975), cert. dismissed as improvidently granted, 424 U.S. 903 (1976) (employment of teaching assistant who is mother of illegitimate child).

92. Equal protection challenges recently have been mounted against sex-
segregated public schools in Philadelphia and Los Angeles by the American
Civil Liberties Union. See, for example, Vorcheimer v. School Dist. of
Phila., 400 F. Supp. 326 (E.D. Pa. 1975), rev'd 532 F.2d 880 (3d Cir. 1976),
in which the lower court finding of a violation of equal protection in the maintenance of separate academic high schools for boys and girls was overturned
by the circuit court. The United States Supreme Court has taken certiorari.
On the issue of whether a private university has enough state involvement to
bring it under the scrutiny of civil rights laws, see Rackin v. University of
Pennsylvania, 386 F. Supp. 992 (E.D. Pa. 1974), in which the employment
policies of the university were found to involve "state action." Contra, Cohen
v. Illinois Inst. of Technology, 524 F.2d 818 (7th Cir. 1975). Title IX of the

Education Amendments of 1972, the primary federal statutory prohibition against sex discrimination in education, currently exempts private undergraduate institutions, public elementary and secondary schools (other than vocational schools), and single-sex public undergraduate institutions from complying with regulations requiring nondiscrimination in admissions.

93.   20 U.S.C. §§ 1681-86 (1974); and regulations at 45 C.F.R. pt. 86 (1975). For a concise discussion of these amendments, see M. Dunkle and B. Sandler, Sex Discrimination Against Students: Implications of Title IX of the Education Amendments of 1972 (Assoc. of Amer. Colleges, 1974).

94.   See, for example, N.J. Stat. Ann. tit. 18A, § 36-20 (1968), as enacted by L. 1973, ch. 380, § 1. See also Mass. Gen. Laws Ann. ch. 76, § 5 (1969), as amended by Stats. 1971, ch. 622, § 1, Stats. 1973, ch. 925, § 9A.

95.   Ill. Ann. Stat. ch. 122, §§ 24-4, 27-1, 34-18(1) (Smith-Hurd 1962); as amended by Acts 1975, No. 79-597, § 1; and Ill. Ann. Stat. ch. 122, §§ 34-18(1), (7) (Smith-Hurd 1962).

96.   See Cal. Educ. Code § 91 (1969), as added by Stats. 1974, ch. 182, § 1; Cal. Educ. Code §§ 9001-9002 (1975), as amended by Stats. 1973, ch. 571, § 2; and L. 1975 (1st Ex. Sess.), ch. 226, adding a new chapter to Wash. Rev. Code tit. 28A. Section 4 of the Washington statute provides a private cause of action for persons aggrieved by violations of the statute.

97.   Alaska Stat. § 14.40.880 (1962).

98.   Alaska Stat. § 14.50.050 (1962).

99.   See the section on athletics below.

100.   See, for example, Me. Rev. Stat. Ann. tit. 5, §§ 4681 et seq. (1964), as added by L. 1975, legis. doc. 516, which establishes an affirmative action standard for all state agencies and contractors.

101.   Hawaii Laws 1974, ch. 188. An unsuccessful Michigan proposal would have funded scholarships for low-income women in higher education. H.B. 4483 (1973).

102.   Cal. Educ. Code §§ 8553, 8576, as amended by Stats. 1973, ch. 764, §§ 1-2; Hawaii Laws 1974, ch. 218; Iowa Code § 257.25, 280.3-280.17, 280A.33 (1973), as amended by Acts 1974, ch. 1168; Mich. Comp. Laws § 340.361a (1976), as enacted by Acts 1974, No. 353, § 1. Two other Michigan proposals would have required instruction in the problems and solutions of discrimination (H.B. 4680 [1973]) and created a biennial review of educational materials for racial and sex stereotyping (H.B. 4806 [1973]).

103.   California State Department of Education, Guidelines for Evaluation of Instructional Materials for Compliance with Content Requirements of the Education Code (Sept. 12, 1974), implementing Cal. Educ. Code § 9002 (1975), as amended by Stats. 1973, ch. 571, § 3, at 1094.

104.   Iowa Code § 257.25 (1972), as amended by Acts 1974, ch. 1168, § 1, adds family law to required curriculum of high school social studies.

105.   California A.B. 104 (1975) would have required teaching of family health, child development, legal and financial aspects of marriage, and parenthood.

106.   See, E. Gerber, J. Felshin, P. Berlin, and W. Wyrick, The American Woman in Sport, ch. 4 (1974).

107. Wilmore, <u>They Told You You Couldn't Compete with Men and You,
Like a Fool, Believed Them. Here's Hope</u>, 1 <u>Womensports</u>, June 1974,
at 43.

108. Comment, <u>Sex Discrimination in Interscholastic High School Ath-
letics</u>, 25 <u>Syracuse L. Rev.</u> 535, 550n.109 (1974) [hereafter cited as <u>Dis-
crimination in Athletics</u>].

109. See DeWolf, <u>The Battle for Coed Teams</u>, 1 <u>Womensports</u>, July
1974, at 63, discussing new regulations proposed by John Pittenger, Pennsylvania's Secretary of Education, which, among other things, would encourage
sex-integrated teams.

110. Fourteenth Amendment equal protection challenges: Brenden v.
Independent School District, No. 742, 477 F.2d 1292 (8th Cir. 1973), <u>aff'g</u>
342 F. Supp. 1224 (D. Minn. 1972) (tennis and cross country); Morris v.
Michigan State Bd. of Educ., 472 F.2d 1207 (6th Cir. 1973) (tennis); Reed
v. Nebraska School Activities Ass'n, 341 F. Supp. 258 (1972) (golf); Harris
v. Illinois High School Ass'n, Civil No. S. Civ. 72-25 (S.D. Ill. March 21,
1972) (tennis); Bucha v. Illinois State High School Ass'n, 351 F. Supp. 69
(N.D. Ill. 1972) (swimming); Ritacco v. Norwin School Dist., 361 F. Supp.
930 (W.D. Pa. 1973) (tennis); Seldin v. State Board of Educ. of New Jersey,
Civil No. 202-72 (filed January 31, 1972) (tennis); Haas v. South Bend Community School Corp., 259 Ind. 515, 289 N.E.2d 495 (Sup. Ct. 1972) (golf);
Gregorio v. Board of Educ. of Asbury Park, No. A-1277-70 (N.J. Super Ct.
App. Div. April 5, 1971) (tennis); Hollander v. Connecticut Interscholastic
Athletic Conference, Inc., Case No. 12-49-27 (New Haven Co. Super. Ct.
Mar. 29, 1971) (cross country); and Gilpin v. Kansas State High School Activities Ass'n, 377 F. Supp. 1233 (1974) (track). See also Darrin v. Gould,
540 P.2d 885 (Sup. Ct. 1975), in which two high school girls sued under the
state ERA to be allowed to join the interscholastic football team. Due to a
number of unreported and temporarily settled cases, this list should not be
considered exhaustive.

111. Note, <u>Sex Discrimination in High School Athletics</u>, 57 <u>Minn. L. Rev.</u>
339, 351-57 (1972); and <u>Discrimination in Athletics</u>, supra note 108, at 548-
53.

112. See Brenden v. Independent School District No. 742, 477 F.2d 1292
(8th Cir. 1973), <u>aff'g</u> 342 F. Supp. 1224 (D. Minn. 1972); Haas v. South Bend
Community School Corp., 259 Ind. 515, 289 N.E.2d 495 (Sup. Ct. 1972);
Morris v. Michigan State Bd. of Educ., 472 F.2d 1207 (6th Cir. 1973); Reed
v. Nebraska School Activities Ass'n, 341 F. Supp. 258 (1972); and Gilpin v.
Kansas State High School Activities Ass'n, 377 F. Supp. 1233 (1974). See
also Commonwealth of Pennsylvania v. Pennsyl:.:'a Interscholastic Athletic
Ass'n, 334 A.2d 839 (Com. Ct. 1975), ruling that u.: state ERA prohibits
PIAA from barring coeducational interscholastic teams, inter alia because
where no girls' team exists such a rule deprives girls of all opportunity to
compete interscholastically.

113. See Gregorio v. Board of Educ. of Asbury Park, No. A-1277-70
(N.J. Super. Ct. App. Div. Apr. 5, 1971); Bucha v. Illinois State High
School Ass'n, 351 F. Supp. 69 (N.D. Ill. 1972); and Ritacco v. Norwain

School Dist., 361 F. Supp. 930 (W.D. Pa. 1973). In addition, relief was denied to a female tennis player in Harris v. Illinois High School Ass'n, Civil No. S. Civ. 72-25 (S.D. Ill. Mar. 21, 1972), on the grounds that participation in interscholastic athletics is a privilege, not a right. In Hollander v. Connecticut Interscholastic Athletic Conference, Inc., Case No. 12-49-27 (New Haven Co. Super. Ct. Mar. 29, 1971), the court, in upholding the association rule against coed competition, completely ignored the lack of a female program in the sport (cross-country).

114. For a discussion of several of these settlements, see Discrimination in Athletics, supra note 108, at 541.

115. This account of the background of the lawsuit is based on Henderson, "Sports Victory in the Court of Law," 4 Modern Times, Jan. 1974, at 2. The attorney was Michael Avery of Williams, Avery, and Wynn, New Haven, Connecticut.

116. 20 U.S.C. § 1681(a) (1974).

117. These regulations appear at 45 C.F.R. pt. 86 (1975). Section 86.41 contains provisions particular to athletics.

118. Cal. Educ. Code § 10930 (1975), as added by Stats. 1974, ch. 1525. § 1, and § 22504.7, as added by Stats. 1974, ch. 1526, § 1.

119. Ky. Rev. Stat. Ann. § 157.350 (1971), as amended by Acts 1974, ch. 349, § 1.

120. Kan. Laws 1974, ch. 15.

ANTIDISCRIMINATION LAWS

Credit

Bingaman, A. K. "Federal Credit Regulations and State Law." Women Law Reporter 1 (May 15, 1975): 211–15.

_____. "Impact of the Equal Rights Amendment on Married Women's Financial Individual Rights." Pepperdine Law Review 3 (Winter 1975): 26–41.

Comment. "Discredited American Woman: Sex Discrimination in Consumer Credit." U.C.D. Law Review 6 (1973): 61–82.

Comment. "Equal Rights: Promise or Reality?" Harvard Civil Rights–Civil Liberties Law Review 11 (Winter 1976): 186–216.

Comment. "Women and Credit." Duquesne Law Review 12 (Summer 1974): 863–90.

Gates, M. J. "Credit Discrimination Against Women: Causes and Solutions." Vanderbilt Law Review 27 (April 1974): 409–41.

Geary, A. J. "Equal Credit Opportunity—An Analysis of Regulation B." Business Lawyer 31 (April 1976): 1641–58.

Littlefield, N. O. "Current Comment on Women's Unequal Access to Credit." Commercial Law Journal 80 (March 1975): 111–16.

_____. "Sex-Based Discrimination and Credit Granting Practices." Connecticut Law Review 5 (Spring 1973): 575–97.

Note/Comment. "Consumer Protection: The Equal Credit Opportunity Act." Oklahoma Law Review 28 (Summer 1975): 577–85.

This bibliography follows the practice of the Law Journal's style sheet and uses the following abbreviations: U.C.L.A., University of California at Los Angeles; U.C.D., University of California at Davis; and UMKC, University of Missouri at Kansas City.

Polikoff, N. "Legislative Solution to Sex Discrimination in Credit: An Appraisal." Women's Rights Law Reporter 2 (December 1974): 26–33.

U.S., Bureau of the Census. Marital Status and Family Status. Current Population Reports, 20 Series P-20, no. 212, Table 5 (March 1970).

_____. Marital Status and Family Status. Current Population Reports, 20 Series P-20, no. 223, Table 8 (1971).

                                   Education

Berlin, P.; Felshin, J.; Gerber, E.; Wynck, W. The American Woman in Sport. Chicago, Ill.: Addison and Wesley, 1974.

Browning, R. S., and Perle, L. E. "Student Classifications and Equal Protection: Marriage and Sex." Journal of Legal Education 3 (January 1974): 93–100.

Buek, A. P., and Orleans, J. H. "Sex Discrimination—A Bar to a Democratic Education: Overview of Title IX of the Education Amendments of 1972." Connecticut Law Review 6 (Fall 1973): 1–27.

Comment. "Constitutional Law—Equal Protection—Sex Discrimination in High School Athletics Unreasonable." New York Law Forum 19 (Summer 1973): 166–74.

Comment. "Equality in Athletics: The Cheerleader v. the Athlete." South Dakota Law Review 15 (Spring 1974): 428–46.

Comment. "Implementing Title IX: The New Regulations." University of Pennsylvania Law Review 124 (January 1976): 806–42.

Comment. "Sex Discrimination in Interscholastic High School Athletics." Syracuse Law Review 25 (Spring 1974): 535–74.

Comment. "Sex Discrimination, the Textbook Case." California Law Review 62 (July–September 1974): 1312–43.

Comment. "Title IX of the 1972 Education Amendments: Preventing Sex Discrimination in Public Schools." Texas Law Review 53 (December 1974): 103–26.

DeWolf, R. "The Battle for Coed Teams." Womensports, July 1974, p. 63.

Dunkle, M., and Sandler, B. Sex Discrimination Against Students: Implications of the Title IX of the Education Amendments of 1972. Washington, D.C.: Association of American Colleges, 1974.

Gallagher, M. "Desegregation: The Effects of the Proposed Equal Rights Amendment on Single-Sex Colleges." St. Louis University Law Journal 18 (Fall 1973): 41–74.

Henderson, L. "Sports Victory in the Court of Law." Modern Times, January 1974.

Note. "Constitutional Law—Due Process—Equal Protection—Mandatory Leave Rules for Public School Teachers." North Dakota Law Review 50 (Summer 1974): 757–62.

Note. "Constitutional Law—Equal Protection—Sex Discriminatory Admission Policies in Public Schools Subject to Stringent Judicial Review." St. Mary's Law Journal 6 (Winter 1974–75): 917–25.

Note. "Constitutional Law—Fourteenth Amendment—Public School Maternity Leave." Ohio State Law Journal 35 (1974): 1004–27.

Note. "Constitutional Law—School Board Regulation Barring Married Students from Extra-Curricular Activities Is Unconstitutional." Texas Tech Law Review 6 (Fall 1974): 215–22.

Note. "Education: Sports, Sex Tracking, In Loco Parentis, Dress Codes." Women's Rights Law Reporter 2 (Spring 1972): 41–43.

Note. "Sex Discrimination and Intercollegiate Athletics." Iowa Law Review 61 (December 1975): 420–96.

Note. "Sex Discrimination in High School Athletics." Minnesota Law Review 57 (1972): 339–71.

Note. "Sex Discrimination—The Enforcement Provisions for Title IX of the Education Amendments of 1972 Can Be Strengthened to Make the Title IX Regulations More Effective." Temple Law Quarterly 49 (Fall 1970): 207–22.

Note. "Sex Restricted Scholarships and the Charitable Trust." Iowa Law Review 59 (April 1974): 1000–29.

Sandler, B. "Sex Discrimination, Educational Institutions and the Law: A New Issue on Campus." Journal of Law and Education 2 (October 1973): 613–35.

Shelton, D. L. "Sex Discrimination in Vocational Education: Title IX and Other Remedies." California Law Review 62 (July–September 1974): 1121–61.

Wilmore, J. H. "They Told You You Couldn't Compete with Men and You, Like a Fool, Believed Them. Here's Hope." Womensports, June 1974, p. 43.

Housing

Note. "Pioneering Approaches to Confront Sex Bias in Housing." Cleveland State Law Review 24 (Winter 1975): 79–106.

U.S., Department of Housing and Urban Development, Office of the Assistant Secretary for Fair Housing and Equal Opportunity. Women and Housing: A Report on Sex Discrimination in Five American Cities. Washington, D.C.: U.S. Government Printing Office, June 1975.

Insurance

Cary, E. "Pregnancy Without Penalty." Civil Liberties Review 1 (Fall 1973): 31–48.

Comment. "Gender Classifications in the Insurance Industry." Columbia Law Review 75 (November 1975): 1381–403.

Comment. "Pregnancy Disability Benefits Under State Administered Insurance Programs." Catholic University Law Review 24 (Winter 1975): 263–93.

BACKGROUND MATERIALS/SEX DISCRIMINATION

Babcock, B.; Freedman, A.; Norton, E.; Ross, S. Sex Discrimination and the Law: Causes and Remedies. Boston: Little, Brown, 1975.

Babcock, B. A.; East, C.; Norton, E. H.; Rawalt, M. "Impact of the Equal Rights Amendment: A Symposium." Human Rights 3 (Summer 1973): 125–54.

Baxter, I. Marital Property. Rochester, N.Y.: Lawyers Cooperative, 1973.

Bingaman, A. K. A Commentary on the Effect of the Equal Rights Amendment on State Law and Institutions. Sacramento: California Commission on the Status of Women's Equal Rights Amendment Project, 1975.

Blackstone, W. Commentaries on the Laws of England. Philadelphia: J. B. Lippincott, 1874.

Brown, B.; Emerson, T.; Falk, G.; Freedman, A. "The Equal Rights Amendment: A Constitutional Basis for Equal Rights for Women." Yale Law Journal 80 (1971): 955–62.

Bunkle, P. "Sex Discrimination and the Law." New Zealand Law Journal, June 17, 1975, pp. 246–54.

Comment. "Constitutional Law: Ameliorative Sex Classification and the Equal Protection Clause." Washburn Law Journal 14 (Winter 1975): 127–33.

Comment. "Equal Rights Amendment and the Military." Yale Law Journal 82 (June 1973): 1533.

Comment. "Sex Discrimination and Equal Protection: An Analysis of Constitutional Approaches to Achieve Equal Rights for Women." Albany Law Review 38 (1973): 66–83.

Conlin, R. B. "Equal Protection v. Equal Rights Amendment—Where Are We Now?" Drake Law Review 24 (Winter 1975): 259–335.

Davidson, K. M.; Ginsburg, R. B.; Kay, H. H. Sex-Based Discrimination. Text, Cases and Materials. St. Paul, Minn.: West Publishing, 1974.

Dunlap, C. "Equal Rights Amendment and the Courts." Pepperdine Law Review 3 (Winter 1975): 42–81.

Erickson, N. S. "Women and the Supreme Court: Anatomy Is Destiny." Brooklyn Law Review 41 (Fall 1974): 209–82.

Ferrell, R. M. "Equal Rights Amendment to the United States Constitution—Areas of Controversy." Urban Lawyer 6 (Fall 1974): 853–91.

Flexner, E. Century of Struggle. New York: Atheneum Press, 1970.

Foote, C.; Levy, R. J.; Sander, F. E. A. Cases and Materials on Family Law. Boston: Little, Brown, 1966.

Furay, M.; Hauser, R. E.; Weaver, A. T. "Equal Rights Amendment: A Symposium." Human Rights 1 (July 1971): 54–85.

Ginsburg, R. B. "Gender and the Constitution." University of Cincinnati Law Review 44 (1975): 1–42.

_____. "Need for the Equal Rights Amendment." Women's Law Journal 60 (Winter 1974): 4–15.

Greenberg, H., ed. Impact ERA: Limitations and Possibilities. Millbrae, Calif.: California Commission on the Status of Women, Les Femmes, 1976.

Hale, M., and Kanowitz, L. "Women and the Draft: A Response to Critics of the Equal Rights Amendment." Hastings Law Journal 23 (1971): 199.

Kanowitz, L. Women and the Law: The Unfinished Revolution. New Mexico: New Mexico Paperbacks, 1969.

Karabian, W. "Equal Rights Amendment: The Contribution of Our Generation of Americans." Pepperdine Law Review 1 (1974): 327-54.

Krauskopf, J. M. "Equal Rights Amendment: Its Political and Practical Contexts." California State Bar Journal 50 (March-April 1975): 78-79.

Lombard, F. K. "Sex: A Classification in Search of Strict Scrutiny." Wayne Law Review 21 (1975): 1355-70.

National Commission on the Observance of International Women's Year, 1976. " . . . To Form a More Perfect Union . . . ": Justice for American Women. Washington, D.C.: U.S. Government Printing Office, 1976.

Norton, E. H. "The Impact of the Equal Rights Amendment." Human Rights Law Review, 1973, p. 125.

Note. "Emerging Bifurcated Standard for Classifications Based on Sex." Duke Law Journal, 1975, pp. 163-87.

Note. "Recent Developments in the Area of Sex-Based Discrimination—The Courts, the Congress and the Constitution." New York Law Forum 20 (Fall 1974): 359-80.

Note. "Supreme Court 1974 Term and Sex-Based Classifications: Avoiding a Standard of Review." St. Louis University Law Journal 19 (Spring 1975): 375-94.

Note. "Supreme Court Avoids Considering Sex-Based Classifications." Nebraska Law Review 55 (1975): 133-43.

O'Neil, W. L. The Women's Movement: Feminism in the United States and England. Chicago: Quadrangle Paperbacks, 1969.

Oakley, A. "Sex Discrimination in Legislation." British Journal of Law and Society 2 (Winter 1975): 211-17.

Ross, S. C. The Rights of Women, ACLU Handbook. New York: Avon Books, 1973.

Wheeler, L. A. "Women Under the Law: The Pedestal or the Cage." Journal of the Kansas Bar Association 43 (Spring 1973): 25–29.

CONSTITUTIONAL LAW/UNITED STATES
SUPREME COURT

Comment. "Aiello v. Hansen—A Step Toward a Sex Blind Constitution."
New England Law Review 9 (Spring 1974): 606–14.

Comment. "Constitutional Law—Due Process—Federal Law Conclusively
Presuming Spouse of Serviceman to Be His Dependent While Rebuttably
Presuming Servicewoman's Spouse Not to Be Her Dependent Violates
Due Process Guarantee of Fifth Amendment." Florida State University
Law Review 2 (Winter 1974): 166–78.

Comment. "Constitutional Law—Equal Protection—Denying Social Security
'Mother's Insurance Benefits' to Fathers Violates Equal Protection
Component of Fifth Amendment Due Process Clause." Florida State
University Law Review 3 (Summer 1975): 427–37.

Comment. "Constitutional Law—Gender Based Classifications—Provision of
Social Security Act Which Provided Less Insurance Protection to Females Than to Males Denied Equal Protection of the Law as Secured by
the Due Process Clause of the Fifth Amendment." Hofstra Law Review
4 (Fall 1975): 149–59.

Comment. "Due Process and the Pregnant Worker: The New Weapon in the
Equal Rights Arsenal." Emory Law Journal 23 (Summer 1974): 787–
810.

Comment. "Geduldig v. Aiello—Pregnancy Classifications and the Definition
of Sex Discrimination." Columbia Law Review 75 (March 1975): 441–
82.

Comment. "Sex Discrimination in the 1970's: The Supreme Court Decisions."
Texas Tech Law Review 6 (Fall 1974): 149–67.

Comment. "Waiting for the Other Shoe—Wetzel (Wetzel v. Liberty Mutual
Insurance Co.) and Gilbert (Gilbert v. General Electric Co.) in the
Supreme Court." Emory Law Journal 25 (Winter 1976): 125–61.

Erickson, N. S. "Kahn (Kahn v. Shevin), Ballard (Schlesinger v. Ballard)
and Wiesenfeld (Weinberger v. Wiesenfeld): A New Equal Protection
Test in 'Reverse' Sex Discrimination Cases?" Brooklyn Law Review
42 (Summer 1975): 1–54.

Johnston, J. D., Jr. "Sex Discrimination and the Supreme Court—1971–
    1974." New York University Law Review 49 (November 1974): 617–92.

_____. "Sex Discrimination and the Supreme Court—1975." U.C.L.A. Law
    Review 23 (December 1975): 235–69.

McNamara, E. M. "State v. Chambers (NJ)." Catholic University Law Re-
    view 23 (Winter 1973): 389–94.

Note. "Barefoot and Pregnant—Still: Equal Protection for Women in Light
    of Geduldig v. Aiello." St. Louis Law Journal 16 (1975): 211–40.

Note. "Constitutional Law: Economic Discrimination, Denial of Social Se-
    curity Benefits Premised on Gender Based Classification Is Unconstitu-
    tional, Violates Equal Protection." Akron Law Review 9 (Summer 1975):
    166–74.

Note. "Constitutional Law—Equal Protection—Discrimination Based on Sex
    in the Provision of Armed Services Dependents' Benefits." Case West-
    ern Reserve Law Review 24 (Summer 1973): 824–45.

Note. "Constitutional Law—Equal Protection—Federal Statute Guaranteeing
    Female Naval Officers Thirteen Years Commissioned Service Does
    Not Violate Due Process." Memphis State University Law Review 6
    (Fall 1975): 133–37.

Note. "Constitutional Law—Tax Exemption for Widows Upheld over Sex
    Discrimination Challenge." North Carolina Law Review 53 (February
    1975): 551–60.

Note. "Frontiero v. Richardson: Characterization of Sex-Based Classifica-
    tions." Columbia Human Rights Law Review 6 (Spring 1974): 239–47.

Note. "Impact of Geduldig v. Aiello on the EEOC Guidelines on Sex Discrimi-
    nation." Indiana Law Journal 50 (Spring 1975): 592–606.

Note. "Irrebuttable Presumption Doctrine in the Supreme Court." Harvard
    Law Review 87 (1974): 1534–56.

Note. "Irrebuttable Presumptions: An Illusory Analysis." Stanford Law Re-
    view 27 (January 1975): 449–73.

Note. "Kahn v. Shevin—Sex: A Less Than Suspect Classification." Univer-
    sity of Pittsburgh Law Review 36 (Winter 1974): 584–601.

Note. "Lafleur v. Cleveland Board of Education: An Unarticulated Applica-
    tion of the New Approach to Equal Protection." University of Pittsburgh
    Law Review 35 (Fall 1973): 141–57.

Note. "Liberty Mutual Insurance Co. v. Wetzel: New Rights for Pregnant
    Workers?" New England Law Review 11 (Fall 1975): 225–48.

Note. "Preferential Economic Treatment for Women: Some Constitutional
    and Practical Implications of Kahn v. Shevin." Vanderbilt Law Review
    28 (May 1975): 843–78.

Note. "Pregnancy and Sex–Based Discrimination in Employment: A Post–
    Aiello (Geduldig v. Aiello) Analysis." University of Cincinnati Law
    Review 44 (1975): 57–80.

Note. "Sex Discrimination: Ad Hoc Review in the Highest Court." Louisiana
    Law Review 35 (Spring 1975): 703–10.

Note. "Sex Discrimination—Sex Found a Permissible Classification for Spe-
    cial Tax Treatment." Kansas Law Review 23 (Spring 1975): 534–44.

Note. "Stanton v. Stanton." Harvard Law Review 89 (November 1975): 98–
    103.

Note. "Stanton v. Stanton." Texas Tech Law Review 7 (Fall 1975): 161–69.

Note. "Taylor v. Louisiana." Loyola Law Review 21 (Fall 1975): 995–1003.

Note. "Taylor v. Louisiana." St. Louis University Law Journal 20 (1975):
    159–80.

Note. "U.S. v. Reiser." Houston Law Review 13 (October 1975): 198–200.

Note. "Weinberger v. Wiesenfeld: Equal Protection and Sex Classifications
    in Government Benefit Programs." New Mexico Law Review 5 (May
    1975): 335–44.

Note/Comment. "Constitutional Law: Sex Discrimination in the Statute Gov-
    erning the Sale of Beer to Minors." Oklahoma Law Review 27 (Winter
    1974): 32–39.

Randolph, D. "Sex Discrimination in the Family Benefits Sections of the
    Social Security Act." Clearinghouse Review 8 (December 1975): 235–65.

Recent Development. "Constitutional Law—Equal Protection—Providing So-
    cial Security Survivor's Insurance Benefits to Widows but Not Widowers
    While Caring for Children Held Unconstitutional." Mississippi Law
    Journal 45 (September 1974): 1056–63.

Recent Development. "Constitutional Law—Social Security Act Granting Bene-
    fits to Women Only, Violates Equal Protection." Fordham Law Review
    44 (October 1975): 170–79.

CRIMINAL LAW

Adult Prisons/Female Offenders

Comment. "Prisoner-Mother and Her Child." Capital University Law Review 1 (1972): 127-44.

Comment. "Sexually Integrated Prison: A Legal and Policy Evaluation." American Journal of Criminal Law 3 (Winter 1975): 301-30.

Comment. "Study in Neglect: A Report of Women Prisoners." Yale Law Journal, 1972.

Comment. "Women's Prison." Wisconsin Law Review, 1973, pp. 210-33.

Haft, M. G. "Women in Prison: Discriminatory Practices and Some Legal Solutions." Clearinghouse Review 8 (May 1974): 1-6.

Note. "Denial of Work Release Programs to Women: A Violation of Equal Protection." Southern California Law Review 47 (August 1974): 1453-90.

Note. "Female Offenders: A Challenge to Courts and the Legislature." North Dakota Law Review 51 (Summer 1975): 827-53.

Note. "Sex Discrimination in the Criminal Law: The Effect of the Equal Rights Amendment." American Criminal Law Review 11 (1973): 469-511.

Note. "The Sexual Segregation of American Prisons." Yale Law Journal 82 (1973): 1229.

Note. "Title VII: A Remedy for Discrimination Against Women Prisoners." Arizona Law Review 16 (1974): 974-1000.

Pennsylvania Program for Women and Girl Offenders. Report on the Employment of Personnel by Race and Sex in Pennsylvania Criminal Justice Agencies. Philadelphia, 1975.

Singer, L. "Women and the Correctional Process." American Criminal Law Review 11 (1973): 295-308.

Juvenile Justice

Bayh, B. "A Symposium: Juveniles and the Law." American Criminal Law Review 12 (1974): 1-32.

Children's Bureau. Statistics on Public Institutions for Delinquent Children. Washington, D.C.: U.S. Department of Health, Education and Welfare, 1968.

Davis, S., and Chaires, S. "Sex Discrimination in Juvenile Law." Georgia Law Review 7 (1973): 494–532.

Davis, S. M. "Equal Protection for Juveniles: The Present Status of Sex-Based Discrimination in Juvenile Court Law." Georgia Law Review (Spring 1973): 494–532

Gold, S. "Equal Protection for Juvenile Girls in Need of Supervision in New York State." New York Law Forum 17 (1971): 570–98.

Note. "Constitutional Law—State Statute Granting Juvenile Court Proceedings to Female Defendants Under the Age of Eighteen but Limiting Such Proceedings to Male Defendants Under the Age of Sixteen Held Violative of Equal Protection Clause." Fordham Urban Law Journal 1 (Fall 1972): 286–97.

Stiller, S., and Elder, C. "PINS: A Concept in Need of Supervision." American Criminal Law Review 12 (Summer 1974): 33–26.

Prostitution

Comment. "Prostitution and the Law: Emerging Attacks . . . the 'Women's Crime.'" UMKC Law Review 43 (Spring 1975): 413–28.

Comment. "Victimless Crime Laws." North Carolina Central Law Journal 6 (Spring 1975): 528–74.

Haft, M. G., "Hustling for Rights." The Civil Liberties Review 1 (1974): 8–26.

Rosenbleet, C., and Pariente, B. "Prostitution of the Criminal Law." American Criminal Law Review 11 (1973): 373–428.

Rape

Curry, P. M. "Police Processing of Rape Complaints: A Case Study." American Journal of Criminal Law 4 (Winter 1975–76): 15–30.

Eisenberg, R. L. "Abolishing Cautionary Instructions in Sex Offense Cases: People v. Rincon-Pinedal." Criminal Law Bulletin 12 (January–February 1976): 58–72.

Note. "Criminal Law—Rape—Cautionary Instruction in Sex Offense Trial Relating Prosecutrix's Credibility to the Nature of the Crime Charged Is No Longer Mandatory; Discretionary Use Is Disapproved." Fordham Urban Law Journal 4 (Winter 1976): 419–30.

Note. "Criminal Procedure—Instruction to Jury That Rape Is Easy to Charge and Difficult to Disprove Is No Longer to Be Given." Texas Tech Law Review 7 (Spring 1976): 732–37.

Note. "Evidence—Rape Trials—Victim's Prior Sexual History." Baylor Law Review 27 (Spring 1975): 362–69.

Note. "Indicia of Consent? A Proposal for Change to the Common Law Rule Admitting Evidence of a Rape Victim's Character for Chastity." Loyola University Law Journal (Chicago) 7 (Winter 1976): 118–40.

Note. "If She Consented Once, She Consented Again—A Legal Fallacy in Forcible Rape Cases." Valparaiso University Law Review 10 (Fall 1976): 127–67.

Note. "Rape Reform Legislation: Is It the Solution?" Cleveland State Law Review 24 (1975): 463–503.

Note. "Recent Statutory Developments in the Definition of Forcible Rape." Virginia Law Review 61 (November 1975): 1500–43.

Note. "The Rape Corroboration Requirement: Repeal Not Reform." Yale Law Journal 81 (1972): 1364–91.

Washburn, R. B. "Rape Law: The Need for Reform." New Mexico Law Review 5 (May 1975): 279–309.

Sentencing

Cargan, L., and Coates, M. A. "Indeterminate Sentence and Judicial Bias." Crime and Delinquency 20 (April 1974): 144–56.

Comment. "Constitutional Law—Sex Discrimination—Disparate Sentencing of Male and Female Offenders Violates Equal Protection." Suffolk University Law Review 8 (Spring 1974): 830–42.

Dershowitz, A. "Let the Punishment Fit the Crime." New York Times Magazine, December 28, 1975.

Note. "Constitutional Law—Equal Protection—Disparate Statutory Sentencing Schemes for Males and Females Declared Unconstitutional." Catholic University Law Review 23 (Winter 1973): 389–94.

Note. "Constitutional Law—Equal Protection—Sex Discrimination in Sentencing Criminal Offenders Is Unconstitutional." North Dakota Law Review 50 (Winter 1974): 359–63.

Note. "State v. Chambers: Sex Discrimination in Sentencing." New England
Journal of Prison Law 1 (Spring 1974): 138–47.

Schreiber, A. M. "Indeterminate Therapeutic Incarceration of Dangerous
Criminals: Perspective—Problems." Virginia Law Review 56 (1970):
602–34.

Task Force Report. Crime and Its Impact—An Assessment. Washington,
D.C.: President's Commission on Law Enforcement, Administration
of Justice, 1967.

Temin, C. Discriminatory Sentencing of Women Offenders." The Argument
for ERA in a Nutshell." American Criminal Law Review 11 (1973):
355–58.

DOMESTIC RELATIONS

General

Asche, A. "Changes in the Rights of Women and Children Under Family Legislation." Australian Law Journal 49 (July 1975): 387–99.

Clark, H. H. Law of Domestic Relations. St. Paul, Minn.: West Publishing
Company, 1968.

Comment. "Equal Rights Amendment: Constraint or Discretion in Family
Law." Buffalo Law Review 22 (Spring 1973): 917–46.

Comment. "Uniform Marriage and Divorce Act: New Statutory Solutions to
Old Problems." Montana Law Review 37 (Winter 1976): 119–30.

Fleischmann, K. "Marriage by Contract: Defining the Terms of Relationship." Family Law Quarterly 8 (Spring 1974): 27–49.

Levy, R. J. "Comments on the Legislative History of the Uniform Marriage
and Divorce Act." Family Law Quarterly 7 (Winter 1973): 405–12.

Massip, J. "Rights of the Wife in the Matrimonial Regime." Tulane Law
Review 50 (March 1976): 549–56.

Note. "Marriage as Contract: Towards a Functional Redefinition of the
    Marital Status." Columbia Journal of Law and Social Problems 9
    (Summer 1973): 607-45.

Parnas, R. I. "Prosecutorial and Judicial Handling of Family Violence."
    Criminal Law Bulletin 9 (November 1973): 733-69.

Washburn, C. K., ed. Women in Transition: A Feminist Handbook on Sep-
    aration and Divorce. New York: Charles Scribners, Son, 1975.

Weitzman, L. J. "Legal Regulation of Marriage: Tradition and Change."
    California Law Review 62 (July-September 1974): 1169-1288.

Zuckman, H. L. "ABA Family Law Section v. The NCUSL: Alienation,
    Separation and Forced Reconciliation over the Uniform Marriage and
    Divorce Act." Catholic University Law Review 24 (Fall 1974): 61-74.

Age of Majority/Age of Marriage

Note. "Divorce Law—Effect of Change in Age of Majority upon Parent's Duty
    of Support." Kansas Law Review 23 (Fall 1974): 181-88.

Weitzman, L. J. "Legal Regulation of Marriage: Tradition and Change."
    California Law Review 62 (July-September 1974): 1169-1288.

Alimony/Support

Branca, J. G. "Dischargeability of Financial Obligations in Divorce: The
    Support Obligation and the Division of Marital Property." Family Law
    Quarterly 9 (Summer 1975): 405-34.

Carter, H., and Glick, P. C. Marriage and Divorce: A Social and Economic
    Study. Cambridge, Mass.: Harvard University Press, 1970.

Comment. "Male Alimony in the Light of the Sex Discrimination Decisions
    of the Supreme Court." Cumberland Law Review 6 (Winter 1976):
    589-610.

Editorial Note. "Economics of Divorce: Alimony and Property Awards."
    University of Cincinnati Law Review 43 (1974): 133-63.

Fisher, M. S., and Saxon, D. B. "Family Support Obligations: The Equal
    Protection Problem." New York State Bar Journal 46 (October 1974):
    441-46.

Freed, D. J., and Foster, H. "Taking out the Fault but Not the Sting." Trial 12 (April 1974): 10–12.

_____. "Economic Effects of Divorce." Family Law Quarterly 7 (Fall–Winter 1973): 275–343, 453–54.

Krauskopf, J. M., and Thomas, R. C. "Partnership Marriage: The Solution to an Ineffective and Inequitable Law of Support." Ohio State Law Journal 13 (1974): 558–600.

Labovitz, I. D. "Alimony . . . A Rose by Any Other Name May Not Provide the Same Cent." Commercial Law Journal 80 (August 1975): 359–61.

Note. "Alimony Awards Under No Fault Divorce Statutes." Nebraska Law Review 53 (1974): 126–36.

Note. "Constitutional Law–Divorce–Pendente–Counsel Fees–Costs–Alimony–Effects of Equal Rights Amendment." Akron Law Review 8 (Fall 1974): 171–79.

Note. "Determination of Fault for Purposes of Permanent Alimony." Loyola Law Review 21 (Fall 1975): 1012–19.

Note. "Divorce–Relitigation of Fault for the Purpose of Alimony." Tulane Law Review 49 (May 1975): 1161–67.

Note. "Family and Domestic Relations Law–Divorce–Fault Is Relevant in Determination of Alimony in Divorce Action Brought Under No Fault Prolonged Separation Statute." Harvard Law Review 87 (May 1974): 1579–89.

Note. "Marriage Contracts for Support and Services: Constitutionality Begins at Home." New York University Law Review 49 (December 1974): 1161–249.

Parry, M. L. "Having Regard to Their Conduct–Financial Provision on Divorce." New Law Journal 125 (1975): 960–62.

Recent Development. "Domestic Relations–Increase or Decrease of Permanent Alimony and Child Support–Granted Without the Necessity of Showing a Change in the Circumstances of Both Parties." University of Baltimore Law Review 3 (Spring 1974): 328–34.

Child Custody

Bodenheimer, B. M. "Rights of Children and the Crisis in Custody Litigation: Modification of Custody in and out of State." University of Colorado Law Review 46 (Summer 1975): 495–508.

Callow, W. G. "Custody of the Child and the Uniform Marriage and Divorce Act." South Dakota Law Review 18 (Summer 1973): 551-58.

Comment. "Custody Rights of Unwed Fathers." Pacific Law Journal 4 (July 1973): 922-42.

Comment. "Father's Right to Child Custody in Inter-Parental Disputes." Tulane Law Review 49 (November 1974): 189-207.

Duncan, N. K. "Child Custody, Preference to the Mother." Louisiana Law Review 34 (Summer 1974): 1881-89.

Gatz, M. J., and Marschall, P. H. "Custody Decision Process: Toward New Roles for Parents and the State." North Carolina Central Law Journal 7 (Fall 1975): 50-72.

Mhookin, R. H. "Child Custody Adjudication: Judicial Functions in the Face of Indeterminacy." Law and Contemporary Problems 39 (Summer 1975): 226-93.

Note. "Avowed Lesbian Mother and Her Right to Child Custody: A Constitutional Challenge That Can No Longer Be Denied." San Diego Law Review 12 (July 1975): 799-864.

Note. "Child Custody: Paternal Authority v. Welfare of the Child." Louisiana Law Review 35 (Summer 1975): 904-13.

Note. "Constitutional Law—Custody Proceedings—Due Process—Equal Protection—Unwed Father Is Entitled to a Hearing as to His Fitness as a Parent." Hofstra Law Review 1 (Spring 1973): 315-23.

Note. "Male Parent Versus Female Parent: Separate and Unequal Rights." UMKC Law Review 43 (Spring 1975): 392-412.

Note. "Paternal Custody of Minor Children." Memphis State University Law Review 5 (Winter 1975): 223-34.

Child Support

Bernet, M. F. "Child Support Provisions: Comments on the New Federal Law." Family Law Quarterly 9 (Fall 1975): 491-526.

Freed, D. J., and Midonick, M. L. "Child Support: The Quick and the Dead." Syracuse Law Review 26 (Fall 1975): 1157-94.

Goodman, A. "Rights and Obligations of Child Support." Southwestern University Law Review 7 (Spring 1975): 36-67.

Note. "Domestic Relations: The Expanding Role of the Mother in Child Support." Arkansas Law Review 27 (Spring 1973): 157–61.

Note. "Parent and Child—Criminal Responsibility for Non–Support—Enforcing Obligation for Support on Father Initially and on Mother Secondarily Is Not a Denial of Equal Protection." Santa Clara Lawyer 14 (Fall 1973): 148–53.

Consortium

Hume, R. G. "Liability to Wife for Loss of Consortium: An Update." Federation of Insurance Counsel Quarterly 24 (Summer 1974): 36–49.

Note. "Equal Rights Amendment: A Woman's Right to Recover for Loss of Consortium." Washington University Law Quarterly, 1975, pp. 507–13.

Note. "Husband and Wife—Wife's Action for Loss of Consortium—Discrimination on the Basis of Sex." North Dakota Law Review 44 (1968): 276–80.

Note. "Wife's Right to Consortium." Washburn Law Journal 14 (Spring 1975): 309–20.

Divorce Grounds

Atkins, M. B. "Developing Divorce Reform Law." New York State Bar Journal 45 (December 1973): 545–51.

Case Note. "In Re Marriage of Cary—Equitable Rights Granted to the Meretricious Spouse." University of San Francisco Law Review 9 (Summer 1974): 186–205.

Domicile

Comment. "College Residency Requirements, Spousal Domicile Requirements and the Fourteenth Amendment." Journal of Family Law 14 (1975): 85–96.

Freed, D. J., and Foster, H. H. "Durational Residency Requirements as Prerequisites for Divorce Jurisdiction." Family Law Quarterly 9 (Fall 1975): 555–71.

Palmer, N. "Married Woman's Domicile—How Independent?" New Law Journal 124 (January 1974): 49–133.

Illegitimacy/Natural Fathers

Comment. "Custody Rights of Unwed Fathers." Pacific Law Journal 4 (July 1973): 922–42.

Comment. "Decision of Illogitimacy: A Quest for Equality." University of Pittsburgh Law Review 34 (Spring 1973): 472–85.

Comment. "Family Law: Putative Father Denied Custody Under Restrictive Interpretation of His Rights." University of Richmond Law Review 9 (Winter 1975): 384–93.

Comment. "Family Law: Rights of Illegitimate Children, Rights of Unwed Fathers." Annual Survey of American Law, 1973–74, pp. 233–53.

Comment. "Illegitimate Children and Constitutional Review." Pepperdine Law Review 1 (1974): 266–86.

Comment. "Putative Father—The Evolving Constitutional Concepts of Due Process and Equal Protection." Western State University Law Review 2 (Spring 1975): 261–80.

Comment. "Putative Father's Rights in Adoption Proceedings." Missouri Law Review 39 (Fall 1974): 573–89.

Kass, M., and Shaw, M. W. "Illegitimacy, Child Support and Paternal Testing." Houston Law Review 13 (October 1975): 41–62.

Krause, H. D. "Uniform Parentage Act." Family Law Quarterly 8 (Spring 1974): 1–25.

Lee, R. E. "Changing American Law Relating to Illegitimate Children." Wake Forest Law Review 11 (October 1975): 1–16.

Note. "Constitutional Law—Civil Rights—Unwed Parenthood Held Not to Be Grounds for Teacher Dismissal in Fifth Circuit." Memphis State University Law Review 6 (Fall 1975): 129–33.

Note. "Constitutional Law—Custody Proceedings—Due Process—Equal Protection—Unwed Father Is Entitled to a Hearing as to His Fitness as a Parent." Hofstra Law Review 1 (Spring 1973): 315–23.

Note. "Constitutional Law—Due Process and Equal Protection—Classifications Based on Illegitimacy." Wisconsin Law Review, 1973, pp. 908–14.

Note. "Constitutional Law—Equal Protection—Descent and Distribution—Illegitimates—Statute That Prohibits Inheritance by Illegitimates from

Father Denies Equal Protection." University of Cincinnati Law Review 44 (1975): 415–25.

Note. "Constitutional Rights of a Putative Father to Establish His Parentage and Assert Parental Rights." Marquette Law Review 58 (1975): 175–83.

Note. "Decedents Estates—Descent and Distribution Statutes—Statute Allowing Inheritance by Illegitimate Children Through the Mother but Silent on Inheritance Through the Father Held Invidious Discrimination Under the Equal Protection Clause of the Fourteenth Amendment." Indiana Law Review 8 (1975): 732–38.

Note. "Domestic Relations—State Statute May Not Forbid a Putative Father from Suing for the Wrongful Death of His Illegitimate Child." Buffalo Law Review 22 (Spring 1973): 111–27.

Note. "Equal Protection for Illegitimate Children in State Welfare Programs." Pepperdine Law Review 1 (1974): 291–96.

Note. "Family Law: Child Support for Illegitimates." UMKC Law Review 43 (Fall 1974): 105–11.

Note. "Illegitimacy and Equal Protection." New York University Law Review 49 (October 1974): 479–531.

Recent Development. "Adoption of Illegitimate Children—Constitutional Law —Provision of State's Adoption Law Which Requires the Consent of the Natural Mother but Not the Natural Father Is Reasonable, Not Arbitrary, and Does Not Constitute a Denial of Equal Protection of the Law." Hofstra Law Review 4 (Winter 1976): 473–91.

Recent Development. "Constitutional Law—Fourteenth Amendment Equal Protection—Rights of the Unwed Father—Consent to Adoption." Cornell Law Review 61 (January 1976): 312–38.

Recent Development. "Constitutional Law—Statute Permitting Adoption of Illegitimate Child Without Father's Consent Is Not a Violation of Equal Protection." Fordham Law Review 44 (December 1975): 646–57.

Recent Development. "Illegitimate Children and Parental Rights Act." Washington Law Review 49 (February 1974): 647–83.

Schwartz, V. E. "Rights of a Father with Regard to His Illegitimate Child." Ohio State Law Journal 36 (1975): 1–16.

Soifer, A. "Parental Autonomy. Family Rights and the Illegitimate: A Constitutional Commentary." Connecticut Law Review 7 (Fall 1974): 1–55.

Teneso, P., and Wallach, A. "Vindication of the Rights of Unmarried
Mothers and Their Children: An Analysis of the Institution of Illegiti-
macy, Equal Protection, and the Uniform Parentage Age." Kansas
Law Review 23 (Fall 1974): 23-90.

Intestate/Succession

Comment. "Gifts in Fraud of the Rights of the Wife." Baylor Law Review
26 (Winter 1974): 85-90.

Wenig, M. M. "Sex, Property and Probate." Real Property, Probate and
Trust Journal 9 (Winter 1974): 642-52.

Marital Property

Barham, M. E. "Introduction: Equal Rights for Women Versus the Civil
Code." Tulane Law Review 48 (April 1974): 560-66.

Baxter, I. F. Marital Property. Rochester, N.Y.: Lawyers Co-operative
Pub., 1973.

Bingaman, A. K. "Community Property Act of 1973: A Commentary and
Quasi-Legislative History." New Mexico Law Review 5 (November
1974): 1-51.

Bronstein, E. H. "No Fault Divorce, Alimony and Property Settlement."
New York State Bar Journal 45 (October 1972): 241-45.

Comment. "Division of Marital Property on Divorce: A Proposal to Re-Use
Section 3.63." St. Mary's Law Journal 7 (1975): 209-27.

Comment. "Equal Management and Control of Community Property: The
Dawning of a New Era." University of San Fernando Valley Law Review 3 (1974): 91-103.

Comment. "Marital Property: A New Look at Old Inequalities." Albany
Law Review 39 (1974): 52-86.

Comment. "Origins of Law Reform: The Social Significance of the Nineteenth-
Century Codification Movement and Its Contribution to the Passage of
the Early Married Women's Property Act." Buffalo Law Review 24
(Spring 1975): 683-760.

Comment. "Tenancy by the Entirety." North Carolina Law Review 47 (1969):
963-71.

Glendon, M. A. "Is There a Future for Separate Property? Family Law Quarterly 8 (Fall 1974): 315–28.

Huber, R. G. "Creditors' Rights in Tenancies by the Entireties." Boston College Industrial and Commercial Law Review 7 (1960): 197–207.

Johnston, J. "Sex and Property: The Common Law Tradition, the Law School Curriculum and Developments Towards Equality." New York University Law Review 47 (1972): 1033–92.

Ledbetter, J. W. "Community Property Laws . . . Revisited." Practical Lawyer 20 (April 1974): 39–52.

Miller, J. G. "Creditors and the Matrimonial Home." Solicitors' Journal 119 (August 29, 1975): 582–84.

Note. "Community Property—Community's Liability for Husband's Antenuptial Debts." Loyola Law Review 20 (1973–74): 355–60.

Note. "Implied Partnership: Equitable Alternative to Contemporary Methods of Postmarital Property Distribution." University of Florida Law Review 26 (Winter 1974): 221–35.

Note. "Painter v. Painter: Equitable Distribution of Marital Assets upon Divorce." Temple Law Quarterly 48 (Winter 1975): 397–413.

Note. "Property—Community Property—Community Property Subject to the Joint Management of Both Spouses Cannot Be Encumbered by One Spouse Acting Without the Other's Consent." Texas Tech Law Review 6 (Spring 1975): 1185–91.

Note. "Property Law—Tenancy by the Entireties—Common Law Disability of Coverture Abolished." Memphis State University Law Review 6 (Fall 1975): 137–41.

Powell, R. R. On Real Property. New York: Matthew Bender, 1975.

Randall, G. C. "Community Property Agreements, Joint Tenancies and Taxes." Gonzaga Law Review 10 (Fall 1974): 109–20.

Sassower, D. L. "Matrimonial Law Reform: Equal Property Rights for Women." New York State Bar Journal 44 (October 1972): 406–09.

_____. "No Fault Divorce and Women's Property Rights: A Rebuttal." New York State Bar Journal 45 (November 1973): 485–89.

Student Symposium. "Community Property and the Homestead." St Mary's Law Journal 7 (1975): 151–64.

Thiede, E. "Community Property Interest of the Non-Employee Spouse in Private Employee Retirement Benefits." University of San Francisco Law Review 9 (Spring 1975): 635-63.

Wiley, T. W. "Community Property in a Common Law State." Practical Lawyer 21 (January 1975): 81-93.

Younger, J. T. "Community Property, Women and the Law School Curriculum." New York University Law Review 48 (May 1973): 211-60.

                                         Names

Bysiewicz, S. R. "Married Women's Surnames." Connecticut Law Review 5 (Spring 1973): 598-621.

Comment. "Married Woman's Right to Her Maiden Name: The Possibilities for Change." Buffalo Law Review 23 (Fall 1973): 243-62.

Comment. "Premarriage Name Change, Resumption and Re-Registration Statutes." Columbia Law Review 74 (December 1974): 1508-27.

Comment. "Right of Women to Use Their Maiden Names." Albany Law Review 38 (1973): 105-24.

Comment. "Woman's Right to Her Name." U.C.L.A. Law Review 21 (December 1973): 665-90.

Daun, R. G. "Right of Married Women to Assert Their Own Surnames." University of Michigan Journal of Law Reform 8 (Fall 1974): 63-102.

Lamber, J. C. "Married Woman's Surname: Is Custom Law?" Washington University Law Quarterly (Fall 1973): 779-819.

Note. "Constitutional Law—Equal Protection and Right of Suffrage Prohibits State from Cancelling Voter Registration of Newly Married Women—Women upon Marriage Do Not Necessarily Abandon Maiden Name." Kansas Law Review 21 (Summer 1973): 588-601.

EMPLOYMENT/SOCIAL INSURANCE

Disability Insurance

Comment. "Current Trends in Pregnancy Benefits—EEOC—Guidelines Interpreted." De Paul Law Review 24 (Fall 1974): 127-42.

Comment. "Disability Benefits for Pregnant Employees Under Title VII of
the Civil Rights Act of 1964." Creighton Law Review 9 (December
1975): 360–72.

Comment. "Due Process and the Pregnant Workers' New Weapon." Emory
Law Journal 23 (Summer 1974): 787–810.

Comment. "Pregnancy and Employment Benefits." Baylor Law Review 27
(Fall 1975): 767–76.

Comment. "Pregnancy and the Constitution: 'The Uniqueness Trap.'" California Law Review 62 (December 1974): 1532–66.

Comment. "Pregnancy Disability Benefits Under State Administered Insurance Programs." Catholic University Law Review 24 (Winter 1975):
263–93.

Kistler, C. H., and McDonough, C. C. "Paid Maternity Leave—Benefits
May Justify the Cost." Labor Law Journal 26 (December 1975): 782–94.

Larson, A. "Sex Discrimination as to Maternity Benefits." Duke Law Journal, September 1975, pp. 805–49.

Note. "Civil Rights—Sex Discrimination—Employer's Denial of Disability
Benefits Held to Violate Title VII of the 1964 Civil Rights Act." University of Richmond Law Review 10 (Winter 1976): 380–86.

Note. "Civil Rights—Sex Discrimination—Pregnancy Must Be Treated as a
Temporary Disability for Job-Related Purposes." Texas Tech Law
Review 7 (Fall 1975): 142–50.

Note. "Constitutional Law—Equal Protection and the Mandatory Maternity
Leave Cases." University of Toledo Law Review 5 (Winter 1974): 366–
81.

Note. Constitutional Law—Equal Protection—Exclusion of Pregnancy-Related
Disabilities from State Salary Compensation Insurance Program Denies
Equal Protection to Pregnant Employees." Vanderbilt Law Review 27
(April 1974): 551–60.

Note. "Constitutional Law—Equal Protection—Under Compulsory Unemployment Disability Insurance System, A State May Exclude from Coverage
Disability Resulting from Normal Pregnancy." Journal of Urban Law
52 (Winter 1974): 591–601.

Note. "Constitutional Law—Gender Based Classifications—Provision of Social Security Act Which Provided Less Insurance Protection to Females

Than to Males Denied Equal Protection of the Law as Secured by the Due Process Clause of the Fifth Amendment." Hofstra Law Review 4 (Fall 1975): 149–59.

Note. "Exclusion of Pregnancy from Coverage of Disability Benefits Does Not Violate Equal Protection." Houston Law Review 12 (January 1975): 488–95.

Note. "Sex Classifications in the Social Security Benefits Structure." Indiana Law Journal 49 (Fall 1973): 181–200.

Note. "Sex Discrimination in Employee Fringe Benefits." William and Mary Law Review 17 (Fall 1975): 109–39.

Recent Development. "Sex Discrimination—State Disability Insurance Program—Pregnancy-Related Disabilities—Equal Protection—Exclusion of Pregnancy and Childbirth Disabilities from State Disability Insurance Program Does Not Violate the Equal Protection Clause." Hofstra Law Review 3 (Winter 1975): 141–54.

Schair, S. "Sex Discrimination: The Pregnancy-Related Disability Exclusion." St. John's Law Review 49 (Summer 1975): 684–712.

Weyand, R. "Baring the Cost of Bearing." Trial 11 (May–June 1975): 86–87.

Job Classifications/Promotion

Beans, H. C. "Sex Discrimination in the Military." Military Law Review 67 (Winter 1975): 19–83.

Callis, P. E. "Minimum Height and Weight Requirements as a Form of Sex Discrimination." Labor Law Journal 25 (December 1974): 736–45.

Note. "Height Standards in Police Employment and the Question of Two Defenses for a Neutral Employment Policy Found Discriminating Under Title VII." Southern California Law Review 47 (February 1974): 585–640.

Protective Labor Laws/Title VII

Hillman, J. J. "Sex and Employment Under the Equal Rights Amendments." Northwestern University Law Review 67 (1973): 133–57.

Kanowitz, L. "The Equal Rights Amendment and the Overtime Illusion." New Mexico Law Review 1 (1971): 461–78.

Note. "Employment Practices and Sex Discrimination: Judicial Extension
of Beneficial Female Protective Labor Laws." Cornell Law Review
59 (November 1973): 133–57.

U.S., Congress, Senate. Committee on the Judiciary. Equal Rights for Men
and Women. 92d Cong., S. Report no. 92–689, 1972.

U.S., Department of Labor. Employment Standards Administration, Women's
Bureau. Highlights of Women's Employment and Education. May 1975.

_____. 1975 Handbook on Women Workers. Bulletin 297, 1975.

_____. State Labor Laws in Transition: From Protection to Equal Status for
Women. Pamphlet 15, 1976.

Public Employment/Pensions

Clinebell, D. R. "Dependents of Public Pensioners: The Forgotten Spouse."
Clearinghouse Review 9 (February 1976): 694–702.

Ferrell, R. M.; Finkelher, M. K.; Picker, J. M. "Symposium on Sex Discrimination and Local Government." Urban Law 5 (Spring 1973): 307–
58.

Note. "Mortality Tables and the Sex–Stereotype Doctrine: Inherent Discrimination in Pension." Notre Dame Law 51 (December 1975): 323–32.

Note. "Sex Discrimination in Employee Fringe Benefits." William and Mary
Law Review 17 (Fall 1975): 109–39.

Williams, L. G., and Bernstein, M. C. "Title VII and the Problem of Sex
Classification in Pension Programs." Columbia Law Review 74 (November 1974): 1203–30.

Unemployment Compensation/Worker's Compensation

Griffiths, M. W. "Sex Discrimination in Income Security Programs." Notre
Dame Lawyer 49 (February 1974): 534–43.

Note. "Presumption of Dependence in Worker's Compensation Death Benefits
as a Denial of Equal Protection." University of Michigan Journal of
Law Reform 9 (Fall 1975): 138–62.

Recent Development. "Unemployment Compensation—Spouse's Relocation
Due to Employment Is a Compelling Personal Reason Constituting Good

Cause for Voluntary Termination." Washington Law Review 51 (March 1976): 391–404.

Samuels, C. The Forgotten Five Million: Women in Public Employment. Brooklyn, N.Y.: Faculty Press, 1975.

U.S., Department of Labor. Unemployment Insurance. Benefit Series Service, Report 304 (International Women's Year Special Supplement), September 1975.

U.S., Department of Labor. Bureau of Labor Statistics. U.S. Working Women: A Chartbook. Bulletin 1880, pt. 3, 1975.

Veterans Preference

Note. "Limiting Veteran's Preference: Rahill v. Bronstein." Albany Law Review 38 (1974): 265–80.

PUBLIC OBLIGATION/CIVIL RIGHTS

Jury Service

Comment. "Twelve Good Persons and True: Healy v. Edwards and Taylor v. Louisiana." Harvard Civil Rights–Civil Liberties Law Review 9 (May 1974): 561–97.

Morrow, W. G. "Women on Juries." Alberta Law Review 12 (1974): 321–26.

Nagel, S. S., and Weitzman, L. J. "Women as Litigants." Hastings Law Journal 22 (1971): 193–97.

Note. "Constitutional Law—Sixth Amendment—Systematic Exclusion of Women from Jury Service Violates the Sixth and Fourteenth Amendments." Fordham Urban Law Journal 3 (Spring 1975): 733–48.

STATE-SPECIFIC MATERIALS

Alabama

Note. "Torts—Women Allowed the Right to Recover for Loss of Consortium in Alabama." Cumberland Law Review 6 (Spring 1975): 275–81.

California

Comment. "California's New Community Law—Its Effect on Interspousal Mismanagement Litigation." Pacific Law Journal 5 (July 1974): 723–37.

Comment. "Credit Equality for the California Women?" University of San Fernando Law Review 3 (1974): 125–42.

Comment. "Credit for Women in California." U.C.L.A. Law Review 22 (April 1975): 873–902.

Comment. "Equal Management and Control Under Senate Bill 569: 'To Have and To Hold' Takes on New Meaning in California." San Diego Law Review 11 (June 1974): 999–1025.

Comment. "Female Surnames and California Law." U.C.D. Law Review 6 (1973): 405–21.

Comment. "Intestate Succession Claims of Illegitimate Children in California." U.C.D. Law Review 6 (1973): 217–39.

Comment. "Management and Control of Community Property: Sex Discrimination in California Law." U.C.D. Law Review 6 (1973): 383–404.

Comment. "Plight of the Putative Father in California Child Custody Proceedings—A Problem of Equal Protection." U.C.D. Law Review 6 (1973): 1–25.

Comment. "Prospective Changes in California's Community Property Law." Pepperdine Law Review 2 (1974): 101–16.

Comment. "Toward True Equality: Reforms in California's Community Property Law." Pepperdine Law Review 2 (1974): 101–16.

Frimmer, P. N., and Kahn, A. D. "California Probate of Community Property: The Final Picture Emerges." California State Bar Journal 50 (July–August 1975): 260–64.

Gabler, R. G. "Impact of the ERA on Domestic Relations Law—Specific Focus on California." Family Law Quarterly 8 (Spring 1974): 51–90.

Note. "California Rape Evidence Reform: An Analysis of Senate Bill 1678." Hastings Law Journal 26 (May 1975): 1551–73.

Porter, E. M. "Evolutions of California's Child Custody Laws: A Question of Statutory Interpretation." Southwestern University Law Review 7 (Spring 1975): 1–35.

The California Commission on the Status of Women's Equal Rights Amendment Project, ed. ERA Conformance: An Analysis of the California State Codes. Sacramento: California Commission on the Status of Women's Equal Rights Amendment Project, 1975.

Connecticut

Balbirer, A. E., and Schoonmaker, S. V., III. "Survey of 1974–1975 Developments in Connecticut Family Law." Connecticut Bar Journal 49 (March 1975): 1–23; 50 (March 1976): 67–80.

McAherney, R. M., and Schoonmaker, S. V., III. "Connecticut's New Approach to Marriage Dissolution." Connecticut Bar Journal 47 (December 1973): 375–415.

Note. "Amendment to the State Constitution Prohibiting Discrimination on Account of Sex." Connecticut Bar Journal 49 (September 1975): 463–68.

State of Connecticut. General Assembly, Office of Legislative Research. The Potential Impact of the Proposed Equal Rights Amendment on Connecticut Statutes. No. 15, March 7, 1973.

District of Columbia

District of Columbia, City Council. Memorandum of the Report of the Public Safety Committee Task Force on Rape. July 9, 1975, pp. 48–50.

Florida

Starling, J. "The Tenancy by the Entireties in Florida." University of Florida Law Review 14 (1961): 111–54.

State of Florida, Senate Judiciary Committee. Florida Statutes Potentially Affected by the Equal Rights Amendment. January 1973.

Georgia

Note. "Protection of the Surviving Spouse Against Disinheritance: A Search for Georgia Reform." Georgia Law Review 9 (Summer 1975): 946–62.

Idaho

Comment. "First Look at the Community Property Agreement in Idaho."
Idaho Law Review 12 (Fall 1975): 41–57.

Young, M. S. "Joint Management and Control of Community Property in
Idaho: A Prognosis." Idaho Law Review 11 (Fall 1974): 1–10.

Illinois

Gherardini, G. A. "Methods of Implementing the Equal Rights Amendment,
If Adopted." Illinois Legislative Council. Mimeographed. January 1973.

Legal Committee, National Organization for Women. Illinois Statutes of Interest to Feminists. Chicago: Legal Committee, National Organization for Women, March 1972.

McAnany, P. D. "Imprisonment Under the Illinois Unified Code of Corrections: Due Process, Flexibility and Some Future Doubts." Chicago-
Kent Law Review 49 (Fall–Winter 1972): 178–98.

Note. "Impact of Stanley v. Illinois on Custody Proceedings for Illegitimate
Children: Procedural Parity for the Putative Father." New York University Review of Law and Social Change 3 (Winter 1973): 31–55.

Note. "Stanley v. Illinois: The Legitimate Birth of the Out-of-Wedlock
Father's Right to Be Heard at Custody Proceedings." Capital University Law Review 2 (1973): 149–63.

Indiana

Note. "Alimony in Indiana Under No Fault Divorce." Indiana Law Journal
50 (Spring 1975): 541–66.

Riddle, C. N., and West, M. S. "The Effect of the Equal Rights Amendment
on Selected Indiana Laws." Bloomington: Indiana University School of
Law, 1972. Mimeographed.

Iowa

Recent Case. "Divorce—Alimony—Under Iowa's No Fault." University of
Cincinnati Law Review 42 (1973): 127–36.

Kentucky

Note. "Kentucky's New Dissolution of Marriage Law." Kentucky Law Journal 61 (1971-73): 980-1002.

Louisiana

Barham, M. E., and Younger, J. T. "Community Property: Symposium on Equal Rights." Tulane Law Review 48 (April 1974): 560-626.

Bilbe, G. L. "Constitutionality of Sex Based Differentiations in the Louisiana Community Property Regime." Loyola Law Review 19 (1972-73): 373-99.

Note. "Community Property—Equal Credit Opportunity in Louisiana." Tulane Law Review 50 (January 1976): 403-11.

Note. "Taylor v. Louisiana: The Jury Cross Section Crosses the State Line." Connecticut Law Review 7 (Spring 1975): 508-28.

Riley, J. M. "Women's Rights in the Louisiana Matrimonial Regime." Tulane Law Review 50 (March 1976): 557-76.

Younger, J. T. "Louisiana Wives: Law Reform to Their Rescue." Tulane Law Review 48 (April 1974): 567-90.

Maryland

Governor's Commission to Study Implementation of the Equal Rights Amendment. 1976 Legislative Analysis, ERA Commission Sponsored Bills. Annapolis, Md.: Governor's Commission, May 1976. Mimeographed.

Note/Comment. "Discrimination on the Basis of Illegitimacy in Maryland's Wrongful Death Statute." University of Baltimore Law Review 3 (Spring 1974): 251-69.

Massachusetts

Commonwealth of Massachusetts. Special Study Commission on the Equal Rights Amendment. October 19, 1976.

Glendon, M. A. "Tenancy by the Entirety in Massachusetts." Massachusetts Law Quarterly 53 (1974): 58-59.

Inker, M. L.; Perocchi, P. P.; Walsh, J. H. "Alimony and Assignment of Property: The New Statutory Scheme in Massachusetts." Suffolk University Law Review 10 (Fall 1975): 1-24.

Note. "Interspousal Contracts: The Potential for Validation in Massachusetts." Suffolk University Law Review 9 (Fall 1974): 185-224.

Michigan

Note. "Impact of Michigan's Common-Law Disabilities of Coverture on Married Women's Access to Credit." Michigan Law Review 74 (November 1975): 76-105.

Minnesota

Note. "The Effect of the Equal Rights Amendment on Minnesota Law." Minnesota Law Review 57 (1973): 771-805.

Mississippi

Comment. "Analysis of Mississippi's Criminal Law Under the Equal Rights Amendment." Mississippi Law Journal 47 (April 1976): 279-301.

Missouri

Comment. "Control of Family Assets in Missouri." UMKC Law Review 47 (Spring 1975): 360-81.

Comment. "Equal Rights Amendment: Its Meaning and Its Impact on Missouri Law." Missouri Law Review 39 (Fall 1974): 553-72.

Comment. "Female Exemptions from Jury Service in Missouri." UMKC Law Review 43 (Spring 1975): 382-91.

Comment. "Rights of Illegitimate Children in Missouri." Missouri Law Review 40 (Fall 1975): 631-51.

Comment. "Taylor v. Louisiana: Constitutional Implications of Missouri's Jury Exemption Provisions." St. Louis University Law Journal 20 (1975): 159-80.

Ferns, F.; Fowler, R.; Krauskopf, J.; Rubland, R. G.; Speca, J. M.; Shapiro, L. S.; Thayer, C. P. "Dissolution of Marriage Under Missouri's New Divorce Act." Missouri Bar Journal 29 (November–December 1973): 495–541.

Montana

Note. "Equality for Men and Women, Three Approaches: Frontiero v. Richardson, The Equal Rights Amendment and the Montana Equal Dignity Provision." Montana Law Review 35 (Summer 1974): 325–39.

New Jersey

Recent Case. "Divorce—New Jersey's Decision on the Eligibility of Assets for Equitable Distribution." Dickinson Law Review 79 (Spring 1975): 526–38.

New Mexico

Bingaman, A. K. "Community Property Act of 1973: A Commentary and Quasi-Legislative History." New Mexico Law Review 5 (November 1974): 1–51.

_____. "The Effect of an Equal Rights Amendment on the New Mexico System of Community Property; Problems of Characterization, Management and Control." New Mexico Law Review 3 (1973): 11–56.

University of New Mexico Law Students, New Mexico Equal Rights Legislation Committee. A Report of Possible Effects of the Equal Rights Amendment. Mimeographed. April 5, 1972.

New York

Comment. "Impact of the Equal Rights Amendment on the New York State Alimony Statute." Buffalo Law Review 24 (Winter 1975): 395–418.

Comment/Note. "Sex Based Discrimination in New York Statutory Law: A Road Map for Legislative Reform." St. John's Law Review 50 (Fall 1975): 152–78.

Foster, H. H., and Freed, D. I. "Marital Property Reform in New York: Partnership of Co-Equals?" Family Law Quarterly 8 (Summer 1974): 169–205.

State of New York, Law Revision Commission. Recommendation of the Law Revision Commission to the 1976 Legislature. Draft no. 5. Mimeographed.

North Carolina

Comment. "Illegitimate Child v. The State of North Carolina: Is There a Justifiable Controversy Under the New Constitutional Standards?" North Carolina Law Journal 6 (Spring 1975): 207–26.

Ohio

Miller, M. E. A Report by the Ohio Task Force for the Implementation of the Equal Rights Amendment. Columbus, Ohio, July 1975.

Note. "Family Law: Construing Ohio Revised Code 3109.05." Capital University Law Review 4 (1975): 283–90.

Note. "Ohio Divorce Reform of 1974." Case Western Reserve Law Review 25 (Summer 1975): 844–75.

Oklahoma

Lilly, O. R. "Oklahoma's Troublesome Coverture Property Concept." Tulsa Law Journal 11 (1975): 1–25.

Reynolds, O. M., Jr. "Co-Ownership of Property in Oklahoma." Oklahoma Law Review 27 (1974): 585–620.

Oregon

Comment. "Oregon's New Age of Majority Law and Existing Child Support Decrees." Willamette Law Review 11 (Winter 1974): 70–86.

Pennsylvania

Beck, P. W. "The Equal Rights Amendment: The Pennsylvania Experience." Mimeographed. Philadelphia: Temple University School of Law, 1975.

Comment. "Illegitimacy in Pennsylvania." Dickinson Law Review 78 (Summer 1974): 684–722.

Comment. "The Support Law and the Equal Rights Amendment in Pennsylvania." Dickinson Law Review 77 (1974): 254–76.

Commonwealth of Pennsylvania, Commission for Women. The Impact of the State Equal Rights Amendment in Pennsylvania Since 1971. Mimeographed, 1976.

Note. "Domestic Relations: Pennsylvania Declares the Wife's Right to Divorce from Bed and Board and Alimony Pendente Lite Unconstitutional in Light of the Equal Rights Amendment." Dickinson Law Review 78 (Winter 1973): 402–14.

Note. "Pennsylvania Constitution—Equal Rights Amendment—Sex Discrimination—Interscholastic Sports." Duquesne Law Review 14 (Fall 1975): 101–10.

Note. "The Administration of Divorce: A Philadelphia Study." University of Pennsylvania Law Review 101 (1953): 1204–25.

Pennsylvania Commission on the Status of Women. Credit Report. August 31, 1973.

Pennsylvania Program for Women and Girl Offenders. Proposed Pennsylvania Criminal Justice Goals and Standards for Women. Philadelphia, 1975.

Recent Development. "Domestic Relations—Pennsylvania Equal Rights Amendment Reverses the Common Law Presumption That Husband, Because of His Sex, Should Bear the Primary Duty of Support." Tulsa Law Journal 10 (1975): 485–92.

Tennessee

State of Tennessee, Tennessee Commission on the Status of Women. The Equal Rights Amendment and the Tennessee Code. Mimeographed. 1973.

Texas

Comment. "ERA and Texas Marital Law." Texas Law Review 54 (March 1976): 590–615.

Comment. "Overview of the Equal Rights Amendment in Texas." Houston Law Review 11 (October 1973): 136–67.

Comment. "Presumptions of Legitimacy in Texas." Baylor Law Review 27 (Spring 1975): 340–52.

Comment. "Section 5.22 of the Texas Family Code: Control and Management of the Marital Estate." Southwestern Law Journal 27 (December 1973): 837–64.

Dawson, L. D.; Huie, W. D.; McKnight, J. W.; Sampson, J. J.; Smith,
    E. E.; Smith, E. L.; Steele, W. W. "Texas Family Code Symposium."
    Texas Tech Law Review 5 (1974): 377–88.

Huie, W. D. "Divided Management of Community Property in Texas." Texas
    Tech Law Review 5 (1974): 623–30.

McConnell, M. T.; Raggie, L. B.; Rasor, R. G.; Smith, E. L. "Anatomy
    of a Family Code." Family Law Quarterly 8 (Summer 1974): 105–68.

Sampson, J. J. "Texas Equal Rights Amendment and the Family Code.:
    Litigation Ahead." Texas Tech Law Review 5 (1974): 631–43.

Weddington, S. "Rape Law in Texas: H.B. 284 and the Road to Reform."
    American Journal of Criminal Law 4 (Winter 1975–76): 1–14.

                                    Utah

Note. "Constitutional Law—Equal Protection—Utah Statute Setting Different
    Ages of Majority for Males and Females Is Unconstitutional." Texas
    Tech Law Review 7 (Fall 1975): 161–69.

                                  Vermont

State of Vermont, Governor's Commission on the Status of Women. The
    Equal Rights Amendment and Its Effect on Vermont Statutes and Law.
    Mimeographed. 1972.

State of Vermont, Joint Committee to Study Equal Rights of Women. Report
    of the Joint Committee to Study Act No. R-97 of the 1971 Adjourned
    General Assembly. October 1972.

                                Washington

Cross, M. "Community Property Law in Washington." Washington Law Re-
    view 49 (May 1974): 729–844.

Dybwad, L. H. "Implementing Washington's ERA: Problems with Wholesale
    Legislative Revision." Washington Law Review 49 (May 1974): 571–602.

Note. "Rights of Putative Fathers in Custody and Adoption Proceedings—
    Washington's Law in Perspective." Gonzaga Law Review 9 (Spring
    1974): 826–44.

Wisconsin

MacDougall, P. R. "Women's Names in Wisconsin: In Re Petition of Kruzel."
    Wisconsin Bar Bulletin 48 (August 1975): 30–35.

State of Wisconsin, Legislative Council. Report to the 1973 Legislature on
    Equal Rights. February 1973.

ABOUT THE AUTHORS

The Women's Law Project is a nonprofit feminist law office dedicated to achieving legal equality for women through litigation, public education, research, and writing. For the past three years, the Project has been carrying out research and providing technical assistance to public officials and private advocacy groups concerning the impact of the Equal Rights Amendment on state laws. During the time this book was written all of the authors were staff attorneys with the Project. Currently, Barbara A. Brown is a private attorney with the Philadelphia firm of Litvin, Blumberg, Matusow and Young; Ann E. Freedman is an attorney with the Defender Association of Philadelphia; Harriet N. Katz is an attorney with the Public Interest Law Center of Philadelphia; and Alice M. Price is Managing Attorney with the Women's Law Project.

Other works on the ERA by the authors include "The Equal Rights Amendment: Constitutional Basis for Equal Rights for Women," a Yale Law Journal article that Ms. Brown and Ms. Freedman co-authored in 1971 with Gail Falk and Professor Thomas Emerson, which has become an integral part of the legislative history of the ERA, and chapters in Impact ERA: Limitations and Possibilities, a publication of the California Commission on the Status of Women. Ms. Freedman is also the coauthor of a textbook on women and the law entitled Sex Discrimination and the Law: Causes and Remedies.

The first chapter of this book was written by Hazel Greenberg, editor of Impact ERA: Limitations and Possibilities, and director of research for the Institute for Studies in Equality, a nonprofit project that evolved from the Equal Rights Amendment Project of the California Commission on the Status of Women. A national nonprofit women's information exchange located in Sacramento, California, the Institute collects, develops, and disseminates a wide range of materials and resources on scholarly, political, and sociocultural activities concerned with women.

FEDERAL EQUAL EMPLOYMENT OPPORTUNITY:
Politics and Public Personnel Administration
David H. Rosenbloom

*PUBLIC LAW AND PUBLIC POLICY
edited by John A. Gardiner

SEX AND CLASS IN LATIN AMERICA
edited by June Nash and
Helen Icken Safa

TRADE UNION WOMEN: A Study of Their Participation in New York City Locals
Barbara M. Wertheimer and
Anne H. Nelson

WOMEN AND WORLD DEVELOPMENT: With an Annotated Bibliography
edited by Irene Tinker,
Michele Bo Bramsen, and
Mayra Buvinic

WOMEN IN ACADEMIA: Evolving Policies Toward Equal Opportunities
edited by Elga Wasserman,
Arie Y. Lewin, and
Linda H. Bleiweis

WOMEN'S INFERIOR EDUCATION: An Economic Analysis
Blanche Fitzpatrick

WOMEN'S WORK IN SOVIET RUSSIA: Continuity in the Midst of Change
Michael Paul Sacks

*Also available in paperback as a PSS Student Edition